NATURE AND CREATURE
Thomas Aquinas's Way of Thought

STUDIEN UND TEXTE ZUR GEISTESGESCHICHTE DES MITTELALTERS

HERAUSGEGEBEN VON

Dr. ALBERT ZIMMERMANN

PROFESSOR AN DER UNIVERSITÄT KÖLN

BAND XXI

NATURE AND CREATURE
Thomas Aquinas's Way of Thought

NATURE AND CREATURE

Thomas Aquinas's Way of Thought

BY

JAN AERTSEN

E.J. BRILL

LEIDEN · NEW YORK · KØBENHAVN · KÖLN

1988

Published with financial support from the Netherlands Organization
for the Advancement of Pure Research (Z.W.O.)

Translated from the Dutch by
Herbert Donald Morton

Library of Congress Cataloging-in-Publication Data

Aertsen, Johannes Adrianus.
  [Natura en creatura. English]
  Nature and creature: Thomas Aquinas's way of thought/Johannes
Adrianus Aertsen; translated from the Dutch by Herbert Donald
Morton.
    p. cm.—(Studien und Texte zur Geistesgeschichte des
Mittelalters. ISSN 0169-8125; Bd. 21)
  Translation of: Natura en creatura.
  Rev. version of thesis (Ph.D.)—Free University in Amsterdam,
1982.
  Bibliography: p.
  Includes index.
  ISBN 90-04-08451-7 (pbk.)
  1. Thomas, Aquinas, Saint, 1225?-1274—Contributions in doctrine
of nature. 2. Thomas, Aquinas, Saint, 1225?-1274—Contributions in
doctrine of the creature. 3. Nature. 4. Creation. I. Title.
II. Series.
B765.T54A6713   1987
189'.4—dc19   87-21896
                                                              CIP

ISSN 0169-8125
ISBN 90 04 08451 7

PRINTED IN THE NETHERLANDS BY E. J. BRILL

CONTENTS

LIST OF ABBREVIATIONS

Comp. Theol.	Compendium Theologiae
De ente	De ente et essentia
De pot.	Quaestiones disputatae De potentia
De quat. opp.	De quatuor oppositis
De spirit. creat.	Quaestio disputata De spiritualibus creaturis
De subst. separ.	De substantiis separatis
De verit.	Quaestiones disputatae De veritate
De virt. card.	Quaestio disputata De virtutibus cardinalibus
In Boeth. De trin.	In librum Boethii De trinitate expositio
In De div. nomin.	In librum Dionysii De divinis nominibus expositio
In De generat.	In libros De generatione et corruptione Aristotelis expositio
In De hebdom.	In librum Boethii De hebdomadibus expositio
In Ethic.	In decem libros Ethicorum Aristotelis expositio
In Matth.	In Evangelium Matthaei expositio
In Metaph.	In duodecim libros Metaphysicorum Aristotelis expositio
In Meteor.	In libros Meteorologicorum Aristotelis expositio
In Perih.	In libros Peri Hermeneias Aristotelis expositio
In Phys.	In octo libros Physicorum Aristotelis expositio
In Polit.	In libros Politicorum Aristotelis expositio
In Post. Anal.	In libros Posteriorum Analyticorum Aristotelis expositio
In Sent.	Scriptum super Sententiis magistri Petri Lombardi
Quodl.	Quaestiones de quodlibet
S.c.G.	Summa contra Gentiles
S. Th.	Summa Theologiae

PREFACE

The study presented here is the revised version of a doctoral dissertation that was submitted to the Central Interfaculty (Faculty of Philosophy) of the Free University in Amsterdam in fulfillment of the requirements of the Doctorate of Philosophy and defended publicly on April 16, 1982. That this dissertation was originally published at a Protestant university may be considered a sign of common responsibility for a Doctor of the still undivided western Christendom.

With gratitude I remember the supervisors of my doctoral research program. Prof. dr. M.C. Smit (Free University Amsterdam) did not live to see the completion of my dissertation. Following a long illness, he passed away on July 16, 1981. My interest in the world of the medieval mind and particularly in the thought of Thomas Aquinas was awakened through his teaching. After Professor Smit's death, Prof. dr. Th. van Velthoven (University of Amsterdam) was prepared to act as supervisor. To him I am deeply indebted for his encouragement and assistance at crucial moments. His tragic passing in May 1986 meant a profound loss for me personally. Philosophically, too, he has meant much to me, for he provided a stimulating example of thinking philosophical problems through from the perspective of a metaphysics of being.

Professor van Velthoven was also the one who took the initiative to have this study of Thomas made available in an international language. Scholars from the Netherlands and Belgium supported this undertaking; to them I am grateful. The Board of Directors of the Free University made it possible for me to experience *in actu* the international atmosphere of present-day research on Thomas. I was privileged to spend the academic year 1983 – 84 at the "Thomas-Institut" of the University of Cologne and at the Pontifical Institute of Mediaeval Studies in Toronto.

Grateful acknowledgements for financial support must be made to The Netherlands Organization for the Advancement of Pure Research (Z.W.O.), whose munificent grant made it possible to translate and to publish this study.

Amsterdam, The Netherlands   Jan A. Aertsen
October 31, 1986

INTRODUCTION

This study arose from involvement with the works of Thomas Aquinas (1224/5 – 1274) that was not only intensive, but also extensive in the time devoted to it. As to the latter, certainly a factor is that Thomas's *oeuvre* is voluminous—taking up dozens of hefty folios in the critical Leonine edition. The main reason is however that in the reading of his writings a difficulty develops that attends the study of many medieval thinkers. In their works the intelligibility of what is is unveiled by means of a multiplicity of determinations, principles, and distinctions—a diversity that may initially confuse rather than enlighten the reader. Consider two examples, taken from the beginning of the *Summa Theologiae*. In q. 2, art. 3 Thomas sketches five ways (*quinque viae*), which prove the existence of God. All are causal arguments. They end in the Unmoved Mover, in the first efficient cause, in what is Necessary by itself, in the "maximum," and in the final cause. Yet what causality is and the manner in which it is differentiated (what is the difference, for example, between the first way and the second way?) remains unstated. In q. 3 Thomas speaks of the simplicity of God by denying of Him various kinds of composition: the composition of matter and form, of subject and essence, of essence and being, of subject and accident. What the meaning of these diverse forms of composition is, what composition is in the internal structure of a being, is not indicated but presupposed.

The order, meaning, and systematic coherence of the intelligible structures are not immediately graspable, because Thomas's writings are often constructed according to the so-called "scholastic" method. On account of a concrete question certain possibilities of thought are proved; here these principles are advanced, there other ones. It is "piecework," from which an imposing edifice is built up "summarily." A systematic exposition of the foundations and joints is only seldom presented expressly. One who would understand Thomas must go in quest of these, must wonder what the fundamentals and the ruling principles of the architectonic are. Is Thomas's thought a continuation of Aristotelianism (as most older monographs maintain)? Or is it dominated by the Platonic notion of participation (FABRO, KREMER)?[1]

---

[1] C. Fabro, *Participation et Causalité selon S. Thomas d'Aquin* (Louvain and Paris, 1961), p. 196: "... les thèses les plus caractéristiques du thomisme soient exprimées et commandées par la notion platonicienne de participation." K. Kremer, *Die neuplatonische Seinsphilosophie und ihre Wirkung auf Thomas von Aquin* (Leiden, 1971).

It could be rightly objected that such descriptions do not touch what is proper to Thomas's view. Even so, however, is his philosophy then a Christian philosophy (GILSON), [2] a philosophy of synthesis which attempts to reconcile the impossible (Reformational philosophers), [3] or a first step towards modern anthropocentrism (RAHNER, METZ)?[4]

A first aim of this study is to disclose avenues whereby, on the basis of a close reading and analysis of the texts, an interpretation can be presented of the inner coherence and direction of Thomas's thought. To this end, three "ways" will be traversed.

(1) To the driving forces of Thomas's philosophizing we come closer by tracing and pondering his way of thought. By this I do not mean a reconstruction of an individual "history of development" in the sense in which that has become prevalent in studies of Aristotle. Although there have been attempts to discover some notable development or "turn" in Thomas's thought, there is something forced about them. What we intend is more general and fundamentally philosophical in character. Characteristic of man as man is a dynamics towards knowing. Aristotle put this into words in the renowed opening sentence of his *Metaphysica*: "All men by nature desire to know." What matters is to discern this tendency in its character as a way (*S.c.G.* III, 143: *per viam intelligibilem*) and to analyze it in its beginning and end, in order to be able to fathom its motives.

The intelligibility which is sought of that which is is determined by its origination. Philosophy turns out to be an urge towards the origin. Thinking comes to rest when it has reduced things to an 'archè' whence they originate. "Origin" (*origo*) means, so Thomas says, *via quaedam a re, vel ad rem* (*S. Th.* I, 40, 2), a certain way from something, or to something, a movement from a principle or to an end. Our thesis is that in Thomas this originality is twofold, that of *nature* and *creature*.

(2) "Nature" is the Greek answer to the problem of being. The 'physis' is the 'ousia', the essence of things (*Phys.* II, 1). "What is by nature," so Aristotle says in his *Ethic. Nic.* V, c. 10, "is unvariable and has everywhere the same power." 'Physis' is a notion that was developed in the Hellenic world during the transition from mythos to logos. It is a conception "that in one way or another lies at the foundation of the whole of Greek philosophical thought,"[5] a conception that, as no other,

---

[2] See 5.3.2.

[3] See 3.7.2.

[4] J.B. Metz, *Christliche Anthropozentrik, Über die Denkform des Thomas von Aquin* (Munich, 1962), with an "Einführender Essay" by K. Rahner, who is stamped by Fabro as "deformator thomisticus radicalis" (in *Divus Thomas* 74 (1971): 338).

[5] E. Frank, "Der Wandel in der Beurteilung der Griechischen Philosophie," in *Wissen, Wollen, Glauben, Gesamm. Aufsätze zur Philosophiegeschichte und Existentialphilosophie* (Zu-

is distinctively and essentially Greek.[6]

"What is natural in each thing is the most powerful."[7] The originality of nature is also the horizon of Thomas's understanding of the world and of man. "What belongs to a thing naturally (*naturaliter*) must be the foundation and principle of all else" (*S. Th.* I, 82, 1). By nature man desires to know, the natural is presupposed for the ethical (*naturalia praesupponuntur moralibus*), [8] by nature all things tend towards God.

In *Phys.* II, c. 1 Aristotle thematizes the question concerning the 'physis'. There he presents, in the judgement of HEIDEGGER, who devoted a searching study to this text, "the explanation of 'physis', which bears and guides all subsequent interpretation of the essence of nature."[9] For this reason, and because of the 'auctoritas' accredited to Aristotle as "the Philosopher ," we shall take as our point of departure for the clarification of the natural origin Thomas's lectio of this text.[10]

In Thomas's commentary on *Phys.* II, 1 (lect. 1 and 2)—hereafter referred to as the first basic text—we encounter in the explanation of nature a number of central philosophical notions such as cause, principle, definition, movement, 'per se', matter and form, potency and act, as well as the character of nature as a way. These notions will be unfolded gradually in the chapters to come. Here I only indicate them briefly in their context.

In response to the question "What is nature?" (*quid sit natura*) Aristotle begins by saying that of all beings, some are by nature and some are by other causes. "By nature" are animals, plants, and the elements. These natural beings differ from non-natural beings because the former are seen to have in themselves a principle of movement. From this Aristotle concludes the definition of nature: it is a principle and cause of motion in that in which it is 'per se'. Nature is an intrinsic principle of movement. This can be twofold, namely, matter and form. Aristotle's thematizing of the 'physis' is unmistakably a synthesis of ancient thought on the origin of things. The form, to be sure, is the nature "more" than matter is, for every thing is more what it is when it is in act than when it is in potency. Nature is also "end." Nature (in the etymological sense of 'genesis') is the

---

rich and Stuttgart, 1955), p. 44.

[6] O. Gigon, *Grundprobleme der antiken Philosophie* (Bern, 1959), p. 154.

[7] *S. Th.* I–II, 31, 6: Manifestum est quod id quod est naturale in unoquoque, est potentissimum.

[8] *De correctione fraterna* q. un., a. 1 ad 5.

[9] "Vom Wesen und Begriff der 'Physis', Aristoteles' Physik B, 1," in *Wegmarken* (Frankfurt am Main, 1967), p. 313.

[10] For this manner of philosophizing, which is typical of medieval philosophy, see W. Kluxen, "Charakteristik einer Epoche: zur Gesamtinterpretation der Philosophie des lateinischen Mittelalters," *Wissenschaft und Weltbild* 28 (1975): 83ff.

4 INTRODUCTION

way (Aristotle uses the term 'hodos') towards nature (*via in naturam*). This
way, which reveals the nature of nature, is the second dynamics we shall
follow, in connection with the first, which is the desire to know. ''. . .
[T]he true philosophical problem upon which the historian of the Middle
Ages must reflect is first of all that of the significance of nature.''[11]

(3) At the beginning of Thomas's era, the 'auctoritas' of the Philosopher was suspect. ''Lecturing'' on precisely the writings on natural philosophy from the corpus Aristotelicum was forbidden on the ecclesiastical
side on pain of excommunication.[12] As late as 1228 Pope Gregory IX
sent a warning to the University of Paris. Let the theologians not deviate
''to the doctrines of the natural philosophers'' and not falsify the Word
of God with ''the fictions of philosophers.''[13] Obviously, the Aristotelian
concept of nature was considered a threat to a Christian understanding
of reality from the Origin.[14]

Already by the first sentence in the Bible, in the book of Genesis, it is
revealed that the world is *creature*, a term which means ''all that is by God''
(*De pot.* 3, 3 ad 2). The Judaeo-Christian idea of creation plays a central
role in Thomas's thought. If one had to provide him with a by-name,
then, as J. PIEPER says, it would have to be: *Thomas a Creatore*. That the
world is qualified by creatureliness—''to have sustained and thought to
the end this conception with all consequences is indeed something that for
Thomas Aquinas . . . is utterly distinctive.''[15]

The idea of creation is worked out philosophically by Thomas in his

---

[11] A. Forest, in *Bulletin thomiste* III, 837. A comprehensive explanation of this basic
term in Thomas is lacking. Cf. L. Oeing-Hanhoff, ''Mensch und Natur bei Thomas von
Aquin,'' *Zeitschrift für katholische Theologie* 101 (1979), 302, n. 4.

Worthy of mention are the studies by J.A. Weisheipl, ''The Concept of Nature,'' *The
New Scholasticism* 28 (1954): 377–408; R. Pannikar, *El concepto de naturaleza, Analisis historico
y metafisico de un concepto*, 2nd ed. (Madrid, 1972); M.-J. Nicolas, ''L'idée de nature dans
la pensée de Saint Thomas d'Aquin,'' *Revue thomiste* 74 (1974): 533–90.

[12] H. Denifle & A. Chatelain, *Chartularium Universitatis Parisiensis* vol. 1, p. 70: Nec libri Aristotelis de naturali philosophia nec commenta legantur publice vel secreto, et hoc
sub pena excommunicationis inhibemus.

[13] *Ibid.*, 114–15.

[14] That they are inconsistent with each other is argued by C.J. Dippel, ''De inconsistentie tussen scheppingsgeloof en natuurbegrip,'' in *Geloof en Natuurwetenschap*, vol. 1
(The Hague, 1965), p. 186.

[15] J. Pieper, ''Kreatürlichkeit, Bemerkungen über die Elemente eines Grundbegriffs,'' in *Thomas von Aquin 1274/1974*, ed. L. Oeing-Hanhoff (Munich, 1974), p. 47. He
follows here the suggestion made by G.K. Chesterton.

It is remarkable that also this basic idea of Thomas's has been relatively seldom the object of systematic reflection. I would mention the studies by A.D. Sertillanges, *L'idée de
création et ses retentissements en philosophie* (Paris, 1945); J.F. Anderson, *The Cause of Being, The
Philosophy of Creation in St. Thomas* (St. Louis and London, 1952); L. Dümpelmann, *Kreation
als ontisch-ontologisches Verhältnis* (Freiburg and Munich, 1969).

writing *De substantiis separatis*, c. 9—[16] hereafter referred to as the second basic text. It likewise contains a number of central philosophical notions, such as "another mode of causing," participation, resolution, and being (*esse*). Here I again only indicate them briefly in their context. Thomas observes that with regard to the mode of existing of the separate, that is, immaterial substances, certain people have deviated from the truth by taking away from spiritual substances the origin (*originem*) by the first Author. This opinion seems to proceed from the fact that the intellect cannot be raised to see another mode of causing than the one which is suited to material things. In all things, however, a resolution must take place, in the sense that each of them is resolved by the intellect into that which is, and its being. For this reason, it is necessary to conceive another origin than that whereby form comes to matter, an origin according as "to be" is bestowed upon things. This other, metaphysical origin is interpreted by Thomas as "participation." The way of creation (*via creationis, S.c.G.* III, 69) relates to what is innermost in each thing, namely, being.[17]

The ways which are investigated in order to see through Thomas's thought refer likewise to a concrete historical situation. They are directly related, as was already noted above, to the intellectual historical circumstances of the thirteenth century. The university, one of the most important innovations of the Middle Ages,[18] was determinative for the life of Thomas Aquinas. It left its stamp on his work as well, not just qua ("scholastic") form but also qua intellectual task. In this center of study and education the two principal sources of Western culture, the classical heritage and Christianity, had come into confluence.

On the one side, the desire to know led to the reception of an extensive body of Greek and Arab science. Under its influence, the propaedeutic faculty of arts developed during the course of the thirteenth century into a philosophy faculty where students received lengthy education in pagan philosophy, especially in Aristotle. On the other side, in the theology faculty there was a deepened interest in the Bible and in the tradition determined by this 'auctoritas'. How to connect the Christian interpretation of the meaning of reality with Greek philosophical rationality was the epochal task thought through by Thomas Aquinas.[19]

---

[16] See for this writing (datable to 1270–1273): F.J. Lescoe, "*De Substantiis Separatis*: Title and Date," in *St. Thomas Aquinas 1274–1974: Commemorative Studies*, vol. 1 (Toronto, 1974), pp. 51–66.

[17] *In II Sent.* 1, 1, 4: Operatio Creatoris magis pertingit ad intima rei.

[18] On the medieval university, see: A.B. Cobban, *The Medieval Universities, Their Development and Organisation* (London: 1975); H. Grundmann, *Vom Ursprung der Universität im Mittelalter*, 2nd ed. (Darmstadt, 1960); G. Leff, *Paris and Oxford Universities in the Thirteenth and Fourteenth Centuries: An Institutional and Intellectual History* (New York, 1968).

[19] Cf. the commendatory opening address by M.-D. Chenu at the international con-

What follows is an unfolding and justification of what has only been indicated here. It can be read as an "itinerary," as a description of a "way." Along the way the motives of the train of thought will gradually come to light and the "hodo-logy"—the rationale of the way—will become graspable. The moment of tension in this investigation is the question to what extent the ways of nature and of creature come together. It is this 'concursus' which determines the distinctive character and problems of Thomas's way of thought.

---

gress commemorating the seventh centennial of Thomas Aquinas's death (Rome and Naples, 1974): "S. Thomas innovateur dans la créativité d'un monde nouveau."

CHAPTER ONE

FROM QUESTIONING TOWARDS KNOWING

The question posed in the first basic text (*In II Phys.*, lect. 1, 141) mentioned in the Introduction is: What is nature (*quid sit natura*)? That is a question which must be thought in terms of its own, that is Greek, nature. So the question is to be elucidated, from the desire to know (1.1.-1.2.), as question posed (1.3.); as "what" question (1.4.); and as question concerning nature (1.5.).

This mode of questioning puts us upon a specific way. The motive behind such questioning may itself become "questionable," that is, worthy of inquiring into. Did not Augustine speak of an unvirtuous desire to know, of "curiosity"? In confrontation with this authority, it is necessary for Thomas to legitimate the desire to know (1.6.).

In his justification Thomas introduces the motif of circulation (1.7.): the process from and towards God. Orientation to this Origin opens up new room for philosophical questioning. It is no longer the *nature* of that which is but the being as *creature* that Thomas poses as the task of thought (1.8.) in the second basic text, that of *De substantiis separatis*. Thereby the order and direction of the traditional questions acquire a twofold sense (1.9.).

1.1. *"All men by nature desire to know"*

"All men by nature desire to know." With this arresting statement Aristotle opens the *Metaphysica* (A 1, 980 a 21). He does not furnish a strict proof for this assertion, but only what he himself calls a "sign": an indication of man's natural desire to know is his disinterested esteem for sensation. "For even apart from their utility, the senses are appreciated for themselves, most of all the sense that functions by means of the eyes." Why this preference for seeing above the other senses? "Because sight most enables us to know reality." The advancement, by way of verification, of both these elements—the priority of sight, and disinterestedness—makes sense only if there is a correlation between them and the nature of the knowledge envisioned—a "vision" (*theoria*) pursued for its own sake.

The renowned opening statement of the *Metaphysica* plays an important role in Thomas's work. In numerous loci he refers to it, especially (see 1.9.) in his account of the "natural desire" for the vision of God (*visio Dei*). From this it may be inferred that for Thomas the dictum puts into words something essential. It will therefore be important to view the various elements in the dictum more closely.

In the first place, the statement suggests a dynamics; for, formally speaking, *desire* is a tendency towards a good that one does not yet possess. That which desires has its end—by which it is made perfect—outside itself. Desire is a movement towards something other.[1]

Moreover, this tendency is oriented. The end and goal in which the desire is fulfilled and comes to rest is "to know" (*scire*), that is, apprehension of the intelligible structure of reality. "Science" in the ancient and medieval tradition is defined as knowledge of the causes of a thing. "Then do we deem ourselves to know perfectly," according to Aristotle, "when we know the cause of something." To know perfectly by knowing the causes or principles of the thing is to know by the same token the truth of the thing; for "the principles of being of the thing and the principles of its truth" (*principia esse rei et veritatis ipsius*) are identical. Finally, science is certain knowledge; it concerns the necessary (*scientia est de necessariis*), the non-contingent, that which cannot be otherwise than it is.[2] As a consequence, the process towards knowledge finds three tracks, which we shall explore in due course: the tendency towards knowledge moves via causality (ch.3); truth (ch.4); and necessity (ch.6).

Desire (to know) as a tendency towards a good that one does not yet possess implies a prior not-knowing. Yet this ignorance is not a pure negation but rather a privation.[3] For there is an attendant awareness that the lack of knowledge is a shortcoming—an awareness that finds positive expression in the desire to know.[4] Both moments, the negative and the positive, are inseparably connected in wondering (*admiratio*); for it is wondering which makes that which is an object of inquiry.[5] All men acknowledge that there exist sensible substances, such as earth, water,

---

[1] *In II Sent.* 1, 2, 1: Desiderium enim est rei non habitae; ad 2: Illud quod agit propter desiderium finis, habet finem extra se quo perficitur; *S. Th.* I, 73, 2: Desiderium in aliud tendens quidam motus dicitur; *S. Th.* I-II, 3, 4: Desiderium finis . . . est motus ad finem. Cf. A. Peperzak, *Der heutige Mensch und die Heilsfrage: eine philosophische Hinführung* (Freiburg, 1972), pp. 95ff. ("Formalelemente des Verlangens").
  For the 'desiderium naturale' see also 8.1.2.

[2] See the definition of 'scire' ('simpliciter') in *In I Post. Anal.*, lect. 4, 32–34.

[3] Cf. *De malo* 3, 7: Nescientia enim simplicem *negationem* scientiae importat. *Ignorantia* vero quandoque quidem significat scientiae *privationem*; et tunc ignorantia nihil est aliud quam carere scientia quam qui natus est habere: hoc enim est de ratione privationis cuiuslibet.

[4] Plato expressed this double aspect vividly in his *Symposion*: Eros is the son of Poros (wealth) and Penia (poverty). "Between wisdom and ignorance he stands in the middle (204 B).

[5] On wonder as the origin of philosophy see Plato, *Theaetetus* (155 D); Aristotle, *Metaphys.* A, 2; Thomas, *S.c.G.* III, 25, Amplius; *In Matth.* c. 5, lect. 2: Naturale autem desiderium est, quod homo videns effectus inquirat de causa: unde etiam *admiratio* philosophorum fuit *origo philosophiae*, quia videntes effectus admirabantur, et quaerebant causam.
  In 7.1.1.3. we shall see that Thomas also relates the *miraculum* to "wondering."

and the other elements; and, further, in an ascending order of nobility, plants; animals and their parts; heaven and the stars (*In VIII Metaph.*, lect. 1, 1683)—precisely those things which are named natural things in the first basic text.[6] Yet, however, indubitable the existence of these sensible substances may be, they lose their self-evidence to the wondering eye: the *causes* of what is seen are hidden.

The desire to know is "by *nature*"—a basic term that now becomes itself the object of the desire for knowledge. And strikingly, as we shall see in this inquiry, the three dimensions of intelligibility just mentioned—causality, truth, and necessity—constitute the ratio of nature.

Because the desire to know is "natural," an intimate connection is established between the "subject" of the desire and its final end. *Man*, precisely because he is man, intends knowledge as his perfection. This connection is apparent in yet another manner: wonder is a specifically human experience of reality. This is so decidedly the case that Thomas derives an argument for the human nature of Christ from the Scripture text, "When Jesus heard it, he marvelled" (Matthew 8:10). Wonder cannot be ascribed to God, because wonder entails ignorance, and that must be denied of God. Neither is wonder ascribable to animals, since a sensitive nature does not concern itself about the knowledge of causes. Wonder at that which appears is a characteristic proper to man alone.[7]

Man marvels in the first instance at that which is directly in view, later at that which is more hidden, such as the properties of the moon, sun and stars, and finally at the origin of the entire universe. One who marvels is ignorant but is already on the way to real knowledge, for such a one desires to flee not-knowing. Wonder is the way to inquire into the truth (*quasi via ad inquirendum veritatem*); wonder is interpreted by Thomas simply as "a desire to know" (*S. Th.* I-II, 32,8). In wondering—not in methodically posed universal doubt—lies the origin of philosophy, which is to say, the motive that moved man to philosophize (*ex admiratione moti sunt ad philosophandum*).[8] The termination of this movement lies, as in the case of every other process, in the opposite of that from which it originated:

---

[6] Celestial bodies, although they are not mentioned as beings "by nature" in the first passage of this basic text, do belong to this enumeration, as is clear from the continuation of the first passage (*In II Phys.*, lect. 1, 142).

[7] *S.c.G.* IV, 33, Praeterea.

[8] A good summary is presented in *In I Metaph.*, lect. 3, 54f.; 55: Ipsi etiam philosophi ex admiratione moti sunt ad philosophandum. Et quia admiratio ex ignorantia provenit, patet quod ad hoc moti sunt ad philosophandum ut ignorantiam effugarent. Et sic deinde patet, quod scientiam studiose quaesierunt, solum ad cognoscendum, et non causa alicuius utilitatis.

that is, in science.[9] Both *termini*, the end and the beginning of the way, deserve closer scrutiny.

1.2. *The natural desire to know the causes*

Men began to philosophize because they inquired into the causes of things (*In I Metaph.*, lect. 17, 259). The objective of philosophy is to know the causes.[10] It is in such knowledge that the desire to know is fulfilled. "In all men there is a natural desire to know the causes of whatever is seen."[11]

In the first basic text nature is referred to as *causa* and also as *principium*—a first indication of the signalized connection between nature and intelligibility. In the second basic text there is an appeal for another mode of causing (*modus causandi*) than the prevalent one. There is therefore every reason to state broadly even at this early juncture what is revealed by the causes and principles.

"Those are said to be the *principles* and *causes* of natural things from which they are and come to be 'per se', and not 'per accidens'" (*In I Phys.*, lect. 13, 111). Even though "principle" and "cause" are often used interchangeably, there is still a conceptual distinction.[12] Already in the work of his youth, *De principiis naturae* (c.3), Thomas establishes— having wrestled his way through Aristotle's contradictory texts—that "principle" has a wider extension: every "cause" is "principle," but the reverse is not the case.

In *Phys.* I, three characteristics of principles are summed up: they are not "from something other," they are not "from each other," and all the rest is "from them."[13] A principle must be something first, a 'primum', not reducible to something other. Theological considerations, particularly the doctrine of the Trinity, provide Thomas with the occasion to emphasize that, properly speaking, "principle," although it is derived from priority, signifies "origin."[14] As such, it implies an order towards

---

[9] *In I Metaph.*, lect. 3,66: Nam unusquisque motus terminatur ad contrarium eius a quo motus incipit. Unde, *cum inquisitio sit motus quidam ad scientiam, oportet quod terminetur ad contrarium eius a quo incipit.*

[10] *In I Metaph.*, lect. 3,67: Erit ergo finis huius scientiae in quem proficere debemus, ut causas cognoscentes, non admiremur de earum effectibus; *S.c.G.* III, 50: Non quiescit igitur sciendi desiderium ... nisi, cognitis substantiis effectuum, etiam substantiam causae cognoscant.

[11] *S.c.G.* III, 25.

[12] See *In I Sent.* 12, 1, 2 ad 1; 29, 1, 1; *De principiis naturae* c.3; *In I Phys.*, lect. 1, 5; *In V Metaph.*, lect. 1, 749f.; *S. Th.* I, 33, 1 corp. and ad 3; *Super Ioannem* cap. 1, lect. 1,34; *De pot.* 10,1 ad 9.
This distinction will prove to be of importance for the definition of "natura" (cf. 7.1.1.4.).

[13] Cap. 5 (lect. 10,77).

[14] See, for example, *S. Th.* I, 33, 1 ad 3: Licet hoc nomen "principium" quantum ad

something. "Principle" indicates that from which something proceeds in any way. It is the first, be it in being, be it in becoming, or be it in knowing of the thing: that is Thomas's concluding observation in his lectio on "principle" (*In V Metaph.*, lect. 1,761).

Every cause has the character of principle (and thus entails a certain order), but adds something to the latter notion. To express this, Thomas employs in his commentary on the *Metaphysica* a terminology of Neoplatonic provenance: "The term 'cause' implies some influence on the being of the thing caused (*influxum quemdam ad esse causati*)."[15] Causality is influx of being, it implies an ontological dependence and substantial diversity of the effect with respect to the cause. Causes are called "those on which things depend in their being or becoming" (*In I Phys.*, lect. 1,5). Not every principle has, however, such an "influence" on the being of that which is principled; a first term of motion, for example, is a "principle," but it is not a "cause."

"Those are said to be the principles and causes of natural things from which they *are* and *come to be* 'per se.'" In the knowledge of causes, philosophy intends clarification of being; through the principles and the causes, the becoming, the being, and the operations of things are rendered intelligible. The order of the universe is woven together by the order and connection of causes (*De verit.* 11,1). And because in knowledge the knower is conformed to the known, the ultimate perfection which man can attain according to the philosophers is that in him "is described the whole order of the universe and its causes."[16]

In book I of his *Physica* and *Metaphysica* Aristotle investigates the view of those who have philosophized before him. They seem without exception to have thought in too restricted a sense about the causes of what is. The first philosophers staked everything on material principles. The Platonists regarded natural things as mathematical entities because they ignored the principle and end of movement.[17] Thomas recapitulates the gist of Aristotle's analysis in an exposition of his own in *In II Phys.*, lect. 10,240. The causal influx of being yields to four-fold differentiation. For the being of whatever has a cause can be considered in two ways. First,

---

id a quo imponitur ad significandum, videatur a prioritate sumptum; non tamen significat prioritatem, sed *"originem."*

[15] *In V Metaph.*, lect. 1,751. For the Neoplatonic background of this terminology, see, for example, *In De causis* prop. 1: Omnis causa primaria plus est *influens* super suum causatum quam causa secunda universalis.

[16] *De verit.* 2,2. Thomas continues: In quo etiam finem ultimum hominis posuerunt, qui secundum nos, erit in visione Dei (cf. 1.9.).

[17] *In I Metaph.*, lect. 17,259: Sed Platonicis praetermittentibus huiusmodi causas facta sunt naturalia, ac si essent mathematica sine motu, dum principium et finem motus praetermittebant. Cf. lect. 12,182; lect. 15,226.

it can be considered in an absolute manner: then the cause of being is the "form" by virtue of which something *is* in act. Secondly, it can be considered insofar as it receives being, that is, insofar as it *comes to be* in act from potency. Now, everything that is in potency is actualized by something that is already actual. From this it follows that there must be two other causes as well: the "matter" and the "agent." The action of the latter tends towards something determinate, for every agent effects what is suitable to it. That towards which the operation of the agent tends is called the "final cause." "Therefore, there must be four causes (*Sic igitur necesse est esse causas quatuor*)."

This doctrine of the four causes is so well known, yes has become so hackneyed, that to explicate it seems superfluous. Yet it is striking that all attention is generally focussed on the fourfold differentiation;[18] the ground on which these causes concur is not explicitly thought.

From Thomas's summary it appears that the differentiation of the causes is attuned to substances, which have matter and hence bear within themselves the possibility of becoming and change. Immaterial substances are, as pure forms, "absolute."[19] It is therefore of importance that in the second basic text "another mode of causing" is sought precisely for these immaterial substances. The motives underlying the *alius modus causandi* can be dealt with systematically only later; yet the vindication as such can mean nothing other than that causality itself, the influx of being, is in its own turn thought and motivated from a deeper "originality"—by which we mean the 'archè' or principle to which thought owes its direction and things their meaning and being. If this (tentative) inference is correct, then the origin meant must appear from the very outset, at least implicitly, in the progress of the desire to know.

1.3. *"All that can be questioned or known can be reduced to four questions"*

The origin of philosophy is wonder at that which is, an ignorance but at the same time a desire to know. The first form in which this desire expresses itself is questioning.

The metaphysical importance of the question has been pointed out by

---

[18] Thus, for example, J. Hirschberger, *Geschichte der Philosophie*, vol. I (Basel, Freiburg, and Vienna, 1974), p. 185: "Aristoteles nähert sich dem Sein *von vier Gesichtspunkten her* (italics added, J.A.A.), den vier ersten Ursachen oder Prinzipien, und versteht unter letzteren, was auch noch Thomas von Aquin damit meint, nämlich 'das, woraus etwas irgendwie hervorgeht.'"

[19] Thomas himself remarks here (*In II Phys.*, lect. 10,240): Sed quia forma est causa essendi absolute, aliae vero tres sunt causae essendi secundum quod aliquid accipit esse; inde est quod in immobilibus non considerantur aliae tres causae, sed solum causa formalis.

RAHNER especially, following HEIDEGGER. "Man questions. This is something final and irreducible." This irreducible fact in human existence contains its ontological turn within itself. "But this necessity can only be grounded in the fact that being is accessible to man at all only as something questionable, that he himself *is* insofar as he *asks about being*, that he himself exists as a question about being."[20] Thomas's way of thought, too, commences with questioning, but with a different accent. Man questions because he is not yet that which he ought to be. Questioning is based on an imperfection, the nonidentity with the good that is suitable to him. Through wondering inquiry, in which man manifests himself as man, a way to knowledge is opened: *de his quaestiones facimus, quae ignoramus (In II Post. Anal.*, lect. 1,408).

This opening, this room needs to be used in a certain manner: it requires questions which interrogate being in a specific direction. The question posed must be "worthy of being known." In the second book of the *Posteriora Analytica*, "philosophical" questioning is systematized. All that can be questioned or known (*quidquid est quaeribile vel scibile*) can—so we read in Thomas's commentary—be reduced to four questions: the "that" question (*quia*): Is it a fact that it is such? the "why" question (*propter quid*): Why is it such? the "if" question (*si est* or *an est*): If it is? and the "what" question (*quid est*): What is it?[21]

The first two questions are complex; they concern a composition of a subject and a predicate. Thus we pose the "that" question when we ask if a certain thing is "this" or "that"—for example, if man is an animal. The moment we know that it is so, we ask "Why?" The latter two questions are simple. For example, when we inquire concerning whether a centaur is or not, then the question is simply whether it exists. The moment the existence is affirmed, the subsequent question becomes "What is it?" "These then and so many are the things we ask; and when we have found the answer, we are said to know scientifically (*scire*)."[22]

There is an intrinsic connection between these questions on the one side and science and causality on the other. When Aristotle wants to show that there are no more than the four causes enumerated, he is satisfied to point out that the "why" question is answered only by these.[23] All men desire to know. Those who know the cause and the "why" are more knowing (*scientiores*) than those who only know the "that."[24]

To gain insight into the motives of this desire to know, it will therefore

[20] *Spirit in World* (Montreal, 1968), p. 57.
[21] *In II Post. Anal.*, lect. 1,408. Cf. *In VII Metaph.*, lect. 17,1651.
[22] *In II Post. Anal.*, lect. 1,409–11.
[23] *In II Phys.*, lect. 10,239.
[24] *In I Metaph.*, lect. 1,24.

be useful to clarify the structure, presuppositions, and sense of this questioning in a detailed analysis. The basis for it is provided by *In II Post. Anal.*, lect. 1 and *In VII Metaph.*, lect. 17. The close coherence between these two texts is in itself an indication of the onto-logical character of that which is sought.

1.3.1. *Every question is in a certain sense a 'quaestio medii'*

In the beginning of the second book of the *Post. Anal.* (90 a 5), Aristotle claims: "every question is a question of the middle term (*medium*)." This statement seems odd at first glance, but implicitly it indicates the framework that is determinative for the finality and structure of questioning: *demonstrative* knowledge.

After "to know" has been defined in *In I Post. Anal.*, lect. 4 in terms of causality, truth, and necessity, the text continues: "to know" is the end or the effect of the demonstrative syllogism; "to know" is, namely, nothing other than having insight, through demonstration, into the truth of a conclusion. Demonstration is a syllogism that produces scientific knowledge.

That of which knowledge is sought through a demonstrative proof is a conclusion, in which something is predicated of something, or more precisely: in which an essential property is predicated of a subject. Scientifically knowable in the proper sense are the conclusions of demonstrations, in which necessary properties are predicated of subjects (*proprie scibilia dicuntur conclusiones demonstrationum, in quibus passiones praedicantur de propriis subiectis*).[25]

The knowledge of the conclusion follows from the knowledge of the principles, which function as premises. Science has what one might call an "*ex*"-structure, the structure of being "out of" or from something; it concerns conclusions deduced from principles: "*scientia, quae est de conclusionibus deductis ex principiis immediatis*" (*In II Metaph.*, lect. 4,325). Because science means to know the cause, truth, and necessity of the thing, demonstrative knowledge must proceed *ex veris*, *ex primis*, and *ex immediatis*, from propositions that are true, primary, and im-medi-ate, which is to say, that are not proven by a middle but that are self-evident; further, *ex notioribus*, *ex prioribus*, and *ex causis*, from the better known, the prior, and the causes of the conclusion.[26] The demonstrative syl-logism would never effect scientific knowledge if the 'logoi' were not of this nature.

---

[25] *In I Post. Anal.*, lect. 10,89; *Post. Anal.* I, 7, 75 a 42; *In I Post. Anal.*, lect. 2,14: Id cuius scientia per demonstrationem quaeritur, est conclusio aliqua in qua propria passio de subiecto aliquo praedicatur: quae quidem conclusio ex aliquibus principiis infertur.

[26] *In I Post. Anal.*, lect. 4,37.

In cap. 1 of the second book of the *Post. Anal.* Aristotle begins the inquiry concerning the principles of the scientific syllogism. That whereby it is demonstrated that a predicate necessarily belongs to a subject is the middle term of the syllogism. The 'medium' of the proof is the reason for the composition of the subject with a predicate in the conclusion.

It is at this moment that Aristotle establishes the connection with "questioning." "In demonstrations, a middle is employed in order to make known something concerning which there might be doubt or question" (lect. 1,407). For demonstrative knowledge is acquired about that which was previously unknown. Now, concerning that which we do not know, we pose questions which are reducible to the four mentioned earlier. The posing of questions, as becomes clear, serves to carry us back to the logically prior.

Only from this perspective does it become understandable that Aristotle can argue that what *all* four questions have in common is their inquiring concerning the middle term of the syllogism: *Omnis quaestio est quodammodo quaestio medii.* [27] In a certain sense (*quodammodo*)—on Thomas's nuance; for while inquiry is indeed made concerning the middle term, it is not made according to the form of the question but as a consequence (*ex consequenti*) of it. When we ask, for example, whether the sun is eclipsed, we do not inquire as such whether there is a middle. Yet, whenever the question is answered affirmatively, it follows that a middle term can be found to demonstrate what is asked. In this "medi-ation" towards demonstrative knowledge, the "that" and "if" questions are to be taken together on the one hand: they ask whether there is a middle; on the other hand the "why" and "what" questions are to be taken together: both inquire concerning what the middle is, the reason of the asked. [28]

Why is it a "consequence" that the questions bear upon the middle term? It is a consequence because, so Thomas says, they all pose the question concerning the *cause*. The cause is the middle term in the demonstration that produces knowledge; for 'scire' is knowing the cause of the thing. And what is sought in all four questions is the cause. [29] Science is knowledge "from" the cause.

---

[27] *In II Post. Anal.*, 2,418; 1,417.

[28] *S.c.G.* III, 50, Adhuc: Sicut se habet quaestio propter quid ad quaestionem quia, ita se habet quaestio quid est ad quaestionem an est; nam quaestio propter quid quaerit medium ad demonstrandum quia est aliquid, puta quia luna eclipsatur; et similiter quaestio quid est quaerit medium ad demonstrandum an est.

[29] *Post. Anal.* B,c.2,90 a 6–7; *In II Post. Anal.*, lect. 1,414: Manifestum est enim quod causa est medium in demonstratione, quae facit scire, quia scire est causam rei cognoscere. Causa autem est quod quaeritur in omnibus praedictis quaestionibus; *Ibid.*, lect. 9,491: Quia scire opinamur cum sciamus causam ..., demonstratio autem est syllogismus faciens scire; ita consequens est quod medium demonstrationis sit causa.

From the analysis as it has been carried through to this point, what
stands out first is the close connection between questioning and the deductive structure of knowledge. The objective of questioning is to arrive at
scientific certainty concerning an effect through a resolution ("analytica") to the prior, to the principles, that is, to the conditions mentioned
earlier in this section.[30] In this re-duction logical anteriority *(medium)* and
onto-logical anteriority *(causa)* interpenetrate.

1.3.2. *The "katallel" structure of questioning and of the being "questionable"*

Knowable in the strict sense is a conclusion in which something is predicated of something, the subject. The question as question is closely tied
to this structure of science. Thomas's commentary on *Metaph.* VII is illuminating in this respect. "To ask something about something other *(aliquid de alio)* is to ask something" (lect. 17, 1664); the question asks why
something is predicated of something other (Greek: *kat'allou; Metaph.* VII,
4, 1030 a 11). Questioning possesses, as R. Boehm formulates it with
reference to the Greek terminology, a "katallel" structure.[31]

The posing of a question takes place in a com-position of two non-
identical moments, which particularly finds expression in the complex
"that" and "why" questions. "To ask why a thing is itself, for example,
why man is man, is to ask nothing" (lect. 17, 1651). For what never can
be ignored is that everything is identical with itself and therefore can be
predicated of itself.

Composition as the condition for questioning "presupposes" something (the subject) about which "something other" is asked. This subject must have been established before the causal reduction to the prior
starts: "in every question in which it is asked "why," there must be
something which is evident *(manifestum)* and something which has to be
sought *(quaesitum)* and which is not evident" *(Ibid.,* 1651). What is manifest is confirmed by the "that" question. Whenever we ask, "Why is
the moon eclipsed?" it must be evident that there is an eclipse. Questioning is only possible with respect to what is, to a being: "then something is asked, when a question is posed about that which is *(de eo quod
est)*"(1665).

---

[30] In the prologue to his commentary on the *Post. Anal.,* Thomas writes: Pars autem
Logicae, quae primo deservit processui (sc. rationis), pars *Iudicativa* dicitur, eo quod
iudicium est cum certitudine scientiae. Et quia iudicium certum de effectibus haberi non
potest nisi resolvendo in prima principia, ideo pars haec *Analytica* vocatur, idest
resolutoria.
[31] *Das Grundlegende und das Wesentliche, Zu Aristoteles' Abhandlung "Über das Sein und das
Seiende" (Metaphysik Z)* (The Hague, 1965), especially pp. 177ff.

Conversely, being, to be "questionable," must itself be understood as composite, as proportional to the structure of "something of something."[32] What is questionable is characterized by a composition. Composed being is "later" than its components. In questioning, this intrinsic composition is "resolved" into the prior and the simple; that is, it is reduced to the cause of the composite's being. The "why" question asks "why something belongs (*inest*) to something other" (1650). Sometimes the "why" question inquires about the cause which is the form in matter, namely, the formal cause (1656), and sometimes about the cause of the form in matter, namely, the efficient and the final cause (1657). In this progress, three things become quite clear.

First, it corroborates that the "katallel" structure of questioning envisions the structure of being itself in its nonidentity. Now, there are many forms of composition.[33] But they all go back to one and the same scheme. The composition is that of something under-lying (*subjectum, substantia, suppositum*) with "something other." This "other," which is asked of the "subject"—taken in a broad sense and as such as applicable to both actual and potential being (matter)[34]—is the form: "the concept of form stands over against that of subject."[35]

Secondly (and that is directly linked to the previous observation), we see that in the reduction to the cause by means of the "why" question, the entire fabric of the four causes is, indeed, at issue, but the focus is on the composition "form in matter." What remains presupposed is an ontological subject.

Thirdly, the limits of this questioning become manifest, precisely because it is restricted to composed being. In the case of a simple substance, there is no room for any question. This conclusion is drawn explicitly:

> He [Aristotle] draws a corollary from what is stated. Since in all questions something is asked about something (*aliquid de aliquo*), as about the cause of matter, which is the formal cause, or about the cause of the form in matter, namely, the final and the efficient cause, it is clear that with regard to simple substances, which are not composed of matter and form, there is no question (possible) (*non est aliqua quaestio*).[36]

---

[32] See E. Tugendhat, *TI KATA TINOS, Eine Untersuchung zu Struktur und Ursprung aristotelischer Grundbegriffe* (Freiburg and Munich, 1958), pp. 5ff.

[33] *De verit.* 16,1 ad 16: Compositio philosophica et naturalis est multiplex. Cf. the many forms of "composition" that are denied of God in *S. Th.* I,3.

[34] *In II De anima*, lect. 1,220: Ut accipiatur hic large subjectum, non solum prout subjectum dicitur aliquid ens actu, per quem modum accidens dicitur in subjecto, sed etiam secundum quod materia prima, quae est ens in potentia, dicitur subjectum; *In VII Metaph.*, lect. 13,1568; *De principiis naturae*, c.1.

[35] *De spirit. creat.* q.un.,a.1 ad 1.

[36] *In VII Metaph.*, lect. 17,1669: Infert quoddam corollarium ex dictis; dicens quod ex

1.3.3. *The "katallel" structure of the "what" question*

The complex "that" and "why" questions satisfy of themselves the katallel structure of questioning, because they have a subject and predicate.[37] But what about the "if" and "what" questions, in which we are primarily interested? Were they not both typified as "simple questions"?

In the first lectio of *Post. Anal.* II (412), the distinction between the complex and simple questions is underscored by a reference to generation— that reference is, as we shall see later (chapter 3), not merely an illustration but a comparison that is exemplary for the origination to which this thought is oriented. When a man becomes white, then it is not said that he is generated absolutely but only that he is generated in a certain respect (*secundum quid*). Similarly, the statement "man is white" signifies not the being of man in its entirety but being something. When, however, a man comes "to be," then it is said that he is generated as such; similarly, by the statement "man is," his being is signified absolutely. The "if" and "what" questions pertain to being as such.

They are therefore the fundamental questions and belong to the domain of the philosopher, who considers being as being. Every particular science supposes (*supponit*) of its subject that and what it is and demonstrates from this knowledge the properties that belong to the subject.[38] The question "What is nature?" (*quid est natura*) is accordingly not a "physical" question but an ontological one, which in natural science is supposed as known.[39]

That the "katallel" structure, which first makes the question as question possible, causes a difficulty with respect to the "what" question (*quid est*) is signalized expressly in *In VII Metaph.*, lect. 17 (1662). That in every question "something" is asked "of something other" seems doubtful with regard to questions in which not "something" is predicated of "something other"—the Greek text uses the term "katallèloos" (1041 a 33). The question "What is man?" namely, concerns one simple

---

quo in omnibus quaestionibus quaeritur aliquid de aliquo, sicut de materiae causa, quae est formalis vel causa formae in materia, ut finis et agens; palam est, quod in substantiis simplicibus, quae non sunt compositae ex materia et forma, non est aliqua quaestio.

[37] They can be brought to knowledge by means of the two types of demonstration, which are called *demonstratio quia* and *propter quid*. See *Post. Anal.* I, c. 13 (lect. 23).

[38] *In VI Metaph.*, lect. 1,1151: Eiusdem scientiae est determinare quaestionem *an est*, et manifestare *quid est*. Oportet enim quod quid est accipere ut medium ad ostendendum an est. Et *utraque est consideratio philosophi, qui considerat ens inquantum ens*. Et ideo quaelibet scientia particularis supponit de subiecto suo, quia est, et quid est, ut dicitur in I Post. (see *In I Post. Anal.*, lect. 2).

For the notion of 'suppositio' in science, see *In I Post. Anal.*, lect. 5,50.

[39] This is affirmed very clearly in *In VIII Phys.*, lect. 5,1006.

thing (*de aliquo uno simplici*); the subject, or supposit, to which it belongs to be a man is not expressed. It is therefore necessary to "correct" such a question; otherwise it would seem that nothing is being asked (*Ibid.*, 1664).

This correction consists in the transformation into the katallel structure. The "what" question, too, analyzes a composition, is directed to something other of something, the subject; it does not inquire from the subject away towards something that is separate from it. "What is it?" can be transformed into "Why is it?" For the "what" question inquires why that about which this question is asked is predicated of each of its subjects. "What is man?" is identical to asking: "Why is this, namely Socrates, man?" In the mediation towards scientific knowledge, the "why" and "what" questions do, in a certain sense (see also 2.2.3.), coincide (*Ibid.*, 1663). A distinction remains insofar as the composition that is brought to unity is of a different character. Knowledge of the "what" question concerns the being as such of something, not the inherence of a property in a subject.[40]

If the question "What is?" can be transformed into the katallel structure, then here, too, "something" must be presupposed of which "something other" is asked.[41] That which is presupposed must be evident and is disclosed through the question "if it is." Whenever it is asked "What is man?" then it must be known that man truly exists (otherwise nothing would be asked). "Being" is presupposed for the "what" question (*esse est praesuppositum ad hoc quod quaeritur quid est; ibid.*, 1666).

There is this definite order: "the question concerning 'what' something is follows upon the question concerning 'if' something is."[42] The causal reduction can only effect clarification of being after a confirmation of being. There is science only of that which is (*S. Th.* III, 10, 3). Thomas, too, follows this way: "The knowledge whereby something can be known is twofold. By the one, one knows of the thing 'if it is' . . . By the other 'what it is.'"[43]

He who poses the "what" question already knows: "Whenever we know if it is, we ask what it is."[44] Before proceeding to inquire more precisely into the sense of the "what" question, our analysis must therefore

---

[40] *In II Post. Anal.*, lect. 1,417: Scire *quid est*, refertur ad scientiam qua scimus de aliquo quod simpliciter sit, non autem quod aliquid insit alicui; sed *propter quid* refertur ad cognitionem eorum quae insunt.

[41] *In VII Metaph.*, lect. 17,1665.

[42] *In IV Phys.*, lect. 10,507.

[43] *De verit.* 18,5.

[44] *In II Post. Anal.*, lect. 1,412; 411: Scientes de aliquo *quia* est simpliciter, quaerimus *quid* sit illud.

focus first on the "if" question, which sets in motion the desire to know the cause. "Those who know if something is desire by nature to know what it is."[45]

1.3.4. The "if" question ('an est') and the order of questioning

According to M.-D. PHILIPPE the most fundamental question for Thomas, following Aristotle, is the "if" question. The other questions are founded on this one.[46] Yet is this judgement in agreement with the finality of this questioning? Is the question "if it is" really the fundamental one? For an answer we have to investigate thoroughly what is affirmed by way of the "if" question, in three respects. First, with respect to the nature of the "being" that is affirmed—all the more so since in exegeses of Thomas's thought, ontological maxims that fail to do justice to the complexity of Thomas's expositions on this point are rather easily linked to the distinction, so characteristic of the Aristotelian conception of science, between the "if" and "what" questions;[47] secondly, with respect to the nature of the knowledge that something is; and, thirdly, with respect to what it is in this affirmation that motivates the order of questioning noted in the preceding section, the progression to the "what" question.

(1) In the second book of the *Posteriora Analytica* Aristotle says only this: "Whenever we know if something is, we ask what it is." The "if" question is twice dismissed in this manner in passing.[48] Thomas speaks more extensively of it in various loci in his writings and places the answer to the question *an est* within a dichotomy of being, namely, extra-mental and intra-mental being.[49]

'Ens' or 'esse' (in this context Thomas uses the terms indifferently) is said in two ways. In a first way it signifies "the entity of the thing according to its division by the ten categories" (*S. Th.* I, 48, 2 ad 2); "the essence of the thing or the act of being" (*De pot.* 7, 2 ad 1); "the nature of the

---

[45] *S.c.G.* III, 50: Videmus autem quod videntes naturaliter quia est aliquid, scire desiderant propter quid; ergo et cognoscentes an aliquid sit, naturaliter scire desiderant quid est ipsum . . .

[46] M.-D. Philippe, "Analyse de l'être chez saint Thomas," in *Atti del Congresso Intern. (Roma-Napoli, 12–24 aprile 1974) Tommaso d'Aquino nel suo settimo centenario*, vol. 6 (Naples, n. d.), p. 16.

[47] J.J. Sanguineti, *La filosofía de la ciencia según Santo Tomás* (Pamplona, 1977), p. 320: "La composición de ser y esencia en los entes se traduce en la ciencia en la dualidad y mutua pertenencia de la cuestion del *an est* y del *quid est*."

[48] 89 b 38–90 a 1; 90 a 8ff.

[49] See *S. Th.* I, 3, 4 ad 2 and 48, 2 ad 2; *S.c.G.* III, 9; *De pot.* 7, 2 ad 1; *De malo* 1, 1 ad 19; *Quodl.* IX, 2, 2; *De ente*, c. 1; *In I Sent.* 19, 5, 1; *In II Sent.* 34, 1, 1; *In V Metaph.*, lect. 9.

ten genera" (*De malo* 1, 1 ad 19); "what is divided by the ten genera, and so being signifies something existing in nature, whether a substance, such as man, or an accident, such as color" (*In II Sent.*, 34, 1, 1); and "what is outside the soul (*extra animam*), divided by the ten categories" (*In V Metaph.*, lect. 9, 889). In a second way "being" signifies what is "only in the mind" (*ibid.*); means "the truth of a proposition that exists in a composition the mark of which is the verb 'is'" (*S. Th.* I, 48, 2 ad 2). And this text continues: "In this sense being is what answers the question "if something is'" (*hoc est ens quo respondetur ad quaestionem 'an est?'*). Similarly, in *De malo* 1, 1 ad 19: "being" is said in a second way, "according as it answers the 'if' question."

In keeping with these two modes, "being" (*ens*) is predicated in different ways. When it is taken in the first way, it is a substantial predicate and belongs to the "what" question. For the being that each thing has in its own nature is substantial: "And therefore when it is said that Socrates is, if the 'is' is taken in the first way, it belongs to the class of substantial predicates; for being is a higher predicate with reference to any (particular) being, as animal with reference to man." Being is a "higher" predicate because it is more general; it is that which is divided by the ten categories. If "being" is taken, however, in the second way, it is an accidental predicate—here Thomas adopts an idea from Averroes' commentary on the *Metaphysica*—and belongs to the "if" question. This "being" is purely in the mind, which joins a predicate to a subject: the proposition "x is" is true.[50]

The reasons for this distinction become clear especially when attention is given to the problems it means to resolve.

What "is" according to the first way is also "being" according to the second mode; for an affirmative proposition—e.g., "man is"—can be formed about whatever has natural being. Yet the reverse is not the case. Whatever is in itself a non-being, such as a privation, can be regarded as a being by the intellect and affirmed in a statement—e.g., "evil is." This does not imply, however, that evil is something in reality, that is, *is* according to the first mode of "being."[51] The possibility of affirming

---

[50] *In II Sent.* 34, 1, 1: Ens autem secundum utrumque istorum modorum diversimode praedicatur: quia secundum primum modum acceptum, est *praedicatum substantiale*, et pertinet ad quaestionem "*quid est?*" Sed quantum ad secundum modum est *praedicatum accidentale*, ut Commentator dicit, et pertinet ad quaestionem "*an est?*"; In III Sent. 6, 2, 2; *In V Metaph.*, lect. 9,896: Esse vero, quod in sui natura unaquaeque res habet, est substantiale. Et ideo, cum dicitur "Socrates est," si ille "est" primo modo accipiatur, est de *praedicato substantiali*. Nam ens est superius ad unumquodque entium, sicut animal ad hominem. Si autem accipiatur secundo modo est de *praedicato accidentali*.
For the reference to "the Commentator," see *Averrois in librum V Metaphysicorum Aristotelis Commentarius*, ed. R. Ponzalli (Bern, 1971), c. 7, 132.
[51] *In I Sent.* 34, 1, 1; *In V Metaph.*, lect. 9, 896; *De ente*, c. 1.

privations and negations is therefore a first reason to regard the answer
to the question "if it is" as a purely logical, predicative synthesis.

A still more important motive becomes apparent at the beginning of the
Summa Theologiae. After Thomas in q.1 has shown that sacred doctrine is
a science, he asks and affirms in the very first place (q.2), in conformity
with the order of questioning: "if God exists" (*an sit Deus*). When it is subsequently inquired in q.3, art.4 whether 'essentia' and 'esse' are identical
in God, then the objection arises (obj.2): "We can know 'if God is', as
has been explained above. 'What He is', however, we cannot know.
Therefore there is a nonidentity between God's being (*esse*) and his essence
(*quod quid est eius*)." To this objection Thomas responds with the dichotomy of "being" just mentioned. It may mean the act of being, or it may
mean the composition of a proposition effected by the mind in joining a
predicate to a subject. Taking "being" in the first sense, we cannot understand God's being; but only in the second sense.[52] This reply raises,
however, various questions. Let us have a closer look at it.

In the first place, the objection suggests that the "if" and "what"
questions imply a composition of "being" (*esse*) and "essence" in that
which can be questioned. In 1.3.2., however, we saw that this questioning
was, indeed, restricted to composed things, but then to a thing that is
characterized by the composition of form and matter. What would have
to be explained first, therefore, is how the order of the questions is related
to the composition of 'esse' and 'essentia' (cf. 1.9.).

From this remark there follows directly a second point that is usually
give too little consideration. The preliminary question must be whether
this mode of questioning is at all possible with respect to God. Are the limits of this questioning not overstepped in the question "if God exists?"
For with regard to a simple being, there is no room for any question
(1.3.2.).

After drawing this corollary in his commentary on the *Metaph*. (VII,
lect. 17, 1671), Thomas adds that what is required here is another mode
of questioning (*alter modus quaestionis*). For we come to knowledge of simple
substances only from the sensible ones, of which the first are in a certain
sense the causes. "Therefore we make use of sensible substances as that
which is known, and through them we inquire concerning the simple
substances." That is precisely the method that Thomas follows in his

---

[52] *S. Th.* I, 3, 4 ad 2: Esse dupliciter dicitur: uno modo, significat actum essendi; alio
modo, significat compositionem propositionis, quam anima adinvenit coniungens praedicatum subiecto. Primo igitur modo accipiendo esse, non possumus scire esse Dei, sicut
nec eius essentiam; sed solum secundo modo. Scimus enim quod haec propositio quam
formamus de Deo, cum dicimus: Deus est, vera est.

"ways" to the existence of God. It must, however, be realized that this mode of questioning is not the "analysis" of an *inner* composition but the reduction to the *extrinsic* cause of sensible things. In Thomas's reply the important structural difference between the two modes of questioning is by-passed, so that the necessity arises to regard the answer to the "if" question as, simply, propositional truth.

Two considerations evidently lead Thomas to reduce the answer to "if" question to something purely mental (*Quodl.* IX, 2, 2: *tantum in actu animae componentis et dividentis*), namely, the affirmation of privations, which are not "something"; and the affirmation of immaterial substances, of which the being-something is unknown to us. With regard to both, it is accordingly impossible to ask: "What is it?"

From this negative conclusion there results an important positive insight: as question, the "if" cannot be separated from the "what" *onto-logically*. But this implies that in both the cases mentioned, the "if" question fails to reach its end. The affirmation of negations and of immaterial substances would therefore have to be distinguished expressly from an affirmation in which the sense of the "if" question is really fulfilled.

Such is the case whenever what is affirmed is not merely an accidental predicate, but means "being" in the first way, which is already connected with the "what" question. One can affirm that "evil is"—insofar as answer is given to the "if" question—but this does not mean that evil is "something," because "being something signifies *not only* what answers to the 'if' question *but also* what answers to the 'what' question" (*De malo* 1, 1 ad 19). The sense of the 'if' question (*an est*) is to manifest the subject as 'ens', as "that which is," a substantial predicate, a "being something" that has its sequel in the "what" question.

(2) Wonder at that which is is the motive of the desire to know: the causes of what is seen are hidden from us. The desire to dispel this ignorance expresses itself in questions in which inquiry is made into the cause.

The question "if something is" may be regarded as an attempt by Aristotle to provide a place for initial wondering in the system of science. *Omnis quaestio est quoddammodo quaestio medii* (1.3.1.). *Every* question, also the "if" question, serves the seeking of the middle term, a search that is only completed in the knowledge of the "what" (*quod quid est*). Upon this "what" is centered the entire inquiry in the *Posteriora Analytica*. M.-D. PHILIPPE's view that the question *an est* is the fundamental one must be considered to be incorrect; the finality of *this* questioning is a reduction of that which is to the logically and onto-logically prior. The relation of the "if" question to the "what" question is understood as that of effect to cause: *Idem est scire quid est, et scire causam quaestionis an est.* The reason for this identity is that there must be a cause of the fact that the thing is.[53]

Yet demonstrative knowledge is not the framework within which the answer to the "if" is revealed. It is significant that the question *an est* is not really thematized as question in the *Posteriora Analytica*. The knowledge "if it is" is an im-medi-ate experience of the sensible, that puts one onto the way towards science, towards the causes of what is *seen*.[54]

An sit natura? In the first lectio of *Phys.* II Thomas comments: it is manifest for the senses that many things are by nature. It is ridiculous, he adds, if anyone attempts to prove this existence; one who would do that is "uncritical," that is, lacks the capacity to distinguish a truth that is known by itself from what is grasped only through rational inquiry. One who would demonstrate that nature is treats a self-evident beginning as if it were an unknown terminus. Whoever does not *see* that nature is is as one born blind who reasons about the harmony of colors. And there are those who are blind to 'physis', not by birth but by "logical" closedness to the phenomena (cf. 6.1.).

"That" nature is is self-evident (*per se notum*) insofar as natural things are manifest to the senses. But what the nature of each thing is is not evident. This ignorance raises the decisive, properly philosophical question concerning "what" nature is.[55]

(3) This order of questioning is not itself called further into question. For what is affirmed in the "if" question belongs already to "what" something is: being as substantial predicate. This is likewise, however, the most general that can be predicated of something, and it therefore stands open for determination: "What is it that is?" The "if," as question and answer, is ordered from the outset to the "what." The relation between the two questions is sometimes such that we know that a thing is without knowing *perfectly* what it is; sometimes we know both at the same time. However, a third possibility is excluded, namely, that we should know "what something is" and be ignorant "if it is" (*tertium est impossibile, ut scilicet sciamus quid est, ignorantes si est; In II Post. Anal.*, lect. 7, 474).

---

[53] *In II Post. Anal.*, lect. 7, 471.

[54] Thomas states categorically in *In III Sent.* 23, 1, 2: Similiter *an res sit*, tripliciter cognoscit. Uno modo quia cadit sub sensu. Alio modo ex causis et effectibus rerum cadentibus sub sensu, sicut ignem ex fumo perpendimus. Tertio modo cognoscit aliquid in seipso esse ex inclinatione quam habet ad aliquos actus.

With regard to the standard example for the questions, the solar eclipse, it is said in *In I Post. Anal.*, lect. 6, 54: Quaedam conclusiones sunt quae sunt notissimae, utpote per sensum acceptae, sicut quod 'sol eclipsetur'. Cf. *In II Post. Anal.*, lect. 1, 412.

[55] *In II Phys.*, lect. 1, 148: Naturam autem esse, est per se notum, inquantum naturalia sunt manifesta sensui. *Sed quid sit uniuscuiusque rei natura,* ... hoc non est manifestum. ... Sed ignorantia ... non impedit quin naturam esse sit per se notum, ut dictum est.

The sense of the "if" question is fulfilled in the manifestation of the first mode of "being," which is divided by the ten categories, the categorical being. This is further qualified as "natural being" (*In II Sent.* 34, 1, 1); and as "being that each thing has in its nature" (*In V Metaph.*, lect. 9, 896). *That* being is established in this sense, namely, as categorical and natural being, is something primary; it accordingly cannot be understood in any other way than as its originality. And this primacy determines the room and the direction in which this being can be questioned. For *because* being is established in this sense, the reduction of that which is to its cause occurs in and through the question: "What is it?"

1.4. *The sense of the "what" question ('quid est')*

The "what" question possesses a certain ambiguity that needs to be cleared away, especially with respect to that which is questioned in the first basic text, nature. For it is precisely the modern, extensional concept of nature that interferes with the original philosophical sense of the "what" question.

1.4.1. *"The 'what' question . . . sometimes inquires into the supposit"*

"What . . . ?" can be taken in two different manners—in modern terminology, it can be taken as reference or it can be taken as sense. "Sometimes it inquires into the supposit (*suppositum*), as when we ask 'What swims in the sea?' and answer: 'A fish.' "[56] The question refers to a concrete and visible subject. And this appeal to observation is usually envisioned in the case of nature as well. "What is nature? Nature is that which we observe in perception through the senses," according to the English philosopher Whitehead.[57] It is the object of the senses. For Kant, too, in his *Metaphysische Anfangsgründe der Naturwissenschaft*, nature—"taken in the *material* sense"—is "the whole of all things, insofar as they can be objects of our senses, and thus also of experience."[58]

In nonphilosophical usage "nature" is employed equally frequently in a collective sense. When, for example, Baudelaire is asked to contribute to an anthology on "Nature," he writes: "My dear Desnoyers, you ask me for verses on Nature, is it not so? On the woods, the great oaks,

---

[56] *In I Sent.* 23, 1, 3 ad 4: "Quid" . . . quando quaerit ipsum suppositum, ut cum quaeritur, quid natat in mari? Piscis respondetur.
Similarly in *S. Th.* I, 29, 4 ad 2.
[57] A.N. Whitehead, *The Concept of Nature* (Cambridge, 1920), p. 3.
[58] Immanuel Kant, *Werke in zehn Bänden*, ed. W. Weischedel, vol. 8: *Metaphysische Anfangsgründe der Naturwissenschaft*, (Darmstadt, 1975), Foreword, p. 11.

the verdure, the insects—the sun, undoubtedly?''[59] Constitutive for this
collective concept of nature is usually the opposition to what man has cul-
tivated. From this point of view a material diversity of sensible objects is
gathered.

In his *Grundbegriffe der Physik im Wandel der Zeit* B. HELLER argues that
it is in the Middle Ages that "the concept of 'physis' with its translation
by 'natura' has been fundamentally changed." For "nature" already
means "the collective representation (*Sammelvorstellung*) of all things to be
found in the universe."[60] This assertion cannot, in its generality, be upheld. Thomas's articulation of the main senses of nature, presented in
various texts,[61] does not mention the meaning objected to. Further consideration of the "what" question can corroborate that what is questioned
is "collected" in another sense.

When it is asked in this first manner "What is (nature)?" then the
"what" (*quid*) is a "that which is" (*quod est*), and the "what" is identical
to that to which it refers. The structure of the question is a predication *per
identitatem*; the predicated is said *ratione suppositi*.[62] Yet from 1.3. it has become clear that the "what" question must not be posed in this extensional
sense; it asks in a "katallel" way, it asks something other of something
that is; the question is a reduction to the ontologically prior. As a matter
of fact, it can be inferred from the first basic text that animals, plants, and
the elements are not nature, but are "by nature" (*a natura*).

1.4.2. *"The 'what' question sometimes inquires into the essence"*

"What" asks, in a second manner, about the *essentia*.[63] This inten-
sional way of questioning was initiated by Socrates. It is the Greek mode
of questioning, which has been of decisive importance for the further
development of Western philosophy. This "maieutics" is also meant, in
a manner still to be specified (1.5.), in the "what" question with respect
to nature.

In his writing *De ente et essentia* Thomas argues that the term "essence"
cannot be derived from the intramental mode of being (*ens*), for in this
sense some things are called beings that do not have an essence, as is
clear in the case of privations. Rather, essence is derived from the mode

---

[59] As quoted by C. Pichois in "Baudelaire et la nature," in *L'Homme moderne et son
image de la nature*, ed. R. Chenu (Neuchâtel, 1974), p. 13.
[60] (Braunschweig, 1970), pp. 8–9.
[61] *In III Sent.*, 5, 1, 2; *S.c.G.* IV, 35; *S. Th.* I, 29, 1 ad 4; *De unione verbi incarnati* q.un.,
art. 1; *S. Th.* III, 2, 1. Cf. for the discussion of the senses of nature section 6.5.2., below.
[62] For this improper way of predicating, see *In III Sent.*, d. 5, *Expos. textus*.
[63] *In I Sent.* 23, 1, 3 ad 4: "Quid" quandoque quaerit essentiam, ut cum quaeritur:
Quid est homo? . . . Quando quaerit ipsum suppositum.

of being, which posits something in reality—the order of questioning carries over into the terminology. Essence is that "through which, and in
which, that which is has being."[64]

Essence, the answer to the question *quid est*, is the translation of the
Greek 'ousia', introduced by Plato as a philosophical term. As a reaction
to Plato's ontology, Aristotle's emphasis on the "katallel" structure
("something of something") precisely of the "what" question (1.3.3.),
which in itself suggests something subsistent, becomes understandable.
The essence which is inquired after is "what something was to be" (*quod
quid erat esse*)—a construction by means of which the Stagirite wants to express that the questioned is not separate from the thing but is rather "that
which it is *for* this or that to be what it is"—or as Thomas explains: "that
which makes a thing to be what it is."[65]

The direction in which the inquiry into the essence goes becomes clear
from the important Book VII of the *Metaphysica*, where Aristotle investigates the essence of the sensible substances. The Philosopher tries, so
Thomas says, to clarify this essence logically in the first instance, namely,
from the mode of predicating (*ex modo praedicandi*), an approach entirely
appropriate to the structure of questioning (cf. ch. 2, below). Not just any
predication provides a suitable answer to the "what" question. For example, if it is asked, "What is man?" one cannot respond "musician" or
"the sitting," for this is predicated of man accidentally (*per accidens*). Only
what is said *per se* belongs to the essence, the "what" of something.[66] For
in such a proposition the predicated is identical with its subject. The logical "analysis" brings an inner multiplicity of something to identity.

That logical and ontological anteriority interpenetrate in the "what"
question becomes clear in the last chapter of Book VII, where Aristotle
examines what essence "really" is (cf. ch. 3, below)—it is the same
chapter 17 that we used in 1.3. for the analysis of the structure and direction of philosophical questioning. From questioning itself it is shown that
the essence is a "principle" and "cause" of something.[67] The "what"

---

[64] *De ente*, c. 1: Ens per se dicitur dupliciter: uno modo quod dividitur per decem
genera, alio modo quod significat propositionum veritatem. ... Sed primo modo non
potest dici ens nisi quod aliquid in re ponit ... Nomen igitur essentiae non sumitur ab
ente secundo modo dicto, ... sed sumitur essentia ab ente primo modo dicto ... Sed
essentia dicitur secundum quod per eam et in ea ens habet esse.

[65] *Ibid.*, c. 1; cf. *In VII Metaph.*, lect. 3, 1310. On the complex terminology Aristotle
uses with regard to 'ousia', see J. Owens, *The Doctrine of Being in the Aristotelian Metaphysics*
(Toronto, 1963), pp. 186ff. and E. Tugendhat, *TI KATA TINOS*, pp. 13ff.

[66] *In VII Metaph.*, lect. 3, 1308f.

[67] *Ibid.*, lect. 17, 1648; 1649: Illud, de quo non quaeritur per quaestionem propter
quid, sed in ipsum alia quaesita reducuntur, oportet esse principium et causam: quaestio
enim propter quid, quaerit de causa. Sed substantia quae est quod quid erat esse, est

question is transformable into the "why" question, and "why" inquires, as we saw (1.3.2.), sometimes about the cause, which is the form in matter, and sometimes about the cause of the form in matter, namely, the efficient or final cause.

What kind of cause is meant in the "what" question? Thomas makes in his commentary a remark that is important for the sense of the question. The logician, who considers the mode of predicating, will regard all that is answered to the "what" question as the essence, whether it is intrinsic or extrinsic. But the philosopher, who inquires about the existence of things (*qui existentiam quaerit rerum*), will include only the *intrinsic* causes under the constitutive whatness (lect. 17, 1658). That is, the transformation of the "what" question is only intended in the direction of the "why," which inquires concerning formal causality: "through the formal cause, which is the substance of the thing, is known what each thing is" (*In I Metaph.*, 4, 70).

In *De ente* Thomas observes that the essence is also called "form," because form signifies the determination of each thing. Does this mean that form alone is the essence? Aristotle is not clear on this point, and as Thomas notes elsewhere, there is also a difference of opinion in the commentaries on Aristotle by Avicenna and Averroes.[68] That is connected to the fact that each composition is, indeed, conceived according to the scheme of subject and form but that the formal causality differs in proportion to the character of the "subject." Whenever this is the matter that is brought to actuality by the form, then at issue is the so-called *forma partis*, the substantial form as an integral part of the thing resulting from this composition. Whenever, on the other hand, an actual subject or supposit is reduced to its specific form, then at issue is the so-called *forma totius*, embracing form *and* matter, not, it is true, the individuating matter but the common matter. Thomas's remark that the philosopher of being includes the intrinsic causes, matter and form, under the essence, is an indication that he—with Avicenna— wishes to conceive essence in this sense of the whole. Other texts corroborate this conclusion.[69] In the "what" question, a multiplicity of particular things is reduced to a unity of essence. This essence can be designated as form in-

---

huiusmodi. Non enim quaeritur propter quid homo est homo, sed propter quid homo est aliquid aliud. Et similiter est in aliis. Ergo substantia rei, quae est quod quid erat esse, est principium et causa.

[68] Cf. *In VII Metaph.*, lect. 9, 1467–9.

[69] See especially *De ente*, c. 2. Cf. *In V Metaph.*, lect. 10, 904: Essentia enim et forma in hoc conveniunt quod secundum utrumque dicitur esse illud quo aliquid est. Sed *forma* refertur ad *materiam*, quam facit esse in actu; *quidditas* autem refertur ad *suppositum* quod significatur ut habens talem essentiam; *ibid.*, 902: Ipsa autem quidditas vel essentia rei includit omnia essentialia principia.

sofar as it is the cause of the subject "in the manner of a form" (*per modum formae*).[70]

The nonidentity of subject and essence in composed things is also indicated by Thomas with the distinction *quod est* and *quo est*[71]—a distinction inspired by Boethius. In a writing which in the Middle Ages was commonly called *De hebdomadibus*, Boethius formulated a number of propositions, the second of which is: "Being (*esse*) and that which is (*id quod est*) are different. For being itself is not yet, but that which is is and exists when it has received the form which gives it being (*forma essendi*)." "That which is" is the individual, subsisting being; "that by which something is" is the essence.[72]

One can consider this essence *in concreto*, in its concretion with the subject, in which case the essence is signified in the manner of a whole (*per modum totius*), as *quod est*, for example, "man." A concrete term contains in its concept the essential principles of something, without thereby excluding the possibility that further (accidental) principles belong to the individual subject. However, one can also consider the essence *in abstracto*, in abstraction from that which is constituted by it, in which case it is signified in the manner of a part (*per modum partis*), inasmuch as everything alien to the essence is cut away, or "prescinded."[73] An abstract term, for example, "humanity," signifies something that does not subsist but that by nature is nevertheless prior to the concrete thing, namely, the *quo est*, that whereby man is man.[74]

This raison d'être is at the same time the ground of knowability; the whatness is the "principle of knowing'," because hereby is known what the thing is. For this "in-form-ative" the term *quidditas* was coined in the Middle Ages. In the quiddity the desire to know comes to rest: "what a thing is is known when its quiddity is comprehended."[75] In the (ques-

---

[70] Cf. *S.c.G.* I, 21.

[71] *In I Sent.* 8, 5, 2: In compositis autem ex materia et forma *quo est* potest dici tripliciter. Potest enim dici "quo est" ipsa *forma partis*, quae dat esse materiae. Potest etiam dici "quo est" ipse actus essendi, scilicet esse. . . . Potest etiam dici "quo est" ipsa natura quae relinquitur ex conjunctione formae cum materia, ut humanitas; praecipue secundum ponentes quod *forma, quae est totum*, quae dicitur quidditas, non est forma partis, de quibus est Avicenna.

[72] Cf. M.D. Roland-Gosselin, *Le "De ente et essentia" de S. Thomas d'Aquin*, 2nd ed. (Le Saulchoir, 1948), pp. 142–45.

[73] In his commentary on the second proposition of *De hebdomadibus* (lect. 2), Thomas explains this distinction. See further *De ente*, c. 3; *In I Sent.* 23, 1, 1; 33, 1, 2; *Quodl.* IX, 2, 1 ad 1; *S.c.G.* I, 30; *In VII Metaph.*, lect. 5, 1378; *S.Th.* I, 13, 1 ad 2.

[74] *In III Sent.* 5, 3, 1 ad 4: Quamvis humanitas non sit sine homine, tamen est prius naturaliter quam homo, quia per eam dicitur aliquis esse homo.

[75] *In I Metaph.*, lect. 12, 183: . . . quod quid est, inquantum est principium cognoscendi, quia per eam scitur quid est res; *In III Sent.* 23, 1, 2: Quid autem res est cognoscitur, dum ipsius quidditas comprehenditur. Cf. *In Boeth. De trin.* 6, 3.

tion concerning the) quiddity is centered the (question concerning) intelligibility: *Intelligibile enim in unaquaque re est quidditas.*[76]

Of importance is that this intelligible determination is precisely the *natura* of the thing.[77] Thus Thomas can equally say that the "what" question inquires (in the second manner) into the "nature," this word taken in the first of the four senses summed up by Boethius in his *De duabus naturis*: "all that can be grasped by the intellect in any way."[78] With this last statement it is affirmed that what is here questioned appeals to another view than that of the senses. It is the insight of the intellect that attains to the "whatness" of the thing. "The proper object of the intellect is the quiddity, which is not separated from the things."[79]

What is added in the last quotation emphasizes again the "katallel" structure as an *intrinsic* feature of what is. In *Metaph.* VII, c. 6 (lect. 5) Aristotle argues that two illogicalities follow from Plato's idea that the essence is a subsisting Form. In the first place, when the science of each thing consists in its essence being known, then Plato's "hypothesis" implies that the concrete thing itself is not knowable; for the exemplary Form is extrinsic to the thing. Furthermore, how can things be being if that by which are should be separate from them? Therefore the constitutive essence is not to be sought in the direction of 'species ideales'. In order that things are and are known it is sufficient that the essence is identical with the thing itself, that they are one in being (*essendo*) and in knowing (*sciendo*).[80] Sciences concern not separate forms but the quiddities, which are in the things.[81]

---

[76] *In I De anima*, lect. 8, 116.

[77] *In VII Metaph.*, lect. 2, 1270; *S. Th.* III, 2, 1: Sic ergo nunc loquimur de natura, secundum quod natura significat essentiam, vel quod quid est, sive quidditatem speciei; *In III Sent.* 5, 1, 2.

[78] *S. Th.* I, 29, 4 ad 2: "Quid" quandoque quaerit de natura . . . ut cum quaeritur: "Quid est homo." *De ente*, c. 1: Hoc (sc., essentia) etiam alio nomine "natura" dicitur accipiendo naturam secundum primum modum illorum quattuor modorum, quos Boëthius in libro De duabus naturis assignat secundum scilicet quod natura dicitur omne illud, quod intellectu quoquo modo capi potest.

Cf. Boethius, *Contra Eutychen et Nestorium*, ed. and trans. H.F. Stewart, in Boethius, *The Theological Tractates. The Consolation of Philosophy* (London, and Cambridge, Mass., 1973), p. 78: Natura est earum rerum quae, cum sint, quoquo modo intellectu capi potest.

[79] *De verit.* 10, 6 ad 2: Intellectus vero pervenit ad nudam quidditatem rei; *In II Post. Anal.*, lect. 5, 459: Quod quid est non est obiectum sensus, sed intellectus, ut dicitur in III De Anima; *In Boeth. De trin.* 5, 2 ad 2; etc.

The basic text, which is referred to repeatedly, is *De anima* III, c. 4, 429 b 10f.; Thomas, lect. 8, 705–19, especially 717: Proprium objectum intellectus est *quidditas rei, quae non est separata a rebus.*

[80] *In VII Metaph.*, lect. 5, 1367: Ad hoc enim quod res sint scitae, et quod sint entes, hoc est sufficiens, scilicet quod quod quid erat rei sit idem cum re . . . ; 1371: Ex his itaque rationibus manifestum est, quod unum et idem non secundum accidens, unumquodque et quod quid erat esse eius. Et similiter in sciendo, idem est scire unumquodque, et scire quid est eius.

[81] *De spirit. creat.*, q.un., a.9 ad 6: Sed Plato quidem dixit scientias esse de formis separatis, Aristoteles vero de quidditatibus rerum in eis existentibus.

For the moment we have now sufficiently indicated the way of this questioning. It can be marked off as follows:

(1) The origin of philosophy is wonder at that which is seen. Wonder motivates inquiry; it is a desire for knowledge, which is sought for its own sake. Its terminus is the science of the causes.

(2) The desire to know (*desiderium sciendi*) commences with questions. The questioning is an "analytica," a resolution into the "ex"-structure of science, a re-duction to the logical and ontological prior, the origin and cause.

(3) The structure of the question is "katallel" (*aliquid de alio*); questioning occurs in a composition. Therefore this questioning is, strictly speaking, restricted to a being that is itself composed, that is characterized by the intrinsic composition of form and matter.

(4) The questions concerning the being of something can be reduced to the "if" (*an est*) and the "what" (*quid est*)—and then in this order: "the question what something is follows on the question if it is." Before the reduction to the whatness, it must be established that the thing is. There is science only of beings, of "that which is."[82]

(5) The meaning of the "if" question is fulfilled in the manifestation of being (*id quod est*) as substantial predicate, that is, of being that each thing has in its own nature. The "if" as question is substantially related to the "what"; onto-logically, it cannot be separated from the latter: What is it that is?

(6) The "what" question inquires not into something separate from the subject but into the intrinsic causes, into the *quo est*, which is the sufficient reason of something. The thing is reduced to the cause of being, to the essence. "Through it, and in it, that which is (*ens*) has being (*esse*)" (*De ente*, c. 1).

(7) This entire desire for knowledge issues in the basic question, in what was for Aristotle "the question raised of old and now and ever and that again and again embarrasses us: namely, what is being, that is, what is the essence?"[83] This finality must already be implicit in the initial wondering. The progression of the desire towards the essence is motivated from an originality which opens up the room for this direction of questioning and knowing. Is it possible to make this 'archè' more explicit? In the reduction to this origin the question *quid sit natura* turns out to be at home.

1.5. *The question: What is nature?*

The difficulty with respect to the "what" question is, as we saw

---

[82] *S. Th.* I, 44, 3 ad 3: ... scientia et definitio sint solum entium.
[83] *Metaph.* VII, 1, 1028 b 2–4.

(1.3.3.), its simplicity. It can, however, be transformed into the "why" question. For the "what" inquires why that about which this question is asked is predicated of each of its subjects. A reflection on this point can be a first step to clarify the distinctive character of the question "What is nature?" raised in the first basic text.

The fact is that this question does not yield simply to the required transformation. Already in connection with the first manner in which the "what" question inquires (1.4.1.), we observed that nature is not a predicate of certain supposits, taken separately or collectively. The impossibility of a transformation in this case is an indication that, despite lingual similarities, the question "What is nature?" differs, even in the way in which the questioned is signified, from a question such as "What is man?"

To account for this difference, we must recall the distinction made in the preceding section between concrete and abstract terms. Concrete terms signify a complete subsisting thing, a *quod est*. Because they denote a composite thing, they can be predicated of their inferiors and questioned in a "katallel" way. In contrast, abstract terms are not predicable, for they signify something not as subsisting but as that whereby a thing is.[84] They result from the "intensification" of that which is to its intelligibility. With the help of this distinction the signalized problem of transformation can be accounted for: in the question "What is nature?" nature is signified abstractly as *quo est*, as that whereby a being is a natural being.[85] Even though the abstract mode of signifying may suggest subsistence, the inquiry into the 'ratio' of nature is possible only in relation to those beings *of* which the questioned is constitutive.

This finding is of importance for indicating more substantially the distinctive character of the present question. "Of all beings, some are by nature," we read in the first basic text. What is inquired into is therefore not the nature of nature as of a subsisting thing, such as of a plant, animal or stone—albeit such reification is not unknown, as is clear from the title of Thomas's writing *De principiis naturae*. The question is directed to nature in the sense of cause and principle of (some) beings: "nature has the aspect of principle" (*natura habet rationem principii*).[86]

This originality of nature was already implied upon the way of Greek

---

[84] *S. Th.* I, 13, 1 ad 2; III, 16, 1; *In De hebdom.*, lect. 2.

[85] See, for example, *Quodl.* II, 2, 2 (ad illud vero quod in contrarium obiicitur): Natura dicitur constituere suppositum etiam in compositis ex materia et forma, non quia natura sit una res et suppositum alia res ..., sed quia secundum modum significandi natura significatur ut pars, ... suppositum vero ut totum; natura significatur ut *constituens*, et suppositum ut constitutum; *De pot.* 2, 3 ad 6: Natura intelligatur esse principium *quo* res subsistit.

[86] *In II Phys.*, lect. 2, 152; *ibid.*, lect. 1, 145: Nomen naturae importat habitudinem principii. Even stronger in *In I Sent.* 34, 2 ad 3: Natura semper habet rationem principii.

desire to know. The order of the questions, we may recall, was that in the "if," something is manifested as a being, namely, as a being that is categorical and natural (1.3.4.). Because being is established in this sense, it is subsequently, in the "what" question, reduced to its essence and quiddity; and this intelligible determination was precisely the nature of the thing (1.4.2.).

From this it follows that the question "What is nature?" is an "intensification" of the inquiring into the ontologically prior of that which is. "The composite of matter and form is not nature itself, but is something by nature."[87] This question is a reduction to that primordiality which is determinative for the meaning of being and the direction of this questioning and knowing.

1.6. *The legitimacy of the desire to know*

"All men by nature desire to know." Yet the desire to know expressed in this authoritative statement does not seem to be justified simply as a matter of course. Throughout the Middle Ages, especially in the monastic setting, there was a strong tradition which discerned in human yearning an unvirtuous desire to know, curiosity (*curiositas*). What is the criterion, then, that legitimates the knowledge sought as meaningful?

May you know with what order and with what end man must know things, writes Bernard of Clairvaux. As for order, first that which is more appropriate for salvation; as for end: not curiosity, but edification. For there are people who want to know solely for the sake of knowing and that is "scandalous curiosity" (*turpis curiositas*). Curiosity is the reaching out towards the "tree of knowledge," by which man fell; it is the root of pride.[88] Thomas's contemporary, Bonaventure, warns against "the curiosity of science" as well. "Curiosities" lead us astray from the way of salvation (*via salutis*), involve us in endless questions.[89]

---

[87] *In II Phys.*, lect. 2, 152: Compositum ex materia et forma, non est ipsa natura, sed est aliquid "a natura."

[88] *Super Cantica Canticorum*, Sermo 36: Sunt namque qui scire volunt eo fine tantum, ut sciant: et turpis curiositas est (*S. Bernardi Opera* II, ed. J. Leclercq, C.H. Talbot, H.M. Rochais (Rome, 1958), p. 5). *De gradibus humilitatis et superbiae* X, 28: Primus itaque superbiae gradus est curiositas (*ibid.*, III (Rome, 1963), p. 38).

[89] *Collationes in Hexaemeron* III, 27 (*Opera Omnia* V, 347); *ibid.* XIX, 4 (*Opera Omnia* V, 420) the reference to Bernard; *De decem praeceptis*, collatio 5 (*ibid.*, 523): "Utilia" autem dirigunt nos in viam salutis; sed "curiosa" distrahunt nos a via salutis et dissipant intelligentiam nostram. *In II Sent.*, prooemium (*ibid.* II, 5): Unde intelligentia, avertendo se a summa veritate ignara effecta, infinitis quaestionibus se immiscuit per curiositatem.

Cf. Vincent of Beauvais, *Speculum doctrinale* I, 26. For the Late Middle Ages see John Gerson, *Contra curiositatem studentium* (*Oeuvres complètes* vol. 3, ed. P. Glorieux (Paris, 1962), pp. 224–49); *De imitatione Christi* I, 2: "Every man by nature desires to know, but of what use is knowledge without the fear of God?"

Knowledge that is an end in itself is set over against saving knowledge. Normative for the human desire to know is a knowledge that is subservient to the way of salvation. This norm sets limits on science.[90] The authority of this tradition is Augustine, whose *De doctrina christiana* especially had a great influence on the medieval order of knowledge.

1.6.1. *Augustine: Unvirtuous desire to know (curiosity)*[91]

In many loci in his writings, the Bishop of Hippo speaks of "curiosity." He deals with it at length in Book X of the *Confessiones*, where the various kinds of vices are discussed according to a scheme derived from I John 2:16: "For all that is in the world, the lust of the flesh, and the lust of the eyes, and the pride of life, is not of the Father, but is of the world." Cap. 35 is devoted to the lust of the eyes (*concupiscentia oculorum*), which is identified with "curiosity." It is a vain and curious desire cloaked in the name of science (*nomine cognitionis et scientiae palliata*).

Why is curiosity called the lust of the eyes? Because in the striving for knowledge, sight has the priority. While for Aristotle the appreciation of seeing was a positive indication of the natural desire to know, for Augustine it is rather a sign of the worldly, fallen man, who tries everything out of a desire for experience and knowledge. The temptation of curiosity is to seek knowledge for the sake of knowledge: "all that is called curiosity—what does it seek other than joy in the knowledge of things?"[92]

The perversion of knowledge, which becomes an end in itself, must be understood from a fundamental distinction in Augustine's thought,

---

[90] When this perspective is no longer accepted, these limits immediately become offensive: they become a sign of man's not yet having come of age. NIETZSCHE regards a mark of the new era to be its "uncompromising curiosity" ("rücksichtslose Neugierde"; *Jenseits von Gut und Böse* VIII, 188). Cf. H. Blumenberg, *Der Prozess der theoretischen Neugierde* (Frankfurt am Main, 1973; this is an enlarged and revised version of *Die Legitimität der Neuzeit*, vol. 3). For a reaction to this study, see H.A. Oberman, *Contra vanam curiositatem. Ein Kapitel zwischen Seelenwinkel und Weltall* (Zurich, 1974).
   Criticism of the modern ideal of science should be accompanied by fundamental reflection on the "legitimacy of Modern Times"—not in order to put the "legitimacy of the Middle Ages" in its place, but in order to call again to mind a way of knowing that respects the meaning of the origin of things.
   [91] See H.-I. Marrou, *Saint Augustin et la fin de la culture antique*, 4th ed. (Paris, 1958), pp. 148–55, 278–79, 350–52, 683–86; R. Lorenz, "Die Wissenschaftslehre Augustins," *Zeitschrift für Kirchengeschichte* 67 (1955–56): 29–60, 213–51; H. Blumenberg, "Augustins Anteil an der Geschichte des Begriffs der theoretischen Neugierde," *Revue des études augustiniennes* 7 (1961): 35–70; H. Blumenberg, *Der Prozess der theoretischen Neugierde*, pp. 103ff.
   [92] *De vera religione* 49 (94); cf. *Epist.* 118 to Dioscorus, in A. Goldbacher, ed., *S. Aurelii Augustini Hipponiensis Episcopi Epistulae* II, C S E L 34 (Vindobonae, 1898), pp. 665ff.; *De trinitate* XII, 15.

namely, that between *uti* ("to use") and *frui* ("to enjoy"). This distinction is featured prominently in *De doctrina christiana*, too. "To enjoy anything means to cling to it with affection for its own sake. To use is to employ what we have received for use to obtain what we want."[93] That alone which may be enjoyed is God, the final end of our striving. All the rest must be used, that is, brought into reference to this enjoyment. The meaning of things lies in their referential character, which is the expression of their creatureliness. "Every human perversion, which is also called vice, is wanting to use what is meant to be enjoyed and to enjoy what must be used. Conversely, every ordering, which is also named virtue, is to enjoy what must be enjoyed and to use what must be used."[94] What makes a desire to know unvirtuous is the denial of this order; it wants to enjoy what must be used. Knowledge becomes an end in itself and thereby results in delay, or even deviation, on man's way to salvation.[95]

From this determination of the place of curiosity, it also follows that Augustine's conception of science is no longer the classical ideal of disinterested 'theoria'. In "the Christian doctrine," science has an instrumental meaning: it is oriented to the knowledge of God and qualified by its utility for this religious end. "I certainly did not attribute to this science whatever can be known by man in human things, where needless vanity and harmful curiosity are excessively abundant, but only that whereby the most wholesome faith, which leads to true beatitude, is begotten, nourished, protected and strengthened."[96]

This orientation entails a reduction of what is worth questioning and knowing, but one which is essentially different in character from the reduction of all that can be questioned to the "if" and "what" questions described in 1.3. The most obvious trait in the attitude of the Christian philosopher, according to GILSON, is that he effects a choice between philosophical problems.[97] Thus Augustine himself concentrates on a twofold question: "The first concerns the soul, the other concerns God.

---

[93] *De doctrina christiana* I, 4, 4: Frui enim est amore alicui rei inhaerere propter seipsam. Uti autem, quod in usum venerit ad id quod amas obtinendum referre.

[94] *De div. quaestionibus* LXXXIII, 30: Omnis itaque humana perversio est, quod etiam vitium vocatur, fruendis uti velle, atque utendis frui. Et rursus omnis ordinatio, quae virtus etiam nominatur, fruendis frui, et utendis uti.

[95] *De doctrina christiana* I, 3, 3: Si eis quibus utendum est frui voluerimus, impeditur cursus noster, et aliquando etiam deflectitur, ut ab his rebus quibus fruendum est obtinendis vel retardemur, vel etiam revocemur, inferiorum amore praepediti.

[96] *De trinitate* XIV, 1, 3.

[97] *The Spirit of Mediaeval Philosophy*, 2nd ed. (London, 1950), p. 37. The sense in which GILSON understands this "spirit" is clear from the opening sentence of this classic work: "It would be hard to imagine any expression more naturally apt to occur to the mind of the historian of mediaeval thought than *Christian philosophy*."

The first effects that we know ourselves, the other that we know our origin.''[98] Self-knowledge related to knowledge of the Origin—that is what is worthy of knowing, and what should move man.

From this perspective Augustine critizes the inquiry of philosophers, which leads to the impious pride of self-exaltation: "So early can they foresee a coming eclipse of the sun, but their own present eclipse they do not see, for they do not seek with a devout mind *(non enim religiose quaerunt)* whence it is that they possess this skill by which they seek out these things" *(Confess.* V, 3, 4). From this optics, too, the investigation of nature is placed within the framework of curiosity in *Confess.* X, 35. "Because of this morbid curiosity . . . men proceed to search out the secrets of nature, things outside ourselves, to know which profits us nothing, and of which men desire nothing but the knowing *(et nihil aliud quam scire homines cupiunt).*''

Of what importance is it to know "the nature of things"? "There is no call to investigate the nature of things as those do whom the Greeks call physicists *(physici).*'' For the Christian, after all, another origination obtains: "For a Christian it is sufficient *(satis est Christiano)* to believe that the cause of created things . . . is none other than the goodness of the Creator.''[99] Therefore, ''while we approve of that line of Virgil, 'Happy is he who has the skill to search out nature's causes [*Georgica* II, 490], we ought not to suppose that it concerns our attainment of happiness that we should know the causes of the great corporal movements in the universe, such as are hid at the most secret bounds of nature.''[100]

''Men desire nothing but the knowing.'' Augustine's formulation is reminiscent of the opening sentence of Aristotle's *Metaphysica.* However, the legitimating ''by nature'' is eliminated here. The desire to know is stigmatized as the vain curiosity of man, whose questioning is ''not devout'' *(non religiose).*

1.6.2. *Thomas Aquinas: 'Studiositas' and 'curiositas'*[101]

How does Thomas manage to harmonize the two ''authorities,'' Aris-

---

[98] *De ordine* II, 18, 47. Cf. *Soliloquia* I, 2, 7: Deum et animam scire cupio. Nihilne plus? Nihil omnino.

[99] *Enchiridion* III, 9.

[100] *Ibid.*, V, 16: Quae cum ita sint (refers to the passage cited from III, 9) quando nobis Maronis ille versus placet ''Felix qui potuit rerum cognoscere causas,'' non nobis videatur ad felicitatem consequendam pertinere, si sciamus causas magnarum in mundo corporalium motionum, quae abditissimis naturae sinibus occuluntur. Cf. *De doctrina christina* II, 29, 46.

[101] The theme of 'curiositas' in Thomas generally receives little attention. Yet, here is an interesting case for his relationship to Augustine and the Augustinian tradition, a relationship that has yet to be the subject of a comprehensive study.

totle (the natural desire to know) and Augustine ("curiosity" as perverted desire to know)? Immediately after the discussion of original sin he takes up the subject of curiosity in the *S. Th.* II–II, q. 166–67. Fundamental in his exposition is the distinction in q. 167, 1: "one must judge differently about the *knowledge* itself of the truth and about the *striving* and assiduity to know the truth."

In this very distinction the distance from Augustine's conception is already apparent. Even GILSON must acknowledge that Thomas did not adopt Augustine's formulations. In his opinion Aquinas did, however, put into practice the selective attitude of the Christian philosopher. For the originality of his thought shines forth especially in those areas where the influence of the Biblical revelation is felt.[102] Yet in this way substantially different motivations are too easily reduced to the same denominator. For what is the purport of the distinction introduced by Thomas? That in science itself there is no room for curiosity: "knowledge of the truth is as such good" *(ibid.).*

This judgement may be clarified in the light of Thomas's exposition of Aristotle's dictum, "All men by nature desire to know." Unlike the Stagirite, Thomas in his Commentary on the *Metaphysica* advances three "apriori" arguments,[103] that is, the desire to know is founded and legitimated from the nature of man. In this section we want to concentrate on the first two arguments; the third argument will be taken up in 1.7.

> [Aristotle] says, first, that the desire to know belongs by nature to all men.
> Three reasons can be given for this. The *first* is that each thing naturally desires its own perfection. Hence matter is also said to desire form as any imperfect thing desires its perfection. Therefore, since the intellect, by which man is what he is, considered in itself is all things potentially, and becomes them actually only through knowledge, because the intellect is none of the things that exist before it understands them, as is stated in Book III of *De Anima* [4, 429 a 23]; so each man naturally desires knowledge just as matter desires form.
> The *second* reason is that each thing has a natural inclination to perform its proper operation, as something hot is naturally inclined to heat, and something heavy to be moved downwards. Now the proper operation of man as man is to understand, for by reason of this he differs from all other things. Hence the desire of man is naturally inclined to understand, and therefore to know.[104]

---

[102] *The Spirit of Mediaeval Philosophy*, p. 38.

[103] This expression is used by Duns Scotus in connection with Thomas's arguments (although Thomas is not mentioned by name), in his Prologue to *Quaestiones subtilissimae super libros Metaphysicorum Aristotelis (Opera Omnia* VII, p. 2).

[104] *In I Metaph.*, lect. 1, 1–3: Proponit [Aristoteles] igitur primo, quod *omnibus homi-*

Both arguments rest upon the same ontological foundation. What all strive after, what all by nature desire, is the good *(bonum)*. Something is desirable insofar as it is perfect, for all desire their perfection. Something is perfect insofar as it is in act. Thus everything tends towards its good as end, that is, towards its complete actualization.[105]

What does this mean for human being? That by which man is man is his intellect. His intellective soul is "as wide as all reality," has an intentional openness to all things; but, in itself, it is only knowing in potency. Therefore the human intellect—indeterminate, like matter—desires by nature actual knowledge as its perfection. Therefore, too, the operation proper to man is "to understand," for in this act he realizes his good.

No other conclusion is possible than that *all* knowledge is good *(omnis scientia bona est)*, since this is the good of man as man, the fulfillment of his natural desire.[106] It is against this background that Thomas claims in the part of the *Summa Theologiae* mentioned at the beginning of this section that the study of philosophy is legitimate and praiseworthy in itself: *studium philosophiae secundum se est licitum et laudabile* (II–II, 167, 1 ad 3).

Science is the perfection of man, given his nature (man is man through his intellect). On the basis of this view, it is impossible in principle to discriminate against certain questioning as *non religiose*, as unvirtuous.[107] "Curiosity" accordingly plays no essential role in Thomas's work, which bears the stamp of the thirteenth-century university setting. Human questioning is legitimated "by nature." In a study entitled "Réflexions sur la controverse S. Thomas—S. Augustin," GILSON contends, too, that "the difference between the ideas which St. Augustine and St.

---

nibus naturaliter desiderium inest ad sciendum.

Cuius ratio potest esse triplex: *Primo* quidem, quia unaquaeque res naturaliter appetit *perfectionem* sui. Unde et materia dicitur appetere formam, sicut imperfectum appetit suam perfectionem. Cum igitur intellectus, a quo homo est id quod est, in se consideratus sit in potentia omnia, nec in actum eorum reducatur nisi per scientiam, quia nihil est eorum quae sunt, ante intelligere, ut dicitur in tertio *de Anima*: sic naturaliter unusquisque desiderat scientiam sicut materia formam.

Secundo, quia quaelibet res naturalem inclinationem habet ad suam propriam *operationem*: sicut calidum ad calefaciendum et grave ut deorsum moveatur. Propria autem operatio hominis inquantum homo, est intelligere. Per hoc enim ab omnibus aliis differt. Unde naturaliter desiderium hominis inclinatur ad intelligendum, et per consequens ad sciendum.

[105] Cf. *S. Th.* I, 5, 1. See 8.1., below ("The good is what all desire").

[106] *In I De anima*, lect. 1, 3: Quod autem omnis scientia sit bona, patet; quia bonum rei est illud, secundum quod res habet esse perfectum: hoc enim unaquaeque res quaerit et desiderat. Cum igitur scientia sit perfectio hominis, inquantum homo, scientia est bonum hominis.

[107] While for Augustine investigating nature, *quae praeter nos est*, was a form of curiosity, *(quae scire nihil prodest)*, there is for Thomas nothing unvirtuous about a study *De occultis operibus naturae*.

Thomas formed of nature is the first cause of their further philosophical divergences.''[108]

What can be misdirected according to Thomas is not the knowledge itself of the truth but exclusively the *striving* towards knowing *(aliter autem est judicandum . . . de appetitu et studio veritatis cognoscendae).* To elucidate this, he begins in *S. Th.* II – II, 166, 2 to put the Aristotelian statement in a field of tension. "Now just as man by nature desires the delights of food by virtue of his *corporeal* nature, so by virtue of his *soul* does he desire to know something. Therefore the Philosopher says in Book I of the *Metaphysica* that 'all men by nature desire to know.'''

As a result of sin, a disharmony has arisen within human nature between soul and body. "With regard to knowledge, there is within man a contrary inclination. For from the side of the soul, man inclines to desire the knowledge of things . . . but from the side of corporeal nature he inclines to avoid the labor of seeking knowledge.''[109] It is therefore man's concern to regulate his appetite.

With respect to this regulation Thomas adopts a central concept of Aristotelian ethics, that of virtue as the "middle" between two extremes. The contrary inclination just referred to makes it possible, with the help of this scheme, to interpret curiosity as a vice. It is one of the two extremes that can occur in the desire to know.[110] This desire must be conducted into reasonable channels by the virtue of "devotion to learning" *(studiositas)*, which is a potential part of the cardinal virtue of temperance.

Augustinian "curiosity" is thereby placed under the regime of the 'studiosus', the Aristotelian 'virtuosus'. It is nothing else than an "excessive" form of an in itself legitimate desire to know. This disorder can assume various shapes. One of these is that man desires to know the truth about creatures without relating it to the obligatory end, namely, the knowledge of God *(S. Th.* II – II, 167, 1).

Striking here is the introduction of a moment that seeks a connection with Augustine. The truth about the creaturely is not brought into reference to the knowledge of God. The unvirtuousness of the desire manifests itself in a science that fails to inquire "fundamentally" into the causes; hence it is an imperfect realization of man's good. All knowledge is good, but there is a hierarchy in knowledge as there are degrees in the

---

[108] In *Mélanges Mandonnet* I (Paris, 1930), p. 375.

[109] *S. Th.* II – II, 166, 2 ad 3.

[110] See *De malo* 8,2: Appetitus sciendi est homini naturalis; unde si scientiae intendat secundum quod recta ratio dictat, erit virtuosum et laudabile; si vero transcendat aliquis regulam rationis, erit *peccatum curiositatis*; si vero deficiat, erit peccatum negligentiae.

good.[111] In this manner Augustine's religious motivation of "curiosity" is transposed into the hierarchy of the *theoretical* view.

1.7. *The natural desire to know and the idea of circulation*

This transposition becomes apparent in the third argument Thomas advances in his lectio in support of the opening statement of the *Metaphysica*. It is as follows:

> The third reason is that it is desirable for each thing *to be united to its principle*, since it is in this that the perfection of each thing consists. This is also the reason why circular motion is the most perfect motion, as is proved in Book VIII of the *Physica*, because its terminus is united to its starting point. Now it is only by means of his intellect that man is united to the separate substances, which are the principles of the human intellect and that to which the human intellect is related as something imperfect to something perfect. It is for this reason, too, that the ultimate happiness of man consists in this union. Therefore man naturally desires to know.[112]

1.7.1. *"It is desirable for each thing to be united to its principle": The Neoplatonic motif of circulation*

Duns Scotus suggests in the prologue of his commentary on the *Metaphysica*[113] that this argument of Thomas's , derived from the highest intelligible object, is also traceable to Aristotle (*Ethic. Nic.* X).[114] Yet something more than that is said in the argument: namely, it is desirable for each thing to be united to its *principle*. Even though Thomas refers to the *Physica* with regard to the perfection of circular movement, the connection of this movement with the desire to know, which he introduces into his lectio, is a motif that is no longer Aristotelian. That in itself is sufficient to make this last argument philosophically the most interesting of the three.

Notable in the first place is that in this argument circular motion is introduced as a general feature of things. That from which the thing comes

---

[111] *S. Th.* II-II, 167, 1 ad 1.

[112] *In I Metaph.*, lect. 1, 4: Tertio, quia *unicuique rei desiderabile est, ut suo principio coniungatur*; in hoc enim uniuscuiusque perfectio consistit. Unde et motus circularis est perfectissimus, ut probatur octavo *Physicorum*, quia finem coniungit principio. Substantiis autem separatis, quae sunt principia intellectus humani, et ad quae intellectus humanus se habet ut imperfectum ad perfectum, non coniungitur homo nisi per intellectum: unde et in hoc ultima hominis felicitas consistit. Et ideo naturaliter homo desiderat scientiam.

[113] *Opera Omina* VII, p. 3.

[114] Cf. Thomas Aquinas, *In De causis*, prooemium: Sicut Philosophus dicit in X Ethic., ultima felicitas hominis consistit in optima hominis operatione quae est supremae potentiae, scilicet intellectus, respectu optimi intelligibilis.

forth turns out to be its end. The final end of each thing is its assimilation to its principle. The dynamics of reality is a circulation characterized by the identity of beginning and end.

This doctrine of circulation is of Neoplatonic provenance. It was known to Thomas from, among others, Proclus[115] and Pseudo-Dionysius. In his commentary on De divinis nominibus Thomas writes:

> It must be kept further in mind that every effect reverts (convertitur) upon the cause whence it came forth, as the Platonists say (ut Platonici dicunt). The reason for this is that every thing reverts upon its good by desiring it. Now, the good of the effect derives from its cause. Therefore every effect reverts upon its cause by desiring it. Therefore Dionysius, having said that all is deduced (deducuntur) from the Godhead, goes on to add that all things revert upon Him through desire.[116]

For Neoplatonism, reality is governed by a twofold process. On the one hand, there is an "emanation," a flowing out from the first Principle, called by Plotinus the One or the Good, which must necessarily communicate of itself. This emanation may be characterized as a step by step descent which manifests itself in an ever greater diverseness from the One. Yet, simultaneously there is a return to the Origin, which is a turning back, or "conversion." All that is emanated reverts, in accordance with its nature, upon that from which it has originated, the Good. For in the likeness to that lies the perfection of everything.

Striking in the third argument in the second place is that Thomas straightaway posits that the "separated substances" are the principles of the human intellect. This formulation is rather vague: substantia separata is a generic term for immaterial beings including the human soul, purely spiritual beings (the so-called "intelligences"—in the Christian tradition identified with angels), and God;[117] it will become clear presently that Thomas expresses himself in general terms here deliberately.

Man, precisely because he is man, can be directly connected with the

---

[115] "Elementatio theologica translata a Guilelmo de Moerbeke," ed. C. Vansteenkiste, Tijdschrift voor Filosofie 13 (1952): 263ff.; prop. 31: Omne procedens ab aliquo secundum essentiam convertitur ad illud a quo procedit; prop. 32: Omnis conversio per similitudinem efficitur eorum quae convertuntur ad quod convertuntur; prop. 33: Omne procedens ab aliquo et conversum, circularem habet operationem.

[116] In De div. nomin. c. 1, lect. 3, 94: Est autem ulterius considerandum quod omnis effectus convertitur ad causam a qua procedit, ut Platonici dicunt. Cuius ratio est quia unaquaeque res convertitur ad suum bonum, appetendo illud; bonum autem effectus est ex sua causa, unde omnis effectus convertitur ad suam causam, appetendo ipsam. Et ideo postquam dixerat quod a Deitate deducuntur omnia, subiungit quod omnia convertuntur ad Ipsum per desiderium. Cf. c. 9, lect. 4, 842; c. 10, lect. 1, 857.

[117] De ente, cap. 5: ... in substantiis separatis, scilicet in anima, intelligentiis et causa prima.

separated substances through his intellect. For knowing is the conforma-
tion of the knower to the known.[118] The desire to know is the 'eros' towards the principle which is proper to man; in the knowledge of the immaterial substances, the desire is fulfilled. In this union with his principle
consists man's highest perfection, that is, his happiness. The ultimate end
of human life is the operation of the highest faculty, the intellect, with
respect to the most intelligible object, whereby man is united with his
principle and the circle is closed.

1.7.2. *The desire to know in Thomas's reinterpretation of the circulation*

The fact that Aquinas introduces the idea of circulation into his exposition of the desire to know has generally attracted little attention in studies
on Thomas. Yet it is significant that his account culminates in this ontological dynamics. From this perspective, various texts in his *oeuvre* acquire
extra relief and coherence. Notice, for example, the manner in which
Thomas integrates the circulation into his view of reality in the *S.c.G.* II,
46:

> An effect is most perfect when it returns to its principle; thus the circle is the
> most perfect of all figures, and circular motion the most perfect of all moti-
> ons, because in their case a return is made to the beginning. It is therefore
> necessary that creatures return to their principle in order that the universe
> of creatures may attain its ultimate perfection.[119]

The introduction of the motif of circulation is all the more striking since
the straight line has at present come to be regarded as the most adequate
symbol for the Christian conception of history.[120] Is it perhaps in connection with this tendency that the important place of the idea of circulation
in Thomas's thought—and in medieval thought generally—is still insufficiently discerned? In following Thomas's way of thought we shall encounter it, however, repeatedly.

Fundamental to all that is is the double dynamics from the Origin and
towards the Origin. Yet, at the same time, this circular movement is

---

[118] See, for example, *De verit.* 10, 7: Sed in cognitione ipsa qua mens ipsum Deum cognoscit ipsa Deo conformatur, sicut omne cognoscens, inquantum huiusmodi, assimilatur
cognito.

[119] *S.c.G.* II, 46: Tunc enim effectus maxime perfectus est quando in suum redit principium; unde et circulus inter omnes figuras, et motus circularis inter omnes motus, est
maxime perfectus, quia in eis ad principium reditur. Ad hoc igitur quod universum creaturarum ultimam perfectionem consequatur, oportet creaturas ad suum redire principium.

[120] See especially O. Cullmann, *Christus und die Zeit. Die urchristliche Zeit- und Ge-
schichtsauffassung* (Zurich, 1946); *Christ and Time: The Primitive Christian Conception of Time
and History*, trans. F.V. Filson, 2nd ed. (London, 1962).

reinterpreted by Thomas in the direction of the conception of Christian faith, with respect both to the egress (*exitus*) and the regress (*reditus*) of things.[121]

Things come to existence because they are all created by God. Rejected is any emanation from natural necessity, any step-by-step coming forth, in which a higher substance would be in each case the direct principle of the lower. The "authority" of the *Liber de causis* is, so Thomas says, not to be followed in its idea that the lower creatures are created by God by means of the higher ones.[122] The creaturely stands in an im-mediate relation of origin to God. The being of the created must be understood as "deduced" from the divine being.[123]

In view of the identity of Origin and final End, the latter also will have to be reinterpreted. In the lectio on Aristotle's *Metaphysica*, Thomas had spoken in a generic sense of separate substances, which were posited as the principles of the human intellect. Undoubtedly, he had deliberately chosen such a general formulation since in this manner the conceptions of Arab philosophers could also be included. Thus it was Averroes' doctrine, for example, that the highest to which man can attain is that he is united or "continued" (*continuatur*) with the lowest of the separated substances, namely the "agent intellect," which is the direct (cosmic) principle of man.

Yet a differentation must now be made within these separate substances. For Thomas only God, the creating Origin of all, can be the ultimate end of man.

> The ultimate perfection of each individual agent is that it can attain to its principle. Now the ultimate perfection or beatitude of man is according to his intellectual activity, as the Philosopher also says in Book X of the *Ethica*.

---

[121] For the 'circulatio' in Thomas, see also *In IV Sent*. 49, 1, 3, 1: Et quia omnia procedunt a Deo inquantum bonus est . . ., ideo omnia creata secundum impressionem a Creatore receptam inclinantur in bonum appetendum secundum suum modum, ut sic in rebus quaedam *circulatio* inveniatur; dum, a bono egredientia, in bonum tendunt; *In I Sent*. 14, 2, 2: In exitu creaturarum a primo principio attenditur quaedam *circulatio* vel regiratio, eo quod omnia revertentur sicut in *finem* in id a quo sicut *principio* prodierunt; *S. Th*. I, 63, 4; *S. Th*. I, 12, 1.

The motif of circulation has been raised thus far almost exclusively in the discussion about the structure of the *S. Th*. inaugurated by Chenu. M. Seckler writes, rightly, in *Das Heil in der Geschichte. Geschichtstheologisches Denken bei Thomas von Aquin* (Munich, 1964), pp. 29-30: "Es ist erstaunlich, dass diese Konzeption bisher kaum Beachtung gefunden hat, weder im Sinne der Zustimmung noch in der eher zu erwartenden Form der Ablehnung, denn sie steht in einem eklatanten Widerspruch zu dem, was sich gemeinhin als christliche Deutung der Wirklichkeit ausgibt."

[122] *De pot*. 3, 4 ad 10: Error iste expresse in libro De Causis invenitur, quod creaturae inferiores creatae sunt a Deo superioribus mediantibus; unde in hoc auctoritas illius non est recipienda.

[123] *De pot*. 3, 5 ad 1: . . . esse, quod in rebus creatis inest, non potest intelligi nisi ut *deductum* ab esse divino.

If, then, the principle and cause of the intellectuality of men were some other
separated substance, it would have to be the case that the ultimate beatitude
of man would consist in that created substance; and those who hold this view
clearly assert this: for they assert that the ultimate felicity of man is to be
"continued" with the agent intellect. Now the true faith asserts that the ultimate beatitude of man is in God alone.[124]

The "deduction" of the created being from the divine being (*esse*) has as
counterpart the "reduction" to God, who "transcends all separate
substances" (*S.c.G.* III, 47).[125]

In Thomas's reinterpretation of the final end, there remains an important moment of continuity in the orientation: man's natural desire is a desire to *know*, that is, in the genuine Aristotelian sense, to know the causes.
Yet at the same time, the terminus of knowing is extended further. Aristotle's definition of to know (*scire*)—"then do we deem ourselves to know perfectly when we know the cause"—is related by Thomas to knowledge of
the first cause, God. This is expressed very clearly in *S.c.G.* III, 25:

> By nature there is in all men the desire to know the causes of whatever is
> seen. So from wonder at that which is seen but whose causes were hidden,
> men first began to philosophize; and when they found the cause, they rested.
> Nor does the search cease until it comes to the first cause; for "then do we
> deem ourselves to know perfectly when we know the *first* cause." Therefore
> man naturally desires, as his ultimate end, to know the first cause. Now the
> first cause of all things is God. Therefore man's ultimate end is to know
> God....
>
> Now the ultimate end of man and of every intellectual substance is called
> happiness or beatitude; for it is this that every intellectual substance desires
> as final end and for its own sake alone. Therefore the ultimate beatitude of
> any intellectual substance is to know God.[126]

---

[124] *De spirit. creat.* q. un., art. 10: Ultima perfectio uniuscuiusque agentis est quod possit pertingere ad suum principium. Ultima autem perfectio sive beatitudo hominis est secundum intellectualem operationem, ut etiam Philosophus dicit X *Ethic.* Si igitur principium et causa intellectualitatis hominum esset aliqua alia substantia separata, oporteret
quod ultima hominis beatitudo esset constituta in illa substantia creata; et hoc manifeste
ponunt ponentes hanc positionem: ponunt enim quod ultima hominis felicitas est continu-
ari intellectui agenti. Fides autem recta ponit ultimam beatitudinem esse in solo Deo.

[125] Noteworthy is the ambiguous relationship between God and the generic concept of
"separate substances." In the text from *De spirit. creat.* just cited, there is mention of an
"*alia* substantia separata," but in *S.c.G.* III, 47 it is said that God transcends all separate
substances. In *De verit.* 10, 6 we read: Quod quidem lumen intellectus agentis in anima
rationali procedit, sicut a prima origine, a substantiis separatis, *praecipue a Deo.*

See also the correction of the motif of circulation in *S. Th.* I-II, 3, 7, obj. 2 and ad 2.

[126] *S.c.G.* III, 25: Naturaliter inest omnibus hominibus desiderium cognoscendi
causas eorum quae videntur; unde propter admirationem eorum quae videbantur, quorum causae latebant, homines primo philosophari coeperunt, invenientes autem causam
quiescebant. Nec sistit inquisitio quousque perveniatur ad primam causam: et *tunc perfecte
nos scire arbitramur quando primam causam cognoscimus.* Desiderat igitur homo naturaliter cognoscere primam causam quasi ultimum finem. Prima autem omnium causa Deus est. Est
igitur ultimus finis hominis cognoscere Deum....

As an expression of the circulation, man's desire to know is the natural desire to attain to the first cause of things (*naturale etiam hominis desiderium, quod est perveniendi ad primam rerum causam*).[127] The re-duction to be realized in thought must be adequate to the ontological de-duction. This origin motivates the "analytica" and opens new room for philosophical questioning.

1.8. *The order of the questions 'an est' and 'quid est' and being as creature*

In 1.3.4. we encountered the statement from *In II Post. Anal.* (lect. 7, 471) that "to know what something is is identical to knowing the cause of the question if it is" (*Idem est scire quid est, et scire causam quaestionis an est*). The desire to know is fulfilled in the knowledge of the quidditative causes. "If someone should come to know fully what the things are, would he not then know *all* about them?"[128] But this identity can itself still be put in question. For, is all that can be questioned really exhausted with the order of the questions directed towards the quiddity?

The order of the questions can itself become worthy of questioning again, from wonder not at what it is that is, but at that that which is *is*, the "wonder of all wonders." "Why is there any Being at all—why not far rather nothing?"[129] The meaning, the direction of *this* "basic" question is another than that of the inquiry into the essence, the "ousiology," since it entails another origination than nature.[130]

Ultimus autem finis hominis, et cuiuslibet intellectualis substantiae, felicitas sive beatitudo nominatur: hoc enim est quod omnis substantia intellectualis desiderat tanquam ultimum finem, et propter se tantum. Est igitur beatitudo et felicitas ultima cuiuslibet substantiae intellectualis cognoscere Deum.

[127] *In I ad Corinth.*, c. 13, lect. 4, 803; *De virtutibus in communi* q. un., a. 10: Naturale hominis desiderium in nullo alio quietari potest, nisi in solo Deo. Innatum est enim homini ut ex causatis desiderio quodam moveatur ad inquirendum causas; nec quiescit istud desiderium quousque perventum fuerit ad primam causam, quae Deus est.

[128] L. de Raeymaker, *Vergelijkende studie over de betekenis van het "Zijn" in de metafysiek van Avicenna en die van Thomas van Aquino* (Brussels, 1955), p. 5.

[129] M. Heidegger, "Was ist Metaphysik?" *Wegmarken* (Frankfurt am Main, 1967), p. 19: "Die Grundfrage der Metaphysik . . . .: Warum ist überhaupt Seiendes und nicht vielmehr Nichts?" Cf. Heidegger, "What is Metaphysics?" *Existence and Being*, (with an Introduction by Werner Brock; Chicago, 1949), p. 349; "Nachwort zu 'Was ist Metaphysik?" in *Wegmarken*, p. 103: "Einzig der Mensch unter allem Seienden erfährt, angerufen von der Stimme des Seins das Wunder aller Wunder: *Dass* Seiendes ist."

[130] Cf. K. Löwith, *Heidegger, Denker in dürftiger Zeit*, 2nd ed. (Göttingen, 1960), p. 25: "Dass diese Frage aber überhaupt nur gefragt werden kann, weil ihr die biblische Schöpfungsgeschichte vorausgeht, der zufolge das Ganze des Seienden, als eine Schöpfung aus Nichts, auch nicht sein könnte, kommt Heidegger nicht in den Sinn, obwohl es doch zu bedenken gäbe, dass und warum diese 'ursprünglichste Frage' von dem ursprünglichen Denken der Griechen nie gefragt worden ist."

Cf. also A. Zimmermann, "Die 'Grundfrage' in der Metaphysik des Mittelalters," *Archiv f. Gesch. der Philos.* 47 (1965): 141-56.

1.8.1. *Another mode of questioning*

For this desire to know, we take as our starting point *De ente et essentia*, one of Thomas's earliest writings, which in its approach bears a great resemblance to Book VII of the *Metaphysica*. The question of the essence and intelligibility of composed substances is dealt with in the first chapters. Going beyond the "authority," Thomas takes up in the fifth chapter the essence of the separate substances.

This theme itself deserves special attention, since it turns out to be the locus where the deepest intentions of Thomas's philosophy can be recovered. For the issue at stake is substances that are "separate" from materiality. Because they are pure forms, they are "absolute," for the cause of being is the form by which something is in act (see 1.2.). Because these substances are simple, the katallel structure of questioning lacks a real basis with respect to them. "It is clear that with regard to simple substances, which are not composed of matter and form, there is no question (possible)" (1.3.2.). Yet for Thomas, precisely this substance becomes questionable in its being.   .

For although such substances are pure forms without matter, there is nevertheless no complete simplicity in them.[131] The argumentation Thomas advances in *De ente* for this is remarkable:

> Everything that does not belong to the concept of an essence or quiddity comes to it from outside and enters into composition with the essence.... Now, every essence or quiddity can be understood without knowing anything about its being (*esse*). We can know, for instance, what (*quid est*) a man or a phoenix is and still be ignorant whether is has being in reality (*an esse habeat in rerum natura*).

On the basis of this distinction Thomas concludes simply: "From this it is clear that being (*esse*) is other than essence or quiddity."[132]

This reasoning is remarkable because it represents in several respects a turn in comparison to the Greek mode of questioning that we followed in 1.3. and 1.4.

(1) The desire to know expresses itself in questions that can be reduced to the "if" and the "what." The relation between the two questions was

---

[131] *De ente*, c. 5 starts with the rejection of universal hylemorphism. For the rejection of this doctrine of Avicebron's, see also *De subst. separ.*, c. 5.

[132] *De ente*, c. 5: Quidquid enim non est de intellectu vel quiditatis hoc est adveniens extra et faciens compositionem cum essentia.... Omnis autem essentia vel quiditas potest intelligi sine hoc quod aliquid intelligatur de esse suo: possum enim intelligere quid est homo vel phoenix et tamen ignorare an esse habeat in rerum natura. Ergo patet quod esse est aliud ab essentia vel quiditate.

such that it was excluded that we should know what something is and be ignorant if it is (see 1.3.4.). What was there considered impossible is now actually affirmed in *De ente*: "We can know, for instance, what a man is ... and still be ignorant whether it has being in reality."[133]

(2) In the previous perspective the "if" question could not be separated onto-logically from the "what" question. The sense of the former question was to manifest "being" as a substantial predicate, which is specified in the progression to the"what." In this reasoning the distinction between the two questions ends up in a real difference: "being is *other* than essence." At the same time, the "katallel" order has been changed: the "other" that is asked of something is not the "essence" but the "being."

(3) From this it follows that in *De ente* another mode of questioning is employed. For the only mode previously considered possible with regard to simple substances was to inquire into the extrinsic cause of the composed thing, which is the separate substance. Now, the questioning does imply an inner composition in the immaterial substance. This compositeness is again indicated by Thomas with Boethius's distinction between *quod est* and *quo est* (cf. 1.4.2.); but this time the "that whereby something is" is related to the *esse*.[134] Through this nonidentity, the separate substance itself becomes worthy of questioning.

The main concern of Thomas's argumentation here is that there is no absolute simplicity in the separated substances.[135] The background of this concern is Thomas's reinterpretation of the circulation of things. It was from this that the necessity arose to differentiate within the separated substances (cf. 1.7.2.).

1.8.2. *The origin of things and the question of being*

This is the moment at which the second basic text, taken from *De substantiis separatis*, must be introduced. In cap. 9 of this work, Thomas traces

---

[133] Likewise *In II Sent.* 1, 1, 1; *ibid.* 3, 1, 1: Quaedam enim natura est de cujus intellectu non est suum esse, quod patet ex hoc quod intelligi potest esse *cum hoc quod ignoretur an sit*, sicut phoenicem, vel eclipsim, vel aliquid hujusmodi.

In I Sent. 8, 4, 2 refers to Avicenna as the source of this reasoning: Tertia ratio subtilior est Avicennae. Omne quod est in genere, habet quidditatem differentem ab esse, sicut homo; humanitati enim ex hoc quod est humanitas, non debetur esse in actu; *potest enim cogitari humanitas et tamen ignorari an aliquis homo sit.*

[134] *De ente*, c. 5. Cf. *Quodl.* IX, 4, 1; *In I Sent.* 8, 5, 2; *In Boeth. De trin.* 5, 4 ad 4.

[135] Cf. *S.c.G.* II, 52: Non est autem opinandum, quamvis substantiae intellectuales non sint corporeae nec ex materia et forma compositae ..., quod propter hoc divinae simplicitati adaequentur. Invenitur enim in eis aliqua compositio.

the progress of human inquiry into the origin of things (*paulatim enim humana ingenia processisse videtur ad investigandam rerum originem*). This investigation reaches its completion only when the necessity is recognized that "... above the mode of coming to be by which something becomes when form comes to matter, we must preconceive another origin of things (*praeintelligere aliam rerum originem*) according as 'to be' (*esse*) is bestowed upon the whole universe of things by the first Being (*a primo Ente*)."

Another mode of questioning—the reduction of that which is to its being—correlates to another mode of causing than that which belongs to material things, one that pertains to everything. These other modes are motivated from another origination. Determinative for this other mode of questioning in the Middle Ages, as is clear from the context of this ninth chapter, is the idea of creation. For to bring forth being in the absolute sense is the mark of creation: "To produce being (*esse*) absolutely, and not merely as this or that being, pertains to the essence of creation."[136]

In his commentary on Aristotle's *Phys.* (VIII, lect. 2, 987), creation is also described by Thomas as "the production of all being by the first cause of being." This influx of being, in contrast to the cause of being discussed in 1.4., is no longer to be sought in the thing itself. "Being," according to *De ente*, c. 5, "cannot be caused by the form or quiddity of a thing." It must be reduced to an extrinsic principle: "Everything whose being is distinct from its nature must have being from another" (*esse ab alio*). Creation requires a *supernatural* agent[137]—a significant term, since it renders transparent how closely bound this reflection still remains to the category it means to transcend. The counterpoint of the basic texts is not artificial; it is in conformity with the movement of thought itself.

The meaning of the question concerning being surpasses the horizon of the whatness, the *nature* of that which is, namely, towards a being as *creature*, taken in the general sense of all that is by God (*accepto communiter nomine creaturae pro omni eo quod est a Deo*).[138] Instructive in this regard is the discussion in *Quodl.* II, 2, 1—again a text that deals with the separated substances ("Whether an angel is composed of essence and being in the manner of a substance"). Thomas argues in this article that all that is creaturely participates in being (see for this point 2.5.); precisely as something participated in, the being of the creaturely does not belong to its essence. It is for

---

[136] *S.Th.* I, 45, 5.
[137] *De pot.* 3, 1 ad 1; cf. *ibid.*, 3, 8.
[138] *De pot.* 3, 3 ad 2.

this reason that the "if" question is different from the "what" question (*et ideo alia quaestio est 'an est' et 'quid est'*). And because all that falls outside the essence of the thing is called "accident," the *esse* that pertains to the "if" question is merely accidental. The text continues:

> Therefore, the Commentator [i.e., Averroes] says on *Metaph.* Book V that this proposition 'Socrates is' is an accidental predication, insofar as it signifies *either* a thing's entity *or* the truth of a proposition.[139]

Here again we encounter a remarkable discrepancy with an earlier finding, namely, with what we established in 1.3.4. concerning the different ways in which 'ens' can be predicated. If "being" is said in the first way (i.e., signifying a thing's entity), it is a substantial predicate and belongs to the "what" question. If, however, it is taken in the intramental way (i.e., signifying the truth of a proposition), it is an accidental predicate and belongs to the "if" question. Now, in *Quodl.* II, 2, 1, both ways are stamped as accidental, because the being of what is creaturely falls outside its essence.[140]

"All that something has, not through itself, but from another is *outside* its essence." Because that which is created has being "from another," Avicenna—an important source of inspiration for Thomas's account— regarded this being as something accidental, as something added to the essence "in the manner of an accident."[141] Normative for anyone who analyzes in this way remains the perspective of the "what" question.

Yet in the same *Quodlibet*, in the response to the second objection, a turn occurs, the laboriousness of which is suggested by the two *quasi*'s:

---

[139] *Quodl.* II, 2, 1: Unde, cum omne quod est praeter essentiam rei, dicatur accidens; esse quod pertinet ad quaestionem *an est*, est accidens. Et ideo Commentator dicit in V Metaph., quod ista propositio 'Socrates est' est de accidentali praedicato, secundum quod importat vel entitatem rei, vel veritatem propositionis.

[140] It it true that Thomas subsequently asserts: "Sed verum est quod hoc nomen 'ens', secundum quod importat rem cui competit huiusmodi esse, sic significat *essentiam rei*, et dividitur per decem genera." However, this meaning of "being" is not pertinent to the distinction between the "if" and "what" questions emphasized here. Cf. also *In II Post. Anal.*, lect. 6, 462.

[141] *De verit.* 8, 8: Omne autem quod aliquid habet non a seipso, sed ab altero, est ei praeter essentiam suam. Et per hunc modum probat Avicenna, quod esse cuiuslibet rei praeter primum ens est aliquid praeter essentiam ipsius, quia omnia ab alio esse habent.

For Avicenna's doctrine, see G. Verbeke, "Introduction doctrinale," in *Avicenna Latinus: Liber de Philosophia prima sive Scientia Divina*, ed. S. van Riet (Louvain and Leiden, 1977), pp. 62ff. ("La dimension existentielle").

Thomas's critique is to be found in *In IV Metaph.*, lect. 2, 556f.; 558: Esse enim rei quamvis sit aliud ab eius essentia, non tamen est intelligendum quod sit aliquod superadditum ad modum accidentis, sed quasi constituitur per principia essentiae.

> Being (*esse*) is an accident, not as though (*quasi*) related accidentally to a
> substance, but as (*quasi*) the actuality (*actualitas*) of any substance.

This "to be" is called accident not because it belongs to the genus accident
but by virtue of a certain similarity to it: neither forms part of the essence.[142] For Thomas, however, there is a profound difference; for "to be"
(*esse*) is that whereby reality is given to the essence, is the "actuality" of
every substance (cf. 6.7.).

What we have found so far we may summarize as follows. The desire
to know finds expression in questions. The question is an "analysis,"
a reduction. In the previous progression of the "if" towards the "what"
a composed thing was reduced to the cause of being, the *quo est*, which is
the *essentia* (1.4.2.). In the present order of questioning, the same formulations are employed, but with an altered content. The "if" question is
directed to a *quo est* that is the *actus essendi* whereby a being is being and
not rather nothing.[143] This "to be" of things, which "enters into composition with the essence," needs to be reduced to the logical and ontological prior, the cause of being, which is God. "The being (*esse*) that is
in created things can only be understood as deduced from the divine
being."[144]

1.9. *The twofold sense of questioning*

In this chapter we have examined the motives of philosophical questioning. Two main modes of questioning have been distinguished.

(1) The first mode is explicitly restricted to things composed of matter
and form. In that case the order of the questions is that the "what" questions follows on the "if." "Whether something is" serves as the starting
point for the decisive question concerning the intrinsic essence. In the
quiddity is centered the intelligibility of that which is. This Greek mode
of questioning that which is (*ens*) is connected with a meaning of being motivated through the origination of nature.

Within the scope of this first mode is the mode of inquiring into a
substance that is separated from matter. Here the katallel structure of

---

[142] *De pot.* 5, 4, ad 3: Esse non dicitur accidens quod sit in genere accidentis, si loqua-
mur de esse substantiae (est enim actus essentiae), sed per quamdam similitudinem: quia
non est pars essentiae, sicut nec accidens.

[143] *In I Sent.* 8, 5, 2: In compositis autem ex materia et forma "quo est" potest dici tripliciter. Besides the *forma partis* and *forma totius* mentioned in 1.4.2. (n. 71), there is still
a third: Potest etiam dici "quo est" ipse *actus essendi*, scilicet esse, sicut quo curritur, est
actus currendi.

[144] *De pot.* 3, 5 ad 1 (see n. 123).

questioning leaves only this room: what is sought is the extrinsic cause of the composed, sensible substance. This cause of the form in matter functions as answer to the question "if" the separated substance is.

(2) The other mode of questioning pertains to everything that is, including the separated substances, because they are also marked by the composition of essence and being (*esse*). Here the "if" question is directed to the 'esse': "Being itself (*ipsum esse*) is related as act to both composite and simple natures.... Now, being seems to pertain to the question 'if it is.'"[145] This basic question is connected with a meaning of being as creaturely and cannot be answered by the "what" question, because "being" is "outside the essence."

How must the twofold onto-logical sense of questioning be interpreted? Does it imply a "turn" in Thomas's thought? A. KELLER is of the opinion that in Thomas's later work there is indeed just such a turn: the priority of the "if" question to the "what" question would acquire an ever stronger accent.[146] But the arguments he advances are not solid.

The order of questioning is that the "what" question is preceded by the "if" question (1.3.3.). But Thomas recognizes that we cannot know of anything "if" it is unless we also know the "what" in some way. Of something which is entirely unknown to us we cannot inquire and know if it is.[147] When at the beginning of the *Summa Theologiae* it is asked if God exists (*an Deus sit*), an objection says (I, 2, 2 obj. 2): the middle term of demonstration is the essence (*quod quid est*). But of God we cannot know what He is (cf. 5.3.4.). Therefore we cannot demonstrate that God exists. In the response Thomas states:

> In order to prove that something is, it is necessary to accept as a middle term what the name signifies (*quid significet nomen*), not the essential what (*quod quid est*). For the "what" question follows on the "if" question.[148]

KELLER's view that in Thomas there is a "turn" in the order of the questions "if it is" and "what it is" is based on texts like these, in which it is said that for the inquiry into the "if" precognition of the "what" is necessary. He neglects, however, the different levels in the ques-

---

[145] *De spirit. creat.* q. un., art. 8 ad 3.

[146] A. Keller, *Sein oder Existenz?* (Munich, 1968), pp. 231ff.; especially pp. 234 and 236.

[147] *In Boeth. De trin.* 6, 3; *In II Post. Anal.*, lect. 8, 484: De eo enim quod est nobis penitus ignotum, non possumus scire si est aut non.

[148] It is against this background that the (generally somewhat neglected) conclusion of the 'viae' to the existence of God must be understood: Hoc *dicimus* Deum (cf. 6.5.4.).

Cf. *In IV Phys.*, lect. 2, 415: Principium autem ad investigandum de aliquo 'an sit', oportet accipere 'quid est', saltem quid significetur per nomen; lect. 10, 507; *In I Post. Anal.*, lect. 2, 17: Unde quaestio 'an est' praecedit quaestionem 'quid est'. Sed non potest ostendi de aliquo an sit, nisi prius intelligatur quid significatur per nomen.

tioning.[149] The knowledge of the "what" that precedes the "if" question relates not to the essence of something but to the signification of the name.

What should count still more heavily is the continuity in the orientation of the desire to know, as is evident from Thomas's own descriptions of the final end. In *S. Th.* I-II, 3, 8 he sketches the dynamics of the human mind in these terms:

> If an intellect knows the essence of some effect but through it cannot know the essence of the cause, that is, know the "what it is" of the cause, then the intellect cannot be said to attain the cause absolutely, although it may be able to know through the effect "that the cause is" (*an est*). Therefore there remains in man by nature, if he knows an effect and knows that it has a cause, the desire to know of the cause, too, "what it is" (*quid est*). And that desire arises from wonder and causes inquiry, as is said at the beginning of the *Metaphysica*. For example, if someone observes a solar eclipse and understands that this issues from some cause, which he does not know as to "what it is," he wonders about it and, from wonder, inquires. And this inquiry does not cease until he comes to know the essence of the cause.
>
> If therefore the human intellect knows the essence of some created effect and knows of God only "that He is" (*an est*), then the perfection of that intellect does not yet reach the first cause absolutely, and there still remains in it the natural desire to inquire into the cause.[150]

We shall return to the main idea of this text more extensively later (5.3.4.). In the present context it is of importance to see wherein the natural desire to know is fulfilled. Man's beatitude can only consist in the contemplation of God's essence, in the "vision of God," in the knowledge of the first cause, in which the answer to the question "what it is" is seen. In this progression, the final terminus continues to be determined by the ideal of ancient "theory," by the contemplation of what things are *in themselves*.

So the two modes of questioning, which in each case involve different reductions of that which is, are found to point to two senses. On the one

---

[149] Cf. H. Weidemann, *Metaphysik und Sprache* (Freiburg and Munich, 1975), pp. 130f.

[150] *S. Th.* I-II, 3, 8: Si ergo intellectus aliquis cognoscat essentiam alicujus effectus, per quam non possit cognosci essentia causae, ut scilicet sciatur de causa '*quid est*'; non dicitur intellectus attingere ad causam simpliciter, quamvis per effectum cognoscere possit de causa '*an sit*'. Et ideo remanet naturaliter homini desiderium, cum cognoscit effectum, et scit eum habere causam, ut etiam sciat de causa '*quid est*'. Et illud desiderium est admirationis, et causat inquisitionem, ut dicitur in principio Metaph. Puta si aliquis cognoscens eclipsim solis, considerat quod ex aliqua causa procedit, de qua, quia nescit quid sit, admiratur, et admirando inquirit. Nec ista inquisitio quiescit, quousque perveniat ad cognoscendum essentiam causae.

Si igitur intellectus humanus, cognoscens essentiam alicujus effectus creati, non cognoscat de Deo nisi '*an est*'; nondum perfectio ejus attingit simpliciter ad causam primam, sed remanet ei adhuc naturale desiderium inquirendi causam.

hand, the knowledge of the ''what'' is the fulfillment of the desire to know, which started with the ''if'' question establishing that which is (*quod est*). Yet in what manner is the origin of the creaturely—an origination which must be preconceived, according to *De substantiis separatis*—retained in the progression of this knowing? On the other hand, the answer to the ''if'' question is expressly placed outside the quiddity: it aims at a *quo est*, which is the act of every essence. Then the problem arises of what intelligibility this ''to be'' (*esse*) actually adds to the perfection of the essence.[151]

Questioning has put us upon a way towards knowing. Along that way various moments have come to the fore that need to be developed further. In particular, it remains to be seen to what extent the two senses of questioning lead to two tracks.

---

[151] J. van de Wiele states, in *Zijnswaarheid en Onverborgenheid* (Louvain, 1964), p. 118, that ''the intelligibility of *esse* . . . can only be situated *outside finite being itself.*'' Yet, it must be asked how this is possible, since it is only through *esse* ('quo est') that a being is being.

BY THE WAY OF PREDICATION
(PER VIAM PRAEDICATIONIS):
DEFINITION AND PARTICIPATION

Questioning opens a way towards knowing. The object of knowing is to understand that which is (*ens*). The desire to know expresses itself in questions about being in which something is asked of something (*aliquid de alio*). Being, to be questionable, must itself be proportional to this katallel structure (1.3.2.).

To state something of something other is to predicate. Therefore the question of being may be pursued *per viam praedicationis*. The way of predication gives the direction both to the questioning of being and to the mode of being of that which is worthy of being questioned. We can observe in history that philosophy has taken this way. "The modes of being are proportional to the modes of predicating" (*Modi essendi proportionales sunt modis praedicandi*).[1] These words express a common conviction of Greek philosophy. The mutually divergent onto-logies of Parmenides, Plato, and Aristotle converge in the determinant role of the predicative logos. This role Thomas briefly indicates in his *Scriptum* on the *Sententiae*. Various ancient philosophers have derived their judgement of natural things from "intentions" in the intellect (*ex intentionibus intellectis*). If they found that certain things agree in a single concept, they wanted them to agree in a single thing. Thus Parmenides, perceiving that 'ens' is predicated of everything, spoke of "being" as if it were really one. And Plato asserted that there is just one man *per essentiam*, which is predicated of all men.[2]

Aristotle's account of predication must be understood as a reaction to these ontologies: "being is said in many ways." Thomas follows this model in the inquiry into the essence of that which is. In the predication *per se* and *per accidens* being *per se* and *per accidens* is disclosed. Being *per se* is, according to the modes of predication, divided into ten predicaments, of which substance is the fundamental one. This first category is said in two manners: as subject and as essence (2.1.).[3]

---

[1] *In III Phys.*, lect. 5, 322.

[2] *In II Sent.* 17, 1, 1: Et inde ortus est error Parmenidis et Melissi, qui *videntes ens praedicari de omnibus*, locuti sunt de ente sicut de una quadam re, ostendentes ens esse unum et non multa. . . .

Ex hoc etiam secuta est opinio Pythagorae et Platonis, ponentium mathematica et intelligibilia principia sensibilium: . . . quia Socrates et Plato sunt homo, quod sit unus homo per essentiam, *qui de omnibus praedicatur*.

[3] This summary is according to the order in *Metaph.* V, c. 7 (lect. 9).

Cor-responding to the "what" question, as its answer, is the defining logos. Thus Thomas himself, in the first basic text (*In II Phys.*, lect. 1, 141), identifies the question "What is nature?" directly with an inquiry into the definition of nature. This questioning terminates in a knowing (*scire*) by the way of definition (*per viam diffinitionis*), a way that is determined by the predication model *per se / per accidens*. Within the "horizon" of definitional thinking, being is reduced to its essence (*nature*) (2.2. and 2.3.).

However, is the way of definition on which we are put by the question "What is nature?" really a passable way, precisely with regard to nature (2.4.)? Cicero's statement in *De Inventione* (I, 24, 34) that it is difficult to define "nature" was repeated throughout the Middle Ages—e.g., by Hugh of St. Victor, Gilbert de la Porrée, and John of Salisbury.[4]

If definition is the perfection which the desire to know seeks to attain, then it is necessary to examine how this terminus is related to the mode of questioning analyzed in 1.8. To the question concerning the being of that which is corresponds for Thomas another mode of predicating. In the reduction of being as *creature* he follows, as is clear from the second basic text (*De subst. separ.*, c. 9), the Platonic model of *per essentiam / per participationem* (2.5.). The way of predication turns out to have two tracks, in conformity with the two senses of questioning (2.6.).

2.1. *"Being is said in many ways" ('Ens multipliciter dicitur')*

The *via praedicationis* is, Thomas states in *In VII Metaph.* (lect. 2, 1287), the method proper to logic. This "way " is, however, not a purely logical procedure, as will appear from the following sections. Predication is an onto-logy in a literal sense: that which is is revealed by the logos. It was also precisely (see 1.4.2.) the mode of predicating that was used in the first place to clarify the essence of sensible substances. The structure of questioning—something other is asked of the subject—drives the inquirer to this approach. Therefore, the meaning of being in which the first mode of questioning is anchored is to be investigated along the path of predication.

---

[4] Hugh of St. Victor, *Didascalicon* I, 10 (ed. C.H. Buttimer, Washington, 1939, 18); Gilbert de la Porrée, *Expositio in Boethii Librum contra Eutychen et Nestorium* c. 1, 1 (ed. N.M. Haring, in AHDLMA 29 (1954), 258); John of Salisbury, *Metalogicon* I, 8 (ed. C.C.J. Webb, Oxford, 1929, 24).

Marius Victorinus, in his commentary on the writing by Cicero just alluded to (*Explanationes in rhetoricam Ciceronis* I, 24), has thematized the finding that the definition of nature is so difficult. The reason is the dispute between the philosophers, which is prior: *deus an natura* (ed. Halm, *Rhetores latini minores*, 215).

2.1.1. *Predication ('per se' and 'per accidens') and being ('per se' and 'per accidens')*

To say relates to what is said primarily *per modum enuntiationis* (*S. Th.* II-II, 76, 1). In the e-nunciation, being is ex-pressed, the mode of being of that which is is manifested. By (affirmatively) predicating "something" "of something other," we say that "this" *is* "that" (*Praedicando enim aliquid de aliquo altero, dicimus hoc esse illud*).[5] This "expressing" bears two marks: composition and identity.

A predicative statement has a katallel structure: "something" is attributed to "something." In and through the enunciation, being is laid out into two moments: the predicate and that of which this is said (the subject). Even in a proposition in which the same is predicated of itself, the plurality of subject and predicate points to a diversity.[6]

To this katallel structure of predication ("man is an animal," "man is white"), corresponds a composition in the thing.[7] That the "logos" is not to be taken in a purely "logical" sense but rather as related to reality is clear from Aristotle's reflections on predicating put forward in *Post. Anal.* I, 22 (lect. 33). One can say in truth both "something white is a log" and "the log is white." Yet there is a difference between these two modes of predicating. The meaning of the first statement is not that "white" is the subject of a log; what is signified is that there is "something other" that is white and also happens to be a log. For, so Aristotle argues, a subject becomes what is predicated of it as subject, either according to its totality or according to a part. But the white, as white, does not become a log. If I say "the log is white," however, not something other is the subject, but the log which, as log, has become white. Only in this case can one speak of genuine predication: "Only those things are said to be predicated which are said in this way, namely not in virtue of some other subject" (lect. 33, 282). Only then, namely, is the predicate said of a subject that is really its bearer.[8] The subject term always has a material function; the predicate term is taken formally: *praedicatum comparatur ad subjectum ut forma ad materiam*.[9]

---

[5] *In III Phys.*, lect. 5, 322.

[6] *S. Th.* I, 13, 12.

[7] *S. Th.* I, 85, 5 ad 3: Compositioni et divisioni intellectus respondet quidem aliquid ex parte rei.
For the coherence between logic and ontology see also 4.2.1., below.

[8] In his commentary on *Post. Anal.* I, 22 W.D. Ross writes (*Aristotle's Prior and Posterior Analytics*, Oxford, 1949, 577): "As a logical doctrine this leaves much to be desired; it must be admitted that all these assertions are equally genuine predications." This judgement disregards, however, Aristotle's logos, in which the distinction in predication is onto-logical.

[9] *In I Perih.*, lect. 8, 98; *S. Th.* III, 16, 7 ad 4: Terminus in subjecto positus tenetur

In the predicative statement, a thing is laid out; but at the same time, its identity is expressed. "What, namely, is predicated of something is signified to be identical with that."[10] Identity is a unity or—taken in its active sense—a union.[11] In the composition the subject acquires through the predicate, which has the function of form, a determined being. Aristotle's argument for genuine predication was: "a subject *becomes* what is said of it." Predication means "in-formation."[12] Thereby a diversity and a multiplicity are brought to identity and unity.

But this identity may not be considered simply as absolute. That is apparent from Aristotle's exposition of "the same" in *Metaph.* V, c. 9. He immediately distinguishes two modes: "essentially" (*per se*) and "accidentally" (*per accidens*)—a distinction that plays an important role in the work of the Stagirite. Because identity follows "by the way of predication," the distinction in identity is to be reduced to predication *per se* or *per accidens*. In this predication being is manifested as *per se* or *per accidens*: "the division of being into essential being and accidental being is based on the fact that something is predicated of something *per se* or *per accidens*."[13]

In the *praedicatio per accidens* there is—as in every statement—an identity of subject and predicate, but this is purely material in character. What is enunciated is not founded in the *ratio* of the subject itself. "Man is white" is a predication *per accidens* because "white" does not belong to "man" in virtue of the latter's own determination, but happens to it. What is composed in the statement is a diversity of forms that have no intrinsic connection with each other. The 'accidens praedicabile'—which is to be distinguished from accident as a category—says something of a being which belongs to it contingently and not necessarily. A predication of this kind is accordingly never universal (not every man is white). It discloses an *ens per accidens* ("a white man").[14]

Praedicatio per se, however, indicates a causal relationship, that is, an in-

---

materialiter, idest pro supposito; positus vero in praedicato tenetur formaliter, idest pro natura significata; *In IX Metaph.*, lect. 11.

[10] *In V Metaph.*, lect. 11, 908. Cf. *S. Th.* I, 13, 12: Huic vero diversitati quae est secundum rationem, respondet pluralitas praedicati et subjecti; identitatem vero rei significat intellectus per ipsam compositionem; *De ente*, c. 4.

[11] *Ibid.*, 912: Identitas est unitas vel unio.

[12] *In III Sent.*, d. 5, Exp. textus: Quando autem (substantiva praedicantur) ratione formae, dicitur (praedicatio) per denominationem sive informationem. Et haec est magis propria praedicatio, quia termini in praedicato tenentur formaliter.

[13] *In V Metaph.*, lect. 9, 885.

[14] For the 'praedicatio per accidens', see *In I Post. Anal.*, lect. 31, 259; 33, 281ff. In *In V Metaph.*, lect. 9, 885ff. this predication is connected with *ens per accidens*, in *In V Metaph.*, lect. 11, 908 with *idem per accidens*.

Three modes are distinguished. In the first, an accident is predicated of an accident ('iustus est musicus'); in the second, an accident of a subject ('homo est musicus'); in the

telligible order, between subject and predicate. In this predication there
is a formal identity; a predicate is attributed to a subject in virtue of the
form of the subject ("man is an animal"). Between the subject form and
the predicate form there is a necessary relation. "Animal" belongs to man
as man.[15] "That which belongs to a thing through itself (*per se*) is necessarily in it always and inseparably" (*S.c.G.* II, 55).

Predication *per se* manifests essential being (*ens per se*): that which
something is through itself. Following the passage just cited from *S.c.G.*
II, 55, Thomas goes on to elucidate this identity: "Now, being is consequent upon form through itself, for by "through itself' (*per se*) we mean
insofar as 'that thing is such', and each thing has being insofar as it has
form."[16] Each being ("white-being," "human-being") is through an inherent form. Hence the forms of being are manifested in what is said *per se*.

2.1.2. *The division of 'ens per se' into the predicaments of substance and accident*

In *Metaph.* V, c. 7 (lect. 9), after the division of being into *per se* and *per
accidens*, essential being is differentiated further. Being *per se* is divided according to the modes of predication (Aristotle speaks here of "category").[17] Being *per se* has as many meanings as there are different categories. This thesis features a polemical point against Parmenides' ontology.
The sage of Elea had transposed into reality the fact that 'ens' is predicated of everything: being is one. Against such a view Aristotle never tires
of repeating that "being is said in many ways."[18] This multiplicity is
that of the diverse categories. To the *modi praedicandi* the *modi essendi* are
proportional. Therefore the diverse modes of being (*genera entis*) manifested in the logos are called "predicaments."[19] Only about this categorical being, as we saw (1.3.4.), can the "what" question be posed. With

---

third, a subject of an accident ('musicus est homo'). In all these cases, 'esse' means
nothing other than 'accidere' (*In V Metaph.*, lect. 9, 887). It is noteworthy that both proper
and improper forms of saying are rubricized under predication 'per accidens'.

[15] *De pot.* 8, 2 ad 6: Per se praedicatur aliquid de aliquo, quod praedicatur de eo
secundum propriam rationem; quod vero non secundum propriam rationem praedicatur,
sed propter rei identitatem, non etiam praedicatur per se; *In III Sent.* 12, 1, 1 ad 6.
    See also 2.2.1. for the *modi dicendi per se*.

[16] *S.c.G.* II, 55: Esse autem per se consequitur ad formam: 'per se' enim dicimus
'secundum quod ipsum'; unumquodque autem habet esse secundum quod habet formam.

[17] *Metaph.* V, 7, 1017 a 22–24.

[18] See the critique of Aristotle in *Phys.* I, c. 2 and 3.

[19] *In III Phys.*, lect. 5, 322: Ens dividitur in decem praedicamenta non univoce (sicut
genus in species), sed secundum diversum modum essendi. Modi autem essendi proportionales sunt modis praedicandi. Praedicando enim aliquid de aliquo altero, dicimus hoc
esse illud: unde et decem genera entis dicuntur decem praedicamenta.

regard to the categories, three things are noteworthy. First, "being" is it-self not a category but is transcendental. Secondly, the categories are not ontically equivalent. And finally, "being" is predicated of the categories "analogically."

(1) The predicaments must not be conceived as additions to "being" comparable to the addition of differences to a genus, as a result of which species originate. "Being" is no genus; for it cannot be specified by the addition of something that is outside being; outside being is nothing.[20] 'Ens' goes beyond the categories; it is transcendental. However, the em-phasis falls in this predicative account not on the transcendentality of being but on the fact that 'ens' is immediately contracted to the diverse categories or genera:

> Being must then be contracted (*contrahitur*) to diverse genera according to the diverse modes of predication, which are consequent upon the different modes of being; for something is signified to be in just as many ways as something is predicated. And for this reason the classes into which being is first divided are called predicaments, because they are distinguished accord-ing to different modes of predicating.[21]

The transcendental character of being makes clear why in the first mode of questioning the "if" question is distinguished from the "what" ques-tion. However, the contraction to categorical being makes clear why *an est* can not be separated from *quid est* ontologically. What is affirmed in the "if" question—a subject as 'ens'—is a predicate that asks for a sequel, for determination. "Being" is at once from the very beginning (*a principio*) substance or quantity or quality, etc.[22]

(2) Each category has its own mode of being and its own mode of predi-cating.[23] The most general genera of being are not, however, ontically equivalent. Aristotle shows this from the different relations of the predi-cate to the subject in predication. Thomas, too, in a discursion of his own in his commentary on the *Phys.* (*III*, lect. 5, 322), gives a deduction of the categories on the basis of predication. As a result, the exposition acquires a somewhat confused character. For the objective is to show the dif-

---

[20] *In V Metaph.*, lect. 9, 889. Cf. *S. Th.* I, 3, 5.

[21] *In V Metaph.*, lect. 9, 890: Unde oportet, quod ens contrahatur ad diversa genera se-cundum diversum modum praedicandi, qui consequitur diversum modum essendi; quia ... quot modis aliquid praedicatur ... tot modis significatur aliquid esse. Et propter hoc ea in quae dividitur ens primo, dicuntur esse praedicamenta, quia distinguuntur secun-dum diversum modum praedicandi.

[22] *In VIII Metaph.*, lect. 5, 1763: Manifestum est quod ens non expectat aliquid addi-tum ad hoc quod fiat hoc, idest substantia, vel quantum, vel quale; sed statim a principio est vel substantia, vel quantitas, vel qualitas; *In V Metaph.*, lect. 9, 890.

[23] *S.c.G.* IV, 11: ... proprium modum essendi; *In I Sent.* 22, 1, 3 ad 2: Unicuique ge-neri debetur proprius modus praedicandi.

ferentiation of the modes of being *in themselves*.[24] But this "absolute" consideration interferes with the different relations of the subject to the predicate in the statement.[25] That is also evident from the dual way in which the proposition "man is white" functions in the exposition. On the one hand, it is used to make clear that what is manifested here is not an essential being but a being *per accidens* ("a white man"). But on the other hand, this same example is used to manifest white-being in itself as a category within the division of essential being (*per se*).

Some predicates signify essentially the subject of which they are said; they are predicated *in quod quid est* and belong to the category of "substance." Predicates which do not signify the essence—that is, are said of something that is not essentially the predicate—are "accidents," for example, "white" as said of "man." For man is not essentially "white" but rather "animal." These accidents must be said of something "underlying," namely, the subject which sustains them. It is not possible that there is something white that is white without being (also) something other.[26]

In the realm of being the fundamental dichotomy is that of "substance" and "accident." The substantial form gives being absolutely (*esse simpliciter*), the accidental form gives being in some respect (*secundum quid*): it causes a secondary being, a being added (*superadditum*) to that of the substance.[27] There are accidents that stand in a necessary connection with the subject. Other accidents do not have such a relation.[28] But for all accidents it holds true that their being is to be in something (*inesse*).[29] An accident entails in its concept incompleteness: its being is dependent-being and composed-being with a subject.[30] The substance is being "in virtue of itself" (*In VII Metaph.*, lect. 1, 1251). It is the most perfect genus: as *per se existens*, substance is the foundation of all beings.[31]

(3) 'Ens' is called what has "being." The categories are the first par-

---

[24] *In V Metaph.*, lect. 9, 885: . . . secundum absolutam entis considerationem.

[25] Cf. the critical assessment of the Aristotelian model of predication by K. Flasch, *Die Metaphysik des Einen bei Nikolaus von Kues, Problemgeschichtliche Stellung und systematische Bedeutung* (Leiden, 1973), pp. 47ff.

See also L.M. De Rijk, "On Ancient and Mediaeval Semantics and Metaphysics," *Vivarium* 15 (1977): 81–110; 16 (1978): 81–107; 18 (1980): 1–62. In this series of articles a new view is developed of the Aristotelian categories: they are to be characterized sooner as classes of *names* than as classes of predicates.

[26] *Post. Anal.* I, 22, 83 a 24ff. (lect. 33, 283ff.).

[27] Cf. *S. Th.* I, 77, 6; *De ente*, c. 7.

[28] For the two meanings of 'accidens,' see *In V Metaph.*, lect. 22, 1139ff.

[29] *In V Metaph.*, lect. 9, 894: Nam accidentis esse est inesse; *S. Th.* I, 28, 2.

[30] *In I Sent.* 8, 4, 3: Ratio autem accidentis imperfectionem continet: quia esse accidentis est inesse et dependere, et compositionem facere cum subjecto per consequens.

[31] *In IV Metaph.*, lect. 1, 543; *De verit.* 14, 2 ad 1.

ticularizations of being, not reducible to each other. They are also related to being in different ways. "Being" is said first of the substance and in a secondary respect (*per posterius*) of the accidents.[32] "The diverse relation to being impedes any univocal predication of being."[33] *Ens multipliciter dicitur*. But in this diversity there is a unity of a special character. "Being" is predicated "analogically" of substance and the other categories, that is, in accordance with the relation and order to one thing.

The doctrine of analogy occupies a modest place in Thomas's work; only in the Scholastic tradition does it gradually receive greater metaphysical elaboration. The framework in which Aquinas places analogy already in his first writing, *De principiis naturae*, is that of predication. Something can be said of various things in three ways: univocally (*univoce*) when the essential concept is completely identical; equivocally (*aequivoce*) when the name but not the essential concept is the same; and analogically when something is predicated of various things of which the essential concepts are different but which are related to one and the same. The last is the case when "being" is said of the substance and the accidents. For their concepts are not entirely (*ex toto*) the same—"having being through itself" stands over against "being in something"—but they are all called 'ens' because of the fact that they are related to one of them. "Being" is said of the accident because its being refers to the substance, of which being is predicated primarily.[34] Science, which deals with "being," must therefore be focussed first of all on this primary category.[35]

That substance is the "first being" (*In VII Metaph.*, lect. 1, 1246) is also corroborated by the cognitive order. Each thing is known better when its substance is known than when its quality or quantity is known. We know things best when the "what" is known. Therefore, the basic question of philosophy is: *quid est substantia rerum?* (*ibid.*, 1260).

The primary category, to which the question of being must be reduced, deserves further attention. For in the exposition on substance a duality can be noticed. As predicate it is the essence of the subject, but by the same token it is the subject that is the bearer and foundation of the accidents.

2.1.3. *"Substance is said in two ways"*: *'Subjectum'* and *'essentia'*

The essentially predicated is not said of something other but deter-

---

[32] *De ente*, c. 1.

[33] *De pot.* 7, 7: Diversa habitudo ad esse impedit univocam praedicationem entis.

[34] *De principiis naturae*, c. 6. Cf. *De pot.* 7, 7; *S.c.G.* I, 34; *S. Th.* I, 13, 6; *In IV Metaph.*, lect. 1, 535.

[35] *In IV Metaph.*, lect. 1, 546.

mines the subject itself. It is therefore likewise the category of the subsisting. Substance turns out to have a dual structure. It is both the category of what is essentially predicated of something, of the ''what'' (*quid est*)
and the category of the subsisting, ''this something'' (*hoc aliquid*), the subject that is not predicated of something other.[36] This dual structure is signalized by Thomas in *De pot.* 9, 1:

> The Philosopher holds that substance may be said in two ways. In one sense
> it is the *ultimate subject* which is not predicated of another; and this is the parti-
> cular in the genus of substance; while in another sense it is the *form* or *nature*
> of a subject. [37]

Thomas goes on to indicate the reason for this distinction: several subjects
may agree in having a common nature, as several men agree in having
the one nature ''man.'' Therefore that which is one must be distinguished
from that which is multiple. Whatever in the thing belongs to the common
nature is called the ''essence,'' or quiddity. If all that is in the particular
substance belonged to this common nature, no distinction would be possible between particular substances having the same essence. It is the polari-
ty of unity and multiplicity which leads to substance being said in two
ways and to Aristotle's speaking, in his *Categoriae*, of ''first'' and ''second'' substance (*ousia*).

This distinction arises, as the descriptions of substance already show,[38]
from the way of predication, which is marked by composition and identity. In a statement, being is laid out in a subject and a predicate. In this
model of predication an ultimate subject, a ''this'' or a ''that'' which is
no longer said of something other, is necessary as a point of reference.
The mode of being of the subject (*subjectum, suppositum*) is ''subsistence,''
a mode of being that, very typically, is interpreted as ''not in another.''
The proper meaning of subsistent being can be expressed in this analysis
not positively but only by a negation (*non in alio existens*).[39] This subsis-

---

[36] *In VII Metaph.*, lect. 1, 1247: Quoddam ens significat ''quid est'' et ''hoc aliquid,''
idest substantiam; ut per ''quid'' intelligatur essentia substantiae, per ''hoc aliquid'' suppositum. See in particular *Metaph.* V, c. 8 (lect. 10).

[37] *De pot.* 9, 1: Philosophus ponit substantiam dupliciter dici: Dicitur enim uno modo
substantia *ipsum subiectum* ultimum, quod non praedicatur de alio: et hoc est particulare
in genere substantiae; alio modo dicitur substantia *forma vel natura* subiecti.

[38] Cf. further *De unione verbi incarnati* q. un., a. 3: Substantia secundum duos modos dicitur, scilicet suppositum, quod *de alio non praedicatur*; et forma, vel natura speciei, quae
de supposito praedicatur.

[39] In the Reformational philosophy there has been sharp criticism of the concept of
substance. In his book *Wijsbegeerte* (Kampen, 1970), Hendrik van Riessen writes that in
Thomas there is a remnant of being which, although created, can exist in and through itself. On the Thomist standpoint there would be such substances in autonomous nature
(p. 170). ''In fact, God's omnipotence is restricted in Thomas, and on his standpoint it
is in a certain respect no longer true that 'of Him, and through Him, and to Him, are

tent is the particular in the genus of substance.

The predicate that is said of subjects essentially is the universal form or essence. It is non-subsisting, an 'abstractum', from which the determination of being comes forth.[40] The essence is the *quo est*, the intrinsic cause of being; it relates itself as form to the particular subject. This composition of subject and essence is the condition of the possibility of transforming the "what" question into a katallel structure and is determinative for the intelligibility of being. As the predicate is the more principal part of the enunciation because it in-forms,[41] so the *second* substance, which is manifested in the predicate, is the ontologically *prior*. This substance is sought in the "what" question: *substantia significat essentiam vel quidditatem rei, vel 'quid est'.*[42]

In essential predication there is a formal identity of what is stated with the subject. 'Socrates' *is* essentially "man." Yet, this identity is not total. 'Socrates' is not the essence, the human nature ('humanitas'), but has it. There is something "outside" (*praeter*) the essence.[43] Hence, there arises the problem of the "other."

In *De pot.* 9, 1 Thomas argues that in individual substances the essence is not completely identical with the subject. This nonidentity comes from their composition of matter and form. "Outside the common nature is the individual matter, the principle of the singularity."[44] The principle of individuation is outside the essence or form and must therefore be located in matter. But this cannot be matter as the principle of indetermination. What is postulated is an "individual" matter—Thomas's exposition does not make clear, however, where this individuation stems from. Because the common form is received in this matter as underlying subject, it is limited and individuated.[45]

---

all things'" (p. 46; cf. Romans 11:36). This critique has radically misunderstood Thomas. That things, although created, would be able to exist in and through themselves, is for Thomas an intrinsic impossibility (cf. 6.3.2.). In this criticism, furthermore, it has been insufficiently discerned that the concept of subsistence must be understood negatively (*non in alio*). More relevant to a critical assessment is therefore the difficulty Aquinas has in reaching a positive meaning of subsistence. For such a positive meaning, see 6.4.

[40] Cf. the duplexity in the following text: Subsistere duo dicit, scilicet esse et determinatum modum essendi; et esse simpliciter non est nisi individuorum, sed determinatio essendi est ex natura vel quidditate generis vel speciei (*In I Sent.* 23, 1, 1 ad 2).

[41] *In I Perih.*, lect. 8, 96: Praedicatum autem est principalior pars enunciationis, eo quod est pars formalis et completiva ipsius.

[42] *Quodl.* II, 2, 2.

[43] Cf. *S.c.G.* I, 21.

[44] *De pot.* 9, 1: Hoc autem quod est in substantia particulari praeter naturam communem, est materia individualis quae est singularitatis principium.... Et ideo in rebus, ex materia et forma compositis, essentia non est omnino idem quod subiectum. Cf. *In VIII Metaph.*, lect. 3, 1710.

[45] *Quodl.* III, 2, 1; *S. Th.* I, 3, 2 ad 3: Formae quae sunt receptibiles in materia, indi-

In simple beings there is no difference between subject and essence, because in them there is no matter, which individuates the common nature. Thus, separated substances are their essence. "The quiddity of the composite is however not the composite itself."[46] As a result of this nonidentity, the thing composed of matter and form can be questioned.

The analysis of the modes of predicating and the modes of being has shed further light on the sense and meaning of the question *quid est*.

(1) The "what" question is anchored in categorical being; it is the basic question because it inquires primarily into the essence of the "first being," substance.[47]

(2) The "what" question asks "something of something other." But this "katallel" structure of subject and form remains within the first category itself. The unity is not outside the multiplicity, the quiddity not separated from that which is. The Platonic model of predication, in which that which is said essentially (*per essentiam*), the Idea, is separated from that which is predicated through participation (*per participationem*), the concrete, is rejected.[48] Aristotle's discussion of predication in *Post. Anal.* I, 22 culminates in a sharp critique: "We must say farewell to the Ideas. They are empty sounds, are not relevant. For the demonstrative sciences are about such predicates as we have mentioned."

(3) The "what" question takes up the philosophical problem of the many and the one. Inquiry is made into the essential unity of a numerical multiplicity. In the "what" question an inner compositeness is reduced to an identity, which is the substantiality of substance.

2.2. *In search of identity: 'Scire per viam diffinitionis'*

What has to be sought, accordingly, is the statement that expresses the intrinsic identity of subject and predicate. "For every being, that is the logos of the essence, which says the predicate without the being itself appearing in it (as subject)."[49]

This logos, this *ratio quidditativa* is, in the line of the Socratic method, the *ratio diffinitiva*:[50] "the definition is a word string signifying what

---

viduantur per materiam, quae non potest esse in alio, cum sit primum subjectum.

[46] *De pot.* 9, 1; *In III Sent.* 5, 1, 3: Quidditas vero compositi non est ipsum compositum. Cf. *S.Th.* I, 3, 3; *Quodl.* II, 2, 2.

[47] On the extent to which 'quid est' can be asked of the other categories, see the two solutions in *In VII Metaph.*, lect. 3 and 4.

[48] Cf. Thomas's criticism of the 'opinio Platonis' in *In II Sent.* 17, 1, 1.

[49] *Metaph.* VII, 4, 1029 b 19ff.; lect. 3, 1313.

[50] *In II Phys.*, lect. 5, 179: Et hoc (sc. forma, species) dicitur causa inquantum est *ratio*

something is" (*definitio est oratio significans quod quid est; In II Post. Anal.*, lect. 2, 419).[51] The essence of something is made known through the definition; only through the (essential) definition is the thing intelligible. Each thing is not comprehended until one knows its definiton.[52] Therefore the "quest" for the definition. This is the terminus of the desire to know: "The natural desire of the rational creature is to know everything that perfects the intellect, namely, the species and genera of things, and their essences (*rationes*)" (*S. Th.* I, 12, 8 ad 4).

The "what" question terminates in a knowing (*scire*) *per viam diffinitionis*.[53] This way can be opened up further through consideration of the definition as *oratio*, or "logos" (2.2.1.) and as "horizon" (2.2.2.), a term which is related etymologically to the Greek word for "definition."

2.2.1. *"The definition consists of what is predicated 'per se'"*

The definitional logos of that which is follows the Aritotelian model of predication, in which the relation of subject and predicate is determined in the modes of predication *per se* and *per accidens*. Irrespective of the nature of the thing to be defined, it holds that: "The definition consists of what is predicated *per se*" (*Definitio constat ex his quae praedicantur per se*).[54] For in this predication there is more than a purely material identity. 'Per se' points as we saw to a causal relationship between subject and predicate, in contrast to what is said 'per accidens'. Only when the subject (or a part of it) is itself the cause of the predicate that is attributed to it does one speak of predication 'per se'.[55]

For this reason, all that is predicated of something 'per accidens' has first to be eliminated from the way of definition. It can neither be the object of any science nor is it of any importance for science. "Nothing of what is predicated of something 'per accidens' belongs to its quiddity."[56]

---

quidditativa rei: hoc enim est per quod scimus de unoquoque quid est; lect. 2, 151: . . . *ratio definitiva rei*; per quam scilicet scimus quid est. . . .

Cf. *Metaph.* I 6, 987 b 1ff., where Aristotle says of Socrates "that he was the first who directed his attention to definitions."

[51] The first mark of the perfect definition is that it manifests what something is, "nam definitio est oratio indicans quid est res"(*In IV Phys.*, lect. 5, 447). Cf. *In V Metaph.*, lect. 2, 274; *In I Sent.* 33, 1, 1 ad 1.

[52] *In I De anima*, lect. 1, 10; *De ente*, c. 1: Non enim res est intelligibilis, nisi per definitionem et essentiam suam; *De verit.* 20, 5: Tunc enim unaquaeque res comprehenditur, quando eius definitio scitur; definitio enim est virtus comprehendens rem.

[53] *In Boeth. De trin.* 6, 4: Nihil potest sciri in scientiis speculativis neque per viam demonstrationis neque *per viam diffinitionis* nisi. . . .

[54] *In VIII Metaph.*, lect. 1, 1685. Cf. *In I Post. Anal.*, lect. 33, 279.

[55] *In I Post. Anal.*, lect. 10, 83: Quando subiectum vel aliquid eius est causa eius, quod attribuitur ei, et hoc significat per se. Cf. P. Hoenen, *La théorie du jugement d'après S. Thomas d'Aquin*, 2nd ed. (Rome, 1953), pp. 107ff.

[56] *In VII Metaph.*, lect. 3, 1309.

Proper to demonstrative science is the predication 'per se' (*In I Post. Anal.*, lect. 35, 299).

Yet, not everything that is predicated 'per se' enters into the definition of the essence. Even in this predication there can still be a nonidentity of subject and predicate.[57] Within predication 'per se' the causal relation between subject and predicate can be further differentiated. Thomas, following Aristotle, sums up four 'modi dicendi per se', the first two of which are of special interest to us. The others, in fact, can be reduced to these two.[58]

In the second mode of saying 'per se', the 'per' signifies the relationship of a material cause, in the sense that the subject, to which something is attributed, is the proper matter of the predicated (as for example, "number" is the proper matter of "odd" when we say of a number that it is odd). In this mode of saying, a property is predicated of its proper subject, for this subject is stated in the definition of the predicate, which is the subject's proper accident (for example, "number" in the definition of "odd"). It is this mode of predicating that belongs to demonstrative science, for in the conclusion of a syllogism, a property is predicated of its proper subject (cf. 1.3.1.).

In the first mode of saying 'per se', the predicated belongs to the form of the subject. The predicate expresses that to which it is attributed in its complete essence, or with regard to a part of it (for example, "man is an animal"). In this mode of saying, the subject is no longer stated in the definition of the predicate (for example, "man" in the definition of "animal"), but reversely the predicate in the definition of the subject. The distinction within the necessary proposition, which the saying 'per se' is, is based on the categorical distinction of substance and accident. In chapter 3 its onto-logical significance will become apparent.

In the first mode of saying 'per se', what is essentially predicated *is* the subject. This saying is the definition sought for:

> The first mode of saying something *per se* is when that which is attributed to a subject pertains to its form. And because the form and essence of a thing

---

[57] *Ibid.*, lect. 3, 1311: Excludit ab eo quod est quod quid est, quod praedicatur secundum se, sicut passiones de subiectis; dicens: neque etiam hoc omne quod praedicatur secundum se de aliquo, pertinet ad hoc quod quid erat esse eius.

[58] For the four modes of saying 'per se', see particularly *In I Post. Anal.*, lect. 10, 84ff.; *In II De anima*, lect. 14, 400ff.; *In V Metaph.*, lect. 19, 1054ff. Actually, only three modes are in question, for the third is, as Thomas remarks, not a 'modus praedicandi' but a 'modus existendi' (*In I Post. Anal.*, lect. 10, 88). That they can be reduced to the first two modes is stated in *In I Post. Anal.*, lect 35, 301.

Further reference may be made to a number of texts where Thomas operates with these modes: *S. Th.* I, 76, 3; *S.c.G.* II, 58; *De anima* q. un., art. 11.

are signified by its definition, the first mode of that which is *per se* is when the definition itself or something expressed in the definition is predicated of the thing defined.[59]

In the definition which signifies the "what" of something, subject and predicate are identical. Yes, in the definition of the essence, no subject is any longer stated: *Illa pertineant ad quod quid est, in quorum definitionibus 'non ponuntur subiecta'* (*In VII Metaph.*, lect. 2, 1313). For this reason the definition is not a "normal" proposition. It is in the strict sense not an "enunciation" because in it something is no longer said of something "other."[60] The definition is for Thomas an *oratio*—a term which we have translated as "word string"—of the constitutive "whatness"; it signifies that which is exclusively in its essence. In the saying of this identity, being and the thought which thinks this being are determined and delimited.

2.2.2. *Definition as "horizon"*

The definition is not an assumption that one stipulates at the outset but something that one seeks. It is the terminus of speculative reason.[61] One who would define will have to traverse all that is essentially predicated of the subject to be defined.[62] "That which belongs to your essence is that which is predicated of you *per se*, such as 'man', 'animal', 'substance', etc."[63]

Defining is delimiting and determining, the definition is *terminus* in the pregnant sense.[64] The multiplicity of essential predicates can therefore not be unlimited, but must come to an end. A progress ad infinitum would render the forming and knowledge of definitions impossible; the "way of definition," because of the receding horizon, would be in-terminable. *Non est procedere ad infinitum, neque in sursum neque in deorsum* (*In I Post. Anal.*, lect. 34, 291): One cannot proceed infinitely, either by ascen-

---

[59] *In I Post. Anal.*, lect. 10, 84: Primus ergo modus dicendi per se est, quando id, quod attribuitur alicui, pertinet ad formam eius. Et quia definitio significat formam et essentiam rei, primus modus eius quod per se est, quando praedicatur de aliquo definitio vel aliquid in definitione positum.

[60] *In II Post. Anal.*, lect. 2, 428; *In I Post. Anal.*, lect. 19, 165.

[61] *In I De anima*, lect. 8, 119: Speculativae etiam intelligentiae finem habent, scilicet rationes; omnes enim terminantur ad aliquas rationes: quae quidem rationes, aut sunt "definitio" ... aut "demonstratio."

[62] *In I Post. Anal.*, lect. 34, 291: Oportet definientem intelligendo pertransire omnia illa, quae substantialiter praedicantur de definito.

[63] *In VII Metaph.*, lect. 3, 1310.

[64] *In I Perih.*, lect. 4, 37: Definitio ideo dicitur terminus, quia includit totaliter rem; *Comp. Theol.* I, 20; *S.c.G.* III, 49.

ding (that is, towards the more universal predicate) or by descending (that is, towards the more particular). The definition must have a beginning and an end; otherwise, one would never come to perfect knowledge of the thing.[65] What is perfect is "finite" (*finitum*): the definition is a typical expression of the Greek way of thought (cf. 8.5.2.).

The principle of all definitions is what is simple. In the ascent to the generic coherence of the definiendum, the upper limit is the *genus generalissimum*. There, the quest finds the first, for something still more universal can not be predicated of the most general genus. In the descent by means of differences towards the specific, the inquiry comes to an end in the *species specialissima*. There, the generic knowledge of a thing is specified in perfect knowledge.[66]

The "horizon" of the definition is that which is constituted of genus and the specific difference. Therefore there is only a definition of the species (*et ideo solius speciei est definitio*). To this conclusion is added, quite tersely: "For species alone seem not to be predicated according to participation and property, or as an accident" (*In VII Metaph.*, lect. 3, 1327). The definitional logos excludes two kinds of predication. The mark of the first mode of saying 'per se' was that the predicate does not relate to the subject as property or accident. Excluded from this model of predication is further something said by participation. The genus is not predicated of its species *per participationem* but *per essentiam*. "Man," for example, is not "animal" through participation in the Idea 'animal' but in virtue of his essence (*ibid.*, 1328). The definition consists of univocal predication, in which the predicate expresses the subject essentially.[67] Hence there is a definition only of the species. The identity therein stated is that of the being according to its specific essence. Within this horizon definitional thinking moves and is established, that is, comes to a stand.

For notice: the uppermost limit is the most general genera of being, the categories. That these are the principle is a "logical" result of the way of predication. For "being" is contracted to diverse categories according to the diverse modes of predicating; in this predicative account, "being" is

---

[65] On the necessity of a "status" in predication, see particularly *Post. Anal.* I, 22 (lect. 33–35) and *In II Metaph.*, lect. 4, 320ff.

[66] *In I De anima*, lect. 8, 121: Definitiones etiam habent principium et finem, quia non est ascendere in infinitum in generibus, sed accipitur quasi primum genus generalissimum, nec etiam est descendere in infinitum in speciebus, sed est stare in specie specialissima. Unde genus generalissimum est principium, species vero specialissima sicut terminus seu finis in definitionibus; *In II Post. Anal.*, lect. 14, 538: Oportet enim omnium definitionum esse principium id quod simplex est, idest genus commune.

[67] Cf. *In VII Metaph.*, lect. 2, 1288: ... de univoca praedicatione, secundum quod genera praedicantur de speciebus, in quarum definitionibus ponuntur; quia non est aliud per essentiam animal et homo.

from the very beginning either substance or quality, etc. (2.1.2.). "Being" itself adds nothing of its own to the forms of being, to the predicaments.[68] What interests the definitional logos is that which is categorically determined, not its *being* as such.

Below the lowest limit falls the *singular*, which is not predicated of something still lower.[69] What "counts" definitionally is the universal, the substance in the sense of form, not the individual subject. When Aristotle says in *Metaph.* II, c. 2 (994 b 21): "it is impossible to have scientific knowledge until we come to what is undivided (*individuum*)," then Thomas hastens to explain in his commentary:

> In this place "undivided" cannot be taken as the singular, because science does not deal with singulars (*scientia non est de singularibus*). But "undivided" can in one sense be called the concept of the last species, which cannot be divided further by essential differences.[70]

For thought, the species is the eido-logical limit whereby things are themselves de-fined and con-fined with regard to others. The definition states this ultimate difference (*differentia specifica*), in which something is comprehended in its being determined.[71] The definition joins together what is gathered in the Greek 'logos': word, concept, and the intelligibility of things.

Thinking and being correspond. With regard to science, the universal is "more" being than the particular, because the everlasting is "more" being than the corruptible. The individual comes to being and passes away, but the universal species is permanent.[72] On the way of definition what matters is to know (*scire*): therefore there is no definition of what is contingent: *definitio est non corruptibilium, sed sempiternorum*.[73] The horizon of the onto-logy, which motivated the "what" question, is the unchangeable, specific persistence, not the particular, corruptible existence.

2.2.3. *The way towards definition: 'Per viam divisionis'*

The horizon of the "what" question is a knowing *per viam diffinitionis*. But what is the way that leads to knowledge of the definition? How can the

---

[68] Cf. H. Berger, *Op zoek naar identiteit* (Nijmegen and Utrecht, 1968), pp. 149; 106.

[69] *In I Post. Anal.*, lect. 34, 291: Singularia, quae non praedicantur de aliquibus inferioribus, non contingit definire.

[70] *In II Metaph.*, lect. 4, 323: Non autem accipitur hic individuum singulare, quia scientia non est de singularibus. Sed individuum potest dici uno modo ipsa *ratio speciei specialissimae*, quae non dividitur per essentiales differentias.

[71] Cf. *In II Metaph.*, lect. 4, 328; *In I Post. Anal.*, lect. 38, 335.

[72] *In I Post. Anal.*, lect. 37, 330.

[73] *Ibid.*, lect. 16, 138. See further *In VII Metaph.*, lect. 15, 1610.

definition be brought to light? In every inquiry concerning what something is, the first difficulty—so Thomas remarks in connection with the
"quest" for the definition of the soul—is that we do not know "by what
way one must proceed towards definition" (*per quam viam procedendum [sit]
ad definitionem*).[74]

In the first basic text (*In II Phys.*, 1, 145), the result of the inquiry set
in motion by the question "What is nature?" is that the "definition of nature" is *concluded*—going beyond Aristotle's literal text—from premises.[75] But is a definition really demonstrable, or is definitional knowledge
deductive?

The direction of the movement of thought induces this objection. For
in 1.3.1. we saw that questioning is determined by the framework of demonstrative knowledge. Philosophical inquiry is a reduction to the middle
term of the syllogism, from which one demonstrates that a predicate necessarily belongs to a subject. "Every question is in a certain sense a
'quaestio medii.'" Now, if the "what" question asks what the medium
of the demonstration is, and the essential definition corresponds to this
question, then the definition must be the sought middle term: "definition ... serves as the middle term in a demonstration, which is a syllogism producing science."[76] By means of the definitional logos of the
essence—the first mode of saying 'per se'—it is shown in the syllogism
"why" a predicate belongs to a subject.

The place which the definition has in the syllogism entails consequences
for knowledge of the definition. From the "ex"-structure of scientific
knowledge, it follows that a definition which signifies the essence is ultimately undemonstrable.[77] "Since demonstration causes science, science
cannot possibly be the principle of science, in the sense that the principles
of the sciences would be known through science."[78] To bring about
science, the syllogism must proceed *ex propositionibus primis et immediatis* (cf.
1.3.1.)—"immediate" because these propositions are not demonstrated
by a middle term but are self-evident; and "primary" in relation to

[74] *In I De anima*, lect. 1, 9.

[75] Earlier in the Middle Ages we find such a deduction in the commentary of Robert
Grosseteste, which is one of the first expositions in the Occident of Aristotle's *Physica*. Cf.
R.C. Dales, ed., *Robert Grosseteste episcopi linconiensis: Commentarius in VIII libros Physicorum
Aristotelis* (University of Colorado Press, 1963), pp. 31ff. This commentary is datable to
c. 1228/9 (*ibid.*, ix).

[76] *In VII Metaph.*, lect. 15, 1610.

[77] *In II Post. Anal.*, lect. 8, 481: Definitio autem quae datur secundum causam forma-
lem, non potest ulterius demonstrari per aliquod principium intrinsecum rei, quod proprie pertinet ad quod quid est, utpote intrans essentiam rei.

On the limited possibility of demonstrating a definition, see *In II Post. Anal.*, lect. 8, 481;
488; *In IV Sent.* 3, 1 ad primam quaestionem (*quid sit baptismus*).

[78] *In II Post. Anal.*, lect. 20, 596.

other propositions demonstrated through them.

Should knowledge of the medium of the demonstration, the definition, be demonstrative, then this knowledge would again have to be mediated by another "what is," which would lead to an infinite regress. As a result every definition and all science would be eliminated, since an infinite series is not traversable. It is necessary—as with the "horizon" of the definition—to come to a stand at something that is im-mediate and hence undemonstrable.[79] The essential definition is the condition of the possibility of demonstrative knowledge; it is 'principium sciendi'.[80] For this reason, too, a distinction is explicitly made between knowing *per viam diffinitionis* and knowing *per viam demonstrationis*.[81]

If definition is "the principle of science" and there is therefore no demonstrative knowledge of it, then how can it be brought to light? There must be "some other method by which definitions are made known."[82] In *Post. Anal.* II, c. 12 (lect. 14 and 15) the method of the quest for the definition is indicated: *per viam divisionis*. Along the way of division that which is predicated essentially is to be investigated and arranged hierarchically. *Via ad inveniendum definitiones convenientissima est per divisiones.*[83] This is also the way that will be taken towards forming the definition of nature (cf. 3.1.).

This method is in line with the "horizon" of the definition. "Through knowing what a thing is, one knows it as distinct from others (*ab aliis distincta*). That is why the definition, which signifies what a thing is, distinguishes the thing defined from all others."[84] The definition states the ul-

---

[79] *In II Metaph.*, lect. 4, 325; *In I Post. Anal.*, lect 4, 41; lect. 35, 307.

[80] *In I Perih.*, lect. 1, 4: Quia enim demonstrationes definitiones praesupponunt, ex quibus concludunt . . .; *In VI Metaph.*, lect. 1, 1156: Cum enim definitio sit medium demonstrationis, et per consequens principium sciendi, oportet quod ad diversum modum definiendi, sequatur diversitas in scientiis speculativis.

In view of the central role played by definition in medieval science, a work of general synthesis on this subject is a desideratum.

[81] See the two texts already cited: *In Boeth. De trin.* 6, 4: Ex quo patet quod nihil potest sciri in scientiis speculativis neque per viam demonstrationis neque per viam diffinitionis nisi . . .; *In I De anima*, lect. 8, 119 (see n. 61, above).

To these two ways there correspond different ways of knowing. Cf. *In I Post. Anal.*, lect. 36, 318: Unde intellectus respondet immediatae propositioni; scientia autem conclusioni, quae est propositio mediata; *In II Metaph.*, lect. 4, 325; *In I Phys.*, lect. 1, 5: Quod autem dicit intelligere, refertur ad definitiones; quod vero dicit scire, refertur ad demonstrationes; *In I Post. Anal.*, lect. 22, 184.

[82] *In VI Metaph.*, lect. 1, 1150; the continuation of this text presents this method: "scilicet *divisione.*"

[83] *In III Phys.*, lect. 1, 279 (in connection with the definition of motion). Additional concrete examples are to be found in, among other places, *In II De anima*, lect. 1, 212: Praemittit quasdam divisiones, ex quibus habetur via ad investigandum definitionem animae; *In II Phys.*, lect. 8, 207; *In IV Phys.*, lect. 6, 455; *In II Ethic.*, lect. 5, 289.

[84] *S.c.G.* III, 46.

timate difference whereby the thing is delimited and determined (2.2.2.).

The most appropriate way of investigating what must be put in the definition is through the division of the genus, which is the principle of every definition. From the common genus the "descent" to the differences can begin. Therefore, prior to this division, it must already be known in some way what this genus is. In 1.9. we observed that the supposed precognition concerns the signification of the name.[85]

The dihaeretic mehod, as it was set forth by Plato in the *Sophistes* and *Politicus*, has according to Aristotle's judgement no demonstrative efficacy.[86] In the division, it is every time more asserted than proven that a certain predicate belongs to the subject. Yet even if the "what" of something cannot be demonstrated by the way of division, it remains true for the Stagirite too that, if a number of conditions are met, this method is an appropriate way towards the definition of the essence.

In forming a definition *per viam divisionis* one must be attentive to three things.[87] First, only that must be included which is predicated essentially, that is, which is always and universally (*per se*) said of the thing but which does not extend beyond its genus. Secondly, these essential determinations must be placed in the required order of the categorically earlier and later. Thirdly, all that which belongs to the essence must be included and nothing left out. That the entirety of the higher genus falls under the parts of the division is assured whenever the first and immediate differences are taken. When the division is carried out in the correct way, that is, descending from the more to the less general according to the essential differences, then all preceding parts will be included in the ultimate difference. *Ultima differentia erit tota substantia, et tota definitio.*[88]

2.3. *Definitional thinking: 'Definitiones sunt sicut numeri'*

The way that was opened by questioning went via "predication," "definition," and "division." What "counts" on the way to definitional knowledge is summed up well in a comparison found frequently not only in Thomas but in many other Scholastic writers: definitions of things are like numbers (*sicut numeri*). This "analogy" is derived from Aristotle (*Metaph.* VIII, 3, 1043 b 32 – 1044 a 11) and to the medieval mind was authorized by the saying in Wisdom 11:21: "Thou hast ordered all things

---

[85] For the distinction between the definition and the 'ratio' that explains the name, see *In VII Metaph.*, lect. 4, 1339; *In II Post. Anal.*, lect. 8, 484; lect. 6, 1466.

[86] *Priora Anal.* I, 31; *Post. Anal.* II, 5 (cf. lect. 4, 443ff.).

[87] *In II Post. Anal.*, lect. 15, 547ff.

[88] *In VII Metaph.*, lect. 12, 1555.

in measure, and *number*, and weight, Lord'' (*Omnia in mensura et numero et pondere disposuisti, Domine*).[89]

The comparison of definitions to numbers contains several moments. Among these moments there is a speculative coherence which makes apparent the direction of the movement of thought.

(1) Through the "what" question, that which is is reduced to its essence signified by the definition. Only of the species is there a definition, which is composed necessarily of a number of parts ('genus' and 'differentia')— necessarily, because the thing to be defined (e.g., "man") is not sufficiently made known according to its essential principles by a single name (e.g., "animal").[90] From this finding arises the question: What brings about the unity of the definition (*quomodo definitio ex partibus existens, possit esse una*)? Is the 'ratio diffinitiva' a sum of component parts, and in this sense a number?[91]

A first moment of the statement "definitions are like numbers" envisions the *unity* of both. Number has in virtue of itself (*per se*) unity and definiteness, just as the thing composed of matter and form. And for the same reason that the substance which is signified by the definition is one, the definition is one, namely *per se*.[92] The way in which composed being is one is the real foundation for the solution to the problem of the definitional composition.

Proper to the substantial form is that it gives "being as such" to matter. What comes to matter that is already actual is an accident, causing a "secondary being." Through the essential form the thing is what it is, has determinate being. Between the substantial form and the matter there cannot be something other, a 'medium', giving specific being. Through the form each thing is therefore also immediately one. The form is the 'ratio' of the unity: from the same source something is "being" (*ens*) and it is one.[93]

---

[89] Cf. *S. Th.* I, 5, 5, obj. 1 and corp. art.

[90] *In VII Metaph.*, lect. 9, 1460: Unum enim nomen non potest esse definitio, quia definitio oportet quod distincte notificet principia rerum quae concurrunt ad essentiam rei constituendam; alias autem definitio non sufficienter manifestaret essentiam rei; lect. 15, 1614.

[91] *In VII Metaph.*, lect. 12; *In VIII Metaph.*, lect. 5, 1755ff. Cf. J. de Tonquédec, *La critique de la connaissance* (Paris, 1929), p. 334: "Définir ... c'est poser une équation où un même objet est signifié, ... par une somme dont les diverses parties sont énumérées selon le rapport qui les unit: A = a + b + c; 'l'homme est l'animal raisonnable mortel.'" In this statement there is an inconsistency, for on the basis of the preceding "sum" the definition of "man" would really have to be: animal *and* reasonable *and* mortal.

[92] *In VIII Metaph.*, lect. 3, 1725ff.

[93] *De anima* q. un., a.9; *De spirit. creat.* q. un., a.3; *S. Th.* I, 76, 3: Nihil enim est simpliciter unum nisi per formam unam, per quam habet res esse: ab eodem enim habet res quod sit ens, et quod sit una.

This unity is implied in the model of predication, to which definitional thinking is tied. "The definition consists of what is predicated *per se*" (2.2.1.). All that can be stated essentially of something is, as such, one.[94] Should the essential predicates be said according to a real diversity of forms, then the first mode of saying would not be followed. For Thomas, accordingly, a decisive argument against the doctrine of the plurality of essential forms advanced by his contemporaries is "the mode of predication."[95]

In the determination by one and the same form, various grades of definiteness can be distinguished, e.g., "being," "body," "animal." In the ascent towards the genus of what is to be defined, and in the descent by means of differences, numerically the same form is sought, which is laid out *secundum rationes intelligibiles*.[96] The concept of the more general determination relates to that of the ultimate as matter relates to form. For in the order of thought, genus is conceived as the underlying determinable, as being that is imperfect and material in relation to specific being. From the composition of genus and differentia the species is constituted.[97] The horizon of the definition is the species, which is really one: *species* [*sit*] *una natura*.[98]

(2) In what is predicated 'per se', the thing and its essence are identical. For in the first mode of saying 'per se,' that which is essentially predicated *is* the subject. Yet Thomas points out that in the strict sense, this statement of Aristotle applies only to the immaterial substances.[99] In material things there is a nonidentity, namely, of the individual subject and the specific nature (cf. 2.1.3.). 'Homo' is not 'humanitas' (*De pot.* 7, 4). There is something "outside" the essence, namely, the particular, but precisely this lies beyond the horizon of the definition. The identity sought by definitional thought concerns the thing in its specific essence. For what is known must be true not now and then but always. "Certain" knowledge desires a "fixedness" of things in their specific persistence.

---

[94] *De subst. separ.*, c. 11, 108: Omnia quae substantialiter de aliquo praedicantur sunt per se et simpliciter unum.

[95] *S. Th.* I, 76, 3: Hoc apparet impossibile ex modo praedicationis. Similarly in *S.c.G.* II, 58; *De anima* q. un., a.1.

[96] *De spirit. creat.* q. un., art. 3 ad 3; *De anima* q. un., a.9: Oportet igitur dicere, quod eadem numero forma sit per quam res habet quod sit substantia, et quod sit in ultima specie specialissima.

[97] *De spirit. creat.* q. un., a.1 ad 24. For predication and for definition it holds alike: praedicatum comparatur ad subiectum ut forma ad materiam, et similiter differentia ad genus: ex forma autem et materia fit unum simpliciter (*In I Perih.*, lect. 8, 98).

For the coherence between the composition of form and matter and that of genus and difference, see also the extensive expositions in *De ente*, c. 3; *In Boeth. De trin.* 4, 2.

[98] *In VII Phys.*, lect. 8, 947.

[99] *In VII Metaph.*, lect. 11, 1535.

In the determination of the definition, the essence is made known *per aliqua certa*, to which nothing can be added or taken away.[100] Therefore, definitions are "like numbers." The addition or subtraction of anything, no matter how slight, alters the *identity*, effects another definition and another specific nature. If, for example, the difference "rational" is added to "besouled sensitive substance," the species "man" is constituted; if, however, "sensitive" is subtracted, the species "plant" results.[101]

(3) In the moment of identity expressed in the comparison with numbers, it is likewise implied that *discreteness* is a characteristic of definitional thinking. The definition states the ultimate 'differentia' in virtue of which the thing is distinguished from all others. The differences do not differ from each other by further differences, they are diverse (*diversa*). "Diverse" is said absolutely; "different" is said in a certain respect. Where there is a difference, there is also agreement.[102]

Therefore the method of division was the most suitable for forming a definition. It required in the first place that only what is always and universally predicated of something but which does not extend beyond its genus would be included in the definition. 'Ens' does not meet this requirement, for being extends to everything and things are not distinct in it.[103] The horizon is categorical being. Primary in this predicative account is formal diversity.

(4) Finally, definitions are "like numbers" because they form a *series*, an order. As in the case of numbers each next one contains the preceding and something that goes beyond it, so the diverse definitions and the essences they signify stand in a hierarchy.

Everything is determined by its form and species to a special grade of being, which is its perfection.[104] Formal diversity therefore presupposes different grades of perfection, a hierarchical order of being.[105]

---

[100] *In II Post. Anal.*, lect. 4, 448.

[101] *In VIII Metaph.*, lect. 3, 1723ff. Cf. *De verit.* 20, 1.

[102] *S. Th.* I, 3, 8 ad 3: Homo enim et equus differunt rationali et irrationali differentiis: quae quidem differentiae non differunt amplius ab invicem aliis differentiis. Unde, si fiat vis in verbo, non proprie dicuntur differre, sed diversa esse; nam secundum Philosophum X Metaph. (c. 3), diversum absolute dicitur, sed omne differens aliquo differt; *De pot.* 7, 3 ad 2.

[103] *In II Post. Anal.*, lect. 13, 529.

[104] *S. Th.* I, 50, 2 ad 1: Unumquodque autem constituitur in specie, secundum quod determinatur ad aliquem specialem gradum in entibus; quia "species rerum sunt sicut numeri", qui differunt per additionem et subtractionem unitatis, ut dicitur VIII Metaph.

[105] *In II Metaph.*, lect. 4, 321; *S. Th.* I, 76, 3: Inveniuntur enim rerum species et formae differre ab invicem secundum perfectius et minus perfectum.

There cannot be a difference among forms unless because one thing exists more perfectly than another. That is why Aristotle likens definitions, through which the natures of things and forms are signified, to numbers, in which species are varied by the addition or subtraction of unity; so, from this, we are made to understand that the diversity of forms requires different grades of perfection. This is quite clear to one who observes the nature of things.[106]

In reality one discovers a scale of increasing nobility: inanimate bodies, plants, irrational animals, and intellectual substances. This order requires a principle, in relation to which the gradation is thought. This principle is matter. The counting starts here: arranged as the first species is the form that gives the lowest grade of perfection to matter. Each that follows is more perfect because it ''in-forms'' in a richer way. For by one and the same form man is essentially a ''being in act,'' a ''body,'' a ''living being,'' an ''animal,'' and a ''man.''[107] The composition of genus and difference in the definition articulates this hierarchical order of reality.

The four moments thus distinguished have a cumulative effect. What ''counts'' on the way of definition, which corresponds to the ''what'' question, is the essential form. Unity, identity, discreteness, and perfection, it is in each case the form that guarantees these for a thing. In the onto-logy the matter is the ''other'': the principle of indefiniteness, mutability, and imperfection. The ''virtus essendi'' follows on the triumph of form over matter (*victoriam formae super materiam*).[108] The relation of form and matter even acquires a dialectical streak because the formal component of being is qualified as something divine (cf. 4.4.).[109]

2.4. *The definition of nature*

The ''what'' question inquires primarily into the whatness of the first category, since this is the essentially predicated and the subsistent

---

[106] *S.c.G.* III, 97: In formis differentia esse non potest nisi per hoc quod una perfectior existit quam alia; propter quod Aristoteles diffinitiones, per quas naturae rerum et formae signantur, assimilat numeris, in quibus species variantur per additionem vel subtractionem unitatis; ut ex hoc detur intelligi quod formarum diversitas diversum gradum perfectionis requirit. Et hoc evidenter apparet naturas rerum speculanti.

[107] *De anima*, q. un., art. 7: Ubicumque enim est diversitas graduum, oportet quod gradus considerentur per ordinem ad aliquid unum principium. In substantiis igitur materialibus attenduntur diversi gradus speciem diversificantes in ordine ad *primum principium, quod est materia.* Et inde est quod primae species sunt imperfectiores, posteriores vero perfectiores et per additionem se habentes ad primas; *S.Th.* I, 76, 4 ad 3; 76, 6 ad 1.

[108] *S.c.G.* II, 30.

[109] *In II Sent.* 15, 1, 2: Secundum quas [sc. formas substantiales] est esse specificum, quod divinum esse dicitur.

(2.1.3.). Definition applies in the proper sense only to what possesses the *ratio entis* perfectly, to what is complete in its being and species, namely, the substance. *Quidditas, et essentia, et definitio est simpliciter tantum substantiarum.*[110] For only substance has an absolute quiddity, that is, it is not dependent, in its essence, on something other. Only the concrete subsisting thing, a *quod est* such as "man" and "stone," for example, possesses an absolute being. It is precisely on the basis of this absoluteness that this thing can be determined definitively through its principles.[111]

In the introduction to this chapter it was noticed that the way of definition with regard to "nature" was considered to be difficult to traverse. The "absoluteness" of the horizon would seem to be a first obstacle. For nature, as has been explained (1.5.), is signified 'in abstracto' as something non-subsisting, as *quo est*. No more than substantial form and matter do does it possess absolute being of itself (*per se esse absolutum*). For this reason the forming of a perfect, that is, "absolute" definition of nature will not be possible. The determination of what has no absolute being will be characterized by the "addition" of something. In such a definition, its subject—more precisely: the proper subject—must be stated.[112]

Nature, however, stands in an even more telling sense over against what is "absolute."[113] It is not only non-subsistent but has always, moreover, the character of principle. Now, "principle is said in relation (*relative*) to that which proceeds from it."[114] Nature is a *nomen relativum*. But then the definition of nature cannot ignore the relationship of principle and cause. Three examples will serve to make clear that various medieval thinkers themselves felt that this relationality presented a difficulty to defining nature.

Thomas Aquinas criticizes (*In II Phys.*, lect. 1, 145) those who wanted to correct Aristotle's definition; they tried, namely, to define nature through something absolute (*per aliquid absolutum*), saying that nature is an inherent force in things (*vis insita rebus*)— a first step on the way to the modern view of nature.[115] R. PANIKKAR is incorrect, in his study *El con-*

---

[110] *In I Sent.* 25, 1, 4 ad 2; *In VII Metaph.*, lect. 1, 1257ff.; *In II De anima*, lect. 1, 213.

[111] *In VII Metaph.*, lect. 4, 1352: Simpliciter per prius, nullius erit definitio nisi substantiae, nec etiam quod quid erat esse . . . Substantia enim quae habet quidditatem absolutam, non dependet in sua quidditate ex alio; *Quodl.* XI, q.2; *In II Sent.* 3, 1, 6.

[112] *De ente* c. 7; *In II De anima*, lect. 1, 213. The prototype of such a determination is the definition of the "soul."

[113] Cf. *De potentia* 9, 4 ad 10 for the two meanings of 'absolutum': Substantia prima dicitur absoluta, quasi ab alio non dependens. Relativum autem in divinis non excludit absolutum quod est ab alio [adde: non] dependens; sed excludit absolutum quod ad aliud non refertur.

[114] *S.c.G.* II, 11.

[115] This expression occurs, among other places, in Avicenna, *Sufficientia* I, 58 (*Opera*

cepto de naturaleza, in seeing as the background of Thomas's criticism the idea that the first principle of the operations of a thing must be sought insofar as these operations are its own and not insofar as God intervenes in each act.[116] The matter at issue is not the opposition between "immanence" and "divine intervention." What appears here—as is clear from the entire context—is the tension between being absolute, which is required by the definition, and being principle.

This interpretation is corroborated by a similar train of thought, reported in Albert the Great's commentary on the *Physica*. Some desired— and, it may be added, actually tried—to define nature *secundum esse absolutum*, and not insofar as it is principle. For, so their argument goes, each thing is more what it is in itself than what it is in relation to something other.[117] In the *Summa Physicorum*, probably written by Robert Grosseteste, the objection is raised that nature is not a principle because a principle belongs to the accidental category of the relation. Nature is in the genus of substance and the substance is an *ens absolutum*.[118] Time and again we see in these objections, in which no adequate distinction is drawn between the relation as an accidental category and the foundation of the relation, the urge to absolutization.

Thomas, normally reserved about using disqualifications, wastes few words on the attempt to define nature through something "absolute." He derides it as "ridiculous" (*deridendi sunt*; *In II Phys.*, 1, 145). Categorically, he asserts that "the name 'nature' implies the relation of principle." Nature is not a thing alongside other things; it has the character of origin. It was precisely that which formed the distinctive character of the question concerning nature (1.5.). This question is an "intensification" of the inquiring into the ontologically prior of that which is. It is a reduction to that origination, which is determinative for the direction of this questioning and knowing.

----

philosophica, Venice, 1508); Hugh of St. Victor, *Quaestiones in epistulam ad Romanos*, q. 119 (Migne PL 175, 463 B); John of Salisbury, *Metalogicon* I, 8 (Migne PL 199, 835 C); Albert the Great, *In II Phys.*, tract. I, c.7 (*Opera Omnia*, ed. A. Borgnet, III, 103): Est enim natura vis insita rebus naturalibus ex similibus secundum naturam similia procreans.

For the mechanistic conception of nature as 'vis', see E.J. Dijksterhuis, *De mechanisering van het wereldbeeld* (Amsterdam, 1950), p. 342ff.; R.G. Collingwood, *The Idea of Nature*, (Oxford, 1945), p. 101.

[116] *El concepto de naturaleza, Analisis historico y metafisico de un concepto*, 2nd ed. (Madrid, 1972), p. 179.

[117] Albert the Great, *In II Phys.*, tract. I, c.3 (*Opera Omnia* III, 97).

[118] *Summa Physicorum* II (ed. J.E. Bolzán y Celina Lértora Mendoza, *Suma de los ocho libros de la "Física" de Aristóteles* (Buenos Aires, 1972)), p. 62: Dubitatur de definitione naturae. Videtur quod non sit principium, quia principium est in genere relationis, cum principium cuiusdam, aut quorundam sit principium. Sed natura, cum sit substantia, non est in genere relationis: quia substantia est ens absolutum, ergo natura non est principium.

Therein too lies the core of the difficulty of defining nature. Those who define intend a resolution of what is to be defined to its principles.[119] But nature *is* this determination, is the very horizon of the definitional logos. "'What' sometimes inquires into the nature signified by the definition."[120] The definition of nature has a meta-character. What is signified by the definition corresponding with the "what" question is nature.

In the progress of the way of definition the coherence between nature and definition is confirmed. The division terminates in the specific difference, and of this it is said: *ultima differentia erit tota substantia rei, et tota definitio* (2.2.3.). At this juncture, reference must be made to the semantic development of the term "nature," which Thomas sketches in various places (cf. 6.5.2.). The last signification is one derived from Boethius: "Nature is the specific difference which informs each thing." Thomas adds to this: "For the specific difference completes a definition and is taken from the proper form of a thing."[121] Nature is the specific difference, and the ultimate difference is the complete definition and essence. The sense of the question "What is nature?" is the direction of definitional thinking (see 7.1.1.4.).

2.5. *Predication 'per essentiam' and 'per participationem'*

In his important study *Toward Understanding Saint Thomas*, M.D. CHENU contrasts Augustine's approach ("a philosophy of participation wherein attention is focussed on beings in their 'degrees' rather than in their autonomy, in the exemplary reasons ... rather than in the internal causes") to Scholastic logic ("one concerned with the determining and the identifying of things. Its main work is to arrive at a definition").[122] This opposition compels us to inquire further. For is there in Thomas not equally a philosophy of participation?[123] And how does this interfere with

---

[119] *In VII Metaph.*, lect. 15, 1615: Resolutio autem definiti in sua principia, quod definientes facere intendunt ...; *In I De anima*, lect. 1, 10: Definitio enim notificat essentiam rei, quae non potest sciri nisi sciantur principia.

[120] *S. Th.* I, 29, 1 ad 4: 'Quid' quandoque quaerit de natura, quam significat diffinitio; *Quodl.* II, 2, 2.

[121] *S. Th.* I, 29, 1 ad 4. Cf. *De unione verbi incarnati* q. un., a.1; *S. Th.* III, 2, 1; *In V Metaph.*, lect. 5, 822.

[122] *Toward Understanding Saint Thomas* (Chicago, 1964), p. 173.

[123] L.-B. Geiger, *La participation dans la philosophie de S. Thomas d'Aquin* (Paris, 1942), p. 451: "la philosophie de S. Thomas peut être appelée à juste titre une philosophie de la participation." GEIGER, together with C. FABRO, has inaugurated an important renewal in Thomas studies by highlighting the great significance of the idea of participation. See the latter's *La nozione metafisica di partecipazione secondo S. Tomaso d'Aquino*, 2nd ed. (Turin, 1950); *Participation et Causalité selon S. Thomas d'Aquin* (Louvain and Paris, 1961).

the logic of identity, which is, after all, not merely formal in character?

In 1.8.2. ("The origin of things and the question of being"), we called attention, in connection with the other mode of questioning *an est* and *quid est*, to a passage from *Quodl.* II, 2, 1. Careful reading of this entire text shows that in Thomas this other mode of questioning is connected with a model of the predicative logos different from the previously discussed predication *per se* and *per accidens*. We shall follow the exposition closely in the following sections and attempt to grasp its philosophical intentions.[124]

2.5.1. *Another mode of predicating*

> It must be said that something is predicated of something in two ways— essentially or by participation.'Light' is predicated of an illumined body in the manner of participation, but if there were some separated light then it would be predicated of it essentially.[125]

The terminology and the (hypothetical) example Thomas uses to elucidate this mode of predication allow no room for doubt that the Platonic model of predication is introduced here. This was known to Thomas from, among other sources, the writings of the keen critic of this ontology, Aristotle. In his commentary on the *Metaphysica* Aquinas finds himself repeatedly confronted with this other mode of predicating; he speaks of it in a manner that goes far beyond the literal text of the Stagirite.[126]

In *In I Metaph.*, lect. 10, 154 he describes Plato's position: "there are many individuals which have the same species predicated of them, and this by participation. For the species or 'Idea' (of man) is the specific nature itself by which there exists man essentially (*per essentiam*). But an individual is man by participation inasmuch as the specific nature is participated in by this designated matter." After presenting this opposition of the species (Idea) and what participates in the species, Thomas continues with a general circumscription of participation. "That which is something in its entirety does not participate in it but is essentially identical

---

[124] C. Fabro, in *Participation et Causalité*, p. 597, entitles *Quodl.* II, 2, 1 as "l'exposé plus mûr et synthéthique de la participation." The way in which he reads this text is characteristic, however, of the rather unproblematic manner in which he analyzes Thomas's thought in this study.

[125] *Quodl.* II, 2, 1: Dupliciter aliquid de aliquo praedicatur: uno modo *essentialiter*, alio modo *per participationem*. Lux enim praedicatur de corpore illuminato participative; sed si esset aliqua lux separata, praedicaretur de ea essentialiter.

[126] Cf. H.H. Berger, "Der Partizipationsgedanke im Metaphysik-Kommentar des Thomas von Aquin," *Vivarium* 1 (1963): 115-40.

with it, whereas that which is not something completely but has another thing joined to it, is said properly to participate." To participate means to be something without being totally identical to what one is.[127] Supposing there should be some separated light—the example from *Quodl.* II, 2, 1—then light could be essentially predicated of it. This self-subsisting light would not be said to participate in light, for it would be nothing other than light; it *is* (essentially) light. But if light is said of an illuminated body, it is predicated by participation: there is in this illuminated thing something other than light. Or—to take up the example from the commentary on the *Metaphysica*—if the separate Idea of man has nothing other than the nature of the species, then it is essentially man and is therefore called man-in-itself (*per se homo*). But an individual possesses, in addition to the specific nature, a designated matter as individuating principle; Plato therefore says that it participates in the species.[128]

Particularly from the examples cited, it is clear that the Platonic model of predication has to be situated within the same movement of thought as the Aristotelian. In both cases the terminus of the desire to know is knowledge *per viam diffinitionis*. Here again we find the motive of unity, the "reduction" to identity. "For the Platonists wish to reduce all that is composed or material to simple and abstract principles" (*reducere in principia simplicia et abstracta*).[129] What is found in a plurality of things must be reduced to a first, that is such through its essence, while the remainder are such through participation in it.[130] The horizon is always the *species*, which is in virtue of itself (*per se*) and which as such has per-sistence. What is predicated *per essentiam* is uni-form, completely identical, and discrete: all characteristics of the definitional logos, in which the essence is disclosed.

However, in this "reduction" to the logically and onto-logically prior, Plato's conception of what is identical differs from Aristotle's. The "what" question inquires into something separate from the subject. The Idea sought is outside the sensible thing, for the latter is particular, non-identical, and mutable, in short, by participation. Therefore, this falls entirely beyond the "horizon."[131] Platonic science concerns separate

---

[127] *In I Metaph.*, lect. 10, 154: Quod enim totaliter est aliquid, non participat illud, sed est per essentiam idem illi. Quod vero non totaliter est aliquid habens aliquid aliud adiunctum, proprie participare dicitur.

[128] *In I Metaph.*, lect. 10, 155.

[129] *In De div. nomin.*, prooemium.

[130] *In De causis*, lect. 16: Secundum autem platonicas positiones, omne quod in pluribus invenitur oportet reducere ad aliquod primum, quod per suam essentiam est tale, a quo alia per participationem talia dicuntur.

[131] *In I Metaph.*, lect. 10, 153.

forms, 'species ideales',[132] which are something "abstract" (*abstractum*). We have encountered this term earlier (1.4.2.): the essence can be considered in "abstraction" from the subject which is constituted by it. But for Plato this is not a mode of viewing the essence, but its mode of being. An "abstractum," and only an "abstractum," is truly, since it is subsistent and totally form—in Thomas's terminology, a "separate perfection."[133]

Not only in his commentaries on Aristotle but also in his other works Thomas speaks of the predication *per essentiam* and *per participationem*. In his *Scriptum* on the *Sententiae*, he takes it up with reference to a statement by Augustine (*De trinitate* V, 10): "For God is not great through that greatness which is not Himself" (*Deus enim non est magnus ea magnitudine quae non est quod ipse*).

Augustine wants to demonstrate here, according to Thomas, that greatness is said essentially (*substantialiter*) of God. For what is not essentially great is called great through participation in a greatness that is not its essence. Now, the greatness in virtue of which something else is called great through participation is greater than that which is great through it. There is something greater, therefore, than all that is not essentially great. However, nothing is greater than God. Ergo, He is essentially great.

Is this reasoning valid? Thomas asks himself. Can it be said that greatness is great? A concrete term is not predicated of an abstract term, is it? Consequently, it seems that greatness is not greater than that which is great through participation.

This objection gives Thomas the opportunity to clarify the meaning of predication 'per essentiam.' In Augustine's reasoning, it is necessary to accept as middle term: *abstractum praedicetur magis quam concretum*. But what matters here is the correct understanding of "more" (*magis*). What is meant by that, in the case of greatness, is that "greater" is what possesses with more truth the 'ratio' of greatness. Similarly, "whiteness" is whiter, not because it has more whiteness, but because the essence of whiteness belongs to it more truly. Predication *per essentiam* is always more important than that *per participationem*. For in the former, the perfect identity of subject and predicate is expressed.[134]

---

[132] *De spirit. creat.* q. un., a. 9 ad 6.

[133] *De subst. separ.*, c. 14: Si autem sit aliqua forma separata, nihil quod ad rationem illius formae pertinere potest ei deesset, sicut si albedo esset separata, nihil quod sub ratione albedinis comprehenditur ei deficeret.

On the 'perfectio separata', see also *De ente*, c. 5 and *S.c.G.* II, 52.

[134] *In I Sent.* 22, 1, Exp. textus: Semper autem principalior praedicatio est per essentiam, quam quae est per participationem. Et ideo albedo quae recipit praedicationem al-

One gains the impression that Thomas, with the formulation of this general proposition—*semper autem principalior praedicatio est per essentiam, quam quae est per participationem*—at the same time ascribes a certain validity to this model of predication. With that, we have arrived along the way of predication at a truly tense moment. This seems an appropriate moment to continue the reading of *Quodl.* II, 2, 1.

2.5.2. *Every creature is being by participation ('Omnis creatura est ens participative')*

Therefore, we must say that 'being' (*ens*) is predicated essentially of God alone, inasmuch as divine being (*esse*) is subsistent and absolute being. However, it is predicated of any creature by participation, for no creature is its being but rather is something which has being. So also God is said 'good' essentially because He is goodness itself, but creatures are said 'good' by participation because they have goodness. For anything is good inasmuch as it is, according to what Augustine says in *De doctrina christiana* I, that inasmuch as we are, we are good.[135]

We can notice that Thomas adopts the model of predication "essentially"/"by participation," but not—it must immediately be added —its Platonic application to the relationship of univocal species to their inferiors. The original step that Thomas takes is that what is said in this way is not the specific being of a thing but "being" as such (*ens*).

Aquinas advances no explicit arguments for the scope of this validity. However, they can lie nowhere else but in the all-encompassing universality of the predicated: "Being is said of everything that is."[136] Thomas's step must be motivated through the insight that "being" is "transcendental," that is, that it goes beyond the genera, the diverse categories (2.1.2.). So in the cited text, essential and participatory predication are also applied to the transcendental "good" (cf. 8.1.1.).[137]

---

bedinis vere per modum essentialem, ut dicatur albedo est albedo, dicitur magis vere praedicationem albedinis recipere, quam res alba; quamvis non eodem modo recipiat, quia rem albam dicimus albam, sed albedinem dicimus albedinem.

[135] *Quodl.* II, 2, 1: Secundum ergo hoc dicendum est, quod ens praedicatur de solo Deo *essentialiter*, eo quod esse divinum est esse subsistens et absolutum; de qualibet autem creatura praedicatur *per participationem*: nulla enim creatura est suum esse, sed est habens esse. Sic et Deus dicitur bonus essentialiter, quia *est* ipsa bonitas; creaturae autem dicuntur bonae per participationem, quia *habent* bonitatem: unumquodque enim, in quantum est, bonum est, secundum illud Augustini in I Doctrina Christiana, quod in quantum sumus, boni sumus.

[136] *S.c.G.* II, 15: Esse autem dicitur de omni eo quod est.

[137] See especially *In De div. nomin.*, prooemium: Nec solum huiusmodi abstractione Platonici considerabant circa ultimas species rerum naturalium, sed etiam *circa maxime communia*, quae sunt bonum, unum et ens. Ponebant, enim, unum primum quod est ipsa

"Things are not distinguished from each other in having being, because in that respect they agree."[138] This did not "count," accordingly,
for definitional thinking. The definition states the ultimate difference,
whereby something is manifested in its determinate being. For Thomas,
however, just being itself, over against which there is "nothing," is what
must be considered as worthy of questioning. The question with respect
to being itself requires a different onto-logy than the saying *per se* of the
definition; in Thomas it is connected with the Platonic logos. This becomes apparent in the second basic text (cf. 1.8.2.), where participation
does not come up until in connection with an origin "according as 'to be'
(*esse*) is bestowed upon the whole universe of things by the first Being (*a
primo ente*)."

In predication *per essentiam / per participationem*, a multiplicity can be reduced to unity at the transcendental level. For the mark of this model of
predication was that the composed thing is said with reference to the separated species, which is uniform and completely identical. Applied to
"being," this means that all that is in any way is reduced to what is essentially.

This being *per essentiam* can only be unique, because it is an "abstract
being" and "separate perfection."[139] It cannot be multiplied by the addition of a difference (in the way the genus is multiplied in species), or by
the reception of the form in different parts of matter (as the species is multiplied in individuals). These possibilities would impair the perfect identity of pure being (*esse tantum*).[140] This unique being *per essentiam* is God;
"the divine being"—thus *Quodl.* II, 2, 1—"is subsistent and absolute
being."

This predicative account entails that "being" is said of all others by
participation. Immediately, as a matter of course, this mode of being is
identified with creatureliness: *omnis autem creatura est ens participative* (*S. Th.*
I, 104, 1). Not one creature *is* its being, but is what *has* being. The same
conclusion is found in *De subst. separ.* c. 9: "Necessarily all other things,
which are under it [i.e., subsistent being], must be as participating in
being." This "having being" expresses the nonidentity that is characteristic of the creaturely condition.

---

essentia bonitas et unitatis et esse, quod dicimus Deum et quod omnia alia dicuntur bona,
vel una vel entia per derivationem ab illo primo.

[138] *S.c.G.* I, 26: Res ad invicem non distinguuntur secundum quod esse habent, quia
in hoc omnia conveniunt.

[139] *De subst. separ.*, c. 14, 121: Id quod abstractum est non potest esse nisi unum in
unaquaque natura. Si enim albedo posset esse abstracta, sola una esset albedo, quae
abstracta esset; omnes aliae albedines essent eam participantes. Sic igitur, sicut sola Dei
substantia est *ipsum abstractum esse*, ...

[140] *De ente*, c. 5.

Quodl. II, 2, 1 continues:

> However, whenever something is predicated of another in the manner of participation, it is necessary that there be something in the latter outside that in which it participates. And therefore, in any creature the creature itself which has being and its very being are other, and this is what Boethius says in *De hebdomadibus*, that 'being and that which is are diverse in all entities except the first'.[141]

That something is predicated of something *per essentiam* or *per participationem* means that in the former case a simplicity and in the latter a composition is expressed. For, to participate means: not to be something completely (*totaliter*) but to have something other added—in the Platonic model, matter. Because the creature is a being through participation, there must be something here "outside" (*praeter*) what is participated in. The index of creatureliness is the composition of that which participates and being that is participated in: "In whatever is created, the nature which participates in being and its being itself (*ipsum esse eius*) are other."[142]

This compositeness is indicated by Thomas in the conclusion of *Quodl.* II, 2, 1 as the "composition of essence and being"; and in another way (in the passage just cited) with the help of Boethius's distinction between 'quo est' (or: "being") and 'quod est'("that wich is"). It applies also to the separated substances, which—although pure forms—nevertheless possess no perfect simplicity and therefore can be questioned concerning that "other" which is their being (cf. 1.8.1.).

The direction of this mode of predication emerges clearly, also in its distinction from the Aristotelian model. It is true that predication *per essentiam* / *per participationem*, too, stands in a movement of thought in which compositeness and multiplicity are reduced to identity and unity, but at a different level.

(1) This mode of predicating corresponds to the question concerning the being of that which is (1.8.). Therein, the categorical meaning of being is transcended into 'ens' as transcendental.

(2) As a result, the reduction to identity also has another character. The horizon of definitional thought was the species, whereby the thing is distinguished from other beings. Primary in this account is not the formal diversity but the transcendental unity of being. All that is is reduced to the "first" being, which most truly is because it *is* in a fully identical way.

---

[141] *Quodl.* II, 2, 1: Quandocumque autem aliquid praedicatur de altero, per participationem, oportet ibi aliquid esse praeter id quod participatur. Et ideo in qualibet creatura est aliud ipsa creatura quae habet esse, et ipsum esse eius; et hoc est quod Boëtius dicit in lib. *De Hebdom.*, quod 'in omni eo quod est citra primum, aliud est esse et quod est'.

[142] *De spirit. creat.* q. un., art. 1. Cf. *In De div. nomin.* c. 4, lect. 14, 476; *De ente*, c. 5.

(3) That of which being is predicated *per essentiam / per participationem* is identified with God and creature. This mode of predicating marks the distinction and the relationship between God and created reality. What is being by its essence is that unique separated substance which is God. The creature is being through participation. "Being" is said differently of God and of the creaure. But in this diversity there is a unity. The manner in which the diversity of the categories of being was brought to unity is now transposed to this level. The diverse relationships of substance and accident to being impede any univocal predication of "being"; it is said "analogically" (2.1.2.). Likewise, God is related to being in another way than is the creature; namely, He is His being. Therefore, "being" is not predicated of God and the creature univocally but analogically. "Being" is said of the creature because its being refers to the first, subsistent being.[143] Creaturely being must be understood in relationship to God.

2.5.3. Predication 'per participationem' and 'per se'

In what preceded, we noted several times that Aristotle has subjected the Platonic model of predication to a sharp critique—a critique shared by Thomas.[144] Aristotelian predication *per se* does not move from the subject away towards something separate but seeks to manifest the *intrinsic* essence of the subject. That things are and are known finds its sufficient reason in the identity of the essence and the thing itself (1.4.2.).

Unavoidable becomes then the question of how the predication of being 'per essentiam / per participationem' relates to the Aristotelian first mode of saying *per se*, which is determinative for the definition.[145] The continuation of the text in *Quodl.* II, 2, 1 is therefore of importance, even though Thomas does not explicitly thematize the relationship between the two modes of predication:

> But it must be known that something is participated in in two ways. In one way it is participated in as though belonging to the substance of the thing participating, as a genus is participated in by a species of it. However, a creature does not participate in being this way for that belongs to the substance of a thing which enters into its definition, but being (*ens*) is not stated in the definition of a creature because it is neither a genus nor a difference. So it is participated in as something not belonging to the thing's essence. And therefore the "if" question (*an est*) is different from the "what"

---

143 *De pot.* 7, 7; *S.c.G.* I, 32 and 34; *S. Th.* I, 13, 6.
144 Cf. sections 2.1. and 2.2.2.; *In II Sent.* 17, 1, 1; *S. Th.* I, 6, 4.
145 Cf. L.-B. Geiger, *La participation*, pp. 122ff.

question (*quid est*). So, since all that is outside a thing's essence may be called an accident, the being which pertains to the "if" question is an accident.[146]

Two modes of participation are distinguished. What is participated in according to the first way belongs to the essence of the thing and enters into its definition; adduced as an example is the genus, which is participated in by the species. This very example, however, requires clarification. For the definition consists of what is predicated 'per se'. That is why the horizon of definitional thinking was the 'species'; for, according to Aristotle, the species is never said by participation, but essentially (2.2.2.). Yet the two perspectives, which seem mutually exclusive, are brought together here.

For understanding this, one should start from the general circumscription of participation in *In I Metaph.* (lect. 10, 154): What is not something completely, but has something other added to it, participates in this quality. In a similar way, the notion of participation is established in Thomas's commentary on *De hebdom.* (c. 2): "To participate is, as it were, to take part (*quasi partem capere*); so when something receives partially what belongs to another in a universal way, it is said that it participates in it." Presented as a first instance is the participation of the species in the genus and of the individual in the species: "so 'man' is said to participate in 'animal', because 'man' does not possess the ratio of 'animal' according to its entire communality; and for the same reason, 'Socrates' participates in 'man.'"[147] What is common to both cases is that the subject is not identical with the predicate, because it possesses a general perfection in a particular way. One genus is specified in a multiplicity of species, one species particularized in a multiplicity of individuals.[148] Yet *this* manner of participation, according to Thomas's judgement, can coincide very well with the Aristotelian predication *per se*.

---

[146] *Quodl.* II, 2, 1: Sed sciendum est, quod aliquid participatur dupliciter. Uno modo quasi existens de substantia participantis, sicut genus participatur a specie.
Hoc autem modo esse non participatur a creatura. Id enim est de substantia rei quod cadit in eius definitione. Ens autem non ponitur in definitione creaturae, quia nec est genus nec differentia. Unde participatur sicut aliquid non existens de essentia rei; et ideo alia quaestio est *an est* et *quid est*. Unde, cum omne quod est praeter essentiam rei, dicatur accidens; esse quod pertinet ad quaestionem *an est*, est accidens.

[147] *In De hebdom.*, lect. 2: Est autem participare quasi partem capere; et ideo quando aliquid particulariter recipit id quod ad alterum pertinet universaliter, dicitur participare illud [For this reading, see L.-B. Geiger, *La participation*, p. 48, n. 2.]; sicut homo dicitur participare animal, quia non habet rationem animalis secundum totam communitatem; et eadem ratione Socrates participat hominem.

[148] Cf. *S.c.G.* I, 32: Omne quod de pluribus praedicatur univoce, secundum participationem cuilibet eorum convenit de quibus praedicatur, nam species participare dicitur genus, et individuum speciem.

The subject in *De hebdomadibus* is the question posed to Boethius: "whether beings are good through their essence or through participation." In his lectio (c.3) Thomas observes that this question suggests an absolute opposition (*considerandum est, quod in ista quaestione praesupponitur quod aliquid esse per essentiam, et per participationem sint opposita*). Yet that is not always the case, as is shown by the manner in which the species participates in the genus. To be sure, for Plato there is an opposition here— the Idea "animal" is different from the Idea "man"—but not for Aristotle. "According to Aristotle's view ... there is nothing to prohibit that what is said by participation is predicated substantially" (*nihil prohibit, id quod per participationem dicitur, substantialiter praedicari*). Man is truly "animal," because this generic term expresses something that belongs to the definition of man's essence. This first manner of participation is not incompatible with the Aristotelian predication 'per se', since for the latter it suffices that the predicate express the subject according to a part of its essence (2.2.1.).[149]

This manner of participation, however, was not the one that Thomas had in mind in his application of the Platonic model of predication. He meant a participation in *being*, and such participation can not be brought together with predication 'per se'. "Being" is not participated in by the creature in the first way, for, so *Quodl.* II, 2, 1 stipulates, 'ens' is not stated in the definition of the creature.

This argument is characteristic of the twofold sense of the movement of thought. It originally belongs in the framework of definitional thought, for in the predicative account corresponding to such thought, "being" is contracted immediately to the diverse categories. 'Ens' is no genus and is therefore not stated in the definition of something. Now the same argument acquires a meaning that breaks through the "horizon": being, as transcendental, possesses an act which forms no part of the essence.

This is also indicated as the reason why the "if" question is different from that concerning the "what." Since what is participated in is something not belonging to the thing's essence, the "being" that pertains to the "if" question is an accident. That is still thought entirely in terms of the essence and its definition. What falls "outside" the essence is accidental.[150] It was Avicenna's view: *opinio Avicenna fuit, quod unum et ens sem-*

---

[149] Cf. *In III Sent.* 10, 1, 2: Ad hoc quod aliqua praedicatio sit per se, non oportet quod praedicatum per se conveniat subjecto secundum omne quod in nomine subjecti implicatur; sed sufficit si secundum aliquid eorum sibi per se conveniat.

[150] *S.c.G.* I, 21 Adhuc: Solum illud videtur esse praeter essentiam vel quidditatem rei, quod non intrat diffinitionem ipsius. Diffinitio enim significat quid est res. Sola autem accidentia rei sunt, quae in diffinitione non cadunt. Sola igitur accidentia sunt in re aliqua, praeter essentiam ejus.

per praedicant accidens (*Quodl.* XII, 5, 5). But Thomas's "turn" consisted precisely in this (1.8.2.), that for him this being is the "actuality" of every substance.[151]

2.6. *The two tracks of predication*

In chapter 1 it was shown that questioning has a twofold sense. This was found to be connected to a different composition in that which is, and to be motivated by a distinct origination. These earlier findings have been confirmed and deepened "by the way of predication." The way of predication led, as it turned out, to two tracks, characterized by different reductions of the multiplicity to identity.

In the first, Aristotelian model of predication, a multiplicity of particular subjects is reduced to the unity of their essence and species. The "what" question terminates in the definition, which consists of what is predicated *per se*. In predication *per se* the subject is identical to its essential being, as Thomas observes in the following article (2) of the same *Quodl.* (II) that we analyzed in the preceding sections: "the Philosopher determines that in what is said *per se* a thing and its quiddity are identical, but in what is said *per accidens* they are not the same. For a man is nothing other than that which is essential to man."

In definitional thinking being is regarded solely for what it is in *itself*. "Each thing is mainly defined according to what belongs to it primarily and 'per se.'"[152] This "*per-se*-ity" is the natural persistence of something. "That which belongs to a thing through itself (*per se*) must be in it universally; as for man to be rational and for fire to tend upwards."[153] That is what "counts" on the "way of definition."

To deepen the import of this, it is of importance to consider a remark made by Thomas that suggests this way is efficacious precisely with respect to the creaturely. Our intellect can represent this according to its complete perfection and so define it.[154] Yet it must be asked whether in this manner the creature is represented as *creaturely*? All creatures are said in relation (*relative*) to God, because in their being they are dependent upon Him.[155] Yes, this relation is so essential for the creature that the

---

[151] Cf. *In I Perih.*, lect. 5, 73: Hoc verbum 'est' ... significat enim primo illud quod cadit in intellectu per modum actualitatis absolute: nam 'est' simpliciter dictum, significat in actu esse.

[152] *S.Th.* III, 60, 4 ad 1: Unumquodque praecipue denominatur et definitur secundum id, quod convenit ei primo et per se.

[153] *S.c.G.* II, 6.

[154] *De verit.* 2, 1.

[155] *S.c.G.* II, 11.

dependence belongs to its very nature.[156] Because the "prior" enters into the definition of the "later" (as substance into the definition of an accident), it is not without grounds that A. HAYEN writes: "That is why St. Thomas is not afraid to affirm virtually that *Deus ponitur in definitione omnium entium* [God is put in the definition of all beings], without troubling himself to make explicit the precise conditions."[157]

The *virtual* character of this affirmation may not, however, elude us. More expressly than in HAYEN, the pretension that the things are defined "integrally" must be tested precisely with respect to the transcendental relation.[158] Does the "horizon" (of nature) also include the thing as *creature*?

Being as *creature* is involved in another mode of questioning, which goes beyond the horizon of the "what" or *nature* of that which is. Then the "if" question is directed to that by which a thing is in act. To this mode of questioning Thomas's application of the Platonic model of predication correlates. *Per participationem* expresses a nonidentity, which stamps every being as creature. This predication can not be brought together with the saying 'per se'. "Being" which is said through participation falls outside the quiddity and essence of the thing (2.5.3.). The expressed nonidentity, which can only be understood in relation to the being *per essentiam*, lies in what is outside the definitional terminus: the creature insofar as it *is*. "Creature" expresses a having being from another (*ab alio*), which breaks through the limits of the *per-se*-ity. The "horizon" itself of definitional thinking is an impediment to "actually" putting God in the definition of each being. In the treatise on creation (*S. Th.* I, 44, 1 ad 1), Thomas states that the relation to the cause does not enter into the definition of a being that is caused (*habitudo ad causam non intret definitionem entis quod est causatum*).[159]

"The modes of being are proportional to the modes of predicating." In the distinct modes of questioning and saying, different compositions in

---

[156] *S. Th.* I, 28, 1 ad 3: Sed in creaturis est realis relatio ad Deum: quia creaturae continentur sub ordine divino, et in eorum natura est, ut dependeant a Deo.

[157] *L'intentionnel dans la philosophie de S. Thomas* (Louvain, 1942), pp. 246–47: C'est pourquoi saint Thomas ne craint pas d'affirmer virtuellement que *Deus ponitur in definitione omnium entium*, sans se soucier d'expliciter les précisions nécessaires." Cf. *S. Th.* I, 13, 6: In omnibus nominibus quae de pluribus analogice dicuntur, necesse est quod omnia dicantur per respectum ad unum: et ideo illud unum oportet quod ponatur in definitione omnium.

[158] The expression 'integraliter definisse' is used in *In II Post. Anal.*, lect. 14, 541.

[159] This text continues: "yet this relation follows as a result of what belongs to its essence"—the second mode of saying 'per se' (tamen sequitur ad ea quae sunt de ejus ratione: quia ex hoc quod aliquid est ens per participationem, sequitur quod sit causatum ab alio).

that which is are revealed.[160] What is expressed on the one hand is the composition of a subject or supposit with the form or essence; "outside" the essence is the individual. What is expressed on the other hand is the composition of 'essentia' and 'esse'; "outside" the essence is being.

"By the way of predication" the composed is reduced to the identity of, respectively, the definitional logos and what is said essentially. This reduction is of more than a merely logical character. That precisely these tracks of predication are taken must be connected to the ontologically prior that is stated. With regard to definitional thinking, this connection has already been expressly noted (2.2.2.). The horizon is the specific persistence. For the universal species is "more" being than the particular subject, because the imperishable is "more" being than the corruptible. To the two tracks of predication correlate different ways of understanding being, which Thomas himself indicates: "The Philosopher does not take being insofar as it means the act of that which is ... but he takes being for the quiddity or essence signified by the definition."[161]

This correlation provides the motivation for the course of the further inquiry. What is desired to be known is the ontologically prior which the two tracks of predication presuppose, that is, the causes of being. For "cause" is that "first" which "influences" the being of things. Thus the way along which the twofold "analysis" of that which is must be carried forward is the *via causalitatis*.

---

[160] On the 'duplex compositio' see *S.c.G.* II, 54. Cf. *De pot.* 7, 4 ('duplex differentia').
[161] *In III Sent.* 8, 5 ad 2: Philosophus non accipit esse secundum quod dicitur *actus entis* ... sed accipit esse pro *quidditate vel ratione quam significat definitio.* Cf. *In I Sent.* 33, 1, 1 ad 1.

CHAPTER THREE

BY THE WAY OF CAUSALITY (PER VIAM CAUSALITATIS)[1]

Questioning opens a way towards knowing. That into which the question "really" (*secundum rem*) inquires is the "principle" and the "cause" (1.4.2.). The desire to know is first of all a yearning to know the causes of whatever is seen. Through the causes, the becoming and the being of that which is are rendered intelligible (1.2.).

In the first basic text, "nature," "art," and "chance" are named as causes of beings. These three are the causes of the *generatio* of things. Generation (*genesis*) is to be understood in a broad sense here, as *via in esse*, the way along which something comes to being, i.e., exists. Becoming is form-ation of the subject, from which the composition "form in matter" results. In generation we find the same structural moments as in predication. Generation can be differentiated in a manner parallel to the division (*per se* / *per accidens*) on the (Aristotelian) way of predication—Thomas even speaks of an "application" of the logical view to natural things.[2] Determinative for this division of generation are the order and regularity in the process, which are reducible to the cause *per se* / *per accidens*. Of the causes 'per se', nature is "basic": it is the cause of substance, the first being. In natural generation there is, qua species, identity (univocity) of principle and end. The way of nature is a circulation (*circulatio*). In the origination *per viam naturae* becomes visible the common motive of the first sense of questioning, to which the definitional logos corresponds, and of the dynamics of being (3.1.–3.4.).

The other sense of questioning (than that of ousiology) correlates with another mode of becoming (than that of generation), with the origination of being in general. The way towards "being" in the transcendental sense is *emanatio*. Because this coming to being is not a formation, an *alius modus causandi* is at issue here—as is stated in the second basic text. This "other mode of causing" is contained in the other (Platonic) mode of predicating: "that which is said to be so by virtue of its essence is the cause of everything said to be so by participation" (*S.c.G.* II, 15). The essen-

---

[1] For this terminology cf. *In Boeth. De trin.* 6, 2: ... per viam causalitatis, sicut ex effectu causa perpenditur.
[2] *In VIII Metaph.*, lect. 1, 1681: Dicit ergo primo quod, cum multa dicta sint in septimo (Metaph.) logica consideratione circa substantiam, oportet syllogizare ex his quae dicta sunt, ut *applicentur* quae secundum *considerationem logicam* dicta sunt, *ad res naturales existentes*.

tial being, God, is the cause of all other being. This origin Thomas also designates with the Judaeo-Christian notion of "creation out of nothing." *Per viam creationis* the divine "givenness" of being as creature is revealed. This being-created is primarily interpreted, in keeping with the Platonic model of predication, as participation (3.5.–3.6.).

Per viam naturae and *per viam creationis*, that which is is reduced to different origins, which qualify the meaning of being. This is the root of the twofold sense of questioning, of the two tracks of predication and of the distinct modes of causing. There is however also a "con-currence" of these ways: they come together in the intelligibility of that which is. This "complication" can be shown via causality—the hierarchical order of the causes—and via predication—the twofold composition in that which is (3.7.)

3.1. 'Per viam divisionis': Cause

The text from *Phys.* II opens with a division of all beings (*inter omnia entia*). "We say that of all beings some are by nature, some are by other causes, as art (*ars*) and chance (*casus*)." The extension of natural things is, albeit not exhaustively,[3] delineated: "by nature" are earth, fire, air, and water ("elementary" beings), plants (vegetative beings), and animals (sensitive beings)—the inquiry into what nature is is only possible in relation to those concrete things of which the questioned is constitutive (1.5.).

This opening is to A. MANSION's judgement *ex abrupto*;[4] qua method, however, it is entirely in keeping with what was sketched in chapter 2. The most suitable way of investigating what must be put in the definition is *per viam divisionis* (2.2.3.). This way is prevalent precisely in thought about nature: philosophical tradition has bequeathed us numerous oppositions—nature versus mind, history, the supernatural, and so forth.

The principle of every definitional determination is the common genus. One qua genus is that which has one mode of predicating.[5] Now, of all that is, we "say" that some beings are by nature, some by other causes. What is specifically divided in the enunciation is the genus *causa* (and *principium*). In this division a starting point is offered for the way of causality, along which the analysis must be continued.

That nature is "cause" is said only indirectly in the text of *Phys.* II, but we find it stated explicitly elsewhere. The most telling instance is perhaps

---

[3] Thus the 'mixta' do not appear and it is only in the continuation of the passage cited that there is any reference to the celestial bodies.

[4] A. Mansion, *Introduction à la physique aristotélicienne*, 2nd ed. (Louvain and Paris, 1946), p. 80.

[5] *In V Metaph.*, lect. 8, 878: Unum vero genere sunt, quae conveniunt in figura "praedicationis," idest quae habent unum modum praedicandi.

Thomas's introduction (lect. 1, 749) to book V of the *Metaphysica*, Aristotle's lexicon of philosophical terms. There, Aquinas endeavors to establish a coherence between the successively discussed terms. "First, Aristotle distinguishes names which signify causes in general [namely, 'principium', 'causa', and 'elementum']. Secondly, he distinguishes a name which signifies a cause in particular (*quamdam causam in speciali*), namely, *natura*." The question "What is nature?" as it again turns out, is an "intensification" of the inquiring into the ontologically prior, the cause.

In the division, nature is opposed especially to art (*technè*). It is remarkable to note, however, that nature is not conceived as the antithesis, the other, of mind (Hegel), but as the prior to which the "other causes" are contrasted. This is a decisive beginning and consequently a point of view in a double sense: the division furnishes a look, discloses a perspective, and is a choice, an option.

To get on the track of what is decisive in this view, it is of importance to consider respectively the reason for the division (3.2.), its parts (3.3.), and the prior in this division (3.4.).

3.2. *The reason for the division: The cause of generation ('via in esse')*

In the seventh book of the *Metaphysica*, which has already proven to be of great importance for the "what" question, the same division can be found as in *Phys.* II, 1. But here the reason for this division is also immediately indicated. The division is taken from "that which is generated and the mode of generation" (*accipitur penes ea quae generantur, et modum generationis*). What is disclosed in it is the different modes of coming to be, which are reducible to the distinct causes of generation. "Of things which come to be (*fiunt*), some come to be by nature, some by art, and some by chance." The reason for the division is the *causa generationis*.[6]

This means that the phrase "some *are* by nature" in the text of the *Phys.* must be understood dynamically. This "to be" is not to be regarded as "absolute" but as the terminus of a coming to be. For generation is nothing other than *via in esse*.[7] By the question "What is nature?" we are put not only upon a way of thought but likewise upon the way towards being.

That "to be" is to be regarded not as "absolute" but as "come to be"

---

[6] *In VII Metaph.*, lect. 6, 1381. Likewise in *In XII Metaph.*, lect. 3, 2444: Omnes enim substantiae, quae generantur, *generantur* aut a natura, aut ab arte , aut a fortuna . . . aut a casu.

[7] See, e.g., *S.c.G.* I, 26: Generatio, per se loquendo, est via in esse; *S. Th.* I, 90, 2; I, 110, 2: Cum fieri nihil aliud sit quam via in esse; *In I De generat.*, lect. 9, 68: Generatio est via de non esse ad esse.

implies (cf. 1.2.) that the entire fabric of the four causes is involved. Thus in *In VII Metaph.* (lect. 6), directly after the division just mentioned, a second division is presented, taken from what is required for every generation (*sumitur penes ea, quae ad generationem requiruntur*):

> For everything which comes to be, comes to be by some agent, and from something as its matter, and also becomes something, which is the terminus of generation.... (1383)
> And the reason for this division is that in every generation something which was previously potential becomes actual. Now a thing can be said to proceed from potency to act only by reason of some actual being, which is the agent by which the process of generation is brought about. Now potency pertains to the matter, from which something is generated, and actuality pertains to the thing generated. (1384)[8]

In this division are contained both the character of generation as process and the differentiation of the causal influx of being.

Every becoming is "ex aliquo ad aliquid" (*De principiis naturae*, c.2). "Out of something" (*ex aliquo*), for generation, like predication, presupposes a subject. It is impossible for anything to become unless there is something that pre-exists. "For the common opinion of the philosophers of nature was that out of nothing comes nothing" (*ex nihilo nihil fit*) (*In VII Metaph.*, 1412).[9] In generation, something becomes actual that was previously in potency. This underlying indeterminate is matter. Even if it is said that change is "from non-being to being" (*ibid.*, 1388), then this "non-being" is not to be understood as an absolute "nothing" (*quod nullo modo est*), but is to be related to matter, which is in itself not a being in act. From such a non-being (i.e., a non-actual) proceeds the generation 'per se'.[10] "Every generation is out of something, namely, matter" (*S.c.G.* III, 69).

Generation is *via ad formam*, a process towards the form as terminus, because through the form the thing is constituted in its determinate being.[11] The form is always the act of the subject.[12] "Every generation is ... to something, namely, form" (*S.c.G.* III, 69).

Besides matter and form, generation requires an "active" principle.

---

[8] *In VII Metaph.*, lect. 6: Omnia enim quae fiunt, fiunt ab aliquo agente, et ex aliquo, sicut ex materia, et iterum fiunt aliquid quod est terminus generationis.... (1383)

Et huius divisionis ratio est, quia in omni generatione fit aliquid actu, quod prius erat in potentia. Nihil autem potest dici de potentia in actum procedere, nisi per aliquod ens actu, quod est agens, a quo fit generatio; potentia vero pertinet ad materiam, ex qua aliquid generatur; actus vero ad id quod generatur. (1384)

[9] Cf. *De subst. separ.*, c. 9, 93. This presupposition will be dealt with further in 7.4.3.

[10] *In XII Metaph.*, lect. 2, 2437; *De quat. opp.*, c. 5. Cf. Aristotle, *Phys.* I, 8, 191 b 13ff.

[11] *De pot.* 8, 3: ... Socrates est homo sua generatione, quae est *via ad formam*, qua formaliter constituitur.

[12] *De spirit. creat.*, a. 1 ad 1 (cf. 1.3.2.).

Something can only be brought from potency to act by a being in act, which is the "agent." Furthermore (cf. 1.2.), the operation of an agent tends towards something determinate. What the agent intends in its operation is that for the sake of which the generation takes place, the "final cause." That this condition for generation is not expressly stated in *In VII Metaph.*, lect. 6 is connected with the fact that what this text wants to show in the continuation is precisely that the end is determinative for the operation of the agent.

In the way to being we find the same structural moments as in predication: the composition "form in matter." In generation the subject acquires determinate being through the form: "generatio quae est via ad esse est per acquisitionem formae."[13] In predication, being is made manifest through the intellect, in that a predicate is said of a subject. In this composition, the predicate is what "in-forms" the subject. According to Aristotle's judgement (see 2.1.1.), there is predication in the proper sense only if "the subject *becomes* what is predicated of it."

Parallel to the division (*per se / per accidens*) of predication, it is possible to elaborate from the second division (the conditions of the process of generation) the first division in which the genus "cause" is specified in "nature," "art," and "chance."

3.3. *Division of the causes of generation*

> Of things which come to be, some come to be by nature (*a natura*), some by art (*ab arte*), and some by chance (*a casu*) or "automatically," i.e., by itself without purpose.
>
> The reason for this division is that the cause of generation is either a cause *per se* or a cause *per accidens*.
>
> For if it is a cause *per se*, either it is ... nature ... or it is art.
>
> But if it is a cause *per accidens*, then it is chance and fortune. (*In VII Metaph.*, lect. 6, 1381–82)

3.3.1. *'Causa per se' versus 'causa per accidens' (chance)*

The reason for the division is the cause of generation. This is either a *causa per se*—as in the case of 'natura' and 'ars'—or a *causa per accidens*. As such, reference is sometimes made to 'casus' alone, and at other times to 'casus' and 'fortuna'. The distinction between them is of no essential importance to the division; in fact, the terms are used interchangeably. It will therefore suffice to speak of them by the single term "chance."[14]

---

[13] *In De causis*, lect. 26.

[14] 'Casus' is the broader of the two concepts: casus est in plus quam fortuna (*In II Phys.*, lect. 10, 227); the distinction between them will be touched upon later in this section.
Aristotle's exposition of chance is found in *Phys.* B, c. 4–6; Thomas, *In II Phys.*, lect.

In this primary differentiation of the causes, the character of nature is disclosed further in the sense that "nature" and "art' are found to be placed *together* as causes over against "chance." For an understanding of nature it is of great importance to realize that this juxtaposition is "prior" to the opposition that is emphasized in the text from the *Physica*.[15]

"Those are said to be the principles and causes of things, from which they are and come to be 'per se' and not 'per accidens'" (*In I Phys.*, lect. 13, 111; cf. 1.2.). This distinction of *per se* and *per accidens* reminds us directly of the identical distinction in the modes of saying according to the Aristotelian model of predication (2.1.1). There the criterion was the manner in which the predicate relates to the subject. 'Per se' expresses an intelligible order between the two in contrast to what is said 'per accidens'. "That which belongs to a thing 'per se' is necessarily in it, always and inseparably." Therefore whatever is said of something 'per accidens' had first to be eliminated from the way of definition.

In proportion to the modes of predication *per se* / *per accidens* the modes of generation can be divided. Determinative for this division is the order in becoming, which is reducible to the different relations between cause and effect, to the modes of causing.

In the process of generation some things come to be always or as a rule, others only seldom. Only what happens by way of exception can be called casual: *esse a fortuna* and *esse in paucioribus* are interchangeable expressions.[16] As in predication 'per accidens' something is said of something as belonging to it contingently, so the exceptional effect is ascribed to a cause 'per accidens', namely, "chance." The onto-logical coherence is established in *In V Metaph.*, lect. 22:

> Accident means that which is in a thing and which is truly affirmed of it, not, however, necessarily or in the majority of cases, but in a minority. (1139)
> And it should be borne in mind that of the kind of accident here mentioned there is no determinate cause, but only "a contingent cause" or "a chance cause," i.e., a fortuitous one, which is an indeterminate cause. (1141)[17]

---

7 – 10. Cf. A. Mansion, *Introduction à la physique aristotélicienne*, pp. 292 – 314; P. Michaud-Quantin, "Notes sur le hasard et la chance," in *La Filosofia della natura nel medioevo*, (Milan, 1966), pp. 156 – 63.

[15] This versus H. Leisegang: "Diese anderen Ursachen aber werden unter den Begriff der Techne zusammengefasst, der damit von der Physis scharf getrennt wird" (in: *Paulys Real-Encyclopädie der classischen Altertumswissenschaft*, 39th Halbband (Stuttgart, 1941), p. 1148.

[16] *In II Phys.*, lect. 8, 208. Cf. *S.c.G.* III, 3; *In VI Metaph.*, lect. 2, 1184.

[17] *In V Metaph.*, lect. 22: Accidens dicitur id quod inest alicui, et quod contingit vere affirmare, non tamen ex necessitate, nec . . . ut in pluribus, sed ut in paucioribus. (1139) Et sciendum, quod accidentis hoc modo dicti, non est aliqua causa determinata, 'sed

If the effect occurs constantly or frequently, then one cannot speak of chance. What participates in order is intelligible, is not 'per accidens'. A first characteristic of every cause 'per se' is that it has a fixed and determinate order to its effect.[18]

The phenomenal distinction in regularity is to be deepened. There must be a reason why the agent brings forth not an arbitrary but a "determinate" effect. The active principle must be directed towards a fixed terminus as final end: "to produce a determinate effect the agent must be be determined towards something definite, which has the character of an end (*quod habet rationem finis*)."[19] The constancy must come forth *ex intentione finis*.[20] A second characteristic of every cause 'per se' is that it intends its effect, that it operates for an end—a feature, therefore, which applies to both what is by art and what is by nature.[21] Since generation is, as we saw, *via ad formam*, form and end coincide in this movement.

There is also a correspondence between the "principle" and "end" of generation. The active principle is the cause of the end with respect to its being, but the end is the cause of the agent with respect to its causality. The end (to be realized) is the prior which motivates the agent.[22] Yet, this is only possible if the form is already present in some way in the efficient cause. "The agent acts only for the sake of the form, insofar as the likeness of the form is in it."[23] A third characteristic of the cause 'per se' is that it always effects something that is alike to itself. What comes to being is in its formal determination similar to that which brings forth: man generates man. The thing generated and the generator are numerically not the same, certainly, but specifically they are.[24] Consequently, in the process of generation, three causes coincide: efficient, final, and formal.

---

contingens' . . . vel . . . causa fortuita, quae est causa indeterminata. (1141)

[18] In *De malo* 1, 3 three characteristics of the *causa per se* are enumerated, including: Omnis causa per se, habet certum et determinatum ordinem ad suum effectum. Cf. *In VI Metaph.*, lect. 3, 1204ff.; *In II Phys.*, lect. 7, 206: Secundum quod aliquid participat rationem vel ordinem, recedit a ratione fortunae; lect. 9, 220: Omnis enim causa per se producit effectum suum vel semper, vel ut frequenter.

[19] *S. Th.* I-II, 1, 2. Cf. *S. Th.* I, 44, 4.

[20] *De verit.* 5, 2: Ea enim quae casu accidunt, proveniunt ut in minori parte; videmus autem huiusmodi convenientias et utilitates accidere in operibus naturae aut semper, aut in maiori parte; unde non potest esse ut casu accidant; et ita oportet quod procedant *ex intentione finis*.

[21] *De malo* 1, 3: Illud quod per se causam habet, est intentum a sua causa; quod enim provenit praeter intentionem agentis, non est effectus per se, sed per accidens; *S. Th.* I-II, 85, 5; *S.c.G.* III, 3.

[22] *In V Metaph.*, lect. 2, 775. Cf. *In IX Metaph.*, lect. 8, 1857.

[23] *S. Th.* I, 15, 1: In omnibus enim quae non a casu generantur, necesse est formam esse finem generationis cujuscumque. Agens autem non agit propter formam nisi inquantum similitudo formae est in ipso. Cf. *S.c.G.* III, 2.

[24] *De malo* 1, 3; *S.c.G.* III, 19: Agens dicitur esse finis effectus inquantum effectus tendit in similitudinem agentis; unde forma generantis est finis generationis.

Outside this "concurrence" remains matter, since it is a being in potency; in the fabric of causes there is an irreducible duality of form (act) and matter (potency).[25]

Becoming is a process of assimilation. Generation is the more perfect as the effect becomes more similar to the form of its principle. "All effects are most perfect when they become most like their efficient causes—a house when it most closely resembles the art by which it is produced, and fire when it becomes most fully similar to its generator."[26] Generation by a cause 'per se' is ruled by the law of "univocity," in virtue of which there is a likeness between the form of the fire generated and the form of the generating fire, and between the form of the house in the builder's mind and the form of the house built. What is generated originates from what in the Greek is called "the synonymous" and in the Latin "the univocal" (*ex agente univoco*), which is to say it originates from what is alike with respect to the form, from what is nominally *and* conceptually identical.[27]

The (logical) terminology in which this "ex"-structure of generation is formulated is significant. "Univocity" points back directly to predication 'per se' and to the definitional logos. For on the way of definition the univocal predication obtained, in which the predicate expresses the subject essentially (2.2.2.).

Regularity, operation for an end, univocity: what is by chance has no part in these three characteristics. A man digs a grave in the earth and finds buried treasure. This "rare" find is connected 'per accidens' with the intended effect.[28] Casual is that which happens *in* an operation for an end outside the intention of an agent, whether through the coincidence of two causes (of which the one is not subordinate to the other), or through the deficiency of the agent, or also through the indisposition of

---

[25] *In VII Metaph.*, lect. 6, 1391ff. Cf. *In II Phys.*, lect. 11, 242: Dicit ergo quod multoties contingit quod *tres causae concurrunt in unam*, ita quod causa formalis et finalis sint una secundum numerum ... Sed causa movens est eadem secundum speciem utrique earum ... Materia vero non est nec idem specie nec idem numero cum aliis causis; quia materia inquantum huiusmodi est ens in potentia, agens vero est ens in actu inquantum huiusmodi, forma vero vel finis est actus vel perfectio.

[26] *S.c.G.* II, 46. Cf. *S. Th.* I, 33, 2 ad 4: Generatio accipit speciem a termino, qui est forma generati. Et quanto haec fuerit propinquior formae generantis, tanto verior et perfectior est generatio. Sicut *generatio univoca* est perfectior quam non univoca. Nam de ratione generantis est quod generet sibi simile secundum formam.

[27] In *Metaph.* XII, c. 3 (lect. 3, 2444ff.) the division of the causes into 'natura', 'ars', 'casus', and 'fortuna' is introduced in order to show that "res acquirunt formam ex agentibus similibus; dicens quod quaecumque substantia fit 'ex agente univoco', idest simili secundum formam."

[28] For this standard example, see *In I Sent.* 46, 1, 2, ad 3; *De pot.* 3, 6 ad 6; *In V Metaph.*, lect. 3, 789; *In VII Metaph.*, lect. 8, 1443.

matter as a result of which the intended form is not incorporated.[29] Therefore, what is by "chance" is called "auto-matic," a term which is explained by Thomas in keeping with the etymology presented by Aristotle in *Phys.* II, 6 (lect. 10, 234) as *per se vanum*, or "vain of itself."

Only *in relation to* the causes, which operate for an end, does this absence of determinateness occur. For that is "vain of itself" which is directed to an end and does not reach it. "Both chance and fortune are found in those things which are done for the sake of something, when some effect results besides the one intended by a cause 'per se'" (*In VII Metaph.*, lect. 6, 1382). A cause 'per accidens' is an indeterminate cause which must be reduced to a cause 'per se': nature or art. In this reduction lies the differentiation between 'fortuna' and 'casus'. 'Fortuna' must be traced to the intellect as efficient cause, and 'casus' to nature.[30]

'Casus' and 'fortuna' are deficient modes, "privations," of 'natura' and 'ars'. Chance is nothing other than *natura agens praeter intentionem*,[31] an expression strikingly indicative of the prevalence of teleology on the way towards being.

3.3.2. *Division of the causes 'per se': 'Ars imitatur naturam'*

With reference to the relationship between art and nature, Aristotle asserts in *Phys.* II, 2 without any explanation: "art imitates nature." How is this imitation to be interpreted?

Often it is interpreted in a "naturalistic" way, because the meaning of what is imitated is no longer understood. Sometimes—as in A. MANSION[32]—the thesis of imitation is taken to be a purely pedagogical scheme meant to facilitate the analysis of what is less familiar, nature, through the analysis of what is more familiar to us. Left unanswered then, however, is the question of what actually legitimates the transfer of the *technè* model to the domain of *physis*. If we would come closer to the Greek meaning of *physis* and its relation to *technè*, then we must see the imitation thesis in the first place as a manifestation of an *identical logos* in the becoming of things.[33]

---

[29] Thomas's own enumeration in *In VI Metaph.*, lect. 3, 1210; cf. *S.c.G.* III, 74.

[30] Cf. *In II Phys.*, lect. 10, 237; *S.Th.* I-II, 75, 1: Omnis autem causa per accidens reducitur ad causam per se.

[31] *In XII Metaph.*, lect. 3, 2445: Fortuna et casus sunt quasi defectus et privationes naturae et artis. Nam fortuna est intellectus agens praeter intentionem, et casus natura agens praeter intentionem; *S.Th.* II-II, 64, 8; *In I Sent.* 43, 2, 1.

[32] *Introduction à la physique aristotélicienne*, p. 229, n. 7.

[33] For the relation of 'physis' and 'technè', see: H. Meyer, *Natur und Kunst bei Aristoteles* (Paderborn, 1919); W. Schadewaldt, "Natur–Technik–Kunst," and "Die Begriffe

At various places in his work, Thomas offers an interpretation of Aristotle's adagium in which he emphasizes the structural agreement between the operation of nature and the operation of art: "Art imitates nature *in its operation.*"[34] The manners in which the two operate on the way towards being are similar: for nature and art are causes 'per se' (3.3.1.). As such they both operate for an end.[35] Therefore there is constancy and an intelligible order in generation.

An intimate connection exists between art and knowledge.[36] As an intellectual habit art is defined as the right reason of things to be made (*recta ratio factibilium*).[37] Art is an ordering of reason (*ordinatio rationis*) whereby human acts arrive via certain means at the intended end (*In I Post. Anal.*, prooem.). Yet natural generation too is ruled by the logos. Nature is *causa ordinationis*; namely, we see that nature advances in an orderly way from the one to the other.[38]

Because nature and art are causes 'per se', becoming by them is ruled by the law of synonymy. The end pre-exists, in a univocal way, in the principle "from" which generation begins. In this "ex"-structure (cf. 1.3.1.) the process of being conforms to the process of demonstrative science. "So that, just as in syllogisms, the essence is the principle of everything; for syllogisms commence from what is the essence, as do generations" (*Metaph.*, VII, 9, 1034 a 30).

In scientific demonstration the principle is the definition of the essence (cf. 2.2.3.). In the natural process the principle is likewise derived from

---

"Natur" und "Technik" bei den Griechen," in *Hellas und Hesperien*, vol. 2 (Zurich and Stuttgart, 1970), pp. 497–512, an 512–24; H. Happ, *Studien zum aristotelischen Materie-Begriff* (Berlin and New York, 1971), pp. 6ff.; K. Flasch, "Ars imitatur naturam: Platonischer Naturbegriff und mittelalterliche Philosophie der Kunst," in *Parusia* (Festgabe für J. Hirschberger; Frankfurt am Main, 1965), pp. 265–306.

[34] *S.c.G.* III, 10. Cf. *In I Post. Anal.*, proemium, 5; *S.c.G.* II, 75.

[35] *In II Post. Anal.*, lect. 9, 503. This basic structure is worked out in *Phys.* B, 8 (lect. 13 and 14). Cf. 8.2.1.

[36] *In VI Metaph.*, lect. 1, 1153: Hoc autem principium rerum artificialium … est primo intellectus, qui primo artem adinvenit; et secundo ars, quae est *habitus intellectus*; et tertio aliqua potentia exequens.

'Ars' may be translated by the term "art" as long as it its kept in mind that the medieval concept was much broader than the modern, aesthetically qualified concept (cf. R. Assunto, *Die Theorie des Schönen im Mittelalter* (Cologne, 1963), p. 12). The term should be thought of rather in the sense of such formulations as "the art of healing," already in Aristotle the preferred paradigm for discussions of technè. The term "culture," which is sometimes used to translate 'ars', is too suggestive of an objectification, analogous to the modern use of "nature."

[37] *In VI Ethic.*, lect. 3; *In I Metaph.*, lect. 1, 34. See also *S. Th.* I-II, 57, 4 for the difference between 'prudentia' (*recta ratio agibilium*) and 'ars'.

[38] *In VIII Phys.*, lect. 3, 993: Natura est causa ordinationis. Videmus enim naturam in suis operibus ordinate de uno in aliud procedere: quod ergo non habet aliquem ordinem, non est secundum naturam; *De pot.* 6, 1 ad 10.

the definition. For the end of generation is the specific form, which is signified by the definition. The same order appears in artefacts. The builder
takes the definition as the principle of his art of building: since the definition of "house" is such and such, this must occur and that must be in order that the house may become.[39] *Scientia, natura*, and *ars*: in their processes, the definitional logos is again and again the ruling principle, even
when in generation it is the terminus.

The definition consists of what is predicated 'per se'. In this kind of predication, however, two modes of saying 'per se' were found to be distinguishable, according to the different causal relationships between subject
and predicate (2.2.1.). A corresponding differentiation can be found in
the reduction of generation to the causes 'per se', nature and art. This division is indicated as follows in *In VII Metaph.*, lect. 6, 1381:

> If it is a cause 'per se', it is either the principle of motion intrinsic to a
> thing, and then it is nature, or it is extrinsic to the thing, and then it is art.
> For nature is a principle of motion in that in which it exists, but art does not
> exist in the thing produced by art but in something other.[40]

The causes are divided according to the differing degrees of univocity
which exist between principle and terminus in the coming to be. This is
not complete in the case of art. Art is a "productive form" which pre-
exists in the mind of the maker in an immaterial, or "exemplary,"
way.[41] The artefact comes to be through assimilation to this idea; in what
is produced, the form is externalized, materially realized. Art is an extrinsic principle, extrinsic to the thing produced, and is in that sense "in
something other." There is indeed a likeness between the productive
principle and the terminus with respect to the form, but not with respect
to the being of the form.

In natural generation the univocity is complete. There is full conformity between the form of the agent and the form of the terminus in the mode
of being: they are alike in their nature. Nature is an intrinsic principle;
the principle of motion is in the natural thing itself.[42]

The degree of identity between the principle and the end in the mode

---

[39] *Phys.* B, 9 200 a 30ff.; *In II Phys.*, lect. 15, 274.

[40] *In VII Metaph.*, lect. 6, 1381: Si enim est causa per se: vel est principium motus in
quo est, et sic est natura vel est extra ipsum, et sic est ars. Natura enim est principium
motus, in eo in quo est. Ars vero non est in artificiato quod fit per artem, sed in alio.

[41] *Ibid.*, lect. 6, 1404; 1407; *S. Th.* I-II, 93, 1: Ratio rerum fiendarum per artem vocatur ars, vel exemplar rerum artificialium.

[42] Cf. *In VII Metaph.*, lect. 8, 1444–5; *S. Th.* I, 15, 1; 41, 3.

The same differentiation is found in the basic text from *Phys.* II: Et *differunt* haec omnia
ab his quae non sunt a natura, quia omnia huiusmodi videntur habere in se principium
alicuius motus et status. For nature as 'principium intrinsecum', see also 7.1.1.

of generation correlates to the degree of identity between the subject and the predicate in the mode of predication. In the first mode of saying 'per se', the predicated belongs to the form of the subject, the essentially predicated *is* the subject. For the second mode, it is characteristic that 'per' signifies the relationship of a material cause, in the sense that the subject, to which something is attributed, is the proper matter of the predicated. This distinction between the two modes is based on the distinction of substance and accident (2.2.1.). Similarly, the modes of generation of the two causes 'per se' differ categorically. For art operates on that which has already been constituted in being by nature. So it is said that "the matter and substance of artefacts are natural things" (*In II Phys.*, 1, 142). Nature is the precondition of the possibility for art, is literally "basic," since art operates on the basis of the matter, for which nature provides.[43]

This need for the presence of the natural thing qualifies the ontological status of the artefact. The form which is realized through art is an accidental one. Art is deficient in comparison with the operation of nature, for nature gives the essential form. It is only thanks to the latter that artefacts are substances.[44] Although nature is not an efficient principle with respect to the forms of artefacts, such forms still do not go beyond the order of nature. Rather, each natural thing is more noble (*nobilius*) that the artefact. "More noble," which is to say, having a greater perfection of being; the natural is the principle of the artificial.[45] *Ars imitatur naturam.*

The investigation 'per viam divisionis' of the causes of generation leads to the following finding.[46] If it is possible to distinguish a threefold cause of the way towards being, namely, nature, art, and chance; if chance is a cause 'per accidens' that must be reduced to the causes 'per se', that is,

---

[43] *De principiis naturae*, c. 1: Ars enim non operatur nisi supra id quod iam constitutum est in esse a natura; *S.c.G.* III, 65: Opus artis praesupponit opus naturae, nam materia artificialium est a natura; *In II De Anima*, lect. 1, 218: Ars enim operatur ex materia quam natura ministrat.

[44] *S. Th.* III, 2, 1; 66, 4: Ars autem deficit ab operatione naturae: quia *natura dat formam substantialem*, quod ars facere non potest, sed *omnes formae artificiales sunt accidentales*; *In II De anima*, lect. 1, 218; *In I Perih.*, lect. 4, 40.

[45] *De pot.*, 3, 8 ad 5; *In II De anima*, lect. 1, 218: Corpora naturalia sunt principia artificialium.

[46] Schematically presented:

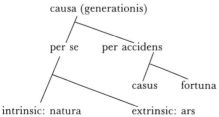

nature or art; and if of the causes 'per se' nature is the presupposition for art, then the meaning—and by the same token the importance—of the question "What is nature?" is that it inquires into *the* originating cause that effects the coming-to-be of things. In the desire to know the causes, that is, in philosophy, nature is the fundamental cause. 'Physis' was for the Greeks the basic word in the new interpretation of reality that they developed in the transition from 'mythos' to 'logos'.[47]

3.4. *'Per viam naturae'*[48]

The order of nature is an *ordo originis*. Nature has the character of origin.[49] "The process of nature is always the principle and origin of every other process, because all that is by art, will, or intellect comes forth from what is according to nature."[50] For the originating character of nature relates to the first category, substance. For Thomas too it holds: "What belongs to a thing naturally and immoveably must be the foundation and principle of all else, since the nature of a thing is the first in everything."[51]

This "naturalism" has its effect on many different domains. A good example is Thomas's view of the origin of kingly government (*regni originem*) in his *De regimine principum*. In the first chapter he argues that people "by nature" form communities and refers to Aristotle's statement in the *Politica*: "Man is naturally a social and political animal." If it is natural for man to live in community, government is necessary to the end that multiplicity not break up into diversity. The political community is "natural." This origination has far-reaching consequences. It has in essence desacralized the early medieval idea of the Christian commonwealth.[52]

---

[47] M. Pohlenz, "Nomos und Physis," *Hermes* 81 (1953): 426: "Der Begriff der Physis ist eine Schöpfung der ionischen Wissenschaft, die in ihm ihr ganzes neues Weltverständnis zusammenfasste"; W. Schadewaldt, "Natur–Technik–Kunst," in *Hellas und Hesperien*, vol. 2, p. 505: "'physis' ... ist eine der grossen Weltvisionen, mit denen die Griechen sich schon ganz früh die andrängende Wirklichkeit gedeutet haben."
See also 3.4.3. for Plato's view and Aristotle's critique of it.

[48] *S. Th.* III, 28, 1 ad 4; *In VIII Phys.*, lect. 2, 987.

[49] *In I Sent.* 20, 1, 3.

[50] *De pot.* 10, 5: Nam semper processio naturae est principium et origo cuiuslibet alterius processionis; omnia enim quae per artem et voluntatem vel intellectum fiunt, procedunt ab his quae secundum naturam sunt.

[51] *S. Th.* I, 82, 1: Oportet enim quod id quod naturaliter alicui convenit et immobiliter, sit fundamentum et principium omnium aliorum: quia natura rei est primum in unoquoque. Cf. *S. Th.* I, 60, 2.

[52] Cf. G.B. Ladner, "Aspects of Mediaeval Thought on Church and State," *Review of Politics* 9 (1947): 403–22; F.J.A. de Grijs, "Mensenmacht, Enige aantekeningen bij

The acts and movements of people are ruled by laws. There are laws that are implanted in reason itself. These laws provide the first measure of every human act. They are called *ius naturale*.[53] From this normative natural law, positive man-made law takes its rise. Once again nature proves to be basic, the "prior" for what is made by art.

3.4.1. *'Natura . . . est via in naturam': Circulation*

It remains for us to establish more fully the order of what comes to being *per viam naturae*. The term 'natura' is etymologically derived from the verb *nascor*, "to be born." Therefore this name is first imposed to signify the generation of living things (see 6.5.2.). That is, the origin of the meaning of nature points towards generation, towards the 'via in esse'. More precisely: nature signifies the generation of the living, or birth. Now, in *Phys.* II the "inorganic," the elements, are also counted among natural things. Thomas clarifies this broadening of the signification by referring to the metaphorical character of language. "Denominations are habitually taken from the more perfect. . . . Because in the whole corporeal nature living things are the most perfect, the name 'nature' has been transferred from living things to all natural things" (*S. Th.* I, 115, 2).

The etymological meaning of *natura* is used by Aquinas to indicate that nature is not only principle but also end. Nature in the sense of generation is *via in naturam* (*In II Phys.*, lect. 2, 155). Natural becoming is the way towards nature as terminus.[54] The end of such becoming is nature, for the nature of each thing is what belongs to it when the genesis has been completed. The intention of nature is directed to the form or specific nature.

A characteristic of nature as cause 'per se' is that it always effects something similar to itself; in natural becoming there is a complete univocity between the end and the efficient principle (3.3.1.). The final terminus and the agent are identical qua species; this synonymy is expressed in a programmatic manner in the thesis: "man generates man." The way of nature is therefore a circulation (*circulatio*):

> As the Philosopher says in Book II of *De generatione*, there is in generation a circulation which however does not return to what is numerically identical

'De Regno' van Thomas van Aquino," *Bijdragen* 35 (1974): 250–97.

[53] Cf. *In III Sent.* 37, 3.

[54] *S. Th.* III, 35, 1 says that the intended terminus of birth is the 'forma' or the 'natura speciei'. Therefore 'nativitas' is called: *via in naturam*. Nature is to nativity as terminus is to movement (*S. Th.* III, 35, 2). Cf. *In VII Metaph.*, lect. 6, 1390; *In XII Metaph.*, lect. 3, 2446: Natura autem rei est in quam terminatur naturalis generatio; *In VII Ethic.*, lect. 11, 1474: Generatio est *via in finem*; lect. 12, 1493: Generatio est *via in naturam*.

but to what is identical qua species: man generates man, not Socrates Socrates. Hence that which is generated is assimilated to that which generates in
all that pertains to the nature of the species.[55]

For the second time we come upon the doctrine of circulation based on
the identity of principle and end. Earlier (1.7.) we encountered this motif
in Thomas's exposition of the opening sentence of Aristotle's *Metaphysica*.
"In all men there is by nature a desire to know, because it is desirable for
each thing to be united to its principle." Fundamental to all that is in Thomas's interpretation of this motif was the dynamics from God as origin
and towards God as final end. On that account, the desire to know seeks
the reduction to the first Cause.

In the present circulation, nature is principle and end. Through the
eternal return of the same, reality is conserved and acquires permanence
(*In II Phys.*, lect. 12, 254: *Propter hoc enim est generatio et corruptio mutua in
istis inferioribus, ut conservetur perpetuum esse in eis*). This intrinsic persistence
is nature. "For through the reproduction of its individuals the species re-
news itself continuously and so maintains itself in the everlasting process
of the 'natura naturans' "[56]

Yet in this circulation of nature there is also, as we shall see in greater
detail later (6.5.3.), a relation to the divine. The cause of the circulation,
in which the same specific perfection is realized again and again, cannot
lie in the corruptible itself. The eternal cycle of generation must be
reduced—as is shown in *Phys.* VIII and *Metaph.* XII—to the uniform and
continuous movement of the celestial sphere. This is set in motion by the
unmoved Mover, which is pure form, pure act, and therefore completely
identical, God. He moves without Himself being moved. For He moves
as final cause, that is, by being the object of desire. This separated
substance is the extrinsic cause of the composition form in matter. Because of its force of attraction, the non-identity of form and matter is overcome cyclically in generation.

Through this circulation natural things, too, take part, according to the
measure of their possibility, in the divine and immortal. They cannot as
individuals become alike unto the divine and everlasting—for they are

---

[55] *In II Sent.* 20, 2, 3: Sicut dicit Philosophus in II *De Generat.*, in generatione est quaedam *circulatio*, quae tamen non redit in idem numero, sed ad idem specie: *homo enim generat
hominem*, non Socrates Socratem; et inde est quod generatum generanti assimilatur in omnibus illis, quae ad naturam speciei pertinent.

[56] K. Oehler, *Ein Mensch zeugt einen Menschen: Über den Missbrauch der Sprachanalyse in der
Aristotelesforschung* (Frankfurt am Main, 1963), p. 38: "Denn durch die Fortpflanzung ihrer Individuen erneuert sich die Art ständig und hält sich so im immerwährenden Prozess
der natura naturans durch."

corruptible—but in the permanence of the species, they can.[57] This is what "counts."

3.4.2. The common motive of both the way of thought and the way of being

From the originality of *natura*, the common motive of the Aristotelian mode of questioning as the way towards knowing (ch. 1); of the mode of predication and the way of definition (ch. 2); and of the mode of generation and the way of causality (ch. 3) can be grasped through "re-flection," that is, through a retrospective view. The movement of thought—determined by the question "What is it?"—and the movement of being converge.

(1) The way towards being is generation (ch. 3). The etymology of "natura" also refers to this coming to be. In generation, all four kinds of causes are involved. The cause of being in the absolute sense is the form, whereby something is in act. The process from a being in potency to an actual being requires in addition an agent, a final cause, and matter—"out of nothing comes nothing." Three of these causes coincide in being act, so that the fundamental non-identity is that between act (form) and potency (matter). Generation is form-ation of the subject, from which the composition form in matter results.[58] The cause of their union is that which effects the actuality of what is potential. "And this is the agent in all that in which there is generation."[59]

The intention of nature is directed to the species, not to the individual. Becoming is *via ad distinctionem et constitutionem*—a being-under-way towards the essence, which, with respect to the particular subject, has the character of formal cause.[60] "The species and substance is called nature because it is the end of the process of generation. For generation termi-

---

[57] In *II De anima*, lect. 7, 314: Et ulterius secundum speciem tale animal facit tale animal, ut homo generat hominem, et oliva olivam. Ideo autem est naturale viventibus facere alterum tale quale ipsum est, ut semper participent, secundum quod possunt, divino et immortali, id est ut assimilentur ei secundum posse. 315: . . . ipsum esse perpetuum est cujus causa agitur, vel res habens perpetuitatem, cui naturalia intendunt assimilari per generationem, in quo scilicet est perpetuitas, vel etiam ipsa generatio, qua perpetuitatem adipiscuntur.

[58] In *II Phys.*, lect. 4, 175: Ad hoc enim terminatur generatio ut forma sit in materia; *De anima*, q. un., art. 6 ad 8.

[59] In *VIII Metaph.*, lect. 5, 1759. For this reason the definition, which signifies the quiddity of something, is also one: Unde, cum hoc sit quod quid erat esse significatum per definitionem, scilicet id quod est in potentia fieri actu, manifestum est quod agens est causa in rebus generabilibus et corruptibilibus, quare quod quid erat esse, una est definitio (*ibid.*). Cf. lect. 5, 1767.

[60] *De pot.* 8, 3: . . . *via ad distinctionem et constitutionem*, sicut si diceremus quod Socrates est homo sua generatione, quae est *via ad formam*, qua formaliter constituitur. Patet ergo quod origo alicuius non potest intelligi ut constitutiva et distinctiva eius, nisi propter hoc quod formaliter constituit et distinguit. Cf. *S. Th.* I, 85, 3 ad 4.

nates in the species of the thing generated, which results from the union
of form and matter.''[61]

The end preexists univocally in the principle. Nature is an intrinsic
principle of motion. The process of nature is a circulation. Circular
movement is characterized by uniformity—there is permanence and
regularity—and by identity. Such movement is from the same to the
same.[62] The way of nature is *via in naturam*, and it acquires through this
identity the highest degree of intelligibility.

(2) The way of definition (ch. 2) is coherent with the origination of
nature.

> In the same manner in which something belongs to the perfection of nature,
> it belongs to the intelligible perfection. Singular things belong to the perfec-
> tion of nature not of themselves but on account of something else, namely,
> that in them the species are preserved which nature intends. For the inten-
> tion of nature is the generation of man, not of this man. . . . Therefore the
> knowledge of the species of things belongs to the intelligible perfection.[63]

That is intended 'per se' in nature which is lasting and enduring: *omne
perpetuum est per se intentum in natura.*[64] This perfection of the specific persistence is precisely the ''horizon'' of the definition. Nature terminates in
that which is the *ratio diffinitiva* itself. The sense of the question ''What is
nature?'' is the direction of definitional thinking (2.4.).

There is no definition of what is particular and of what is contingent:
definitio est non corruptibilium, sed sempiternorum. The definitional logos states
the identity of that which is in its specific essence. The expression of this
onto-logy is determined by predication 'per se'. For along this way of predication the substantial identity of subject and predicate becomes manifest: in the first mode of saying 'per se', what is predicated belongs to the
form of the subject.

(3) The origination of nature also motivates the direction of questioning and knowing (ch. 1), the resolution to the logically and ontologically prior. Philosophical questioning is centered from the outset upon the

---

[61] *In V Metaph.*, lect. 5, 822.

[62] *In De div. nomin.* c. 4, lect. 7, 371: Est autem in motu circulari duo considerare:
unum, scilicet quod est uniformis; aliud vero, quod motus circularis est sine principio et
fine; *De verit.* 10, 8 obj. 10: Circulus autem motus est ab eodem in idem.

[63] *De anima* q. un., a. 18: Unde considerandum est quod, eo modo quo aliquid est de
perfectione naturae, eo modo ad perfectionem intelligibilem pertinet. Singularia namque
non sunt de perfectione naturae propter se, sed propter aliud: scilicet ut in eis salventur
species quas natura intendit. *Natura enim intendit generare hominem, non hunc hominem*; nam
in quantum homo non potest esse, nisi sit hic homo. . . . *Unde et cognoscere species rerum pertinet
ad perfectionem intelligibilem.*

[64] *In II Sent.* 20, 1, 1; *S. Th.* I, 98, 1. Cf. *De quat. opp.*, c. 4: Homo generat hominem:
natura enim manet una secundum rationem naturae, cum definitio sit una.

"what" question (*quid est*). For in that question, inquiry is made into the intrinsic determination whereby the thing is what it is, its nature. In the quiddity, the natural desire to know the causes is fulfilled.[65]

3.4.3. *The prior and later in the division of the causes*

Decisive for the division of the causes of generation is what is posited as the (ontologically) prior and what is posited as the later. The primary difference was found to be the division between cause 'per se' and cause 'per accidens', that is, chance. This division obtains extra relief when it is set in a historical context which was unknown to Thomas Aquinas but which was not on that account strange to him philosophically (cf. 4.3.2.).

In the tenth book of the "Laws" (*Nomoi*), in an argument against people who deny the existence of God, Plato brings up a recent doctrine.

> Some assert that of all things that have come to be and are coming to be now and shall come to be, some are by nature, some by art, some by chance. (888 E)

This tripartite division is practically identical in its formulation to the opening of Aristotle's *Physica* II, which was discussed in 3.1. and 3.2. What matters, however, is to see where the primary differences are laid. Plato continues:

> It is evident, they claim, that nature and chance produce the grandest and finest things, but art the meanest; art takes over from nature the genesis of the grand and primary works, and fashions then all the minor works. (889 A)

In this doctrine, as in Aristotle's, nature is regarded as the prior. Yet what is striking is that nature is posed *together* with chance as the prior over against art. "Fire, water, earth and air are all by nature and chance, none of them by art" (889 B). It is owing to the inherent dynamics of the elements that heaven, earth, all living beings and plants were constituted. All this came to be "neither through an intelligent mind, nor through a god or art but, as said, through nature and chance" (889 C). The order of the world is the product of a chance mixing of the inanimate elements.

Precisely in this connection of nature with chance, in Plato's judgement, lies the "godlessness" of this explanation of the world. That which is the first cause of all coming to be and passing away—and what to Plato's mind really deserves the name of "nature" (*physis*)—is regarded by this doctrine not as the prior but as the later; that, however, which be-

---

[65] *S. Th.* I, 12, 8 ad 4. (Cf. ch. 2.2.)

came later is regarded as the prior (891 E). The godlessness consists in a reversal of the "later" and "prior," which is to say in the priority of the 'physis' of the elements over 'technè'. Prior to and more original than the material nature, however, so Plato holds, is the soul (*psyche*) and what belongs to it: mind, art, and law (*nomos*) (892 A ff.). For the first motion is that which moves itself and likewise sets the other things in motion. This motion is proper to the soul.

Plato's entire effort is aimed at showing that what is named 'physis' by those thinkers possesses no priority but is dependent upon and reducible to art, and to the mind which confers order and intelligibility (cf. 892 B). The art to which the grand and primary works of the world are reducible is not, however, a (human) art starting from existing natural things, but the divine productive art. The "'archè' of motion" (896 B), the "metaphysical" principle of the way towards being is the World-Soul, which is the source of the cosmic order.[66]

If we recall the Aristotelian division of the causes of generation, then the agreement with Plato's train of thought is that nature ('physis') verifies the claim of its name: it is a cause of order and rationality and is opposed together with art to chance (as cause 'per accidence'), as a result of which nature is released from blind chance.

Yet a significant difference appears as well. In Aristotle this intelligible operation of nature is not effected in a divine art or intelligence. When he speaks of 'technè', he always means *human* art; to this, the work of nature is primary. And when in the first basic text nature is opposed to "other" causes, then it is *infra*-natural causes that are meant. Nature *itself* as a generating principle has a demiurge function,[67] is itself 'nomos', autonomous; nature itself operates for an end.

The Aristotelian concept of nature—together with the thought about the origin implied in it—thereby acquires at the same time a polemical function. Two points are particularly instructive in this regard. Plato's definition of the Soul is applied by Aristotle to nature. This is now defined as "intrinsic principle of motion." And secondly, what deserves attention is the philosophical motive that induces Aristotle to introduce a discussion of "nature," "art," and "chance" into *Metaph.* VII (c. 7–9; Thomas: lect. 6–8)—the very text that was central in the elucidation of nature (cf. 3.2.–3.3.). His analysis of the causes of generation, of which

---

[66] For the broader background, see D. Mannsperger, *Physis bei Platon* (Berlin, 1969).

[67] See, e.g., *De partibus animalium* I, 5, 645 a 9; II, 9, 654 b 31; *De generatione animalium* I, 23, 731 a 24; II, 6, 743 b 23.

Cf. F. Solmsen, "Nature as Craftsman in Greek Thought," *Journal of the History of Ideas* 24 (1963): 473–96, where it is observed (p. 495) that many passages in Aristotle would be more convincing if "Demiurge" were read instead of "nature."

nature was the fundamental one, is meant to refute Plato's thesis that separate species are necessary in order to explain the generation of sensible beings. Ideas or exemplary Forms are no more necessary for the becoming of composed beings than they are for their knowability and essence (lect. 6, 1381). In natural generation the efficient cause and the final cause correspond. The generator and the generated are specifically identical: man generates man (7, 1432). Plato had assimilated the coming forth of natural things to the way in which artefacts are made (*Plato productionem rerum naturalium assimilavit factioni rerum artificialium; In I Metaph.*, 15, 231). Here the artificer looks to an idea in order to produce something similar to it. But to Aristotle the hypothesis of an ''exemplar'' is utterly superfluous for natural becoming. For in the operation of natural things we see that the alike is generated by the alike, as man by man (*ibid.*, 232). *Homo generat hominem* is not merely an aphoristic illustration of this view but the paradigm of this origination.[68]

Similarly, in *Metaph.* XII, c.3 the doctrine of the separate Forms is criticized on the basis of the division of the causes of generation. ''The Platonists said that is was necessary to posit Ideas in order that particular substances might be formed in likeness to them. But this is not necessary, because in the realm of sublunar things one finds an adequate cause (*causa sufficiens*) of everything that comes to be. For the natural agent produces something like itself. Man generates man.''[69] Things have a causality and an efficiency of their own, by their very nature.

This sufficiency of nature goes so far that in various adages found throughout Aristotle's entire work, 'physis' appears as if it were a subsisting power, in disregard of the ''abstract,'' non-subsistent character of nature. ''Nature always does what is best,'' ''nature does nothing superfluous,'' ''does not fall short in the necessary,'' etc.[70]

This polemical function of the concept of nature verifies to just how great an extent the division of the causes is a point of view in the double sense—a perspective and a choice (3.1.). It is this option that determines the ways of questioning, of predication, and of causality that we have followed thus far.

---

[68] See, e.g., *In VII Metaph.*, lect. 6, 1391; *De principiis naturae*, c. 4; *S. Th.* I, 3, 8; 4, 3; 100, 1; I-II, 81, 2; *Comp. Theol.* I, 197. Cf. *De pot.* 3, 8.

[69] *In XII Metaph.*, lect. 3, 2454.

[70] There is an echo of this in Thomas. Thus he argues in an exposition of his own in the commentary on the *Phys.* (III, lect. 5, 332) and in *De regime principum* (I, 1) that nature has sufficiently given the other living beings the means they need to preserve their lives—horns for self-defense, fur for protection, etc. In this respect, man is a *Mangelwesen*, a being with a lack; he does not possess such things. But this lack is his prerogative: he is free of 'determinata instrumenta'. They *could* not be given to man *by nature* because they would not fit his possession of reason.

3.5. *Another mode of causing ('alius modus causandi')*

In 1.8.1. we saw that for Thomas there is another mode of questioning, which concerns the being (*esse*) whereby that which is is. In 2.5.1. we saw that Thomas connects with it another mode of predicating. In the predication 'per essentiam' and 'per participationem', a multiplicity is reduced to unity at the level of being. In coherence with these other modes, an *alius modus causandi* needs to be looked into now.

3.5.1. *The necessity of another mode of becoming*

In the second basic text (*De subst. separ.*, c.9), at the beginning of the chapter, Thomas observes that with regard to the mode of existing (*modum existendi*) of the separate substances, certain people have deviated from the truth by taking away from immaterial substances the origin by the first Author (*auferentes earum originem a primo et summo auctore*). Some of them asserted that these substances had absolutely no cause of their being.

The conception of these thinkers is entirely consistent with the natural origin from which the operation of the four causes is thought. Within the framework of causality, oriented as it is to generation, it is necessary to deny any "being caused" of the separate substances. Immaterial beings bear no possibility of becoming in themselves. They are, as pure forms, "absolute" (1.2.). The arguments advanced in *De substantiis separatis* for this "an-archy" (originlessness) are accordingly all derived from the conditions of generation.

This *via in esse* is, we saw in 3.2., *ex aliquo*, namely, from something underlying, *ad aliquid*, namely, to the form, whereby something is in act. In the first argument the point of departure is taken from the "common supposition" of the natural philosophers: "out of nothing comes nothing." Whatever has a cause of its being must become from another, matter. If, therefore, spiritual substances have no matter, it seems to follow that they have absolutely no cause of their being. Only what is composed of matter and form can come to be.[71]

The second argument arrives at the same conclusion, on the basis of the consideration that every becoming requires a pre-existing subject. The third reasons, on the contrary, from the terminus of generation. When the form is acquired, the substance *is* a being. If then something is through itself form, this does not become a being, but it is subsistent. "Therefore spiritual substances do not have a cause of their being in the sense of having been made by another." In *S.Th.* I, 61, 1, where the

---

[71] Cf. *De anima* q. un., art. 6 ad 8: Generans naturale non nisi ex materia generat.

same problem is at issue (*Utrum angeli habeant causam sui esse*), in the second objection a statement of Aristotle's is cited from *Metaph.* VII, c. 6 which underlines once more the tie of causality to hylomorphism. "If any substance be a form without matter, straightaway it has being and unity of itself, and has no cause of its being and unity." The conclusion seems inescapable that the angels, which are immaterial forms, have no cause of their being.

But is this inference compelling? It is on this crucial point that Thomas opens up a new perspective in *De substantiis separatis*: "the present opinion seems to proceed from the fact that the intellect cannot be raised to see another mode of causing (*alium modum causandi*) than the one which is suited to material things." It is necessary, however, beyond this mode of becoming, the generation, to posit another and higher one.[72] Thomas advances several arguments for this necessity. The first one is based on the "other" predication model of *per essentiam* and *per participationem*. The reasoning is as follows.

The first principle must be the most simple (*simplicissimum*); it must be understood as being itself (*ipsum esse existens*). This subsistent being can only be one, because (see 2.5.2.) it is pure being by its essence. From this it follows that all other things, which are under it, must be as participating in being. Participation expresses the non-identity of that which is with its being. In all such things a common resolution (*resolutio*) must take place, in the sense that each of them is resolved by the intellect into that which is, and its being. For this reason, concludes the first argument, above the mode of coming to be by which something becomes when form comes to matter, we must preconceive another origin of things according as 'to be' is bestowed (*attribuitur*) upon the whole universe of things by the first Being, which is its being (cf. 1.8.2.).

This other origin—other, namely, than nature—needs to be examined, more extensively than it is in this argumentation, in connection with the three moments mentioned in the conclusion: the "being" (*esse*), the universal attribution, and the reduction to the first Being, which is its being.

3.5.2. *The necessity of an origin of being in general: 'Emanatio'*

The universal attribution of being is central in another argument, which is advanced in *De subst. separ.*, c. 9 to elucidate the necessity of another mode of causing. What is by accident (*per accidens*) must be reduced

---

[72] Thomas adds: *secundum sententiam Platonis et Aristotelis.* See for this 5.2. and 5.3.2.

to that which is through itself (*per se*). In every change or mutation there comes to be that which is this or that being 'per se'; but being, taken in its generalness (*ens autem communiter sumptum*), becomes accidentally; for it does not become from "non-being" as such but from "non-being *this*." Therefore—so it is concluded once again—it is necessary to consider in things an origin according to which being, taken in its generalness, is 'per se' granted to things—which transcends all change and motion.[73]

This reasoning, which is also to be found in *S.c.G.* II, 21 and *In VIII Phys.*, lect. 2, 975, is striking in its simplicity, but its import is transcendent in more respects than the one indicated in the conclusion. The opening is reminiscent of the division of the causes of generation (3.3.). The primary difference in that division was the distinction between cause 'per se' and cause 'per accidens'. The latter had to be reduced to the causes 'per se', of which nature was the basic one. But in the reasoning just cited, that division is exceeded, because the analysis is carried further, towards the cause of being as being. From this point of view it must be said that the generative causes are causes of being 'per accidens' and not 'per se'.[74]

Thomas reaches this conclusion by radicalizing Aristotle's thought in *Phys.* I, 8 (lect. 14, 125). When a particular being, for example a man, comes to be, then it is a "man" that comes to be 'per se', because as human being, it was not before; in such a generation, however, it is a "being" that comes to be 'per accidens', because it does not become out of absolute non-being. Always there is presupposed a preexistent subject. This structure conveys Thomas from the categorical level (this or that being) to the transcendental plane. He even carries the parallel with the way of generation so far that in *S.c.G.* II, 21 he speaks of "to produce being from non-being pre-existing" (*producere ens ex non-ente 'praeexistente'*). Only when a being becomes out of an absolute nothing does a "being" become 'per se', that is, as being.[75]

Because Thomas deepens the "non-being in a certain respect" to a radical "nothingness," the origin of what is can no longer be the *generatio*. One of the essential conditions of generation, the subject, the potential being "out of" which something becomes, is missing. In the various arguments in *De subst. separ.*, c. 9, he again and again emphasizes that this coming forth is not to be conceived as a mutation or motion from potency

---

[73] *De subst. separ.*, c. 9, 96.

[74] *S.c.G.* II, 21: Hoc autem est primum ens solum quod est causa entis, in quantum hujusmodi est; alia vero sunt causa essendi per accidens et non per se.

[75] Cf. *In VIII Phys.*, lect. 2, 975: Sed si fit totum ens, quod est fieri ens inquantum ens, oportet quod fiat ex penitus non ente.

to act. Things have received being through an *emanatio* from the first principle.[76] Because this coming forth is not a formation, but terminates in being, which transcends all categories, "the mode of causing" must be another one than in the case of generation. In his commentary on *De causis* Thomas writes:

> There is namely a twofold mode of causing (*duplex modus causandi*). In the first, something becomes, while something else is presupposed; and we say that in this way something becomes *per informationem*, because what comes later is related to what was presupposed in the manner of a form. In another mode, something is caused while nothing is presupposed . . .[77]

In that latter mode of causing there is not an irreducible duality of form and matter. At issue here is not a cause which produces a specific (and therefore definable) effect, that is, a particular cause, but a transcendental one, the *causa universalis totius esse*.[78]

On this other mode of causing is based the reply to the previously (3.5.1.) cited objection against the separate substances' being caused. A subsistent form is at once "being" and "one"; it has no agent that moves it from potency to act. Yet it has a *causam influentem ei esse*.[79] "Over and above the mode of becoming whereby something comes to be through change, there must be a mode of becoming or origin of things without any mutation or motion through the influx of being (*per influentiam essendi*)."[80] It is worthy of notice that Thomas employs here the (Neoplatonic) terminology with which he had defined the notion of cause in general (1.2.): "some influence on the being of the thing caused." It is only in the influx of being that the authentic meaning of cause is fulfilled.

It is necessary to posit an origin of "being, taken in its generalness." This influx of being requires a universal cause, because being is the most general.[81] Yet because of this universal attribution, is it not at the same time the most imperfect? For it must be determined by, i.e., contracted

---

[76] *Ibid.*, 974: Et quia omnis motus indiget subiecto, ut hic Aristoteles probat et rei veritas habet, sequitur quod productio universalis entis a Deo non sit motus nec mutatio, sed sit quaedam simplex emanatio; *ibid.*, 988: Per emanationem a primo rerum principio.

[77] *In De causis*, lect. 18: Est enim *duplex modus causandi*: unus quidem quo aliquid fit praesupposito altero, et hoc modo dicitur fieri aliquid per informationem, quia illud quod posterius advenit se habet ad illud praesupponebatur per modum formae; alio modo causatur aliquid nullo praesupposito. . . .

[78] *In VIII Phys.*, lect. 2, 987. The second argument in *De subst. separ.*, c. 9 (95) for an 'alius modus causandi' is based on the opposition of 'causa particularis' and 'causa universalis'.

[79] *De spirit. creat.* q. un., art. 1 ad 5; cf. *S. Th.* I, 61, 1 ad 2.

[80] *De subst. separ.*, c. 9, 95.

[81] *Ibid.*, c. 8, 87: Ipsum esse quod est communissimum.

116 CHAPTER THREE

to the categories.[82] It was to "being" in this sense that the "if" question (*an est*) was directed in the progression to the "what" question (*quid est*).

Thomas does not follow this direction here, however, for he reverses the order: "being" (*esse*) is the most perfect of all. That can only be understood against the background of the Neoplatonic view of reality. For pseudo-Dionysius "Being itself" is the highest idea of the intelligible world, and it therefore stands closest to the Highest Principle, God. In the ontology of Proclus the central thought is that the more universal a principle is, the more powerful it is. What is most universal, Being, is the most real, for it is the richest in content. All that is participates in the fullness of Being.[83]

Yet Thomas introduces a new element into this understanding of being: he connects the idea of being with that of actuality. "Being" (*esse*) is the most perfect because it is act. Every form is act of the subject, to be sure, but it is only actual insofar as it *is*. Being relates to every perfection as its actualizing act.[84] "What I call 'being' is the actuality of all acts, and for this reason it is the perfection of all perfections."[85] Avicenna is criticized by Thomas for construing 'esse' as accident. It is rather the actuality of every substance. This perfection was aimed at in the other way of posing the "if" question (1.8.2.): "Being itself (*ipsum esse*) is related as act to both composite and simple natures.... Now, being seems to pertain to the question 'if it is' (*an est*)."[86]

3.5.3. *"That which is said to be so by virtue of its essence is the cause of everything said to be so by participation"*

To "being as such" Thomas applies the Platonic model of *per essentiam / per participationem*. Being *per essentiam* is said of God. He alone is Being, is subsistent Being. For Neoplatonism Being was indeed the summit of the intelligible world, but it was still derived from the One. Thomas, however, identifies the fullness of being with the first Principle, God.

This theo-ontology is confirmed, Thomas believes, in the words of

---

[82] Cf. *De pot.* 7, 2 obj. 9: Esse est imperfectissimum, sicut prima materia: sicut enim materia prima determinatur per omnes formas, ita esse, cum sit imperfectissimum, determinari habet per omnia praedicamenta; *S. Th.* I, 4, 1 obj. 3.

[83] See K. Kremer, *Die neuplatonische Seinsphilosophie und ihre Wirkung auf Thomas von Aquin* (Leiden, 1971), 205ff. (re Proclus), 293f.; 353 (re pseudo-Dionysius).

[84] *S. Th.* I, 4, 1 ad 3: Ipsum esse est perfectissimum omnium: comparatur enim ad omnia ut actus. Nihil enim habet actualitatem, nisi inquantum est: unde ipsum esse est actualitas omnium rerum, et etiam ipsarum formarum.

[85] *De pot.* 7, 2 ad 9. See also section 6.7. ("*Esse* is 'the actuality of all acts'")

[86] *De spirit. creat.* q. un., art. 8 ad 3.

Exodus 3:14. God's essence is his Being. "This sublime truth"— Thomas is, for him, unusually lyrical in *S.c.G.* I, 22—God himself has revealed unto Moses. "When Moses asked our Lord: 'if the children of Israel say to me: What is His name? What shall I say to them?' The Lord replied: 'I AM WHO AM. Thou shalt say to the children of Israel, He who is hath sent me unto you.' By this our Lord showed that his own proper name is 'QUI EST' (HE WHO IS)." Thomas continues: "Now, names have been devised to signify the natures or essences of things. It remains, then, that the divine being is God's essence or nature." HE WHO IS is the most proper name of God.[87]

This revelation of God's name plays an important role in GILSON's studies of the character of medieval philosophy in general and of Thomas's philosophy in particular. The Christian revelation had a decisive influence on the development of metaphysics: "Exodus lays down the principle from which henceforth the whole of Christian philosophy will be suspended": the identity of essence and being in God. GILSON even speaks of a "metaphysics of Exodus": "There is but one God and this God is Being, that is the corner-stone of all Christian philosophy, and it was not Plato, it was not even Aristotle, it was Moses who put it in position."[88]

In Exodus is laid down "the corner-stone of Christian philosophy." Various questions can be raised with regard to this view of GILSON's (see also 5.3.2.). These are not suggested primarily by the fact that present-day Biblical exegesis understands this passage in a different (more "Jewish") sense and does not hear a "definition" of God in the text of Exodus. In the verse that follows (Ex. 3:15) God says to Moses: "Thus shalt thou say unto the children of Israel, The Lord God of your fathers, the God of Abraham, the God of Isaac, and the God of Jacob, hath sent me unto you." The promise of faithfulness ("Certainly I will be with thee," v. 12) is connected with the Name.

GILSON does acknowledge that there is not a word of metaphysics *in* Exodus, but there is nevertheless a "metaphysics *of* Exodus."[89] The question, however, is whether this really means a radical—"Christian"— renewal of philosophical thought. GILSON, and many others

---

[87] *In I Sent.* 8, 1, 1; *S. Th.* I, 13, 11; *S.c.G.* II, 52; *De pot.* 2, 1; *Super Ioannem* c. 8, lect. 3, 1179.

Cf. E. Zum Brunn, "La 'métaphysique de l'Exode' selon Thomas d'Aquin," in *Dieu et l'Etre: Exégèses d'Exode 3, 14 et de Coran 20, 11–24* (Paris, 1978), pp. 245–69.

[88] *The Spirit of Mediaeval Philosophy*, pp. 51, 63; *Le Thomisme*, pp. 99ff.; *Introduction à la philosophie chrétienne*, pp. 45ff.

[89] *The Spirit of Mediaeval Philosophy*, p. 433, n. 9. Cf. C.J. de Vogel, *Antike Seinsphilosophie und Christentum im Wandel der Jahrhunderte* (Baden-Baden, 1958), p. 16.

with him, may be said to have answered this question affirmatively too quickly and uncritically. In historical perspective one must say that the cornerstone of this metaphysics was laid by the ancient logos in which the perfect identity is predicated of the first Principle. The medieval exegesis of the text in Exodus builds systematically upon a tradition of thought that culminates in Neoplatonic philosophy. W. BEIERWALTES writes correctly: "The so-called *Exodusmetaphysik* is the most unsuitable subject ... for wanting to demonstrate a genuine 'Christian philosophy.'"[90] Thomas's exposition, too, of Exodus 3:14 has its place within the continuous movement of philosophy towards intelligibility.

God is being 'per essentiam'; all other things participate in being. If this having being is to be intelligible, then it must be reduced to the ontologically prior, to the first being, which is its being. Thomas carries out this reduction in *S. Th.* I, 44, 1:

> It must be said that everything, that in any way is, is from God. For whatever is found in anything by participation must be caused in it by that to which it belongs essentially, as iron becomes heated by fire. Now it has been shown above (I, 3, 4) when treating of the divine simplicity, that God is self-subsisting being itself, and also that subsisting being can be only one.... Therefore all beings other than God are not their own being, but are beings by participation. Therefore, it must be that all things which are diversified by the diverse participation of being, so as to be more or less perfect, are caused by one first Being, Who is most perfectly. Hence Plato said that unity must come before every multitude; and Aristotle said that whatever is greatest in being and greatest in truth is the cause of every being and of every truth.[91]

By means of participation, an intimate relation is established philosophically between God and being. All that in any way is refers in its raison d'être to the Origin of being. This "re-duction" is marked by three features.

First, it is a causal reduction. In the "other" predication model of *per essentiam / per participationem* is contained the meaning of the other mode of

---

[90] *Philosophische Rundschau* 16 (1969): 149. Cf. K. Kremer, *Die neuplatonische Seinsphilosophie*, pp. 391, 396.

[91] *S. Th.* I, 44, 1: Necesse est dicere omne quod quocumque modo est, a Deo esse. Si enim aliquid invenitur in aliquo per participationem, necesse est quod causetur in ipso ab eo cui essentialiter convenit; sicut ferrum fit ignitum ab igne. Ostensum est autem supra (I, 3, 4), cum de divina simplicitate ageretur, quod Deus est ipsum esse per se subsistens. Et iterum ostensum est quod esse subsistens non potest esse nisi unum.... Relinquitur ergo quod omnia alia a Deo non sint suum esse, sed participant esse. Necesse est igitur omnia quae diversificantur secundum diversam participationem essendi, ut sint perfectius vel minus perfecte, causari ab uno primo ente, quod perfectissime est. Ut et Plato dixit quod necesse est ante omnem multitudinem ponere unitatem. Et Aristoteles dicit, in II *Metaph.*, quod id quod est maxime ens et maxime verum, est causa omnis entis et omnis veri.

causing. *Quod per essentiam dicitur est causa omnium quae per participationem di-cuntur.* Whatever is by participation must be reduced to what is by its essence, as cause.[92] Causation, in the proper sense, is influx of being. This metaphysical causality is derived from the principle of participation: "from the fact that a thing is being by participation, it follows that it is caused by another."[93] Participation in being implies causal dependence upon what is essentially.

Secondly, it is a reduction of multiplicity to unity. Significant for this point (and for the moment of continuity with ancient thought) is the reference to Plato's dictum at the end of *S. Th.* I, 44, 1: before every multitude there must be unity. Prior to the multiplicity of beings is a unique being. In the prologue to this commentary on the Gospel of John, Thomas expressly observes that this reduction was typical for the (Neo-) Platonists. For they saw that "all that is by participation is reduced to that which is such by its essence, as the first and highest.... And this is God, who is the most sufficient, most dignified, and most perfect cause of all being, and through whom all that is participates in being."[94]

Thirdly, in the causal reduction a compositeness is brought to identity. What has being and is not being is a being through participation. But what is characterized by the composition of essence and being has a being that is caused by another (*ab alio*). This extrinsic cause is the first being that is wholly simple, because being and essence are identical in it.[95]

3.6. 'Per viam creationis'[96]

In 3.5. we saw that Thomas considers the necessity of another mode of becoming and causing, the necessity of an origin of being in general, an *emanatio*. This origin he also designates with the Judaeo-Christian notion of *creatio*: "Emanationem totius entis a causa universali ... designamus nomine creationis" (*S. Th.* I, 45, 1). To create is, properly speaking, to cause or produce the being of things (*causare sive producere esse rerum*).[97]

---

[92] *S.c.G.* II, 15. Cf. *In II Metaph.*, lect. 2, 296.

[93] *S. Th.* I, 44, 1 ad 1. See also *De subst. separ.*, c. 3; *S. Th.* I, 61, 1: Omne autem quod est per participationem, causatur ab eo quod est per essentiam; sicut omne ignitum causatur ab igne; *Comp. Theol.* I, 68.

[94] *Super Ioannem*, prologus, 5.

[95] *S. Th.* I, 3, 4: Oportet quod illud cuius esse est aliud ab essentia sua, habet esse causatum ab alio; 3, 7 ad 1.

[96] *S.c.G.* III, 69.

[97] *S. Th.* I, 45, 6.

3.6.1. *'Creatio ex nihilo'*

"In the beginning God created the heaven and the earth." At a very early time—first in the "Pastor" of Hermas, one of the so-called Apostolic Fathers (*Mandata* I, 1)—Christianity tried to verbalize the uniqueness and totality of this origination in the expression "creation out of nothing" (*creatio ex nihilo*). This wording may have been inspired by late Jewish tradition: in any case, it is to be found in II Macc. 7:28, where the Vulgate reads that God made heaven and earth and man *ex nihilo*. Expression was thereby given to a radical antithesis with the philosophical speculation about the origin of reality. The common supposition of the ancient philosophers was: *ex nihilo nihil fit*.[98] For does becoming not always require a subject?

In continuity with the Christian tradition of faith, Thomas states: *creare est ex nihilo aliquid facere* (*S. Th.* I, 45, 1 sed contra). He takes great pains to attain to a pure understanding of the "out of nothing," called by SCHELLING "the cross of the intellect."

The point of departure for his reflection is everyday language.[99] If it is said that "something becomes out of nothing," then that can have a twofold sense. The first possibility is that the negation contained in the "nothing" also includes the preposition "out of"; in which case one intends to say that something does *not* become *out of something* because there does not preexist something out of which it becomes. Likewise it is said that someone speaks about "nothing" because he does not speak about something. The second possibility is that the negation is included by the "out of"; in that case one expresses that something becomes *out of nothing* because it becomes *after* nothing (*post nihilum*), as when it is said: "out of" the morning becomes midday, that is, "after" the morning. Both meanings are "verified" (*verificatur*) in the expression 'creatio ex nihilo'. The first meaning is a negative one: denied is the relation to something preexisting (*negatio neget ordinem creationis . . . ad aliquid praeexistens*). The second is an affirmative one: it affirms the relation of the creation to nothing preexisting (*remaneat ordo creationis ad nihil praexistens natura affirmatus*), in the sense that by nature the creaturely has non-being prior to its having being.[100]

With regard to this exposition a critical question arises. Is the expression 'creatio ex nihilo' really "verified" by the semantics of "nothing"

---

[98] Cf. *De pot.* 3, 1 obj. 1; *S. Th.* I, 45, 2 obj. 1; *S.c.G.* II, 16.

[99] See *S. Th.* I, 45, 1 ad 3 and *De pot.* 3, 1 ad 7, of which the following presentation is a summary.

[100] *In II Sent.* 1, 1, 2.

in everyday language? For Thomas himself observes (*In VIII Phys.*, lect. 2, 974) that " 'to become' and 'to make' are said equivocally in the universal production of things and in the other productions." In his argument, J.F. ANDERSON disregards the decisive point of this equivocalness: "There is a rational or logical relation of indeterminate proportion between the being of anything whatever and its 'antecedent' non-being. In this sense . . . all productions are 'from nothing', i.e., from the prior non-being of the thing produced." In this way, creation is subsumed under productions in general: "true of all productions, creation included."[101] Indeed, every becoming has as 'terminus a quo' non-being; but this is precisely not an *absolute* nothing. Creation differs in principle from intraworldly processes.

Is it, therefore, possible to give 'creatio ex nihilo' an intelligible meaning by interpreting the expression as creation *after* nothing, as illustrated by the example of the midday which becomes "out of" (that is, "after") the morning? Nothing is clarified in this way: "before" and "after" are relations having validity only within creaturely reality. They presuppose a temporal continuity which also makes itself felt in Thomas's formulation that creation has an order to a 'nihil *praeexistens*'.[102]

Although the quest for insight is difficult, Aquinas in his reflection on the two senses of 'creatio ex nihilo' has still gained two important characteristics of the idea of creation.[103] "The first is that creation presupposes nothing in the thing that is created: in this it differs from other changes." "Creation" expresses the absolute sovereignty of God, His power which presupposes nothing. Every duality inherent to a *formatio* is cut off radically.

"For of Him, and through Him, and to Him, are all things." In his exposition of the doxology of Rom. 11:36 Thomas writes: "to indicate the causality of God (*causalitas Dei*), the Apostle uses three prepositions."[104] "Out of" (*ex*) cannot signify a material cause, for the world is not made out of preexisting matter. "Therefore it is said, not that all that is created is out of something, but that it is *ex nihilo*; for it was nothing be-

---

[101] J.F. Anderson, *The Cause of Being: The Philosophy of Creation in St. Thomas* (St. Louis and London, 1952), pp. 10, 9.

[102] It is remarkable that, in *De pot.* 3, 2, Thomas criticizes this representation of creation, including the example: "secundum imaginationem tantum."

[103] *In II Sent.* 1, 1, 2: Sciendum est autem quod ad rationem creationis pertinent duo. *Primum* est ut nihil praesupponat in re quae creari dicitur: unde in hoc ab aliis mutationibus differt. . . . *Secundum* est, ut in re quae creari dicitur, prius sit non esse quam esse.

[104] *In Epist. ad Romanos*, cap. 11, lect. 5. Cf. J.A. Aertsen, " 'Uit God zijn alle dingen': Enkele overwegingen bij de 700-ste sterfdag van Thomas van Aquino," *Philosophia Reformata* 39 (1974): 102–55.

fore it was created to be.'' The meaning of ''of'' in this text is that all
things are of God as the first agent (*Ex Deo sunt omnia sicut ex primo agente*).
At the same time, it is expressed that the creatures do not come forth from
God as being alike in essence to him (*ei consubstantiales*): they are not *de ipso*
but only *ex ipso*. A radical difference remains between the Creator and the
created.

As Creator, God reveals Himself as the absolute and integral Origin of
all things. Therefore creation is different from any becoming. It is no
''mutation'' of something into something else. ''Creation is more perfect
than and prior to generation and alteration, because the terminus is the
whole substance of the thing. That, however, which is understood as the
begin term is absolute non-being.''[105]

Accordingly, another mode of causing is at issue here than in the case
of generation. ''In another way something is caused when nothing is
presupposed; and in this way it is said that something becomes *per creationem*'' (*In De causis*, lect. 18). The creating cause is total cause.[106]

> The causality of that which generates or alters does not extend to all that is
> found in the thing, but to the form, which is brought from potency to act.
> But the causality of that which creates extends to all that is in the thing. And
> therefore it is said that creation is from nothing, since there is nothing that
> preexists before the creation, as though it were not created.[107]

The second characteristic of the idea of creation, which is mentioned in
In II Sent. 1, 1, 2, is that in the creaturely, non-being is prior to being (*prius
sit non esse quam esse*). What is meant by this it not a temporal but an ontological priority, in the sense ''that the creature would fall into non-being if
left to itself. For it only has being from the influence of a higher cause.''
The terminus of creation, because it is *ex nihilo*, is 'esse' in the absolute
sense. The being of things is a datum in the deeper sense of ''gift.''[108]

This origin motivates another meaning of being than is revealed *per
viam naturae*. The horizon of the nature of what is, the per-se-ity, is broken
open towards being as creature. Creature expresses an integral origination *ab alio*. The relation to God is essential for the creaturely: ''every

[105] *S. Th.* I, 45, 1 ad 2.
[106] *In De div. nomin.* c. 5, lect. 1, 624: Deus . . . est causa . . . creatrix omnium existentium, quia scilicet non producit substantias ex aliquo praeexistente, sed simpliciter omne
existens ex virtute Ipsius provenit.
[107] *In II Sent.* 1, 1, 2: *Causalitas generantis* vel alterantis non sic se extendit ad omne illud
quod in re invenitur, sed ad formam, quae de potentia in actum educitur. Sed *causalitas
creantis* se extendit ad omne id quod est in re; et ideo creatio ex nihilo dicitur esse, quia
nihil est quod creationi praeexistat, quasi non creatum.
[108] *In I Sent.* 37, 1, 1: Creare autem est dare esse.

creature in regard to its entire being naturally belongs to God" (*S. Th.* I, 60, 5).

In the perspective of creation, the traditional order of questioning, which is directed to the definitional 'quid est', also becomes subject to questioning (1.8.). What gives rise to wonder is that that which is *is*: "Why is there any being at all—why not far rather nothing?"

3.6.2. *Creation and participation*

From the origin of the creation, the common motive of the movement of thought (initiated through the other mode of questioning) and the way towards being (the other mode of becoming and causing) becomes visible. Of philosophical importance is that in this approach Thomas interprets 'creatio ex nihilo' as participation. That already became apparent "by the way of predication": "being is predicated of any creature by participation" (2.5.2.).

The idea of creation is pre-eminently connected by Thomas with the Platonic doctrine of participation. The treatise on creation in *S. Th.* I, 44, 1 commences with the question: "Whether it is necessary that every being is created by God?" From the 'corpus articuli', quoted in 3.5.3., it appears that the entire question—in keeping with the first argument in *De subst. separ.*, c. 9 for the necessity of another origin—is dealt with exclusively in terms of participation. K. KREMER goes so far as to say that the terminology of Creator and creature in Thomas is often only a "signboard" which in reality is interpreted from participation.[109] In the created is "received or participated being." God, however, is his subsistent Being.[110] The divine Being is the *ratio creandi*, for through creation all things participate in being.[111]

The identification of "creation" and "participation in being" is made without qualification. But what does this identification imply, and is it really so self-evident? These questions are usually not asked. For example, C.J. DE VOGEL writes without a trace of hesitation, "To create is to bestow part in Oneself."[112] But is the counterpart of this "to

---

[109] K. Kremer, *Die neuplatonische Seinsphilosophie*, p. 347.

[110] *De verit.* 21, 5: Ipsa autem natura vel essentia divina est eius esse; natura autem vel essentia cuiuslibet rei creatae non est suum esse, sed esse participans ab alio. Et sic in Deo est esse purum, quia ipse Deus est suum esse subsistens; in creatura autem est esse receptum vel participatum.

[111] *De quat. opp.*, c. 4: Esse namque divinum proprie est ratio creandi, quia per creationem omnes res communiter accedunt ad participandum esse quantum est eis possibile; *S. Th.* I, 8, 1; *S. Th.* I, 45, 6.

[112] C.J. de Vogel, "De Griekse wijsbegeerte en het Christelijk scheppingsbegrip," in *Theoria: Studies over de Griekse wijsbegeerte* (Assen, 1967), p. 199.

bestow part in Oneself'' not that to be created is ''to have part in God Himself''? In what follows it will be made clear that there is good reason indeed to give critical attention to the implications of the idea of participation.

Thematizing the idea of creation as participation in being introduces a problem into the relation of Creator and creature, and that problem acquires still added sharpness in Thomas. For, in a departure from the Neoplatonic tradition, he identifies 'Esse' with God Himself. Often this departure is presented as a slight modification (e.g., by KREMER),[113] but in fact it is not unimportant for the very character of the participation.

For Neoplatonism Being was the summit of the intelligible world, but still derived from the First Principle. That is also the true sense of the fourth proposition in the book *De causis*: ''The first of created things is being, and nothing else is created before it.'' For pseudo-Dionysus, too, *ipsum esse* is the highest Idea, certainly, but not God Himself. That for him ''being'' has a mediating position is acknowledged by Thomas in his commentary on *De divinis nominibus* (c. 5, lect. 2, 660):

> Next, Dionysus shows how 'esse' is related to God, and he says that *ipsum esse* is from the first being, which is God. From this it follows that the *esse commune* is related to God in a different way than all else that exists, in three respects.
>
> First, all else that exists depends on the *esse commune*, but God does not; the *esse commune* depends rather on God....
>
> Secondly, all that exists is contained under the *esse commune*, but God is not; the *esse commune* is contained rather under his power (*continetur sub eius virtute*)....
>
> Thirdly, all else that exists participates in being, but God does not; *ipsum esse creatum* is rather a certain *participatio Dei* and likeness to Him.

One can see how here the (created!) *esse commune* occupies a place between God and existing things. In Thomas, however, this mediation is dropped. Is the consequence not a direct participation of the created in the divine Being?

Some scholars have shied away from drawing this conclusion. How in that case would Thomas be able to avoid monism and preserve the boundaries between the divine and the creaturely? To W. WEIER's insight ''there can be no question of participation in being in the sense of participation in the divine being as such in Thomas.''[114] It seems to be

[113] K. Kremer, ''Die Creatio nach Thomas von Aquin und dem Liber de Causis,'' in *Ekklesia: Festschrift für Bischof Dr. Matth. Wehr* (Trier, 1962), 329: ''Neu ist gegenüber dem Neuplatonismus *nur* (italics added, J.A.A.), dass es nicht mehr wie bei diesem *ens ab alio*, sondern *ens a se* ist.''
[114] W. Weier, ''Seinsteilhabe und Sinnteilhabe im Denken des hl. Thomas von

WEIER's own systematic considerations, however, that shore up this assessment.

That there is a question of participation in the divine being in Thomas is beyond doubt as far as K. KREMER is concerned. As he sees it, it is precisely through participation that the metaphysical distinction between Creator and creature is guaranteed. That which participates always remains deficient with respect to that which is participated in because it receives being only in a particularized way.[115] Typical of every philosophy of participation is the duality of *per essentiam* and *per participationem*.

Yet however great the distance between essential being and being through participation may be, there remains at the basis of this distinction a transcendental unity. That is directly apparent in the text from *Quodl.* II, 2, 1 that was analyzed in 2.5.1: "being (*ens*) is predicated essentially of God alone...; it is predicated of any creature by participation." "Being" is said *secundum prius et posterius*, that is, predicated analogically of God and creature. This unity of being comes out even more clearly when Thomas argues that being caused does not belong to being as such. Otherwise, each being would be caused by another, so that the series of causes would be infinite. There must be a thing that is uncaused.[116]

Whatever is by participation is caused by what is essentially, "as everything fiery is caused by fire" (*sicut omne ignitum causatur ab igne*) (*S. Th.* I, 61, 1). There is a likeness between the creature and God because "from being are beings" (*ab ente sunt entia*).[117] There is also "synonymy" in this coming to be—every agent produces something like itself— and that is the reason creatures can be called beings. Created being participates in the "nature of being" (*natura essendi*) that belongs to God alone infinitely, that is, without any limitation.[118]

The transcendental unity of being ('natura essendi') makes it necessary to situate the distinction between God and the creaturely in a "con-

---

Aquin," *Salzburg. Jahrbuch für Philosophie* 8 (1964), 97–98. Cf. L. Dümpelmann, *Kreation als ontisch-ontologisches Verhältnis* (Freiburg and Munich, 1969), pp. 23ff.

[115] K. Kremer, *Die neuplatonische Seinsphilosophie*, p. 449.

[116] *S.c.G.* II, 52; *S. Th.* I, 44, 1 ad 1.

[117] *In II Sent.* 16, 1, 2 explains the two modes of "synonymy": "Similitudo operis potest dici ad operantem dupliciter: aut quantum ad id quod habet in natura sua, sicut homo generat hominem; aut quantum ad id quod habet in intellectu suo, sicut artificiatum ab artifice in similitudinem artis suae procedit."

Now, according to the first mode "procedit creatura a Deo in similitudinem ejus ... quia *ab ente sunt entia*."

[118] *S. Th.* I, 45, 5 ad 1: Quodcumque ens creatum participat, ut ita dixerim, *naturam essendi*: quia solus Deus est suum esse; *Quodl.* III, 1, 1: Cum autem Deus sit ipsum esse subsistens, manifestum est quod *natura essendi* convenit Deo infinite absque omni limitatione et contractione.

finement'' of the fullness of being in whatever is created. A text fom *De spirit. creat.* (q. un., art. 1) shows this with great clarity:

> It is manifest that the first being, namely God, is infinite act. For it has in it the entire fullness of being that is not contracted to a generic or specific nature ... because then it would be limited (*finiretur*) to this nature.
> This cannot be said, however, of anything else. So all that comes after the first being has, because it is not its being, received being in something, whereby being itself is contracted. And so in whatever is created, the nature of the thing that participates in being is other (*aliud*) than being itself, which is participated in.[119]

What is entailed in interpreting creation as participation in being appears here in sharp relief. Creation is *contraction* of being, without the subsistent Being itself being limited. There was mention of contraction of being already in 2.1.2.; but there, ''contraction'' had a different sense: in Aristotle's account of predication, the universal 'ens' was contracted directly to the diverse categories, the particular modes of being. Now, however, the point of departure is the infinite fullness of being which is contracted to a finite being.

Creation is limitation of the fullness of being. It is accordingly understood by interpreters like FABRO and KREMER in a true Neoplatonic manner as a ''fall.''[120] A *malum metaphysicum* adheres to the divine gift of being. The creatures have an imperfect being, because they only participate in being.[121] Hereupon rests the natural desire for the Origin. For every thing it is desirable to be united to its principle (1.7.1.) ''The perfection of every effect consists in the assimilation to its cause'' (*De subst. separ.* c. 12, 112). All the creaturely desires by nature the perfect source from which it has originated. The de-duction of the created from the divine 'esse' has as its counterpart the re-duction to the being that is truly and essentially.

---

[119] *De spirit. creat.* q. un., art. 1: Manifestum est enim quod primum ens, quod Deus est, est actus infinitus, utpote habens in se totam essendi plenitudinem, non contractam ad aliquam naturam generis vel speciei ... quia sic finiretur ad illam naturam. Hoc autem non potest dici de aliquo alio....
Omne igitur quod est post primum ens, cum non sit suum esse, habet esse in aliquo receptum, per quod ipsum esse contrahitur; *et sic in quolibet creato aliud est natura rei quae participat esse, et aliud ipsum esse participatum.*
[120] K. Kremer, *Die neuplatonische Seinsphilosophie*, p. 423: ''Denn was Gott schafft, ist immer von geringerer Seinsfülle als er selbst und deshalb, aber auch nur deshalb, Abfall von Gott.'' C. Fabro, *Participation et Causalité selon St. Thomas d'Aquin*, p. 243: ''L'étant au sens propre indique la première et fondamentale 'chute' de l'*esse*.... L'étant est ce qui est, le réel ... mais il paie son affirmation de réalité du lourd prix de n'être point l'*esse*.''
[121] *S. Th.* I-II, 2, 5 ad 2: Sed si consideretur ipsum esse prout participatur in hac re vel illa, quae non capiunt totam perfectionem essendi, sed habent esse imperfectum, sicut est esse cujuslibet creaturae; *De spirit. creat.* q. un., a. 1.

The unity of being must evoke dialectically in the created "something other" (*aliud*), whereby being is limited and determined. In the concluding statement of the text just cited from *De spirit. creat.*, it is said: "And so in whatever is created, the nature of the thing that participates in being is other than being itself, which is participated in." The index of creatureliness is the non-identity, the composition, of essence and being whereby the distinction between God and the created remains guaranteed. This otherness in the structure of that which is must engage our attention more thoroughly.

3.7. 'Con-cursus'

3.7.1. 'Per viam naturae'—'per viam creationis'

"Way refers to being-under-way, that is, to motion (*Via ad motum refertur*)."[122] The preceding chapters have been an inquiry, have been literally an "investigation" of this way.[123] Two main "tracks" have been followed: *per viam naturae* and *per viam creationis*.

"The fulfillment of every motion lies in its end."[124] The terminus of generation is the intrinsic nature or essence of the thing. The final term of the corresponding way of thought is the definition, which determines that which is in its specific essence. The terminus of creation is being (*esse*). The creature has its being from another. Creation is a gift of God.

It was established in 3.4. that: "What belongs to a thing naturally and immovably must be the foundation and principle of all else, since the nature of a thing is the first in everything" (*S. Th.* I, 82, 1). But from the perspective of creation it is affirmed in *De aeternitate mundi*: "What belongs to a thing in itself is naturally in it prior to what it only has from another. Now, the creature has being from another; left to itself, it is, considered in itself, nothing. So in the creature, nothing is naturally prior to being."

In both statements the point of departure is that what belongs to something naturally is prior to what it has from another. From this it is concluded in the first statement that the *nature* is therefore the persistent foundation and principle of all else. In the second statement the conclusion is that, consequently, the *creature* is by nature "nothing." The distinguishing mark of the idea of creation is that in the creaturely, non-being is prior to being (3.6.1.). In the order of creation, there is a radical re-

---

[122] *In Job*, lect. 38.
[123] *In De div. nomin.* c. 1, lect. 1, 34: Nam investigare proprie est per vestigia alicuius euntis per viam, ad viae terminum perduci.
[124] *De verit.* 1, 2: Complementum autem cuiuslibet motus est in suo termino.

versal of the "prior" and "later" as these are found in the order of nature.

This is the radix of the twofold sense of questioning, of the two tracks of predication, and of the different modes of causing.[125] Although the terms "nature" and "creature" are often used interchangeably in discussions,[126] we have shown through the analysis of their backgrounds that in these notions is centered a different primordiality, which qualifies the meaning of being and the direction of thought.

Nature says what being is *in itself*, its specific essence, which is preserved by the circulation of things. It is a typical espression of Greek philosophical rationality, as that had acquired form in Aristotelian thought and was passed on to the thirteenth century.

Creature says *being-related* to God. The Biblical idea of creation expresses both the radical distinction between God and the created and the religious directedness of all that is to the Origin. That the world is created is an essential moment of the Christian faith (cf. 5.3.1.: "Creation as an article of faith").

3.7.2. 'Duplex ordo'

It is the divergent tendencies of the ways of nature and creation that have been exposited in our investigation thus far. There is also, however, a "concurrence." This is true even in a merely external sense: the two movements can both be followed in Thomas's work. H. MEYER writes in his extensive monograph on Thomas:

> The viewpoints from which a thinker sees a problem and approaches its solution are not a matter of indifference to him. For Thomas it is characteristic that he seeks to interpret the natural becoming on the basis of Aristotelian principles and the genesis of the world on the basis of the Christian worldview.[127]

Such an exposition is unsatisfactory even as a summary. Have we not just seen how Platonic moments affect Thomas's thematization of the idea of creation? But what is philosophically of greater importance is the question whether the issue can simply be left at such a juxtaposition. For nature implies an ontology and aitiology, yes even a theology ("Unmoved

---

[125] Cf. *In I De caelo*, lect. 29, 287: Nos autem secundum fidem catholicam ponimus quod incoepit esse, non quidem per generationem quasi *a natura*, sed effluens *a primo principio*.

[126] See, e.g., D. Dubarle, "Dignité de la nature terrestre et mission cosmique de l'homme," in *L'homme moderne et son image de la nature*, ed. R. Chenu (Neuchâtel, 1974), p. 125: "Ceci m'oblige à introduire immédiatement une distinction de vocabulaire: par le mot nature, je signifierai en réalité la création."

[127] H. Meyer, *Thomas von Aquin, Sein System und seine geistesgeschichtliche Stellung* (Paderborn, 1938), p. 274.

Mover''), of which is must be inquired how these relate to the meaning of being as creature.[128] It is to this question that the further investigation must be directed.

Thomas speaks in *De subst. separ.* c. 8, 89 of a *duplex ordo* in that which is composed.[129] One is the order of the matter to the form; this is realized in generation. Here we have to do with the order of nature, which is constitutive for categorical being. The other order is that of the composite thing itself to the 'esse' participated in.

At this stage the meaning of this "twofold order" cannot yet be fully fathomed (7.4.4.). Nonetheless, it opens up the possibility of a twofold assessment of that which is. Taking this tack is the interpretation of L.-B. GEIGER. Because participation is creative, it in no respect diminishes the substantial value and the autonomy of being. The *same* beings are *per se* (the Aristotelian model of predication) and *per participationem* (the Platonic model). They are real substances and independent natures; and they are the emanation and deficient likenesses of a first, perfect Principle. Between these two viewpoints there is no contradiction, because they are no longer on the same philosophical level. Aristotle's viewpoint applies whenever created beings are considered on a horizontal level, without concern for their relation to the first Being.[130]

Different points of view, different levels.... The entire "duplexity" is summed up in this text of Thomas's: "Created being is not through something other (*per aliquid aliud*) whenever 'per' means the intrinsic formal cause." This perseity was intended in the definition: for a thing is defined through its intrinsic principles, i.e., its nature. "But whenever 'per'"— thus Thomas—"means the extrinsic formal cause or the efficient cause, then the created is through the divine being and not *per se*."[131]

Yet the assertion that there are different viewpoints can hardly be the final word, given among other things the polemical sense of Aristotle's concept of nature (cf. 3.4.3.). What matters is the concurrence of the distinct originations. The question is, how do the categorical and transcendental levels cohere? Hence, what must be shown is the manner in which the meaning of that which comes to be *per viam naturae* is related to the Origin.

Is there not, however, a price to be paid for this effort? It seems ap-

---

[128] Cf. also Augustine's critique of the concept of nature: V. de Broglie, *De fine ultimo humanae vitae* (Paris, 1948), app. 1: De notione augustiniana 'naturae'.

[129] *De subst. separ.* c. 8, 89: Invenitur igitur in substantia composita ex materia et forma *duplex ordo*: unus quidem ipsius materiae ad formam; alius autem ipsius rei jam compositae ad esse participatum.

[130] L.-B. Geiger, *La participation dans la philosophie de St. Thomas d'Aquin*, 443ff.

[131] *In I Sent.* 8, 1, 2 ad 2.

propriate to mention at this juncture the view of the Dutch Reformational philosopher H. DOOYEWEERD. To him, medieval philosophy is "synthesis philosophy." The term has a pejorative connotation; it smacks of "compromise."

Thomas would have attempted to synthesize in his philosophy what are in reality unreconcilable: the ground motives of the Christian religion and of Greek thought—an impossible synthesis, for the former stands, already in its motive of creation, in a radical antithesis to ancient philosophy.[132] According to DOOYEWEERD, the dialectical character of the Thomistic synthesis manifests itself most sharply precisely where it seeks its point of contact: in the idea of creation, "in the attempt to reconcile the Greek (especially Aristotelian) concept of the 'nature' (*physis*) of things, which is entirely dominated by the dualistic form-matter theme, with the scriptural idea of the nature of the creatural, which is grounded in the divine order of creation."[133] Such a reconciliation can result at most in a mutual "accommodation," "because the confession of the absolute sovereignty of God over all that is created tolerates no unreconciled dualism in the Origin of the creation."[134]

Thomas's adaption thus had far-reaching consequences: "the Biblical creation-motive was deprived of its original and radical character."[135] "The principles of form and matter are both withdrawn from God's creational sovereignty. The latter extends only to concrete, created things." Form and matter "are the two metaphysical principles of all perishable existence, but with respect to their origin Thomas was silent."[136]

DOOYEWEERD's merit has been to put the discussion on the level at which it must be carried on: that of the *origin of things*. The way, however, in which he worked the problem out vis-à-vis the Middle Ages is less satisfying.[137] The notion of "synthesis" that he uses is too static and limited. There is more going on in Thomas than a combining of antithetical elements, more than "accommodation." The concept of "synthesis" introduces a discordance in thought in advance. As regards content, too, the synthesis seems taken too narrowly, in that DOOYEWEERD interprets Thomas too exclusively in terms of Aristotle. At the end of *Reformatie en*

---

[132] H. Dooyeweerd, *Roots of Western Culture* (Toronto, 1979), pp. 28–29.

[133] *Reformatie en Scholastiek*, vol. 1, p. 36.

[134] "De vier religieuze grondthema's in den ontwikkelingsgang van het wijsgeerig denken van het Avondland," *Philosophia Reformata* 6 (1941): 169.

[135] *A New Critique of Theoretical Thought*, vol. 1 (Amsterdam and Philadelphia, 1953), p. 180.

[136] *Roots of Western Culture*, p. 118. Cf. *Reformatie en Scholastiek*, vol. 1, p. 59.

[137] I have dealt with the matter more extensively in my article, "'Uit God zijn alle dingen'" (see n. 104).

Scholastiek [Reformation and Scholasticism] he writes (I, 491–92): "That Thomas had the honest intention of accommodating Aristotelian metaphysics to the ecclesiastical doctrine of creation I do not at all doubt. The question is only if this was possible *within the framework of an accommodated Aristotelian philosophy*" (italics added, J.A.A.). It is still very much the question, however, if with this question Thomas's way of thought has been sufficiently fathomed.

3.7.3. *Intelligibility*

There is in Thomas a 'con-cursus' of the ways of nature and creation. The Latin term contains—for the moment not unhappily so—a certain ambiguity. "Concursus" can mean "collision," but it can also signify "coming together" into an integrated unity.[138]

The precondition for, and the character of, this "concurrence" in Thomas can be approached by noting the direction of the movement of thought in the preceding chapters. The desire to know is a reduction towards the logically and ontologically prior, a regress into what we have called the "ex"-structure of science, by which a multiplicity is brought to unity and a composition to identity. It is in this movement towards the *intelligibility* of reality that the ways of nature and creature concur.

"A thing is only intelligible through its definition and essence" (*De ente*, c. 1). The intelligibility of what is is centered in the quiddity. And this determination is precisely the *nature* of the thing (1.4.2.). Nature is 'causa ordinationis'. The intention of nature is directed towards the species and essence. "In the same way in which something belongs to the perfection of nature, it belongs to the intelligible perfection" (cf. 3.4.2.). Thinking and being correspond. Science and nature: in their processes, the definition is the principle (3.3.2.). Demonstration and generation start from the essence (*ex 'quid est'*).

Into this tendency towards intelligibility the interpretation of *creature* as participation fits completely. That can be amplified through an exposition in *De pot.* 3, 5, where Thomas asserts that the statement of the Catholic faith that all things are created by God can be proven by three arguments.

The *first* runs as follows: if in a number of things something is found that is common to all, then this must be the effect in them of one cause. Now, because being is found to be common to all things, which are distinct from each other in what they are, it follows necessarily that being is imparted to them not of themselves but by one cause (*ab aliqua una causa*

---

[138] Cf. *S. Th.* I-II, 12, 3 ad 2: Aliqua duo concurrunt ad integrandum aliquid unum; *In V Metaph.*, lect. 3, 793: Plures causae concurrunt ad unius rei constitutionem.

esse attribuatur). "Seemingly this is *Plato's* argument, since he required every multitude to be preceded by some unity not only as regards number but also in the nature of things."

The *second* argument maintains that whenever something is found that is participated in by a number of things in different manners, then it must be imparted by the one in which it is found most perfectly to all the others in which it is found imperfectly. For where something is said positively of things according to degrees of perfection, then this is owing to the measure of their approximation to one thing. Hence if the property were to belong to each thing of itself, there would be no reason for its being found more perfectly in one of these than in another. Thus it is necessary to posit one being that is the most perfect and the most true (*est autem ponere unum ens, quod est perfectissimum et verissimum ens*). That is proven from the fact that there is a mover altogether immovable and absolutely perfect. Therefore all other less perfect things must receive being from this being. And this is "the proof of the *Philosopher* in the second book of the *Metaphysica*."

Finally, the *third* argument: all that is through another is reduced (*reducitur*) to that, as cause, which is *per se*. If there were a *per se* heat, then this would be the cause of all hot things, which have heat by way of participation. Now, a being must be posited that is its own being (*ipsum suum esse*). That is proven from the fact that there must be a first being that is pure act in which there is no compostion. "Hence from that one being all other beings that are not their own being, but have being by participation, must proceed. This is the argument of *Avicenna*." And Thomas concludes: "Thus reason proves and faith holds that all things are created by God" (*Sic ergo ratione demonstratur et fide tenetur quod omnia sint a Deo creata*).

Two things are striking in this argumentation. In the ontological interpretation of creation, a direct continuity is established with ancient philosophy. With patterns of thought which according to Thomas himself are derived from non-Christian philosophers, the intelligibility of reality as creation is substantiated (see also 5.3.). And it is the intelligibility that is at issue, for all three arguments are a reduction to that whereby being as being is intelligible. That which is is reduced to the cause of being that is one (the first argument), perfect (the second argument), and essential (the third argument). From this the creaturely is "deduced."

The concurrence of what is revealed *per viam naturae* and *per viam creationis* consists in the intelligibility of that which is. This intelligibility was previously analyzed in terms of causality and predication. Hence a renewed consideration of both will enable us to show the concurrence.

3.7.4. *Grades of causality*

"Whatever is caused reverts upon its cause through desire."[139] This turning back, this "conversion" follows from the essence of causality. For the character of cause belongs first of all to the good (cf. 8.1.).[140] And there are two reasons for this. The first is that the good has the character of end, for "the good is what all desire." Now, the end has primarily the character of cause. Thus we saw (3.3.1.) in connection with the analysis of the cause 'per se' that the end is the prior that motivates the agent. The second reason is that the agent effects something like itself. The agent has this capacity only insofar as it is a perfect being. But the perfect has the character of "good." That is why it is worth striving after. Every generation is therefore a process of assimilation. "All effects are most perfect, when they become most like their efficient causes" (*S.c.G.* II, 46).

Whatever the differences between the ways of nature and creation, there is a structural agreement in their movements: both are a circulation based on the causal identity of principle and end. Nature is *via in naturam*. Through this circulation, reality is sustained and acquires permanence (3.4.1.) The creature, too, desires by nature towards the Origin whence it came forth (1.7.2. and 3.6.2.). "An effect is most perfect when it returns to its principle.... It is therefore necessary that creatures return to their principle in order that the universe of creatures may attain its ultimate perfection" (*S.c.G.* II, 46).

The circulation is the most perfect of all motions, because it connects the end with the beginning. It proceeds from the same to the same, and it acquires through this identity the highest degree of intelligibility.

The operation of nature as cause 'per se' is characterized by regularity, directedness towards an end, and univocity. But in connection with the division of the causes of generation, we found that in the circulation of nature something can happen that is not intended as such. What happens by chance has no part in order; it is 'per accidens' (3.3.1.).

Already in his commentaries on Aristotle, Thomas calls explicit attention to the "relativeness" of this view. At the close of a long excursus in *In VI Metaph.*, lect. 3, Thomas establishes that Aristotle is speaking of the contingent events which occur "here" (that is, in the sublunar world) in relation to *particular* causes (1216).[141] The reasoning that leads to this conclusion is dominated by the problem of intelligibility.

---

[139] *In De div. nomin.* c. 4, lect. 2, 296.
[140] *Ibid.*, c. 3, lect. 2, 227.
[141] Cf. *In II Phys.*, lect. 10, 238.

The starting point is the thesis that the higher the cause, the more extensive is its causality and the more universal its effect. The order found in effects is proportional to the order of causality. For it is characteristic of the cause 'per se' to produce certain effects in an "orderly" way. Now, "when effects are referred to a lower cause, they seem to be unrelated and to coincide with each other merely 'per accidens'; however, when they are referred to some higher common cause, they are found to be related and not accidentally connected but to be produced simultaneously by one cause 'per se'" (1205).

This view is then concretized. In reality there are three grades of causes (*invenitur autem in rebus triplex causarum gradus*). Causes of the third grade are particular, because they are determined to proper effects of a single species: fire generates fire, man generates man (1207)—a statement which, as we saw, is exemplary for the "way of nature." The cause of the second grade is the celestial body, which plays a large role in Thomas's world picture (cf. 7.2.). Its operation is more universal because its causality extends not to a single species but to everything that comes to be and passes away again (1208). "First cause" is God; the cause of this degree is fully universal, for its proper effect is 'esse' (1209). Because this causality extends to everything insofar as it is, there can be nothing that escapes its order. Its causality cannot be hindered by the indisposition of the material, for that too cannot be outside the order of the agent that operates by giving being (*per modum dantis esse*). From this it appears that "in the sphere of lower bodies no efficient cause can be found which is not subject to the order of the first cause" (1215). "This is why the Catholic faith says that nothing in the world happens by chance" (1216).

In the ultimate reduction to the first cause, to God, all that comes to be is found to exist in an ordered way and not 'per accidens'. Herein lies according to DECLOUX the main renewal of Thomism as over against Aristotelianism: "All, absolutely all, is reintegrated by Aquinas into the domain of intelligibility."[142] In the same spirit GILSON writes in his *The Spirit of Mediaeval Philosophy*: "If their conception [i.e., the medieval conception of nature, put on a par by GILSON with the Christian conception of nature] differed from the Greek it was not because it contained less determinism, but rather because it contained more."[143]

Distinctive of the Christian conception of nature is the greater measure

---

[142] S. Decloux, *Temps, Dieu, Liberté dans les commentaires aristotéliciens de St. Thomas d'Aquin: Essai sur la pensée grecque et la pensée chrétienne* (Brussels, 1967), p. 111.

[143] *The Spirit of Mediaeval Philosophy*, p. 367; cf. p. 370: "Thus, where Greek thought tolerates an indetermination resulting from a certain lack of rationality, Christian thought tightens the bonds of natural determinism by reducing the apparent disorder of nature to the laws of a higher reason."

of *rational* determination, through elimination of chance *sub specie causae primae*, without, however, a denial of its reality from the viewpoint of the particular causes.[144] In the same context GILSON speaks of "how profoundly the Greek conception of nature was transformed by the Christian doctrine of creation and providence" (p. 372). This transformation through the doctrine of creation seems to consist especially of an increase in the rationality of 'physis' (nature).

Thomas's exposition in the commentary on the *Metaphysica* confirms in the first place that the way of creation, like the way of nature, is viewed in the perspective of intelligibility. But at the same time, another trait becomes apparent: the concurrence of the two ways is thought as a *hierarchy* of causes. Because of this gradation, there remains continuity in the desire to know. For science is knowledge of the causes. The hierarchy of causes is determined by the degree of generalness. There is a universal cause, God, whose causality extends to the *esse*. The necessity of "another mode of causing" pertained, we recall, to the origin of being in general (3.5.2.).[145] Below this first cause stand particular causes, which produce specific (and hence definable) effects. The causality of nature extends to the *species*.

This order of the causes according to the scheme of "universal-particular" evokes a problem, however. The first argument for the createdness of things in *De pot.* 3, 5 (see 3.7.3.) was: "Now, because being is found to be common to all things, which are distinct from each other in what they are, it follows necessarily that being is imparted to them not of themselves but by one cause." "Being" is the most general effect—it transcends every specification—and is therefore to be reduced to the first cause.[146] Yet precisely because all things agree in being, this did not "count" for definitional thinking. Within the horizon of the definition appears the "datum" of being as a *universal* condition not touching the specific essence. Thus there must necessarily arise in this ordering of the causes according to the degree of their universality the question concerning the relation to the Origin of the formal diversity of things, of their being what they are. By considering the structure of what is caused, in which the 'esse' is the participated that is contracted through "something

---

[144] See, e.g., *S.c.G.* III, 74.

[145] Cf. *In De causis*, lect. 19: Universalitas enim causalitatis propria est Deo.

[146] The same reduction appears in *S.c.G.* II, 15: Secundum ordinem effectuum oportet esse ordinem causarum, eo quod effectus causis suis proportionati sunt; unde oportet quod, sicut effectus proprii reducuntur in causas proprias, ita *id quod commune est in effectibus propriis reducatur in aliquam causam communem.* . . . Omnibus autem commune est *esse*. Oportet igitur quod supra omnes causas sit aliqua causa, cujus sit dare esse. Prima autem causa Deus est.

other," this problem can be articulated even more sharply.

3.7.5. *'Subiectum — essentia — esse': The problem of the "other"*

It belongs to the essence of what is caused to be in some way composite.[147] What comes to be through generation is marked by the composition form in matter. To be through participation means: not being something totally, but having something other added.

From this it becomes understandable why the *via praedicationis* set the direction for the intelligibility of that which is. By predicating something of something other—what we called the "katallel" structure—a composition is brought to identity. And "the law of intelligibility is that of identity."[148]

The first track of predication was the Aristotelian model of *per se/per accidens*. In predication *per se* there is a formal identity of predicate and subject. Yet in individual substances the essence is not totally identical to the subject (cf. 2.1.3.). Man is not humanity (*homo enim nec est humanitas*). "Man" can possess something that does not belong to the ratio of "humanity."[149] Because of the composition of matter and form, there is a nonidentity of predicated form and particular subject, a composition of *subjectum/suppositum* and *natura/essentia/forma*. They are related as potency and act: "Every subject relates to that of which it is the subject, as potency to act."[150] To the essence or form nothing can be added that is foreign to it. That appears from the fact that definitions, which signify the essences of things, are like numbers: an addition of something changes the species. A definition consists of what is predicated 'per se'; the identity expressed in it is that of the thing according to its essence.

We find the same framework of thought in the other mode of predicating, too. To predicate something of something *per essentiam* or *per participationem* is to say that in the first case a simplicity and in the second a composition is expressed (2.5.2.). The creature is a being through participation. The index of creatureliness is the composition of essence and being.

This structure too is conceived according to the scheme of subject and form:

---

[147] *S. Th.* I, 3, 7 ad 1: Est autem hoc de ratione causati, quod sit aliquo modo compositum: quia ad minus ejus esse est aliud quam quod est.

[148] J. Peters, "De wijsgerige waarde van St. Thomas' participatieleer," in *De vraag naar het zijn* (Kampen, 1984), p. 81.

[149] *De pot.* 7, 4.

[150] *De spirit. creat.* q. un., art. 1 ad 1.

> Being itself (*ipsum esse*) is not signified as the subject of being (*subiectum essen-di*).... Being itself is not yet ... but that which is is, when it has received the form of being (*forma essendi*), namely, through taking up the act of being (*actus essendi*)....[151]

Mention is made of 'subiectum' and 'forma (essendi)': therefore the relation of potency and act can also be applied here: "Hence the nature itself is related to its own being as potency to act."[152] 'Esse' is the actuality of every substance.

Already in *De ente et essentia* (c. 5), where Thomas for the first time shows the nonidentity even in the separate substances (1.8.1.), the composition of essence and being is interpreted in this way. Everything that receives something from another is potential with regard to what it receives, and what is received in it is its actuality. Therefore in the immaterial substance too the quiddity or form "must be potential with regard to the being (*esse*) it receives from God, and this being is received as an actuality (*per modum actus*)."[153] The composition of act and potency has therefore greater extension than that of form and matter. The latter is limited to material substances, whereas potency and act divide "common being."[154]

In each of the two modes of predicating there becomes apparent a different compositeness. Correlating with the two tracks of predication is a "twofold composition" (2.6.).[155] In *De pot.* 7, 4 Thomas sketches this nonidentity. In the composed creatures is found a twofold difference (*duplex differentia*). For the individual subject is neither the nature of the species nor its being. *Homo enim nec est humanitas nec esse suum*. In simple substances there is only one difference, namely, that of essence and being. In God there is no distinction at all. He is his nature and his being. What is divided in creatures is one in God.[156]

From this text it is apparent that there is a 'concursus' of both tracks,

---

[151] *In De hebdom.*, lect. 2.

[152] *S. Th.* I, 50, 2 ad 3.

[153] Cf. for the interpretation of the composition of 'essentia' and 'esse' through the notions of 'potentia' and 'actus': *In II Sent.* 3, 1, 1; *In VIII Phys.* lect. 21, 1153; *Quodl.* III, 8, art. un.; *Ibid.*, VII, 3, 2; *In Boeth. De trin.* 5, 4 ad 4; *S.c.G.* II, 53; *De subst. separ.*, c. 3, 59: Omne participans ens, oportet esse compositum ex potentia et actu. Id enim quod recipitur ut participatum, oportet esse actum ipsius substantiae participantis.

[154] *S.c.G.* II, 54.

[155] *S.c.G.* II, 54; *De spirit. creat.* q. un., art. 1; *S. Th.* I, 50, 2: Quod quidem manifestum potest esse ex consideratione rerum materialium, in quibus invenitur *duplex compositio*. Prima quidem formae et materiae ex quibus constituitur natura aliqua. Natura autem sic composita non est suum esse, sed esse est actus ejus.

[156] Likewise in *S.c.G.* IV, 11.

whereby the structure of being becomes "more complicated." "Man is neither humanity nor his being." The structure of that which is (*ens*) becomes, in Thomas, *threefold*: 'subjectum – essentia – esse'. The degree of identity between these three moments is decisive for the place in the hierarchy of being. This "complication" deserves special attention, because there is a direct coherence with the threefold gradation of causality discussed in the preceding section.

A being is first reduced to the specific essence in which the many particular subjects agree. Next it is reduced to the 'esse'. The 'esse' is to be distinguished from the essence, because being is common to all that is. The result of this "analytica" is a threefold structure, in which the essence has, and is, the middle.

On the one hand, the essence is for the subject the intrinsic cause, the *nature* of a thing, to which the definition corresponds. Falling outside it is the singular (2.1.3.).[157] But on the other hand, the essence is for the thing as *creature* the limiting potency in regard to the 'esse' whereby this act is contracted. 'Esse' "comes to an essence from outside and enters into composition with the essence," is "other (*aliud*) than the essence or quiddity" (*De ente*, c. 5), is "outside (*praeter*) the quiddity" (*In II Sent.* 3, 1, 1). That "being" is participated in as something that does not belong to the essence of the thing is also clearly apparent from the text (*Quodl.* II, 2, 1) that served as the model for the other mode of predicating (cf. 2.5.2.):

> Whenever something is predicated of another in the manner of participation, it is necessary that there be something in the latter outside (*praeter*) that in which it participates. And therefore, in any creature the creature itself which has being and its very being are other (*aliud*).

On two sides something falls "outside" the essence. As a consequence, in thought in which the essence has the middle, there arises the problem of the "other." This finding renders the "reduction" that evokes this 'aliud' problematical in itself. The gradation of causes according to the "universal-particular" scheme raised the question concerning the relation of the formal diversity of things to the Origin. Here a similar apory arises, since being is posited *outside* the essence. GEIGER observes, "Such a limitation can easily be understood in the perspective of the participation through composition, in which the emanation of 'esse', the proper effect of the *Esse per se subsistens*, is received and limited by quiddities

---

[157] Cf. further *In III De anima*, lect. 8, 706: Nam natura speciei individuatur per materiam: unde principia individuantia et accidentia individui sunt *praeter* essentiam speciei.

independent (italics added, J.A.A.) in their ontological content from the action of the First Being." The essential determinations must be provided by other causes.[158]

K. KREMER believes that only Thomas's way of expression moves in the representational scheme of composition.[159] When it is said in *Quodl.* II, 2, 1 that 'esse' is something other than the creature participating in being, then by 'esse' is intended, in his opinion, *ipsum esse subsistens*. "Outside that" is the creaturely. What would be indicated is the duality required for every philosophy of participation: *esse subsistens* and *entia*.[160] But this interpretation is not correct. Thomas concludes: "And therefore, in any creature the creature itself which has being and its very being (*ipsum esse eius*) are other." This 'eius' indisputably refers to the creature's *inner* composition of 'essentia' and (participated) 'esse' which marks whatever is created.[161]

"If something can exist only when several elements come together (*nisi concurrentibus pluribus*), it is composite. But no thing in which the essence is other than being can exist unless several elements come together, namely, the essence and the being" (*S.c.G.* I, 22). In these components, different originations "concur" in that which is: one that is natural and intrinsic, and another that is extrinsic. "All that something has, not through itself, but from another, is outside its essence" (*De verit.* 8, 8).[162] The essence is set apart; so, too, is the origin of being.

That brings to a close a first phase in the inquiry concerning the "concursus" of nature and creature. Both are concerned with the intelligibility of that which is. The "concurrence" appears in the hierarchy of the causes and in the threefold structure of that which is. In this coming together there arises, however, the problem of the "other." The proper effect of the first cause is "being"; the 'esse' is "outside" the essence. Because of this difference, the need arises to analyze the relation of the essence to

---

[158] L.-B. Geiger, *La participation*, pp. 199, 201.

[159] K. Kremer, *Die neuplatonische Seinsphilosopie*, p. 426.

[160] *Ibid.*, pp. 435–36; 458.

[161] See also, e.g., *In II Sent.* 3, 1, 1: Omne quod non habet aliquid ex se, sed recipit illud ab alio, est possibile vel in potentia respectu ejus, ideo ipsa quidditas est sicut potentia, et *suum esse acquisitum* est sicut actus. Cf. L.M. de Rijk, *Middeleeuwse wijsbegeerte*, p. 217 (French trans.: *La philosophie au moyen âge*, p. 171).

[162] A telling formulation of this duality appears in Meister Eckhardt: Quia igitur in omni creato aliud est esse et *ab alio*, aliud essentia et *non ab alio*, propter hoc alia est quaestio an est, quaerens de anitate sive de esse rei, alia quaestio quid est, quaerens, ut dictum est, de quiditate sive essentia ipsius rei (*Expositio libri Exodi* cap. 3, 14, in *Die lateinischen Werke* II, 1, 23). Remarkable is the term formed as an analogy of 'quidditas': "anitas" (if-ness), which is otherwise rare in the Middle Ages.

the Origin and to consider the identity of the different components in created being. If "being" is really comprehensive, is transcendental, then the formal diversity cannot be "outside" it. The progress of the analysis will therefore have to focus on opening up still further the perspective on the origin, precisely as it pertains to this point.

CHAPTER FOUR

THE WAY OF TRUTH (*VIA VERITATIS*)

In the preceding chapters we followed the movement of thought—"from questioning towards knowing"—and the dynamics of being—generation and creation. At the same time, we analyzed the correspondence of the two movements. This coming together (*convenientia*) is called "truth." The end of the natural desire to know is to know the truth. Thus one can speak of the "way of truth."[1] It is a process of knowing by which the intellect conforms itself to that which is. The way of truth is likewise a dynamics of being whereby things are knowable for the intellect, are "unhidden." "Everything is knowable insofar as it has being" (*S. Th.* I, 16, 3).

The analysis of the "true" in this chapter follows logically upon the analysis of "being." "Something is prior logically insofar as it is prior in the apprehension of the intellect. Now, the intellect first apprehends being itself." This apprehension presupposes that being as such is knowable. It could not be grasped by the intellect if it were not intelligible. Insofar as being is of itself disposed to produce true knowledge, it is called "true." "Secondly, the intellect apprehends that it understands being ... Hence the notion of 'being' is first, that of 'true' second."[2]

Decisive for the direction of the "way of truth" is Parmenides' statement: "It is the same thing that can be thought and can be."[3] In the question of truth, the intelligibility of being is explicitly thematized. In Thomas we find the thesis that "being and true are convertible." These transcendental terms are not, however, synonymous. "True" adds something conceptually to "being": the "conformity" to intellect. It is precisely because intelligibility and transcendentality are connected with the notion of the "true" that the further investigation must proceed along the way of truth (4.1).

In book I of the *Physica* and in book I of the *Metaphysica* Aristotle discusses the opinions of those who have investigated the nature of beings and who have philosophized about truth before him.[4] The first philosophers turned away radically "from the way of truth and from the natu-

---

[1] Cf. *Super Ioannem*, c. 14, lect. 2, 1868 with reference to Christ's saying 'Ego sum via, veritas et vita'; *In I Sent.* 39, 2, 2: Haec quaestio ab omnibus sapientibus ventilata est, et ideo oportet diversorum positiones videre, ut erroribus evitatis, *viam veritatis* teneamus.

[2] *S. Th.* I, 16, 4 ad 2; 16, 3 ad 3.

[3] See for the difficult translation of *Fragm.* B, 3 W.K.C. Guthrie, *A History of Greek Philosophy*, vol. 2 (Cambridge, 1969), p. 14.

[4] *In I Metaph.*, lect. 4, 72.

ral way'' (*a via veritatis et a via naturali*). For they said that nothing comes
to be and passes away, a claim which is contrary both to truth and to nature.[5] In the second basic text (*De subst. separ.*, c. 9) Thomas observes that
with regard to the mode of existing of the separated substances, some have
deviated (*deviasse*) from the truth. Their deviation consisted in the elimination of the divine origin of things. That precisely these ''wrong tracks''
are advanced indicates that the measure of the truth of that which is the
order of nature and the order of creation. This measure entails a twofold
reduction of the ''true'' (4.2. and 4.3.).

The two perspectives of the truth of things coincide in the *species*, which
is as extrinsic measure the *exemplar* and as intrinsic measure the *forma*.
Through this coincidence, the 'concursus' of nature and creature acquires
a new dimension (4.4.). It is for a very specific reason that we pose the
question of truth after the question of being. In the ''concurrence'' of the
causes whereby things come to be, there arose the problem of the ''other''
(*aliud*): ''being'' (*esse*) was posited *outside* the essence. In the analysis of
what is (*ens*), the relation of the formal diversity of things to the Origin
became problematical. This relation is expressly affirmed in the reduction
of the ''true.'' Thus there results a twofold metaphysical reduction (4.5.).

4.1. *Intelligibility of being: Truth*

4.1.1. *The desire to know and truth*

In all men there is by nature a desire to know. The desire to know is
directed towards the knowledge of the causes. To know (*scire*) was defined
as to know the cause of the thing. This perfect knowledge likewise grasps
the truth of the thing: *eadem enim sunt principia esse rei et veritatis ipsius* (cf.
1.1.). As a basis for this assertion, reference is made to the second book
of the *Metaphysica*,[6] a central text (as we shall see in 4.3.1.) for the coherence of truth and causality.

The origin of philosophy is wonder, an ignorance that motivates inquiry. From this it also becomes clear that the ''natural desire'' must be a
desire for knowledge which is sought for its own sake and not for the sake
of some use it might have.[7] A ''theoria'' which is an end in itself is no
idle curiosity (cf. 1.6.: ''The legitimacy of the desire to know''). For

---

[5] *In I Phys.*, lect. 14, 121.

Still, *ipsa rei evidens natura* showed them the way to the knowledge of the truth (*dedit eis
viam ad veritatis cognitionem*; *In I Metaph.*, lect. 5, 93).

[6] *In I Post. Anal.*, lect. 4, 32: Considerandum est quod scire aliquid est perfecte cognoscere ipsum, hoc autem est perfecte apprehendere veritatem ipsius: eadem enim sunt
principia esse rei et veritatis ipsius , ut patet ex II Metaph.

[7] *In I Metaph.*, lect. 3, 55.

science is man's good. Considered in itself, the intellect, by which man is man, is all things only potentially, and it becomes them actually only through knowledge. Therefore each desires by nature to know as his perfection. For science is the assimilation of the knower to the known, an identity which is effected in the knower. It is the perfection of the knower as knower that, in knowledge, another thing is in him.[8] It is for this reason that Thomas regards the intellect as more exalted than the will. For it is simply more perfect to have the nobility of another thing in oneself than to be directed towards a noble thing outside oneself.[9]

The perfection man desires is that the order of the causes should be inscribed in his soul. This perfection can also be described as "the science of the truth" (*In II Metaph.*, lect. 2, 290). At the beginning of book II of the *Metaph.* (993 b 19) Aristotle writes: "Philosophy is rightly called the knowledge of the truth; for the end of theoretical knowledge is truth, that of practical knowledge is action."[10]

The practical intellect intends as its end not truth as such but its application to some determinate particular and to some determinate time.[11] The practical intellect is concerned with operable things, which are singular and contingent, but not with necessary things, with which the theoretical intellect is concerned.[12] A science can be called "speculative," or theoretical, firstly in relation to the things known (*ex parte rerum scitarum*); its objects are not operable by the knower; such is the case in man's science of natural and divine things.[13]

As a consequence, the theoretical intellect has another "mode of knowing" (*modus sciendi*). In its consideration a form is not applied to matter; a composite is resolved into its universal formal principles. Our following the "methods" of definition and division in chapter 2 was implicit—as it now appears—in the progress *per viam scientiarum speculativarum* (*S.c.G.* III, 44): this way proceeds by defining and dividing.[14]

---

[8] *De verit.* 2, 2.

[9] *De verit.* 22, 11.

[10] For the distinction between 'speculativus' and 'practicus', see *In II Metaph.*, lect. 2, 290; *S. Th.* I, 14, 16; *In Boeth. De trin.* 5, 1 and ad 4; *In III De anima*, lect. 15, 820; *De verit.* 3, 3; *In I Polit.*, lect. 1.

[11] *In II Metaph.*, lect. 2, 290: ... ad aliquod determinatum particulare et ad aliquod determinatum tempus.

[12] *S. Th.* I–II, 91, 3 ad 3.

[13] *S. Th.* I, 14, 16: Sciendum est quod aliqua scientia potest dici speculativa tripliciter. *Primo, ex parte rerum scitarum*, quae non sunt operabiles a sciente: sicut scientia hominis de rebus naturalibus vel divinis.

[14] *Ibid.*: *Secundo, quantum ad modum sciendi*: ... operabile enim est aliquid per applicationem formae ad materiam, non per resolutionem compositi in principia universalia formalia ... quidquid enim in rebus nos speculative cognoscimus *definiendo et dividendo* ...

The distinction between "theoretical" and "practical" knowledge culminates, as Aristotle indicates, in the end intended. The end of the speculative intellect is the consideration of truth.[15] The theoretical intellect intends knowledge for the sake of knowledge, is ordered to truth as such. It is precisely because of this finality that man's happiness consists not in active domination but in contemplation. Towards this end points the dignity both of man's intellectual faculty and of the objects that specify the act of knowing.[16]

"No desire leads us so high as the desire to know the truth".[17] *Veritas* must be the ultimate end of the universe, Thomas writes at the beginning of the *S.c.G.* (I, 1).

4.1.2. *Being and true are convertible ('Ens et verum convertuntur')*

The first question which Thomas poses in *De verit.* (1,1) is: What is truth (*quid sit veritas*)? The way in which he tackles this question is remarkable. He does not, like Anselm of Canterbury in his dialogue *De veritate*, analyze the meanings which "truth" has in various fields but investigates the conditions of the possibility for every inquiry into "what something is." He attempts as it were to recover the inception of thought, and he does this through the method of "reduction."

Every inquiry into what something is (*quid est*) requires a reduction (*reductio*) to principles which are known to the intellect immediately (*per se*). The argument for this reduction is the same one used in connection with the forming of definitions: the impossibility of an infinite regress. An infinite regress would entirely eliminate science and the knowledge of things.[18]

That which the intellect first conceives, as best known (*notissimum*), and into which it resolves all its concepts, is "being" (*ens*); in 5.4. we shall deal more extensively with this Archimedean point. All other concepts must therefore be arrived at by an addition to being. Now nothing, however, can be added to being that is alien to it: every nature is essentially "being"

---

[15] *Ibid.*: *Tertio, quantum ad finem*: nam intellectus practicus differt a speculativo fine, ut dicitur in III *De anima*. Intellectus enim practicus ordinatur ad finem operationis; finis autem intellectus speculativi est *consideratio veritatis*.

[16] Cf. *S.Th.* I–II, 3, 5 (Utrum beatitudo sit operatio speculativi, an practici); *In X Ethic.*, lect. 10ff.

[17] *S.c.G.* III , 50: Nullum desiderium tam in sublime fert sicut desiderium intelligendae veritatis; *De malo* 9, 1: Est enim homini naturale quod appetat cognitionem veritatis, quia per hoc perficitur eius intellectus.

[18] *De verit.* 1, 1: Sicut in demonstrabilibus oportet fieri reductionem in aliqua principia per se intellectui nota, ita investigando quid est unumquodque: alias utrobique in infinitum iretur, et sic periret omnino scientia et cognitio rerum.

(*quaelibet natura est essentialiter ens*)—a statement which confronts us again with the problem of the "other," which arose at the end of the preceding chapter. The addition to "being" must therefore be understood in this sense, that the other concepts express a mode of being, which is not made explicit by the name "being" (*ens*) itself.

That expression can take two directions. First, what is expressed may be a special mode of being (*specialis modus entis*). These particularizations are the categories to which being (according to the modes of predicating) is contracted. Secondly, the expression can concern a general mode of being (*modus generaliter consequens omne ens*). Concepts of this kind express a determination which pertains to every being. In virtue of their universal extension, they go beyond the categories; they are transcendental. Among these concepts, as the following shows, is the "true."

The manner in which Thomas deduces the various transcendentals we shall not discuss in detail here. Noting the main division will suffice. The general modes of being, which are made explicit by the transcendental determinations, are of two kinds. The first pertains to every being in itself (*in se*); to this kind belong "thing" (*res*) and "one" (*unum*). The second pertains to every being in relation to another (*in ordine ad aliud*). The mode of being expressed here is the "coming together" (*convenientia*) of one being to any thing else. The condition for it is something whose nature it is to accord with every being. Such is the human soul which, as Aristotle says in *De anima* III, c. 8 "is in a certain sense all things" (*quodammodo est omnia*). The specific faculties of man are the intellect and the will. The 'convenientia' of being with the appetitive power is expressed by the name "good" (*bonum*), the 'convenientia' with the intellect by "true" (*verum*).

Now, all knowledge is brought about through the assimilation of the knower to the thing known. For that, being must correspond to the intellect. This correspondence is called "the adequation of thing and intellect." Therein, the essence of "truth" is formally fulfilled. What "true" as concept adds to "being" is the conformity (Thomas speaks also of commensuration) of being and intellect.[19]

In this renowned text from *De verit.* 1, 1 three points merit attention. First, "true" is a transcendental determination. *Ens et verum convertuntur.* Yet it will prove meaningful to pose the question of truth after the question of being, precisely because "true" adds something to "being." Being is called "true" insofar as it is ordered to the intellect, is con-form-able, is

---

[19] *Ibid.*: Prima ergo comparatio entis ad intellectum est ut ens intellectui concordet: quae quidem concordia adaequatio rei et intellectus dicitur; et in hoc formaliter ratio veri perficitur. Hoc est ergo quod addit verum super ens, scilicet conformitatem, sive adaequationem rei et intellectus.

naturally constituted to bring about a true estimation of it.[20] In "true" the intelligibility of being is understood.[21]

The second point of importance is that "true" belongs to the relational transcendentals. Truth is a relation between thought and reality. Even with regard to the "ontological" truth, Thomas takes the relational character seriously: the true is always *per respectum ad intellectum*.[22] "Being is called true insofar as it is conformed or conformable to the intellect; therefore all who define 'the true' correctly incorporate the intellect into its definition."[23] For Thomas "the truth of things" expressly includes two elements: first, the entity (*entitas*) of things, but this is not taken in itself, for truth adds to it a relation of adequation to the intellect.[24]

Thirdly, in *De veritate* it is in relation to the human power of knowing, the intellect, that the determination "true" is situated. In the question concerning the essence of the truth, a being is involved which is intentionally "as wide as all reality." Human being is characterized by a transcendental openness, in virtue of which it can "come together" with every being (cf. ch. 5).

The relation between intellect and being, which is truth, is first realized in knowledge.[25] In *S. Th.* I, 16, 1 Thomas writes: "The true names that towards which the intellect tends." Every process finds its completion in the terminus. Now, the terminus of knowledge is in the intellect itself. For knowledge is, in distinction from appetite, the interiorization of the thing as known. For this so-called logical truth, Thomas always refers to Aristotle, who in *Metaph.* VI, 4 (1027 b 30ff.) says that good and evil reside in things, but the true and the false in the intellect.

Truth is twofold:[26] it applies to the knowledge and to the things. Each

[20] *In I Sent.* 19, 5, 1: Unde res dicitur vera quae nata est de se facere veram apprehensionem; *De verit.* 1, 2; *S. Th.* I, 16, 1; 16, 5: Veritas invenitur in intellectu, secundum quod apprehendit rem ut est, et in re, secundum quod habet esse conformabile intellectui.

[21] *In I Sent.* 19, 5, 1 ad 2: Verum non est in ratione entis, sed ens in ratione veri; sicut potest aliquis intelligere ens, et tamen non intelligit aliquid de *ratione intelligibilitatis*; sed nunquam potest intelligi intelligibile, secundum hanc rationem, nisi intelligatur ens.

[22] *In I Perih.*, lect. 3, 29.

[23] *De verit.* 21, 1.

[24] *De verit.* 1, 8: Veritas rerum existentium includit in sui ratione entitatem earum, et superaddit habitudinem adaequationis ad intellectum humanum vel divinum.

See for the ontological truth: J. Vande Wiele, *Zijnswaarheid en onverborgenheid, Vergelijkende studie over de ontologische waarheid in het Thomisme en bij Heidegger* (Leuven, 1964); J. Pieper, *Wahrheit der Dinge, Eine Untersuchung zur Anthropologie des Hochmittelalters*, 4th ed. (Munich, 1966).

[25] *In I Sent.* 19, 5, 1: In ipsa operatione intellectus ... completur relatio adaequationis, in qua consistit ratio veritatis; *De verit.* 1, 2.

[26] *Super Ioannem*, c. 18, lect. 6, 2365: ... duplicem veritatem; unam scilicet in ipsis rebus, ... et aliam ... in animabus nostris.

of the two is convertible with "being," but in different manners. "True" taken ontologically is interchangeable with "being" by predication ("every being is true") or substantially. "True" taken as predicated of the intellect is convertible with (the extra-mental) "being," not by predication but by consequence: to every true intellect there must correspond some being.[27]

4.1.3. "Measure"

Truth is the adequation or commensuration of thing and intellect. Therefore the concept of "truth" implies a "measure" (mensura) of the right relation between being and intellect.[28] This notion of measure—generally rather neglected in studies of truth—deserves further attention.

Truth is a relation. The essence of the relation is the being-to-something-other (ad aliud), the ordering of the one thing to the other. By what is the one related to the other? Thomas, following Aristotle, distinguishes two foundations of the real relation: on the one hand, quantity; on the other, action and passion.[29]

On quantity is based a static relation. Through it, one thing is related to another in the sense of measure and measured (De pot. 7, 10). Quantity implies the concept of measure.[30] Through the measure, what is measured is known. Measure is originally a principle of knowing the discrete quantity, the number. From quantity, the concept was extended to other categories as well. Similarly, the phrase "take one's measure" also does not have a purely quantitative meaning. Quantity acquires the character of "perfection," forms a "criterion."[31] "Measure" is the first, the most simple, and the most perfect in every genus. So circulation is the measure of movement. For of all movements, circular movement is the most uniform, regular, and perfect.[32]

---

[27] De verit. 1, 2 ad 1; S.Th. I, 16, 3 ad 1.
Corresponding with this twofold meaning of "true" is the division of "being" into extra-mental and intra-mental, a dichotomy which Thomas introduced in connection with the "if" question (1.3.4.).
[28] In I Sent. 19, 5, 2 ad 2: Cum veritas sit quaedam rectitudo et commensuratio, oportet quod in ratione veritatis intelligatur mensura.
[29] De pot. 7, 9: Ordinatur autem una res ad aliam vel secundum quantitatem, vel secundum virtutem activam seu passivam. Ex his enim solum duobus attenditur aliquid in uno, respectu extrinseci; S.Th. I, 28, 4; Secundum Philosophum (in V Metaph.), relatio omnis fundatur vel supra quantitatem, ut duplum et dimidium, vel supra actionem et passionem, ut faciens et factum; In V Metaph., lect. 17. Cf. A. Krempel, La doctrine de la relation, pp. 195ff.
[30] De virt. card. q. un., a. 3: Quantitas autem importat rationem mensurae, quae primo quidem invenitur in numeris.
[31] Ibid.: Dupliciter potest eius quantitas seu perfectio considerari. Cf. S.Th. I, 42, 1.
[32] For the notion of 'mensura' see In V Metaph., lect. 8, 872ff.; In X Metaph., lect. 2,

The basis of a dynamic relation is movement, change. This is signified by the categories of "action" and "passion." For the same movement can be regarded both in that which undergoes the movement, that is, in what is mobile, and in its origin, that is, the mover which causes the action (cf. 6.5.3.).

Besides the static relation and the dynamic relation yet a third kind is introduced by Aristotle in his discussion of relation in *Metaph.* V, c. 15; rather confusingly, however, he signifies it, too, with the terms "measure" and "measurable." This type will have to be distinguished from the first mode, based on quantity. Here "measure" and "measurable" are not taken "according to quantity" but "according to the mensuration of being and truth" (*secundum mensurationem esse et veritatis*).[33] At issue is the measure which is determinative for the truth. This relation is distinguished as a separate type because of its special nature. It has no real reciprocity: there is a one-sided dependence of the one term upon the other. Only the relation of the measured to the measure is real.[34]

The first task will now be to make explicit the measure for the "coming together" of being and intellect. A reduction of the true is thereby set in motion which agrees structurally with that into the logically and ontologically prior, the cause, in the question of being. This agreement comes to expression in the fact that the question concerning that whereby something is true is also a regress into the so-called "ex"-structure (cf. 1.3.1.).

4.2. *"Measure": Truth and nature*

4.2.1. *Science is "from what is true" ('ex veris')*

"Truth" is a relation between thought and reality. This relation is first realized in knowledge (4.1.2.). The intellect that composes in its judgment what is combined in reality is true. He who regards as composed what is combined in things (e.g., that man is an animal) is true in his opinion. But whoever conceives the thing otherwise than it is in its nature perpe-

---

1937ff.; *In I Sent.* 8, 4, 2 ad 3: Mensura proprie dicitur in quantitatibus ... Exinde transumptum est nomen mensurae ad omnia genera, ut illud quod est primum in quolibet genere et simplicissimum et perfectissimum dicatur mensura omnium quae sunt in genere illo eo quod unumquodque cognoscitur habere de veritate generis plus et minus, secundum quod magis accedit ad ipsum vel recedit. For the 'circulatio' as 'mensura' of movement, see *In IV Phys.*, lect. 23, 635; *In VIII Phys.*, lect. 20, 1137.

[33] *In V Metaph.*, lect. 17, 1003. Cf. H. Seidl, "Bemerkungen zu Erkenntnis als Massverhältnis bei Aristoteles und Thomas von Aquin," in *Mass, Zahl, Zahlensymbolik im Mittelalter*, vol. 1, ed. A. Zimmermann (Berlin and New York, 1983), pp. 32–42.

[34] *In V Metaph.*, lect. 17, 1004: Ordinatur autem una res ad aliam, vel secundum esse, prout esse unius rei dependet ab alia, et sic est tertius modus.

trates an untruth. "The disposition of the thing is the cause of truth both in thought and in speech," says Thomas in *In IX Metaph.*, lect. 11 (1897).

In this lectio he makes clear that the judgment of the intellect has what we earlier termed a katallel structure: the predicate term has a formal function with regard to the other term.

> When the intellect makes a composition, it receives two concepts, one of which is related to the other as a form; hence it takes one as being present in the other, because predicates are taken formally.[35]

If such an act of the intellect, in order to be true, must be reduced to the disposition of the thing as its cause, then a composition in reality itself must correspond to the predicative judgment.

> Therefore, if such an operation of the intellect should be reduced to a thing as its cause, then in composite substances the composition of form to matter, or of what is related in the way of matter and form, or also the composition of accident to subject, must respond as the foundation and cause of the truth (*fundamentum et causa veritatis*) to the composition which the intellect makes in itself and expresses in words.[36]

Ontological compositeness is the foundation of logical truth—a confirmation of what we found earlier (2.1.1.) with respect to predication. "When I say, 'Socrates is a man,' the truth of this enunciation is caused by the composition of the form of man with the individual matter" (1898). The composition of subject and essence or form is the measure.

The 'locus' proper to truth is therefore, according to Thomas, the judgment—that is, that operation of the intellect which in the Scholastic tradition is called "composition and division." For in a judgment it is affirmed or denied that some form signified by the predicate belongs to a thing signified by the subject. There is therefore no truth in the proper sense in the intellect, which knows what a thing is (*quid est*), i.e., in that operation of the intellect which is called "simple apprehension" (*simplex apprehensio*). For the definition of the essence is, as we saw, not a predication in which something is said of something other, is not an enunciation. From this it follows—a conclusion which Thomas expressly draws—that the definition in itself has no truth value. "Truth and falsity are properly

---

[35] *In IX Metaph.*, lect. 11, 1898: Cum autem intellectus compositionem format, accipit duo, quorum unum se habet ut formale respectu alterius: unde accipit id ut in alio existens, propter quod praedicata tenentur formaliter.

[36] *Ibid.*, 1898: Et ideo, si talis operatio intellectus ad rem debeat reduci sicut ad causam, oportet quod in compositis substantiis ipsa compositio formae ad materiam, aut eius quod se habet per modum formae et materiae, vel etiam compositio accidentis ad subiectum, respondeat quasi *fundamentum et causa veritatis*, compositioni, quam intellectus interius format et exprimit voce.

found in the second operation [of the intellect, namely judgment] or in the sign of it, namely, the enunciation, and not in the first [that is, in simple apprehension], or in the sign of it, namely, the definition.''[37]

Thomas tries to escape the apory that the answer to the "what" question is in itself not true and consequently not knowable—"there is only knowledge of the true"[38]—by relating definitional knowledge too to the truth of judgment.

> Truth is found prior in the composition and division of the intellect; and it is said to be *secondarily* and *posterior* in *the intellect forming definitions*. Consequently, a definition is said to be true or false by reason of a true or false composition.[39]

Truth appears to be attributable to definition too, insofar as a true or false judgment is implied in it.[40]

Yet with regard to this determination of the place of definitional truth and its derivation from the truth of the judgment, a critical objection could be raised. Does this solution fit the "reduction" prevalent in the earlier ways towards intelligibility? In the first mode of "questioning," of "predicating," and of "causing," a composite being was reduced to the logically and ontologically prior, to substantial identity. Generation, just like demonstrative science, is *ex quid est*, starts from the quiddity signified by the definition (3.2.2.). The re-duction is each time a regress into the "ex"-structure. Since the "true," too, as we saw, is marked by composition, one might expect that the way of truth would proceed similarly.

And indeed, science must proceed not only "from" what is "first" and "immediate" (1.3.1. and 2.2.3.) but just as much "from what is true" (*ex veris*). Thomas's explanation of this last point (*In I Post. Anal.*, lect. 4, 40) underscores once again the ontological import. The demonstration that produces knowledge must proceed "from the true," for there is no

---

[37] *In I Sent.* 19, 5, 1 ad 7; cf. *S. Th.* I, 16, 2: Et ideo proprie loquendo veritas est in intellectu componente et dividente, non autem . . . in intellectu cognoscente quod quid est; *De verit.* 14, 1; *In I Perih.*, lect. 3, 25; *In III De anima*, lect. 11, 746.

[38] After Thomas has summed up, in *In II Post. Anal.*, lect. 1 (409), the four questions to which all that can be questioned or known can be reduced, he goes on to comment: "*Cum scientia non sit nisi veri*, verum autem significetur solum per enunciationem, oportet solam enunciationem esse scibilem, et per consequens quaeribilem."

There is science only of the true. The true is signified only through the enunciation, in which "something" is said "of something." Therefore only this statement—defined as the *oratio, in qua verum vel falsum est* (*In I Perih.*, lect. 7, 83)—is knowable and hence "questionable."

[39] *De verit.* 1, 3: Veritas per prius invenitur in compositione et divisione intellectus. Secundario autem dicitur verum et per posterius in intellectu formante definitiones; inde definitio dicitur vera vel falsa, ratione compositionis verae vel falsae.

[40] Cf. *S.c.G.* I, 59.

knowledge of what is not. Yet what is not true, is not: "to be and to be true are convertible" (*esse et esse verum convertuntur*). Therefore what is known must be true. The demonstrative syllogism, however, would not be able to produce scientific knowledge if its 'logoi' were not true. "For we cannot know what is true through what is false, but only through something other which is true" (*In II Metaph.*, lect. 2, 291).

In the line of this reduction, it is consistent that this "other" be not in a secondary sense but "more" knowable and true. "Always, that whereby something is, is that more, just as that whereby we love something is the more loved." Such is the argument that Aristotle advances to show that we know the principles "better" than the conclusion, for we know the conclusion on the basis of the principles.[41] This "prior" is the measure of demonstrative knowledge.[42]

That the definition is true in a manner "prior" to the composition of judgment appears from the continuation of the exposition in *In IX Metaph.*, lect. 11 (1901ff.), with which we began this section. The true is not present in the same manner in simple being and in composed being. That is not surprising: the true follows being (*verum consequitur ens*). What is not similar in being is not similar in truth, either (1903). The separated substance is pure form, it is not generated, not brought from potency to act, it *is* in act. Since truth most consists in the act, there is no room for untruth with regard to the simple substance (1915). There is either a true insight—then the intellect grasps the essence of that which is—or complete ignorance. For it is impossible to know something of it and to be ignorant of something else of it, since in this being there is no composition. And this conclusion is extended in the text likewise to the quiddity and the definition of the composed substance.[43]

Science is "from" the true, the first, and the immediate: namely, from the definition. This is the measure of science. For definitions, which signify the essences of the things, are like numbers: any addition changes the species (2.3.). And that to which nothing can be added and from which nothing can be taken away is a certain measure. To this knowledge 'per viam diffinitionis' corresponds the ontological way of truth, which we must now examine.

---

[41] *In I Post. Anal.*, lect. 6, 55.

[42] *In I Post. Anal.*, lect. 36, 318: Syllogismi autem principia sunt propositiones; unde oportet quod propositio simplicissima, quae est immediata, sit unum, quod est mensura syllogismorum.

[43] *In IX Metaph.*, lect. 11, 1905; 1907.

4.2.2. 'Per viam naturae': 'Termini stabiliti' as truth

Being is called true insofar as it is conformable to the intellect. Of this ontological truth Thomas says in *S.c.G.* I, 60: "Although according to the Philosopher, the true is properly not in things but in the intellect, a thing is at times said to be true when it reaches in a proper way *the act of its own nature*. Hence Avicenna says in his *Metaph.* (Tr. VIII, c. 6) that 'the truth of a thing is the property of the being of each thing which has been established in it' (*veritas rei est proprietas esse uniuscuiusque rei quod stabilitum est ei*)."[44] With the 'proprietas esse . . . stabilitum' is meant the proper essence of the thing.[45] This interpretation is confirmed by the explanation Thomas gives of Avicenna's definition of truth in one of his *Quodlibeta*:

> The truth of each thing, as Avicenna says in his *Metaphysica*, is nothing else than the property of its being which has been established in it. So that is called true gold which has properly the being of gold and attains to the established determinations of the nature of gold. Now, each thing has properly being in some nature because it stands under the complete form proper to that nature, whereby being and species in that nature is.[46]

The actualization through the form is the truth, the cognitive conformability, of the thing. A thing is true insofar as it has the form proper to its nature, its specific essence.[47] Mention is made of *terminos stabilitos*: "that is called true gold which . . . attains to the established determinations (*terminos stabilitos*) of the nature of gold."[48] In this "stability" the *via veritatis* and the *via naturalis* concur.

The coming-to-be that generation is is "information" of the subject. In the form, the movement terminates, because the form is cause of being in the absolute sense (3.3.1.). Nature in the sense of generation is *via in*

---

[44] Thomas directly adds an element to this ontological determination: *inquantum talis res nata est de se facere veram aestimationem*. The relation to the intellect must be incorporated into the definition of "true" (4.1.2.).

[45] Cf. J. Vande Wiele, "Le problème de la vérité ontologique dans la philosophie de saint Thomas," *Revue philosophique de Louvain* 52 (1954): 532ff.

[46] *Quodl.* VIII, q. 3, art. un.: Veritas autem uniuscuiusque rei, ut dicit Avicenna in sua Metaph., nihil est aliud quam proprietas sui esse quod stabilitum est ei; sicut illud quod proprie habet esse auri attingens ad *terminos stabilitos* naturae auri, dicitur esse vere aurum. Unumquodque autem proprie habet esse in aliqua natura per hoc quod substat completae formae propriae illius naturae, a quo est esse et ratio speciei in illa natura.

[47] *S.Th.* I, 16, 2: Cum autem omnis res sit vera secundum quod habet propriam formam suae naturae; *De verit.* 1, 10 ad 3: Prima perfectio est forma uniuscuiusque, per quam habet esse . . . Ex prima autem perfectione resultat ratio veri in rebus. Cf. *In IX Metaph.*, lect. 10, 1894: Quando aliqua reducuntur de potentia in actum, tunc invenitur earum veritas.

[48] Likewise in *In I Sent.* 8, 1, 3.

THE WAY OF TRUTH

naturam. The intention of nature is directed to the form or nature of the species (3.4.1.). This species "relates to matter as the measure to the measured, because of the fact that the form is the end of matter."[49]

Intended 'per se' in nature is that which is lasting and enduring. The natural circulation tends towards those 'termini stabiliti' which constitute the unchangeable "truth of nature."[50] "That according to which a thing receives its species must be something fixed and permanent (*fixum et stans*) and as it were indivisible" (*S. Th.* I – II, 52, 1). This permanence 'per viam naturae' is the intrinsic measure for the truth of that which is.[51] Through its specific form, that which is is con-formable to the intellect.

With the dynamics of being, the way of definition concurs. The definition is the "terminus of knowledge," on the one hand because in it one has come to a perfect knowledge of the thing; on the other hand because the definition determines the intelligibility of the thing. This terminus of knowledge must likewise be the "terminus of the thing," for knowledge is brought about through the assimilation of the knower to the known.[52]

"The true names that towards which the intellect tends." Therefore Thomas can also say: "the proper object of the intellect is the true."[53] Earlier (1.4.2.) we saw that the quiddity was signified as the proper object of the intellect. The intelligibility of that which is centered in the quiddity. With the reduction of "being" to the essence by means of the "what" question goes together the reduction of the "true" to the intrinsic truth of the species. "The truth of what exists consists radically in the apprehension of the quiddity of things."[54]

4.2.3. *The natural thing as the measure of the truth of knowledge*

The way of truth is a process of knowing and a dynamics of being. For their conformity there must be a "measure" (4.1.3.). In *De verit.* 1, 1 it is said that the entity of the thing (*entitas rei*) is the basis for truth as adequation; and that knowledge is a certain effect of truth in the mind. The manner in which the basis and the effect of the relation of truth are pre-

---

[49] *In I De generat.*, lect. 15, 107.

[50] For 'veritas naturae' see *S. Th.* I, 119, 1; *S.c.G.* III, 26; *In IV Sent.* 44, 1, 2, 4.

[51] Cf. for the coherence between 'physis' and 'alètheia' also M. Heidegger, *Einführung in die Metaphysik* (Tübingen, 1953), p. 78.

[52] *In V Metaph.*, lect. 19, 1048: ... substantia rei, quae est essentia et definitio significans quod quid est res, dicitur terminus. Est enim *terminus cognitionis* ... Si autem est terminus cognitionis, oportet quod sit *rei terminus*, quia cognitio fit per assimilationem cognoscentis ad rem cognitam.

[53] *S. Th.* I – II, 3, 7; cf. I – II, 2, 8; I, 54, 2.

[54] *In De div. nomin.*, c. 7, lect. 2, 713: Veritas enim existentium radicaliter consistit in apprehensione quidditatis rerum.

sented here suggests a general validity. But this relation proves to be still more complex.

The measure of the relation of the thing to the intellect is, so Thomas says in *De verit.* 1, 2, twofold. Sometimes the thing is related to the intellect as the "measured" to the "measure." That is the case with the practical intellect. The science of the artificer is a cause of things and is therefore the measure of the artifacts. They are called true insofar as they are in conformity with the art.

For the theoretical intellect the relation is the reverse: the thing is the measure because it is "prior." And thus do the natural things relate to the human speculative intellect.

> The speculative intellect, being receptive of things, is in a certain way moved by things themselves, and in consequence things measure it. From this it is evident that the natural things from which our intellect receives knowledge measure our intellect.[55]

Natural things are the measure of the intellect, not in the sense that the thing known is in the knowing subject according to its natural mode of being. As far as knowledge is concerned, the faculty of knowing is the measure.[56] However, as far as the *truth* of science is concerned, not man, as Protagoras thought, but the natural thing is the measure.[57] "Not because we know something is it true in the nature of things. But because it is so in the nature of things, that is why we know something truly."[58]

In the measure of the relation between the thing and the intellect we find "verified" the order of origin that was established in 3.3. along the way of causality. Nature and art are causes 'per se,' but nature is the primary cause whereby things come to be and are intelligible.

This order is also the basis of the distinction between "theoretical" and "practical" knowledge. Three differences were mentioned earlier (4.1.1.): they concern the objects, the mode of knowing, and the end. But these differences go back to one and the same source: the different originations.

---

[55] *De verit.* 1, 2: Intellectus speculativus, quia accipit a rebus, est quodammodo motus ab ipsis rebus et ita res mensurant ipsum. Ex quo patet quod res naturales, ex quibus intellectus noster scientiam accipit, mensurant intellectum nostrum. Cf. *In I Perih.*, lect. 3, 29: Considerandum autem quod aliqua res comparatur ad intellectum *dupliciter.* Uno quidem modo, sicut *mensura ad mensuratum*, et sic comparantur res naturales ad intellectum speculativum humanum ... Alio autem modo, res comparantur ad intellectum, sicut *mensuratum ad mensuram*, ut patet in intellectu practico, qui est causa rerum; *S. Th.* I, 21, 2; *S.c.G.* I, 62; *In X Metaph.*, lect. 2, 1959; *De virtutibus in communi*, q. un., art. 13.

[56] *In III Sent.* 27, 3, 3 ad 2.

[57] *In X Metaph.*, lect. 2, 1959.

[58] *Ibid.*, lect. 2, 1957.

With regard to what is by nature, the human intellect is only cognitive; the investigation of nature is not directed towards operation, not towards domination by man, but exclusively towards science. That natural science is not "practical" appears from the fact that the principle of motion is in the natural things themselves.[59] Contemplation of the order not made by human reason belongs to natural philosophy, in this sense—it is said in addition (*In I Ethic.*, lect. 1, 2)—that metaphysics, too, is to be included under it! Our science of natural things presupposes their preexistence (*scientia nostra de rebus naturalibus esse non potest nisi res ipsae praeexistant*)[60] and is therefore called "speculative."

With regard to what is by art, the human intellect is cognitive and operative. The knowledge of the artificer precedes the things known, because they are constituted as artifacts by human reason itself. His science is therefore called "practical."[61]

In spite of this productive "more" the practical intellect does not have priority, because art is a later cause than nature (*Ars imitatur naturam*). In the distinction between "theoretical" and "practical," the priority of what is "by nature" appears once again. This originality is upheld in the *theoria*, which receives the measure of its truth from what is natural.

The relation of "measure" and "measured" was found to be of a special nature (4.1.3.): it has no real reciprocity. It is a so-called "mixed" relation, characterized by the one-sided dependence of the one term, the measured, upon the other.

These mixed relations "arise from the movement of the one without any change of the other. That occurs in those things, of which one is dependent on the other, but not the other way around, e.g., science in relation to knowable things."[62] Science stands in a real relation to the thing known: it is dependent upon it; its truth is measured by it. The reverse, however, does not apply; there is no real relation of the natural thing to science—it undergoes nothing by the operation of the intellect. There is a relation of the natural thing to science only in thought. The

---

[59] *In II Phys.*, lect. 5, 176; *In VI Metaph.*, lect. 1, 1153: Quod autem scientia naturalis non sit factiva, patet; ... principium motus rerum naturalium est in ipsis rebus naturalibus.

[60] *De verit.* 2, 8.

[61] *In I Polit.*, lect. 1: Ex quo patet quod ratio humana eorum quae sunt *secundum naturam* est cognoscitiva tantum; eorum vero, quae sunt *secundum artem* est et cognoscitiva et factiva: unde oportet quod scientiae humanae, quae sunt de rebus naturalibus, sint speculativae; quae vero sunt de rebus ab homine factis, sint practicae, sive operativae secundum imitationem naturae ... Scientiae practicae speculativis distinguantur in hoc quod speculativae ordinantur solum ad *scientiam veritatis*, practicae vero ad opus. Cf. *In I Ethic.*, lect. 1.

[62] *In III Sent.*, 5, 1, 1, 1.

knowable thing is thought in relation to science not because it has reference itself but because science refers to it.[63]

The "relation-lessness" of things expresses their transcendence with
respect to science. The condition for a real mutual relation is that both
terms be of the same order. Just this condition is missing here. Natural
things, according to Thomas, are not really related to knowledge, for considered in themselves they are outside the order of intelligible being (*extra
ordinem esse intelligibilis*).[64] The natural thing is in no way touched in its
essence by the act of the theoretical reason. The thing stays as it is,
whether it is understood or not. Its being known is accidental to it.[65]

In Thomas's reflection on the order between the intellect and being, the
limitations of this way of thinking about relation likewise become apparent, as we shall see even more clearly in 4.3.3. First, it is presupposed
that a real relation expresses dependence of the subject term of the relation
on the other term and as such implies imperfection. Yet, is that correct?
The essence of relation is to "be-to-something-other." The terms stand
in a relative opposition to each other, the only kind of opposition which
does not imply a denial of perfection. They exclude each other solely in
the "being-to."[66]

Secondly, the foundations of the dynamic relation are action (*actio*)
and passion (*passio*). But these categories are ontologically inadequate
to explain the "communication," the being-together of the relata in
knowledge. This inadequacy becomes clear when we confront the argument for the "relation-lessness" of natural things—"considered in themselves they are outside the order of intelligible being"—with "true" as a
transcendental property of "being." Why is the natural thing knowable?

---

[63] *In V Metaph.*, lect. 17, 1003; 1026ff.; *De verit.* 21, 1: Scientia enim dependet a scibili,
sed non e converso. Unde relatio qua scientia refertur ad scibile, est realis; relatio vero
qua scibile refertur ad scientiam, est rationis tantum; dicitur enim scibile referri, secundum Philosophum, non quia ipsum referatur, sed quia aliud refertur ad ipsum. Et ita est
in omnibus aliis quae se habent ut mensura et mensuratum; *S.c.G.* IV, 14.

[64] *S.Th.* I, 13, 7; *De pot.* 7, 10: Ipsa res quae est extra animam, omnino est *extra genus
intelligibile.*

[65] *In V Metaph.*, lect. 9, 896; *S.c.G.* IV, 14.

[66] *S.Th.* I, 28, 3; *S.c.G.* IV, 14: Propria relationis ratio consistit in eo quod est ad alterum; *De pot.* 7, 8 ad 4: Oppositio relationis in duobus differt ab aliis oppositionibus:
quorum primum est quod in aliis oppositis unum dicitur alteri opponi, inquantum ipsum
removet ... Non autem est hoc in relativis ... Et ex hoc causatur secunda differentia,
quia in aliis oppositis semper alterum est imperfectum ... Hoc autem in relativis non
oportet, immo utrumque considerari potest ut perfectum.

Cf. B.A.M. Barendse, "Intersubjectief verkeer en lichamelijkheid; De bemiddeling
van het lichaam," in *Zich door het leven heendenken* (Kampen, 1982), pp. 76–97. This is a
pioneering essay in view of its interpretation of the multiplicity of intersubjectivity as a
"relative opposition"; Th. van Velthoven, *Ontvangen als intersubjectieve akt* (inaugural
address; Amsterdam, 1980).

Because it is being, and as such true. "True" is convertible with "being" by predication or substantially. "True" is always said, however, *per respectum ad intellectum* (4.1.2.). The relation to the intellect is therefore not something that comes to belong to the thing afterwards, but a perfection of the thing as being. Insofar as something is in act, it *gives* itself to be known. Correlative to this is the re-cognition of the intellect, the act of the *receiving* subject. The distinction of the terms of the relation is based solely on the "being-to." And this was precisely the mark of the relative opposition.

4.3. *"Measure": Truth and creature*

That whereby being discloses itself, whereby it becomes intelligible, is its specific form, its nature. This constitutes the truth of the things. "The truth of what exists consists radically in the apprehension of the quiddity of things." This "horizon" of truth is sharply criticized by Bonaventure in his *Collationes in Hexaemeron*. The philosophers know only the *nature* of things; they do not know them as a vestige (*ut vestigium*), i.e., in their reference to the Origin. They are closed to the reflection of the divine exemplarity in reality as creaturely reality. The entire world is a shadow of, a way to, and a vestige of the exemplary forms. When the soul sees the book of the world, it feels itself compelled to go from the shadow towards the light, from the way towards the terminus, from the vestige towards the truth.[67]

Such a view seems to be proper to Franciscan Augustinism; but one can also find it, with identical metaphors, in Aquinas himself. "If it is said that every creature, regarded in itself, is darkness or falsity or nothing, then this must be understood in the sense that it only has being, light, and truth through something other. Hence if it be considered without that which it has from another, it is nothing and darkness and falsity (*si consideretur sine hoc quod ab alio habet, est nihil et tenebra et falsitas*)."[68] Things are in themselves "nothing," for in the creaturely nonbeing is prior to being (3.6.1.). Things are in themselves darkness: it is only through the first cause, which makes them to be in act, that they are lucid and trans-parent.[69] Therefore things also have no truth of them-

---

[67] *Collationes in Hexaemeron* XII, 15 (*Opera Omnia* V, 386).

[68] *De verit.* 8, 7 ad 2 (2 ae. ser.).

[69] See the remarkable text in *In De causis*, lect. 6, 168: Per lumen corporale visibilia sensibiliter cognoscuntur, unde illud per quod aliquid cognoscitur, per similitudinem dici potest lumen. Probat autem Philosophus in IX Metaph., quod unumquodque cognoscitur per id quod est in actu et ideo *ipsa actualitas rei est quoddam lumen ipsius*. Et quia effectus habet quod sit in actu per suam causam; inde est quod illuminatur et cognoscitur per suam

selves.[70] The analysis of the truth of things leads Thomas to the discovery of something that goes beyond natural truth: "the truth of a thing is something created."[71]

4.3.1. *"There is the same disposition of things in being and in truth"* (*'Eadem est dispositio rerum in esse et veritate'*)

For a good insight into Thomas's further analysis of the true, the second book of the *Metaph.*, c. 1 is of great importance. It is the text referred to when in connection with the definition of "to know" it was said that the knowledge of the causes likewise grasps the truth of the thing. It is in this same chapter that Aristotle writes: "Philosophy is rightly called the knowledge of the truth." What is true, however, we do not know unless through the cause: *scientia de vero non habetur nisi per causam.*

> From this it is apparent that the true things with which a science deals have causes which also have truth. For we cannot know what is true through what is false, but only through something other which is true. This is also the reason why demonstration, which produces science, begins "from what is true" (*ex veris*), as is stated in Book I of the *Posteriora Analytica.*[72]

From this observation an ontological reduction is set in motion towards that true "from which" the subsequent is true. The course of Aristotle's argument is articulated precisely by Thomas in his lectio. The starting point is a universal proposition.

> In each case that which causes something in other things that is predicated of them univocally is said to be that attribute maximally. Thus fire is the cause of heat in compounds. Therefore, since heat is predicated univocally both of fire and of compound bodies, it follows that fire is the hottest.[73]

The key words in this thesis are "predicated," "maximally," and "causes." They have a mutual coherence which agrees structurally with the other mode of predicating (2.5.), which implied another mode of

---

causam. Causa autem prima est actus purus nihil habens possibilitatis adiunctum et ideo ipsa est lumen purum a quo omnia alia illuminantur et cognoscibilia redduntur.

[70] *Ad Romanos* c. 3, lect. 1, 255: Similiter, secundum quod accipitur veritas ex parte rei, homo de se non habet veritatem, quia natura sua vertibilis est in nihilum.

[71] *De verit.* 1, 4 ad 4: Veritas rei est aliquid creatum.

[72] *In II Metaph.*, lect. 2, 291: Ex quo apparet, quod eorum verorum, de quibus est scientia aliqua, sunt aliquae causae, quae etiam veritatem habent. Non enim potest sciri verum per falsum, sed per aliud verum. Unde et demonstratio, quae facit scientiam, ex veris est, ut dicitur in I *Post. Anal.*

[73] *Ibid.*, 292: Unumquodque inter alia *maxime* dicitur, ex quo *causatur* in aliis aliquid univoce *praedicatum* de eis; sicut ignis est causa caloris in elementatis. Unde, cum calor univoce dicatur et de igne et de elementatis corporibus, sequitur quod ignis sit calidissimus.

causing (3.5.). When this other mode was elaborated, it was ascertained that that which is in virtue of participation must be reduced to that which is in virtue of its essence as cause, as iron becomes fiery by fire. Now it is posited: what is the cause of a property which is said univocally of other things, is the *maximum* of that attribute. This last point is a new moment. That this causality of the 'maximum' is to be correlated, however, with the causality of that which is essentially appears from the fact that both are illustrated with the example of fire and heat. What is something maximally is that property completely and therefore the measure of what participates in it.[74]

The continuation of the lectio shows the agreement with the "other" mode of predicating in still another respect. For we saw that the scope of its validity was tied to the all-encompassing universality of the predicated: namely, "being" (2.5.2.). Now we read:

> The term 'truth' is not proper to one species of beings only, but is applied universally to all beings. Therefore, since the cause of truth is one having the same name and intelligible structure as its effect, it follows that whatever causes subsequent things to be true is itself most true.[75]

Truth is not limited to any one species but is transcendental. Hence, in virtue of the universal proposition, what causes the subsequent to be true must itself be the most true; it has the perfection maximally within the transcendental unity. To this observation Thomas links a conclusion directly reminiscent of a finding with regard to causality (3.7.4.). There, according to the degree of generalness, a gradation of causes was distinguished: God—the celestial bodies—the specific nature. Here it is concluded that there is a *hierarchy* in truth; which is, indeed, already implicit in the notion of a 'maximum.'

> From this he again concludes that the principles of things which always exist, i.e., the celestial bodies, must be most true. He does this for two reasons.
> First, they are not "sometimes true and sometimes not true," and therefore surpass the truth of things subject to generation and corruption, which sometimes exist and sometimes do not.
> Second, these principles have no cause but are the cause of being of other things. And for this reason they surpass the celestial bodies in truth and in being . . .[76]

---

[74] Cf. *Quodl.* V, q. 4, art. un.: Id quod per essentiam dicitur, semper est mensura illius quod dicitur per participationem.

[75] *In II Metaph.*, lect. 2, 294: Nomen autem veritatis non est proprium alicui speciei, sed se habet communiter ad omnia entia. Unde, quia illud quod est causa veritatis, est causa communicans cum effectu in nomine et ratione communi, sequitur quod illud, quod est posterioribus causa ut sint vera, sit verissimum.

[76] *Ibid.*, 295: Ex quo ulterius concludit quod principia eorum, quae sunt semper,

The principles of what is lasting are necessarily the most true. For although the celestial bodies are incorruptible, they are nevertheless transcended in truth and being by these principles. For the latter have no cause but are themselves the cause of being for other things. With that, the ground is laid for an ultimate corollary.

> Since those things which are the cause of being of other things are true in the highest degree, it follows that each thing is related to truth in the same way as it is to being; for things which do not always have being in the same way do not always have truth in the same way, and those which have a cause of their being also have a cause of their truth.[77]

There is the same disposition of things in being and in truth.[78] "Being" and "true" are convertible. The things which have a cause of their being also have a cause of their truth. The first principle is "maximally" true and therefore the "measure" of all that is true.[79]

This argument must have had a strong appeal to Thomas: he makes use of it at crucial points in his work. It is not difficult to discover where this attraction lies. The reasoning is dominated by the motive of unity. A renewed confirmation of our interpretation is that this motive results here, too, in a regress into the "ex"-structure, in which logical anteriority and ontological anteriority interpenetrate.[80] Just as in 4.2.1. there was a reduction to the prior and simple (the quiddity and definition) "from which" the rest is deduced, so there is a reduction here, too, to the first

---

scilicet corporum caelestium, necesse est esse verissima. Et hoc duplici ratione. Primo quidem, quia non sunt 'quandoque vera et quandoque non,' et per hoc transcendunt in veritate generabilia et corruptibilia, quae quandoque sunt et quandoque non sunt. Secundo, quia nihil est eis causa, sed ipsa sunt causa essendi aliis. Et per hoc transcendunt in veritate et entitate corpora caelestia ...

[77] *Ibid.*, 298: Cum enim ita sit, quod ea, quae sunt aliis causa essendi, sint maxime vera, sequitur quod unumquodque sicut se habet ad hoc quod sit, ita etiam se habet ad hoc quod habeat veritatem. Ea enim, quorum esse non semper eodem modo se habet, nec veritas eorum semper manet. Et ea quorum esse habet causam, etiam veritatis causam habent.

[78] For the concept of 'disposition', see *De verit.* 1, 1 ad 5: Dispositio non accipitur ibi secundum quod est in genere qualitatis, sed secundum quod importat quemdam ordinem; cum enim illa quae sunt causa aliorum essendi sint maxime entia, et illa quae sunt causa veritatis aliorum sint maxime vera, concludit Philosophus, quod *idem est ordo alicuius rei in esse et veritate.*

[79] Cf. *In I Sent.* 24, 1, 1: Illud quod est *maximum*, est principium in quolibet genere, sicut maxime calidum omnis calidi, ut dicitur II Metaph., et illud quod est simplicissimum, est *mensura* in quolibet genere, ut X Metaph. dicitur.

This citation shows that Thomas links the Aristotelian texts on 'mensura' and 'maximum.'

[80] Cf. *Comp. Theol.* c. 219: Cum Ipse [sc. Deus] sit veritas prima, a quo omnis alia veritas certitudinem habet, sicut secundae propositiones a primis principiis in scientiis demonstrativis.

truth, the *veritas mensurans*, which is the origin of all that is true.[81]

The first truth is God, who is also the first being.[82] Although in the text of *Metaph.* II there is mention of a plurality of principles, this first principle can only be "unique", for the same reasons that being *per essentiam* is unique. Multiplication would impair the uniformity and the absolute identity of the *maximum*.[83]

On this insight is based Thomas's fourth "way" to the existence of God (*S. Th.* I, 2, 3), taken "from the gradation found in things." Among things there are some "more" and some "less" good and true; the same holds for other, similar properties (i.e., of perfections, which have a universal extension). Now, "more" and "less" are predicated of different things according as they resemble in different ways something which is the 'maximum.' Thomas provides the standard example: a thing is said to be hotter according as it more nearly resembles what is hot maximally. There is therefore something that is the most true and, consequently, maximally being, for those things that are greatest in truth are greatest in being, as is said in *Metaph.* II. That this maximum involves causality is stated explicitly by Thomas in the last part of his argument: "The maximum in any genus is the cause of all in that genus, as fire, which is the maximum of heat, is the cause of all hot things. Therefore, there must also be something which is to all beings the cause of their being and every other perfection; and this we call God."

Christ's saying, "I am the way and the truth ..." (John 14:6) must, according to Thomas, be understood to mean that Christ according to his human nature is the way (*via*) to the truth; for the end of human desire is knowledge of the truth. Yet at the same time, Christ is the terminus of the way, for according to his divinity he *is* the Truth.[84]

The origin of the true from God is conceived of as *participatio*. All other things participate in the one, maximal Truth. Now, there is the same disposition of things in being and truth. Therefore, so Thomas says, the

---

[81] *Super Ioannem* c. 18, lect. 6, 2365: Veritas increata et intellectus divinus est veritas non mensurata nec facta, sed veritas mensurans; *S.c.G.* I, 1: Sed et primam philosophiam Philosophus determinat esse scientiam veritatis, non cujuslibet, sed ejus veritatis, quae est *origo omnis veritatis*, scilicet quae pertinet ad primum principium essendi omnibus; unde et sua veritas est omnis veritatis principium. Sic enim est dispositio rerum in veritate, sicut in esse.

[82] *In I Sent.* 19, 5, 1: Utraque autem veritas, scilicet intellectus et rei, reducitur sicut in primum principium, in ipsum Deum; quia suum esse est causa omnis esse, et suum intelligere est causa omnis cognitionis. Et ideo ipse est prima veritas, sicut et primum ens: unumquodque enim ita se habet ad veritatem, sicut ad esse. Cf. *S.c.G.* I, 62.

[83] *De verit.* 1, 5: Haec autem veritas prima non potest esse de omnibus nisi una. Cf. *In I Sent.* 19, 5, 2.

[84] *Super Ioannem* c. 14, lect. 2, 1868ff.

separated substances cannot be the final end of the desire to know the truth, in which man's beatitude consists. For beings by participation are true by participation. Only the contemplation of God, who is truth by essence, makes man perfectly blessed.[85] It is only then that man is united with his Principle, and that the circle is closed. The desire towards truth—just like the desire to know the causes (3.7.4.)—is extended to and fulfilled in the knowledge of the first truth.[86]

The coming forth of the true, just like that of being, is also signified as *creatio*. When by means of the doctrine of participation Thomas has shown in *S. Th.* I, 44, 1 that all beings are created by God, he closes with a reference to *Metaph.* II: "Hence . . . Aristotle said that whatever is maximally being and maximally true is the cause of every being and of every truth."[87]

4.3.2. *'Per viam creationis: Natura imitatur artem (divinam)'*

The other mode of causing and the other origination also affect the question of truth. The truth of things is a participation in the maximal Truth, is qualified by creatureliness. There is the same order in truth as in being. Yet in the analysis of truth as compared to the analysis of being new elements gradually emerge.

God is the first Truth. What does this mean? Truth is a relation of thing and intellect. The thing that the divine intellect first understands is its Essence, through which it at the same time understands all other things. There is no "adequation" here, however, in which the one is the measure of the other, for in God intellect and essence are absolutely identical. Therefore in God truth means primarily the equality (*aequalitas*) of the divine intellect and the thing which is his Essence.[88] Intellect and Being are one in the Origin. God *is* Truth.

To the divine truth the truth and intelligibility of things must be re-

---

[85] *S. Th.* I–II, 3, 7.

[86] Cf. *S. Th.* II–II, 167, 1 ad 1: Bonum hominis consistit in cognitione veri: non tamen summum hominis bonum consistit in cognitione cujuslibet veri, sed in perfecta cognitione summae veritatis.

[87] Cf. *S.c.G.* II, 15; *De pot.* 3, 5, the second argument, summarized in 3.7.3.

In *In VIII Phys.*, lect. 3, 996 Thomas stipulates that on the basis of the thesis "eadem est dispositio rerum in esse et in veritate," it is also Aristotle's insight that God is the cause of being of the world.

[88] *De verit.* 1, 7: Ideo et veritas in Deo principaliter importat *aequalitatem* intellectus divini et rei, quae est essentia eius, et consequenter intellectus divini ad res creatas. Intellectus autem divinus et essentia divina non adaequantur ad invicem sicut mensurans ad mensuratum, cum unum non sit principium alterius, sed sint omnino idem. Cf. *S. Th.* I, 16, 5; *S.c.G.* I, 62.

duced. This reduction of things to the divine intellect as first Principle has as its counterpart that the emanation of things from God must be understood according to the model of art. And what is created by the divine art is the natures:

> The emanation of creatures from God is as the coming forth of artifacts from the artificer. Therefore, just as from the art of the artificer the artificial forms flow into matter, so also do all natural forms and virtues flow from the ideas in the divine mind.[89]

This perspective is rather striking because in 3.4.3. we came to the conclusion that in Aristotle the concept of nature—and the idea of origin it implies—had a clear polemical function against Plato. The intelligible operation of nature is not effected in the divine art or intelligence. *Physis* itself has a demiurge function, nature is cause of ordering. *Ars imitatur naturam* (3.3.2.), because human art imitates in its operation the order that rules in natural becoming. But in Thomas's reduction of the "true" the limited view of the Aristotelian division of the causes is "verified." His analysis of the true leads to the recognition that nature has been originated, that it has been effectuated by creative art. Nature itself stands in its own turn in a relation of dependence to an art, i.e., the divine art: "All natural things were produced by the divine art, and so in a sense are God's works of art."[90]

Here the "complication" of nature and creature becomes palpable. And that has not happened as the result of the incorporation of a foreign (Platonic) element or of a theological conception into a reflection on nature based on the commentary on *Phys.* II. It is the outcome of Thomas's own analysis of the 'auctoritas'. For at the end of his exposition concerning this book, he concludes: "Therefore it appears that nature is nothing other than the 'ratio' of some art, namely the divine, which is implanted in things."[91]

In the Aristotelian division of the causes 'per se', nature was the primary and fundamental cause. For art works on that which has already been constituted in being by nature. Nature is basic for the causality by art (3.3.2.). Now above the causality by nature there is put a third level:

[89] *In II Sent.* 18, 1, 2: Emanatio creaturarum a Deo est sicut exitus artificiatorum ab artifice; unde sicut ab arte artificis effluunt formae artificiales in materiam, ita etiam ab ideis in mente divina existentibus fluunt formae et virtutes naturales.
[90] *S.Th.* I, 91, 3. One finds this representation at countless places in Thomas's work. See, e.g., *S.c.G.* III, 100: Unde tota natura est sicut quoddam artificiatum divinae artis; *S.c.G.* II, 24: Res creatae sunt a Deo sicut factae. Factibilium autem ratio est ars, sicut dicit Philosophus. Comparantur ergo omnes res creatae ad Deum sicut artificiata ad artificem; *S.Th.* I, 27, 1 ad 3; I–II, 13, 2 ad 3.
[91] *In II Phys.*, lect. 14, 268 (cf. 8.2.2.).

"As the operation of art presupposes the operation of nature, so the operation of nature presupposes the creative operation of God."[92]

Nature is located between two arts: the divine, which is the basis for the
intelligibility of natural things; and the human. From this it appears that
for Thomas the generic concept of "art" contains a perfection that is
sublimated in the divine art: namely, the productive "a priori." Implied
in this view in principle is a revaluation of the practical intellect: "The
Creator's knowledge of creatures and the artificer's knowledge of artifacts
naturally precede the things known."[93] The actual consequences of this
productive "a priori" for human knowing will be drawn only later in history, namely, in the thesis of Vico (1668–1744) that "the true and the
made are convertible" (*verum et factum convertuntur*).[94] For Thomas's reflection on the question of truth it is of importance that with the interpretation of creation as art a new aspect of the other mode of causing
appears.

Aristotle's analysis of the causes of becoming was a reaction against
Plato's thesis that exemplary forms are necessary in order to explain the
generation of sensible beings. The hypothesis of an exemplar for natural
becoming is superfluous: "man generates man." The idea of origin implied in "nature" is a rejection of the reduction of reality to an ideality
extrinsic to it. Plato incorrectly "assimilated the coming forth of natural
things to the way in which artifacts are made" (3.4.3.).

Having mentioned this criticism of the Philosopher in his commentary
on the *Metaphysica*, Thomas feels compelled to add a marginal note. This
reasoning, he goes on to say, does not alter the fact that the divine science
is the exemplar of all things (*non tamen removet divinam scientiam esse rerum
omnium exemplarem*).[95]

Yet why is it necessary to posit divine ideas or exemplars? It belongs
to the essence of the Idea to be the form or species imitated by something
else. This imitation is 'per se' intended by the agent. Characteristic for
this efficient cause is its acting by intellect, i.e. setting the end for itself.[96]

Thomas takes up this exemplary causality in his treatise on creation

---

[92] *S.c.G.* III, 65.

[93] *De verit.* 2, 8.

[94] Cf. K. Löwith, *Vicos Grundsatz: Verum et factum convertuntur, Seine theologischen Prämisse
und deren säkulare Konsequenzen* (Heidelberg, 1968).
In *S. Th.* I–II, 3, 5 ad 1 Thomas asserts that the likeness of the practical intellect with
God is "according to proportionality," that of the speculative "according to union or
representation, which is a much greater likeness."

[95] *In I Metaph.*, lect. 15, 231.

[96] These three moments are dealt with together in *De verit.* 3, 1: Haec ergo videtur esse
ratio ideae, quod idea sit forma quam aliquid imitatur ex intentione agentis, qui determinat sibi finem. Cf. *S. Th.* I, 15, 1; *In De div. nomin.* c. 5, lect. 3.

(*S. Th.* I, 44, 3). For the production of anything an exemplar is necessary, in order that the effect may receive a determinate form. Here the model of art presents itself: the artificer produces a determinate form in matter by reason of the exemplar which he beholds. Now, it is manifest that what becomes by nature receives determinate forms. Natural generation is a final process, and it is ruled by the law of "synonymy"; however, the natural generator does not determine the end of its operation deliberatively. The "determination" of natural forms must be reduced to a first intellective principle that predetermines the end of nature, to the divine wisdom. Therefore we must say that the Ideas of all things, the exemplary forms, exist in the divine intellect. God is, as the efficient cause, likewise the first exemplary cause of all things.[97]

So Thomas is able to clarify the likeness of the creature to the Creator not only with the synonymy between the natural agent and its effect (*ab ente sunt entia*) but also with the univocity which obtains in becoming through art. The creaturely comes forth from God according to his likeness, because it comes forth from *rationes ideales*.[98]

Since imitation belongs to the essence of the exemplar, Thomas can also invert Aristotle's thesis of imitation (*ars imitatur naturam*) and say: *Natura imitatur artem divinam.* "Because all natural things are related to the divine intellect as artifacts are to art, every thing is consequently called true insofar as it possesses the proper form according to which it imitates the divine art (*secundum quam imitatur artem divinam*). And in this way 'being' and 'true' are convertible, because every natural thing, through its form, is conformed to the divine art."[99]

Nature imitates art; in its orderly operation it fulfills the intention of the divine Logos. That being the case, Thomas can give a new interpretation of the traditional adagium "art imitates nature." The natural things are imitable by (human) art, because the nature of each is ordained to its end by an intellective principle, so that the "work of nature" is the "work of an intelligent substance" (*opus intelligentiae*).[100]

---

[97] *S. Th.* I, 44, 3. Cf. *De verit.* 3, 1: Operatio naturae, quae est ad determinatum finem, praesupponit intellectum, praestituentem finem naturae, et ordinantem ad finem illum naturam; *In I Metaph.*, lect. 15, 233.

[98] *In II Sent.* 16, 1, 2 ad 2 (cf. 3.6.2.).

[99] *In I Perih.*, lect. 3, 30. Cf. *S. Th.* I, 14, 12 ad 3; *S. Th.* I, 66, 1 obj. 2.

[100] *In II Phys.*, lect. 4, 171. For the statement "opus naturae est opus intelligentiae," see also *In I Sent.* 35, 1, 1; II, 25, 1, 1; III, 32, 5; *De verit.* 3, 1; 5, 2; *S.c.G.* III, 24; *De pot.* 1, 5; 2, 3 ad 5; 3, 15; *De operationibus occultis naturae*, n. 447.
It is noteworthy that after Book II of the Commentary on the *Sententiae*, Thomas no longer associates the dictum with the 'Philosophus' but with the 'philosophi' in general. The axiom does not appear in Aristotle's work, but can be read in it because Thomas, as we saw, in his Commentary on the *Physica* understands 'natura' as 'ratio artis divinae' (see also section 8.2.2.).

4.3.3. *God's science as the measure of the natural thing*

"True" always implies a relation to the intellect. A thing understood may be in relation to an intellect essentially (*per se*) or accidentally (*per accidens*). A thing is related "essentially" to an intellect on which it depends for its being, but "accidentally" to an intellect by which it is solely knowable. Now we do not judge of a thing by what belongs to it 'per accidens' but by what belongs to it 'per se.' Hence, so Thomas concludes, everything is said to be true absolutely, insofar as it is related to the intellect on which it depends.[101]

After our previous criticisms of the manner in which the relationality added by true to being is conceived by Thomas, it may be clear that we consider the terms "essentially" and "accidentally" unfortunate. To be true as knowability is not something accidental to being. This does not mean, however, that Thomas's distinction lacks any basis whatsoever. With respect to the actuality of being known, a thing can be related to the intellect in different ways.

The truth of artifacts is essentially fulfilled in relation to *our* intellect, since the science of the artificer is the cause of the things and therefore the measure of artificial things. They are called true insofar as they are in conformity to his art, insofar as they acquire the likeness of the form in the mind of the artificer (4.2.3.).

But natural things "can *not* be said to be essentially true in relation to our intellect." For the natural thing is said to be true in relation to the theoretical intellect not *essentialiter* or *formaliter*, but *effective*.[102] To Thomas's insight the relation to the human intellect is accidental to the truth of the natural thing. Even in the absence of such an intellect, the thing would still continue in its essence.[103]

The measure of the truth of natural things can only be a being-bestowing intellect, just as the knowledge of the artificer is the measure of artifacts. As such a cause, the divine science relates, as we saw, to

---

'Opus naturae est opus intelligentiae' is a much quoted saying in the Middle Ages. See for Albert the Great: J.A. Weisheipl, "The axiom 'Opus naturae est opus intelligentiae' and Its Origins," in *Albertus Magnus, Doctor Universalis 1280/1980*, ed. G. Meyer and A. Zimmermann (Mainz, 1980), pp. 460ff. See further Jean de Sècheville, *De principiis naturae*: Totiens clamat philosophia quod opus naturae est opus intelligentiae (ed. R.-M. Giguère (Paris, 1956), p. 196); Meister Eckhardt, *Exp. libri Genesis* II, n. 214 (Lat. Werke I, 690); *Quaestiones parisienses* I, n. 5 (*ibid.*, II, 42); Nicolaus Cusanus, *Compendium* XI, n. 35; *De docta ignorantia* II, 9, n. 147.

[101] *S.Th.* I, 16, 1.

[102] *In I Perih.*, lect. 3, 29.

[103] *De verit.* 1, 4: Veritas autem quae dicitur de rebus in comparatione ad intellectum humanum, est rebus quodammodo *accidentalis*, quia, posito quod intellectus humanus non esset nec esse posset, adhuc res in sua essentia permaneret.

everything.[104] "Natural things are measured by the divine intellect, wherein all things are, just as all artifacts are in the intellect of the artificer."[105] God's science is prior to natural things and is their "measure."

> That which is the measure in any given genus is most perfect in that genus ... But the divine truth is the measure of all truth. For the truth of our intellect is measured by the thing outside the soul, since our intellect is said to be true because it is in agreement with the thing that it knows. On the other hand, the truth of a thing is measured by the divine intellect, which is the cause of things ... In the same way, the truth of artifacts comes from the art of the artificer.[106]

Things do not have their being-true from themselves. Thomas's argument in *De verit.* 1, 1 for the convertibility of "being" and "true," namely, the relation to the human intellect, can therefore not be decisive. The transcendental openness of the human mind does not constitute essentially the relation of truth, the conformity of "being" and "intellect." For the truth of things the relation to God is an essential order, a relation 'per se.' Truth as "the adequation of thing and intellect" is ultimately understood by Thomas as the conformity of the thing with the divine intellect. The natural thing is "true" insofar as it acquires the likeness of the species in the divine mind. "True" is said, for example, of the stone that possesses the nature proper to a stone, according to the preconception in the divine Logos.[107]

Thanks to the conformity with their Principle, natural things can be the measure of human knowledge. That science of natural things is "speculative" was traced earlier (4.2.3.) to the fact that its objects are not made by human reason. Now it can be regarded as characteristic of the "theoretical" intellect that it contemplates what is "made elsewhere," namely, in the divine art.[108]

---

[104] *In I Sent.* 38, 1, 1: Sicut est causalitas artificis per artem suam, ita consideranda est causalitas divinae scientiae.

Science is cause, insofar as it is attended by the will to effectuate the end conceived. It is therefore more precise to say that "sua scientia sit causa rerum, secundum quod habet voluntatem conjunctam" (*S. Th.* I, 14, 8). Cf. *De verit.* 2, 14. See also 8.2.2.

[105] *De verit.* 1, 2: Res naturales ... sunt mensuratae ab intellectu divino, in quo sunt omnia, sicut omnia artificiata in intellectu artificis.

[106] *S.c.G.* I, 62: Illud quod est mensura in unoquoque genere, est perfectissimum illius generis ... Sed divina veritas est mensura omnis veritatis. Veritas enim nostri intellectus mensuratur a re quae est extra animam, ex hoc enim intellectus noster verus dicitur quod consonat rei; veritas autem rei mensuratur ad intellectum divinum, qui est causa rerum ...; sicut veritas artificiatorum ab arte artificis.

[107] *S. Th.* I, 16, 1; 14, 8 and ad 3; *De pot.* 7, 10 ad 5.

[108] Cf. *In De caelo*, prooemium, 1: ... in ratione speculativa, cuius consideratio est circa ea quae sunt aliunde facta.

In summary, the natural thing is as well the "measure" as the "measured." It is midway between two intellects: the divine, that is not measured but measure; and the human, which does not measure things but is measured. In virtue of the adequation with both, the natural thing is said to be true, but primarily insofar as it fulfills that to which it is ordained by the divine intellect.[109]

God is the "measure" of what exists.[110] Typical of the continuity in Thomas's analysis of truth is that he immediately thinks it possible to compare this relation with that of the natural thing to science (4.2.3.). "Hence, God is related to the other beings as the knowable to our science, which is measured by the knowable" (S.c.G. II, 12).

The relation, too, between God and the world is a "mixed" relation, is not a real mutual relation. There is a real relation of the creature to God, because it is the effect of His art. The dependence upon Him belongs to the nature of the creature. In God there is however no real relation to creatures, but a relation only in thought, inasmuch as creatures are related to Him.[111]

Why are the relations to the creatures not real in God? In S.c.G. II, 12 Thomas advances the argument, besides the one derived from the relation of the "measure" to the "measured," that such relations cannot exist in God as accidents in a subject, since in Him there is no accident at all. Neither can they be God's very substance. For through a real relation God's substance would depend on something other extrinsic to it, and would not be necessary through itself. Therefore the relation in God to the world is a conceptual one.

In 4.2.3., with reference to the "relation-lessness" of the natural thing, we criticized this way of thinking about relation. And this criticism acquires a special cogency in connection with the denial of a real relation in God to the creaturely. For does this not mean an estrangement from the Biblical language about God? To be sure, there is in Scripture a profound sense of the utter transcendence of God above all that is created. But this in no way conflicts with the word that the Lord has made a covenant with his people. "God is with us": "Immanuel" (Isaiah 8:8, 10), the name of his Son, whom He has given us, and who reveals himself as Love, the relational reality par excellence.

Philosophically, insufficient justice is done the relation between God

---

[109] De verit. 1, 2. Cf. S.Th. I, 14, 8 ad 3.

[110] Thomas can refer for this to pseudo-Dionysius. Cf. In De div. nomin., c. 4, lect. 3, 310.

[111] S.Th. I, 13, 7: Sed in Deo non est aliqua realis relatio ejus ad creaturas, sed secundum rationem tantum, inquantum creaturae referuntur ad ipsum. See also, among other places, De pot. 7, 10; Quodl. I, 2, 1.

and creature by Thomas, because his thought is oriented to a too restricted model of relation. Two remarks may be made at this point.

First, the foundation of a dynamic relation is the categories of action
and passion. These categories obtain in the strict sense for natural movement. On this basis it is necessary to say that God, who produces something without himself being moved, has no real relation to his effect.
Therefore He has a relation only in thought—*tertium non datur*. Already in
4.2.3. we saw that the categories of action and passion are ontologically
inadequate. A fortiori, they fall short as a foundation for the relation of
creation, the relation to a world which is qualified as creature through
God's loving grace. "God loves everything that exists," writes Thomas
in *S. Th.* I, 20, 2. Yet not as we love. For our will is not the cause of the
goodness of things, but rather is moved by it. God's love, however, infuses
and creates goodness in things (*perfundens et creans bonitatem in rebus*). At one
place in his work (*In I Sent.* 30, 1, 3 ad 3), Thomas expressly distinguishes
the relation between science and the knowable from that between the
loving and the loved. The latter relation is a real relation from each of the
two sides (*utrobique relatio realis*). For the relation of love is founded on the
good, which is real in both terms. However, this remained an isolated
reference in Thomas.

The second remark follows directly from the first. Thomas's thought
about the relation of God to that which is moves within the horizon of the
categories. Relation is an *accidental* category. The concept of "accident"
implies imperfection: the being of an accident is "to be in something";
it is being-dependent-on a subject (2.1.2.).[112]

The division of being into the categories of substance and accident is
to Thomas's judgment a "division of created being."[113] Even so, he is
not consistent on this point. Two ways of predicating, he observes, remain
preserved in the divine, namely, *secundum substantiam* and *secundum rela-
tionem*. Even predication "according to relation": for the relation as
relation—not as accident—implies no imperfection; it expresses the
"being-to-something-other."[114]

So we find in Thomas, in comparison to Aristotle, a new elaboration
of the concept of relation: namely, in his exposition of the Trinity. In God
himself there are real relations that constitute the three Persons. These
intra-divine relations of origin are, however, no accidents but subsisting

---

[112] Cf. further *De ente*, c. 7, where Thomas works out the relation between substance
and accident on the basis of the main idea of *Metaph.* II: Illud, quod dicitur maxime et
verissime in quolibet genere, est causa eorum, quae sunt post in illo genere.
[113] *In I Sent.* 8, 4, 2 ad 1.
[114] *In I Sent.* 8, 4, 3. Cf. 33, 1, 1 ad 5.

relations.[115] In other words, being can be relational without being "relative."

This philosophically important thought, however, remained in Thomas outside the metaphysics of creation (cf. 6.6.). That is in a certain sense remarkable, because Thomas himself emphasizes, in his prologue to book I of the Commentary on the *Sententiae*, that the temporal proces of the creatures is derived (*derivatur*) from the eternal process of the Persons. For the first is always the cause of the subsequent—again an allusion to *Metaph.* II. Here lies a starting point for thinking with Thomas beyond Thomas.

His elaboration of relation in the doctrine of the Trinity can be made fruitful for a re-thinking of the relation of creation. For God, to be is to give being—creation is giving being; for the creature, to be is to receive being. The terms stand in a relative opposition to each other. In this opposition their being together is realized. A relative opposition implies as such no imperfection. For we have to do here with "a plurality without imperfection, a plurality which does not have to be eliminated through reduction because it is the unity at its best."[116]

Yet in Thomas all the emphasis falls on the non-reciprocity of the relation.[117] Certainly that has something to do with the framework within which he thinks the creation: the so-called "ex"-structure. The truth of the creature is "derived" from the first being and true.

4.4. 'Con-cursus'

The *via veritatis*, too, has a twofold sense. For the investigation leads to the conclusion that truth is measured by different originations. The measure of the truth of the human intellect is the natural thing. The natural thing is true by an intrinsic truth, the 'termini stabiliti' of its nature. But this intelligibility is to be reduced to the divine intellect, God's productive

---

[115] *S. Th.* I, 28, 1; *De pot.* 8, 1.

[116] B.A.M. Barendse, "Intersubjectief verkeer en lichamelijkheid," p. 85. His analysis of human intersubjectivity has inspired various Dutch philosophers to re-think Thomas's doctrine concerning the relation of Creator and creature. See J. Hollak, "Wijsgerige reflecties over de scheppingsidee: St. Thomas, Hegel en de Grieken," in *De eindige mens?* ed. C. Struyker Boudier (Bilthoven, 1975), pp. 89–103; H.H. Berger, *Zo wijd als alle werkelijkheid* (Baarn, 1977), pp. 213ff., 230. See also Th. van Velthoven, *Ontvangen als intersubjectieve act*, p. 14.

[117] God's being-free from a real relation Thomas compares, in *De pot.* 7, 8 ad 6, to the accidental relation of the builder to the house: Non enim esse Dei a creatura dependet, sicut nec esse aedificatoris a domo. Unde sicut accidit aedificatori quod domus sit, ita Deo quod creatura. Omne enim dicimus per accidens se habere ad aliquid, sine quo illud esse potest.

science. The extrinsic measure of the truth of things is God, who is the Truth.[118]

These findings must now be connected with the 'concursus' *per viam naturae* and *per viam creationis* which we noted at the close of chapter 3. This coming together appeared in the movement towards intelligibility, in the hierarchical order of the causes, and in the complex composition of being (*subjectum-essentia-esse*). In this "concurrence" there arose the problem of the "other": the relation of the essence to the Origin. With that problem in mind, the inquiry into being was carried on by means of the inquiry into truth. In the analysis of the transcendental property "true," the relation between being and intellect, the order sought comes to light.

For the two reductions of the "true" come together in the intelligibility of the *species*. A thing is called true insofar as it acquires the likeness of the species in the divine intellect, the *exemplar*. Everything is true insofar as it has its specific form.[119] Through closer consideration of the relation of *exemplar* and *forma* or *species* it will be possible both to deepen the philosophical meaning of the foregoing analysis of truth and to show the reduction of the formal diversity of things to a unity in the Origin (4.4.1.).

The order of nature is an *ordo originis*. This "naturalism" is the horizon of understanding in various domains, e.g., in that of law (3.4.). Normative for the acts and movements of people is the natural law. From the analysis of the truth of things, this "natural" is seen in a more fundamental perspective. The divine science creates the natural datum.[120] Nature is founded in the divine art, in the divine Wisdom, which in Christian theology is attributed to the second Person of the Trinity, the Word (the Logos). The Wisdom has the character of art or exemplar or idea, inasmuch as all things are created by it. As moving all things to their due end, it bears the character of law (*rationem legis*).[121] Thomas's relating the natural law to it is an expression of the 'concursus': the natural law is nothing other than the rational creature's participation in the eternal

---

[118] Cf. *De verit.* 1, 5: Veritas adaequationem quandam et commensurationem importat; unde secundum hoc denominatur aliquid verum, sicut et denominatur aliquid commensuratum. Mensuratur autem corpus et mensura *intrinseca* . . . et mensura *extrinseca* . . . Unde et aliquid potest denominari verum dupliciter: uno modo a veritate inhaerente; alio modo ab extrinseca veritate.

[119] *De verit.* 1, 5 ad 2: Res enim ipsa ex specie quam habet, divino intellectui adaequatur, sicut artificiatum arti, et ex virtute eiusdem speciei nata est sibi intellectum nostrum adaequare; *S. Th.* I, 16, 1: Et similiter res naturales dicuntur esse verae, secundum quod assequuntur similitudinem *specierum* quae sunt in mente divina: dicitur enim verus lapis, qui assequitur propriam lapidis *naturam*, secundum praeconceptionem intellectus divini.

[120] Cf. *De pot.* 1, 3 ad 1; Quidquid [Deus] in rebus facit . . . est eis natura, eo quod ipse est conditor et ordinator naturae.

[121] *S. Th.* I–II, 93, 1.

law.[122] To the "complication" of nature and creature by the way of exemplarity attention will be given in 4.2.2.

By the reduction of nature to the divine exemplar, a special philosophical problem arises for Thomas. Are things more true in themselves than in the exemplar, the Word (4.4.3.)?

4.4.1. *The unity of origin of the diversity of forms*

The creaturely is an imitation of the divine exemplar, the measuring Arche-type. We saw that this imitation must be intended 'per se' by the intellective efficient cause. God's intent extends to more, however, than simply the order of creation in general. It is absurd to think that in God there would be only one Idea, namely, of creation *in universali*. For that would mean that the specific distinction of things would be outside His intention, would come about by chance. In relation to particular causes, something can be 'per accidens'; not, however, in relation to the first cause (cf. 3.7.4.). The proper essences of things, from which the order of the universe is constituted, are as such intended by the creating intellect. Therefore it is necessary to accept a plurality of Ideas in God.[123]

This plurality is not repugnant to the divine simplicity. For the Ideas are not to be regarded as likenesses, by which (*quo*) the intellect understands, but as that which (*quod*) is understood. By one and the same principle, many things can be understood; such a plurality implies no composition in the intellect.[124] The one by which God knows is identical with His essence. God's essence is the Idea of everything—not, however, it must be added, the essence as it is in itself, but the essence as it is in relation to the creature, insofar as it is known by God as imitable by this or that creature.[125]

For the creatures imitate the divine essence never fully but always in a deficient way. The "copy" invariably falls short in comparison with the "model." The fullness of God's perfection is represented by every creature in its own way (*secundum proprium modum*). God, in the perfect self-knowledge of his Essence, knows also the diverse proportions to Him of

---

[122] *S. Th.* I–II, 91, 2: Unde patet quod lex naturalis nihil aliud est quam participatio legis aeternae in rationali creatura.

[123] *De verit.* 3, 2; *S. Th.* I, 15, 2.

[124] *S. Th.* I, 15, 2; *De pot.* 7, 1 ad 8: Similiter in intellectu eius sunt multa intellecta per unum et idem, quod est sua essentia. Quod autem per unum intelligantur multa, non inducit compositionem intelligentis; unde nec ex hac parte sequitur compositio in Deo.

[125] *S. Th.* I, 15, 2 and ad 1; 15, 1 ad 3; *In I Sent.* 36, 2, 2: Hoc nomen idea nominat essentiam divinam secundum quod est exemplar imitata a creatura; ad 1: Idea non nominat tantum essentiam, sed essentiam imitabilem.

the things to be created and therein the 'rationes' proper to the creatures. To that extent there is a plurality of Ideas in God. But these Ideas are not really distinct from his essence; for an Idea is the likeness of the divine essence, insofar as it can be participated in by different things in diverse manners.[126]

Two points in this exposition merit further attention: the reduction of the many to unity and the corresponding deduction, which is interpreted as participation.

The exemplar is really identical with God's essence: "there is one thing which is the exemplar of all, namely, the divine essence, which is imitated by all."[127] By means of this exemplarity a plurality can be reduced to unity: "the one first form (*una prima forma*) to which all is reduced is the divine essence considered in itself."[128]

The divine essence contains all things in itself beforehand (*omnia in Seipsa praehabet*), albeit not in the manner in which things are in themselves. For in themselves they are caused and finite, while in God they are infinite. In themselves they have composition, in God the most simple unity. In God all things preexist in a more eminent manner, that of God himself, that is: "supersubstantially." What exists in the effect in composite and multiple fashion, is in the cause simply and unitedly (*S.c.G.* II, 45). In the Origin the multiplicity is "absorbed," just as number is in the one—a comparison that goes back to pseudo-Dionysius and is strongly characteristic for this movement of thought. *Numerus uniformiter praeexistit in unitate*: the "one" is virtually every number. Because everything that is in another is in it in the way of the subject in which it is, it is said that number preexists "uniformly" in the one, namely in the manner of unity. The more the number is removed from the unity, the more it is brought to multitude (*in multitudinem deducitur*).[129]

The creaturely imitation of the divine exemplar is always partial and

---

[126] *Quodl.* IV, q. 1, art. un.; *De verit.* 3, 2: Unde, cum sint diversae rerum proportiones, necesse est esse plures ideas; et est quidem una omnium ex parte essentiae; sed pluralitas invenitur ex parte diversarum proportionum creaturarum ad ipsam; *ibid.*, 2, 4 ad 2; *S.c.G.* I, 54; *In De div. nomin.*, c. 5, lect. 3, 665; *S. Th.* I, 44, 3: Quae [rationes] licet multiplicentur secundum respectus ad res, non sunt tamen realiter aliud a divina essentia, prout ejus similitudo diversimode a diversis participari potest.

[127] *Quodl.* IV, q. 1, art. un.

[128] *De verit.* 3, 2 ad 6. See for the motive of unity especially *In Ad Coloss.*, lect. 4, 37: Platonici ponebant ideas, dicentes, quod quaelibet res fiebat ex eo quod participabat ideam, puta hominis vel alicuius alterius speciei. *Loco enim harum idearum nos habemus unum, scilicet Filium, Verbum Dei.*

[129] *In De div. nomin.*, c. 5, lect. 1, 641; 644 (numerus uniformiter praeexistit in unitate); c.5, lect. 3, 669; c. 8, lect. 3, 770; c. 13, lect. 3, 984: Et omnia praeexistunt in ea (sc. causa), non per modum proprium, sed per modum ipsius Dei, scilicet supersubstantialiter. Cf. *S. Th.* I, 57, 1.

deficient. In order that the likeness of God's essence might be more perfectly communicated to things, it was therefore necessary that there be
diversity in things. So what could not be perfectly represented by one
thing might, in more perfect fashion, be represented by a diversity of
things in different ways (*per diversa diversimode*). What is in God in a unified
and simple manner cannot be in creatures except in a diversified manner.
Now, things are differentiated by their possession of diverse forms from
which they receive their species.[130] This means that the diverse things
"represent, according to diverse forms, the one, simple form of God."[131]

Everything is determined by its form and species to a special grade of
being. Formal diversity therefore presupposes different grades of perfection, a hierarchy. The definitions and the essences signified by them are
"like numbers" because in their discreteness they form a series, an order
(2.3.). This order of being requires a principle, in relation to which the
gradation is thought. This principle, it appeared in 2.3., was matter.
What was counted as the first species was the form which "informs"
matter to the lowest grade of perfection.

On the way of truth which is movement towards the divine Truth, the
order has been changed. As a result, the problem of the "other"—the
relation of the essence of things to the Origin—receives an answer. The
diversity of forms and the different grades of perfection are constituted by
the degree of approximation to the divine exemplar, just as "numbers"
are in relation to "unity". The more a thing approaches to the likeness
of God, the more perfect it is. The order of the grades is viewed in relation
to a First, which possesses all perfections unitedly. In the descent from this
"vertex" these are differentiated in things—including the immaterial
substances.[132]

In this "gradualism"[133] the notions of measure, maximum, hierarchy,

---

[130] *S.c.G.* III, 97: Res autem per hoc diversae sunt quod formas habent diversas, a
quibus speciem sortiuntur.

[131] *De verit.* 2, 1: Quaelibet res imitatur aliquo modo Deum, sed imperfecte; unde et
diversae res diversimode Deum imitantur, et *secundum diversas formas repraesentant unam
simplicem Dei formam*, quia in illa forma unitur quidquid perfectionis distinctim et multipliciter in creaturis invenitur; sicut etiam omnes proprietates numerorum in unitate
quodammodo praeexistunt.

[132] See especially the text which in its entirety is basic to this section, *S.c.G.* III, 97.
In Q.D. *De anima* q. un., a. 7 we find the two orders together: Ubicumque enim est
diversitas graduum, oportet quod gradus considerentur per ordinem ad aliquod unum
principium. In substantiis igitur materialibus attenduntur diversi gradus speciem diversificantes in ordine ad primum principium, *quod est materia* ... In substantiis vero im-
materialibus ordo graduum diversarum specierum attenditur, non quidem secundum
comparationem ad materiam, sed secundum comparationem ad *primum agens*, quod
oportet esse *perfectissimum*.

[133] Delineated as the basic concept of medieval thought in G. Müller, "Gradualis-

and participation which we encountered earlier acquire their metaphysical meaning. They are integrated by Thomas into the 'quarta via' (*S. Th.*
I, 2, 3) and into the argumentation for the createdness of reality in *De pot.*
3, 5 (quoted in 3.7.3.). In his fourth way to the existence of God, Thomas
states: "'more' and 'less' are predicated of different things according as
they approximate in different ways something which is the *maximum*."
The maximum in any genus is the cause of all in that genus (4.3.1.).
"Whenever something is found that is participated in by a number of
things in different ways, then it must be imparted by the one in which it
is found most perfectly to all the others in which it is found imperfectly
... Therefore all other less perfect things must receive being from this
being" (*De pot.* 3, 5). All that is imperfect takes its origin from that which
is perfect.[134]

This origin is a step by step descent, manifesting itself in an ever greater
diversity from the One.

> All perfections of things descend in a certain order from the vertex of things,
> God ... And because perfect unity is found in the vertex of things, i.e., God,
> and the more one the more virtuous and worthy every thing is, the conse-
> quence is that the further one recedes from the first principle, the greater the
> diversity and variety found in things.[135]

This descent is not an emanation in which a higher substance is in every
case the direct principle of the lower. Thomas's correction of the motive
of circulation was that all that is creaturely stands in an im-mediate relation of origin to God (1.7.2.). There is in the production of things a hierarchical order, insofar as diverse grades of perfection are constituted in creatures according to the disposition of the divine art. God effects his likeness
in things *gradatim*, so that some are more nearly like Him than others.[136]
From the One and Simple a multiplicity can come forth immediately—not
because there is any diversity at all in the first cause, but because God acts
through his knowledge: his art brings forth diverse grades of being for the
perfection of the universe.[137] In this connection Thomas again refers to

---

mus," *Deutsche Vierteljahrsschrift für Literatur und Geistesgeschichte* 2 (1924): 681ff.

[134] *In I Sent.*, prol.: Omne imperfectum a perfecto trahit originem.

[135] *S.c.G.* IV, 1: Omnes rerum perfectiones quodam ordine a summo rerum vertice
Deo descendunt ... Et, quia in summo rerum vertice Deo perfectissima unitas invenitur,
et unumquodque, quanto est magis unum, tanto est magis virtuosum et dignius, consequens est ut, quantum a primo principio receditur, tanto major diversitas et variatio
inveniatur in rebus.

[136] *S. Th.* I, 65, 3 ad 1: In rerum productione est aliquis ordo, non quidem ut una
creatura creatur ab alia, hoc enim impossibile est, sed ita quod ex divina sapientia diversi
gradus in creaturis constituuntur; *In I Sent.* 13, 1, 1; *De verit.* 5, 1 ad 9.

[137] *In De causis*, lect. 24; *De pot.* 3, 4; 3, 1 ad 9; *S. Th.* I, 47, 2.

Wisdom 11:21, where it is said: "Thou hast ordered all things in measure, and number, and weight, Lord." In this text, according to Thomas, by "measure" is to be understood the mode or grade of perfection in every thing; and by "number" the diversity of species resulting from the diverse grades of perfection.[138]

In this hierarchical ordering the discreteness of the essences is relativized, the boundaries become more fluid. There is a certain continuity, a "marvelous connection" (*mirabilis connexio*; *S.c.G.* II, 68). For it is always found that the lowest in the higher species touches the highest in the lower species. Lower animals, e.g., enjoy a form of life scarcely superior to that of plants. With special preference, Thomas cites the statement of pseudo-Dionysius: "divine wisdom has united the ends of the higher things with the beginnings of the lower" (*divina sapientia conjungit fines superiorum principiis inferiorum*). The higher nature (*natura superior*) touches in its ends the beginning of the lower nature (*natura inferior*).[139]

Every creaturely perfection is "deduced in an exemplary manner" from the perfection of the Creator, is an imitation of the divine exemplar.[140] This imitation is understood, in truly Platonic fashion, as participation. The "de-duction" is a participation in the likeness of the divine essence. And the "mode of participating" is determinative for the diverse grades of perfection.[141] Because this diversity is a formal diversity, Thomas concludes in *S.c.G.* III, 97 that "form is nothing else than a divine likeness that is participated in things." He goes on to add: "Hence, Aristotle, where he speaks about form in Phys. I (c. 9, 192 a 17) quite appropriately says that it is 'something divine and desirable' (*divinum quoddam et appetibile*)."

---

[138] *S.c.G.* III, 97.

[139] *In De div. nomin.*, c. 7, lect. 4, 733. Thomas applies the Dionysian principle especially to the relation between the human soul and the pure intellectual substance of the angel (see 5.1.). Cf. *S. Th.* I, 78, 2; 108, 6; 110, 3; *S.c.G.* II, 91; III, 97; *De spirit. creat.* q. un., a. 2; *De verit.* 15, 1; 16, 1: Inferior natura attingit in sui supremo ad aliquid quod est proprium superioris naturae, imperfecte illud participans; *ibid.*, 25, 2; *In II Sent.* 39, 3, 1; *In De causis*, lect. 19.

[140] *In I Sent.* 43, 1, 2 ad 1; 42, 1, 2: Quidquid perfectionis in creatura est, totum est exemplariter eductum ex perfectione Creatoris; 22, 1, 2.

[141] For the term "de-duction" see *De verit.* 2, 4 ad 2: ... deducatur a similitudine divinae essentiae.

In *S. Th.* I, 15, 2 it is said alternately of the divine essence that it is *participabilis/imitabilis*. *S. Th.* I, 14, 6; *In I Sent.*, d. 8, exp. primae partis textus: Magis et minus potest dici aliquid dupliciter: vel quantum ad ipsam naturam participatam ...; vel quantum ad *modum participandi*; et sic etiam in essentialibus dicitur magis et minus secundum diversum modum participandi, sicut angelus dicitur magis intellectualis quam homo; *ibid.*, 8, 3, 1 ad 1.

The conclusion in which the exposition results is of great importance for the 'concursus'. For the linking of the form and the divine touches directly the originality of nature.

4.4.2. 'Per viam exemplaritatis'—'per viam naturae'

Nature is the 'ratio' of the divine art. Joining this view, J. PIEPER writes: "One can speak of a nature of things and of man with pretense to precision and exactness only insofar as things and man are expressly seen as *creatura*, as creation". For things can only have a nature if they are designed, i.e., formed according to an exemplar that has its place in a creative, knowing intellect.[142]

Striking here is the assessment that a nature of things can be spoken of *with precision* only on the basis of creation. This judgment agrees with the statement by GILSON that we encountered earlier (3.7.4.): the distinctiveness of the Christian conception of nature lies in the greater measure of rational determination. The creative Logos guarantees this intelligibility.

Where, then, does this rationality manifest itself? "A thing is said to be true because it fulfills that for which it was formed in the divine intellect by retaining its nature" (*retinendo naturam suam*).[143] Yet through this retention is not at the same time the (Greek) ontology, in which coming-to-be is "the way towards nature," "established" in an "exemplary" manner in the divine Logos?

An example of unproblematical concurrence of "naturalism" and "exemplarism" may be found in *Quodl.* VIII, 1, 2. There Thomas poses the question whether the divine exemplars pertain to the creaturely primarily with regard to its singularity or primarily with regard to its specific nature. The *sed contra*—conceded (*conceditur*) at the close of the text—already contains the core of the train of thought: "the ideated, i.e., created thing is more assimilated to the divine exemplar in virtue of the form (*secundum formam*), from which the species is, than in virtue of the matter, which is the principle of individuation." How does Thomas arrive at this thesis?

The answer begins with the comparison between God and the artificer. In the divine intellect are the exemplary forms of all creatures, just as in the intellect of the artificer are the ideas of the artifacts. There is, however, a difference. The ideas of the created artificer produce not the matter but only the form of the artifact. The exemplars of the divine intellect produce

---

[142] J. Pieper, "Wahrheit der Dinge—ein verschollener Begriff," in *Festschrift für Leo Brandt*, ed. J. Meixner and G. Kegel (Cologne and Opladen, 1968), p. 428.
[143] *De verit.* 1, 6 ad 2.

the *entire* thing, not only with regard to the form but also with respect to the matter. Then, however, at this juncture comes the turn: the exemplars still pertain to the creature primarily with regard to the specific nature (*per prius tamen quantum ad naturam speciei*). Thomas advances the following reasoning. An exemplar is that which is imitated by something. It is of the essence of an exemplar that the assimilation of the work to the exemplar is intended by the agent; for otherwise such an assimilation would happen by chance and not *secundum viam exemplaritatis*. What does this way of exemplarity entail? An exemplar pertains primarily to what the agent primarily intends in the work. Now, every agent intends first and foremost what is more perfect in that work. What is most perfect in every individual is the specific nature. Through it, namely, a twofold imperfection is perfected: first, that of matter, the principle of singularity; next, that of the generic nature, still in potency to the specific differences. Therefore, primary in the intention of nature is the *species specialissima*.

It is noteworthy how uncritically the core of the argumentation is shifted to the operation of nature. The continuation of the text also confirms this:

> For the principal intention of nature is not the generation of Socrates. For in that case the order and intention of nature would perish with the destruction of Socrates. But nature intends in Socrates the generation of man.[144]

So the conclusion is: "the exemplar in the divine intellect pertains primarily to the specific nature in every creature."

The question was: What is the intention of the divine work of creation? Yet in the answer, the meaning of being as *creature* is not really articulated; rather, what is asked becomes identified with the intention of *nature*. This identification results in the legitimation of the modes of questioning, predicating, and causing that were motivated by the origination of nature.

The intention of nature is directed to the lasting, the 'termini stabiliti,' which constitute the species. Therefore the knowledge of the species of things belongs to the intelligible perfection (3.4.2.). This knowledge is sought in the "what" question and in definitional thinking. In the definition, being is determined solely according to what it is in *itself*. Beyond the horizon lies the creature, insofar as it (through participation) *is*, i.e., as understood in relation to God (cf. 2.6.). Thus in a recent essay it could be asserted that for Thomas the affirmation of God in a philosophical discourse is relevant "only subsequent to a consideration of things in

---

[144] *Quodl.* VIII, 1, 2: Non enim *natura* intendit principaliter generare Socratem, alias destructo Socrate ordo et intentio *naturae* periret; intendit autem in Socrate generare hominem.

terms of their own proper and intrinsic principles. To his way of thinking the philosophical analysis of a theme is virtually complete before the question of its relationship to a divine principle becomes explicit."[145]

But can the transcendental relation, the being-from-and-to-God, be something added, something to be taken up only after the completion of the philosophical analysis? Is it not rather determinative from the very outset for the true meaning of being? One form of the vice of curiosity was for Thomas (1.6.2.) that "man strives to know the truth about creatures without relating it to its obligatory end, namely, to the knowledge of God" (S. Th. II–II, 167, 1). The pretension that things are grasped "integrally" by the way of definition is not verified. The truth of things is fulfilled only in the relation to God.

The way of nature is a circulation: "man generates man." Through the permanence of the species, natural things, according to the measure of their possibility, take part in the divine (3.4.1.). Outside the essence or quiddity is the individual matter, the principle of singularity (2.1.3.).[146]

This horizon forces Thomas, in De verit. q. 3, to pose in succession the questions, "Does primary matter have an Idea in God?" (art. 5) and "Does the singular have an Idea in God?" (art. 8). This last question is answered in the negative by Plato: there are only Ideas of species. One of his attendant considerations, so Thomas says, was that there is an Idea only of what is intended 'per se'. Now, the intention of nature is directed primarily to preserving the species (ad speciem conservandum). Thomas concludes this article: "We, however, posit that God is the cause of the singular with regard to the form as well as with regard to the matter." That he leaves it as this antithesis is, however, not satisfactory. The origin of creation—the Ideas are creativae et productivae rerum[147]—should prompt a renewed consideration of the constitution of the individual.[148] It is no coincidence that later medieval thinkers, especially Duns Scotus, undertook this task.

Yet in Thomas's work, too, expositions can be found that lend nuance to the picture as it was sketched in Quodl. VIII, 1, 2. In S. Th. I, 98, 1 he

---

[145] P. Masterson, "The Coexistence of Man and God in the Philosophy of St. Thomas Aquinas," in Images of Man, Studia G. Verbeke dicata (Leuven, 1976), p. 338.

[146] Cf. In III De anima, lect. 8, 706: Nam natura speciei individuatur per materiam: unde principia individuantia et accidentia individui sunt praeter essentiam speciei.

[147] De verit. 3, 1 ad 5.

[148] In De verit. 3, 4 the Idea is circumscribed as "forma, quae est principium formationis alicuius rei." The question of whether there are in God Ideas of the first matter and the singular things brings Thomas to emphasize that "idea proprie dicta respicit rem secundum quod est producibilis in esse" (De verit. 3, 5 and 3, 8 ad 2). In that sense one Idea corresponds both to the singular and to the species and the genus, which are individualized in the singular thing. With that, room is made for a re-founding of individuality.

again takes the position that nature intends what is lasting (*semper*) and perpetual (*perpetuum*), but now he distinguishes between corruptible and incorruptible creatures. In the corruptible, only the species is permanent; it is for this reason that the good of the species belongs to the principal intention of nature and that generation is directed to the preservation of the species. Incorruptible substances, however, are permanent not only in the species but also in the individual. "And therefore even the individuals belong to the principal intention of nature (*et ideo etiam ipsa individua sunt de principali intentione naturae*). Hence it belongs to man to generate, because of his bodily nature, which is corruptible. But on the part of the soul, which is incorruptible, it is fitting that the multitude of individuals is intended 'per se' by nature, or rather by the Author of nature (*a natura, vel potius a naturae auctore*), who alone is the creator of human souls."

Here it is no longer maintained, as in *Quodl.* VIII, 1, 2, that the intention of nature is directed to the man in Socrates and not to the individual. Yet from the distinction between corruptible and incorruptible substances it appears that time after time the normative framework remains the intention of *nature*, which is again identified with the Creator.

The integral unity of origin of the creaturely is, *per viam naturae*, involved in the dialectic of form and matter, of the perfect and the imperfect. Generation is formation, a movement "from something" "to something," namely, the form, whereby something is in act. In the fabric of the natural causes there is an irreducible duality of form and matter (3.3.1.).

In 4.3.2. we cited Thomas's statement: " 'being' and 'true' are convertible because every natural thing, *through its form*, is conformed to the divine art." He continues with a reference, which we also found at the end of the preceding section vis-à-vis the participation in essential forms: "Therefore the Philosopher, in *Phys.* I, calls the form something divine."[149] While creation "out of nothing" rules out radically every duality inherent to a formation, there now arises in what is because (with ancient thought) the principle of form is related to God a dialectical relation to the other principle, matter. That can be elucidated by directing attention to another aspect of the 'concursus'.

4.4.3. *Are things more true in themselves than in the exemplars?*

The origination of nature was Aristotle's option against the "reduc-

---

[149] *In I Perih.*, lect. 3, 30.

tion" of reality to what is exemplary. The natural thing is in itself knowable, is through an inherent truth conformable to human science. For Thomas that does not mean the end of the "way of truth". In a further analysis nature is reduced to the divine science, which is the measure of all that is true.

This reduction compels Thomas to address the question (*De verit.* 4, 6) of whether things are more true in the divine Ideas, i.e., in the Word, than they are in themselves. Was not the Idea, according to Plato, being in the true sense? Thomas answers with a distinction: "more true" (*verius*) can signify the truth of the thing (*veritas rei*) or the truth of predication (*veritas praedicationis*). If the former is intended, then undoubtedly the truth of the thing in the Word is greater. In the case of the "truth of predication" the reverse is so: for "man" is "more truly" predicated of something insofar as it is in its own nature. What Thomas means by the "truth of predication" he has explained earlier in this text. The caused falls short in its imitation of the cause. Because of the resultant distance between exemplar and copy, something is predicated truly of the caused while it is not said of the cause.

Thomas's exposition is not immediately clear. Why is the truth of predication the reverse of the truth of the thing? The basis of the former still lies in the thing itself (cf. 4.2.1.). The sense of this distinction will have to become clear from the formulated question, which arises from the "concurrence" of the two perspectives of the "truth of things." Apparently, it can be said of one and the same thing, e.g., of "man," that it is in the Word, where it has an *uncreated* being; and that it is in itself, created.[150]

In *S. Th.* I, 18, 4 ad 3 Thomas poses the same question and argues: if matter did not belong to the essence of natural things, then in all respects they would exist more truly in the divine mind, by the ideas of them, than in themselves. But since matter does belong to the essence of natural things, it must be said that they have this particular being, e.g., "man," "more truly" in their own nature than in the divine intellect; for it belongs to the truth of man to be material. Similarly, a house has nobler being in the mind of the artificer than in matter, although the house that is materially realized is called "more true" than the one which exists in the mind.

Strictly speaking, this answer is not complete—it leaves the subsistent forms out of consideration. Moreover, it does not really jibe with Thomas's conception of truth, to the extent that what has "less being"

---

[150] *S. Th.* I, 18, 4 ad 3: ... quia in mente divina habent esse increatum, in seipsis autem esse creatum.

is still called "more true." Yet it does become clear that the question can arise only because there exists between created being and uncreated being a relation of con-form-ity, which evokes an '*aliud*'. The form is "something divine"; the matter must then be this "other." From this it becomes understandable why Thomas in *De verit.* 4, 6 makes a distinction between the truth of the thing and the truth of predication. If the first is meant, the truth in the Word is greater. For every thing possesses being and truth through the form, according to which it imitates the divine art.[151] In the case of the truth of predication, the reverse holds. For in natural things there is a non-identiy of form and subject. This composition, which is the basis of logical truth, derives from the deficiency in imitation.[152]

4.5. *Retrospect*

With the problem of the "other" in the relation to the Origin, we arrive at a point similar to that reached at the end of the preceding chapter. The 'con-cursus' of the orders of origin of nature and of creature seems continually to evoke new complications. It will therefore be useful to look back at the way we have come; to summarize concisely and to evaluate the analysis of "being" and of the "true." Perhaps we shall find in this retrospect prospects for the continuation of the way of thought.

4.5.1. *The reduction to 'Esse' and 'Essentia'*

(1) The principle and end of the natural coming to be are, insofar as the species is concerned, identical. The way of nature is a circulation. Nature in the sense of generation is *via in naturam*. The intention of nature is directed to the specific form. The natural agent is a cause whose efficacy extends to the sort.

In natural genesis the form overcomes matter cyclically. As a result of the composition of form and matter, there is in that which is a nonidentity between subject and essence. Because the form is taken up in matter, it is limited and particularized.

---

[151] *De verit.* 1, 8: Res autem existens extra animam, per formam suam imitatur artem divini intellectus, et per eandem nata est facere veram apprehensionem in intellectu humano, per quam etiam formam unaquaeque res esse habet. Cf. *De verit.* 1, 10 ad 3; *In I Sent.* 1, 1, 1 ad 5: Forma, quae pars est rei, est similitudo agentis primi fluens ab ipso. Unde omnes formae reducuntur in primum agens sicut in principium exemplare; *In II Sent.* 18, 1, 2.

[152] *S. Th.* I, 3, 3 ad 2: Effectus Dei imitantur ipsum, non perfecte, sed secundum quod possunt. Et hoc ad defectum imitationis pertinet, quod id quod est simplex et unum, non potest repraesentari nisi per multa: et sic accidit in eis compositio, ex qua provenit quod in eis non est idem suppositum quod natura.

The origination of nature motivates a specific mode of questioning and knowing. The intelligibility of that which is is sought via the "what" question (*quid est*). In this questioning, a composite being is reduced to the *essentia*, and a multiplicity of particular subjects is reduced to the unity of the species. This is determined by the definition.

Thomas considers it necessary to conceive above the natural becoming another and higher origin pertaining to being as being. "Being" (*ens*) is transcendental; it is attributable to all that is. "Things are not distinguished from each other in having being, for in that respect they agree."[153] The intelligibility sought by the desire to know requires the reduction of this agreement.[154] The *esse* must be reduced to a "supernatural agent" (*De pot.* 3, 1 ad 1), God. The emanation of being from the universal cause is called by Thomas *creatio*. The terminus of creation is "to be," which is the actuality of every substance.

The reduction of being as creature to God is accompanied in Thomas by a reduction of being 'per participationem' to being 'per essentiam.' Every creature is a being through participation. For to participate means not to be something completely, but to have something other added to it. No creature at all, however, is totally being, but has something "outside" (*praeter*) of that in which it participates. That which is by participation must be reduced to that which is by its essence as cause. All that is has to be reduced to the first being, God, who is absolutely simple, because his essence in his *Esse*.[155]

The transcendental unity of being evokes an 'aliud' whereby the fullness of being in the created is limited. "All that comes after the first being has, since it is not its being, received being in something, whereby being itself is contracted" (*De spirit. creat.* q. un., a. 1). This "other" is the essence, which relates as potency to the act of being. The relation between essence and being is similar to the composition of subject and essence (form). Because being is received in the specific essence, it is limited.[156]

As a result every thing desires to return to the first Being. For everything it is desirable to be united with its principle, for therein consists the perfection of each. The way of the creature is a circulation. Origin and End are identical. The being of that which is created is from and to God.

In this analysis of being by means of the participation through composi-

---

[153] *S.c.G.* I, 26.

[154] Cf. *In II Sent.* 1, 1, 1: Unitas enim causati requiritur unitatem in causa per se; et haec est via Avicennae.

[155] Cf. *In II Post. Anal.*, lect. 6, 462: In solo enim primo essendi Principio, quod est essentialiter ens, ipsum esse et quidditas eius est unum et idem; in omnibus autem aliis, quae sunt entia per participationem, oportet quod sit *aliud* esse et quidditas entis.

[156] *S.c.G.* I, 43: Omnis actus alteri inhaerens terminationem recipit ex eo in quo est, quia quod est in altero est in eo per modum recipientis.

tion, the problem must arise of the relation to the Origin of the (finite) essence, of the formal diversity of things.

(2) With this problem in mind, the inquiry was continued with the analysis of the transcendental determination "true."

A thing is true insofar as it has being that is conformable to the intellect. That whereby the thing is true is its specific form, its 'termini stabiliti'. Determinative for this stability is the nature of the thing. Through their forms and species things are determined to a grade of being. The forms differ from each other according to a "more" or "less" in perfection. Formal diversity means gradation in perfection. The intelligibility sought by the desire to know requires the reduction of *this* multiplicity to unity. At just this point the significance of the analysis of truth becomes apparent.

The relation to the human intellect is not the foundation of the truth of the natural thing. The essential forms have to be reduced to an "intellectual agent" whose science is the measure and exemplar of the ontological truth. The exemplary cause of all that is true is God. Nature is an imitation of the divine art.

The reduction of the true as creature to God is accompanied by a reduction of the participated form to the divine *Essentia*. "Every creature has its own proper species, according to which it participates in some way in the likeness of the divine essence" (*S. Th.* I, 15, 2). For "to participate" is defined by Thomas in his commentary on *De hebdomadibus* as "to take part." "So when something receives partially (*particulariter*) what belongs to another in a universal way, it is said that it participates in it" (2.5.3.). Every creature has "partially," since it is particularized through its species to a particular mode of being.[157] It has to be reduced to a first, that is the maximum, as cause. Now, God's essence contains all things in it beforehand unitedly. The unity to which something that participates is reduced is that of the "universal mode of being" of the first Form.

The creaturely is a deficient, since finite, imitation of the exemplar. According to the measure of approximation, the diverse forms are deduced. The divine art has disposed a hierarchical order in the created. The mode of participating is determinative for the grade of perfection. The form is "a divine likeness participated in things."

In this analysis by means of the participation through formal hierarchy, the relation of the essences to the Origin is affirmed.

(3) From this summary it is apparent that the reduction of "being" (*ens*) goes beyond the horizon of the "whatness," or nature of that which is, to the 'esse' of creaturely being, while the reduction of "the true" es-

---

[157] *De subst. separ.*, c. 8, 88.

tablishes the natural determination in an exemplary manner in the divine intellect. In connection with these reductions, the analysis of "that which is" and the analysis of "that which is true" proceed via two different forms of participation.[158] The first concerns the actuality (*esse*) of that which is; the second concerns the being "what," the formality (essence). The first is marked by an inner multiplicity, the composition of subject (*essentia*) and 'esse'. This composition entails as a consequence that being is limited. The second is marked by a formal diversity; the limitation is original. The first is reducible to an efficient causality, the second to an exemplary causality. In the first there is an equality in the datum of being (*per participationem*), in the second a hierarchical order of grades and modes.

4.5.2. *The double metaphysical reduction*

(1) Divergent interpretations of Thomas go back to these different forms of participation. Primary for FABRO is the participation through composition. The central thesis of Thomas's metaphysics is to his mind the real distinction of 'essentia' and 'esse' in every creature. In this ontological difference lies the distinction from God; what one must distinguish (*dirimere*) in the finite is identical in God. Through the fundamental "Diremption"—a term FABRO borrows from HEGEL—of 'essentia' and 'esse,' being by participation is constituted. The terminus of creation is 'esse,' which is taken up in the essence. Here there arises with regard to the essence the problem of the "other" in the structure of that which is.

Characteristic of FABRO's solution of this problem of composition is the double recourse to God. Both—'essentia' and 'esse'—come forth from the causality of God. That must be understood in the sense that each goes back to an "original derivation *of its own*" (italics added, J.A.A.), for from the viewpoint of the transcendental foundation, the position of the essence differs from that of being. "That is to say that what is *esse per essentiam* in God, pure act and totality of perfection, is poured out in the creature through a *double* (italics added, J.A.A.) creation: of the *essentia* and of the *esse*." FABRO speaks not only of a *double* creation but also of a *distinct* creation of 'essentia' and 'esse'.[159] He refers in this regard to *De pot.* 3, 5 ad 2 (but can one really read a "double" creation from this text?):

> From the very fact that being (*esse*) is imparted to a quiddity, not only being but also the quiddity is said to be created: since before it had being, it was

---

[158] Cf. L.-B. Geiger, *La participation*, pp. 26–29.
[159] C. Fabro, *Participation et Causalité*, p. 468; cf. p. 67.

nothing, except perhaps in the intellect of the creator, where it is not a creature but the creating essence.[160]

(2) Primary for GEIGER, WEIER, and KREMER, despite mutual differences, is the participation through formal hierarchy. Yet here, too, when this participation is connected with creation, an "other" appears.

In KREMER's interpretation of Thomas the creaturely participates in the Form of Being itself (*Ipsum esse subsistens*), which contains all perfection in itself. This first Form is received only in a particularized way by that which participates. It is here that the deepest distinction between Creator and creature is to be sought, not in the real distinction of essence and being. For the limitation of the act of being through the essence presupposes a *finite* essence going back to God himself. "The contingency of the creatures is therefore not grounded just by the limited act of being, but the reverse: it is grounded by the limited, i.e., contingent essence."[161] The being that the creatures receive is nothing other than their nature, "to which being self-evidently also belongs, but, to be precise, only 'also belongs'."[162]

Yet in Thomas we read: "Creation has no reference to nature or essence unless by means of the act of being (*nisi mediante actu essendi*), which is the first terminus of creation."[163] But according to KREMER only Thomas's mode of expression moves in the representational scheme of composition. If it is said that "being" is outside the creature which participates, then it must, in his opinion, be the *ipsum esse subsistens* that is meant by the 'esse.' But, as we stated in 3.7.5., this interpretation is faulty. To the creature an *inner* composition of 'essentia' and 'esse' is proper. KREMER solves the problem of the "other" by denying it.

WEIER thinks that in Thomas there is no question of participation in being (*Seinsteilhabe*) in the sense of taking part in the divine Being (3.6.2.). Participation is for Aquinas at bottom participation in meaning (*Sinnteilhabe*), i.e., participation of the essences in the divine meaning, whereby the diversity of things is constituted. The relation of participation in which things stand to the divine Being signifies solely the "relation of foundation" of things in their being through God's power of being.[164] Creation consists herein, that "God joins being and essences, being and meaning

---

[160] *De pot.* 3, 5 ad 2: Ex hoc ipso quod quidditati esse attribuitur, non solum esse, sed ipsa quidditas creari dicitur: quia antequam esse habeat, nihil est, nisi forte in intellectu creantis, ubi non est creatura, sed creatrix essentia. Cf. *De pot.* 3, 1 ad 17: Deus simul dans esse, producit id quod esse recipit.

[161] *Die neuplatonische Seinsphilosophie*, p. 412.

[162] *Ibid.*, p. 413.

[163] *In III Sent.* 11, 1, 2 ad 2.

[164] "Seinsteilhabe und Sinnteilhabe im Denken des hl. Thomas von Aquin," p. 95.

to each other and so assigns being to the creaturely meaning."[165] Notice that creation is a *joining* of 'essentia' and 'esse.' Prior to the composite, however, are the diverse components. How can they be *creaturely* principles of being if creation consists precisely in their composition?

For GEIGER it is certain that participation through composition cannot be primary in the thought of Thomas because it is irreconcilable with the idea of creation. The composition of 'essentia' and 'esse' cannot explain the provenance of finite beings. Creation requires the participation through limitation.[166] Its primacy is implicitly confirmed whenever Thomas explains the finiteness of the creature through the limits of its 'esse,' limits which are themselves dependent on the finite character of the quiddity. "The being of man is limited to the species of man, because it is received in the nature of the human species, and it is just the same with the being of the horse or with any other creature" (*De pot.* 1, 2). Because the natures receive their limits from the divine wisdom itself through a purely formal limitation, this determination is primary.[167]

But GEIGER himself raises the question why Thomas prefers to define the finiteness of the creature through the limitation of its being instead of simply affirming that the essence is necessarily limited. His answer is that only in creation does the form acquire actuality. By creating, God brings possible participations in his Essence to existence.[168] The real composition is not merely a scheme of representation. The 'esse' brings it about that the creature is not merely a divine Idea or a pure possibility. Therefore the limitation of the 'esse' determines formally the condition of the creature.[169]

(3) This critical survey of the manners in which Thomas's thought has been interpreted by some of the foremost scholars makes two things clear. First, the divergent interpretations have a certain basis of justification, insofar as they are founded either on the reduction to the Esse or on the reduction to the Essentia. Both interpretations are possible since Thomas himself did not thematize the relation between the two forms of participation. Secondly, no matter how much these interpretations may vary, there is still a deeper-lying agreement to be discerned in them. For in the problems they evoke, they indirectly affirm that in Thomas the structure of that which is has become threefold (3.7.5.). It is this complexity that needs further consideration.

---

[165] *Ibid.*, p. 99.
[166] *La participation*, pp. 392ff.
[167] *Ibid.*, pp. 394–95, n. 2.
[168] *Ibid.* p. 105, n. 2.
[169] *Ibid.* p. 395n.

Our investigation of Thomas's way of thought followed the order of the transcendentals "being" and "true." These terms are convertible; they refer to the same subject or supposit. Although "being" and "true" are the same really, however, they differ in idea. They are not identical as concepts. "True" adds something to being, namely, the relation to the intellect. This nonidentity deserves more attention than it usually receives. For in it the difference between 'essentia' and 'esse' in that which is comes to expression.[170] Unlike "being," "true" primarily refers to the essence. The ontological truth of the thing is its specific nature, which is a participation in the divine essence. The "act of being" was not at issue in the reduction of the "true." There are, indeed, texts in which Thomas reduces the intelligibility of that which is to "being" as act. For clarification he then uses the metaphor of light. Just as in the sensible world colors are rendered knowable by light, so a thing is rendered knowable to the intellect by that through which it is in act. The thing is lucid and transparent only through its actuality (*ipsa actualitas rei est quoddam lumen ipsius*).[171] But the 'esse' always remains on the periphery of the consideration of the true. In the participation concerning the essence, the form is something "divine." Through the form something is knowable. This inner clarity is obscured in corporeal creatures by the "other," matter; they are intelligible only in potency.[172]

The 'duplex ordo' in that which is—that of *subjectum/essentia* and that of *essentia/esse*—follows the twofold analysis through which Thomas desires to understand reality as nature and creature. The ontological difference is presented expressly by Thomas in *S.c.G.* IV, 11. In the creatures are different (*aliud*) 'essentia,' 'esse,' and (in some) 'what subsists in its nature': "this man is not his humanity nor his being." What is divided in creatures is fully one in God: "God is his essence and his being." Yet in Him is all that belongs to the concepts of subsistence, essence, and being itself (*ipsius esse*). For to God belongs "not being in something other (*non esse in aliis*), insofar as He is subsistent; being what (*esse quid*), insofar as He is essence; and being in act (*esse in actu*), in virtue of His Being." The striking thing about this text is that while it is meant to mark the differences, it still shows implicitly where the components come together. For in all three there is mention of 'esse.'

In a twofold metaphysical reduction the components of what is created—'essentia' and 'esse' (as act)—are as really different from each other

---

[170] One of the few who have noticed this is L.-B. Puntel, *Analogie und Geschichtlichkeit*, vol. 1 (Freiburg, Basel, and Vienna, 1969), pp. 193ff.

[171] *In De causis*, lect. 6 (see n. 69).

[172] *In De div. nomin.*, c. 4, lect. 16, 501.

related to God, in Whom they are identical. The duality is thought right into God Himself.

> In the thing are two, i.e., the quiddity of the thing and its being ... Similarly, too, in God Himself one has to consider His *natura* and also His *esse*. And just as His nature is the cause and exemplar of every nature, so also is His *esse* the cause and exemplar of every being.[173]

Through the twofold recourse to God the "difference" of 'essentia' and 'esse' in the creaturely is thought, to be sure, but not the "being" in which subsistence, essence, and act come together.[174]

It therefore seems attractive to regard the twofold reduction to the Origin, to which different forms of participation are connected, not as alternatives but as complementary.[175] For God is "the first exemplary and effective cause." Now, what in itself is one our reason can regard successively from the viewpoint of the efficient and of the exemplary causality.[176] Undoubtedly, more justice is done Thomas's intentions in this way: "through one and the same, God is in the concept of diverse causes" (*De pot.* 7, 1 ad 3). This may all seem somewhat self-evident; but it must be realized that a solution of this sort must also be fraught with consequences for the unity of origin of the effectuated, for the identity of being in the creaturely, in short, for the problem of the "other." It therefore needs to be asked whether the unity and diversity in the causal relation of God to that which is do not go back to something more than just a complementary view.

(4) I believe there is the suggestion of a deeper meaning in the question Thomas poses in his analysis of truth (4.4.3.): "Are things more true in themselves than in the Word?" Moreover, in his thesis that the temporal process of the creatures is derived from the eternal process of the divine Persons (4.3.3.), and in his remark that instead of the Platonic Ideas "we

---

[173] *In I Sent.* 38, 1, 3: Cum in re duo sint, quidditas rei, et ejus esse ... Similiter etiam in ipso Deo est considerare *naturam* ipsius, et *esse* ejus; et sicut natura sua est causa et exemplar omnis naturae, ita etiam esse suum est causa et exemplar omnis esse.

C. Fabro, *Participation et Causalité*, p. 479 observes in connection with this text: "La *resolutio* de cette première composition réelle de la créature ... est à faire dans la première dualité *notionelle* (italics added, J.A.A.) que notre intellect institue dans la plénitude divine quand nous y considérons le contenu de l'essence ... et sa forme ou acte." Such a statement typifies the focus of this way of thought on the 'differentia' of 'essentia' and 'esse,' of content and act in created being.

[174] It is remarkable that Geiger (*La participation*, p. 199n.) asks for a more synthetical notion that extends to the essence as well as to the existence. He considers such to be the 'virtus essendi.'

[175] Cf. J.-D. Robert, "Note sur le dilemme: 'Limitation par composition ou limitation par hiérarchie formelle des essences,'" *Revue des Sciences philos. et théol.* 49 (1965): 60–66.

[176] Cf. *S. Th.* I, 44, 4 ad 4.

have one something, namely, the Son, the Word of God."[177] From this
it appears that the exemplary causality is connected through appropriation to the second person of the Trinity. "The Son is the sufficient reason
of the temporal process of the created as *word* and *exemplar*" (*De pot.* 10,
2 ad 19). Earlier (4.3.2.) we saw that truth in the divine is "equality";
this too is a name appropriated to the second Person. "Truth," "art,"
"Wisdom," that "whereby" (*per quem*) things are, are attributed to the
Son. The "entity" of things, the efficient causality, the power of creation,
the principle "from which" (*ex quo*) things are, are appropriated to the
Father.[178]

If the twofold metaphysical reduction of that which is (true) becomes
meaningful when viewed in terms of the operation of the tri-une God,
then it may not be too bold to interpret the threefold structure of the
effectuated being in a trinitarian way too. In this way it becomes possible
to think not only the difference in the created, which Thomas analyzes,
but the unity as well. For where there is a difference there is also agreement (cf. 2.3.). The triad 'subjectum-essentia-esse' expresses the 'prin-
cipium-medium-finis' of the creaturely. And it is of the last triad that
Thomas says, it represents the distinction of the divine Persons. The
"middle" of the thing, its truth, is the essential form, which is reducible
to the 'media Persona.'[179]

At this moment, in the analysis of "the true," i.e., in the "middle" of
the way of thought, these considerations cannot yet be definitive. A
"rounded-off" assessment can only be made (cf. 8.5.) when the ways of
nature and of creature have reached their end (*finis*) and man's desire
to know is followed to the end. The task will be to inquire further into
how the 'concursus' of nature and creature is thought philosophically, expressly as 'concursus.' This objective determines the continuation of the
itinerary, to its end.

---

[177] *In Ad Coloss.*, lect. 4, 37 (cf. n. 128, above).

[178] *In II Sent.* 1, 1, 6 ad 1: Ratio principii effectivi appropriatur Patri, sed ratio prin-
cipii exemplaris per modum artis appropriatur Filio, qui est sapientia et ars Patris. Cf.
De verit. 1, 4 (sed contra): Propter quamdam appropriationem entitas rerum refertur ad
Deum ut ad causam efficientem, veritas ut ad causam exemplarem; *ibid.* 1, 7: [Veritas]
appropriatur personae Filii, sicut ars et cetera quae ad intellectum pertinent; 7, 3; *S. Th.*
I, 39, 8; 45, 6 ad 2.

[179] *In I Sent.* 3, 2, 2: In creaturis invenitur principium, medium et finis . . . Et secundum rationem etiam horum trium repraesentatur in creaturis distinctio divinarum
personarum, in quibus Filius est media persona.

CHAPTER FIVE

BY THE WAY OF REASON (*PER VIAM RATIONIS*)

In the preceding chapter the intelligibility of that which is was sought by the way of truth. This quest also points to the intellect that understands, that is, to man. A striking element in Thomas's analysis of the transcendental "true" is that "true" expresses a relation to "something" whose nature it is to accord with every being, the human intellect. It is man who desires to know. It is he who inquires, predicates, and defines. Man's intellect is "under way towards" insight. It is this aspect of the desire to know that is explicated in this chapter.

"The truth of what exists consists radically in the apprehension of the quiddity of things" was a statement from Thomas's commentary on pseudo-Dionysius's *De divinis nominibus* that we read earlier (4.2.2.). This text continues: "yet rational souls do not immediately apprehend the quiddity through itself."[1] Man does not see the truth of things in a simple intuition but attains it only in a process of inquiry, in a "discursion" (*discursus*). His knowledge comes about *per viam rationis* (5.1.).[2]

The way of reason, which is grounded in man's mode of being, is a discursion *from* something *towards* something, is a movement and therefore has a succession, also in the temporal sense.[3] That makes it possible to integrate historical tradition into the way of reason. In the search for truth, time is a "good cooperator," because the philosopher can build on what earlier philosophers have discovered.[4] In the second basic text, Thomas sketches the historical course of the desire to know (5.2.).

This sketch contains various moments that are important for the further inquiry into the intelligibility of reality. These moments will be worked out partly in this chapter and partly in the ones that follow. The moments that are discussed in this chapter will at the same time provide a deepening of a number of themes from the first chapter: the dynamics of the desire to know; the order of questions and the double sense of the "if" question (*an est*); the circulation motif and man's beatitude; Christian faith and the desire to know.

The most important moment in the historical itinerary is that it de-

---

[1] *In De div. nomin.* c. 7, lect. 1, 713: ... quam quidditatem rationales animae non statim apprehendere possunt per seipsam.

[2] The expression "per viam rationis" is used in *De verit.* 11, 3 ad 4; 15, 1.

[3] Cf. *S. Th.* I, 14, 7.

[4] Cf. *In I Ethic.*, lect. 11, 132.

scribes the 'concursus' of the order of nature and the order of creature: the history of philosophical reflection terminates in the idea of creation. That the world is created is, however, not "theoria" first but Christian confession. How is this insight of faith received by reason? In Thomas, what is the relation—a central question in medieval philosophy—between this knowledge *per viam fidei* and knowledge by way of natural reason (5.3.)?

In the strict sense, for Thomas faith begins where reason ends. If the insight of faith does not constitute the starting point of rational discursion, then it may be asked (5.4.) what is the "first" that makes the movement of thought possible. The first known and the condition for all knowledge is being (*ens*). From this Archimedean point, the process of knowledge develops in accordance with the scope which is proper to man: *via ex nobis notioribus* (5.5.).

5.1. *The discursive reason*

"All men by nature desire to know." "Desire" expresses a nonidentity, for desire is a tendency towards that which one does not yet possess, a movement which comes to rest only when the end has been attained (cf. 1.1.). The desire to know in man implies a prior not-knowing. This imperfection must be understood from the human mode of being and its place in the universe.

In what is created there is a gradation of modes of being, a formal hierarchy based on the diverse modes of participation (4.4.1). In this descending series of perfections spiritual substances most nearly approximate to God. Of the intellectual substances, the human soul occupies the lowest grade. Its being is so near to the material things that it is united with a body.[5]

Thomas gives expression to man's special position in the prologue to the commentary on the third book of the *Sententiae*, where he reflects on a text from Ecclesiastes 1:7: "Ad locum unde exeunt, flumina revertuntur, ut iterum fluant." All streams return to the place from whence they arose, in order to flow again. There is nothing new under the sun. Thomas undertakes to give this text a deeper meaning in terms of the circulation motif: all comes forth from God and returns to the Origin. The "streams" are the natural gifts, which God bestows on the creatures, such as "to be," "to live," and "to understand." In created reality outside

---

[5] *De spirit. creat.* q. un., a. 1: Inter omnes autem creaturas Deo maxime appropinquant spirituales substantiae; *In II Sent.* 3, 1, 1; 3, 1, 6 (a text that is basic to this entire section): Ex hoc anima rationalis ab angelis differt, quia ultimum gradum in substantiis spiritualibus tenet, sicut materia prima in rebus sensibilibus . . . Unde quia plurimum de possibilitate habet, esse suum est adeo propinquum rebus materialibus, ut corpus materiale illud esse possit participare, dum anima corpori unitur ad unum esse.

man, these gifts occur separately; in man the three come together. In a sense man unites in himself all that is created. For that reason man is as it were the "horizon" and "confines" of the spiritual and material. For that same reason he is the *medium* between the two. As both spiritual and material being, man is the "middle" of the cosmos.[6]

The perfection of the intellectual substance consists in the knowledge of the truth. The mode of being proper to man entails a special mode of knowing. Because the human soul is the lowest ranking spiritual being, it participates in intellectuality in an imperfect way. The human intellect is in potency to intelligible objects as in the material world primary matter is in potency to sensible forms.[7] Man possesses a transcendental openness, but he must still appropriate reality by actual knowing.

It is in connection with the potentiality of the soul, with this imperfection, that man's knowing is "rational." "It pertains to human nature to use reason in order to know the truth (*Ad hominis enim naturam pertinet ratione uti ad veritatis cognitionem*). It is proper to reason that it does not grasp the truth immediately; therefore, it is proper to man to advance only gradually in the knowledge of truth."[8] Reasoning as he goes, man proceeds from the one to the other. Human knowing occurs *per viam rationis*, with 'ratio' to be taken here in the strict sense as a mode of knowing distinct from 'intellectus.'[9]

P. ROUSSELOT has called attention to the significance of this distinction in Thomas's thought.[10] Its importance is underlined by a striking text in

---

[6] *In III Sent.*, prol.: Ista flumina in aliis creaturis inveniuntur distincta; sed in homine quodammodo omnia congregantur. Homo enim est quasi horizon et confinium spiritualis et corporalis naturae, ut quasi medium inter utrasque. Cf. *S.c.G.* II, 68; *In III Sent.* 2, 1, 1, sol. 1. This middle position of man acquires significance for salvation history in *S.c.G.* IV, 55: Homo enim quum sit constitutus ex spirituali et corporali natura, quasi quoddam confinium tenens utriusque naturae, ad totam creaturam pertinere videtur quod fit pro hominis salute.

See for the broader background: G. Verbeke, "Man as a 'Frontier' according to Aquinas," in *Aquinas and Problems of His Time* (Leuven, 1976), pp. 195–213; Kl. Kremer, "Wer ist das eigentlich—der Mensch? Zur Frage nach dem Menschen bei Thomas von Aquin," *Trierer Theol. Zeitschr.* 84 (1975): 81ff.

[7] *De anima* q. un., a. 7; *De ente*, c. 5; *S.c.G.* II, 68; *S.Th.* I, 14, 2 ad 3.

[8] *In I Ethic.*, lect. 11, 132. Likewise in *S.Th.* I, 58, 4.

[9] Cf. *In II Sent.* 3, 1, 6; *S.Th.* I–II, 5, 1 ad 1: Intellectualis natura excedit rationalem quantum ad modum cognoscendi eamdem intelligibilem veritatem: nam intellectualis natura statim apprehendit veritatem, ad quam rationalis natura per inquisitionem rationis pertingit; *In I Sent.* 25, 1, 1 ad 4.

See also the documented study by J. Peghaire, *Intellectus et ratio selon S. Thomas d'Aquin* (Paris and Ottawa, 1936).

[10] *L'Intellectualisme de saint Thomas*, 3rd ed. (Paris, 1936), p. 56: "On ne saurait exagérer, en philosophie thomiste, l'importance de cette distinction." This is equally valid for the later philosophical development; one may think of Nicolaus Cusanus, and of the

which the distinction is used by Aquinas to clarify the difference between nature and creation.[11] Just as the understanding (*intelligere*) of principles is not concluded "from" something, so too is *creatio* not "from" something; rather, it is principle. The acts of the *ratio*, in contrast, are to be compared to those of *natura*. Just as every natural movement is from something, so too is every conclusion of reason (from nothing follows nothing). Reason proceeds from the one to the other and is in this respect "connatural" to nature. *Ratio imitatur naturam.*[12]

The first mark of rationality is discursiveness. Human souls are called "rational" because as a result of "the weakness of their intellectual light" they acquire the knowledge of truth discursively. The way of reason is a "discursion" from the one towards the other, from what is known earlier towards what is still unknown, as from the knowledge of the effect to that of the cause.

Man's need of such a discursion originates from his mode of being: mind in a body. As incarnated mind, he is dependent upon sense experience. The second mark of the rational process is that the knowledge of intelligible things is derived from what is sensible, is the progression "from what is sensible to what is intelligible."[13] Sense knowledge concerns the external determinations of something, the particular. Therefore multiplicity is proper to reason; it disperses itself in the consideration of many properties in order to gather from the multiplicity the one, simple truth. Its discursion is *collativa* ("collecting") and *cogitativa* (literally, "driving together").[14]

As discursion, the way of reason is a movement: *discursus quemdam*

---

distinction between "Verstand" and "Vernunft" in nineteenth-century German philosophy.

[11] *De pot.* 3, 1 ad 6.

[12] Cf. *In I Post. Anal.*, prooemium; *In Iob*, prooemium.

[13] *In II Sent.* 3, 1, 6: Et sic a sensibilibus in intelligibilia venit, et per hoc ab angelo differt, qui non a sensibilibus discurrendo ad intelligibilia, cognitionem accipit; *S. Th.* I, 58, 3: Animae vero humanae, quae veritatis notitiam per quemdam discursum acquirunt, rationales vocantur. Quod quidem contingit ex debilitate intellectualis luminis in eis; *S. Th.* II–II, 180, 6 ad 2; *In I Post. Anal.*, prooemium, 4; *De verit.* 15, 1; *In Boeth. De trin.* 6, 1.

[14] *In Boeth. De trin.* 6, 1 ad tertiam quaestionem: Differt autem ratio ab intellectu, sicut multitudo ab unitate... Est enim rationis proprium circa multa diffundi et ex eis unam simplicem cognitionem colligere. Unde Dionysius dicit De divinis nominibus (c. 7) quod animae secundum hoc habent rationalitatem quod diffusive circueunt existentium veritatem, et in hoc deficiunt ab angelis; cf. *In De div. nomin.* c. 7, lect. 2, 713.

Collativa: *De verit.* 11, 1 ad 12: Potentia intellectiva, cum sit collativa, ex quibusdam in alia devenit.

Cogitativa: *In I Sent.* 3, 4, 5: Cogitare autem est considerare rem secundum partes et proprietates suas: unde dicitur quasi coagitare; 27, 2, 1 ad 3: In cogitatione est exitus rationis ab uno in aliud per collationem.

motum nominat.[15] A movement from the one towards the other is a 'motus rectus'. It is for this reason that Thomas, inspired by pseudo-Dionysius, compares the intellective operation of the rational soul with a rectilinear movement.[16]

'Per viam rationis' the theme from the beginning of the first chapter, that "all men by nature desire to know," is deepened. The dynamics of the natural desire to know acquires an ontic basis. There is a desire to know, a wondering questioning and seeking into the causes and truth of things, because the subject, man, is by "nature" rational. His soul, the lowest in the hierarchy of spiritual beings, is only knowing in potency. Therefore man desires by nature to know as matter desires form.

Over against the *ratio* stands the *intellectus*, the mode of knowing proper to pure spiritual beings. The separated substances do not know discursively but see immediately, in a single intuition, the truth of things. 'Intellectus' is explained as 'intus-legere', i.e., reading the truth within the essence itself of the thing.[17] The spiritual substances do not have to gather the truth from a multiplicity and diversity of sensible things. Their knowledge is simple and uniform; their understanding is godlike (*deiformis*).[18]

Although the knowledge proper to man is brought about *per viam rationis*, discursively, it still has a certain participation in the simple knowledge which is found in the higher substances: the 'intellectus'.[19] The hierarchical order of the creaturely is marked (4.4.1.) by a "marvellous connection," described by pseudo-Dionysius as follows: "divine wisdom has united the ends of the higher things with the beginnings of the lower." At its top the lower nature touches the bottom of the higher nature. This continuity also finds expression in man's cognition.[20]

The principle and the terminus of the movement of reason are the 'intellectus'. This must be the beginning because "the way of reason" is passable only when the discursion begins from insights which are not acquired through reasoning but which are apprehended immediately: the first contents of thought (*prima intelligibilia*). The terminus, too, is 'in-

---

[15] *S. Th.* I, 58, 3 ad 1. Cf. *S. Th.* I, 79, 9; I–II, 5,1; *S.c.G.* I, 57; *De verit.* 15, 1; *De spirit. creat.*, q. un., a. 10.

[16] *S. Th.* I–II, 180, 6; *In De div. nom.* c. 4, lect. 7, 372; 375.

[17] *De verit.* 15, 1.

[18] *S.c.G.* III, 91; *In II Sent.* 3, 1, 6: Per hoc quod angelus intellectum deiformem habet, convertitur ad quodcumque immobiliter; per quod ab anima dicitur angelus differre, quae non intellectu deiformi, sed per inquisitionem rationis cognitionem habet.

[19] From that it also appears that the definition of man, whereby "man" is determined to a specific grade of being, must sooner be understood in terms of intellectuality (that is, from the order to the first Principle) than in terms of animality (that is, from the order to matter). On these two different principles of ordering, see 4.4.1.

[20] *De verit.* 15, 1; 16, 1; *In I Sent.* 3, 4, 1 ad 4; *In II Sent.* 39, 3, 1.

tellectus'. When reason has finally reduced a multiplicity to unity, when it has arrived by its laborious path at the essence of the thing, it no longer reasons but understands.

Acts of reason and of intellect are not the acts of distinct powers. Reasoning is compared to understanding as movement is to rest, or as acquisition is to possession. Since each natural movement proceeds from something unmoveable and ends in something at rest, hence it is that human reasoning must be reduced to the intellect as its beginning and terminus. Now, "rest" and "movement" are not to be referred to different powers but to one and the same nature (cf. 7.1.1.4.: "The definition of nature"). By the same power we understand and reason: "Reason itself is called intellect insofar as it participates in the intellectual simplicity which is the principle and terminus of its own operation."[21]

Because of its beginning and terminus the movement of the rational soul is not only rectilinear. The inquiry into the truth of things has a circular structure: reason begins from the one and simple, namely, the 'intellectus' of the first principles; and it proceeds through the many in order to terminate in the one. *In processu rationis est quaedam convolutio ut circulus.*[22]

For the third time, we encounter a circulation in our investigation. We found the way of nature and the way of creature to be circular movements, and now man's process of knowing is understood as a circle. In viewing the course, the beginning, and the terminus of the way of reason, a new entry is opened to Thomas's way of thought, to the thinking together of the intelligibility of nature and creature.

5.2. *The historical reason: "The ancient philosophers gradually advanced in the knowledge of truth"*

It is typical of man to make progress in the knowledge of truth only gradually. Man advances to fuller insight step by step. The "way of reason," like the way of nature, goes from the imperfect to the perfect. That is so for the individual but also for mankind as a whole. Thus

---

[21] *De verit.* 15, 1. Cf. *S. Th.* I, 79, 8; II–II, 8, 1 ad 2: Discursus rationis semper incipit ab intellectu et terminatur ad intellectum: ratiocinamur enim procedendo ex quibusdam intellectis, et tunc rationis discursus perficitur quando ad hoc pervenimus ut intelligamus id quod prius erat ignotum; *In II Sent.* 3, 1, 6 ad 2: In homine est intellectus . . . quia ejus cognitio secundum terminum tantum et secundum principium intellectualis est; *In III Sent.* 35, 1, 3, sol. 2; 35, 2, 2, sol. 1; *S.c.G.* I, 57: Supremum in nostra cognitione est, non ratio, sed intellectus qui est rationis origo.

[22] *In De div. nomin.* c. 7, lect. 2, 713. Cf. *De verit.* 10, 8 ad 10.

See also *In De div. nomin.* c. 4, lect. 7; *In I Sent.* 36, 4; *De verit.* 8, 15 ad 3; *S. Th.* II–II, 180, 6 and ad 2, where the intellectual operations are compared with the 'motus circularis', 'rectus', and 'obliquus'.

tradition—history—acquires a place in science. What is dealt with imperfectly by the first philosophers is completed by later ones.[23]

In *De subst. separ.*, c. 9—the second basic text—Thomas sketches this
historical progression, a number of the elements of which we have already
encountered. First, the text *in extenso*:

> For human ability is seen to have progressed slowly in investigating the
> origin of things (*Paulatim enim humana ingenia processisse videntur ad investigan-
> dam rerum originem*). In the beginning (*primo*) men thought that the origin of
> things consisted only in an external change, by which I mean an external ori-
> gin that takes place according to accidental changes. For those who were first
> to philosophize about the natures of things held that to become is nothing
> other than to be altered, so that the substance of things which they called
> matter is a completely uncaused first principle. For they were not able by
> their intellect to surmount the distinction between substance and accident.
> Others, proceeding a little further (*Alii vero aliquantulum ulterius procedentes*),
> likewise investigated the origin of the substances themselves, asserting that
> certain substances had a cause of their being. But because they were not able
> by their minds to see anything beyond bodies, they did indeed reduce sub-
> stances to certain principles but corporeal principles, and they posited that
> other substances come to be through the combining of certain bodies, as
> though the origin of things consisted solely in combining and separating.
>
> Later philosophers proceeded (*Posteriores vero philosophi ulterius processerunt*)
> by reducing sensible substances into their essential parts, which are matter
> and form. Thus they made the "becoming" of physical things to consist in
> a certain change, according as matter is successively made subject to dif-
> ferent forms.
>
> But beyond this mode of becoming, it is necessary, according to the
> teaching of Plato and Aristotle, to posit another and higher one (*Sed ultra hunc
> modum fiendi necesse est, secundum sententiam Platonis et Aristotelis, ponere alium
> altiorem*). For, since it is necessary that the first Principle be most simple, this
> must of necessity be said to be not as participating in being but as being it-
> self. But because subsistent being can be only one . . ., then necessarily all
> other things under it must be as participating in being. Therefore there must
> take place a common resolution in all such things in the sense that each of
> them is resolved by the intellect into that which is, and its being. Therefore,
> above the mode of coming to be by which something becomes when form
> comes to matter, we must preconceive another origin of things according as
> being is bestowed upon the whole universe of things by the first Being that
> is its being.

Thomas sketches a similar itinerary in *De pot. 3, 5; S.c. G.* II, 37; *In VIII
Phys.*, lect. 2; and *S. Th.* I, 44, 2.[24] It contains a number of moments

---

[23] *S. Th.* I–II, 97, 1: Humanae rationi naturale esse videtur ut gradatim ab imperfecto
ad perfectum perveniat. Unde videmus in scientiis speculativis, quod qui primo
philosophati sunt quaedam imperfecta tradiderunt, quae postmodum per posteriores sunt
tradita magis perfecte; *In Iob*, prol.

[24] Cf. E. Gilson, *The Spirit of Mediaeval Philosophy*, pp. 68–69; A. Hayen, *La communica-*

which are decisive for the direction of the inquiry into the intelligibility of reality. We shall first indicate what these are, making use of the texts just mentioned.

(1) "The ancient philosophers gradually, and as it were step by step, advanced in the knowledge of truth" (*Antiqui philosophi paulatim, et quasi pedetentim, intraverunt in cognitionem veritatis; S. Th.* I, 44, 2). The history of philosophy and the systematic order of knowing correlate; the historical reason is the discursive reason. The historical development comes about in keeping with the structure of human knowledge.

> The ancients in their consideration of the nature of things proceeded in accordance with the order of human knowledge. Hence as human knowledge reaches the intellect by beginning with the senses, the early philosophers occupied themselves with sensible things, and thence gradually reached the realm of the intelligible.[25]

The historical way of philosophy proceeds as a rational discursion: it goes from the many to the one; from what is sensible, intelligible truth is gathered. Typical of the progression towards knowledge is the *via ex nobis notioribus* (cf. 5.5.); it develops *per viam sensus* (cf. 6.1.).

(2) The historical way proceeds "by the way of resolution" (cf. 6.4.)— in *De substantiis separatis* the terms "to resolve" and "resolution" are used a number of times. It is a reduction to the ontologically prior. Thomas places the history of philosophy in the perspective of the question concerning the origin of being. Here the circular structure of the way of reason becomes already somewhat discernible, for "being" is the first known (cf. 5.4.). In accordance with the order of knowledge the historical "analysis" proceeds from an extrinsic to a more intrinsic consideration of being, from a particular to a more universal. Those who were the first to inquire into the origin of things restricted themselves solely to "particular makings of beings" (*particulares factiones entium*); only later did philosophers attain to a deeper level of consideration (*S.c.G.* II, 37: *magis intrinsece rerum factionem considerantes*).

(3) In the progress of the analysis, three main phases can be distinguished.[26] Thomas's discussion of the first two relies heavily on Aris-

---

tion de l'être d'après Saint Thomas d'Aquin vol. 2, pp. 38ff.: "L'Achèvement chrétien de la réflection antique"; F. Brunner, "Über die Thomistische Lehre vom Ursprung der Welt," *Zeitschr. f. philos. Forschung* 16 (1962): 251–58; E. Gilson, *Introduction à la philosophie chrétienne* (Paris, 1960), pp. 28–44.

[25] *De pot.* 3, 5: Secundum ordinem cognitionis humanae processerunt antiqui in consideratione naturae rerum. Unde cum cognitio humana a sensu incipiens in intellectum perveniat, priores philosophi circa sensibilia fuerunt occupati, et ex his paulatim in intelligibilia pervenerunt.

[26] Only in *De subst. separ.* does Thomas distinguish four phases, because there he makes a division within the pre-Socratic first phase.

totle's expositions in *Metaph.* I and *Phys.* I. The concrete historical setting
of the third phase is not immediately clear; in the texts the place of Plato
and Aristotle especially is not unambiguous. We shall say more about this
in 5.3.2.

The first step in the historical discursion was taken by the pre-Socratics.
They inquired into the 'archè' of all things. But the first philosophers were
still so tied to the sensible that they believed only sensible, material beings
exist. They could not transcend the distinction between "substance" and
"accident." Because the accidental forms as such are sensible, they asserted that all forms are accidents and that only the matter is the substance
of things (*De pot.* 3, 5). As the principle of all things, the pre-Socratics
posited one or more primary materials which they regarded as never
having become and as incorruptible. To the extent they acknowledged
change in any of these primary materials, it consisted only in an accidental
change (as rarefaction and condensation, combination and separation).
For in this view "becoming" can be nothing other than "alteration,"
since each thing becomes from a being actually existing. These accidental
modifications of a permanent, actual substratum they attributed to causes
like "Friendship" and "Discord" (Empedocles) or "Mind" (Anaxagoras).

A second phase in the clarification of being is reached when the intellect
"resolves" the substance into its essential principles, "matter" and
"form." This distinction makes it possible to acknowledge essential
changes (*S. Th.* I, 44, 2: *secundum formas essentiales*), becomings of substances. Herein consists the great difference from the first phase of the
desire to know. For the pre-Socratics the primary matter was "actual";
therefore, becoming is for them "alteration." Later philosophers,
however, start from a primary matter which is purely potential. Through
the coming of form to this indeterminate subject, it is brought into act.
For these substantial changes ("generation") they accept more general
causes, such as the oblique circle of the sun according to Aristotle (in *De
generat.* II, 10, 336 a 32) or the Ideas according to Plato.

Thomas emphasizes in *S. Th.* I, 44, 2, however, that the decisive and
final step had not yet been taken. For there remains a subject presupposed
that is contracted through the form to a determinate species, just as a substance belonging to a certain species (e.g., "man") is contracted through
an accident (e.g., "white") to a determinate mode of being. The
philosophers of the first and second phases always considered being under
some particular aspect, namely, either as *this* being or as *such* being. As
a result, the causes, too, to which both groups attributed the becoming of
things were particular; they do not produce the total being of things. What
is put at issue is a categorical causality, a causality which is restricted to

a category of being, be it accident (as in the first phase) or substance (as in the second). Even hylomorphism is inadequate to account for the radical origin of things. Generation, whereby a form comes to matter, is "the making of a particular being," which explains the becoming of a being inasmuch as it is *this*, "but not inasmuch as it is, universally" (*non autem in quantum est ens universaliter*), because there preexisted a being that is trans-form-ed into this being (*S.c.G.* II, 37).

Why is there any being at all—why not far rather nothing? This question remains unanswered in the metaphysics of forms. It is necessary to conceive of another origin, that of universal being itself. The third and final step of the itinerary of the desire to know begins, according to Thomas (*S. Th.* I, 44, 2), only when some thinkers (*aliqui*) finally raised themselves to the consideration of being as *being* (*ens inquantum est ens*).[27] In this ultimate, metaphysical analysis that which is is reduced to its "being." These philosophers considered the causes of things not only insofar as the things are *these* beings or *such* beings but also insofar as they are *beings*. They were the only ones to have posited that reality in its totality was brought into being by the first being, God.[28] Human reflection thereby definitively transcends the categorical level of becoming, of particular causality. This procession of all being from the universal cause is not a process of becoming, because it no longer presupposes anything. To produce being absolutely pertains to the essence of creation.

From this survey of the historical way of philosophy it appears that to the three phases in the history of the consideration of being there cor-

---

[27] Who does Thomas really mean with these *aliqui*? It has been suggested that he had himself in mind. Quite a number of other possibilities are advanced as well. According to C. Fabro (*Participation et Causalité*, p. 368, n. 13), he means the "Platonici," i.e., the Neo-Platonists. A.C. Pegis ("A Note on St. Thomas, Summa Theologica I, 44, 1–2," *Mediaeval Studies* 8 (1946): 162, n. 9) believes that Thomas "has in mind those Christian thinkers who listened more to Genesis than to Platonism or to Aristotelianism." E. Gilson (*The Spirit of Mediaeval Philosophy*, pp. 438–41, n. 4; *Le Thomisme*, p. 155) maintains that Thomas means the philosopher Avicenna.

This last view seems to me to have a certain plausibility, though not for the reason Gilson gives. For he refers to the argumentation Thomas advances in *De pot.* 3, 5 for the createdness of reality. Then, however, Plato and Aristotle too could with equal reason be numbered amongst the 'aliqui', since Thomas refers to them *expressis verbis* in the first two arguments. Precisely this possibility, however, is rejected by Gilson (for the pertinent background, see 5.3.2.).

Yet there is at least one text in which Thomas says that *quidam philosophi*, such as Avicenna, have recognized on the basis of demonstration that God is the Creator of things. See *In III Sent.* 25, 1, 2 obj. 2: Deum esse unum est probabile per demonstrationem, et similiter Deum esse creatorem rerum; unde etiam quidam philosophi, *ut Avicenna*, demonstratione moti hoc concedunt.

[28] *De pot.* 3, 5: Posteriores vero philosophi, ut Plato, Aristoteles et eorum sequaces, pervenerunt ad considerationem ipsius esse universalis; et ideo ipsi soli posuerunt aliquam universalem causam rerum, a qua omnia alia in esse prodirent.

responds, in a systematic respect, a threefold distinction in the structure of being, in causality, and in "becoming." In this correspondence the 'concursus' of nature and creature becomes clear.

With regard to the *structure of being*, the analysis yields successively the distinctions between substance and accident, matter and form, and essence and being (*esse*). It is against this background that the fact that in Thomas the structure of that which is has become threefold ('subiectum—essentia—esse') must be understood.

With regard to (efficient) *causality*, there is the progression from a particular towards a universal cause, God. What Thomas sketches here agrees with the earlier finding that there are three grades of causes, distinguished by the degree of generalness (3.7.4).

With regard to "*becoming*", what is discerned successively is accidental change (*alteratio*), substantial change (*generatio*), and the *emanatio* of being. This triad is summarized in *In VIII Phys.*, lect. 2, 975:

> The first philosophers considered only the causes of accidental changes, as they were of the opinion that "to become" is "to be altered". Subsequent thinkers arrived at a knowledge of substantial changes. Later philosophers, however, like Plato and Aristotle, arrived at the knowledge of the principle of all being.[29]

In these different modes of "becoming", the distinct originations of *nature* and *creature* take shape.

(4) It is of importance, finally, to underscore Thomas's objective in presenting the history of human reflection on the origin of things. In *De subst. separ.*, c. 9 his intention is to oppose the idea that the separated substances have no cause of their being (cf. 3.5.1.); in *S. Th.* I, 44, 2 the historical survey serves as an answer to the question "Whether primary matter is created by God, or is an independent co-ordinate principle with Him?" For the historical way of the desire to know terminates in Thomas's view in the idea of creation. It is this moment that needs to be elaborated first of all.

5.3. *"By the way of faith"*—*"By the way of reason"*

In Thomas's version of the history of the inquiry concerning being, the idea of creation is placed in the framework of a gradual advancement in thought. What is followed is *sola rationis via*. The idea of creation ap-

---

[29] *In VIII Phys.*, lect. 2, 975: Quorum [sc. philosophorum] primi consideraverunt causas solarum mutationum accidentalium, ponentes fieri esse alterari; sequentes vero pervenerunt ad cognitionem mutationum substantialium; postremi vero, ut Plato et Aristoteles, perveniunt ad cognoscendum principium totius esse.

pears as the result, yes the crowning of the *internal* development of the
desire to know. Thomas speaks of "the philosophers entering more deeply
into the problem of the origin of things" (*S.c.G.* II, 37).

But that the world is created by God is for the Christian an integral part
of his confession. "Through faith we understand that the worlds were
framed by God, so that things which are seen were not made of things
which do appear" (Hebrews 11:3). The createdness of reality is revealed
per viam fidei.[30] How, in Thomas, is the way of faith related to the way of
reason?

5.3.1. *Creation as an article of faith*

In his commentary on the Apostle's Creed (*In Symbolum Apostolorum*,
c.3) Thomas writes: "For us it is beyond doubt that all that is in the world
is through God." "For us" is an indication of the "we" community of
Christians. The Christian knows from and in his faith that God is the
Creator of heaven and earth, that all is from Him. This confession is
fundamental for the Christian orientation to reality. The world finds its
origin and end not in itself but is, precisely as creational, constituted in
a permanent dependence upon and directedness to the Origin.

The religious-ethical significance of this relation to God is summarized
by Thomas in this commentary in five points. Belief in creation first
brings man to knowledge of the divine majesty, which arouses the fear of
God in his heart; in the second place, it leads him to works of gratitude:
because God is the Creator of all things, it is certain that all we are and
all we have are from Him; thirdly, it gives him patience in adversity, for
God will order all things for good; in the fourth place, belief in creation
obliges man to stewardship, to the correct use of things: for we must use
the creaturely for the ends for which God made it; finally, this belief brings
man to an understanding of his dignity: for God has made all for man and
purposed man to serve Him.[31]

That the relation God-world is one of the Creator to his creature is
therefore not in the first place the result of philosophical 'theoria' but a
matter of *faith* in Revelation. The knowledge of faith affords an insight
which according to Thomas ancient philosophy was never able to achieve.
"Not one philosopher, for all his efforts, was able before the coming of

---

[30] The expressions 'sola rationis via' and 'per viam fidei' can be found in *S.c.G.* I, 4.
[31] *In Symbolum Apostolorum*, c. 3: Ex hujusmodi autem consideratione homo dirigitur ad
quinque. *Primo* ad cognitionem divinae majestatis... *Secundo* ex hoc dirigitur ad gratiarum
actionem... *Tertio* inducitur ad patientiam in adversis... *Quarto* inducimur ad recte utendum rebus creatis... *Quinto* dirigimur ex hoc ad considerationem magnitudinis et dignita-
tis humanae...

Christ to know as much about God and the things necessary for eternal life as an old woman knows through her faith after the coming of Christ (*In Symbolum Apostolorum*, c. 2).

Aquinas himself clearly outlines the distance between the Biblical idea of creation and Greek reflection about the origin of reality, in his treatise on the articles of faith (*De articulis fidei et ecclesiae sacramentis*). In speaking there of the creation of things, he sums up six errors. The first three of these are of special interest to us because they indict the doctrines of the great Greek philosophers.[32]

The first error is that of Democritus and Epicurus. The view of these materialists may be summarized as follows: they know not only no "creation" but also no divine "formation", i.e., the imposition of order and form upon preexistent matter by a transcendent Mind. For they maintained "that neither the matter of the world nor the world itself was composed by God, but that the world was made casually (*casu*) by the convergence of indivisible bodies (atoms) which they regarded as the principles of things. Against them Psalm 32:6 says: 'By the word of the Lord were the heavens made', which is to say according to eternal reason, not however by chance."[33]

The second error is that of Plato and Anaxagoras, "who maintained that the world was made by God but from preexistent matter. Against them Psalm 148:5 says: 'He commanded, and they were created', i.e., made out of nothing." The purport is clear: Plato and Anaxagoras do know a "formation", but no "creation". The question concerning the origin of reality is posed, but not yet radically and totally enough. With regard to Plato, this inadequacy is an ever recurring theme in Thomas's writings. When in *De verit.* 3,5 he raises the question: "Whether first matter has an Idea in God", his answer begins thus: "Plato in the dialogue *De natura*—i.e., the *Timaeus*—has not posited an Idea of first matter, because he maintained that Ideas are the causes of the ideated; first matter, however, was not caused by an Idea but was itself cause, according to him." Thomas goes on to formulate his counterposition with a certain personal emphasis: "We, however, maintain that matter is caused by God; therefore it must be maintained that in some way the Idea of it is in God." A second example may be found in Thomas's

---

[32] Not in order here is the question whether Thomas's interpretation can be called legitimate from the standpoint of modern historical research; the issue primarily at stake is *his* view of ancient philosophy.

For a modern assessment, see C. J. de Vogel, "De Griekse wijsbegeerte en het Christelijk Scheppingsbegrip", in *Theoria, Studies over de Griekse wijsbegeerte* (Assen, 1967), pp. 188–202.

[33] Cf. *Super Ioannem* c. 1, lect. 1, 65.

commentary on the second book of the *Sententiae* (1,1,1); it expresses the distance with equal clarity. Anaxagoras and Plato did not consider an efficient cause to be the principle of matter, although—so Thomas simply establishes—there is such an agent. Plato, moreover, added yet a third originating principle to the Demiurge and first matter, namely, the exemplary Forms: "Through these three the world and the things of which the world consists are caused."[34]

The third error that Thomas sums up in this treatise is that of Aristotle, "who was of the opinion that the world has been made by God but is from eternity. Against this Genesis 1:1 says 'In the beginning, God created the heaven and the earth'." Aristotle does not acknowledge that the created world has a beginning.[35]

The dominant impression one gains from this text is that the Biblical idea of creation is contrasted to what the Greek philosophers thought about the origin of reality. Thomas acknowledges the fundamental discontinuity. The "anti-thesis" appears also in the formal structure of this text: over against the errors of the philosophers Thomas always posits a Bible text: "Against them it is said" (*contra quos dicitur*). It is good to bear in mind that the thirteenth century was not only the century of the introduction of the complete Aristotle but at the same time—as CHENU has pointed out in various studies—the century of renewed interest in and study of the Bible.[36]

In this section we have referred especially to those works of Thomas (*De articulis fidei, In Symbolum Apostolorum*) in which he speaks of the creation *per viam fidei*. That all things are from God is for Thomas in the first place a truth of faith, more certain in its nature than any rational truth whatsoever.[37]

---

[34] Cf. *In II Sent.* 1, 1 exp. textus: Sciendum quod in hoc Plato erravit, quia posuit formas exemplares per se subsistentes extra intellectum divinum, et neque ipsas neque materiam a Deo esse habere.

[35] Cf. the exposition that stems from the same period as *De articulis fidei*, i.e., *In Decretalem I Expositio ad archidiaconum Tridentinum*: Alius error fuit Aristotelis ponentis quidem omnia a Deo producta esse, sed ab aeterno, et nullum fuisse principium temporis; cum tamen scriptum sit Gen. 1:1 "In principio creavit Deus coelum et terram." Thus here, too, Thomas argues that Aristotle erred, but only regarding the eternity of the world. We shall return to Thomas's own view of the idea of creation in relation to the eternity of the world in 5.3.2.

[36] See, e.g., M. D. Chenu, *Introduction*, pp. 199ff.

[37] *S. Th.* II–II, 4, 8 ad 2: Multo magis homo certior est de eo, quod audit a Deo, qui falli non potest, quam de eo, quod videt propria ratione quae falli potest.

5.3.2. *Creation as a truth of reason: Christian philosophy?*

To believe implies, however, no "sacrifice of the intellect." The truth of faith asks for articulation, clarification, explication, and, to the extent possible, insight: What is contained in the idea of creation, what does it mean that things are creaturely? *Fides quaerens intellectum*, this renowned motto of Anselm of Canterbury (d. 1109), which is often regarded as the distinguishing feature of medieval philosophy, has also been seen as the guideline of Thomas's work.[38] Yet such a general typology entails the risk of weakening the distinctiveness of Thomas's way of thought. Precisely with regard to the idea of creation, as was already indicated in 5.2., the 'intellectus' acquires a pregnant sense in Aquinas.

Thomas asserts the rational demonstrability of the creation. "I answer that not only faith holds but also reason proves there is creation" (*Respondeo quod creationem esse non tantum fides tenet, sed etiam ratio demonstrat*).[39] This conviction was relatively new in medieval thought. Thomas's teacher Albert the Great, for example, was of the opinion that this insight can be acquired not through philosophical reflection but only from Revelation.[40] In his student, a significant development appears. After Thomas has described the history of human thought about the question of being in *De pot.* 3, 5, he continues: "The statement of the Catholic belief [that all things are created by God] can be proven by three arguments." These arguments, derived from Plato, Aristotle, and Avicenna, were presented in 3.7.3. Thomas ends the argumentation with the conclusion: "Thus reason proves and faith holds that all things are created by God."

In re-tracing Thomas's way of thought, the question concerning the order of faith and reason is inescapable. What is the significance of Christian faith for philosophical discourse? No one who asks this question can disregard the important interpretation of E. GILSON.

GILSON opens his work *The Spirit of Mediaeval Philosophy* with the statement, "It would be hard to imagine any expression more naturally apt to occur to the mind of the historian of mediaeval thought than *Christian philosophy.*"[41] It is on the basis of historical considerations that GILSON

---

[38] It is the subtitle of B. A. M. Barendse's monograph about Thomas Aquinas: *Een geloof op zoek naar inzicht* (Baarn, 1968).

[39] *In II Sent.* 1, 2.

[40] A. Rohner, *Das Schöpfungsproblem bei Moses Maimonides, Albertus Magnus und Thomas von Aquin, Ein Beitrag zur Geschichte des Schöpfungsproblems im Mittelalter* (Münster, 1913), p. 137.

[41] For the idea of Christian philosophy in E. Gilson, see M. C. Smit's dissertation, *Christendom en Historie* (Kampen, 1950), pp. 142–45 (Eng. tr.: *The Relation between Christianity and History in the Present-day Roman Catholic Conception of History*, tr. by Herbert Donald Morton, Toronto: Wedge Publishing Foundation, forthcoming). In addition to the litera-

arrived at the idea of a Christian philosophy. Elsewhere[42] he reports that
through the study of the history of philosophy, especially that of the
Middle Ages, the conviction grew in him that a special relation exists
between Christianity and philosophy. How has it come about, he asked
himself, that the thought of the Middle Ages is so different from that of
the Greeks? This originality cannot be explained, according to GILSON,
without taking into account the influence exercised by Christianity. In the
work mentioned, he undertakes to substantiate this thesis. He intends to
show with the help of various themes that medieval thought produced
significant renewals in the field of philosophy; important examples of
these are the idea of God (cf. 3.5.3 on the metaphysics of Exodus) and the
idea of creation. These innovations are inconceivable apart from "the
Christian input." Thus it can be said that medieval philosophy is a
"Christian philosophy" as "conceptual translation of what I believe to be
an observable historical object."

What matters now is to determine more precisely the nature of the relation between Christianity and philosophy. There are various philosophies
which have been influenced by Christianity but which are not yet therefore Christian. GILSON desires more: philosophy must be really leavened
with Christian faith if there is to be an intrinsic connection between the
two terms of the expression: "One will never be able to say that here the
philosophical ends and the Christian begins; Christian philosophy will be
integrally Christian and integrally philosophy, or it will not be."[43] His
definition of Christian philosophy is, finally: "If it is to deserve that name
the supernatural must descend as a constitutive element not, of course,
into its texture which would be a contradiction, but into the work of its
construction. Thus I call Christian, every philosophy which, although
keeping the two orders formally distinct, nevertheless considers the Christian revelation as an indispensable auxiliary to reason."[44] Through
Revelation the Christian philosopher is put in possession of a truth of
faith; his reason accepts this as an indispensable aid and transforms it into
a "condition of rationality." Distinctive of Christian philosophy is a
"revelation generating reason."[45]

---

ture mentioned there, note may be made of A. Renard, *La querelle sur la possibilité de la philosophie chrétienne* (Paris, 1941), pp. 37–44; E. Gilson, "La possibilité philosophique de la philosophie chrétienne", *Revue des Sciences religieuses* 32 (1958): 168–96; E. Gilson, *Introduction à la philosophie chrétienne* (Paris, 1960).

[42] *Bulletin de la Société Française de Philosophie* 31 (1931): 72.
[43] *Ibid.*, p. 46.
[44] *The Spirit of Mediaeval Philosophy*, p. 37.
[45] *Bulletin*, p. 39.

In this sense Thomism too has a right to that title.[46] A fine specimen of it is the idea of creation. Thomas seeks as a philosopher to make rationally demonstrable through a process of transformation what was initially only an insight of faith.

GILSON's idea of a Christian philosophy has not gone unchallenged from the Thomist side. At a gathering of the "Société thomiste" MANDONNET argued that Christianity has changed the world, to be sure, but not transformed philosophy.[47]

GILSON: Where did St. Thomas find the idea of creation? In the Greeks? Where did he get it?

MANDONNET: It is he who constituted it. But he knew very well the Neoplatonic theory of emanation, for he gave as title to his treatise on creation: *De emanatione rerum a Deo.*

GILSON: Before him there is still the book of Genesis, from which he quotes...

MANDONNET: Genesis is of no concern to us as philosophers...[48]

Against this extrinsic view GILSON sets his idea of Christian philosophy, in order to express the significance of Christian Revelation for thought. His great merit has been to place Thomas's philosophy were it must be situated: within the perspective of the Christian experience of faith. Faith is of concern to the philosopher because it provides an insight that gives direction to his orientation to reality. It is not for nothing that "above" the history of the question of being (*De pot.* 3,5 sed contra) there stands written the Bible text from Romans 11:36. *Per viam fidei* Thomas "knows" that from, through, and to God are all things.[49]

At the same time, however, we want to point out another crucial moment in GILSON's interpretation, a moment that evokes a tension in his idea of Christian philosophy.[50] The order of faith and the order of thought remain—and must remain—expressly distinguished. Faith is not, as faith, the constitutive point of departure of philosophical reflection: Christian faith is super-natural. Should faith enter into theoretical

---

[46] Characteristic is the title of Gilson's work *Le Thomisme* in the authorized English translation: *The Christian Philosophy of St. Thomas Aquinas*, tr. L. K. Shook (New York, 1956).

[47] In *La philosophie chrétienne - Journées d'Etudes de la Société Thomiste* (Juvisy, 1933), p. 67.

[48] *Ibid.*, pp. 71–72.

[49] Cf. also section 1.7.2., where over against Averroës' view that man's happiness is to be "continued" with the lowest of the separated substances, Thomas asserts: "Fides autem recta ponit ultimam beatitudinem hominis esse in solo Deo" (*De spirit. creat.* q. un., a. 10); and section 3.7.4.: "secundum fidem catholicam dicitur, quod nihil fit temere sive fortuito in mundo" (*In VI Metaph.*, lect. 3, 1216).

[50] Cf. my study "Uit God zijn alle dingen", *Philos. Reform.* 39 (1974): 145ff.

thought, then rational discourse would be de-natured as a result. For philosophy is founded, so Thomas says, on the natural light of reason; from the principles of faith (*ex principiis fidei*) something is proven in the eyes of the faithful, from principles which are naturally known (*ex principiis naturaliter notis*) something is proven in the eyes of all.[51] Since the Moslems and the pagans do not agree with us in accepting the authority of Scripture, "we must have recourse to the natural reason, to which all men are forced to give their assent."[52] This "recourse" governs the way of the historical reason, which ends in the idea of creation. Yet, with the rational proof of the creation, is not precisely the intrinsically Christian character of the idea of creation abolished?

For the question thus raised, it will be useful to have another look at the history of the question of being as Thomas has sketched it. It is among other things the idea of creation that, in the judgment not only of GILSON, distinguishes medieval thought as Christian philosophy in a fundamental way from ancient thought. But how is this to be rhymed with the fact that on such a cardinal point Thomas's placement of Plato and Aristotle is sometimes far from clear?

In *S. Th.* I, 44, 2 he situates them in the second phase of the still particular consideration of being. Or must we be more cautious and say that Aquinas borrows examples for this second stage from Plato and Aristotle? For in some parallel texts the thought of these two protagonists of ancient philosophy is assigned to the third and decisive stage. In the practically contemporaneous disputation *De pot.* 3,5 we read: "Later philosophers, as Plato, Aristotle, and their followers, arrived at the consideration of universal being itself." In *De subst. separ.*, c. 9 Thomas states that *secundum sententiam Platonis et Aristotelis* it is necessary to posit a higher mode of becoming than generation. And in Thomas's commentary on the *Phys.* (VIII, lect. 2), it is said straightforwardly: "Plato and Aristotle arrived at the knowledge of the principle of all being."

SERTILLANGES disposes of this question rather facilely when he writes: "The generalness of these historical classifications, which in themselves were of little interest to our author, leaves room for some vagueness."[53] GILSON took this difficulty more seriously, and not without reason, since his whole idea of Christian philosophy is at stake here. "Surprise is sometimes expressed that St. Thomas should attribute the idea of creation to Plato and Aristotle. But in fact he did nothing of the sort."[54] Thomas's

---

[51] *S. Th.* II–II, 1, 5 ad 2.
[52] *S. c. G.* I, 2.
[53] *Somme Théologique I, 44–49: La Création* (Paris, 1927), p. 237.
[54] *The Spirit of Mediaeval Philosophy*, p. 439.

authentic position is that of the *Summa Theologiae*: the other texts must be harmonized with it. Such a harmonization is possible, GILSON thinks, if *esse* is regarded as having sometimes a strict (and specifically Thomist) sense, that of existing, and at other times a broad (and Aristotelian) sense, i.e., that of substantial being. It is then possible for Thomas to say without contradicting himself that "Aristotle had elevated himself to a first *causa totius esse* in the sense of substantial being."[55] But is this solution really reconcilable with the text in the *Physica*? For does this text not clearly distinguish three phases in the history of the question of being: consideration of the accidental changes, then of the substantial ones, and finally the position of Plato and Aristotle, who arrived at the knowledge of the principle of all being?

Certainly Thomas presents a benign interpretation here. For we saw in 5.3.1. that he regards Plato's conception of the origin as an error. But the fact of this interpretation indicates that Thomas views the philosophical tradition somewhat differently from GILSON. The "motive" of the historical 'via' is the natural desire to know, the reduction to that whereby being as being is intelligible. "Creation" is incorporated into the consideration of being as being—a genuine Aristotelian formulation—and interpreted as "participation" (3.6.2.). Because of the philosophical transformation of the originally religious idea of creation, this can be presented as a "higher," more intelligible moment in the reflection on being. At the same time more emphasis thereby comes to lie on the element of continuity than was the case in Thomas's writings on the articles of Christian faith. This continuity lessens the distance from ancient thought and makes it possible to accord Plato and Aristotle "virtually" a share in the definitive solution of the question of being. Thus in *De pot.* 3, 5 the createdness of the world is proven by three arguments, which according to Thomas himself are derived from non-Christian philosophers. The "demonstration" of the creation is an indication of the increasing autonomy of (natural) thought within the religiously founded unity of the experience of reality.

Something else points in the same direction. It is striking that Thomas develops a twofold notion of "creation," a philosophical and a Christian one. He introduces such a distinction in *In II Sent.* 1, 1, 2: "If we accept as belonging to the essence of creation that the created, with respect to duration, too, has non-being prior to being, then the creation cannot be demonstrated, nor is it conceded by the philosophers, but is maintained through faith" (*nec a philosophis conceditur, sed per fidem supponitur*). This

---

[55] *Le Thomisme*, p. 155, n. 6.

duality is expressed still more clearly when later in his commentary on the *Sententiae* Thomas formulates an objection to the fact that creation is a part of the Christian confession of faith. Articles of faith cannot be proven demonstratively. Still, some philosophers, like Avicenna, have recognized on the basis of demonstration that God is the Creator. In his reply, Thomas points out that the philosophers did not know that God is the Creator in the sense in which faith maintains that this is so, namely, that heaven and earth were brought into being after they once were not.[56] This insight of faith remains "outside" philosophy. The philosopher can, indeed, make the *origin* of the world, that is, its being's dependence, rationally transparent, but not its *beginning*. A principle of duration does not belong to the essence of creation *unless* creation is taken as faith takes it.[57]

Against complaints of contemporaries (*contra murmurantes*) Thomas maintains—even devoting a separate writing to it—that, from a philosophical point of view, the createdness of the world, i.e., the relation of total dependence, is not incompatible with the eternity of the world. The world is not necessarily from eternity (against Aristotle); by the same token, however, the notion of creation also does not necessarily entail a "beginning." That the world began is an object of faith but not of science or demonstration (*credibile, non autem scibile vel demonstrabile*); the temporal beginning is a datum of faith, is upheld by faith alone (*sola fide*); it cannot be proved demonstratively (*S. Th.* I, 46, 2).

Sola fide. Yet it must be observed that here the moment of faith is first made explicit in order to complete what philosophy was not able to do. Does this not give the impression that the relation between faith and reason is determined from a framework structured in the first instance by thought? It is only at the *end* of the way of reason that faith begins. This conclusion can be corroborated in a still more systematic manner.

5.3.3. *"Reason," "faith," and "vision"*

To clarify Thomas's view of the relation of faith and reason, it is instructive to have a look at the methodical plan and structure of his *Summa contra Gentiles*. In I, 9 he presents it in these terms: "We shall first seek to make known the truth which faith professes and reason investigates. This we shall do by bringing forward both demonstrative and probable arguments . . . whereby the truth is confirmed and the adversary convinced." In this way, *per viam rationis*, he will proceed in the first three books.

---

[56] *In III Sent.* 25, 1, 2 ad 2.

[57] *De pot.* 3, 14: De ratione vero creationis est habere principium originis, non autem durationis; *nisi* accipiendo creationem ut accipit fides.

"Then, in order to follow the progress from the more manifest to the less manifest, we shall proceed to make known that truth which surpasses reason." This "truth of faith" he will explain in the fourth book.[58]

In the beginning of this book (IV, 1), Thomas considers again the order followed. He now gives a more fundamental motivation that is of great importance. "Because man's perfect good is to know God in some manner, a certain way (*quaedam via*) is given to man whereby he can ascend to the knowledge of God." The direction of this way is determined by the circulation motif. "The perfections of things descend in a certain order from the vertex, God" (cf. 4.4.1.). Man's way is therefore "that he, beginning from the lower and gradually ascending, arrive at knowledge of God. For it is also so with regard to corporeal movements [Thomas here refers to Aristotle's *Phys.* III (202 a 19)] that the way up is identical with the way down, even though they are distinct as to beginning and end."

Yet the knowledge of God to which man can attain along this way is very imperfect; the reason for this is that his intellect is dependent upon sense experience (cf. 5.3.4.). Therefore God out of his immeasurable goodness has revealed to man some truths about Himself that transcend the intellect. In this revelation there exists a certain order, in the sense that here too man advances gradually from the imperfect to the perfect. At the outset the truths are so revealed to man that they are not understood but only believed by him. At the end, however, he will be elevated to insight into what has been revealed.

Human knowledge of the divine is accordingly threefold. The first is the 'via ascensus': man ascends by the natural light of reason by means of the creaturely to the knowledge of God (*prima est secundum quod homo naturali lumine rationis per creaturas in Dei cognitionem ascendit*). The second is the 'via descensus': the divine truth which transcends the intellect descends by means of revelation to man, "not, however, as demonstrated so as to be seen, but as spoken so as to be believed" (*non tamen quasi demonstrata ad videndum, sed quasi sermone prolata ad credendum*). For faith is, according to Romans 10:17, "by hearing." The third is the elevation of the human mind to perfect insight into what has been revealed (*tertia est secundum quod mens humana elevatur ad ea quae sunt revelata perfecte intuenda*). The first Truth is then known not as believed but as seen.

Reason, faith, and vision: the knowledge of faith is midway. In the

---

[58] *S.c.G.* I, 9: Primum nitemur ad manifestationem illius veritatis quam fides profitetur et ratio investigat, inducentes rationes demonstrativas et probabiles ... per quas veritas confirmetur et adversarius convincatur. Deinde, ut a manifestioribus ad minus manifesta fiat processus, ad illius veritatis manifestationem procedemus quae rationem excedit ... veritatem fidei declarantes.

remainder of this section we shall first concentrate on its relation to reason.

For "human philosophy" and "Christian faith" the creaturely is a subject of consideration in different manners, Thomas emphasizes in *S.c.G.* II, 4. The philosopher considers what belongs to creatures in virtue of their own nature (*natura propria*); the believer considers only what belongs to them according as they are related to God—for instance, that they are created by God (*utpote quod sunt a Deo creata*). They also proceed according to different principles. The philosopher takes his argument from the things' own causes, the believer from the first cause. As a result there is also a different order. Philosophy considers first the creatures in themselves and proceeds from there to the knowledge of God; in the doctrine of faith the order is reversed (*primo est consideratio Dei, et postmodum creaturarum*).

What is striking in this elaboration is that all the emphasis is placed on what is distinctive of the "philosopher" and of the "believer." Thus there are in Thomas two approaches between which he wishes to make a careful distinction: a descending from God and an ascending from nature. The ascent bears the mark of the history of the question of being that Thomas sketches. The statement of faith does not enter in any way into the philosophical argumentation. And indeed, structurally, there is also no place for it. For Thomas *himself* has correlated the historical way to the progress of human knowledge: proceeding from the sensible, it arrives at the intelligible. The idea of creation acquires relief only from the analysis of what is, for the natural reason, "prior."

Yet there is identity in the twofold movement. In *S.c.G.* IV, 1 Thomas states: "the natural reason ascends through the creatures to knowledge of God, the knowledge of faith descends, in contrast, through the divine revelation, from God to us; the way of ascent is however the same as the way of descent (*est autem eadem via ascensus et descensus*)." This identity was used as an argument earlier in this chapter, as we saw, but then with another import: man's ascent to God is a counterpart of the *ontological* descent of the perfections. Now the drift is that the ascent of reason is identical with the descent of revelation. This is a matter of fundamental confidence in Thomas. Yet what guarantee is there of this identity?

For the moment (see also 5.4.2.) we can establish that the posited identity is possible without a *cognitive* illumination of the human reason by faith (and by the knowledge that belongs to faith). Absent too is the conviction that faith is the precondition and starting point for the way of reason in the sense of the 'Fides quaerens intellectum'—the traditional order, as one finds it expressed in Bonaventure, for example, with deliberate criticism of the philosophers.[59] Man can, of his own power, by the natural light of reason, arrive at truth about God and the creaturely. This knowledge falls as such outside faith, for what is believed is not seen (*S. Th.* II – II, 1, 5: "All objects of science must needs be, in a manner, seen").[60] What belongs in the strict sense to the domain of faith is that which transcends reason, i.e., the so-called mysteries.

That is not to say, however, that it was superfluous that truths understandable to reason were also revealed *per viam fidei*. For (5.1.) the way of reason is marked by multiplicity since it gathers the intelligible truth from many sensible things; is changeable since it advances discursively from one thing to another; and is defectible (*S.c.G.* III, 91). It is given only to a few to follow this way to the end; moreover, the way of reason requires a great deal of time and is full of error. If the only way open to us for the knowledge of God were that of reason (*sola rationis via*), the human race would remain in the blackest shadows of ignorance. That is why it was necessary for salvation that *per viam fidei* the unshakable certitude and pure truth concerning divine things be made known to men.[61]

But the principal importance of Christian faith will be found to lie for Thomas precisely in its position midway between reason and the third way of knowing God, the vision.

5.3.4. The "distress" of philosophy and the liberation through faith

"All men by nature desire to know because it is desirable for each thing to be united to its principle." The ultimate end of human life is the union of man's intellect with the origin. As principles of the human intellect, the separated substances were posited (1.7.1.). Thomas's reinterpretation of the circulation motif required a differentiation within these substances (1.7.2.). For him only God, the creating Origin of all, can be the ultimate end of man, which is called happiness. "Therefore the ultimate happiness of every intellectual substance is to know God" (*S.c.G.* III, 25).

The central question is accordingly whether human life can actually attain happiness, i.e., reach its highest perfection through union with the Origin. For philosophers this question means: Can the separated substances be attained through the human desire to know? In Thomas's reinterpretation this problem becomes even more pressing: Can the natu-

---

[59] See his sermon "Christus unus omnium magister," n. 15 (*Opera Omnia* V, p. 571).

[60] See this entire question ('Utrum ea quae sunt fidei possint esse scita'). Cf. *S. Th.* I, 12, 13 ad 3.

[61] *S.c.G.* I, 4. Cf. *In Boeth. De trin.*, prol.: Et ideo deus humano generi aliam tutam viam cognitionis providit, suam notitiam mentibus hominum per fidem infundens.

ral desire be fulfilled in the knowledge of God, who "transcends all separated substances" (*S.c.G.* III, 47)? Aquinas himself observes with regard to this question that philosophers and theologians here stand before the same difficulty: "the distance between our intellect and the divine essence or the other separated substances."[62]

In *De verit.* 18, 5 ad 8 Thomas writes that Aristotle left unresolved the question whether the human intellect can attain knowledge of the essences of the separated substances. In his opinion, however, the question must be answered in the negative. This negative answer stems from the specifically human mode of being—spirit in a body—and the mode of knowing based upon it (5.1.). As rational soul, man is dependent upon sense experience. From sensible things reason—including the historical reason (cf. 5.2.)—must gather the knowledge of the intelligible. Science extends only as far as sensible knowledge can lead. Not that the senses are the total cause of science, yet they do provide the material for the discursive reason. From this it follows that the separated substances—immaterial and therefore not knowable by the senses—cannot really be known by man. All that can be known of them on the basis of the visible effects is *that* they are.

This conclusion agrees with what was established in the first chapter. There it was found (1.3.4. and 1.9.) that with regard to simple substances another mode of questioning is required. With respect to them, the katallel structure of the question leaves only this room: of the sensible substance composed of form and matter, the extrinsic cause is sought. This cause functions as answer to the question "if" (*an est*) separated substances exist. The question "what" they are must remain unanswered. Knowledge of their essence remains hidden.[63]

This statute of human knowing is the reason why Thomas in *S. Th.* I–II, 3, 6 asserts that man's perfect happiness cannot consist essentially in the knowledge of the speculative sciences, in philosophical 'theoria'.[64] However, so it is remarked in the second objection of this text, that which is naturally desired by all for its own sake seems to be man's ultimate happiness. Now, such is the knowledge of the theoretical sciences; for as it is said in *Metaph.* I, "all men by nature desire to know"; and shortly thereafter (c. 2) it is added that the theoretical sciences are sought for their own sake. Thomas's response is: "By nature we desire, not only perfect happiness, but also any likeness or participation of it."

---

[62] *In IV Sent.* 49, 2, 1.

[63] *In Boeth. De trin.* 6, 4: Et ideo per nullam scientiam speculativam potest sciri de aliqua substantia separata *quid est*. Cf. *S. Th.* I, 88, 1; *De verit.* 18, 5.

[64] *S. Th.* I–II, 3, 6: Perfecta ergo beatitudo in consideratione scientiarum speculativarum essentialiter consistere non potest.

The desire to know is not fulfilled in scientific knowledge. Through philosophical consideration not true happiness is reached but a likeness of it, i.e., an imperfect realization. The highest knowledge of God which philosophers can attain is the knowledge *that* He is, that He is the extrinsic cause of composed being, even that He is the creating cause.[65] In such knowledge, however, the natural desire to know cannot come to rest. Its end must consist in the knowledge of God which leaves nothing more to be desired.[66]

Man's perfect happiness can only consist in the contemplation of God's essence, in the vision of God (*visio Dei*), in the knowledge of the first cause, in which the answer to the question "*what* this is" is seen. This conclusion Thomas draws in *S. Th.* I – II, 3, 8—a text we quoted at the end of ch. 1.

> If therefore the human intellect knows the essence of some created effect and knows of God only "that He is" (*an est*), then the perfection of that intellect does not yet reach the first cause absolutely, and there still remains in it the natural desire to inquire into the cause. Hence it is not yet perfectly happy.
>
> Consequently, for perfect happiness the intellect must reach the very essence of the first cause. Thus it will have its perfection through its union with God as with that object in which alone man's happiness consists.[67]

With this conclusion, philosophy is caught in a grave crisis. The means at its disposal are inadequate to the final end. There appears to be an unbridgeable discrepancy between the terminus of the 'via ascensus' of reason (the first knowledge of God of *S.c.G.* IV, 1) and the beatific vision of God (the third knowledge of God mentioned there). Philosophy offers no prospect of a fulfillment of human life.

Thomas discusses at length in *S.c.G.* III, 41f. Aristotle's solution and the solutions of the Greek commentators and Arab philosophers.

But someone might say that, since happiness is the good of the intellectual

---

[65] *S.c.G.* III, 49: Per effectus enim de Deo cognoscimus *quia est*, et quod causa aliorum est ...; et hoc est ultimum et perfectissimum nostrae cognitionis in hac vita. Unde Dionysius dicit quod Deo quasi ignoto conjungimur; quod quidem contingit dum de Deo quid non sit cognoscimus, quid vero sit penitus manet ignotum.

[66] *S.c.G.* III, 39: Illa igitur cognitio Dei essentialiter est ipsa felicitas, qua habita, non restabit alicujus scibilis desideranda cognitio. Talis autem non est cognitio quam philosophi per demonstrationes de Deo habere potuerunt, quia adhuc, illa cognitione habita, alia desideramus scire quae per hanc cognitionem nondum sciuntur.

[67] *S. Th.* I – II, 3, 8. Si igitur intellectus humanus, cognoscens essentiam alicujus effectus creati, non cognoscat de Deo nisi "an est"; nondum perfectio ejus attingit simpliciter ad causam primam, sed remanet ei adhuc naturale desiderium inquirendi causam. Unde nondum est perfecte beatus. Ad perfectam igitur beatitudinem requiritur quod intellectus pertingat ad ipsam essentiam primae causae. Et sic perfectionem suam habebit per unionem ad Deum sicut ad objectum, in quo solo beatitudo hominis consistit.

nature, perfect and true happiness is for those in whom the intellectual nature is perfect, namely, in separated substances, and that in man it is imperfect, and by a kind of participation . . . Therefore neither is happiness, in its perfect nature, possible for man; but he has a certain participation of it, even in this life. This seems to have been Aristotle's opinion about happiness. Hence . . . he concludes that those who in this life attain to this perfection are happy *as men*, as though not attaining to happiness absolutely, but in a human manner.[68]

Aristotle's solution is that of resignation. Man attains happiness only in a manner that is possible for him, i.e., incompletely and imperfectly. Alexander of Aphrodisias and Averroës therefore posited that man's ultimate happiness does not consist in scientific knowledge but in the knowledge which is through "continuation" with the separated substance (1.7.2.). They were of the opinion that this is possible for man in this life. Aristotle realized, however, that in this dispensation there is no other human knowledge than that of the theoretical sciences. Therefore he maintained that man does not reach perfect happiness. His solution is telling for the "distress" and "despair" of philosophy. Thomas concludes in *S.c.G.* III, 48: "Hence it becomes sufficiently clear how these great minds suffered from being so straitened on every side."[69] Can we "be freed from these straits" (*ibid.*)?

If the natural desire to know remains ultimately unfulfillable, then man can at no time attain perfect happiness, and human life can never achieve its end.

That, however, is in the first place un-reasonable. Human existence cannot be without meaning and purpose. In the text just cited from *S.c.G.* III, 48, Thomas brings Aristotle's own principles to bear against him: "Natural desire cannot be empty, since 'nature does nothing in vain'. But nature's desire would be empty if it could never be fulfilled. Therefore man's natural desire can be fulfilled . . ." On the basis of this consideration Thomas states repeatedly: "we must conclude that it is *possible* for the divine substance to be seen through the intellect."[70] Because of the re-

---

[68] *S.c.G.* III, 48: Potest autem aliquis dicere quod, quum felicitas sit bonum intellectualis naturae, perfecta et vera felicitas est illorum in quibus natura intellectualis perfecta invenitur, id est in substantiis separatis. In hominibus autem invenitur imperfecta per modum participationis cujusdam . . . Unde nec felicitas, secundum suam perfectam rationem, potest omnibus hominibus adesse; sed aliquid ipsius participant, etiam in hac vita. Et haec videtur fuisse sententia Aristotelis de felicitate; unde in *I Ethic.* (c. 14) . . . concludit illos quibus talis perfectio in hac vita adest, esse beatos ut homines, quasi non simpliciter ad felicitatem pertingentes, sed modo humano.

[69] Likewise in *S.c.G.* IV, 54: Et sic circa inquisitionem beatitudinis homo tepesceret, *ipsa desperatione detentus.*

[70] *S.c.G.* III, 51: Quum autem impossibile sit naturale desiderium esse inane . . .

ceding horizon a kind of dialectic has arisen in the natural desire to know. Even though fulfillment of the desire in the 'visio' is philosophically impossible, the very phenomenon nonetheless indicates a priori its possibility. This basic confidence can only be understood from the motif of circulation. Because the things, through creation, have come forth from the Origin, their "conversion" to the End can not be meaning-less.

Moreover, the impossibility of the *visio Dei* is in conflict with faith. For the possibility of the immediate contemplation of God is promised us in Scripture, which is the foundation of the Christian faith.[71] Through the authority of the Bible we are freed from the distress of philosophy: "we shall be freed from these straits if we hold ... that man is able to reach perfect happiness after this life" (*S.c.G.* III, 48). The Christian has knowledge of a future fulfillment that transcends man's earthly possibilities. The 'via descensus' of faith (the second knowledge of God of *S.c.G.* IV, 1) offers the prospect of overcoming the discrepancy between what can be understood by the natural light of reason and the end of the desire to know, the vision of God.

How "reasonable" this liberation through faith is appears from various passages in Thomas's Bible commentaries. With reference to Matthew 5:8, "Blessed are the pure in heart: for they shall see God," he remarks that some hold that God is never seen in his essence. This is in the first place contrary to Holy Scripture. For in I John 3:2 we read: "we shall see Him as He is" and in I Corinthians 13:12: "For now we see through a glass, darkly; but then face to face." Furthermore, Thomas argues, this view is also contrary to reason,

> because man's happiness is man's ultimate good, in which his desire comes to rest. Now, it is man's natural desire, when he sees an effect, to inquire into the cause of it. Hence the wonder of the philosophers was the origin of philosophy, for seeing effects, they wondered and sought the cause. That desire will not come to rest until man reaches the first cause, God, namely, the divine essence itself. Therefore He will be seen in his essence.[72]

---

necesse est dicere quod *possibile* est substantiam Dei videri per intellectum. Cf. *S.c.G.* III, 44; *S.Th.* I, 12, 1.

This "possibility" will be discussed at greater length in 8.4.3.

[71] *S.c.G.* III, 51: Haec igitur visio immediata Dei repromittur nobis in Scriptura; *S.Th.* III, 55, 5: ... per auctoritatem sacrae Scripturae, quae est fidei fundamentum; *In Symbolum Apostolorum*, 1: Nullus ergo potest pervenire ad beatitudinem, quae est vera cognitio Dei, nisi primo cognoscat per fidem.

[72] *In Matth.*, c. 5, lect. 2: Quia beatitudo hominis est ultimum bonum hominis, in quo quietatur desiderium ejus. Naturale autem desiderium est, quod homo videns effectus inquirat de causa: unde etiam admiratio philosophorum fuit origo philosophiae, quia videntes effectus admirabantur, et quaerebant causam. Istud ergo desiderium non quietabitur, donec perveniat ad primam causam, quae Deus est, scilicet ad ipsam divinam

The *eschatology* of *Christian faith* goes together with the *finality* of the *natural* desire to know. In this synthesis, the Biblical witness concerning the vision of God is interpreted as a contemplation in which God is seen in his essence, in what He is. The terminus of the desire to know may transcend the horizon of philosophical speculation, it is true; but in this transcending it remains essentially determined by the ideal of the 'theoria'.

This interweavement likewise indicates that the revelation from God, though transcending reason, need by no means be conceived of as a denial of man's rationality; it is rather its perfection. For through the Word of God the truth is revealed that is indispensable to man if he is to reach his end as an intellectual being.[73] Faith speaks to the intellect. In a variant of the traditional adage 'Fides quaerens intellectum', it can be said that the human intellect ultimately seeks faith. Where rational discursion terminates, the way of faith opens the prospect of fulfillment of man's desire to know (see also 8.4.).

5.4. *The first known: Being ('ens')*

Human knowing takes place *per viam rationis*. The way of reason is a discursion from the one to the other, from the previously known to the as yet unknown. The historical course of this 'via' led to consideration of the relation of faith and reason in Thomas. This analysis directed our attention especially to the end of the way of reason; but it did not tell us anything about its beginning.

In the methodologically important work *In Boethii De trinitate* Thomas writes that in the speculative sciences we always proceed from something previously known (*ex aliquo prius noto*), both in demonstrating propositions and in finding definitions. So from the concept of the genus and difference, and from the causes of a thing, one comes to know its species. This regression cannot go on, however, to infinity, because then all science would cease, since the infinite cannot be traversed. Therefore inquiry in all the speculative sciences must be reduced to something first (*aliqua prima*), which man does not have to learn or to discover, but which he knows naturally.[74] The principle of the discursive movement cannot itself be acquired through reasoning. The way of reason is only passable when the discursion begins from an 'intellectus', from an immediate

---

essentiam. Videbitur ergo per essentiam.

Similarly in the Commentary on the Gospel according to John 1:18 (lect. 11).

[73] Cf. P.E. Persson, *Sacra doctrina: Reason and Revelation in Aquinas* (Oxford, 1970), ch. 1.

[74] *In Boeth. De trin.* 6, 4.

insight (cf. 5.1). *Ratio sequitur intellectum.*[75]

What is this "first" from which reasoning begins? On the basis of the preceding section one can say negatively of this first that it is not an insight of faith. But how is this first to be determined positively?

In 4.1.2. we saw that in *De verit.* 1, 1, in search of the answer to the question "What is truth?" Thomas sketches the reduction to this first:

> Just as in demonstrables a reduction must be made to principles which are known through themselves to the intellect, so likewise in investigating what anything is; else one would in either case go on *in infinitum*, with the result that the science and knowledge of things will perish utterly. Now that which the intellect first conceives, as best known, and to which it resolves all conceptions, is 'being' (*ens*), as Avicenna says in the beginning of his *Metaphysica.*[76]

"Being" is "that which falls first in the conception of the intellect" (*quod primo cadit in conceptione intellectus*). Every inquiry into the "what" something is proceeds from this conception. Without this insight nothing can be apprehended by the intellect. It is the condition of the possibility of the discursion of the human reason.[77]

Is it possible to clarify still further the nature of the "being" in question? And how does knowledge of this "first" come about?

5.4.1. *The nature of being which is first conceived by the intellect*

The character of the first known becomes somewhat clearer if we bring together a number of texts, scattered through Thomas's writings, in which—otherwise than in *De verit.* 1, 1—a certain motivation is presented.

---

[75] *In De causis*, lect. 18.

[76] *De verit.* 1, 1: Sicut in demonstrabilibus oportet fieri reductionem in aliqua principia per se intellectui nota, ita investigando quid est unumquodque; alias utrobique in infinitum iretur, et sic periret omnino scientia et cognitio rerum.
Illud autem quod primo intellectus concipit quasi notissimum, et in quo omnes conceptiones resolvit, est *ens*, ut Avicenna dicit in principio Metaph. suae.

[77] Cf. *De ente*, prooemium: Ens autem et essentia sunt quae primo intellectu concipiuntur, ut dicit Avicenna in principio suae Metaph.; *In IV Metaph.*, lect. 6, 605; *In X Metaph.*, lect. 4, 1998; XI, lect. 5, 2211; *S. Th.* I, 11, 2 ad 4; *S. Th.* I–II, 55, 4 ad 1; 94, 2: In his autem quae in apprehensione hominum cadunt quidam ordo invenitur. Nam illud quod primo cadit sub apprehensione est ens, cujus intellectus includitur in omnibus quaecumque quis apprehendit; *De pot.* 9, 7 ad 15.
For the reference to Avicenna, see Avicenna Latinus, *Liber De philosophia prima sive Scientia divina*, ed. S. van Riet (Louvain and Leiden, 1977), tract. I, cap. 5: Dicemus igitur quod res et ens et necesse talia sunt quod statim imprimuntur in anima prima impressione, quae non acquiritur ex aliis notioribus se.
Noteworthy is the difference from Thomas. While Avicenna speaks of '*imprimuntur* in anima', Thomas employs the term '*concipiuntur*'.

(a) *De verit.* 10, 11

In the tenth objection it is asserted:

> Just as being that is predicated of all is the first in commonness (*primum in
> communitate*), so being whereby all is caused is the first in causality (*primum
> in causalitate*), namely, God. Now, being that is first in commonness is the
> first conception of our intellect in this earthly life (*in statu viae*). Therefore
> we can in this life also know immediately in its essence being that is first in
> causality.

In Thomas's reply, the parallelism between being that is first in causality
and being that is first in commonness is rejected. The former transcends
all other things; nothing is in proportion to it. Therefore this being cannot
be sufficiently known by means of something else. What is first in commonness, in contrast, stands in a relation of proportionality to each thing.
Because of its universal predicability, it is apprehended in the knowledge
of each thing.

(b) *In I Metaph.*, lect. 2, 46

In simple apprehension, the more universal is the first known; for
"being" comes first in the intellect, as Avicenna says, and "living being"
comes prior in the intellect to "man." For just as in natural being (*in esse
naturae*) that comes from potency to act "living being" is prior to "man,"
so in the process of knowing (*in generatione scientiae*) "living being" is conceived in the intellect prior to "man." What is more universal by predication is earlier known to us.

(c) *S. Th.* I, 5, 2

> The first that falls in the conception of the intellect is being, because every-
> thing is knowable only insofar as it is in act. Hence, being is the proper object
> of the intellect, and is thus the first intelligible, as sound is the first
> audible.[78]

"Being" is the first intelligible, because it refers to the act of being (*De
verit.* 1, 1: *ens sumitur ab actu essendi*). And "to be" (*esse*) is the act par excellence, the actuality of every substance.

In the motivation of the priority of "being," two lines become discernible in these texts: universality and actuality. From this datum the
two senses of the "if" question (*an est*) found in 1.9. acquire added relief.

---

[78] *S. Th.* I, 5, 2: Primo autem in conceptione intellectus cadit ens: quia secundum hoc
unumquodque cognoscibile est, in quantum est actu, ut dicitur in IX Metaph. Unde ens
est proprium objectum intellectus: et sic est primum intelligibile, sicut sonus est primum
audibile.

On the one hand, the question "if" something is serves as the starting point for the question "what" something is, i.e., its essence. This Greek mode of questioning was connected with a meaning of being motivated by the origination of nature. Fitting in with this mode is what is advanced in the texts (a) and (b): predicative universality, the comparison with the prior "in natural being." There is, it is said in *In I Metaph.*, lect. 2, 46, conformity between natural and cognitive becoming. 'Being' is the first known, just as "by way of generation and time" (*secundum viam generationis et temporis*) the more universal comes first in the order of nature.[79]

On the other hand, the "if" question is directed to the 'esse'. Fitting in with this mode is the statement that 'ens' is the first intelligible because it has the primary act of being. Only through its "actuality" is a thing lucid and transparent.

If we add to this motivation from the "universality" and the "actuality" that 'ens', although it is the most general, is nevertheless said in a concrete manner,[80] then this conclusion is justified: that which "falls first in the conception of the intellect" is "being" *constituted* as the composition of 'subiectum—essentia—esse'.[81] This is the Archimedean point of Thomas's thought, from which all else must be understood: "All other conceptions of the intellect must be arrived at by addition to being" (*De verit.* 1, 1).

But is there not in this "first" a presupposition that concerns precisely its origin? "The first of created things is being" (*prima rerum creatarum est esse*). When Thomas cites this proposition from *De causis*, he explains: the word "being" refers to the proper nature of the object of creation. For something is called created because it is a being, not because it is this being (*nam eo dicitur aliquid creatum, quod est ens, non ex eo quod est hoc ens*), since creation is "the emanation of all being from the universal being."[82]

In Thomas the sense is not lacking that 'ens' is a participium, that it is said in the way of "participation." This comes out clearly, for example, in his exposition in *In De causis*, lect. 6: "that which is acquired first by the intellect, is being; that wherein the character of being is not found is not graspable by the intellect." On this ground the Neoplatonists argued

---

[79] Cf. *S. Th.* I, 85, 3 ad 1.

[80] *In De hebdom.*, c. 2: Ea autem quae in omni intellectu cadunt, sunt maxime communia; quae sunt ens, unum et bonum . . . Sed id quod est, sive ens, quamvis sit *communissimum*, tamen *concretive* dicitur.

[81] Thomas never calls 'esse' the first known. The point is noteworthy because in comparative studies about Thomas and Heidegger there is a tendency to ignore this 'Differenz' between 'ens' and 'esse'. See J.B. Lotz, *Martin Heidegger und Thomas von Aquin* (Pfullingen, 1975), pp. 41ff.

[82] *S. Th.* I, 45, 4 ad 1.

that the first cause is supra-intelligible, since it is "above being" (*supra ens*), in keeping with the thesis: "the first of created things is being." Thomas's riposte is:

> In truth, the first cause is above being insofar as it is infinite being; "being" (*ens*), however, is called that which participates in being in a finite way; and this being is proportionate to our intellect.[83]

But does the knowledge of a being that participates in being not presuppose the knowledge of being in its fullness? It is on this point that Bonaventure takes an additional step. "By an intellect that carries out the resolution completely, something cannot be understood unless the first being is understood."[84] For an imperfect being is only known as such by means of the perfect being, since "privations and shortcomings are only knowable by means of the positive determinations." At the foundation of knowledge of the finite as finite must lie knowledge of the infinite, perfect, and absolute being. Now, all the creaturely is being through participation: it is finite, imperfect, and dependent. Therefore, so Bonaventure says, our intellect cannot come to a complete resolution of created being if it is not aided by the insight into the most pure being. This, the divine being, is what comes first into the intellect: *esse igitur est quod primo cadit in intellectu, et illud esse est quod est purus actus . . . est esse divinum.*[85] Astonishing is the blindness of the intellect, which does not consider that which it sees first and that without which it can know nothing:[86] the light of the divine being reflected in the mirror of the soul. "The writer of the *Liber De causis* says: 'the first of created things is being.' But I [Bonaventure] say: 'the first of intellectual things is the first being.'"[87]

For Thomas, God is not the first known. Not being that is the first in causality but being that is the first in commonness is the first conception of our intellect. An immaterial substance can not really be known by man in this life. The knowledge of God is rather the ultimate end, the happiness of man.[88]

---

[83] *In De causis*, lect. 6: Secundum rei veritatem causa prima est supra ens in quantum est ipsum esse infinitum, ens autem dicitur id quod finite participat esse, et hoc est proportionatum intellectui nostro.

[84] *In I Sent.* 28, 1 (*Opera Omnia* I, 504): Intellectu resolvente semiplene, potest intelligi aliquid esse, non intellecto primo ente. Intellectu autem resolvente perfecte, non potest intelligi aliquid, primo ente non intellecto.

[85] *Itinerarium* V, 3 (V, 308/9); *De scientia Christi* IV, fund. 25 (V, 19); *Itinerarium* III, 3 (V, 304): Cum "privationes et defectus nullatenus possint cognosci nisi per positiones" (Averroes, III De Anima), non venit intellectus noster ut plene resolvens intellectum alicuius entium creatorum, nisi iuvetur ab intellectu entis purissimi, actualissimi, completissimi et absoluti.

[86] *Itinerarium* V, 4 (V, 309).

[87] *Collationes in Hexaëmeron* X, 18 (V, 379).

[88] *S. Th.* I, 88, 3; *In Boeth. De trin.* 1, 3.

Yet Bonaventure is not touched by this criticism: for him, too, the *a priori* knowledge of God is not the beatific vision. A direct confrontation occurs only when Thomas continues: For "some" (*aliqui*) God is the first known insofar as the influx of the divine light (*influentia lucis ipsius*) is the first that is known by us. But to Thomas's mind this view is untenable, for two reasons. First, this light is a natural light by which the intellective power is constituted (*lux naturalis per quam constituitur vis intellectiva*). Secondly, this light is not the first object known by the intellect, since much inquiry is needed in order to know what it is.[89]

Thomas acknowledges that God is known implicitly in all that is known,[90] but this knowledge has to be made explicit from the knowledge of being (and not the reverse). That 'ens' is the first known must be directly connected to Thomas's view of the light, "under which" it appears.

5.4.2. The origin of the knowledge of being[91]

About the origin of the knowledge of being we have read in *In Boeth. De trin.* 6, 4: "Inquiry in all the speculative sciences must be reduced to something first, which man does not have to learn or to discover . . . but which he knows naturally." The first conceptions are "implanted" into man, are a permanent habitus of the subject. The knowledge of the first intelligibles is revealed to man "by the light of the agent intellect, which is something natural to him" (*ibid.*).

Our intellect knows being "naturally."[92] That is, this action proceeds from the nature of the human species, belongs to man through a principle formally intrinsic in him. All people share in the power (*virtus*) that is the principle of this action of knowing, namely, the light of the agent intellect.[93] It is not from a separated substance (separated, that is, from man) that the intelligible forms flow into our mind. The human intellect has a light, which is of itself sufficient for knowing intelligible truths (*S. Th.* I – II, 109, 1). Man as man possesses an active power of knowing: "The agent intellect, of which Aristotle speaks, is something of the soul" (*S. Th.* I, 70, 4). Thomas's first argument against the view that the divine light

---

[89] *In Boeth. De trin.* 1, 3.

[90] *De verit.* 22, 2 ad 1: Omnia cognoscentia cognoscunt implicite Deum in quolibet cognito.

[91] Cf. G. Verbeke, "Le développement de la connaissance humaine d'après saint Thomas," *Revue philos. de Louvain* 47 (1949): 437 – 57; D.M. de Petter, "De oorsprong van de zijnskennis volgens Thomas van Aquino," in *Begrip en werkelijkheid* (Hilversum and Antwerp, 1964), pp. 94 – 135.

[92] *S.c.G.* II, 83.

[93] *S. Th.* I, 79, 4; 79, 5 ad 3.

is the first known was, indeed (5.4.1.), that the light whereby the intellective power is constituted is a natural light.

It is typical of Thomas that his attention is directed first of all towards
this origination. In a further analysis it can be said that, insofar as the
natural is derivative in its own turn—that is, is creaturely—God is the
ultimate ground of human knowing. The natural light of reason is ultimately reducible to the divine origin. "The light of the agent intellect in
the rational soul proceeds from, as first origin, separated substances, in
particular from God" (*De verit.* 10, 6). Or more strictly in *De spirit. creat.*,
q. un., a. 10:

> Since this intellectual light pertains to the nature of the soul, it comes from
> Him alone by whom the nature of the soul is created. Now God alone is the
> creator of the soul, and not some separated substance we call an angel . . .
> Hence it is left that the light of the agent intellect is not caused in the soul
> by any other separated substance, but is caused immediately by God.[94]

Shortly thereafter it is said in the same text: "The light of the agent
intellect, of which Aristotle speaks, is impressed upon us immediately by
God." We can observe that in the "intellectual light" both originations
concur.[95] The way of human knowing is natural and creatural. The
natural light, whereby the first intelligibles are known to man, is a participation in the divine light, "a likeness of the uncreated truth that is reflected in us" (*De verit.* 11, 1), "a participated likeness of the uncreated
light" (*S. Th.* I, 84, 5).[96] In this connection Thomas frequently refers to
a text from Psalm 4:7, "Many say: who showeth us good things?" When
the psalmist answers, "The light of thy countenance, O Lord, is signed
upon us," it is because he would say, as it were, that all is shown us by
the seal of the divine light in us (*per ipsam sigillationem divini luminis in
nobis*)[97]—an expression we shall encounter again later in this section.

In the light of the agent intellect all science is in a certain sense originally implanted in us.[98] The universal concepts are the seeds (*semina*) as it

---

[94] *De spirit. creat.*, q. un., a. 10: Cum istud lumen intellectuale ad naturam animae
pertineat, ab illo solo est quo animae natura creatur. Solus autem Deus est creator animae,
non autem aliqua substantia separata, quem angelum dicimus . . . Unde relinquitur quod
lumen intellectus agentis non causatur in anima ab aliqua alia substantia separata, sed *immediate a Deo*.

[95] Cf. *S. Th.* I, 79, 4 ad 5: Nihil prohibet virtutem quae a supremo intellectu participatur . . . ab essentia ipsius (sc. animae) procedere.

[96] Cf. *De verit.* 11, 3; 10, 6 ad 6: Prima principia, quorum cognitio est nobis innata,
sunt quaedam similitudines increatae veritatis; *S. Th.* I, 12, 11 ad 3: Ipsum lumen naturale
rationis participatio quaedam est divini luminis.

[97] *S. Th.* I, 84, 5.

[98] *De verit.* 10, 6: In lumine intellectus agentis nobis est quodammodo omnis scientia
originaliter indita.

were of all that is subsequently known.[99] With that, however, precisely because of the participatory character of man's intellectual light, not yet everything has been said about the origin of the knowledge of being. The created intellect is not related to universal being (*ens universale*) as pure act, as the act of all being. That is proper to the divine intellect alone which is identical with the essence of God, in which all being originally (*originaliter*) and virtually (*virtualiter*) preexists as in its first cause. The relation of the finite intellect to being contains necessarily a moment of potentiality, of receptivity.[100] Human science is partly *ab intrinseco*, partly *ab extrinseco* (*De verit.* 10, 6).

Only against this background does it become understandable that Thomas, in *In Boeth. De trin.* 6, 4, shortly after having said that man knows the first principles "naturally," goes on to assert: "Our knowledge of the above-mentioned principles begins in the senses and memory." The following exposition precedes this assertion:

> These principles are revealed to man by the light of the agent intellect, which is something natural to him; and this light makes things known to us only to the extent that it renders phantasms intelligible; for in this consists the operation of the agent intellect ... Now, phantasms are taken from the senses. So our knowledge of the above-mentioned principles begins in the senses and memory.[101]

Thomas's reasoning is very compact; it needs further elaboration.

For actual knowledge man needs sense perception. The processing of a set of such perceptions by the inner senses results in an image, the so-called "phantasm." This is the abiding basis of intellectual activity.[102] The phantasm is not yet purified, however, of all material (and consequently individual) conditions and is therefore only intelligible in potency. To be intelligible in act, it must be dematerialized. That is the act proper to the agent intellect, which "lights" the phantasm and abstracts the intelligible content.[103] "To abstract the universal from the particular,

---

[99] *De verit.* 11, 1 ad 5: Universales conceptiones, quarum cognitio est nobis naturaliter insita, sunt quasi semina quaedam omnium sequentium cognitorum.

[100] *S.Th.* I, 79, 2.

[101] *In Boeth. De trin.* 6, 4: Huiusmodi autem naturaliter cognita homini manifestantur ex ipso lumine intellectus agentis, quod est homini naturale, quo quidem lumine nihil manifestatur nobis, nisi in quantum per ipsum phantasmata fiunt intelligibilia in actu. Hic enim est actus intellectus agentis ... Phantasmata autem a sensu accipiuntur. Principium cognitionis praedictorum principiorum est ex sensu et memoria.

[102] *Ibid.*, 6, 2 ad 5: Phantasma est principium nostrae cognitionis, ut ex quo incipit intellectus operatio non sicut transiens, sed sicut permanens ut quoddam fundamentum intellectualis operationis. Cf. *S.Th.* I, 84, 7 and the commentary on this text by K. Rahner, *Spirit in World*, 1ff.

[103] *De verit.* 8, 9; *S.c.G.* II, 75.

or the intelligible species from the phantasm, is to say: to consider the nature of the species apart from its individual principles represented by the phantasm.''[104]

For intellectual knowledge, both moments, the *a priori* and the *a posteriori*, are constitutive.[105] The knowledge of being, too, although connatural, becomes actual only through the activity of the agent intellect with regard to sensible things.

> There preexist in us certain seeds of the sciences, namely the first conceptions of the intellect, which immediately by the light of the agent intellect are known through species abstracted from sensible things, whether they be the complex ones such as the axioms, or the incomplex ones, such as the notions of ''being'' (*ens*), ''one,'' and other such, which the intellect immediately apprehends.[106]

The notion of being (*ratio entis*) has as ''medium'' on the one hand the *lumen* of the agent intellect—i.e., that under which (*sub quo*) the intellect views all—and on the other hand the *species intelligibilis*, abstracted from the phantasm, i.e., that whereby (*quo*) the intellect understands.[107] In the origin of the knowledge of being there appears, and we thus find confirmed, the complex structure of being. For the concurrence of 'phantasma—species intelligibilis—lumen', from which the conception of being results, is nothing other than the cognitive side of the composition in that which is of 'subjectum—essentia—esse'.[108]

Illustrative for the relation of the two moments of knowledge is a little noted text (*In Boeth. De trin.* 3, 1 ad 4) in which Thomas points to a similar structure in the knowledge of faith. Faith is ''by hearing,'' namely, the revealed Word of God. But at the same time there is something inner whereby man inclines to assent. That is the light of faith (*lumen fidei*), a habit infused by God, ''a certain seal of the first truth'' (*quaedam sigillatio primae veritatis*). Their relation is the same as that in the knowledge of the first intelligibles. ''As knowledge of the principles is derived from the

---

[104] *S. Th.* I, 85, 1 ad 1.

[105] Cf. *S. Th.* I, 84, 5: Praeter lumen intellectuale in nobis, exiguntur species intelligibiles a rebus acceptae.

[106] *De verit.* 11, 1: Praeexistunt in nobis quaedam scientiarum semina, scilicet primae conceptiones intellectus, quae statim lumine intellectus agentis cognoscuntur per species a sensibilibus abstractas, sive sint complexa, ut dignitates, sive incomplexa, sicut ratio entis, et unius, et huiusmodi, quae statim intellectus apprehendit.

[107] *Quodl.* VII, 1, 1; *In III Sent.* 14, 2, 1.

That this twofold medium does not result in ''mediated'' knowledge is emphasized in *Quodl.* VII, 1, 1.

[108] Cf. L. Oeing-Hanhoff, ''Die Methoden der Metaphysik im Mittelalter,'' in *Die Metaphysik im Mittelalter*, ed. P. Wilpert (Berlin, 1963), pp. 82ff; L.B. Puntel, *Analogie und Geschichtlichkeit*, vol. 1, pp. 236ff.

senses (*a sensu*) and yet the light whereby the principles are known is innate (*innatum*), so is faith by hearing (*ex auditu*) and yet the habitus of faith is infused (*infusus*).'' The two moments, external and internal, together bring about determinate knowledge (*aliqua cognitionis determinatio*).

It is noteworthy that this text uses an expression for the light of faith that was applied earlier to the natural light: *sigillatio primae veritatis*. From this two conclusions can be drawn, which also bear upon the exposition in 5.3. on the relation between faith and reason.

First, Thomas's confidence that the ascending way of reason is identical with the descending way of faith has its basis here. There is "a twofold mode of truth" (*S.c.G.* I, 3) about the divine, certainly, but no "double" truth. For both the light of faith and the light of reason come from the same Source. A contradiction between the truth of faith and the truth of reason is impossible, because then God himself would have to be the cause of one of the two being untrue. But a God who deceives as a "malignant genius" is an absurdity.[109]

At the same time, it is from the Source that the distinction between the two ways has been "sealed." The illumination of reason has been "naturalized." The progress of man's desire to know is qualified by this "naturalization."

5.5. *'Via ex nobis notioribus'*

Being (*ens*) is the first known. A thing is knowable to the extent that it is being. Therefore what is being maximally is the most "true"—"There is the same disposition of things in being and in truth" (4.3.1.)—and by nature the more knowable.[110] Yet we saw earlier that the first being, which is the first Truth, cannot be known essentially by man.

In *I Post. Anal.*, lect. 4, Thomas states that science must proceed "from what is first and immediate" (*ex primis et immediatis*), "from what is true" (*ex veris*), and, furthermore, "from what is better known and prior" (*ex notioribus et prioribus*). For then do we know, when we know the cause; and each cause is by nature "prior" to and "better known" than its effect.[111] But here he introduces a distinction between prior and better known "in reference to us" (*quoad nos*) and "according to nature" (*secundum naturam*).

---

[109] Cf. *In Boeth. De trin.* 2, 3.

[110] *In De causis*, prooemium; *In I Phys.*, lect. 1,7: Sunt autem secundum se notiora, quae plus habent de entitate: quia unumquodque cognoscibile est inquantum est ens. Magis autem entia sunt, quae magis sunt in actu: unde ista maxime sunt cognoscibilia naturae.

[111] *In I Post. Anal.*, lect. 4, 37; 42.

What is better known according to nature is mostly incongruent to what
is better known in reference to us. On the way from questioning towards
knowing (1.3.1.; 2.2.3.; 4.2.1.), we saw that man's desire to know is a
"re-duction," a going back into the "ex"-structure of science, a regress
to the logically and ontologically prior. The first causes are in reference
to us the later known. Our intellect relates to the most intelligible as the
eye of the bat relates to the light of the sun: the lucidity exceeds the capacity to see.[112] The way of inquiry proper to man is presented at the beginning of the *Physica*: "It is natural for us to proceed from what is better
known to us" (*innata est nobis via ex nobis notioribus*).

This *via* is staked out by two marks: on the one hand by the order within
human intellectual knowledge and on the other hand by the dependence
of this knowledge on the senses.[113] These marks evince again the characteristics of the way of reason (5.1.) and of the knowledge of being (5.4.).

Distinctive of the rational soul is, in the first place, discursivity, the
progression from the one to the other, from the earlier known to the as
yet unknown. There is conformity between natural becoming and the
process of science: in both processes the more universal comes first. *Ratio
imitatur naturam*: both advance from potentiality to act, from the imperfect
to the perfect. The better known in reference to us is the more universal—
the knowledge of it is intermediate between potency and act. One knows
the genus of something, to be sure, but this knowledge is not distinct,
is still in potency to a specific knowledge whereby the constitutive differences are actually known. It is not until the ultimate act of the reason
that one attains a complete knowledge in which things are known distinct-
ly and determinately.[114] The *via ex nobis notioribus* goes from the logically
more to the less universal. This sheds new light on the way towards the
definition taken in 2.2. For the "horizon" of definitional knowing was the
species. The "quest" is directed towards this terminus. That implies, as
we can now see, that in the forming of a definition, too, there is a discursion.[115] The most appropriate manner to arrive at the definition was the
method of division (*per viam divisionis*). Now it has become clear that this
method is proper to man; he proceeds by specifying the initially still
indistinct universal.

---

[112] *In De causis*, prooemium: Quamvis huiusmodi primae causae sunt minus et
posterius notae quoad nos: habet enim se ad ea intellectus noster sicut oculus noctuae ad
lucem solis quam propter excedentem claritatem perfecte percipere non potest; *In I Phys.*,
lect. 1, 7.

The comparison with the bat is borrowed from Aristotle, *Metaph.* II, 1, 993 b 9.

[113] See (also for what follows in this section) *In I Phys.*, lect. 1, 6f.; *In I Post. Anal.*, lect.
4, 42f.; *S. Th.* I, 85, 3.

[114] Cf. *In I Meteor.*, lect. 1,1: Manifestum est quod complementum scientiae requirit
quod non sistatur in communibus, sed procedatur ad species.

[115] A clear example in *Super Ioannem*, c. 1, lect. 1, 26.

Distinctive of the rational soul is, in the second place, that he must gather the intelligible truth from sensible things. From this point of view, the first known by us is the particular thing.[116] The historical progress of the desire to know also occurs in accordance with this order of knowledge: the first philosophers occupied themselves with the sensible (5.2.). The *via ex nobis notioribus* goes from the particular to the universal (in causing), to the ontologically prior: *innata est nobis via a posterioribus in priora*.[117]

In his writing *In Boeth. De trin.* 6, 1 Thomas says that the method of natural science is most in conformity with the process proper to man in knowing. For in its progress natural science retains the two features that are characteristic for reason: dependence on the sensible, which is the better known in reference to us, and discursivity.

To assess this conclusion correctly, we may look back at the course of this chapter. Natural for man is the *via rationis*. The principle of the movement of reason is the 'intellectus'. First known, condition of the possibility for the discursion, is 'ens', "that which is." The process of knowledge starts from being, from the one in which all other is included: "all other is somehow included in being, unitedly and indistinctly, as in its principle" (*In I Sent.* 8, 1, 3). Human knowledge of being becomes actual only through the activity of the intellect with respect to sensible things. Through the concurrence of "sense—reason—intellect" in concrete knowledge the inquiry gets caught in the tension of the many to the one. The discursive reason and the historical reason aim to elucidate being by reducing multiplicity to an original unity. In Thomas the idea of creation, too, stands in this perspective of reason in search of understanding.

The way of reason is particularly observed in natural science. Hence physics is most in conformity with the human intellect (*In Boeth. De trin.* 6, 1: *propter hoc scientia naturalis inter alias est maxime hominis intellectui conformis*). The inquiry into the origin and cause, that nature is, *is* the course of the rational discursion. What "better known" points the way for it?

---

[116] *In I Phys.*, lect. 1, 8: Ipsa individua sensibilia . . . sunt magis nota quoad nos, quia sensus cognitio, quae est singularium, praecedit cognitionem intellectus in nobis, quae est universalium; *In I Post. Anal.*, lect. 4, 43; *S. Th.* I, 85, 3. Cf. *In X Metaph.*, lect. 4, 1990.
[117] *In I Sent.*, Epilogus. Cf. *In I Metaph.*, lect. 2, 46: Universalia in causando sunt posterius nota quoad nos, licet sint prius nota secundum naturam; *In I Ethic.*, lect. 4, 52.

CHAPTER SIX

HODO-LOGY

Human knowing takes place *per viam rationis*. The way of reason is a discursion from something to something. In knowledge that proceeds discursively, and only in such knowledge, signs (*signa*) function. For the mark
of a sign is that we are led by it to the knowledge of something other.[1] A
sign, in keeping with Augustine's definition in *De doctrina christiana* (II, 1,
1), expresses something manifest to us by which we are conducted to the
knowledge of something that is hidden. Better known to us is the sensible.
Precisely for this reason, "in us signs are sensible because our knowledge
that is discursive starts from what is sensible."[2]

In the first basic text (*Phys.* II) "seeing" (*phainetai, videntur*) is mentioned as a significative resourse. What is significant is the phenomena.
That which is seen is motion (*motus*), the mark of natural things. Therefore it suits man to have motion show him the way to the intelligible
(6.1.).[3] Physics is most in conformity with the human intellect.

Discursive reason seeks the "logos" of the phenomena, a knowledge of
the "'rationes' of those things which are seen by the senses" (*S. Th.* I,
84, 8). This phenomeno-logy demands that in the movable a "reference"
can be found to necessity as the basis of its knowability: *omne scibile est ex
necessitate.*[4] Scientific knowledge deals with what is necessary. Therefore
natural things need to be reduced to this intelligibility (6.2.).

But is the creature not likewise marked by mutability, by contingency?
Thus in the second basic text (*De subst. sep.*, c. 9) a mode of becoming is
introduced that concerns being itself. In Thomas's view, however, on the
way from the sensible to the intelligible, the creaturely is not primarily a
"sign" that refers to something other but a "thing" (*res*) with its own
principles (6.3.)

Human reason proceeds from the sign to the signified through a process

---

[1] *De verit.* 9, 4 ad 4: Signum proprie loquendo, non potest dici nisi aliquid ex quo de-
veniatur in cognitionem alterius quasi *discurrendo*; et secundum hoc, signum in angelis non
est, cum eorum scientia non sit discursiva; *De verit.* 11, 1 ad 4.

[2] *Ibid.* 9, 4 ad 4. Cf. *In IV Sent.* 1, 1, 1 sol. 2; sol. 1 ad 5; *S. Th.* III, 60, 4 ad 1: Et
inde est quod primo et principaliter dicuntur signa, quae sensibus offeruntur, sicut Au-
gustinus dicit (De doctr. christ. II), ubi dicit quod 'signum est quod praeter speciem quam
ingerit sensibus facit aliquid aliud in cognitionem venire'.

[3] Cf. *S. Th.* III, 60, 4: Est autem homini connaturale ut per sensibilia perveniat in
cognitionem intelligibilium. Signum autem est per quod aliquis devenit in cognitionem
alterius.

[4] *In VI Ethic.*, lect. 3, 1145.

of reduction.[5] Reason's discursion is a "resolution", an "analysis" to the ontologically prior. "By the way of resolution" (6.4.) what is seen is reduced on the one hand to the intrinsic and on the other hand to the extrinsic causes. On these causes depends its necessity.

The double resolution has to be applied first to the basic phenomenon of the "mutation" or movement (6.5.). The analysis is focussed on the immobile, from which the motion is intelligible. It is therefore in a pregnant sense a "hodo-logy," for in the principle and the terminus of motion, that is, of being-under-way, the "ratio of the way" is established. This hodology *is* nature, for nature is—as it appears from the first basic text—an intrinsic principle (and terminus) of motion. The extrinsic cause is in the ultimate analysis the Unmoved Mover, God.

With this analysis, however, the resolution is not at an end. It must be continued, according to the second basic text, with the analysis of that which is to the 'esse', which "is something fixed in that which is."[6] In this meta-physical reduction, the nature of what is is transcended in the direction of being as creature (6.6.). Yet, in this transcendence there is at the same time continuity with the earlier resolution. Both reductions, that of motion as well as that of being, come together in the notion of "act" (6.7.). This convergence makes clear from a systematic standpoint why Thomas can describe the history of philosophical reflection on the origin of reality as a continuous progression towards the idea of creation.

6.1. 'Per viam sensus': The phenomenon of motion

"Some, in order to investigate the truth about the nature of things, have proceeded *ex rationibus intelligibilibus*." This approach, this 'via', was characteristic of the Platonists. They were so intent on the intelligible that they were ignorant of the "existing", that is, of the natural and sensible things. Rather than take the 'via Platonica', others have proceeded *ex rebus sensibilibus* in their investigation of the nature of things. This approach, according to the judgment of Simplicius, was proper to the philosophy of Aristotle.[7]

And it is in this last manner, in Thomas's judgment, that man must

---

[5] *In I Sent.*, dist. 1, exp. textus: Accipiens enim cognitionem procedit de signis ad signata, quasi modo resolutorio, quia signa magis sunt nota quoad ipsum.

[6] *S.c.G.* I, 20: Esse autem est aliquid fixum et quietum in ente.

[7] *De spirit. creat.* q. un., art. 3. The philosophical approach is stamped in this text itself as a "via": quidam vero secundum eamdem viam ingredientes... Cf. R. J. Henle, *Saint Thomas and Platonism* (The Hague, 1956), pp. 296–97.

In I De gener., lect. 3, 25: Causa huius quod Plato minus potuit videre... ea quae sunt omnibus manifesta, fuit inexperientia: quia scilicet, circa intelligibilia intentus, sensibilibus non intendebat, circa quae est experientia... Sed Platonici, qui erant indocti 'existentium', idest circa entia naturalia et sensibilia...

make his way. "It is natural to man to attain to the intelligible through
sensible things, because our knowledge originates from sense."[8] As
'animal rationale' he needs sense experience for knowledge. Earlier it was
established that it is characteristic of reason to derive from the sensible
that is better known *quoad nos* the knowledge of the intelligible that is better
known *secundum naturam* (5.1. and 5.5.). Man, who occupies the lowest
place in the hierarchy of spiritual beings, must gather the truth from multiple things *per viam sensus*.[9] For the senses are given to man not only for
the purpose of procuring the necessaries of life, as is the case with other
living beings, but also for the purpose of knowledge. Hence man's face
is not turned to the ground but he has an upright stature. Thus, chiefly
by sight, he can know sensible things celestial as well as terrestrial from
all sides, so as to gather intelligible truth.[10] Sensible things are 'praeambula' to the intelligible;[11] they are "the way towards knowledge of the intelligible."[12] Theoretical science extends to where the phenomena can
lead (cf. 5.3.4.: "The 'distress' of philosophy").[13]

What is seen? According to the text from *Phys.* II: "motion" and
"rest", common marks of the sensible (*sensibilia communia*).[14] Motion is
the best known to us, since it is evident to the senses. Of the five "ways"
that prove the existence of God, the *manifestior via* is the one from motion.
"It is certain, and evident to our senses, that in the world some things are
in motion" (*S. Th.* I, 2, 3).[15]

"Motion" is not to be taken only as change of place but is to be understood in the broad sense of "process." The Greek sense of motion is *muta-*

---

[8] *S. Th.* I, 1, 9.

[9] *S. Th.* I, 76, 5: Anima intellectiva ... secundum naturae ordinem, infimum gradum in substantiis intellectualibus tenet; intantum quod non habet naturaliter sibi indi-
tam notitiam veritatis, sicut angeli, sed oportet quod eam colligat ex rebus divisibilibus
per viam sensus, ut Dionysius dicit (*De div. nomin.*, c. 7).

[10] *S. Th.* I, 91, 3 ad 3: Homo vero habet faciem erectam, ut per sensus, et praecipue
per visum, qui est subtilior et plures differentias rerum ostendit, libere possit ex omni parte
sensibilia cognoscere, et caelestia et terrena, ut ex omnibus intelligibilem colligat
veritatem.

[11] *In De div. nomin.* c. 4, lect. 9, 414.

[12] *In IV Sent.* 11, 1, 1 ad tertiam quaestionem: via ad cognitionem intelligibilium.

[13] *S. Th.* I, 12, 12: Naturalis nostra cognitio a sensu principium sumit: unde se tantum
naturalis cognitio nostra extendere potest, inquantum manuduci potest per sensibilia.
From the exposition of the origin of the knowledge of being (5.4.2.) it has already appeared that sensible knowledge is not the total cause of intellectual knowledge; it is rather
materia causae (*S. Th.* I, 84, 6). Cf. *De verit.* 10, 6 ad 2. See also K. Kremer, "Der Apriorismus in der Erkenntnismetaphysik des Thomas von Aquin," *Trierer Theologische Zeitschrift*
72 (1963): 105–16.

[14] For the "sensibilia communia," see *S. Th.* I, 78, 3 ad 2.

[15] Cf. *In IX Metaph.*, lect. 3, 1805: Inter alios autem actus, maxime est nobis notus et
apparens motus, qui sensibiliter a nobis videtur.

tio; it is, as this name already indicates, a "mutation" or change from something to something that initially was not.[16] What is moved exists now differently from how it existed before.[17] Motion is being – under – way (*via in ens*),[18] as discursive reason is in a cognitive respect: "Discursus quemdam motum nominat" (5.1.).

However, is what is seen, motion, not phenomenal seeming? In his poem Parmenides opposes the wrong path of the human senses to the divinely revealed way of the "logos" that leads us to the true nature of being. This way of truth is marked by many "signs": Being is ungenerated and imperishable, entire and one, immovable and complete (*Fragm.* B 8). Precisely the immovability confirmed by the onto-logy demonstrates that the senses are an unreliable guide. "Do not let custom . . . force thee to let wander along this road thy aimless eye, thy echoing ear, or thy tongue; but do thou judge by reason (*logos*)" (*Fragm.* B 7, 3 – 5).[19] For Melissus, too, being is according to truth immobile, although sense judges that many beings are moved.[20]

But this opposition of the 'apparentia sensus' to the 'ratio'[21] conflicts with the way of knowing: it is natural for man to attain to the intelligible from the sensible. The reasoning of the Eleatic philosophers is accordingly not in conformity with the truth. An argument *ad hominem* can be levelled against them immediately: the negation of motion refutes itself. For even when the opinion that things are moved is untrue, it follows that there is motion. For opinion is a motion of reason, it demands a discursion.[22]

That there is motion cannot, to be sure, be "demonstrated". Indeed, such an attempt would testify to a lack of critical judgment. Anyone who seeks arguments to prove what is manifest of itself lacks the capacity to discriminate between what is an evident starting point and what is not. "Now it is manifest of itself that some things are in motion." Against its denial there is but one remedy: we see (*videmus*) that there is mobility.[23]

In the first book of the *Physica* it is posited against Parmenides: "That

---

[16] *In V Phys.*, lect. 2, 650.

[17] *S.c.G.* II, 17: In omni mutatione vel motu, oportet esse aliquid aliter se habens nunc quam prius; *S. Th.* I, 9, 1.

[18] E.g., *In II Sent.* 24, 3, 1; *In IV Sent.* 1, 1, 4 ad secundam quaestionem: Motus autem non est ens completum sed est *via in ens*.

[19] Cf. *In I Phys.*, lect. 2 – 3; *In III De caelo*, lect. 2, 552.

[20] *In VIII Phys.*, lect. 6, 1018.

[21] Cf. *In I Metaph.*, lect. 9, 143.

[22] *In VIII Phys.* lect. 6, 1018: Opinio etiam quidam motus est rationis, ex aliquibus ratiocinantibus procedens.

[23] *Ibid.*, lect. 6, 1018 – 19.

natural things are moved can be manifest from induction; for it appears
to the senses (*ad sensum apparet*) that natural things are moved"(*In I Phys.*,
lect. 2, 18). One who with his reason denies that there is motion cannot
be refuted by the physicist: it is the "supposition" (*suppositio*) of his
science.[24] From induction it can be clear, however, that natural things
are marked by mobility.[25] This characteristic is therefore significant for
the essence of what appears, for that whereby the natural is natural: nature. *Per viam motus*, as in the first basic text, the concept of nature has to
be disclosed.[26]

In the first sentence of the third book of the *Physica* Aristotle states that
ignorance of motion results in ignorance of 'physis': *ignorato motu, ignoratur
natura*.[27] He who eliminates motion destroys no small feature of nature.[28]
Therefore the philosophers of Elea are not on the way of truth: the complete elimination of generation and motion is *contra veritatem et naturam* (cf.
ch. 4); they have spoken of natural things in an unnatural manner (*non
naturaliter*). The basic error of Parmenides and Melissus is a "metabasis
eis allo genos". What belongs to the essence of the *super*-natural substances, immobility, they have transferred to the sensible, namely, to the
natural things.[29] This deviation is typical of the tension between the
phenomenon of movement on the one hand and, on the other hand, the
terminus of the desire to know, namely the immovable and necessary.

6.2. *Necessity and nature*

6.2.1. *The desire to know and the necessary*

"All men by nature desire to know." What is desired is not just any
knowledge but certain knowledge (*certa cognitio*). That which can be otherwise than it is can not bring about this certainty. Science must therefore

---

[24] Before the passage cited in the text it is said: In scientia naturali *supponitur* quod
naturalia moveantur vel omnia vel quaedam . . . (*In I Phys.*, lect. 2, 18). Cf. *In VIII Phys.*,
lect. 1, 967.
For the notion of "suppositio," see also 1.3.3.

[25] See for the notion of induction *In II Post. Anal.*, lect. 20, 595: Sic enim, scilicet per
viam inductionis, sensus facit universale intus in anima.

[26] For "per viam motus" see *De subst. separ.*, c. 1; *In VII Metaph.*, lect. 2, 1287: . . .
per viam motus, quae quidem probatio est per viam naturalis philosophiae.

[27] *In III Phys.*, lect. 1, 276.

[28] *In IX Metaph.*, lect. 3, 1803.

[29] *In III De caelo*, lect. 2, 552: Transtulerunt *ea quae pertinent ad rationem supernaturalium
substantiarum*, ad haec sensibilia. . . Et ideo Parmenides et Melissus . . . non tamen quantum ad hoc bene dicebant, quod de rebus naturalibus non naturaliter loquebantur,
attribuentes ea quae sunt substantiarum immobilium, substantiis naturalibus, quae sunt
substantiae sensibiles.

deal with the necessary (cf. 1.1.): science is *de necessariis*.[30]

With necessity, after causality and truth, we arrive at a last dimension of "to know." And it is especially in this intelligible perfection[31] that the motive of the desire to know becomes apparent. For necessary is what always is in the same way. Science provides a grip, gives "certainty," not only in a cognitive respect against shifting opinion, but also in an ontological respect. Science grasps the *certitudo* of each thing, the formal and definitive moment persisting through all changes.[32] And this is the best in things: *optimum in rebus est permanentia* (*In II De caelo*, lect. 18, 468). From the ascertainment that science deals with the necessary it also follows directly for Aristotle that the knowable is the everlasting. Necessity and eternity go together.[33]

In Book V of the *Metaphysica*, his lexicon of philosophical terms, in ch. 5, Aristotle distinguishes the different senses of "necessary". The first and foremost meaning is "what cannot be otherwise" (*quod non contingit aliter se habere*); this is necessary in an absolute sense (*et hoc est necessarium absolute*).[34]

The primary, absolute sense of "necessary" is characteristic of demonstrative knowledge. The conclusion of the syllogism cannot be other than it is: the predicate belongs to the subject necessarily. This necessity is caused by the deduction from the premises. The syl-logism could not produce certain knowledge, however, if the 'logoi' themselves were not necessary. Here, too, we find the "ex"-structure of science: science is from that which is necessary (*ex necessariis*).[35] As an argument, Aristotle adduces the predication 'per se'. The principle of the demonstration that effects science is the definition. The definition is necessary itself, because "the definition consists of what is predicated 'per se'" (2.2.1.). And what is predicated of something 'per se' is necessarily, always, and inseparably in it.[36]

---

[30] *In I Post. Anal.*, lect. 4, 32 and 34; *In VI Ethic.*, lect. 3, 1145; *In Boeth. De trin.* 5, 1; *In I Sent.*, prol., 1, 3, sol. 2.

[31] Cf. *S. Th.* I, 79, 9 ad 3: Unde et [intellectus] necessaria, quae habent perfectum esse in veritate, perfecte cognoscit.

[32] Cf. *De ente*, c. 1: Dicitur [essentia] etiam forma secundum quod per formam significatur certitudo uniuscuiusque rei, ut dicit Avicenna in secundo Metaphysicae suae.

[33] *In I Post. Anal.*, lect. 16; *In VI Ethic.*, lect. 3, 1145: Sic ergo patet quod omne scibile est ex necessitate. Ex quo concludit quod sit aeternum, quia omnia quae sunt simpliciter ex necessitate, sunt aeterna. Hujusmodi autem non generantur neque corrumpuntur. Talia ergo sunt de quibus est scientia.
Cf. for the identity of the necessary and the eternal *De caelo* 1, 12.

[34] *Metaph.* V, c. 5, 1015 a 35ff. (Thomas: lect. 6, 832). On "necessity" in Aristotle, see S. Mansion, *Le jugement d'existence*, 2nd ed. (Louvain, 1976), pp. 62–93; and the older study by J. Chevalier, *La notion du nécessaire chez Aristote et chez ses prédécesseurs* (Paris, 1915).

[35] *In I Post. Anal.*, lect. 13.

[36] *In I Post. Anal.*, lect. 13, 110; cf. also lect. 14 (demonstratio est de his et ex his quae sunt per se).

Demonstrative science is characterized by the so-called "ex"-structure (1.3.1.). The knowledge of the conclusion is deduced from that of the premises. The desire to know proved to be always a regress into this "ex"-structure. Time after time, too, we found that in this reduction logical and ontological anteriority interpenetrate. This emerges perhaps nowhere so clearly as in the necessary. For notice the conclusion that Aristotle draws in *Metaph.* V from the structure of demonstrative science. From the fact that in demonstrations the premises are the cause of the conclusion and that each of the two is necessary, it follows that there are two modes of being necessary. Some things have a cause of their necessity, while others do not; they are necessary of themselves (*propter seipsa*).[37]

From the "ex"-structure of science there is inferred an ontological hierarchy in the "necessary" which is parallel to that in the "true" (4.3.1.). For just as the celestial bodies are always true, but still have a cause of their truth, so there are things that are necessary and everlasting, certainly, but nonetheless have a cause of their permanency.[38] This structure is easily recognizable in the construction of Thomas's third "way" to the existence of God (see 6.3.2.).

But if science is directed to the necessary, then the question arises how in that case there can be a way from the phenomenon of motion, which is typical of the natural, to the intelligible. For that which is in motion is not necessary but contingent: it can be otherwise than it is. The mobility seems to clash with the intelligility sought by the desire to know: "the intelligible insofar as it is intelligible, is necessary and incorruptible" (*S.c.G.* II, 55).

6.2.2. *Necessity and physical contingency*

Motion is a basic phenomenon which, more than any other, disposed the Greeks to wonder. For it has a mixture of being and non-being. All that is moved can as such be and not be. How, then, can mobile being ever be the object of the theoretical reason, since science deals with the necessary and all that is necessary is as such immobile?[39] And how can definitions be established of what is contingent, since *definitio est non corruptibilium, sed sempiternorum* (2.2.2.)?

The discrepancy between what is seen and what is envisioned induced the philosophers of Elea to deny motion as phenomenal seeming. It was

---

[37] *Metaph.* V, c. 5, 1015 b 9ff. (lect. 6, 839).
[38] Cf. *In VIII Phys.*, lect. 3, 995; *In De causis*, lect. 26 (with the rejection of the idea of a *causa sui*).
[39] *In Boeth. De trin.* 5, 1. Cf. 5, 2 obj. 4.

the same difficulty, so Thomas says, that drove Plato to posit his doctrine of ideas. Believing that all sensible things were always in flux, he thought there can be no science concerning them. "So he claimed that there were substances separated from the sensible world, which might be the objects of science and definitions."[40] Science deals with "separated" forms.

With Aristotle, Thomas rejects this solution. There is science of what is subject to becoming and corruption. For a thing that is contingent can be considered in two ways. First, it can be considered insofar as it is contingent. Secondly, it can be considered insofar as something of necessity is found in it: for nothing is so contingent that it has not in it something necessary.[41] This element of necessity is the precondition of the possibility of physics, it enables us "to have an immobile science of mobile things" (*de rebus mobilibus immobilem scientiam habere*).[42] Wherein consists the necessity which the intelligibility of the contingent requires?

In *Metaph*. V the concept "necessary" is taken up directly after "nature". Thomas introduces the discussion with a remark that points to a close connection with causality:

> Having distinguished terms which signify causes, the Philosopher now discusses a term which designates something pertaining to the notion of cause, namely, "necessary"; for a cause is that from which something else follows of necessity (*ad quam de necessitate sequitur aliud*).[43]

A cause has an influx of being that can be differentiated in four ways. To these ways are related diverse modes of necessity.[44]

The primary sense of "necessary" was "what cannot be otherwise". This formulation deserves particular attention. The primary sense of "necessary" must be understood from and in correspondence with the idea of physical contingency, the modality of the being that is in motion. Necessary is not: what cannot not be; necessary is what cannot be *otherwise* than it is. This "absolute necessity" (*necessitas absoluta*) belongs to a thing "by reason of something that is intimately and closely connected with it": the form or the matter or the very essence of a thing.[45] On an *intrinsic* cause depends that which is absolutely necessary. Once again this con-

---

[40] *In Boeth. De trin.* 5, 2; *In I Post. Anal.*, lect. 16, 140.

[41] *S. Th.* I, 86, 3: Contingentia dupliciter possunt considerari. Uno modo secundum quod contingentia sunt. Alio modo, secundum quod in eis aliquid necessitatis invenitur: *nihil enim est adeo contingens, quin in se aliquid necessarium habeat; De spirit. creat.* q. un., art. 10 ad 8.

[42] *S. Th.* I, 84, 1 ad 3.

[43] *In V Metaph.*, lect. 6, 827; cf. lect. 1, 749.

[44] Cf. *S.c.G.* II, 30: Diversimode autem ex diversis causis necessitas sumitur in rebus creatis.

[45] *In V Metaph.*, lect. 6, 833.

firms the importance for philosophy of the "what" question, for this question inquires into the essence of that which is.

Without its essential principles, which are matter and form, a thing cannot be. From these principles results an absolute necessity in a thing with respect to its being.[46] In the next section we will deal with the different roles of these principles more extensively. On account of matter, some things are necessarily corruptible, which is to say they can be otherwise than they are. From the form there results, however, a necessity to be. The form is "something divine" (4.3.2.), because it lends stability and permanence. Since the essential form of what is in motion is, considered in itself, immobile, there are sciences and definitions of contingent things.[47]

That which is necessary not in an absolute sense but in a certain respect (*secundum quid*) depends on an *extrinsic* cause—the end and the agent.[48] Determinative for necessity by the efficient or moving cause is not only the efficient cause itself but also the condition of the recipient of the action. If the agent causes an effect that is contrary to the disposition and receptivity of the patient, there will be necessity of violence (*necessitas violentiae*). This second type of necessity, "coercion", entails the subject's being moved by an extrinsic cause to something for which it has no aptitude by its own nature.[49] For "violent," according to Aristotle's definition in *Ethic. Nic.* III, 1 (1110 b 15 – 17) is "that of which the principle is extrinsic and to which that which has undergone the force confers nothing" (*cuius principium est extra, nil conferente vim passo*).[50] If, on the other hand, the order is such that the effect is not contrary to the disposition of the subject, then there will be not necessity of violence, but natural necessity.[51]

From the final cause there results necessity insofar as the end is the later in being (*posterius in esse*). This is not an "absolute" but a "conditional" (*conditionata*) necessity.[52] It is discussed extensively in the second book of the *Phys.* (c. 9), because this third mode of necessity is found in natural becoming. Aristotle refers to it (199 b 34) as "hypothetical" necessity. It is a question of a necessity that is conditioned by the end to be realized: if this must become, then that must be; the consequence necessitates the

---

[46] *S.c.G.* II, 30.
[47] *In Boeth. De trin.* 5, 2: Formae et rationes rerum quamvis in motu existentium, prout in se considerantur, absque motu sunt. Et sic de eis sunt scientiae et diffinitiones. Cf. *ibid.* 5, 2 ad 4; *In I Post. Anal.*, lect. 16, 141; *In VI Ethic.*, lect. 1, 1123; lect. 3, 1146.
[48] *In V Metaph.*, lect. 6, 834.
[49] *Ibid.*, lect. 6, 835; *S.c.G.* II, 30.
[50] *In III Ethic.*, lect. 1, 387.
[51] For this opposition between "natura" and "violentia" see 7.1.1.1.
[52] *S.c.G.* II, 30.

antecedent. This conditional necessity governs the 'via in naturam'. In the natural process, the necessary results from what are the later causes in being, namely, the end and the form as the end of generation.[53] The character of this necessity implies that in motion directed towards an end something can happen 'per accidens' that is not intended as such (cf. 3.3.1. on "chance" as 'causa per accidens').

What is in motion is to be reduced to that in it which is necessary. In this context it is striking that the absolute necessity, i.e., the necessity from essential principles, is also called by Thomas "natural necessity" (*necessitas naturalis*).[54] "Necessary," "intrinsic cause," and "nature" go together. Implicit in this conjunction is a reference to *nature* as the intelligibility of *mobile* being.

6.3. *Contingency and creature*

6.3.1. *The mutability of the creature*

In his writing *In Boeth. De trin.* (q. 5, art. 2) Thomas raises the following objection. Every creature is mutable, for, as Augustine says in *De civitate Dei* (XI, 10), immutability belongs to God alone. Now, natural philosophy is concerned with what is in motion. Does the consideration of all that is creaturely not therefore belong to natural philosophy? Mutability, so Thomas replies, belongs to all the creaturely, but *this* mutability is not in virtue of a natural motion (*secundum aliquem motum naturalem*) of which the philosophers have spoken but in virtue of the dependence upon God (*secundum dependentiam ad Deum*). And that dependence falls under the consideration of metaphysics rather than under that of natural philosophy.[55]

This metaphysical dependency is expressed philosophically with the term "contingency." B. DELFGAAUW writes in his monograph on Thomas that the core of created being "lies simply and solely in the total dependence on God, the complete contingency of the creature, that can be and not be, in contrast to the being of God, that cannot not be."[56]

"Contingency" is according to H. BLUMENBERG one of the few concepts of specifically Christian provenance in the history of metaphysics.[57] Yet the fact can not be disregarded that the term was derived from Aris-

---

[53] *In II Phys.*, lect. 15, 270; *De principiis naturae*, c. 4; *In I Post. Anal.*, lect. 42, 374.
[54] *S. Th.* III, 14, 2.
[55] *In Boeth. De trin.* 5, 2 ad 7. Cf. *S. Th.* I, 9, 2 ad 1.
[56] *Thomas van Aquino* (Bussum, 1980), p. 63. Cf. E. Gilson, *The Spirit of Mediaeval Philosophy*, p. 71.
[57] In *Religion in Geschichte und Gegenwart* III, 1793, s.v. "Kontingenz."

totelian logic.[58] Through Boethius's translation of the *Perihermeneias* especially, 'contingens' as a rendering of the Greek 'endechomenon' gained entry into medieval philosophy. Thus for its sense, we must accordingly first consult the logic.

In his commentary on *Perih.* I, c. 9 Thomas presents various divisions of the proposition. One of these concerns the modality of the judgment. According to the relation of the predicate to the subject, the categorical proposition can be "modified" in three ways. If the predicate *per se* belongs to the subject (e.g., "Man is an animal"), then their composition is "necessary" or "natural." For "necessary" is what cannot be otherwise than it is. If, however, the predicate is contrary to the ratio of the subject (e.g., "Man is an ass"), then the statement is "impossible." It is "possible" or "contingent" if the relation of predicate and subject is neither *per se* necessary nor *per se* impossible.[59] What is contingent can be and not be. From this explanation by means of the predicative composition, it becomes understandable that in Aristotle's ontology the term "contingent" can be connected with mobile being. The modality of the being in motion is that it can as such be and not be (6.2.2.).[60]

However, in medieval thought, "contingency" acquires a much more radical sense from the perspective of creation: it now determines being as being. The term brings to expression that things in themselves have neither persistence nor the foundation of their existence. For the things are created "out of nothing" and are kept in being only by God's will. It is "perhaps the most far-reaching way in which medieval thought opposed itself to ancient thought."[61] That all that is creaturely is contingent is the central moment in the philosophy of Duns Scotus.[62] R. PANIKKAR indicates as a general mark of the Christian conception that "the Greek horizon of *mobility* is altered into that of *contingency* . . . This sense of contingency is in essence a feeling of *creatureliness*."[63]

---

[58] Particularly *Perih.* I, c. 9 (Thomas: lect. 13–15). Cf. G. Verbeke, ed., *Ammonius, Commentaire sur le Peri Hermeneias d'Aristote, Traduction de Guillaume de Moerbeke* (Louvain and Paris, 1961), pp. xxxviff.: "Contingence et Vérité—La doctrine d'Ammonius et de Saint Thomas."

[59] *In I Perih.*, lect. 13, 166. Cf. Thomas's writing *De propositionibus modalibus* (ed. Leonina t. 43, 421–22).

[60] Thomas makes this connection himself in his commentary on *Perihermeneias* (lect. 14, 181).

[61] L.M. de Rijk, *Middeleeuwse wijsbegeerte*, p. 92; cf. p. 273ff. (in the French tr. *La philosophie au moyen âge*, p. 70; cf. pp. 216ff.).

[62] Cf. C. Solaguren, "Contingencia y creación en la filosofia de Duns Escoto," in *De doctrina Ioannis Duns Scoti*, vol. 2 (Rome, 1968), pp. 297–348, p. 320: "Todo ser creado es essencialmente y existencialmente contingente."

[63] R. Panikkar, *El concepto de naturaleza*, 2nd ed. (Madrid, 1972), p. 106: "El horizonte griego de la *movilidad* se cambia en el de la *contingencia* . . . Este vivencia de la contingencia

There is, according to the Flemish philosopher DE PETTER, an insufficiency that marks all things in this world and hence the world as a whole.
"It lies in the contingency intrinsic to the being itself of all things. It
means that the being of all things in this world appears as completely
gratuitous."[64] This contingency belongs to things, not as a result of
something other, but from themselves. "This immediate datum, in view
of its all-encompassing character with regard to the empirical world, raises
the question which is the metaphysical question *par excellence*: 'Why is there
something and not rather nothing?'"[65]

6.3.2. *Thomas's view of contingency*[66]

Is this also Thomas's view of contingency? Does the core of created
being lie for him in contingency? It must be observed that on this point
Aquinas has either been misunderstood by many interpreters or no longer
followed. For Thomas neither is created being identical with contingent
being nor is the ontological insufficiency an immediate datum nor does he
speak of a contingency intrinsic to the being itself of things. We want to
elaborate this conclusion in four steps.

(1) It is immediately striking that Thomas uses the term "contingent"
exclusively in an Aristotelian sense. That is, he views contingency as an
effect of the *material* mode of being. "Contingency arises from matter, for
the contingent is what can be and not be, and potency belongs to matter.
Necessity, however, results from form."[67] Contingency belongs to something on account of matter, which is as such a being in potency. What can
be, however, can also not be. Matter is in potency to non-being, insofar
as it, existing under one form, is in potency to another form contrary to
that with which it is united. Because of their matter certain things are
necessarily corruptible (*ex ordine materiae necessario res aliquae corruptibiles exis-
tunt*). The form, on the other hand, is act, and through it things exist in
act. Hence from it there results in some things a necessity to be (*necessitas*

---

es en el fondo un sentimiento de *creaturabilidad*." Cf. by the same author (although his
name is written here as R. Paniker): "La novedad que en el concepto de naturaleza
introduce el Christianismo," *Tijdschrift voor Philosophie* 13 (1951): 236–62.
[64] *Naar het metafysische* (Utrecht and Antwerp, 1972), p. 156.
[65] *Ibid.*, p. 161.
[66] See for this view especially C. Fabro, "Intorno alla nozione 'tomista' di contingenza," *Rivista di Filosofia Neoscolastica* 30 (1938): 132–49; and J. Gevaert, *Contingent en Noodzakelijk Bestaan volgens Thomas van Aquino* (Brussels, 1965). Not very profitable is G. Jalbert,
Nécessité et Contingence chez St. Thomas et chez ses prédécesseurs (Ottawa, 1961).
[67] *S. Th.* I, 86, 3: Est autem unumquodque contingens ex parte materiae; quia contingens est quod potest esse et non esse. Potentia autem pertinet ad materiam; necessitas
autem consequitur rationem formae.

ad esse). And this happens for two reasons: either because these things are subsistent forms, so that there is in them no potency to non-being—such is the case with separated substances; or because the form through its perfection completely fulfills the potency of matter, so that there remains in these things no potency to a contrary form nor consequently to non-being—such is the case with the celestial bodies. Both groups of beings are absolutely necessary because they can not be otherwise than they are.[68]

The composition of matter and form structures this conception of contingency. Whatever possesses matter that is subject to contrariety is contingent; it bears in itself the possibility of non-being. From this follows a fundamental dichotomy of the universe: there is a necessary , imperishable part and a contingent, perishable one.[69] Contingency is the mark of the sublunar beings; of them ''corruptible'' is predicated 'per se'.

(2) ''Among the parts of the whole universe, the first distinction to be observed is that between the contingent and the necessary (*prima distinctio apparet secundum contingens et necessarium*). For the highest beings are necessary, incorruptible, and immobile'' (*S.c.G.* III, 94). This bifurcation of the universe is maintained by Thomas in a world that has been created ''out of nothing.'' Instructive in this regard is his exposition in *S.c.G.* II, 30.

Although all things depend on the will of God as first cause, nevertheless absolute necessity is not on this account excluded from things, so that we should have to concede that everything is contingent. True, this might appear to someone to be the case on account of the fact that things have with no absolute necessity proceeded from their cause, for usually an effect is contingent which does not proceed from its cause necessarily. Yet there are some created things whose being is absolutely necessary because in them there is no potency to non-being. Other things, however, were so brought forth by God that there is in their nature the potency to non-being; and this results from the fact that their matter is in potency with respect to another form. Hence things in which there is no matter or—if matter is present—no potency to another form have no potency to non-being; they are simply and absolutely necessary.

Thomas in *S.c.G.* II, 30 accordingly draws the conclusion, ''To be simply necessary is not incompatible with the notion of created being.'' Being created is not identical with being contingent. A few remarks may serve to clarify this striking conclusion. First, we recall the meaning of ''necessary'' in the absolute sense. Necessary is not: what cannot not be; it is:

---

[68] *S.c.G.* II, 30; *De pot.* 5, 3; *De verit.* 5, 2 ad 6.

[69] *S.c.G.* III, 94; III, 72: Ens autem dividitur per contingens et necessarium; et est per se divisio entis; *In X Metaph.*, lect. 12, 2145; *S.Th.* I, 22, 4 ad 3.

what cannot be *otherwise* than it is. From this determination it becomes immediately understandable why in Thomas's view created being and necessary being are not incompatible with each other. For the determination
of necessary is fully applicable to whatever, once it has come into being,
is not susceptible to corruption, is imperishable. In the second place,
Thomas's conviction that necessary being and created being do not conflict is shored up by the idea of a hierarchy in the necessary, which is conceived after the model of demonstrative science: the necessity of the conclusion is caused by the necessary premises (cf. 6.2.1.). Thomas explicitly
makes this connection in *S.c.G.* II, 30:

> To be simply necessary is not incompatible with the notion of created being:
> for nothing prevents a thing being necessary whose necessity nevertheless
> has a cause, as in the case of the conclusions of demonstrations.[70]

Thomas's limited conception of contingency was criticized already in
the Middle Ages. A. MAURER does not share this criticism: "Indeed, the
very possibility of science and philosophy was here at stake, for, as Aristotle shows in his *Posterior Analytics*, these are impossible without necessary
objects."[71] The value of this argument is rather doubtful—why would
the contingency of the world as a whole exclude necessary relations between things? Yet it is in a certain respect representative for the model of
thought that is employed here.

The reason that necessary being and creaturely being are not incompatible Thomas actually gives already in the argumentation of *S.c.G.* II,
30 mentioned above. Necessity and contingency in things are distinguished not with reference to the first cause, God, but in relation to their
next causes, the intrinsic principles of form and matter.[72] Both modes of
being do find their ultimate origin in God. For He is the universal cause
of being, thus also of the differences of being, the contingent and the
necessary. In keeping with the 'lex necessitatis vel contingentiae' (*In VI
Metaph.*, lect. 3, 1222) set by Him, the causality of finite things is ordered.
The creating cause itself transcends this order.[73]

---

[70] *S.c.G.* II, 30: Esse autem necesse simpliciter non repugnat ad rationem esse creati:
nihil enim prohibet aliquid esse necesse quod tamen suae necessitatis causam habet, sicut
conclusiones demonstrationum. Cf. *S.Th.* I, 44, 1 ad 2; 50, 5 ad 3.

[71] A. Maurer, "St. Thomas and Henry of Harclay on Created Nature," in *La Filosofia della natura* (Milan, 1966), p. 545. Henry of Harclay (d. 1317), a student of Duns
Scotus's, sharply criticized Thomas's view of contingency.

[72] See also *S.c.G.* II, 55: Res dicuntur necessariae et contingentes secundum potentiam quae est in eis, et non secundum potentiam Dei.

[73] *De malo* 16, 7 ad 15; *In I Perih.*, lect. 14, 197: Et ... omnes dependeant a voluntate
divina, sicut a *prima causa, quae transcendit ordinem necessitatis et contingentiae*; *In VI Metaph.*,
lect. 3, 1219ff.

Thus it might appear that the bifurcation of the necessary and the contingent is limited to finite being. However, that this is not the case becomes nowhere clearer than in Thomas's third "way" to the existence of God (*S. Th.* I, 2, 3), which is often—but unjustly—called a proof 'ex contingentia mundi'. The point of departure is not the ontological insufficiency of the creaturely as an immediate datum. The demonstration starts from the evident empirical fact of the contingency of material beings ("We find in reality things that are possible to be and not to be, since they are found to be generated, and to be corrupted, and consequently it is possible for them to be and not to be"). This phenomenon sets off a causal reasoning that ends in: "there must be something that is necessary" (*oportet aliquid esse necessarium in rebus*). With that conclusion, however, the proof is not yet at an end, because necessary being is twofold: "But every necessary thing either has its necessity caused by another, or not." By means of the elimination of an infinite series, finally a being is reached that is necessary *per se*: "what all call God."[74]

The Greek division of the universe into a contingent part and a necessary part is retained. For it is within the necessary that the proof differentiates a necessary being *per se* from one "by another." As an argument for this differentiation Thomas in *S.c.G.* II, 30 adduces the hierarchical order of the world. The more distant a thing is from that which is a being by virtue of itself, namely, God, the nearer it is to non-being. The nearer a thing is to God, the further it is removed from non-being. Now, the things that are lowest are near to non-being through having potency to non-being. Therefore what is nearest to God must be such—that the order of things be complete—that it possesses in itself no potency to non-being. Such things are absolutely necessary. Thus, some created things have being necessarily (*Sic igitur aliqua creata de necessitate habent esse*).

It is striking in this reasoning how strongly the order of creation remains tied to Greek cosmology. From the standpoint of Thomas's view it is incorrect to say that finite beings are separated from God "by the

---

[74] An example of the confusion with respect to the "tertia via" is L.M. De Rijk's account in his *Middeleeuwse wijsbegeerte*, p. 164 (French tr. p. 127). He presents the proof as follows: "It is meaningful to interpret the created order as contingent; the concept 'contingent being' is meaningless without that of 'necessary being'; thus there is 'necessary being.'" This conclusion, according to De Rijk, holds for the order of thought, certainly. But "thus there *is* 'necessary being'" by no means follows for the order of being.

This account seems to me untenable simply because Thomas nowhere regards contingency as the creaturely mode of being. Therefore Thomas's argumentation is not directed towards a "necessary being" but towards an *ens necessarium* that is *per se*—a distinction that is ignored in De Rijk's exposition.

abyss which opposes necessary Being and contingent being.''[75]

(3) In Thomas the composition of form and matter remains determinative for contingency. Since he further rejects universal hylomorphism, a contingency affecting created being as such would seem to be excluded. Yet this step may be premature. For the issue at stake is not primarily a term but the philosophical conception behind it. Now, did we not see earlier (cf. 1.8.1.) that Aquinas knows yet another composition, which extends to all the creaturely—including the immaterial substances—namely, that of 'essentia' and 'esse'? Is the metaphysical contingency of created being not implied in that composition? Such is the view of GILSON,[76] among others.

Certainly, there is in the immaterial, simple substance too potentiality of being (*potentia essendi*). For every separated substance after God participates in being. What participates is composed, is marked by the non-identity of participating "essence" and participated "being." 'Essentia' and 'esse' are related as potency and act. Therefore there is in every substance, however simple, a potency to "being" that it has "from another."[77] On the basis of this relation Thomas can say (see 6.3.1.) that mutability belongs to every creature in virtue of the dependence on God. Even the necessary beings are dependent on the influx of being from the first cause.

The relation to God permanently qualifies creaturely being. "For the being of every creature depends on God, so that not for a moment could it subsist, but would fall into nothingness, were it not kept in being by the operation of the divine power" (*S. Th.* I, 104, 1). That things, although created, could exist in and through themselves is for Thomas an intrinsic impossibility. To the question whether "God could communicate to any creature that it is kept in being by itself without God" he says literally that this is a contradiction.[78] Things constantly need divine preservation, which is not a new action but the continuation of the action whereby the Creator gives being.[79]

That is not to say, however, that in the immaterial, simple substance there is also a *potentia ad non esse*, i.e., that it is intrinsically contingent—for

---

[75] Contra L.-B. Geiger, *La participation dans la philosophie de S. Thomas d'Aquin* (Paris, 1942), p. 308.

[76] *The Spirit of Mediaeval Philosophy*, p. 435, n. 1.

[77] *In VIII Phys.*, lect. 21, 1153: Omnis ergo substantia quae est post primam substantiam simplicem, participat esse. Omne autem participans componitur ex participante et participato et participans est in potentia ad participatum. In omni ergo substantia quantumque simplici, post primam substantiam simplicem, est *potentia essendi*; *Quodl.* IX, 4, 1.

[78] *De pot.* 5, 2 and ad 2.

[79] *S. Th.* I, 104, 1 ad 4.

contingent is what can be *and not be*. In *De pot*. 5, 3 Thomas discusses the
view of Avicenna ("all things except God have in themselves a possibility
of being and non-being") and the view of Averroës ("some things are
created in whose nature there is no possibility of non-being"). The latter
opinion he considers "more reasonable" than that of Avicenna, in which
created being is identical with contingent being. Why? Such a possibility
of being and non-being is incompatible with the mode of being of the
simple substance. As pure form the separated substance is "necessitated"
to be. Participation entails composition, certainly, but not contingency:
not every potency relates to opposites. Medieval physics already afforded
Thomas a proof of this thesis; celestial bodies have matter, but nonetheless
not a possibility of non-being. With greater reason the potency of the
simple substances is in virtue of their nature not separable from the act
of being. They have 'esse' necessarily.[80]

(4) But is this conclusion not contrary to the Christian tradition? More
than once Thomas cites in this connection a passage from Johannes
Damascenus's *De fide orthodoxa* (II, 3): "All that is out of nothing is
changeable to nothing" (*Omne quod est ex nihilo, vertibile est in nihil*). Is therefore not every creature changeable to nothing (*S. Th.* III, 13, 2)?

In *S.c.G.* II, 30 Thomas takes up this objection. If it be said that what
is from nothing of itself tends to nothing, it still does not follow that in all
creatures there is a potency to non-being. For created things tend *to*
nothing in the same way in which they are *from* nothing, namely, solely
according to the power of their efficient cause (*secundum potentiam agentis*).
"Consequently, the potency to non-being is not in created things, but in
the Creator there is the power to give them being, or to cease pouring forth
being into them" (*Sic igitur et rebus creatis non inest potentia ad non esse, sed
Creatori inest potentia ut eis det esse vel eis desinat esse influere*). As God alone can
bring things to being, not of natural necessity but by His will, so can He
also bring them again to nothingness.

In *De pot*. 5,3 the question is: "Can God reduce a creature to nothingness?" (*Utrum Deus possit creaturam in nihilum redigere*). Impossible for God
is what is impossible in itself. The simple non-existence of creatures is not
in itself impossible, for otherwise their non-existence would have to involve an inner contradiction. But the statement "The creature does not
exist at all" (*Creatura non est omnino*) does not imply any contradiction, for

---

[80] *De spirit. creat.* q. un., a. 1: Remoto igitur fundamento materiae, si remaneat aliqua
forma determinatae naturae per se subsistens, non in materia, adhuc comparabitur ad
suum esse ut potentia ad actum: non dico autem ut potentiam separabilem ab actu, sed
quam semper suus actus comitetur; *In VIII Phys.*, lect. 21, 1153ff. (a discussion with Alexander of Aphrodisias and Averroës about the cause of the sempiternity of the celestial
bodies).

the creature is not its being but has received it.[81] The "annihilation" of the created world is *possible* if God should will it; it is in His "absolute power" to do this.

But from the standpoint of the 'potentia Dei ordinata' this can no longer be said. At the end of *De pot.* 5, 3 Thomas establishes: it is not impossible for God to reduce things to nothing since it is not necessary that He give things being except on the presupposition of his decree and foreknowledge (*nisi ex suppositione ordinationis et praescientiae*). Now God ordained that He would keep things in being in perpetuity (*in perpetuum*). In His wisdom "He created all things that they might be" (Wisdom 1:14) and not that they might sink again into nothingness.[82] This concrete *reality* is the subject of *De pot.* 5, 4: "The universe of creatures will never be reduced to nothingness." For this certainty Thomas adduces two arguments.

The first argument starts from the divine will, on which the being of creatures depends (*ex divina voluntate, ex qua creaturarum esse dependet*). Although free with respect to the creaturely, God's will still has, in a conditional sense (*ex suppositione tamen facta*), some necessity. Because His will is unchangeable, it is necessary—if it be supposed that He wills something at some time—that He will it always, although it is not necessary that he will to be always that which He wills to be at some time. Now he who wills something for its own sake wills that this be forever. For it is not intended as a means to an end. Now, God wills the created universe "for its own sake."[83] From this it is apparent that He wills the permanence of the creaturely. God remains faithful to His creating will and will not withdraw from things His gift of being.

The second argument Thomas takes from the nature of things (*ex ipsa*

---

[81] *De pot.* 5, 3: Creaturas autem simpliciter non esse, non est in se impossibile quasi contradictionem implicans, alias ab aeterno fuissent. Et hoc ideo est, quia non sunt suum esse, ut sic cum dicitur 'Creatura non est omnino', oppositum praedicati includatur in definitione, ut si dicatur 'Homo non est animal rationale': huiusmodi enim contradictionem implicant, et sunt secundum se impossibilia.

[82] Cf. *Quodl.* IV, 3, 1.
We find here the distinction "potentia Dei absoluta/ordinata" that is to play such an important role in late medieval thought. The difference is, however, significant: Thomas's speculation is not primarily focussed on the idea of the absolute power of God.
For the notion of 'necessitas ex suppositione', see A. Hayen, *La communication de l'être d'après saint Thomas d'Aquin*, vol. 2, pp. 153–77. See also 6.2.2. for the Aristotelian background.

[83] *De pot.* 5, 4: Deus autem creaturarum universitatem vult propter se ipsam, licet et propter se ipsum eam vult esse; haec enim duo non repugnant. Vult enim Deus ut creaturae sint propter eius bonitatem, ut eam scilicet suo modo imitentur et repraesentent ... Unde idem est dictu, quod Deus omnia propter se ipsum fecit ... et quod creaturas fecerit propter earum esse.

rerum natura). God framed each nature in such a way as not to deprive it of its property. The natural mark of the immaterial substances is their sempiternity. That is why He will not take this property from them, lest He act contrary to His decrees.[84]

These two arguments deserve further reflection. For they proceed from different perspectives. The first argument proceeds from the unchangeableness (*immobilitas*) of God's will. Upon it depends the "being" (*esse*) of things, the dependence that marks the *creature*. The second proceeds from the *nature*, whose permanence is the ontological expression of the order willed by God.

6.3.3. *The creature as "sign" and as "thing"*

Thomas's view gains relief when compared to that of his contemporary Bonaventure. A passage from the latter's commentary on the *Sententiae* is instructive in this regard.[85] The mutation that affects the entire substance of the thing is called change (*versio*). Each creature is *vertibilis per naturam*. What does this mean? Nature signifies "the natural origin." The origin of the creature is *ex nihilo* and *ex suis principiis*. Hence something can be "natural" for the creature for two reasons. "Natural" is in the first place what belongs to it on account of its genesis "out of nothing." "Nothing," however, cannot be the positive cause of something. It is the cause of the inner deficiency of the creatures through which they are by nature unable to sustain themselves. For as the reason of their changeability, not an "efficient cause" must be adduced but a "deficient cause." In the second place, that can be called "natural" which belongs to something on account of its own principles. In that sense it cannot be said that the creature is naturally "unchangeable." For natural is what nature can do. But the intrinsic principles are not able to sustain the thing. Only by God's gratuitous goodness are the creatures kept in being. The creatures possess unchangeableness not *per naturam*—that belongs to God alone— but *per gratiam*.[86] It is owing to this "grace," this "surplus" in their being, that in Bonaventure the creatures are significative, that they refer to God.

The Middle Ages are "an era of the symbol, as much as, indeed more

---

[84] Cf. *S.c.G.* II, 55; *S. Th.* I, 105, 6.

[85] *In I Sent.* d. 8, p. 1, art. 2, q. 2 and ad 7, 8.

[86] Cf. J. Ratzinger, "Der Wortgebrauch von natura und die beginnende Verselbständigung der Metaphysik bei Bonaventura," in *Die Metaphysik im Mittelalter*, Misc. Mediaevalia, vol. 2 (Berlin, 1963), p. 496.

than, an era of dialectic'' (CHENU).[87] The visible is the sign of the invisible, the "symbol" of the Origin. A symbol is, in the circumscription of Hugh of St. Victor: "a juxtaposition, that is, a coaptation of visible forms brought forth to demonstrate an invisible thing."[88] The visible "demonstrates" what cannot be seen of God, the natural becomes a theophany. Alanus of Insulis poetized: "Every creature of the world is, for us, like a book and a picture and a mirror as well."[89]

For the mind that reads this book, the way of knowledge becomes an *itinerarium mentis in Deum*. In his writing of that name, Bonaventure states that all creatures of the visible world convey the mind to the eternal God because they are images of that Origin, of that art, because they are God-given "signs." These are brought forth (*proposita*) to human minds so that "through the sensible which they see they are conveyed to the intelligible which they do not see, as by signs to the signified." The creatures signify (*significant*) the 'invisibilia Dei' because God is the origin, exemplar, and end of every creature, and every effect is "sign" of the cause, every copy of the exemplar, and every way of the end to which it leads.[90]

In this signification philosophy stands at a crossroads. The pagan philosophers know only the nature of things; they do not know them as a vestige. They are closed to the reflection of the divine exemplarity in reality as creaturely reality (cf. 4.3.). At this point, where the ways part, a decisive choice must be made. Either one stops—and that is the way of deviation—at the beauty of the creature in order to know it in its own being or one is moved by it to go further. *Aut sistitur in pulchritudine creaturae aut per illam tenditur in aliud. Si primo modo tunc est via deviationis.*[91] The creatures can be considered either as things or as signs (*creaturae possunt considerari ut res vel ut signa*). The deviation of the philosophers consists just in their misappraising the significative character of the creaturely.[92]

Thomas too knows this signification of things.[93] Yet in conjunction

---

[87] "The Symbolist Mentality," in *Nature, Man, and Society in the Twelfth Century* (Chicago, 1968), p. 103.

[88] *Exp. in Hiër. cael. III*, init. (Migne PL 175, 960): ... symbolum, collatio videlicet, id est coaptatio visibilium formarum ad demonstrationem rei invisibilis propositarum.

[89] Alanus de Insulis, *Rythmus* (Migne PL 210, 579): Omnis mundi creatura quasi liber et pictura nobis est et speculum.

[90] *Itinerarium* II, 11 and 12. Cf. U. Leinsle, *Res et signum. Das Verständnis zeichenhafter Wirklichkeit in der Theologie Bonaventuras* (Munich, Paderborn, and Vienna, 1976); L. Piazza, *Mediazione simbolica in S. Bonaventura* (Vicenza, 1978), pp. 65ff.

[91] *In I Sent.* d. 3, p. 1, a. un., q. 2 ad 1.

[92] *In I Sent.* d. 3, p. 1, a. un., q. 3 ad 2. Cf. E. Gilson, *La philosophie de saint Bonaventure* (Paris, 1924), pp. 209ff.

[93] *S. Th.* I, 1, 10: Ipsae res significatae per voces etiam significant aliquid.

with twelfth-century tendencies to put greater emphasis on the proper nature of things,[94] he did not take the path of symbolist thought. That is directly related to the fact that in the investigation of things he regards the 'via Aristotelica' as natural to man as 'animal rationale' (6.2.1.). This way eliminates the "epiphany of the transcendent."[95] It proceeds from the visible to seek the inner essence, determines conceptually what things are in themselves. Science considers in this changeable world a necessity that is intrinsic, an intelligibility that is proper to this world and concentrated in the notion of *nature*.

Typical of Thomas's view is the manner in which he handles the traditional categories in his *Scriptum* on the *Sententiae*. Peter Lombard had structured his work on the basis of the distinctions from Augustine's *De doctrina christiana: uti/frui* and *signum/res*.[96] In 1.6.1. we saw that in Augustine's writing the distinction between "to use" and "to enjoy" has a prominent place. The significative character of things is closely connected with this distinction. For that which alone may be enjoyed is God. All the rest must be used, that is, brought into reference to this end. In his commentary, Thomas takes note of the authoritative framework, but already in the exposition of the text he raises a critical objection. "All creatures are a sign of the divine goodness; and so it seems that almost everything that is dealt with in this science is a sign." He answers:

> Although creatures are a sign of something, they are still not established for that principally. Therefore they are not contained under the signs except in a secondary sense.[97]

The creature is not first of all a reference to something else but a thing (*res*) with an intrinsic, "absolute" meaning.[98] With this conclusion we have to connect the special philosophical sense which the term "thing" has in Thomas. "Thing" belongs to the so-called transcendentals, is a

---

[94] See in particular the studies by M.-D. Chenu, "Nature and Man—The Renaissance of the Twelfth Century," in *Nature, Man, and Society in the Twelfth Century*, pp. 1–48; and T. Gregory, "La nouvelle idée de nature et de savoir scientifique au XIIe siècle," in J.E. Murdoch and E.D. Sylla, eds., *The Cultural Context of Medieval Learning* (Dordrecht and Boston, 1975), pp. 193–218.

[95] Cf. G. Durand, "L'Occident iconoclaste, Contribution à l'histoire du symbolisme," *Cahiers internationaux de symbolisme* 2 (1963): 3–15; M.-D. Chenu, "The Symbolist Mentality," p. 134.

[96] Lib. I. dist. 1, cap. 2 (ed. PP. Collegii S. Bonaventurae Ad Claras Aquas, T. I, p. II (Grottaferrata, 1971) p. 56).

[97] *In I Sent.* d. 1, exp. textus: Quamvis creaturae sint signum alicujus, nihilominus tamen ad hoc principaliter non sunt institutae: et ideo non continentur sub signis, nisi secundum quid.

[98] *Ibid.*: *Signum* enim est quod est institutum ad aliud significandum: *res* autem est quae habet absolutam significationem non ad aliud relatam.

property of being as being, and is convertible with "being." Between
these terms there is only a conceptual distinction, to the effect that "being" (*ens*) is derived from the act of being, while "thing" expresses the
essence or quiddity.[99] In other words, 'res' points to the intrinsic intelligibility of being, as is also evident from the etymology which Thomas
advances: "'res' is called what has a determinate and stable being (*esse
ratum et firmum*) in nature" (*In II Sent.* 37, 1, 1). 'Res' is derived, so
Thomas suggests, from the Latin 'ratum', which means determinate,
stable, valid. That every "being" is a "thing" implies, on the one hand,
that it is fixed and stable through its essence and, on the other hand, that
we are thereby able to "think" the "thing." "For a thing is intelligible
only through its definition and its essence" (*De ente*, c. 1).

Thus we see that Thomas in his *Scriptum* does not follow the division of
Peter Lombard (*de rebus ... de signis*) but advances a scheme of his own:
things shall be considered insofar as they proceed from God as principle
and insofar as they return to Him as end.[100] In the ultimate analysis the
relation to God, the Alpha and the Omega, becomes manifest. Already
in his earliest work Thomas interprets being as creature with the circular
movement of egress and regress.

This circular movement is not a contingency intrinsic in things. Aquinas judges that "the potency to non-being is not in created things, but in
the Creator there is the power to give them being, or to cease pouring forth
being in them" (*S.c.G.* II, 30). The crux of this thesis, in which the
Latin 'potentia' permits a shift from the passive "potency" to the active
"power," is that the "nothingness" of the creature is taken as a property
that comes to it from outside. Therein lies a philosophical difficulty. The
mark of what is created (see 3.7.1.) is that it has being from another and
that it is, regarded in itself, a "nothing," a "non-being."[101] How then
can the "nothingness" of the creature be taken as an extrinsic quality?
How is that to be rhymed with what Thomas himself argues:

> Non-being has no cause 'per se'; for nothing is a cause except inasmuch as
> it is a being, and a being as such is a cause of being. Therefore, God cannot

---

[99] *De verit.* 1, 1; see especially *In I Sent.* 25, 1, 4 and *In II Sent.* 37, 1, 1. Cf. J. Vande
Wiele, " 'Res' en 'ding', Bijdrage tot een vergelijkende studie van de zijnsopvatting in
het Thomisme en bij Heidegger," *Tijdschrift voor Filosofie* 24 (1962): 427–506.

[100] *In I Sent.* dist. 2, divisio textus: Consideratio hujus doctrinae·erit de rebus, secundum quod exeunt a Deo ut a principio, et secundum quod referuntur in ipsum ut in finem
... *Aliter* potest dividi secundum intentionem Magistri, quod in prima determinat de
rebus, in secunda de signis.

[101] Cf. *De pot.* 3, 13 ad 4; *S. Th.* I–II, 109, 2 ad 2. In section 4.3. we cited the statement: Si consideretur (creatura) sine hoc quod ab alio habet, est nihil et tenebra et falsitas
(*De verit.* 8, 7 ad 2; 2 ae. ser.).

be the cause of tending to non-being, but a creature has this tendency of itself, since it is out of nothing. But 'per accidens' God can cause things to be reduced to non-being by withdrawing his action from them.[102]

It is typical of Thomas's view, however, that it is not this inner deficiency that he regards as decisive for the mutability but the dependence on God.[103] That can also be seen from the construction of his exposition in *De pot.* 5, 3. There are two ways in which something is possible in things created by God. The first is exclusively by the power of the agent (*per potentiam agentis*). From this point of view, as we saw, it is not impossible for God to reduce things to non-being. For the creature is not its being but has this from another. The 'esse' is "outside" the essence. As a result of this non-identity the mutability that belongs to the creaturely is only by the power of the Creator (*secundum potentiam Creantis*). In the second way something is possible by the potency inherent to the things made (*per potentiam quae est in rebus factis*). What is pure form is absolutely necessary. What has a material nature is indeed contingent, but matter itself has no potency to complete non-being. It follows that "in the entire created nature there is not such potency whereby something has the possibility of tending to nothingness." Therefore the permanence of nature was an argument that the world of creatures will not be annihilated.

6.4. *"By the way of resolution" ('Per viam resolutionis')*

The phenomenon of movement is characteristic of natural things. It needs to be reduced to that which makes the natural thing intelligible. After this reduction comes the metaphysical question, which seeks to understand the being of the creature. This quest for intelligibility occurs *per viam resolutionis*.[104] "Resolution" is not to be taken in a material sense as it is in *In II Phys.* (lect. 1, 142), where it is said of the so-called ele-

---

[102] *S. Th.* I, 104, 3 ad 1: Non esse non habet causam per se, quia nihil potest esse causa nisi inquantum est ens; ens autem per se loquendo est causa essendi. Sic igitur Deus non potest esse causa tendendi in non esse, sed *hoc habet creatura ex seipsa, inquantum est de nihilo.* Sed per accidens Deus potest esse causa quod res in nihilum redigantur, subtrahendo scilicet suam actionem a rebus.

[103] *S. Th.* I, 9, 2; 75, 6 ad 2: Cum dicitur aliquid vertibile in nihil non importatur in creatura potentia ad non esse, sed in creatore potentia ad hoc quod esse non influat; *S. Th.* I, 104, 3; III, 13, 2; *De spirit. creat.* q. un., a. 5 ad 4.

[104] In M.-D. Chenu's estimation, "It is St. Thomas in one of the most personal pieces of his methodology" (*Towards Understanding St. Thomas*, p. 191). Yet little has been published on this theme. Reference may be made to L.-M. Régis, "Analyse et synthèse dans l'oeuvre de saint Thomas, "in *Studia Mediaevalia in honorem ... R.J. Martin* (Brugge, 1948), pp. 303–30; and L. Oeing-Hanhoff, "Die Methoden der Metaphysik im Mittelalter," in *Die Metaphysik im Mittelalter*, Misc. Mediaevalia, vol. 2 (Berlin, 1963), p. 71–91.

ments that they cannot be reduced further (*quae non resolvuntur in aliqua corpora priora*), but in the sense of a discursive analysis of the phenomena into their necessary causes. In *De subst. separ.*, c. 6 Thomas criticizes the 'via' of Avicebron, which proceeded analytically (*resolvendo*) towards material principles. That is inconvenient, for matter is less being than form, from which necessity of being results. The analysis needs to be directed towards formal principles.[105]

Resolution or reduction is the prevalent method in Thomas's quest for intelligibility. This was the direction "from questioning towards knowing" (ch. 1). "By the way of predication" (ch. 2) a composition was reduced to identity along two tracks: by the way of definition[106] and via the Platonic model of predication. "By the way of causality" (ch. 3) this movement of thought was confirmed: "What is composite and what is by participation must be reduced to what it is by its essence, as cause."[107] "There are two ways to proceed to the knowledge of truth" (*Est autem duplex via procedendi ad cognitionem veritatis*). The one is *per modum resolutionis*, whereby we advance from the composite to the simple. The other way is the *via compositionis*, a process in the opposite direction.[108] But this way is not proper to man.[109] The specifically human "way of reason" (ch. 5) is a *processus resolutorius*: a progression from what is prior in knowledge to what is ontologically prior.[110] This is likewise the course of the historical way of philosophy, which Thomas sketches; the second basic text speaks expressly of "resolution" (see 5.2.).

A systematic exposition of the "way of resolution" is presented by Thomas in *In Boeth. De trin.* 6, 1 (ad tertiam quaestionem). This text deals with the modes of knowing of the theoretical sciences. "Just as the rational method (*rationabiliter procedere*) is attributed to natural philosophy because in it the mode of reason is observed most closely, so the intellectual method (*intellectualiter procedere*) is attributed to the divine science because in it the mode of intellect is observed most closely." Already in 5.5. ("Via ex nobis notioribus") we saw that the method of natural science

---

[105] *De subst. separ.*, c. 6, 67: Unde et Plato investigando suprema entium, processit resolvendo in principia formalia ... Inconvenientissime igitur hic [Avicebron] per contrariam viam processit in principia materialia resolvendo.

[106] Cf. *In VII Metaph.*, lect. 15, 1615: Resolutio autem definiti in sua principia, quod definientes facere intendunt.

[107] *In II Metaph.*, lect. 2, 296.

[108] *Ibid.*, lect. 1, 278.

[109] The "synthetic" method is possible only in the "manifesta mathemata." Cf. *Post. Anal.* I, c. 32, 88 b 17ff. (lect. 43, 391).

[110] *S. Th.* I–II, 14, 5: Si autem id quod est prius in cognitione, sit posterius in esse, est *processus resolutorius*: utpote cum de effectibus manifestis judicamus resolvendo in causas simplices.

is most in conformity with the mode of human knowing. For in its progress, physics retains the two features that are characteristic of reason. In the first place, it derives the knowledge of the intelligible from what is sensible, which is the better known in reference to us. Secondly, it is marked by the discursion from the one to the other, as from the knowledge of the effects to that of the causes.

In the text in question, natural philosophy and the divine science are connected with reason and intellect respectively. This connection enables Thomas to set their relation in the perspective of the multitude versus the unity. "Now reason differs from intellect as multitude does from unity." This idea too we have encountered before (5.1.). Multiplicity is proper to reason; it disperses itself in the consideration of many properties and effects, in order to gather from them the one, simple truth. The knowledge of the pure spiritual substances, however, is simple and uniform. Their understanding is godlike; they see in a single intuition the truth of things.[111]

Although the knowledge proper to man is brought about 'per viam rationis', it still has—as we saw at the end of 5.1.—a certain participation in the mode of knowing proper to the immaterial substances. The principle and terminus of discursive reason are the 'intellectus'. Hence Thomas continues in *In Boeth. De trin.* 6, 1:

> Rational consideration terminates in intellectual consideration, following the way of resolution (*secundum viam resolutionis*), insofar as reason gathers one simple truth from many things. And again, intellectual consideration is the beginning of rational thinking, following the way of composition or discovery (*secundum viam compositionis vel inventionis*), insofar as the intellect comprehends a multiplicity in unity.[112]

The first known is "being" (5.4.). It is "that which the intellect first conceives, as best known, and to which it resolves all conceptions" (*De verit.* 1, 1). The way of resolution, which is typical of man, goes in two directions.

First, there is a resolution in the order of reality (*secundum rem*), a progression from the one thing to the other, a reduction to the *extrinsic* causes ("for causes are more simple, unchangeable, and uniformly permanent

---

[111] *In Boeth. De trin.* 6, 1 ad tertiam quaestionem: Est enim rationis proprium circa multa diffundi et ex eis unam simplicem cognitionem colligere ... Intellectus autem e converso per prius unam et simplicem veritatem considerat et in illa totius multitudinis cognitionem capit, sicut deus intelligendo suam essentiam omnia cognoscit.
[112] *Ibid.*: Rationalis consideratio ad intellectualem terminatur secundum viam resolutionis, in quantum ratio ex multis colligit unam et simplicem veritatem. Et rursum intellectualis consideratio est principium rationalis secundum viam compositionis vel inventionis, in quantum intellectus in uno multitudinem comprehendit.

than their effects"). The ultimate end of this analysis is attained when man arrives at the highest and simplest causes, which are the separated substances. Secondly, there is a resolution in the order of reason (*secundum rationem*), a reduction to the *intrinsic* causes. It proceeds from the more particular to the most universal forms. "Now that which is most universal is common to all beings." The ultimate end of this analysis is therefore the consideration of being (*consideratio entis*).

The consideration in which human reason, following the way of resolution, ends is supremely intellectual. It is attributed to the divine science— not because it does not proceed by reasoning but because its reasoning most closely approaches intellectual consideration.[113] For the object of this science is twofold: being as being, and the highest causes. Therefore the divine science is also called 'meta-physics': its objects are found by the way of resolution "after" physics.[114] In Thomas's sketch of the history of philosophy, this level of consideration distinguishes the third and final phase, when "some" thinkers raised themselves to the consideration of being as being.

This "divine" science is possible for man because of the "reflexivity" of his mind. Since it participates in the intellectuality, the discursive movement is a circulation: starting from "being," a knowledge which man has by nature and in which all else is included, it terminates in the consideration of being. The mark of the spiritual substance is the "complete return" (*reditio completa*) to itself, in which its subsistence is manifested—a substantial being that only here acquires a positive meaning and is understood not merely by a negation (*non in alio existens*; cf. 2.1.3.). Through this return, being as formal object is known.[115]

The discursion of reason is a resolution towards the ontologically prior. This dynamics towards intelligibility which has ruled all the preceding ways must now be made concrete with respect to what was found in 6.2. and 6.3. The method of resolution will first of all be applied to the most notorious, i.e., to movement. It is in physics that the movable is reduced to the immobile. Subsequently, the analysis must be carried on into "the meta-physical," into the consideration of being, into the unitary view of the intellect.

---

[113] *Ibid.*, ad 1.

[114] *Ibid.*: Consideratio intellectualis est terminus rationalis, propter quod dicitur metaphysica quasi trans physicam, quia post physicam resolvendo occurrit; *In Metaph.*, prooem.: Dicitur ... Metaphysica, in quantum considerat ens et ea quae consequuntur ipsum. Haec enim transphysica inveniuntur *in via resolutionis*, sicut magis communia post minus communia.

[115] Thomas speaks in various places (*In De causis*, lect. 15; *S. Th.* I, 14, 2 ad 1) of the "complete return" (*reditio completa*) to itself that is the mark of the spiritual substance. He does not make, however, an explicit connection with the knowledge of being.

6.5. *Resolution of movement*

Movement manifests a multiplicity sharpened to mutability. As the discursive reason seeks science of this phenomenon, consideration must be given to what is necessary in mobile things. The contingent must be reduced to the permanent: "every movement presupposes something immovable."[116]

Now, in every change a double process is to be distinguished, namely, one from the principle towards the terminus and another from the efficient cause, the agent, towards that which undergoes the action, the patient.[117] That leads to a twofold "analysis" (6.5.1. and 6.5.3.), which is nothing other than the two ways of resolution that were described in the preceding section: a reduction *secundum rationem* to the intrinsic causes and *secundum rem* to the extrinsic causes.[118] Different modes of necessity depend on these causes (cf. 6.2.2.). The model for this twofold resolution is Thomas's first "way" to the existence of God (*S. Th.* I, 2, 3).

6.5.1. *Principle and terminus: Matter and form*

Movement is a "mutation" or change from something to something that initially was not. What is moved exists now differently from how it existed before. This being-under-way can be analyzed in five steps.

(1) Every movement occurs between two terms: a *terminus ex quo*, the principle from which the movement begins, and a *terminus in quem*, towards which the movement tends. In this latter terminus, now used in the strict sense of *finis*, the process finds its fulfillment.[119] Movement itself cannot be an end since it always tends towards something other, towards a determination that is not there yet.[120] The beginning and the terminus fix the movement. Neither the principle nor the end is in movement itself. Every process starts from something unmovable and terminates in something in which it comes to rest.[121]

It is not between arbitrary terms but between terms that stand in some

---

[116] *S. Th.* I, 84, 1 ad 3.

[117] *De pot.* 3, 3: In omni vera mutatione et motu invenitur duplex processus. Unus ab uno termino motus in alium . . .; alius ab agente in patiens.

[118] In this analysis the structural moments found for generation in 3.2. will appear again but in a different context. There the comparison with predication was the leading issue, while here the establishment of the immobile is.

[119] *In V Phys.*, lect. 1, 641; *In XI Metaph.*, lect. 11, 2361.
Cf. *In V Metaph.*, lect. 19, 1045–48 (on the different senses of 'terminus').

[120] *S.c.G.* IV, 82: Est enim contra rationem motus quod sit finis, quum omnis motus in aliud tendat; *De pot.* 5, 5.

[121] *S. Th.* I, 46, 3 ad 2: Quod est in principio motus, vel in termino, non est in moveri. Cf. *S. Th.* I, 79, 8, where this thesis is applied to the 'via rationis'.

kind of opposition to each other that movement occurs. Characteristic of
every opposition with the exception of the relative opposition (see 4.2.3.)
is that the one term wholly or partially removes the other. Now, in movement there is a non-identity of the terms, in the sense that there is a mutation from what earlier was not to its opposite, the presence of what was
absent. *Omnis mutatio est ex oppositis* (*In XII Metaph.*, lect. 2, 2428). From
this it also follows that the terms of movement relate to each other as the
imperfect to the perfect. For there is always implied in the privative and
contrary opposition some negation, a non-being of the one opposite.[122]
The ontological meaning of this relation of the imperfect to the perfect will
first become clear in the continuation of this section.

(2) If movement is a mutation from something to something other, then
besides the opposites there must still be a third, for two reasons. In the first
place, the one opposite (e.g., heat) does not itself change to its contrary
(e.g., cold). Moreover, there must be identity in the mutation, lest the
movement disintegrate into discontinuous moments. Movement presupposes a subject common to both opposites that persists throughout the
mutation. "Everything which is moved remains in part as it was, and in
part passes away."[123]

Thus every mutation requires three principles. First, the subject, which
is movable, i.e., which must be receptive of both termini. This is matter,
for it is on account of matter that something can be and not-be. "In everything that is moved, matter must be understood."[124] Secondly, the terminus, the perfection in which the movement terminates. This is the
form. The movement is *via ad formam* (cf. 3.2.). In the form the movement
comes to an end, because through the form the subject is constituted in
its determinate being. Thirdly, the opposite of this determination: the
privation. This principle is numerically one with the subject, certainly,
but it is distinct from it in concept. For in movement matter persists but
the privation does not. This "non-being" is a principle 'per accidens'
inasmuch as the absence of the form happens to the subject from which
the movements begins.[125]

---

[122] *In I Phys.*, lect. 10, 81: Despite the differences between the philosophers, there is
agreement in this, that "quaecumque principia accipiuntur ab eis, unum eorum se habet
ut melius et aliud ut peius ... Et hoc ideo est, quia semper alterum contrariorum habet
privationem admixtam."

[123] *S. Th.* I, 9, 1. Cf. *In I Phys.*, lect. 11 and 12; *In XII Metaph.*, lect. 2, 2429ff.; *De pot.*
3, 2 and ad 4: Id quod non similiter se habet nunc et prius, mutatur, supposita consistentia
subiecti.

[124] *In II Metaph.*, lect. 4, 328: In omni eo quod movetur necesse est intelligere materiam; *In VII Metaph.*, lect. 2, 1285ff.

[125] *In I Phys.*, lect. 12 and 13; *De principiis naturae*, c. 2; *In I Phys.*, lect. 15, 135: Cum
privatio nihil aliud sit quam negatio formae in subiecto.

Already in 1.2. the thesis was reported: "Those are said to be the principles and causes of natural things from which they are and come to be
'per se', and not 'secundum accidens'" (*In I Phys.*, lect. 13, 111). From
the present analysis it follows that there are two principles 'per se' of
coming to be: matter and form. They are also principles of being, since
they enter into the constitution of that which is. These principles are themselves ultimately ungenerated. For a mutation always requires a subject
and form. Should matter and form become, then it would follow that
matter and form must already be before they would become—an obvious
impossibility.[126]

(3) All that is moved remains in part as it was and in part passes away.
"And thus in everything which is moved there is some kind of composition to be found."[127] The mutation comes to an end when the form has
appeared in the subject. What becomes, in the proper sense of the word,
is the composite of matter and form.[128]

Therefore it is precisely with regard to movement that Aristotle can
make fruitful his solution to the problem of the unity of what is multiple,
namely, the "katallel" structure of "something of something other."
Movement and the movable thing are marked by the katallel structure of
subject and form. Movement is not "outside" the predicaments of being.
Every mutation occurs within the horizon of the categories: *omne enim quod
mutatur, mutatur secundum praedicamenta entis*.[129]

From the 'terminus ad quem' in the different categories of being, the
movement acquires its specification. Three kinds of mutations or changes
are distinguished. The first, motion (*motus*) in the strict sense, is the mutation of an actual subject with respect to an accidental form. Here the termini stand in an opposition of contrariety, since the opposites are of the
same genus. Hence motion is in those three categories that admit contrariety, namely, in the genera "quality" (alteration), "quantity" (aug-
mentation and diminution), and "place."[130] The other two species of
mutation are in the first category, "substance," namely, generation and
corruption. Here the termini do not stand in a contrary opposition, since
substance has no contrary. Both mutations are *inter opposita secundum*

---

[126] *In I Phys.*, lect. 15, 139; *In XII Metaph.*, lect. 3, 2443; *De principiis naturae*, c. 2.

[127] *S. Th.* I, 9, 1: Et sic in omni eo quod movetur, attenditur aliqua compositio.

[128] Cf. *In I Phys.*, lect. 13, 111, where the 'resolutio' of the definition is advanced as
an argument: Quod autem id quod fit secundum naturam, fit ex subiecto et forma, probat
hoc modo. Ea in quae resolvitur definitio alicuius rei, sunt componentia rem illam; quia
unumquodque resolvitur in ea ex quibus componitur. Sed ratio eius quod fit secundum
naturam, resolvitur in subiectum et formam.

[129] See for this *In III Phys.*, lect. 1; *In XI Metaph.*, lect. 9, 2291ff.

[130] *In V Phys.*, lect. 3 and 4.

contradictionem (*In V Phys.*, lect. 2, 654). Yet it would be still more accurate to speak of a privative opposition, since the subject of substantial changes, first matter, is not an absolute "nothing" (see point 4, below). And the privation, unlike the contradiction, is no absolute negation but a negation of being in a subject.[131]

All mutations presuppose something immovable. In an accidental mutation the substance, and in a substantial mutation the matter, remains immobile. Even in the contingent there is stability. Therefore we are in a position "to have an immobile science of mobile things" (6.2.2.).

(4) "All these are mere names . . .: coming into being and perishing . . . change of place and alteration of bright color," Parmenides maintains in his poem.[132] For being is, and non-being is nothing. From nothing becomes nothing, nor from being, since in that case it would be before it would come to being. Against the Eleatic ontology Aristotle asserts: "being" is said not in one way but in many ways (*multipliciter*). This multiplicity is in the first instance that of the diverse categories. Being is divided according to the modes of predication. To the "modes of predicating" the "modes of being" are proportional (2.1.2.).

To this division Aristotle adds another: "being" is twofold, namely, in potency (*dynamei*) and in act (*entelecheia*).[133] This distinction, which we have encountered several times in passing in the preceding chapters, is fundamental to an understanding of the dynamics of being. Its neglect was to Aristotle's mind the cause of the errors of the ancient philosophers. For with the help of this distinction the dialectics of being and non-being in movement can be "mediated": "Being in potency is as it were the middle between pure non-being and being in act."[134] Every mutation presupposes being, for if there were no subject then there could be no mutation. By the same token, what is moved *is* not yet completely, precisely because it is mobile.

The name "act" is given first to what is for us the most evident act. By common consent "act" has been conceived first of all as movement. Then the notion has been transferred to what is the principle and the terminus of movement: the act of the form, the *actus primus*.[135] "The concept of

---

[131] For the four forms of opposition, see *De quat. opp.*, c. 1; *In V Metaph.*, lect. 12, 922. For the difference between contradiction and privation: *In X Metaph.*, lect. 6, 2043ff.

[132] *Fragm.* B 8, 38–41 (H. Diels, *Fragmente*, vol. 1, 6th ed. (1951), p. 238).

[133] *Metaph.* V, c. 7, 1017 a 35–1017 b 9 (lect. 9, 897). The entire ninth book of the *Metaph.* is devoted to the doctrine of act and potency.

[134] *In I Phys.*, lect. 9, 60: Et omnes hi decepti fuerunt quia nesciverunt distinguere inter potentiam et actum. Ens enim in potentia est quasi medium inter purum non ens et ens in actu; lect. 14, 127; *In XII Metaph.*, lect 2, 2432ff.

[135] *In IX Metaph.*, lect. 3, 1805: Inter alios autem actus, maxime est nobis notus et

form stands over against that of subject. For every form is as such act; but every subject relates to that of which it is the subject as potency to act.''[136]

The subject, in the respect in which it is moved, is not a being in act; neither is it a non-being, unless 'per accidens', that is, insofar as the privation of the form happens to the subject. Matter is of itself a being in potency to act. It is disposed to the reception of the form, its perfection. Potency is intrinsically ordered to its fulfilling act.[137] The act is the end of the potency, and therefore not something alien to the potency.[138]

The division of being into potency and act makes it possible to understand the ontological character of the mutation as being-under-way. Since all that is moved—as we have seen—is moved in a category of being, movement in the generic sense can only be defined with these modalities of potency and act, which extend to all the predicaments of being.

Motion is nothing else—so Thomas says in his 'prima via'—than the reduction of something from potency to act.[139] What is moved stands midway between potentiality and actuality; it is partly in potency and partly in act. For what is purely in potency is not yet moved, and what is already in complete act is moved no longer. Motion is an "imperfect act."

The "dynamis" of this act must be expounded to two sides. What is moved does not yet have its end within it. Should the "imperfect act" not stand in a relation of potency to a further act, not extend towards the end, then this act, however imperfect it might be, would not be motion but the terminus of the change. Movement is *actus imperfectus* and *imperfecti*: incomplete act of a still imperfect subject.

This act likewise would have the character, if it were considered exclusively in relation to a further act, not of motion but of the principle of motion. Then and then only does the "imperfect act" have the character of motion, when it is related to a further act as potency and to something imperfect as act. Accordingly, Aristotle's renowned definition of motion is: "the act of that which is in potency in the respect in which it is in potency."[140]

---

apparens motus, qui sensibiliter a nobis videtur. Et ideo ei primo impositum fuit nomen actus, et a motu ad alia derivatum est; *De pot.* 1, 1.

[136] *De spirit. creat.* q. un., a. 1 ad 1.

[137] *S. Th.* I, 77, 3: Potentia secundum illud quod est potentia, ordinatur ad actum; *De malo* 1, 2: . . . cum esse in potentia nihil aliud sit quam ordinari in actum.

[138] *In IX Metaph.*, lect. 8, 1857: Actus est finis potentiae; *S. Th.* I–II, 27, 3.

[139] *S. Th.* I, 2, 3: Movere enim nihil aliud est quam educere aliquid de potentia in actum.

[140] *In III Phys.*, lect. 2, 285: Motus est entelechia, idest actus existentis in potentia secundum quod huiusmodi. Precisely this mixture of potency and act, so Thomas observes

(5) In motion a twofold order can be ascertained. First, there is the temporal development from the beginning to the terminus, the order "by way of generation and time." Along this way the imperfect is prior to the perfect, the still indeterminate potency prior to the act which gives the subject specific being. But this order is to be reduced to the "order of perfection or of the intention of nature." For there is motion because the subject's being is still imperfect, still extends towards actualization through the form. The end of the potency is its act. As intended end, act is prior to potency—a precedence that rests on the ontological priority of the perfect over the imperfect.[141]

The end of the first book of the *Physica* is the place where Aristotle makes the statement, cited several times already, that the form "is something divine, is the best and desirable."[142] "Something divine"; for every thing is in act through its form. Therefore the form is a likeness of the divine, that is pure act. The form is "the best" because it is the fulfillment of the potency and its good. What is composed of matter and form is good and perfect through the form. From this it also follows that the form is that which is "desirable"; it is the end of matter. There is a natural desire of what is in potency towards the form; this desire (*appetitus*) of matter is nothing other than its ordering with respect to its end.[143]

6.5.2. 'Per viam motus': Nature

In this first resolution motion was reduced to its two terms, the principle and the final terminus, which fix the way and the movement. In 6.1. we saw that motion is characteristic of natural things and that therefore the concept of nature is to be disclosed *per viam motus*. We can now take an additional step and connect "nature" to the established hodo-logy.

This connection is directly apparent from the development of the meaning of nature, which Thomas sketches at five places in his writings: *In III Sent.* 5, 1, 2; *S.c.G.* IV, 35; *S. Th.* I, 29, 1 ad 4; *De unione verbi incarnati* q. un., a. 1; and *S. Th.* III, 2, 1. The last text follows in full:

(lect. 3, 296), is the reason that it is so difficult to grasp what motion is. Cf. *In XI Metaph.*, lect. 9, 2294ff.

[141] *S. Th.* I, 85, 3 ad 1; 82, 3 ad 2; *De spe* q. un., art. 3. Cf. *In IX Metaph.*, lect. 7 and 8 for the priority of act over potency.

[142] *In I Phys.*, lect. 15, 135: Forma est quoddam divinum et optimum et appetibile.

[143] *Ibid.*, 136ff.

On this dynamics of being is based the first argument for the natural desire to know (cf. 1.6.2.): Quia unaquaeque res naturaliter appetit perfectionem sui. Unde et materia dicitur appetere formam, sicut imperfectum appetit suam perfectionem (*In I Metaph.*, lect. 1, 2).

We have to consider what nature is (*quid sit natura*). The term 'natura' derives from 'nasci' (to be born). Therefore the term 'natura' is first imposed to signify the generation of living things, which is called 'nativity' or 'pullulation', the word 'natura' amounting as it were to 'nascitura' (going to be born).

    Then it is extended to signify the principle of this generation.

    Since the principle of generation in living things is something intrinsic, the term 'natura' is broadened to signify any inner principle of movement, as the Philosopher says, in *Phys.* II, that "nature is a principle of motion in that in which it is 'per se' and not 'per accidens'.

    This principle is either form or matter; thus sometimes form is called 'natura', and sometimes matter is.

    And since the end of the generation in what is generated is the essence of the species, signified by the definition, that essence also is called 'nature'. In this way Boethius defines nature when he says that "nature is the specific difference which informs each thing," that is, which completes the definition of the species.[144]

This process of signification clearly shows nature to be the hodo-logy of what is in motion, that is, the intelligible determination of what is being-under-way. For nature is principle—"that from which motion starts" (*In V Metaph.* lect. 1, 762)—and end, and it is by these two terms that every movement is fixed.

    The process starts with the etymological meaning: "nature" first signifies birth or *generation*. From this act "nature" comes to mean the intrinsic *principle* of generation and—in general—of *movement*.[145] This character of origin is determinative for nature; "it is the foundation and principle of all else" (*S. Th.* I, 82,1). The inner principle of movement is both the *matter* and the *form* of the thing: consequently, both can be called "nature". Nature is twofold.

---

    [144] *S. Th.* III, 2, 1: Ad hujus quaestionis evidentiam, oportet considerare quid sit natura. Sciendum est igitur quod nomen naturae a nascendo est dictum vel sumptum. Unde primo est impositum hoc nomen ad significandum *generationem viventium*, quae nativitas vel pullulatio dicitur, ut dicatur natura quasi nascitura. Deinde translatum est nomen naturae ad significandum *principium hujus generationis*. Et quia principium generationis in rebus viventibus est intrinsecum, ulterius derivatum est nomen naturae ad significandum *quodlibet principium intrinsecum motus*: secundum quod Philosophus dicit, in II Physic., quod 'natura est principium in eo in quo est per se et non secundum accidens'. Hoc autem principium vel forma est, vel materia. Unde quandoque natura dicitur *forma*; quandoque vero *materia*. Et quia finis generationis naturalis est in eo quod generatur, essentia speciei, quam significat definitio, inde est quod hujusmodi *essentia speciei* vocatur etiam natura. Et hoc modo Boetius naturam definit, in libro De duabus naturis, dicens: 'Natura est unamquamque rem informans specifica differentia', quae scilicet complet definitionem speciei.

    The main articulations in the parallel texts are identical. A certain difference appears in the *Scriptum* on the *Sententiae*: nature there refers in its second and third senses to the *principium activum*, while elsewhere the intrinsic character of the principle is always to the fore.

    [145] Cf. *In II Phys.*, lect. 1, 145. Therefore Aristotle can say at the beginning of *Phys.* III: he who ignores motion ignores nature (cf. 6.1.).

The movement goes towards an end. In this regard it holds that nature in the sense of generation is 'via in naturam'. Nature is to generation as the terminus is to the movement.[146] The movement terminates in the species, substance, or *essence*; therefore "nature" is also said of the specific essence.

The 'termini stabiliti' of the essence are signified by the definition. The way of definition terminates in the specific difference, whereby the determination of the thing is completed. The last meaning of "nature" is the *specific difference*, which informs each thing; for this meaning Thomas always refers to Boethius.[147]

In this exposition two things are confirmed: on the one hand, that the differentiation of the four causes is being thought from the originality of nature (cf. 1.2.); on the other hand, that nature and definitional thinking go together (2.4.). In chapters 7 and 8 the philosophical meaning of the semantics of nature will be worked out further.

6.5.3. *Principle and terminus: Agent and end ('finis')*

"Motion" was defined (6.5.1.) as the act of that which is in potency in the respect in which it is in potency. From this it also follows that movement is the act of that which is mobile in the respect in which it is mobile; for this is what is in potency.[148]

But that which is in potency cannot reduce itself to act. This is the point of departure for a second resolution that is focussed on the other process that was distinguished in motion, i.e., that of the agent towards the patient. This hodo-logy can also be established in five steps.

(1) "Being in potency becomes a being in act always through something that is in act,"[149] through an "active" principle. In the process of be-

---

[146] *In II Phys.*, lect. 2, 155: Natura dicta ut generatio . . . se habet ad naturam sicut ad terminum.

[147] In *In II Sent.* 37, 1, 1 Thomas mentions the four senses of nature that Boethius had distinguished: Nomen naturae multipliciter dicitur, ut Boetius in lib. *De duabus naturis et una persona Christi* (cap. 1), dicit. *Primo* enim modo dicitur natura, secundum quod communiter ad omnia entia se habet, prout natura definitur omne id quod intellectu, quoquo modo capi potest. *Secundo* modo prout tantum substantiis convenit: et sic natura dicitur esse quod agere vel pati potest. *Tertio* modo dicitur natura quod est principium motus vel quietis in eis in quibus per se est, et non secundum accidens. *Quarto* modo unumquodque informans specifica differentia dicitur natura.

This last meaning Thomas incorporates into his own summing up, in connection with 'essentia'.

[148] So Thomas also holds that from the formal definition of "motus" the following material definition can be concluded: "Motus est actus mobilis inquantum est mobile" (*In III Phys.*, lect. 4, 297).

[149] *Metaph.* IX, 8, 1049 b 24ff.

coming, the potency of a particular thing is temporally prior to its actualization. But also in a temporal respect, act must have priority over potency
within the same sort.[150]

What is moved is brought towards the terminus of the motion by a
mover which in the respect in which it moves is itself act. For nothing can
be at once both in potency and in act with respect to the same. The impossible consequence would be that the same thing should at once both be and
not be a certain perfection. "Besides matter and form there must be a
principle that acts; this is called: *causa efficiens, vel movens, vel agens, vel unde
est principium motus*.[151] In every change is implied a causal relation of the
mover to the movable.[152]

The principle of causality acquires therefore the following formulation
in Aristotle's *Physica*: "everything that is moved is moved by another"
(*omne quod movetur ab alio movetur*). This thesis likewise occupies a central
place in Thomas's resolution of movement, as appears from his analysis
in *S. Th.* I, 2, 3 and *S. c. G.* I, 13. It can be proven—so Thomas asserts
in *S.c.G.* I, 13—in three ways. The third argument follows the course of
the first "way" towards God in *S. Th.* I, 2, 3:

> The same thing cannot be at once in act and in potency with respect to
> the same thing. But everything that is moved is, as such, in potency. For mo-
> tion is the act of something that is in potency inasmuch as it is in potency.
> That which moves, however, is as such in act, for nothing acts except accord-
> ing as it is in act. Therefore, with respect to the same motion, nothing is both
> mover and moved. Thus, nothing moves itself.[153]

"Nothing moves itself." It is possible to speak of self-movement only
in this sense, that in what moves itself, one part moves (*movet*) and another
part is moved (*movetur*). That a whole cannot move itself follows necessarily—this is the drift of the first argument in *S.c.G.* I, 13—from the relation of potency and act. In the strict sense, the thesis that "everything that
is moved is moved by another" is not proven but made explicit from the
priority of act to potency. "How should something come into motion if
there is no cause in act?"[154]

---

[150] *In IX Metaph.*, lect. 7, 1847–49.

[151] *De principiis naturae*, c. 3.

[152] *In III Phys.*, lect. 1, 280. Cf. Thomas's concluding reflection in *ibid.*, lect. 5, 324:
Sic iam implicatur ratio causae et effectus: nam reduci aliquid de potentia in actum, non
est nisi ab aliqua causa agente.

[153] *S.c.G.* I, 13: Nihil idem est simul in actu et in potentia, respectu ejusdem; sed
omne quod movetur, in quantum hujusmodi, est in potentia, quia motus est actus existentis in potentia secundum quod hujusmodi. Omne autem quod movet est in actu, in quantum hujusmodi, quia nihil agit, nisi secundum quod est in actu. Ergo nihil est, respectu
ejusdem, movens actu et motum; et sic nihil movet seipsum.

[154] *Metaph.* XII, 6, 1071 b 30.

The active principle is therefore a cause that acts on something other inasmuch as it is other, albeit (in so-called self-movement) there can be some kind of identity, as this "other" is part of the same thing as the mover.[155] That which is moved always needs to be reduced, in its being moved, to a 'motor'.

(2) Every agent acts insofar as it is in act. On account of a thing's actuality an active power belongs to it.[156] Now, a thing is in act through its form. The efficient causality is therefore reducible to the formal causality. Every agent is active in virtue of and in accordance with its formal principle; the form is "a moving principle."[157]

To the degree of a thing's actuality, it has activity. Now, every natural thing is partly in act, on the one hand because it is composed of matter and form, on the other hand because its perfection of being is contracted to one genus and species. Accordingly, its activity is "particular," is limited to the specific essence.

From this a further conclusion necessarily follows: "the natural agent needs matter, which is the subject of the mutation."[158] The moving cause needs the movable thing, just as, conversely, that which is movable needs the mover. For this reason it was said in 6.2.2. that the necessity by the moving cause is determined not only by this cause itself but also by the condition of the patient of the action. If the effect is not contrary to the disposition of the subject, there is a natural, not a violent, necessity. The efficient cause needs of itself a corresponding passive power receptive of the action. This receptivity is the potency of matter, which is intrinsically ordered to its fulfilling act.[159]

Hence the natural agent always acts through movement.[160] It can communicate its form only by effecting in that which is movable a change from potency to act. The two processes that were distinguished in every

---

[155] *S.c.G.* II, 7: Potentia enim activa est principium agendi in aliud secundum quod est aliud. Cf. *In V Metaph.*, lect. 14, 955; *In IX Metaph.*, lect. 1, 1776.

[156] See among other places *S. Th.* I, 89, 1; *S.c.G.* II, 6; *S. Th.* I, 25, 1 ad 1: Potentia activa non dividitur contra actum, sed fundatur in eo: nam unumquodque agit secundum quod est actu.

[157] *In III Phys.*, lect. 4, 302: Huiusmodi enim formae sunt causae et principia motuum, cum omne agens movet secundum formam. Omne enim agens agit inquantum est actu ... unde, cum unumquodque sit actu per formam, sequitur quod forma sit principium movens; *S. Th.* I, 42, 1 ad 1.

[158] See the exposition in *De pot.* 3, 1.

[159] *De verit.* 8, 9: Sicut autem forma comparatur ad materiam ut actus ad potentiam, ita agens ad patiens; cum unumquodque agit inquantum est actu, patiatur vero inquantum est potentia. Et quia actus proprius propriam potentiam respicit, ideo et proprio agenti respondet determinatum patiens, et e converso, sicut se habet de forma et de materia; *S.c.G.* II, 16; *In II Sent.* 12, 1, 1.

[160] *De pot.* 3, 1: Agens naturale agit movendo. Cf. *S.c.G.* I, 23.

mutation are in essence one and the same. What is in the moved as patient
and what is by the mover as agent are identical. Only a conceptual distinction can be made between them. The act of movement is in the patient—
for it is the act *of* that which is movable—and is in this respect called "passion." Considered in respect of its origin, however, the same movement
can be called "action," since it is caused by the agent.[161]

Movement establishes a relation between the mover and the moved.
We have already spoken of relation, namely, when we discussed the relation between the natural thing and science (4.2.3.) and that between God
and world (4.3.3.). There we saw that the basis of the relation is twofold,
on the one hand, quantity; and on the other, action and passion. These
latter categories bring about a relation of origin.

(3) Every agent acts for the sake of an end (*propter finem*), intends in its
operation something determinate. Should the efficient cause not be "determined" to a certain effect, then there would be no reason for its effecting precisely this instead of something else. The end to be realized is the
prior that motivates the agent; the agent is active for its sake. In the order
of the causes, the final cause is the first, because it is the cause of the
causality of the agent.[162]

The end of the agent is tied to its inner essence; the efficient cause intends the imparting of its own perfection, the communication of the form
whereby it is in act. "The proximate end of every agent is that it induces
in something else the likeness of its form."[163] Every agent effects something similar to itself (cf. 3.3.2.).

The form is also the terminus of the change in that which is movable;
matter desires it by nature. Mover and moved tend towards the same terminus. Agent and patient have the same end but in the different modes
of giving and receiving.[164]

Act has priority over potency. What is brought to act already preexists
in some way: "Man generates man." There is an eternal return of the
same, not numerically, but qua species. The intention of nature is direct-

---

[161] On motion and the predicaments "actio" and "passio": *In III Phys.*, lect. 5, 314;
320; 324; *In XI Metaph.*, lect. 9, 2312ff.; *In III De anima*, lect. 2, 592ff.; *S. Th.* I, 41, 1
ad 2: Sicut enim motus, prout est in mobili ab aliquo, dicitur passio; ita origo ipsius motus,
secundum quod incipit ab alio et terminatur in id quod movetur, vocatur actio.

[162] *S. Th.* I–II, 1, 2; *In II Sent.* 37, 3, 2; *S. Th.* I, 105, 5: Nam primo quidem principium actionis est finis, qui movet agentem; secundo vero agens; *De principiis naturae*, c. 4.
See also ch. 8.

[163] *S. Th.* II–II, 123, 7. Cf. *De pot.* 2, 1: Natura cuiuslibet actus est, quod seipsum
communicet quantum possibile est.

[164] *S.c.G.* III, 3; *S. Th.* I, 44, 4: Est autem idem finis agentis et patientis, inquantum
huiusmodi, sed aliter et aliter: unum enim et idem est quod agens intendit imprimere, et
quod patiens intendit recipere.

ed towards the everlasting. The end of the process is therefore necessary, for the eternal and the necessary go together. The way of nature is a circulation (cf. 3.4.1.) whereby the contingent world of the sublunary participates in what is the best in things: permanence.

(4) This permanence requires a further resolution. The cause of the sempiternity cannot lie in the sublunary things themselves, since not one of them endures forever. It must be reduced to an *agens perpetuum* which through its uniform and regular movement effects the perpetuity of natural becoming. That is heaven.[165] The circulation of nature whereby reality acquires permanence is reducible to the circulation of the things, which in themselves are imperishable and which to ancient thought were the most divine of sensible things: the celestial bodies.[166]

The first movement is the daily revolution of the sphere of the fixed stars. But this uniform movement alone is not sufficient to explain the cycle of coming to be and passing away. For that, a celestial movement is required that has part in the movement of the first sphere but that nonetheless does not remain completely the same. That is the case with the movement of the sun. Through its annual ecliptical orbit the sun is now closer to the earth and now further from it; that movement is the cause of the periodic coming to be and passing away.[167]

Confirmation of what is observed by looking at the heavens is provided by logical analysis.[168] In *S.c.G.* III, 82 Thomas argues that between the various sorts of movement there is a hierarchical order. Local movement precedes all others. It precedes by nature, because all other processes presuppose it. It is also first in perfection because it brings about change in a thing not in respect of something inherent but only in respect of something extrinsic. Thomas's consideration may seem astonishing at first glance, but it is entirely fitting in a reduction of motion to the immobile. In the perspective of this reduction, it is consistent to call that mode of movement the most perfect which effects the least variation in things.

Among local movements, Thomas continues, circular movement holds the first place. It is first in time, because it alone can be continuous and everlasting; for every other movement occurs between opposites and

---

[165] Thomas refers especially to Aristotle, *De generat.* II, c. 10 and 11. Cf. *Phys.* VIII, c. 6 (258 b 16–259 a 6); *In II De caelo*, lect. 18, 468; *In XII Metaph.*, lect. 6, 2510: Relinquitur igitur, quod oportet aliquid esse perpetuum agens, quod semper uniformiter agat ad perpetuitatem causandam. Et hoc est primum caelum, quod movetur et resolvit omnia motu diurno; *S.Th.* I–II, 109, 1.

[166] Cf. *S.c.G.* IV, 82; *In II Phys.*, lect. 7, 204: Caelum et ea quae sunt diviniora inter sensibilia manifesta nobis, scilicet partes mundi sempiternae.

[167] *In XII Metaph.*, lect. 6, 2511ff.

[168] Cf. *Metaph.* XII, c. 7, 1072 a 22.

comes to an end when the opposite has been reached. The circulation is also prior by nature, because it is more simple and one. Finally, the circulation is first in perfection, because it returns to its principle. The important place which circular movement turned out to have in earlier chapters follows from this analysis of movement. The circulation is the first and most perfect of all movements because it connects the end with the beginning. In 4.1.3. we saw that whatever is first in a genus is the measure and cause of that which comes later. On the basis of this principle it is certain, so Thomas asserts, that the uniform movement of the heavens is the cause of that which comes later.[169]

The argumentation that Thomas advances for this in S. Th. I, 115, 3 shows in still another manner how this conclusion is reached through the resolution towards the immobile. "Every multitude comes from unity." What is unmovable is always uniform, while what is moved is multiform. Hence throughout the whole of nature it can be observed that every movement starts from something unmovable. Therefore, the more unmovable something is, the more it is the cause of what is more movable. Now, the celestial bodies are of all bodies the most unmovable, for they are moved only locally. Hence the multiform movements of the terrestrial bodies must be reduced (reducuntur) to the movement of the celestial body as to their cause.

(5) The celestial bodies approach unmovability more closely than do terrestrial things. For they undergo no change in their substance ("generation") and in their quality ("alteration"). Yet they themselves are moved in their own turn. And "everything that is moved is moved by another."[170]

This regress cannot, however, go on to infinity. This thesis—characteristic of every resolution not only in the order of being but also in the order of knowledge—must be understood against the background of a hierarchically ordered series of movers. In this order the lower cause which moves but is itself moved in its own turn is the "instrument" of the higher cause. An instrumental cause owes its moving power to the principal cause. It needs to be reduced to it, for without the principal cause there would be no movement at all. It is therefore necessary to stop at a "first unmoved mover."[171]

The first principle, to which the analysis finally leads, is the cause of the eternal movement of the heavens without itself being moved. For this

---

[169] This exposition in S.c.G. III, 82 is based on Phys. VIII, c. 7 and 8.

[170] Cf. De verit. 5, 9; Comp. Theol. I, 4.

[171] S.c.G. I, 13; Comp. Theol. I, 3. Cf. E. Gilson, "Prolégomènes à la Prima via," AHDLMA 30 (1963): 53–70.

cause—an aspect that is emphasized in *Metaph.* XII, c. 7—is in no respect in potency, it is immaterial; its essence *is* act. The "Unmoved Mover," called "God" by Aristotle, is simple, hence necessary and eternal.

Yet how can something move without itself being moved?[172] The only possible way is that it do so as end. The end moves as "motive," as being desired. The end can set in motion without itself requiring a prior mover. Only the "desirable" moves without being moved. God is as pure act first in the order of the desirable. Hence He produces motion as "being loved," as final cause; is prime Mover without being moved.[173]

"On such a Principle heavens and nature depend."[174] By the attraction of its essence it brings about the first movement, the circulation of the outermost celestial sphere, which most nearly approximates the immobility of the first Act. Consequently, nature too depends on this Principle, since all natural things depend on heaven. That the operation of nature is directed to the everlasting is possible for nature—so Thomas stipulates—insofar as it acts in the power of God, who is "the prime root of perpetuity" (*prima radix perpetuitatis*).[175]

With the reduction of motion to the Unmoved Mover the analysis has come to the meta-physical. Aristotle states that physics would be the first science if there were no immovable being. Yet since there is such being, the science that considers it is the "first philosophy."[176] He accordingly distinguishes in *Phys.* II, c. 7 two kinds of principles that cause natural movements. One of these, however, is not physical since it has no principle of movement within itself. Such is the prime Mover.[177]

6.5.4. *Movement – Nature – Unmoved Mover*

The resolution of movement towards the immobile, of multiplicity towards unity can be summed up as follows. First (6.5.1.), movement was reduced to the intrinsic principle and terminus: matter and form, causes that relate to each other as potency and act. This hodology *is* nature (6.5.2.). Next (6.5.3.), movement was reduced to the extrinsic causes: the active principle, the agent, and the end. The end is ruled by the law of

---

[172] Every natural movement requires mutual contact of mover and moved and involves a reaction of the latter to the former: *Phys.* III, c. 2, 202 a 3–7.

[173] *Metaph.* XII, c. 7, 1072 a 26ff. Cf. *De pot.* 6, 6; *S. Th.* I, 80, 2. Because motion is in the patient, it is not necessary that every mover be moved: Actus activi et motivi fit in patiente, et non in agente et movente. Et ista est ratio, quare non est necessarium, quod omne movens moveatur (*In III De anima*, lect. 2, 592).

[174] *Metaph.* XII, c. 7, 1072 b 14 (lect. 7, 2534).

[175] *S.c.G.* IV, 82.

[176] *Metaph.* VI, c. 1, 1026 a 27.

[177] *Phys.* II, c. 7, 198 a 35 (lect. 11, 245).

synonymy and by perpetuity. That requires a hierarchy of movers characterized by an increasing degree of immobility. In this cosmic order the
celestial bodies occupy a place of importance. Their movement is reducible to an ultimate, metaphysical cause, God.

In this summary the essential coherence between nature and ontology
comes to the fore. The phenomenon of movement is to be understood
from the duality of matter and form. Both are nature. With the originality
of nature corresponds a "first philosophy" which in its ontology and
aitiology remains bound to this origin. In a world realizing iself by nature,
everything turns on the "what," for everything "revolves" about the
specific essence, which is unchangeable. The formal cause of being is
"something divine" in things. For the first principle is the Unmoved
Mover, pure form and act, which initiates the natural movement towards
perfection.

In the *Scriptum* on the *Sententiae*, Thomas distinguishes two different
meanings of "natural." In a first sense, it is opposite to "being in the
soul" (*ens in anima*). So "natural" is called whatever has a fixed being (*esse
fixum*) in nature. In a second sense, "natural" is opposite to "divine being
which is separated from matter and motion" (*ens divinum, quod abstrahitur
a materia et motu*). In this sense only that is called "natural" which is moved
and ordered upon coming to be and passing away.[178]

In this text what distinguishes God from the natural is located in movement. GILSON accordingly considers no problem more vital to Christian
thought than "that of movement." And because Aristotle's philosophy is
essentially an analysis of becoming and of its metaphysical conditions, it
has become (and will always remain so), GILSON concludes, "an integral
part of Christian metaphysics."[179]

But precisely for GILSON, who speaks of a "metaphysics of Exodus,"
the initial distinction assumed here—and with it, therefore, his conclusion
as well—would have to become problematical. For in terms of such a
"Christian" metaphysics not *movement*, which involves the origination of
nature, but the *being* of that which is movable must be considered the real
problem.

From this perspective of being, a certain embarassment arises regarding Thomas's "first way", which provided the model for the resolution
of movement. J.A. WEISHEIPL is a case in point. If St. Thomas would
prove the existence of God as he understands Him, then he "must have

---

[178] *In II Sent.* 2, 2, 2 ad 4. Cf. section 6.1., where the ontology of the Eleatic
philosophers was subjected to criticism for attributing to natural substances what belongs
to the *super*-natural: immobility.

[179] *The Spirit of Mediaeval Philosophy*, p. 65.

intended the verb *movetur* to be taken in the widest possible sense of any change whatever produced by another. Consequently *movetur* must include every coming into being, even of the whole substance whether it be physical or spiritual.''[180] But this extension of ''being-moved'' to ''being-moved to being'' goes beyond the horizon of the ''first way.'' It requires a further resolution. That brings us to a general observation about the so-called proofs of God.

In apologetics the ''five ways'' have acquired a significance that seems neither historically nor systematically justified. Generally it is ignored that the proofs of God's existence are to be located in and understood from the traditional order of science. After it is shown in q. 1 of the *Summa Theologiae* that ''sacred doctrine'' too is to be regarded as a science according to the Aristotelian model, there follows in q. 2. the preliminary question of science, the ''if'' question: *an sit Deus* (cf. 1.3.4.). This procedure is similar to that followed by Aristotle in *De anima* and in the *Physica* with regard to the soul and nature respectively.

To prove the existence of the ''subject'' of theological science, Thomas advances a number of arguments from the philosophical tradition that are justified qua the *method* of resolution—that is why he rejects Anselm's proof—but that qua result form no more than a first approach (''hoc omnes dicunt Deum''). Only in the further resolution is the relation of being to the Creator made explicit.[181]

6.6. *Metaphysical resolution*

What is moved must be ''being,'' for every mutation is from something to something. The mobile does not owe ''being'' to its mover, but only ''movement.'' It is dependent solely in its being moved.[182] Therein, for Thomas, as we saw in 3.5.1. (''The necessity of another mode of becoming'') and 3.5.2. (''The necessity of an origin of being in general''), lies the necessity to radicalize and intensify the resolution. In his systematic exposition of the method of resolution (6.4.), Thomas already pointed out that its terminus is the consideration of being as being. This intention is

---

[180] J.A. Weisheipl, '''Omne quod movetur ab alio movetur' in Medieval Physics,'' *Isis* 56 (1965): 29.

[181] This point I have worked out more extensively in my essay, ''Der wissenschaftstheoretische Ort der Gottesbeweise in der *Summa Theologiae* des Thomas von Aquin,'' in *Mediaeval Semantics and Metaphysics: Studies Dedicated to L. M. de Rijk*, ed. E. P. Bos (Nijmegen, 1985), pp. 161–93.

[182] *In IV Metaph.*, lect. 17, 747: Omne quod permutatur, necessario est ens; quia omne quod permutatur, ex aliquo in aliud permutatur; *S.c.G.* II, 57: Mobile non habet esse per suum motorem, sed solum motum.

also expressed clearly in the second basic text (*De subst. separ.* c. 9), which
sketches the historic development of philosophy: "There must take place
a common resolution in all such things in the sense that each of them is
resolved by the intellect into that which is, and its being." This analysis
terminates in the idea of creation (5.2.).

"In the origination of all being from one first being, the transmutation
of one being into another is inconceivable. . . . For this reason it is the task
not of the philosopher of nature but of the 'first philosopher' to consider
the origin of things."[183] Here a metaphysical origin is at issue that transcends every movement. God's action, which is called creation, is neither
a motion nor a change, properly speaking,[184] although man tends to understand it in that way.[185] The distinction is always drawn sharply by
Thomas. In this section we would accordingly indicate the transcendence
of the origination of being by means of a comparison with the twofold
resolution of movement that was carried out in 6.5.

Movement is a "mutation" from something to something, terms which
stand in privative or contrary opposition to one another. This means that
in the change there is always a commonness of the extremes, be it in a genus, be it (at least) in a subject.[186] In creation this is not the case. Creation is "out of nothing." Here obtains the contradictory opposition,
which does not allow any mediation. Thus the three phases in the history
of philosophy, marked by different kinds of "becoming" (alteration,
generation, and creation), can be connected with the three forms of opposition, that is, the contrary, privative, and contradictory, respectively.[187]

Movement presupposes a subject common to both opposites that persists throughout the mutation: matter. The terminus is the form, whereby
the subject is constituted in its determinate being. Creation, however,
presupposes no subject;[188] therefore its terminus is not the form, but
"the whole substance of the thing" (*S. Th.* I, 45, 1 ad 2), the 'esse' (*De
pot.* 3, 5 ad 2). From this it also follows directly that creation breaks
through the horizon of the categories, within which every mutation occurs. To produce being absolutely, and not merely as this or that being,
belongs to the concept of "creation."[189]

---

[183] *S.c.G.* II, 37: In hac autem totius entis origine ab uno primo ente, intelligi non
potest transmutatio unius entis in aliud. . .; propter quod nec ad naturalem philosophum
pertinet hujusmodi rerum originem considerare, sed ad philosophum primum.
[184] *S.c.G.* II, 17.
[185] *S. Th.* I, 45, 2 ad 2: Creatio non est mutatio nisi secundum modum intelligendi tantum; *S.c.G.* II, 18; *De pot.* 3, 2.
[186] *S.c.G.* II, 17: Extrema motus vel mutationis cadunt in eundem ordinem.
[187] Cf. *De quat. opp.*, c. 4.
[188] *De pot.* 3, 2.
[189] *S. Th.* I, 45, 5.

Movement was defined as "the act of that which is in potency in the respect in which it is in potency." Creation is not such a transition from potency to act; it presupposes no potency that is receptive of the action.[190] "Before the world existed, it was possible for the world to be, not, indeed, according to a passive potency, which is matter, but according to the active power of God."[191]

Hence there is in creation "another mode of causing" (cf. 3.5.) than in movement. In the resolution towards the extrinsic causes of movement it was established that "everything that is moved is moved by another." The mutation from potency to act is effected by an agent which is described in terms of movement: "causa efficiens vel unde est principium motus." Creation, the total causation of being, requires a new concept of this efficient causality. The "cause of motion" must be transcended towards the "cause of being," towards the origin through the influx of being (*per influentiam essendi*).[192] So Thomas distinguishes between two kinds of efficient cause—a distinction that marks the difference between the first "way" and the second towards the existence of God.[193] This distinction Thomas borrows from Avicenna: there are agents of two kinds: a natural, which is the cause of movement, and a divine, which gives being.[194]

Every agent acts insofar as it is in act. The natural thing is partly in act; therefore its activity too is "particular." "God in contrast is totally act (*totaliter actus*): as well in relation to himself, since He is pure act without admixture of potency, as in relation to the things that are in act, since in Him is the origin of all things. Hence He produces by his action the whole subsisting being (*totum ens subsistens*) . . . And therefore he can make something out of nothing, and this action is called creation."[195]

Every agent acts for an end (*propter finem*). The agent's end is the communication of its own perfection (*omne agens agit sibi simile*). The first agent, which is pure act, does not act, however, for the acquisition of an end that perfects Him. God is not dependent on something other but is Himself the end. He constitutes other things not out of need but out of generosity. He wills them to be partakers in His perfection. Through

---

[190] *S.c.G.* II, 17; *De pot.* 3, 3 ad 8.

[191] *S. Th.* I, 46, 1 ad 1.

[192] *De subst. separ.*, c. 9, 95.

[193] Cf. E. Gilson, "Notes pour l'histoire de la cause efficiente," *AHDLMA* 29 (1962): 23ff.; "Prolégomènes à la Prima via," *AHDLMA* 30 (1963): 55.

[194] *In II Sent.* 1, 1, 2 ad 1: Secundum Avicennam duplex est agens: quoddam naturale, quod est agens per motum, et quoddam divinum, quod est dans esse; *In I Sent.* 7, 1, 1 ad 3; 42, 1, 1 ad 3. Cf. *In VII Metaph.*, lect. 17, 1661.

[195] *De pot.* 3, 1.

creation He communicates being to things, in order to show His good-ness.[196]

To create is the proper action of God alone. For among all effects being itself (*ipsum esse*) is the most universal; and hence it must be the proper effect of the first and most universal cause, God.[197]

How much Thomas attempts to understand creation by eliminating the moment of "movement" appears from a final point of comparison with the prior resolution. Through movement a relation between the mover and the moved is caused. The motion, which is in the moved by something other, is called "passion"; viewed in respect of its origin, it is called "action." Now, if motion is removed from "action" and "passion"—for creation is no mutation—then there remain only the diverse relations. Creation, so Thomas says, belongs solely to the genus of relation.[198]

Creation in the *active* sense is the action of God, which is His essence with a relation to the creature. This relation is, however, for reasons that were discussed critically in 4.3.3., not a real relation but a relation in thought only. There is in God no real relation to the world. Creation in the *passive* sense, the being-created, is the real relation of the creature to its Creator, the dependence on its Origin. "Creation is really nothing else than the relation to God with newness of being."[199]

With this determination of creaturely being as being-related-to-God an insight is attained that can open up a new and fruitful perspective for "being" as "relational being." But the manner in which Thomas elaborates this relation in his metaphysics of creation proves to be rather disappointing. Created being *is* not the relation to the Origin but has this relation.[200] Creation is an accident, which is not caused by the subject, certainly, but which as accident requires an absolute being, a substance

---

[196] *S. Th.* I, 44, 4: Omne agens agit proper finem ... Sed primo agenti, qui est agens tantum, non convenit agere propter acquisitionem alicujus finis, sed intendit solum communicare suam perfectionem, quae est ejus bonitas; I, 19, 2; *In II Sent.* 15, 3, 3 ad 2; *De verit.* 23, 1 ad 3.

[197] *S. Th.* I, 45, 5. See further for the thesis 'creatio est propria Dei actio': *S.c.G.* II, 21; *De pot.* 3, 4; *Comp. Theol.* I, 69.

[198] *S. Th.* I, 45, 2 ad 2: Sed cum actio et passio conveniant in substantia motus, et differant solum secundum habitudines diversas, ut dicitur III Phys., oportet quod, subtracto motu, non remaneant nisi diversae *habitudines* in creante et creato; *S. Th.* I, 45, 3: Subtracto autem motu ab actione et passione, nihil remanet nisi relatio; *S.c.G.* II, 18; *De pot.* 3, 3.

From the texts cited it is evident that Thomas's primary reason for considering creation a relation is the elimination of motion ("subtracto motu").

[199] *De pot.* 3, 3 and ad 2; cf. *S. Th.* I, 45, 3 and ad 3; *In II Sent.* 1, 1, 2 ad 4 and 5; *S.c.G.* II, 18.

[200] Cf. *In III Sent.* 11, 1 ad 7: Creatura non est illa relatio secundum quam dicitur esse a Deo, per quam habet esse.

in which it inheres. That implies that the relation of creation considered ontologically is "later" than the subsisting subject—just as every accident, not only qua concept but also qua *nature* is posterior to the substance.[201]

Bonaventure already realized that creation cannot be fit into the predicamental division of being into substance and accident. For creation as accident cannot precede the substance. To his insight "the relation of the creature to the Creator is not accidental, but essential."[202]

Thomas's elaboration, it must be said, is far from consistent from the standpoint of his own intention as well. Always intent on showing that creation transcends the categorical horizon of motion and becoming, he nevertheless conceives the relation of creation as an accidental category. As accident it is something added (*superadditum*)[203] to the substance, as relation not "intrinsically affixed" to what is subsistent, but "assistant" to it.[204]

In the ontology of nature, the relation to the Unmoved Mover does not affect essentially the substance of things. But the creature's being is received being; being related to God cannot be disengaged from creaturely being. Therefore the manner in which Thomas conceives the relation of creation is an indication that with the transcendence of creation over mutation, all has not yet been said. In the resolution of being, certain principles of the reduction of movement are continued. Such a continuation is possible because the analysis of movement, too, came to the metaphysical. What structures acquire transcendental validity by going beyond the horizon of movement?

6.7. *'Esse' is "the actuality of all acts"*

With this question we approach the end that was formulated at the close of ch. 4: to inquire further into how the 'concursus' of nature and creature is thought philosophically, as 'concursus'.

The prevalent method in the quest for intelligibility is the "way of resolution," the reduction to the ontologically prior, the causes. Two resolu-

---

[201] *De pot.* 3, 3 ad 3: Illa relatio accidens est, et secundum esse suum considerata, prout inhaeret subiecto, posterius est quam res creata; sicut accidens subiecto, intellectu *et natura*, posterius est; *S. Th.* I, 45, 3 ad 3.

[202] *In Hexaemeron* IV, 8; *In I Sent.* d. 30, dub. 4: Talis relatio, quae exprimit ipsam dependentiam, non est creaturae accidentalis, sed magis *essentialis*.

Duns Scotus (*Ordinatio* II, d. 1, q. 4–5, 277) interprets the relation of being created as "relatio transcendens."

[203] *S.c.G.* IV, 14.

[204] *S. Th.* I, 28, 2: Relationes secundum id quod relationes sunt ... inveniuntur esse assistentes, non intrinsecus affixae.

tions have been carried out in the present chapter: that of movement, the way of nature; and thereafter that of being, the way of the creature. Upon closer examination, these two reductions are found to come together in the notion of "act." Herein lies a new point of convergence of the 'concursus'.

To account for mutation, Aristotle introduced the division of being into potency and act. Precisely because these modalities extend to all categories, they can acquire transcendental validity. That is what Thomas actually does in his analysis of being: he applies them to "common being."[205]

(1) The name "act" (6.5.1.) is given first to what is for us the most manifest act, movement. Subsequently, this notion has been transferred to "something other" (*ad alia derivatum*). This "other" is the being in which movement terminates: "*substantia* et *forma* et *species* est actus quidam" (*In IX Metaph.*, lect. 8, 1866). "First act" is the form.

The intrinsic principle and the terminus of the way of nature are matter and form, which are related to each other as potency and act. There is a natural desire of what is in potency towards the act that perfects it.

Act has priority over potency in the "order of perfection or of the intention of nature." One manner in which Aristotle proves this is by comparing the everlasting to the corruptible. The celestial bodies, in contrast to sublunary things, are not in potency to non-being. Now, it is manifest that with respect to perfection the everlasting is prior to the corruptible. Therefore qua perfection act has priority over potency.[206] The same conclusion can also be reached starting from what is necessary (*de necessariis*). What is necessary is always in act, cannot be and not-be. But what is necessary is the first of all, for if what is necessary should be taken away, nothing of the rest would remain.[207] The priority of act is also evident from the intelligibility and truth of things. Only through the act is the thing knowable, is it conformable to the intellect. A thing is said to be true when it reaches the act of its own nature, of its specific form (4.2.2.).

The actualization of what is in potency is always caused by something that is in act. To be in act involves activity. In both resolutions we find the thesis: "Every agent acts insofar as it is in act." Efficient causality is tied to actuality. The end of the activity is the communication of that

---

[205] Cf. 3.7.5.: The composition of act and potency has greater extension than does that of form and matter. The latter is restricted to material substances; "potency" and "act" divide *ens commune* (*S.c.G.* II, 54).

[206] *In IX Metaph.*, lect. 9, 1867.

[207] *Ibid.*, lect. 9, 1873, illustrated with a very characteristic example: Utpote si tollerentur *essentialia praedicata*, quae necessario praedicantur, non possunt inesse accidentalia praedicata, quae contingit esse et non inesse.

whereby the agent is in act. "Every agent effects something similar to itself." Three of the four causes, formal, efficient, and final, coincide in being act.

The intention of nature is directed towards the permanent essence, the act which gives being to the subject.[208] This end requires a hierarchical order of necessary and eternal agents. The "first immobile mover," God, is pure form, *is* therefore act. God is as pure act first in the order of the desirable. He moves "as loved," as final cause. In this way the process of nature is set in motion towards the form, whereby everything is in act.

(2) Terminus *per viam creationis* is 'esse' in the absolute sense. With personal emphasis—something which is relatively rare in his work—Thomas states how he wishes to understand this "being": "What I call 'esse' is *the actuality of all acts*" (*De pot.* 7, 2 ad 9). The expression is a Hebraism, like "king of kings," and striking through the combination of continuity and transcendence in the notion of act. Thomas intends a philosophy of being in which being is understood as act. 'Esse' is the act of acts, is the act also of the form, of the essence. "Being" is the actuality of every substance (1.8.2. and 3.5.2.).

First act is God. He *is* act, namely, *Ipsum Esse*. Thereby He is in three ways the cause of other things. As first Act He is at once the efficient, exemplary, and final cause of all.[209]

"Every being acts insofar as it is in act." In accordance with the order in actuality is the order of agents. Only God is pure act. Therefore God's being is His action.[210] "Every agent effects something similar to itself." The proper effect of the first Act is being itself. God is not only final cause but also Creator—an insight that, for Thomas, follows from the structure of act. Creation is the proper action of God.

"The first act is the universal principle of all acts."[211] All the rest participates in being: it is "effected," is not act. Just as in everything that is moved there is a composition, so also is the creature characterized by a composition of potency and act. What is in potency to being is the essence. In the internal structure of being, the 'esse' participated in is the actuating moment.

---

[208] *In I Sent.* 7, 1, 1 ad 2: Ipsa essentia dat esse habenti: et iste actus est quasi actus primus.

[209] *De pot.* 7, 1 ad 3: Per unum et idem Deus in ratione diversarum causarum se habet: quia per hoc quod est actus primus, est agens et est exemplar omnium formarum et est bonitas pura, et per consequens omnium finis.

[210] *De pot.* 1, 1; *S. Th.* I, 54, 1: Actio enim est proprie actualitas virtutis, sicut esse est actualitas substantiae, vel essentiae ... Solus autem Deus est actus purus. Unde in solo Deo sua substantia est suum esse et suum agere.

[211] *S. Th.* I, 75, 5 ad 1: Primus actus est universale principium actuum omnium ... Unde participatur a rebus.

According to the degree of act and potency all being is ordered hierarchically: from God, pure act, to first matter, pure potency.[212] There is in
all the creaturely a natural desire towards perfection. Something is perfect
insofar as it is in act. Therefore God is the end of the natural desire. In
the union with the Origin consists the perfection of every thing.

Act and potency are the ontology of the hodo-logy. Origin and end lie
in the actuality, the dynamics of what is in the potency to act. This is the
'ratio' of the way of nature and of the way of creature. The resolution of
the movement-nature-Unmoved Mover is continued with that of the
being-creature-Creator.

Thomas's analysis needs to be further concretized and to be worked out
with respect to the ''concurrence'' of nature and creature. That will occur
by focussing on the 'principium' of the hodo-logy (ch. 7) and subsequently
on the 'finis' (ch. 8).

---

[212] *De verit.* 8, 6; *De ente*, c. 5.

CHAPTER SEVEN

PRINCIPIUM

In chapter 5 we saw that in the second basic text Thomas sketches the history of the question of being. The most striking feature in this text is the 'concursus' of the orders of *nature* and *creature*: the itinerary of the historical reason terminates in the idea of creation. Yet in this text the systematic-philosophical background indispensable for the understanding of this progression remains implicit. This background is made explicit in the hodo-logy that was established in chapter 6. The discursion of reason turned out to be a resolution. We followed Thomas in his reductions of movement and of being, which come together in the ontology of act. With the help of these analyses, we shall now in this chapter investigate systematically the different origins and consider the way of nature and the way of creature in their concurrence.

In the history of the question of being, Thomas distinguished three phases. The first two phases, as we have noticed, are dominated by generation, by the causality of motion, and by the origination of nature. Now in the first basic text (*Phys.* II) nature is defined as "intrinsic principle" of motion. This principle is twofold: matter and form (7.1.). The union of matter and form requires an agent, the causality of which needs to be reduced to the heavens, the "universal nature" (7.2.). In the third and final phase being as being and its metaphysical origin are analyzed. The first principle is God, who through creation has given being to things (7.3.).

Characteristic of Thomas's analysis is the continuous dynamics towards intelligibility, the progression from a particular towards a universal consideration of being. In this continuity lies at the same time the special problem of Thomas's way of thought (7.4.).

7.1. *Nature*

7.1.1. *Nature is "principle of motion"*

7.1.1.1. *"Intrinsic principle"*

The most evident act is motion. "With regard to every change, we then know something maximally, when we know the principle of motion."[1] Science requires a resolution to the principles.

In 6.1. it was found that motion belongs to the natural as such. There-

---

[1] *In III Metaph.*, lect. 4, 382.

fore this phenomenon is reducible to the structure of the natural things
themselves. This is the manner in which nature is specified in *Phys.* II.

> All of these things [which are by nature] differ from the things which are not
> by nature because all things of this sort are seen to have in themselves a prin-
> ciple of motion and rest (*in se principium alicuius motus et status*); some accord-
> ing to place, such as the heavy and the light, and also the celestial bodies,
> some according to increase and decrease, such as the animals and plants, and
> some according to alteration, such as the simple bodies and everything which
> is composed of them.
>   But things which are not by nature, such as a bed and clothing and like
> things, which are spoken of in this way, have in themselves no principle of
> mutation, except 'per accidens', insofar as the matter and substance of ar-
> tifacts are natural things.[2]

That which differentiates nature and art is the principle (*archè*) of motion. Natural things have a principle of motion and coming to rest in themselves; artifacts do not have "such an innate tendency to change" (192 b
19), unless 'per accidens'. Not as artifact, but insofar as it is, e.g., of iron,
or of stone—that is, insofar as it is "by nature"—does it have a principle
of motion in itself. Nature is "intrinsic principle of motion." The resolution towards the intrinsic principles is the way to establish what nature is.

According to the terminus, three sorts of natural movement are distinguished in the text, namely, in the categories "place," "quantity," and
"quality." Now *Phys.* II began with the statement "some beings are by nature." In the continuation of the exposition, however, reference is made
exclusively to accidental changes, to processes in already actually existing
subjects. Not mentioned are "generation" and "corruption," the other
two kinds of mutation (cf. 6.5.1.). Does this mean that here "motion" (*motus*) must be taken in the strict sense, to the exclusion of substantial
changes?

This conclusion does not just follow of itself. In the first place, it is con-
spicuous that the distinction between 'motus' and 'mutatio' is not strictly
maintained in the text.[3] It is said that natural things have in themselves

---

[2] *In II Phys.*, lect. 1, 142: Et differunt haec omnia ab his quae non sunt a natura, quia
omnia huiusmodi videntur habere in se principium alicuius motus et status: quaedam quidem secundum locum, sicut gravia et levia, et etiam corpora caelestia; quaedam vero
secundum augmentum et decrementum, ut animalia et plantae; quaedam vero secundum
alterationem, ut corpora simplicia et omnia quae componuntur ex eis. Sed ea quae non sunt
a natura, sicut lectus et indumentum et similia, quae accipiunt huiusmodi praedicationem,
nullius mutationis principium habent in seipsis nisi per accidens, inquantum scilicet materia et substantia corporum artificiatorum sunt res naturales.

[3] On the varying extension of 'kinèsis' in the *Phys.*, see H. Wagner, *Aristoteles, Physikvorlesung*, 2nd ed. (Darmstadt, 1972), p. 446. Cf. *In III Phys.*, lect. 1, 276: Natura est principium motus et mutationis.

a principle of motion (*motus*), and that artifacts have in themselves no principle of mutation (*mutatio*), except 'per accidens'. For "the matter and substance of artifacts are natural things." That recalls the discussion in chapter 3 of the division of the causes into "nature" and "art." The reason for this division was the causes of *generation*, of which nature was the first since it is the cause of the "first being," substance. Already in that analysis the fundamental coherence between generation and the causality of nature became apparent.

Of importance, in the second place, is the process of signification of 'natura' sketched in 6.5.2., for it shows that the Latin term has an even closer connection with generation than does the Greek term 'physis'. The process starts with the etymological meaning: "nature" first signifies generation (of living things) or birth. From this act, 'natura' (and likewise 'physis') has come to signify the intrinsic principle of generation and, by extension, of motion.

The reason that generation is not mentioned amongst the natural movements may have something to do with a problem that will come up in the next section. That reason is definitely not, however, the one adduced by such an authority as Ross. The definition of "nature" is in his opinion appropriate to most natural processes, where a living being produces changes in itself, but not to generation, where the origin of the movement is extrinsic. "The definition of nature really breaks down in the case of generation."[4]

But generation does have to be taken into account. "Man generates man" is an aphorism characteristic of nature as origin. "To generate"—so writes Thomas in his commentary on De anima—is the *opus naturalissimum*, because in it the animate agrees with the inanimate. There is a difference, certainly, and it consists just in this, that the inanimate is generated by an extrinsic principle while living beings are generated "by an intrinsic principle insofar as they are generated from seed that advances to the living thing."[5] It is preeminently from the generation of living things that the character of nature as intrinsic principle is shown. Thomas does this later on in his commentary on *Phys.* II:

> The name 'nature' implies the relation of principle. For those things are said to be born which are generated in conjunction with a generator, as is clear in plants and animals. Thus the principle of generation or motion is called nature.[6]

---

[4] W.D. Ross, *Aristotle's Metaphysics* II (Oxford, 1924), p. 355 (with reference to *Metaph.* XII, c. 3, 1070 a 7).
[5] *In II De anima*, lect. 7, 312.
[6] *In II Phys.*, lect. 1, 145: Nomen naturae importat habitudinem principii. Quia enim

In his commentary on the *Metaphysica*, too, he exerts himself to show
from the structure of generation that nature can never mean an extrinsic
principle.[7] For in the generation of living things there is always, according
to Aristotle's and Thomas's view, a conjunction of the generated with the
generator. "Thus the generator and the generated are as it were one thing.
Therefore, because the name 'natura' is derived from 'nascor' (to be
born), those are said to be by nature of which the principle is within themselves."[8]

The intrinsicality of the origin of nature is what matters. That a movement is natural and does not come from an inner principle involves, so
Thomas says, a contradiction.[9] This insight is determinative for the
differentiation from other principles.

In *Phys.* II nature is opposed especially to *art*. This opposition we have
worked out in 3.3.2. "Art" is a "productive form" which pre-exists in the
mind of the maker. It is a principle extrinsic to the thing produced and is
in that sense "in something other." Nature, in contrast, is a principle of
motion in the natural thing itself. "Nature seems to differ from art in nothing else than that nature is an intrinsic principle and art an extrinsic
principle."[10]

In other places—particularly *De caelo* III, 2—nature is opposed to *violence*. By that is meant an active power of man that requires little or no intellectual deliberation and that is exercised especially in the throwing and
pushing of objects.[11] This principle too we discussed earlier. It is of importance to recall the context of that discussion, since it puts the opposition of
"nature" and "violence" in a broader coherence, that of intelligibility.
"Violence" came up when in 6.2.2., in connection with causality, diverse
modes of necessity were distinguished. Besides "absolute" necessity based
on intrinsic principles—also called "natural" necessity—there is the
necessity through the extrinsic cause, the agent. If the agent brings about
an effect that is contrary to the disposition and receptivity of the patient,
this is necessity of violence. "Violence" entails that the subject is

---

nasci dicuntur ea quae generantur coniuncta generanti, ut patet in plantis et animalibus,
ideo principium generationis vel motus natura nominatur.

  [7] *In V Metaph.*, lect. 5, 815: Ex hoc autem apparet, quia quod nascitur semper est
coniunctum ei ex quo nascitur. Ideo natura numquam dicit principium extrinsecum, sed
secundum omnes suas acceptiones dicit principium intrinsecum.

  [8] *In III Sent.* 8, 1. Cf. *S. Th.* I, 115, 2.

  For a detailed analysis: A. Mitterer, *Die Zeugung der Organismen, insbesondere des Menschen
nach dem Weltbild des hl. Thomas von Aquin und dem der Gegenwart* (Vienna, 1947).

  [9] *De caritate* q. un., a. 1.

  [10] *In II Phys.*, lect. 14, 268.

  [11] Cf. *In VII Metaph.*, lect. 6, 1395.

moved by an extrinsic cause to something for which it of itself has no aptitude. Whenever someone throws up a heavy object, then this is not to be
understood in the sense that a force is pressed into this body whereby it is
moved: ''For then the violent motion would be through an intrinsic principle, which conflicts with the concept of violent motion.''[12] The principle
of a forced movement is entirely extrinsic, and the effectuated is ''contrary
to nature.''

Besides the oppositions to ''art'' and ''violence,'' Thomas knows yet a
third extrinsic principle to which nature is opposed: the *principium supra
naturam*, which works miracles (*miraculosa*), such as making the blind to see
again and raising the dead to life.[13] The need for this last opposition indicates that nature in Thomas is connected with yet another perspective on
the origin, a perspective which is absent in Aristotle. The character of nature as principle—in opposition to these three extrinsic principles—will be
further elaborated in the following sections.

7.1.1.2. *''Active'' and ''passive'' principle*

In the continuation of his commentary on *Phys.* II, Thomas notes an objection to Aristotle's exposition. Is it true that in every sort of mutation of
natural things there is a principle of motion in that which is moved? For
the generation (!) of the so-called elements appears to be entirely from an
external agent.

> Therefore, some say that even in changes of this sort an active principle of
> motion is in that which is moved, not perfectly, but imperfectly, which princi-
> ple helps the action of the external agent. For they say that in matter there
> is a certain inchoateness of form, which they say is privation, the third princi-
> ple of nature. And the generations and alterations of simple bodies are said
> to be from this intrinsic principle.[14]

Everything acts insofar as it is in act. It is actual through its form. A
moveent is natural if its origin is intrinsic. Therefore ''some'' posit regard-

---

[12] *In III De caelo*, lect. 7, 591. Cf. lect. 5, 576.

[13] *In IV Sent.* 43, 1, 1, 3: Est enim aliquis motus sive actio, cujus natura nec est principium nec terminus; et talis motus quandoque est a principio supra naturam, ut patet
de glorificatione corporis, quandoque autem a principio alio quocumque, sicut patet de
motu violento lapidis sursum; *De verit.* 10, 11.

[14] *In II Phys.*, lect. 1, 143: Dicunt ergo quidam quod etiam in huiusmodi mutationibus
principium activum motus est in eo quod movetur; non quidem perfectum, sed imperfectum, quod coadiuvat actionem exterioris agentis. Dicunt enim quod in materia est quaedam inchoatio formae, quam dicunt esse privationem, quae est tertium principium
naturae; et ab hoc principio intrinseco generationes et alterationes corporum simplicium
naturales dicuntur. Cf. *In VII Metaph.*, lect. 8, 1442 a ff.

ing the generation of the elements an active principle in what is moved. Not a complete form, certainly, but an imperfect: there is in matter a "beginning of form" (*inchoatio formae*), which assists the external cause. Through this active principle, also the genesis of the elementary bodies is natural. Among others, Albert the Great and Bonaventure held this view.[15] To Thomas's mind, it comes close to the doctrine of the "hidden-ness of forms" (*latitatio formarum*), which he ascribes to Anaxagoras: forms are in a hidden way actually present in matter.[16] Thomas however rejects this solution on account of the structure of act and potency. The "in-choateness of form" is not act and therefore cannot be an active principle. A form cannot act before it actually exists.[17]

In the arguments pro and contra an active principle, a certain dilemma appears. If the elements have no intrinsic principle of their movement and becoming, then their movement and becoming are not natural but vio-lent. And, moreover, what in that case would be the difference between artificial and natural generation? If, on the other hand, such an active principle must be assumed in the inanimate (in order that its movements be natural), what then would the difference be between the inanimate and the animate? For the mark of living beings is self-motion (*sola viventia in-veniuntur movere se ipsa*).[18] And it is not without reason that the objection centers just on the inanimate: the elementary bodies.

Aristotle had transferred to 'physis' the definition of the Soul given by Plato in his *Nomoi* (cf. 3.4.3.). Does that not recoil upon him here? When the extension of beings that are "by nature" is set off at the beginning of *Phys.* II, the enumeration starts with living beings and ends with the elementary bodies. COLLINGWOOD judges: "The world of nature is thus for Aristotle a world of self-moving things ... It is a living world."[19] Consequently, the problem must arise whether the idea of 'physis' is com-patible with the role of the Unmoved Mover, "when everything that be-longs to nature has been so lavishly endowed with the self-moving capaci-ty."[20] Several modern exegetes of Aristotle have seen a discrepancy here.[21]

---

[15] Albert the Great, *In II Phys.*, tract. I, c. 9; Bonaventure, *In II Sent.* 18, 1, 3.
This view finds modern resonance in W. Charlton, *Aristotle's Physics I, II* (Oxford, 1970), p. 92: Aristotle "thinks that the material of a thing can be a source of change be-cause it has an active tendency to change independent of any external cause."

[16] Cf. *In VII Metaph.*, lect. 7, 1430; 1442 d.

[17] *In II Phys.*, lect. 1, 143.

[18] See *In VII Metaph.*, lect. 8, 1442 b ff. Cf. for the definition of 'vita' *S. Th.* I, 18, 1.

[19] *The Idea of Nature* (Oxford, 1945), p. 82.

[20] F. Solmsen, *Aristotle's System of the Physical World* (Ithaca, 1960), p. 232.

[21] See especially F. Solmsen, *op. cit.*, pp. 94, 101, 232ff. An earlier proponent of this view is H. von Arnim, *Die Entstehung der Gotteslehre des Aristoteles*, Sitzungsberichte der Akademie der Wissenschaften Wien, Phil.-hist. Kl. 212, 5 (Vienna and Leipzig, 1931).

Yet in this interpretation Aristotle's idea of nature is thoroughly misunderstood. More keenly than many a modern interpreter, Thomas has seen that precisely in *Phys*. VIII additional light is shed on the character of nature by the thesis *Omne quod movetur ab alio movetur*. Thus we must turn first to *Phys*. VIII in order thereafter to return to Thomas's exposition of *Phys*. II.

In *Phys*. VIII, c. 4 (lect. 7), Aristotle begins to prove that "everything that is moved, is moved by another." This is the most evident in what is moved by violence. "Violence" is by definition an extrinsic principle. It is also evident in what is moved by itself. For something can only move itself, as we saw in the resolution of motion (6.5.3.), when two parts can be distinguished in it that relate to each other as act (mover) and potency (moved). That is the case in living things and only in them: for they have a soul that moves the body. Self-motion is an act proper to life.[22]

The elementary bodies can accordingly not move themselves. They do not have a body but are it. A non-living thing is a continuous whole, infinitely partitionable, but not into a "first" part that would be the mover of another one.[23] Inanimate bodies are therefore moved by something other.

But here a distinction needs to be made. They have a motion "outside nature" (*extra naturam*) through violence, e.g., when someone throws up a stone. To speak of "violent" motion is meaningful only if there is also a natural dynamics. According to nature (*secundum naturam*) elements are moved to their "proper" places, where they rest. This "natural" place differs from element to element: for light bodies it is above, for heavy ones below—which is why the consideration can be concentrated on the upward and downward movements of the "extreme elements": the light (fire) and the heavy (earth). The task now is to indicate the cause of these natural movements, which cannot be self-movements (lect. 8).

For a movement to be natural and not violent, that which is mobile must itself confer something, that which is moved must be in potency to that which it becomes in act. All that is in potency is moved by that which is in act. But being-in-potency is twofold: the first potency is with respect to the first act, that is, the actuality of the form (e.g., "heaviness" or "lightness"); the second potency, which is connected with the first act, is with respect to the natural place, that is, the accidental act of being low

---

[22] Cf. *In VII Metaph.*, lect. 8, 1442 e: Sola viventia inveniuntur movere seipsa. Et hoc ideo quia inveniuntur habere diversas partes, quarum una potest esse movens et alia mota; quod oportet esse in omni movente seipsum, ut probatur in VIII Phys.; *In De causis*, lect. 5, 136; *S. Th.* I, 78, 1.

[23] *In VIII Phys.*, lect. 7, 1026ff.

or being high. The actualizations of these potencies are fundamentally different from each other. The first potency is actualized by an extrinsic principle, the giver of the form, the generator. The second potency however is actualized not by an efficient cause but directly from the subject itself. Once it has received by generation the form of lightness or heaviness, there follows immediately—unless an impediment occurs—the inclination and motion towards the second act.

This analysis shows that the thesis *Omne quod movetur ab alio movetur* also applies in the case of the heavy and light bodies.[24] For the essential cause (*movens per se*) of their movements is the generator, which "informs" the mobile and thereby imparts to it the inclination towards the proper place. From the first act, accidental processes proceed "by nature" (see also 8.2.3.). That in *Phys.* II these alone are mentioned must be understood from this structure.

The analysis has made clear, furthermore, that none of the heavy and light bodies move themselves. Yet they are moved naturally, since in virtue of an intrinsic principle they have an inclination and dynamis towards their proper places. Their movement is natural because they have a principle of motion in themselves.[25] That was precisely the definition of natural things given in *Phys.* II. The elaboration in *Phys.* VIII shows concretely that nature as "intrinsic principle" is not identical with self-motion.[26] This principle of motion that inanimate bodies have in themselves—so Thomas emphasizes at the end of his lectio—is not active but passive, namely, a natural potency to act. "From this it is apparent that it is contrary to the intention of the Philosopher that there be in matter an active principle (the so-called "inchoateness of form"), which according to some is necessary for a natural movement; for that, a passive principle suffices."[27]

This is the moment to return to Thomas's exposition of *Phys.* II. For in an excursion of his own he introduces here the distinction that is worked out in *Phys.* VIII.

> And so it must be said that a principle of motion is in natural things in the way in which motion belongs to them. Therefore in those things to which it belongs to move, there is an active principle of motion. Whereas in those things to which it belongs to be moved, there is a passive principle, which

---

[24] *Ibid.*, lect. 8, 1036. Cf. *S.c.G.* I, 13.

[25] *In VIII Phys.*, lect. 8, 1035: Nihil horum, scilicet gravium et levium, movet seipsum: sed tamen motus eorum est naturalis, quia habent principium motus in seipsis.

[26] This distinction occurs frequently in Thomas's work. Cf. *De verit.* 24, 1.

[27] *In VIII Phys.*, lect. 8, 1035.

is matter. And this principle, insofar as it has a natural potency for such a form and motion, makes the motion to be natural.[28]

The origination of nature is distinguished into an "active" (formal) principle and a "passive" (material) principle—a distinction that plays an important role in Thomas's work and turns up in the most unexpected places.[29]

The significance of this distinction is twofold. First of all, it makes possible an inner relation between moving things, active and passive, in reality. That a body undergoes an influence of an external cause does not mean ipso facto a violent motion, is not contrary to the concept of nature.[30] For in things there is a natural receptivity to the action of an extrinsic cause.[31] If the relation between agent and patient is such that the effect is not contrary to the disposition of the subject, then there is not a violent but a natural necessity. There is a natural order between active and passive, intrinsic and extrinsic principles, a conclusion that is a corroboration of what was found in the twofold resolution of motion (6.5.). With a natural passive potency corresponds always an active power in nature.[32] Therefore, if the lower things are moved by the higher, that movement is natural; there is in the lower an intrinsic inclination to follow the higher.[33]

The division of the intrinsic principle into an active and a passive capacity makes it possible, furthermore, to extend the natural origin to movements of the inanimate as well. A principle which has a natural potency for a form and for motion renders the motion natural. The generation of

---

[28] *In II Phys.*, lect. 1, 144: Et ideo dicendum est quod in rebus naturalibus eo modo est principium motus, quo eis motus convenit. Quibus ergo convenit movere, est in eis principium *activum* motus; quibus autem competit moveri, est in eis principium *passivum*, quod est materia. Quod quidem principium, inquantum habet potentiam naturalem ad talem formam et motum, facit esse motum naturalem.

[29] In III Sent. 3, 2, 1 ad 6; 22, 3, 2, 1 (Whether the Ascension of Christ was 'violentus'); *In IV Sent.* 43, 1, 1, 3; *In I De caelo*, lect. 3, 22; *In III De caelo*, lect. 7, 590; *In VII Metaph.*, lect. 8, 1442 f: Non enim oportet ad motum naturalem, quod semper principium motus, quod est in mobili, sit principium activum et formale; sed quandoque est passivum et materiale, *S. Th.* I-II, 6, 5 ad 2; III, 32, 4 (Utrum Beata Virgo aliquid active egerit in conceptione corporis Christi).
See also 8.4.3.

[30] *S. Th.* I-II, 6, 4 ad 2; 9, 4 ad 2.

[31] Cf. *S. Th.* I-II, 6, 5 ad 2: Alio modo secundum principium passivum, quia scilicet est in natura inclinatio ad recipiendum actionem ab extrinseco; *In V Metaph.*, lect. 6, 835; *De pot.* 6, 1 ad 17.

[32] *In IV Sent.* 43, 1, 1, 3: Passivum autem principium naturalis generationis est potentia passiva naturalis quae semper habet aliquam potentiam activam sibi respondentem in natura.

[33] *In III De caelo*, lect. 7, 590.

the elements differs from the becoming of artifacts because in the matter of the latter there is not a "natural" potency to the artistic form.[34] So also the motion of the heavy and light bodies is natural.

> However in heavy and light bodies there is a formal principle of motion
> . . . For just as the other accidents are consequent upon substantial form, so also is place, and thus also 'to be moved to place'. However the natural form is not the mover. Rather the mover is that which generates and gives such and such a form upon which such a motion follows.[35]

This exposition contains a difficulty. In *Phys.* VIII it was said that the intrinsic principle of motion of the heavy and light bodies is not active but passive, while in the exposition of *Phys.* II a "formal principle" is introduced that Thomas usually identifies with "active principle."[36] J. STUFLER[37] has called attention to an ambiguity on this point in Thomas's work. While in his early writings he makes of the "form of lightness" an active principle, in his later works the same form is a passive principle.[38] Others, such as K. RIESENHUBER,[39] have concluded from this that in his commentary on the *Physica* and thereafter, Thomas describes nature only as a passive principle. But is this inference correct?

The argumentation in *Phys.* II is directed against the adherents of the "inchoateness of form" and is intended to show that nature as intrinsic principle is not exclusively an active principle but can *also* be a passive one (in 7.1.2. and 7.1.3. this duality will become still more explicit). Moreover, it is hardly plausible that there is a real turnabout in Aquinas on this point. For precisely in the commentary on the *Physica*, the principle of gravitation is called both "passive" (book VIII) and "formal" (book II), identical with "active." These indications express something different, to be sure, but of greater importance is the common basis on which they rest, namely, the insight that the form is no mover (*motor*), no efficient or moving cause, but principle of motion. In the early writings, too, Thomas insists upon this: "Although in the motion of simple bodies the natural form is principle of motion, this is still not the

---

[34] *In II Phys.*, lect. 1, 144. Cf. *In VII Metaph.*, lect. 6, 1389; 8, 1442 f.

[35] *In II Phys.*, lect. 1, 144: In corporibus vero gravibus et levibus est principium formale sui motus (. . .), quia sicut alia accidentia consequuntur formam substantialem, ita et locus, et per consequens moveri ad locum: non tamen ita quod forma naturalis sit motor, sed motor est generans, quod dat talem formam, ad quam talis motus consequitur.

[36] See *In III Sent.* 22, 3, 2, 1; *In I De caelo*, lect. 3, 22; *In VII Metaph.*, lect. 8, 1442 f.

[37] *Gott, der erste Beweger aller Dinge* (Innsbruck, 1936), p. 34.

[38] 'Principium activum': *In III Sent.* 3, 2, 1 and ad 6; 22, 3, 2, 1; *In IV Sent.* 43, 1, 1, sol. 3; *S.c.G.* III, 23; *De pot.* 5, 5; *De verit.* 12, 3. 'Principium passivum': *S. Th.* III, 32, 4; *In I De caelo*, lect. 3, 22; *In V Metaph.*, lect. 14, 995.

[39] *Die Transzendenz der Freiheit zum Guten* (Munich, 1971), p. 22.

mover, but the essential mover is the generator which gave the form."[40]

It is possible to indicate, moreover, the background of Thomas's complex mode of expression. He is wrestling here with the difficulty of fitting this intrinsic principle of motion into Aristotle's notion of 'dynamis' (*potentia*). In *Metaph*. V, c. 12, Aristotle distinguishes different senses of this term. The first is: "principle of motion and change in something other, insofar as it is other." As example Aristotle names architecture. In his commentary Thomas signalizes that there is also a principle of motion *in* what is moved, namely, matter or a formal principle upon which the motion follows as in the case of heavy bodies. Such a formal principle cannot however be called an active potency or efficient cause; for that would imply self-motion. Thomas's conclusion is: "Potency, insofar as it is a principle of motion in that in which it is, is understood not as an active potency, but rather as a passive potency. For heaviness in earth is not a principle of moving, but rather of being moved" (lect. 14, 955). This conclusion is inserted almost literally as a parenthesis in the previously cited passage from *In II Phys*. (lect. 1, 144).[41] Nature as formal principle must be distinguished from matter but is still no "active potency," no 'motor', since it is not a principle of motion in something other.

We have devoted extensive attention in this section to the motion of the heavy and light bodies because its analysis is most illuminating for the understanding of nature as "intrinsic principle." But there is still a second reason. According to the model of this motion, which is reducible to an extrinsic cause and an inner principle, the relation of God and nature is understood.

"An external cause does not move naturally except insofar as it causes an intrinsic principle of motion in the movable thing. Thus, the generator, that gives the form of gravity to the generated body, naturally moves the heavy body downwards."[42] Only what is the cause of something's nature can cause a natural movement.[43] In the same way, so Thomas says in *De pot*. 3, 7, God works in nature.

> It must be observed that one thing may be the cause of another's action in several ways. First, by giving it the power to act: thus it is said in *Phys*. VIII that the generator moves heavy and light bodies, inasmuch as it gives

---

[40] *In II Sent*. 14, 1, 3; cf. *De verit*. 22,3. See also J.A. Weisheipl, "The Concept of Nature," *The New Scholasticism* 28 (1954): 400ff.

[41] *In II Phys*., lect. 1, 144: (sed huiusmodi principium formale non potest dici potentia activa, ad quam pertinet motus iste, sed comprehenditur sub potentia passiva: gravitas enim in terra non est principium ut moveat, sed magis ut moveatur).

[42] *S.c.G*. III, 88.

[43] *S. Th*. I-II, 9, 6: . . . motum naturalem causare non potest, nisi quod est aliqualiter causa naturae.

them the power upon which such a motion follows. In this way, God causes
all the actions of nature, because he gave natural things the powers whereby
they are able to act.[44]

God is the cause of every natural operation insofar as He gives to things
the forms and powers which are the intrinsic principles of their motions.[45] God's action does not eliminate the natural action but rather He
is the cause and sustainer of it.[46] There is no incompatibility between the
action of the external cause and that of the intrinsic principle, but a 'concursus' of God and nature (cf. 6.5.4.).

7.1.1.3. 'Potentia oboedientialis': Nature and miracle

In the first section of this chapter we saw that "nature" is opposed not
only to "art" and "violence" but also to a third extrinsic principle, the
"supernatural cause," God. Since we found at the end of the preceding
section just a 'concursus' of God and nature, the reason of this additional
opposition must lie in the fact that the effect produced by the external
cause is supernatural, a miracle.[47]

The term "miracle" is derived from "admiration" or wonder (*nomen
miraculi ab admiratione sumitur*).[48] Since wonder is the origin of the desire
to know (1.1.), Thomas can place the miracle, too, in the movement
towards intelligibility. Wonder arises when an effect is manifest, whereas
its cause is hidden. Thus one wonders upon seeing an eclipse without
knowing its cause. Now the cause may be known to one and not to
another. A rustic wonders at an eclipse, while an astronomer does not.
Miracle is called what is as it were full of wonder. It is, namely, an effect
that falls "outside" the ordinary course of things, that is "beyond the order of the whole created nature" (*S. Th.* I, 110, 4), yes it occurs in those
things in which a natural order is to a "*contrary* effect" (*De pot.* 6, 2). The
miracle accordingly has a "cause absolutely hidden from all," namely,
God. A miracle is what is done by God outside the causes that are known
to us.[49]

---

[44] *De pot.* 3, 7: Sciendum namque est, quod actionis alicuius rei res alia potest dici causa multipliciter. Uno modo quia tribuit ei virtutem operandi; sicut dicitur in VIII Phys.
quod generans movet grave et leve, in quantum dat virtutem per quam consequitur talis
motus: *et hoc modo Deus agit omnes actiones naturae*, quia dedit rebus naturalibus virtutes per
quas agere possunt.

[45] *De verit.* 24, 14; *De virt. card.* q. un., a. 2.

[46] Cf. *S. Th.* I, 83, 1 ad 3.

[47] *De pot.* 6, 3: In miraculis enim producuntur effectus absque actionibus naturalibus,
a causa supernaturali; *S. Th.* II-II, 178, 1: ... per aliquos supernaturales effectus, qui
miracula dicuntur.

[48] *S. Th.* I, 105, 7. Cf. *De pot.* 6, 2.

[49] *S. Th.* I, 105, 7.

In the miracle, God works not by means of the natural forms He has given, but immediately. On the basis of the preceding analysis of the natural principle the question must then necessarily arise: does this not mean that the divine miraculous works are violent, "contrary to nature"? For violent is according to Aristotle's definition "that of which the principle is extrinsic and to which that which has undergone the force confers nothing." Now, in things there is no natural receptivity for the miracle (*in natura recipiente non sit ordo naturalis ad illius susceptionem*).[50]

To escape this consequence and to render intelligible the breaking through of the natural order of things, Thomas introduces into nature alongside the passive principle yet another capacity, the so-called *potentia oboedientialis*.[51] It is an "obediential" potency to what God 'supra naturam' can do in a thing, to what takes place in a "miraculous way." This potency is inherent in the creaturely condition: every creature obeys God by receiving into itself what the Creator has willed. It is a potency that cannot be realized by a natural agent but by God alone, the "supernatural agent."[52]

Because of this potency, whatever God does in things is not contrary to nature but "natural." If the lower is moved by the higher, that movement is not violent, even if it is not in conformity with the movement that the lower has of itself. An example Thomas likes to use is the ebb and flood of the sea, caused by the moon; that movement is not contrary to nature, even though the natural motion of water goes in but one direction, downwards. Similarly, and even more so, since every creature is naturally subject to God, all that God does is natural, even if it is perhaps not in conformity with a thing's own specific nature, e.g., when He raises one who is dead.[53]

There is still another reason—not from the nature of things but from the divine will—why God cannot act against nature. For nature is the ontological expression of God's creating will (cf. 6.3.2.). Should He act against that, then He would act "against His foreknowledge" (*S. Th.* I, 105, 6).

---

[50] *In IV Sent.* 17, 1, 5, 1.
[51] See *In I Sent.* 42, 2, 2 ad 4; *In II Sent.* 18, 1, 2; *In III Sent.* 1, 1, 3 ad 4; 2, 1, 1; *In IV Sent.* 8, 2, 3 ad 4; 17, 1, 5, 1; *De verit.* 8, 4 ad 13; 8, 12 ad 4; 12, 3 ad 18; *De pot.* 1, 3 ad 1; 6, 1 ad 18; *S. Th.* III, 1, 3 ad 3; III, 11,1; *De virtutibus in communi* q. un., a. 10 ad 13.
[52] *De virtutibus in communi* q. un., a. 10 ad 13: . . . ex eis potest aliquid fieri virtute supernaturalis agentis quod non potest fieri virtute alicuius naturalis agentis; et secundum hoc dicimus, quod in tota creatura est quaedam obedientialis potentia, prout tota creatura obedit Deo ad suscipiendum in se quidquid Deus voluerit.
[53] *In Epist. ad Romanos* c. 11, lect. 3; *De pot.* 1, 3 ad 1; *De malo* 5, 5 ad 4; *S.c.G.* III, 100; *S. Th.* II-II, 104, 4 ad 2.

What stands out in this view is that what is normative for the miracle is the relation to *nature*. Accordingly, creation, though the proper action of God, is for Thomas in the strict sense no "miracle," because the bestowal of being cannot proceed from any other cause. Creation does not fall "outside" the order of nature.[54]

The miracle is a breaking through of the natural order. This determination suggests a 'concursus' in the sense of a "competition" between the natural actions and the operation of God, as if nature had a persistence of its own in relation to God.[55] So J. STUFLER can write: "What becomes and befalls in this cosmos proceeds precisely as it would proceed if there ... were alongside the creatures no Creator."[56]

Just because the miracle is thought primarily from the order of nature, all attention must be concentrated on the formal question of the *possibility* of the miracle. To this question the notion of 'potentia oboedientialis' provides an answer. It expresses above all, to GILSON's judgment, "the distinctive characteristic of a Christian nature, open that is to say towards its Creator."[57] But is this relation to God not minimalized if the openness of nature is that of a potency to miracle, of an obedience to what God wills outside the way of nature?

The *reality* of the miracle is done more justice when another way, that of creature, is given a more central place than it is in Thomas. Along that way the miracle, e.g., of raising the dead, of healing the sick, appears as a sign of the (re-)creating power directed towards the being (whole) of things.[58] Because the miracle is correlated to nature and is thought from this intrinsic principle of motion, it must eventually become a supernatural effect. This "super-naturalism" we shall encounter more often along Thomas's way of thought (see especially 8.4.).

7.1.1.4. *The definition of nature and definitional thought*

After his excursus concerning nature as "active principle" and "passive principle," Thomas concludes[59] "what nature is," arriving at the definition Aristotle (*Phys.* II, c. 1, 192 b 20) gives of nature: "a principle and cause of motion and rest in that in which it is primarily and through

---

[54] *S. Th.* I, 105, 7 ad 1; *De pot.* 6, 2 ad 5.

[55] J.H. Diemer, *Natuur en Wonder* (Amsterdam, 1963), especially pp. 117ff. (partially translated as *Nature and Miracle*, Toronto, 1977).

[56] J. Stufler, *Gott, der erste Beweger aller Dinge*, p. 21.

[57] *The Spirit of Mediaeval Philosophy*, pp. 377, 381.

[58] Cf. *S. Th.* III, 44, 3: Et ideo conveniens fuit ut Christus, particulariter homines miraculose curando, ostenderet se esse universalem et spiritualem omnium Salvatorem.

[59] For (the problem with respect to) this "concluding" see 2.2.3.

itself, not through something that is accidental'' (*principium (et causa) motus et quietis in eo in quo est primo et per se et non secundum accidens*). In the continuation of his lectio (nr. 145) Thomas carefully explains the different parts of the definition. That furnishes the opportunity to delve deeper into this complex determination and in so doing to round off the consideration of nature as intrinsic principle of motion.

In the definition of nature, *principium* is placed as its genus. In opposition to those who wished to correct Aristotle's definition and tried to define nature through something ''absolute'' (as ''a force seated in things''), Thomas maintains that nature always has the character of principle (cf. 2.4.).

Nature is called *principium* and *causa* in order to point out, so Thomas says, that '' in that which is moved nature is not a principle of all motions in the same way, but in different ways.'' Thus we saw in connection with the analysis of the motion of heavy and light bodies that nature is indeed a ''principle of motion,'' but no ''mover,'' no ''efficient cause.'' For understanding the definition of nature it is accordingly useful to recall the distinction made in 1.2. between ''principium'' and ''causa''. ''Principle'' signifies origin, indicates that from which something proceeds in any way. ''Cause'' adds something to this notion, namely influx of being. Causality implies an ontological dependence of the effect in relation to the cause. Not every principle has, however, such an ''influence'' on the being of that which is principled; as an example of this was adduced a ''principle of motion.'' Precisely because ''principle'' is more extensive than ''cause,'' ''principle'' is placed in the definition. By no means is it thereby excluded that nature is also cause: every ''cause'' is ''principle,'' but the reverse is not the case. The heavy or light bodies do have a principle of motion in themselves, not, however, the cause. What A. MANSION writes is therefore incorrect: ''the causality implied in the definition of nature, conceived as inner principle of the movements of the being, appears to have to be understood in the sense of an efficient causality.''[60] It is remarkable that the idea of 'physis' can be misunderstood at such a crucial point.

Nature is 'principium *motus et quietis*'; nature is a principle not only of motion but also of rest. For motion is not an end in itself but happens for the sake of something else. Also the terminus, in which motion attains its end and fulfillment, is natural. What is moved by nature to the proper place likewise rests there by nature. Yet because the motion of the celes-

---

[60] *Introduction à la Physique aristotélicienne*, p. 227; cf. p. 239.

tial bodies is continuous and circular (more on this particular case in 7.2.), Thomas points out that the definition must not be so understood that in everything that is moved by nature, nature is also a principle of rest.

Nature is a principle in that '*in quo est*', in distinction from extrinsic principles, such as art. Because nature is a principle and not something "absolute," it follows that in the definition of nature—as was observed earlier (2.4)—its subject, or more precisely: the proper subject, must be stated. This is indicated in the next part of the definition.

Nature is a principle in that in which it is '*primo*'; Aristotle gives no further explanation of this "primarily," Thomas gives an example by way of clarification. 'Primo' is added

> because even though nature is a principle of motion of composite things, nevertheless it is not such primarily. Hence that an animal is moved downwards is not because of the nature of animal insofar as it is animal, but because of the nature of the dominant element.[61]

How must this "primarily" be interpreted? Must it be inferred from the example that nature is principle of a motion that is common to all mobile things and that is therefore the least perfect?[62]

Indeed there are texts in which nature is taken in this sense. When in his commentary on *De anima* Thomas speaks of "increase" and "decrease" he declines to regard nature as principle of these movements—although in *Phys*. II, 1 "increase" and "decrease" are expressly reckoned among the natural processes. "That this principle is not nature, but the soul, is clear." For nature does not move to opposite places, while plants do not grow only either up or down but in both directions.[63] In *S. Th*. I-II, 31, 7 he speaks of the "nature" in man, insofar as it is opposed to "reason"; it is "that which is common (*commune*) to man and to other things, particularly that which is not obedient to reason." But in the same text it appears that nature can be taken in another sense, "insofar as intellect and reason are principally the nature of man, because by them man is constituted in the species." At one time "nature" is considered to be the common and generic, at another the specifically determinative. In which direction does the definition given in *Phys*. II tend?

The key to the answer lies in *primo*. It has been too little noted that in

---

[61] *In II Phys.*, lect. 1, 145: Quia natura, etsi sit principium motus compositorum, non tamen primo. Unde quod animal movetur deorsum, non est ex natura animalis inquantum est animal, sed ex natura dominantis elementi.

[62] Thus S. O'Flynn Brennan, "'Physis', The Meaning of 'Nature' in the Aristotelian Philosophy of Nature," *Thomist* 24 (1961): 395; 398.

[63] *In II De anima*, lect. 3, 257.

In I Post. Anal. Thomas gives an explanation of this logical term which is decisive for the interpretation of the definition of nature. He observes that "primarily" restricts the predication 'per se'. "Whatever is predicated 'primo' is predicated 'per se', but not the reverse." Something is said "primarily" in relation to what is prior to the subject and contains this. That the sum of the corners of a triangle is 180 degrees is not predicated "primarily" of an equilateral triangle. For this property does not belong to the equilateral triangle as such but is common to all triangles.[64] What belongs to something in virtue of a part does not belong to it "primarily."[65]

Let us now apply this determination to the example Thomas advances in his exposition of the definition of nature. He states that downward movement is not proper to the animal as such but belongs to it on account of the element that is dominant in its body. Because this is "heavy," downward movement is natural for the animal, certainly, but it does not yet belong to it "primarily." That is also evident, as Thomas signalizes elsewhere, from the fact that upward movement is natural for the animate body since it comes forth from an intrinsic principle, but not for the body insofar as it is heavy.[66] The downward motion is predicated "primarily" of the heavy, which in virtue of its nature is determined to this place: "nature is determined to one effect" (*natura determinata est ad unum*).[67] The processes which belong primarily to the animal are sensation and self-movement. These are for the animal as such natural, since their intrinsic principle is the "soul," which is the nature and form of the animal.[68]

From this elaboration of the example given by Thomas the central role of "primarily" in the definition of nature becomes clear. For it effects that nature has always to be related to the subject, of which it is primarily the principle of motion. Nature is not something subsistent. In relation to the subject, to which it belongs primarily, nature again and again acquires a specifically different content. The natural operation of the stone

---

[64] *In I Post. Anal.*, lect. 9, 78ff.; lect. 11, 97.

[65] Cf. *In V Phys.*, lect. 1, 639ff.; *S. Th.* I, 8, 4.

[66] *De motu cordis*: Cum enim animal movetur deorsum quidem est motus eius naturalis et toti animali et corpori, eo quod in corpore animalis elementum grave predominatur. Cum autem animal movetur sursum, est quidem naturalis motus animali, quia est a principio intrinseco ipsius quod est anima; non tamen est naturale corpori gravi; *In III Sent.* 22, 3, 2, 1; *S.c.G.* III, 23; *In VIII Phys.*, lect. 7, 1023.

[67] *De pot.* 3, 13; 3, 15; *S.c.G.* I, 50; II, 83; III, 23; *S. Th.* I, 41, 2; 42, 2 ad 2; I-II, 10, 1 ad 1; 18, 10; 63, 1.

[68] *In VIII Phys.*, lect. 7, 1023: Motus animalis, quo movet seipsum, si comparetur ad totum animal, est naturalis: quia est ab *anima, quae est natura et forma animalis; In II De anima*, lect. 7, 323.

is the movement downwards, that of man is understanding[69]—therefore man desires by nature to know. The notion "motion" in the definition is so broadened that it also comes to embrace spiritual activities. 'Motus' in the strict sense is the act of the imperfect (*actus imperfecti*), i.e., of that which is in potency; sensing and understanding are however the acts of the perfect (*actus perfecti*), i.e., of what is in act.[70] They can be called "motions" in a more general sense, because these operations too imply a transition from potency to act. Through this broadening, nature can also be said of non-physical beings.[71]

Characteristic of the different specifications of nature is that the "determination to one effect" acquires an ever less restrictive character. So the intrinsic principle, whereby the elements are determined to their natural places, becomes in living things the principle of self-movement. In them grades can then be distinguished. The more the living thing moves from and to itself, the higher the grade of life.[72] So sensitive and intellective beings are receptive of intentional forms, which are the cause of their movements and operations.[73] There is in nature a hierarchical order.

Order connotes 'principium'. The principle from which the order is thought continues to be maintained throughout the diversity of natures. As a general basic rule Thomas formulates: that which comes first is always preserved in what comes later (*semper prius salvatur in posteriori*).[74] Nature is always the immovable foundation and principle of everything else (cf. 3.7.1.). This rule holds for man as well.[75] Nature determines the faculties that belong to man "primarily," the intellect and the will. "Naturally" the human intellect knows "being" and the first intelligibles; from this "first known" (cf. 5.4.) is caused the science of conclusions. "Naturally" the will tends towards its last end, happiness; from this natural will ('voluntas ut natura') are caused all voluntary strivings.[76]

---

[69] Cf. *De verit.* 13, 1.

[70] *S. Th.* I, 18, 1: Illa proprie sunt viventia, quae seipsa secundum aliquam speciem motus movent; sive motus accipiatur proprie, sicut motus dicitur actus imperfecti, idest exsistentis in potentia; sive motus communiter, prout motus dicitur etiam actus perfecti, prout intelligere et sentire dicitur moveri. See for this distinction: *In III De anima*, lect. 12, 766. Cf. *De verit.* 24, 1 ad 14; *S. Th.* I, 14, 2 ad 2.

[71] Cf. *S. Th.* I-II, 10, 1. See for the broader background 8.2.3.

[72] See *S. Th.* I, 18, 3.

[73] *S. Th.* I, 41, 2: Voluntas et natura secundum hoc differunt in causando, quod natura determinata est ad unum; sed voluntas non est determinata ad unum. Cujus ratio est: quia effectus assimilatur formae agentis per quam agit. Manifestum est autem quod unius rei non est nisi una forma naturalis per quam res habet esse. Unde quale ipsum est, tale facit. Sed forma per quam voluntas agit, non est una tantum, sed sunt plures, secundum quod sunt plures rationes intellectae; *S. Th.* I-II, 10, 1 ad 1.

[74] *S. Th.* I, 60, 1.

[75] *De motu cordis*: . . . cuiuslibet suae operationis principium naturale est.

[76] *S. Th.* I, 18, 3; 41, 2 ad 2; 60, 2: Semper id quod pertinet ad prius, habet rationem

The last part of the definition of nature is: *per se et non per accidens*. Only of this component does Aristotle give an elucidation. It can happen that a physician is himself the cause of his health; then the principle of his healing lies in himself. By the definition it is excluded, however, that such a principle is natural: for the connection of the physician and the patient is accidental. Natural things have in virtue of their essence a principle of motion within themselves.[77]

The detailed explanation, necessary for the correct understanding of the definition of nature, makes explicit at the same time something of a more general character. The explanation is the way of definitional thought itself. The intelligible marks of nature are those of the definition as such. For the definition is a resolution of the thing to its *principles*. The definitional logos must indicate the *intrinsic* principles as answer to the "what" question. The definition consists of what is predicated *per se* (2.2.1.). "Each thing is mainly defined according to what belongs to it *primo* and *per se*."[78] The forming of the definition presupposes a hierarchical order of perfections (2.3.).

This intelligible coherence acquires still more relief in the continuation of *Phys.* II, 1 where it can be seen that the definition of nature is a condensation of the Greek philosophers' quest for the origin of things. For nature, as Aristotle shows, can be said as well of matter as of form— something Thomas anticipated in his commentary with his distinction of "passive principle" and "active principle." While at first glance it may simply seem a sample of logical ingenuity, the definition of nature in fact comprehends the historical and systematic progress of the desire to know.

7.1.2. *Matter is the nature*

After the definition of nature is established, Aristotle continues (*Phys.* II, c. 1, 193 a 9ff.): to some it appears that the nature and essence of natural things is the "first" constituent of them that is in itself unformed; so the "nature" of a bed is wood. An indication of this is seen by the Sophist Antiphon in the fact that if someone were to bury a bed and if the rotting

---

principii. Unde cum natura sit primum quod est in unoquoque, oportet quod id quod ad naturam pertinet, sit principium in quolibet. Et hoc apparet in homine quantum ad intellectum, et quantum ad voluntatem. Intellectus enim cognoscit principia naturaliter . . . Unde voluntas naturaliter tendit in suum finem ultimum. Omnis enim homo naturaliter vult beatitudinem; *S.Th.* I-II, 17, 9 ad 2; *S.c.G.* II, 83; *De motu cordis.*

[77] In *Phys.* II, 8 (199 b 31ff.) Aristotle again employs the image of the self-healing physician, this time to emphasize not the difference but the agreement between 'physis' and 'technè'. Nature is like the art that is in what is moved, even though it is 'per accidens'.

[78] *S.Th.* III, 60, 4 ad 1.

process were to have the power of sending up a shoot, it would not be a bed that would be generated, but wood. From this he concludes that arrangement through human art is something that belongs to the subject merely accidentally; its essence, in contrast, is what persists continuously throughout the process. If in its own turn this substratum can be resolved into something else (e.g., wood into earth), then according to Antiphon this last is the nature and essence. On the basis of these considerations, so Aristotle observes, some have asserted that fire, air or other elements are the nature of things. For this 'archè' is the whole of substance, imperishable and eternal, all else being its accidental dispositions and modifications, which endlessly come to be and pass away.

This exposition is instructive in two respects. First, it shows the desire to know as a resolution and makes evident what motivates this desire. The analysis is directed to the "essence" and "substance" of things as over against the accidental, to the perpetual in distinction from the corruptible.[79] The science of nature thereby provides certainty in a changeable world. The systematic resolution to the intrinsic principles of motion (6.5.1.) had the same direction: it proved to be a reduction to the immobile terms which make motion intelligible.

In the second place, Aristotle's further thematizing of nature proves to coincide with the historical resolution. It follows in fact the first phase of the history of philosophical reflection about the origin of being, as this was set out in 5.2. in the light of the second basic text. The first philosophers, the pre-Socratics, adduced only material principles as causes; they viewed a primary substance as the 'archè' of all that is. They asserted that all forms are accidents and that only matter is the substance and the principle of things. "Becoming" can accordingly be nothing other than an accidental change, an "alteration," because each thing becomes from a being actually existing.[80]

This view of the pre-Socratics is not fully rejected by either Aristotle or Thomas. Aristotle notes straightforwardly in *Phys*. II: "In one sense 'nature' is thus called matter, as the 'first' substratum of things that have in themselves a principle of motion and change" (193 a 28). Thomas makes an evaluation through a distinction which comes down to the differentiation of nature into an active and a passive principle: the position of the pre-Socratics is in part true and in part false. True is that matter belongs to the nature of things. For matter is principle of becoming, since on the basis of matter a thing is subject to movement and change; and principle

---

[79] Aristotle constantly identifies 'physis' with 'ousia' (193 a 9; 16; 20; 25). Cf. also Thomas, *In II Phys*., lect. 2, 149.

[80] Cf. *In I Phys*., lect. 2, 14; lect. 14, 123.

of being, since it enters into the constitution of that which is. Untrue, however, is that all forms are accidents and that the material substratum is the entire essence of things.[81] The basic error of the first philosophers is that they judged the process of nature according to the model of generation through art. In such becoming the actually existing matter is the substance, and the forms are accidental.[82] But for natural generation this does not hold.

This insight marks the second phase in the history of the question of being. Then a distinction is made between "matter" and "substantial form," whereby it becomes possible to acknowledge essential changes. While for the pre-Socratics the primary matter is "actual," later philosophers start from a primary matter that is pure "potential" and is brought into act through the form. Thomas regards it as Aristotle's great merit that with his doctrine of the potentiality of matter he offered a solution to the difficulty that "becoming" can be only "alteration."[83]

Matter is that nature that is the cause of becoming "in the manner of a mother"[84]—the terms 'materia' and 'mater' are cognate—that is, as receptive subject. Matter is what is of itself neither "substance" nor "quality" nor one of the other categories whereby being is divided and determined.[85] This diversity of matter with respect to all forms of being Aristotle proves not only "by the way of motion" but also "by the way of predication,"[86] a corroboration of the onto-logical coherence found earlier. Motion and mobile being are marked by the "katallel" structure of subject and form—every mutation occurs within the horizon of the categories (6.5.1.); equally determinative for being is the predicative structure of "something of something other" (1.3.2. and 2.1.). There must be a subject of which all substantial forms are predicated, and then such that the essence of that subject is other than that of the categories.[87]

Just like predication, generation always presupposes a subject. It is im-

---

[81] *In II Phys.*, lect. 2, 150.

[82] *In II Phys.*, lect. 2, 149: Et ideo similem opinionem accipiebant de formis naturalibus, sicut de formis artificialibus; *In V Metaph.*, lect. 5, 818. Cf. *In VII Metaph.*, lect. 2, 1284; *S. Th.* I, 76, 4.

[83] *De spirit. creat.* q. un., a. 3: Et Aristoteles eorum dubitationem solvit ponendo materiam esse in potentia tantum, quam dicit esse subiectum generationis et corruptionis simpliciter.

[84] *In I Phys.*, lect. 15, 135.

[85] *In VII Metaph.*, lect. 2, 1285.

[86] *Ibid.*, 1287: Attamen diversitatem materiae ab omnibus formis non probat Philosophus *per viam motus*, quae quidem probatio est per viam naturalis philosophiae, sed *per viam praedicationis*, quae est propria Logicae.

[87] *Ibid.*, 1287. Correctly, Thomas notes in his commentary (1288ff.) that this does not hold for "univocal" predication, but only for what is predicated "denominatively".

possible for anything to be generated unless something preexists (cf. 3.2.). The common opinion of the philosophers of nature was: *ex nihilo nihil fit*. "Out of nothing comes nothing"—this conviction dominates Greek thought about the origin and nature of things. Therefore several pre-Socratics posited an actually existing material principle. Therefore Anaxagoras posited as principle an original mixture from which things came to be through combination and separation. Therefore Parmenides denied the reality of generation and motion. Therefore Aristotle acknowledged as principle matter, which is ungenerated and is incorruptible, and which as being in potency is a middle (*medium*) between absolute non-being and being in act.[88]

7.1.3. Form is the nature "more"

In another manner—so Aristotle continues his exposition in *Phys.* II, 1 (193 a 30ff.)—nature is the "form" (*morphè*) and "species" (*eidos*) from which the 'ratio' of the thing is constituted. He adduces three arguments for this.

The first is based on an analogy with 'technè'. We do not say "this is art" if something is an artifact, e.g., a bed, only in potency and does not yet have the form of a bed. The same is true of natural things. What is flesh or bone in potency does not have its nature until it is actual, until it has received the form according to which the definition of the thing is formed, whereby we know what flesh or bone is. Therefore in a second sense the nature of things having a principle of motion within them is the form, which is inseparable from the material subject except in thought—a polemical rider against Plato's 'chorismos' of the Idea.

The second argument is meant to show that on the basis of Antiphon's argumentation for the view that matter is the nature one can with equal justification arrive at a different conclusion. According to this Sophist, not the form but the material substratum is the essence of things. For a bed, if it could bring forth anything, would generate not a bed but wood. Well then, so Aristotle asserts, even if this is "the nature," then the form is just as much the nature: for man generates man. The natural form returns through generation.[89]

---

[88] Cf. *In VII Metaph.*, lect. 6, 1412; *In I Phys.*, lect. 9, 59: Quod etiam ab omnibus naturalibus philosophis supponebatur, quod scilicet ex nihilo nihil fit. (60) Ut enim non cogerentur ponere aliquid de novo fieri quod prius omnino non esset, posuerunt aliqui omnia prius extitisse: vel in aliquo uno confuso, sicut Anaxagoras et Empedocles; vel in aliquo principio materiali ... Et omnes hi decepti fuerunt quia nesciverunt distinguere inter potentiam et actum. Ens enim in potentia est quasi medium inter purum non ens et ens in actu.

[89] Cf. *In II Phys.*, lect. 2, 154: Sed forma rei naturalis redit per generationem, fit

The third and final argument we have already encountered a number of times before: nature in the (etymological) sense of generation is *via in naturam* (3.4.1.). Every coming to be is from something, matter, towards something, namely form. Therefore, the terminus and end of the way of nature must be the form.

The arguments in this exposition are ruled by the same motive that was determinative for the identification of matter and nature. Here too the way of nature is reduced to what is substantial and permanent. There is an eternal return of the same specific form. What comes to be, properly speaking, is the composite of form and matter, not the form itself.[90] And form, according to Aristotle (193 b 6) is the nature "more" than matter is, for everything is more what it is when it has its end in it, is in act, than when it is in potency. 'Physis' is primarily "eidetic." A thing has its nature only when it has its form. Through the form it is in act; form gives being to matter. Through the form, too, the thing is constituted in its species and completed in its essence; then it has a definable logos.[91]

Nature is twofold, namely, matter and form.[92] In the concept of nature are combined the resolution of motion towards the intrinsic principles, which entail an absolute necessity (6.5.1.)—nature is this hodology (6.5.2.)—and the first two phases of the history of philosophy. Aristotle's thematizing of 'physis' is an attempt to synthesize ancient thought. It brings together the "archaic" tradition of the pre-Socratics, who wanted to reduce reality to a material 'archè', and the tradition inaugurated by Socrates, who sought the intelligibility of reality in the form.

Per naturam ex nihilo nihil fit (De pot. 3, 8). Because of this origination, there is an irreducible duality in nature. "Matter is in a sense cause of form, insofar as it sustains form, and form is in a sense cause of matter, insofar as it gives actual being to matter."[93] Both are "nature." "The principle from which (*ex quo*) natural generation proceeds, namely matter, is called nature ... Again, the principle according to which generation comes about, namely the form of the thing generated, is called nature ...

---

enim ex homine homo: ergo forma rei naturalis est natura.

[90] Cf. *In VII Metaph.*, lect. 7, 1417ff.

[91] Cf. *In V Metaph.*, lect. 5, 820: Ad ponendum autem formam esse naturam, hac ratione inducebantur, quia quaecumque sunt et fiunt naturaliter non dicuntur habere naturam, existente materia ex qua nata sunt fieri vel esse, nisi habeant speciem propriam et formam, per quam speciem consequantur; *In II Metaph.*, lect. 4, 320; *S. Th.* I, 5.5.

[92] *In II Phys.*, lect. 4, 167: Natura dicitur *dupliciter*, scilicet de materia et forma.

From this it is also clear, as indeed it is from the *Physica* in its entirety, that Heidegger's interpretation that the 'morphè' is the only essential determination of 'physis' is incorrect ("Vom Wesen und Begriff der Physis," in *Wegmarken* (Frankfurt am Main, 1967), p. 363).

[93] *De verit.* 28, 7.

For a natural generation is one which is directed towards nature.''[94] The reason that both principles can be called ''nature'' lies in the relation of potency and act, which is the ratio of the way of nature (6.7.).

The way of nature is a process towards perfection. Matter has as being in potency the character of the imperfect: it is the most incomplete.[95] Form is act, and because act is always prior to potency, the eidetic nature is primary. Form is the principle of being and intelligibility; through the form the thing is true (4.4.2.) and perfect.[96] Form is ''something divine'' in things. Therefore there is a natural desire of the imperfect towards this perfection.

7.2. ''Universal nature''

Not only that from and towards which generation proceeds is called nature, but also the principle by which (a quo):

> Again, the principle by which generation comes about, as by an agent, is the specific nature, which is specifically the same as the nature of the thing generated, although it is in something other. For man generates man.[97]

''Man generates man'': natural generation is ruled by the law of univocity.

In *Phys.* II, 2 (194 b 13) Aristotle—in a discussion of the question to what extent form is the object of physics—adds something to this thesis: ''man generates man, and the sun does too.'' It is the only place where Aristotle mentions this ''extra''; an explanation is not provided. Now, Thomas not only cites this statement *Homo generat hominem et sol* many times[98] but also provides an elaborate account of the causality of the sun. In studies of Aquinas's doctrines, one generally finds little about the role of the sun in his world picture. In GILSON's standard work, *The Christian Philosophy of St. Thomas*, for example, the celestial bodies are hardly men-

---

[94] *In VII Metaph.*, lect. 6, 1389–1390.

[95] *De principiis naturae*, c. 4: Materia ex eo quod est ens in potentia, habet rationem imperfecti; *De spirit. creat.* q. un., a. 1: ... materiam primam, quae est incompletissimum inter omnia entia.

[96] *S. Th.* I, 3, 2: Omne compositum ex materia et forma est perfectum et bonum per suam formam.

[97] *In VII Metaph.*, lect. 6, 1391: Et iterum principium, a quo fit generatio, sicut ab agente, est natura dicta secundum speciem, quae scilicet est eiusdem speciei cum natura generati, sed tamen est in alio secundum numerum. Homo enim generat hominem.

[98] Besides *In II Phys.*, lect. 4, 175, see among other places *S.c.G.* II, 76; III, 104; *S. Th.* I, 79, 4; 115, 3 ad 2; *De verit.* 5, 4; *De malo* 4, 3; *De subst. separ.*, c. 10, 105; *Comp. Theol.* I, 170; *In De causis*, lect. 5; *In V Metaph.*, lect. 3, 785; *In VIII Phys.*, lect. 10, 1053. See further for the role of the sun *In De div. nomin.* c. 4, lect. 3, 311ff.; c. 5, lect. 2, 662.

tioned. That in Thomas himself matters are quite otherwise is evident
from the extensive material amassed by TH. LITT in *Les corps célestes dans
l'univers de Saint Thomas d'Aquin*.[99] The philosophical significance of the
celestial spheres is, however, not sufficiently elucidated in this work.

The philosophical meaning of the adage *Homo generat hominem et sol* can
be grasped through an exposition of Thomas's in *De subst. separ.*, c. 10:

> A given nature or form has a twofold cause: one, which is 'per se' and ab-
> solutely the cause of such a nature or form; the other, which is the cause that
> such a nature or form is in such a thing. The necessity of this distinction is
> apparent to anyone considering the causes of the things which are genera-
> ted.[100]

Two causes of a nature must be distinguished. The "univocal agent"
("man," "horse") is indeed the cause that the nature begins to exist in
the thing generated, yet it is not the cause 'per se' of the generated nature.
For that which is the cause 'per se' of a specific nature must be the cause
of that nature in all subjects that have that species. If the generator were
the cause 'per se', then the impossible consequence would be that it is the
cause of itself. The univocal agent has a particular effect; it causes the nature to be in this matter, which is the principle of individuation: the generating horse is the principle of the coming to be of "this horse" insofar
as it is the cause that the nature of horse comes to be in this matter. "It
remains, therefore, that above all those participating in the nature of
horse, there must be some universal cause of the whole species" (*oportet
super omnes participantes naturam equinam esse aliquam universalem causam totius
speciei*).[101]

It is noteworthy that in this statement from *De substantiis separatis* the notion of "participation" is applied in a Platonic sense to the relation of the
particular subjects to their specific nature. In order to understand this we
must refer to section 2.5.3. ("Predication 'per participationem' and 'per
se'"), where two manners of participation were distinguished. According
to the first mode, what is participated in belongs to the essence of the thing
and its definition. For "to participate" can be circumscribed as "to take
part"; "so when something receives partially what belongs to another in
a universal way, it is said that it participates in it" (*De hebdom.*, lect. 2).
Thus one can say of 'Socrates' that he participates in 'man'. For the in-

---

[99] Louvain and Paris, 1963.
[100] *De subst. separ.*, c. 10: Alicuius naturae vel formae duplex causa invenitur: una quidem quae est per se et simpliciter causa talis naturae vel formae; alia vero quae est causa
huius naturae vel formae in hoc. Cuius quidem distinctionis necessitas apparet, si quis
causas consideret eorum quae generantur.
[101] *De subst. separ.*, c. 10. Cf. *S.c.G.* III, 65; *De pot.* 5, 1.

dividual subject is not identical with the predicate but possesses a general perfection in a particular way. To Thomas's mind this manner of participation can, as we saw, coincide very well with the Aristotelian predication 'per se', in which something is said univocally of something else.[102] This participation is realized *per viam generationis*.[103]

To that which participates in a nature, the cause 'per se' of that nature can never be reduced:

> A perfect thing participating in any nature effects a likeness to it, not by absolutely producing that nature, but by applying it to something else. For this (individual) man cannot be the cause of human nature absolutely, because he would then be the cause of himself; but he is the cause that human nature exists in the man generated.[104]

Above all participants must be a universal cause of the species, of the form, as form. What is this? The continuation of *De subst. separ.*, c. 10 provides the answer.

> The Platonists posited as this cause a Form separate from matter in the manner in which the principle of all artifacts is the artistic form that does not exist in matter. According to Aristotle, however, this universal cause must be located in some one of the celestial bodies. Therefore he himself, distinguishing beween these two causes, said that man generates man, and the sun does too (*homo generat hominem, et sol*).[105]

The Platonists considered as this universal cause of things the separate species, the Ideas. Through participation in these, material things acquire their substantial forms. But this view is untenable. Since these examplars are immobile and always identical, they cannot explain the generation and corruption of things. Therefore Aristotle posited a universal principle, which by its movement causes the cycle of coming to be and passing

---

[102] Cf. *S.c.G.* I, 32: Omne quod de pluribus praedicatur *univoce, secundum participationem* cuilibet eorum convenit de quo praedicatur: nam species participare dicitur genus, et individuum speciem ... omne quod participatur determinatur ad modum participantis, et sic partialiter habetur, et non secundum omnem perfectionis modum.

[103] *Comp. Theol.*, c. 255: Nullus autem eorum ex hoc dicitur homo, quod similitudinem participat alterius hominis, sed ex eo solo quod participat essentiam speciei: ad quam tamen participandam unus inducit alium per viam generationis.

[104] *S. Th.* I, 45, 5 ad 1: Aliquod perfectum participans aliquam naturam, facit sibi simile, non quidem producendo absolute illam naturam, sed applicando eam ad aliquid: non enim hic homo potest esse causa naturae humanae absolute, quia sic esset causa suiipsius; sed est causa quod natura humana sit in hoc homine generato.

[105] *De subst. separ.*, c. 10: Quam quidem causam Platonici posuerunt speciem separatam a materia, ad modum quo omnium artificialium principium est forma artis, non in materia existens. Secundum Aristotelem autem hanc universalem causam oportet ponere in aliquo caelestium corporum: unde et ipse has duas causas distinguens, dixit, quod homo generat hominem, et sol.

away. The movement towards the species, generation, must be reduced to the celestial bodies.[106]

The sun has a causality which extends to the entire species and—in distinction from the "univocal agent," whose causality extends to but a single individual—is called the "equivocal agent." Wholly adequate this term is not, since it seems to come into conflict with the principle that "every agent effects something similar to itself." But Thomas wishes to bring to expression with it that the effect is in the cause not in a synonymous manner but in a higher and more universal manner. The equivocal agent comes before the univocal agent, for a universal cause comes before a particular cause, and every multitude must be reduced to a unity.[107]

With the reduction of the nature of a thing to a twofold cause, of which the celestial body is the primary one, many earlier findings are connected.

First, this analysis has as counterpart in the structure of being the composition of 'subjectum' and 'essentia'. In individual substances, the essence is not completely identical with the subject. This distinction was explained in 2.1.3.: several subjects are found to agree in a common nature. Therefore that which is one must be distinguished from that which is multiple. Whatever in the thing belongs to the common nature is called the "essence." 'Socrates' is not the essence, the human nature, but has this: *homo enim nec est humanitas*. This non-identity comes from the composition of matter and form. In material being there is the "katallel" structure of subject and essence or form, which relate to each other as potency to act. This structure of being is now traced to a twofold causality. In this reduction the philosophical significance of the "celestial" cause becomes evident: this is origin of the species, of the essence, the act that gives being to the subject.

Secondly, this analysis confirms the hierarchical order in causality (3.7.4.), truth (4.3.1.), and necessity (6.2.1.), in short in intelligibility. In 3.7.4. ("Grades of causality") we discussed the thesis taken from *In VI Metaph.*, lect. 3—namely, the higher the cause the more universal its effect. The order found in effects is proportional to the order of causality. Univocal causes are particular, since they are determined to proper effects of a single species: "man generates man." The operation of the celestial

---

[106] Cf. *S. Th.* I, 115, 3 ad 2.

[107] *In II Sent.* 18, 2, 1; *De pot.* 7, 7 ad 7: Agens aequivocum oportet esse prius quam agens univocum, quia agens univocum non habet causalitatem super totam speciem . . . sed solum super aliquod individuum speciei; agens autem aequivocum habet causalitatem super totam speciem; unde oportet primum agens esse aequivocum; *De verit.* 10, 13 ad 3; *S. Th.* I, 13, 5 and ad 1: Hoc autem agens universale, licet non sit univocum, non tamen est omnino aequivocum, quia sic non faceret sibi simile; sed potest dici agens analogicum; *In Boeth. De trin.* 1, 4 ad 4; *In VIII Phys.*, lect. 10, 1053.

body is more universal because its causality extends not to a single species but to everything that comes to be and passes away. Thanks to this hierarchy there is a concurrence of the two causes in the bringing forth of the concrete subject.

Thirdly, this analysis confirms the historical resolution. The history of the desire to know is marked by the ascent from a particular towards a universal consideration of being (5.2.). In the second phase of the historical itinerary, substantial changes were acknowledged. More general causes were advanced for these changes, such as the oblique circle of the sun, by Aristotle, or the Ideas, by Plato. That Thomas puts the two solutions together can no longer be surprising after the elaboration in *De subst. separ.*, c. 10. For the celestial bodies have to fulfill the role assigned by Plato to the "separate species."

Fourthly, this analysis confirms the systematic resolution of motion to the extrinsic causes (6.5.3.). Natural becoming requires an 'agens perpetuum' which through its circulation effects the perpetuity of this becoming: "The alterations and corruptions in this world are reducible to the celestial body as first mover."[108] Here too comes to the fore the important place the celestial bodies occupy in Thomas's analysis. One can accordingly not ignore his reflections about them simply because the physics on which they are based is by modern standards obsolete.

The analysis shows from various angles that Thomas's thought is cosmologically oriented and that in following "the way of nature" it remains tributary to Greek thought—which was already apparent in his view of contingency (6.3.). The world is divided into a sublunary (contingent) part and a necessary part. To the latter belong the celestial bodies; they are absolutely necessary, because their potentiality with respect to being is completely fulfilled. Reality is hierarchically structured according to the degree of immobility. In this cosmic order the separated substances come closest to God, who is fully immovable. Directly thereafter follow the celestial bodies.[109] Pseudo-Dionysius had formulated as a general principle that the lower nature touches in its upper ends the beginnings of the higher nature. This continuity takes shape in the celestial body: it touches the spiritual nature in that it has part in incorruptibility.[110]

Yet the ontological position of the celestial bodies is not altogether

---

[108] *Comp. Theol.* I, c. 4. Cf. *S.c.G.* III, 149: Omnis actio particularis agentis originem habet ab universali agente, sicut in istis inferioribus omnis motus praevenitur a motu caelesti.

[109] Cf. *S.c.G.* III, 72; *In I De caelo*, lect. 6, 64.

[110] *De pot.* 6, 6 ad 12: Id quod est supremum in corporibus, attingit ad infimum spiritualis naturae per aliquam participationem proprietatum eius sicut per hoc quod est incorruptibile, non autem per hoc quod ei uniatur.

unproblematical. Thomas signalizes that on this point amongst philosophers and ecclesiastical Doctors there is a diversity of opinions. The background of this diversity is what we established in connection with the definition of nature (7.1.1.4.): in the order of natures "the determination to one thing" acquires an ever less restrictive character. Is therefore living being not higher than corporeal being? Not without reason did the nobility of the celestial bodies bring Plato and Aristotle to regard them as besouled.[111] And must the position of the celestial bodies not be for Thomas himself a fortiori problematical, given the special position he assigns to man, a being who has an intentional openness to all that is?[112] Man forms the "horizon" of the spiritual and material—he unites in himself "to be," "to live," and "to understand"— and is therefore the "middle" of the universe (5.1.). Between *this* "middle" and the middle position of the celestial bodies between the spiritual nature and the corporeal nature there is an imbalance.[113] Here the balance tilts towards the "objective" cosmic order, for we can observe that Thomas wants to guarantee this order by making celestial motion dependent on the separated substances.

Nature always tends to one thing. Now movement as such excludes uniformity; that which is moved is conditioned otherwise now and before. Nature therefore never intends movement for its own sake, but for something that follows from movement; it intends, through movement, rest. So the heavy body is inclined by nature to the movement that leads to its natural place.[114]

The movement of the heavens, however, never comes to rest; it is continuous and circular. From this it follows that this movement cannot be "by nature", which is to say from an active, intrinsic principle. It is rather "voluntary" and "intellectual"; its principle must be an intelligence, a separated substance. That, however, is not to say that the circulation is violent for the heavens. Here Thomas can make fruitful his division of nature into an active and a passive principle. The circular movement of the heavens is natural because they have in their nature an inclination thereto and so have within them a passive principle of movement that is

[111] *De spirit. creat.* q. un., a. 6.
[112] Cf. *S. Th.* I, 14, 1: Unde manifestum est quod natura rei non cognoscentis est magis coarctata et limitata; natura autem rerum cognoscentium habet majorem amplitudinem et extensionem.
[113] For the broader historical background see H. Heimsoeth, *Die sechs grossen Themen der abendländischen Metaphysik*, pp. 90ff.: "Seele und Aussenwelt."
[114] *S.c.G.* III, 23: Natura semper ad unum tendit ... Impossibile est igitur quod natura intendat motum propter seipsum. Intendit igitur quietem per motum, quae se habet ad motum sicut unum ad multa; *De pot.* 5, 5; *De spirit. creat.* q. un., a. 6.

actualized by an external agent.[115] The celestial bodies "touch" the separated substances, because the lowest of the spiritual beings is as *motor* united with them.[116]

The celestial body is moved by an intellectual substance, is the instrument of an intelligent agent.[117] Cosmic movement is the work of an intellect. Earlier is was established that celestial movement is directed towards generation; the celestial body is the cause 'per se' of the specific forms. From these two findings Thomas can now draw a further conclusion. The coming to be of sublunary things originates from the intention of an intellectual agent, and the essential forms are determined by the 'species', which preexist in the intellect of the separated substance (just as the forms of the products of art exist in the mind of the artifex). In this way is verified (*verificatur*) Plato's thesis that the separate Forms are the causes of the forms that exist in matter. Certainly a difference remains, so Thomas says, for according to our view neither do these Forms subsist 'per se' nor do they cause the essential forms immediately, but through the movement of the heavens.[118]

The celestial body is among natural things the "first cause."[119] The heavens, so we read in *S. Th.* I, 82, 4, occupy in nature the place that the king has in the field of politics: both aim at the common good and set their subjects in motion. The univocal agent is a "second" and "instrumental" cause; it is instrument of the celestial body.[120] The generator is the cause that matter acquires a particular form, is only the cause "of becoming." The heavens have on the contrary a more essential influence: they are cause of the form as such and therefore not only the cause of the becoming of the effect, but also the cause of its being (*est causa non solum fiendi sed essendi*).[121]

Homo generat hominem, et sol. These two causes are also described by Thomas (in *S. Th.* I-II, 85, 6) as "particular nature" and "universal nature" (*natura universalis*). The first is "a thing's own power of action and preservation." In respect of this nature death, corruption, and every defect is

---

[115] *S.c.G.* III, 23; *De pot.* 5, 5; *In I De caelo*, lect. 3, 22; *S.Th.* I, 70, 3.

[116] *De spirit. creat.* q. un., a. 6 ad 1. It is to be noted that the celestial body is "united" with the separated substance as the mobile is with the motor, and not through participation as is the case with man. There remains on this point an imbalance in Thomas.

[117] *S.c.G.* III, 23.

[118] *S.c.G.* III, 24. Cf. *In II Sent.* 15, 1, 2; *S.c.G.* I, 44; *S.Th.* I, 65, 4.

[119] *In I Meteor.*, lect. 2, 13: Manifestum est autem corpus caeleste inter naturalia esse primam causam: quod eius incorruptibilitas et nobilitas demonstrat.

[120] *S.c.G.* II, 21: Quidquid est causatum secundum aliquam naturam, non potest esse prima causa illius naturae, sed secunda et instrumentalis; ... et ideo oportet quod generans univocum sit quasi agens instrumentale respectu ejus quod est causa primaria totius speciei; *S.Th.* I, 115, 3 ad 2; *In Boeth. De trin.* 1, 4 ad 4.

[121] *S.Th.* I, 104, 1.

"contrary to nature," since this power intends the being of the thing of which it is the principle. The "universal nature" is "an active power in some universal principle of nature, for instance, in some celestial body; or a power of some superior substance, in which sense God is also called by some the nature that natures (*natura naturans*)." This power intends the good and the preservation of the universe. To this end the cycle of coming to be and passing away is required, for in this way the species is preserved. In respect of the universal nature corruption, then, is natural.[122]

Striking in the text cited from *S. Th.* I-II, 85, 6 is that Thomas leaves open the possibility that the "universal nature" must be identified with God, who by "some" is also called *natura naturans*.[123] He expresses the same suggestion in his commentary on pseudo-Dionysius's *De divinis nominibus*:

> The universal nature is called the universal cause of all that naturally comes to being. Now, God is the universal cause of all that naturally comes to being. Therefore some call Him the nature that natures.[124]

According to WOLFSON[125] Spinoza would have borrowed the term 'natura naturans'—a central notion in his thought (cf. *Ethica* I, prop. 29)—directly from Thomas. Yet the only, and far from compelling, argument is that Spinoza refers to "the Thomists" in his *Korte Verhandeling* (I, 8), where he underscores the difference between their doctrine and his own conception of "the nature that natures."[126]

It needs to be noticed, moreover, that in the two texts in question, which are the only places in Thomas's work in which God is described with 'natura naturans', Aquinas assumes a cautious stance: it is the manner in which "some" speak. In his commentary on Dionysius, he express-

---

[122] Cf. *S. Th.* I, 22, 2 ad 2; *De verit.* 13, 1 ad 2; *In De causis*, lect. 9; *In De div. nomin.* c. 4, lect. 21, 550ff.
In *S. Th.* I, 92, 1 ad 1 (and 99, 2 ad 1) this distinction is applied to the generation of the woman: Per respectum ad *naturam particularem* femina est aliquid deficiens et occasionatum; quia virtus activa quae est in semine maris, intendit producere sibi simile perfectum secundum masculinum sexum ... Sed per comparationem ad *naturam universalem* femina non est aliquid occasionatum, sed est de intentione naturae ad opus generationis ordinata.

[123] See for this notion H.A. Lucks, "Natura naturans. Natura naturata," *The New Scholasticism* 9 (1935): 1–24; O. Weyers, "Contribution à l'histoire des termes 'natura naturans' et 'natura naturata' jusqu'à Spinoza," *Vivarium* 16 (1978): 70–80.

[124] *In De div. nomin.* c. 4, lect. 21, 550: Natura universalis dicitur causa universalis omnium quae naturaliter fiunt. Est autem Deus universalis causa omnium quae naturaliter fiunt; unde et quidam Ipsum nominant naturam naturantem.

[125] *The Philosophy of Spinoza*, I (Cambridge, Mass., 1934), pp. 15ff.

[126] "Gelijk ook de Thomisten bij het zelve God verstaan hebben, dogh haare Natura naturans was een wezen (zy zo noemende) buyten alle zelfstandigheden" *Opera*, vol. 4, eds. J. v. Vloten and J.P.N. Land, 3rd ed. (The Hague, 1914), p. 33.

ly dissociates himself from the idea that the "universal nature" must be identified with God. "But better is to understand the universal nature as the universal cause of what naturally comes to being in the genus of natural things." This universal nature is, so he continues, according to the Platonists a 'species separata', but it is better to say with Aristotle "that the universal nature is the active power of the body, that is first in the genus of the natural causes," which is to say, the heavens.[127]

R. PANIKKAR has analyzed the concept of "nature" in an extensive study in which Thomas's thought is central. To his judgment God as *naturans* represents "the most authentic sense of nature in all Scholasticism."[128] The phrases 'natura naturans' and 'natura naturata'—used for the first time in the Latin translation of Averroës' commentary on *De caelo*—express to his mind in a perfect way the relation of God to the creatures. Participation in the divine nature can appropriately be called "naturing" because it comes forth from a nature. God's act of creation would be "to nature."[129]

This interpretation is not only forced—the phrases used are rather the exception than the rule in Scholasticism—but above all fundamentally incorrect. PANIKKAR's reference to the text from Thomas's commentary on Dionysius, in support of his construction, is misplaced. That such a 'concursus' of nature and creation is foreign to Thomas's way of thought will be evident from what follows.

7.3. *"Creator of the world"*

The universal cause of man is, Thomas states, not man but the sun, and *ulterius Deus*.[130] How is this further reduction to be understood? In 7.2. the philosophical significance of the causality of the heavens was elucidated through a text from *De subst. separ.*, c. 10. The cause 'per se' of a specific nature can not be a particular thing that participates in that nature. The entire drift of the argumentation is now that the same conclusion must hold for being (*esse*) that is the most common:

---

[127] *In De div. nomin.* c. 4, lect. 21, 550. Cf. c. 5, lect. 1, 646; *In II De caelo*, lect. 9, 375: Dicitur autem natura universalis, virtus activa in causa universali, puta in corpore caelesti; *In De causis*, lect. 9; *De pot.* 6, 1 ad 1.
[128] *El concepto de naturaleza*, p. 131: "Dios como *naturans*, lo cual representa . . . el sentido más genuino de naturaleza en toda la Escolástica"; cf. p. 30.
[129] *Ibid.*, pp. 131ff.
[130] *S.c.G.* IV, 7: Sol, qui est extra genus humanum, est universalis causa generationis humanae, et ulterius Deus.

Consequently, the causality [of being] cannot be attributed to any one of the particular beings that participate in being; it must be reduced to the universal and first cause of being, namely God, who is being itself.[131]

In all things is found the "nature of entity" (*natura entitatis*),[132] but in the way of participation, in a particularized way. Here too the notion of "participation" is introduced into the resolution. "Just as an individual man participates in human nature, so every created being participates, so to speak, in the nature of being (*naturam essendi*)."[133] Yet this manner of participation needs to be distinguished from the manner in which an individual participates in the species. In participation in being, what is participated in does not belong to the essence of the thing and to its definition (cf. 2.5.3.).

To what participates in a nature in a finite way, the cause 'per se' of that nature can never be reduced. Above all the participants there must be a universal cause, the cause of being as being. This first principle, to which the "nature of being" belongs without any limitation, is God (cf. 3.6.2.). He brings things to being, not through motion but *per viam creationis*.[134] This universal cause is called—in distinction from the "equivocal agent" whose causality extends to the species—an "analogical agent." That is because the effect, being, possesses an analogical likeness with the cause: for God is being itself.[135]

With the reduction of "being" to its cause, many earlier findings are again connected.

First, this analysis has as its counterpart in the structure of being the composition of 'essentia' and 'esse'. The creature is not its being but has this: *homo enim nec est humanitas nec esse suum* (3.7.5.). The index of creatureliness is the "katallel" structure of essence and being, which relate to each other as potency and act.

Secondly, this analysis confirms the hierarchical order in causality (3.7.4.). Three grades of causes are distinguishable in reality: the univocal agent, the celestial body, and finally the first cause, God. This last cause is fully universal, for its proper effect is 'esse', which transcends every specification.

Thirdly, this analysis confirms the historical resolution. The third and

---

[131] *De subst. separ.*, c. 10, 105: Eius [sc. esse] causalitas attribui non potest alicui particularium entium, quod participat esse, sed oportet quod reducatur in ipsam universalem et primam causam essendi, scilicet Deum, qui est ipsum esse.
[132] *In II Sent.* 1, 1, 1.
[133] *S. Th.* I, 45, 5 ad 1.
[134] Cf. *De subst. separ.*, c. 10, 103 bis; *De pot.* 3, 6; 7, 2.
[135] *In I Sent.* 8, 1, 2.

final phase began, according to Thomas, when "some thinkers" considered being as being. They posited an other origin of things. The historical 'via' of philosophy terminates in the idea of creation.

Fourthly, this analysis confirms the systematic resolution on the metaphysical level (6.6.), a reduction which leads to the cause of being. Every agent effects something like itself. The proper effect of "the first act" is the act of all acts, 'esse'.

The way of thought in this section follows at every turn the same lines as those in the previous section. Just as the specific nature needs to be reduced to a cause 'per se', so too the most general nature of being. Though Thomas also knows, as we shall see later (8.5.3.), another perspective, the "cosmocentric" way of thought is continued in this analysis: "Just as heaven is the universal cause with respect to lower things, so is God the universal cause with respect to all beings. With respect to Him, also heaven itself is a particular cause."[136]

Here too the relation of the causes is thought according to the model of "first" and "second" cause. Just as heaven is the first cause in relation to the "particular nature," so is God the first cause in relation to the "universal nature." For this reason Thomas could assert (7.1.1.3.) that the divine works of wonder are not violent. God has the power to accomplish something "outside" the order of the second causes. This is however not "contrary to nature," but rather "according to the most universal nature" (*secundum naturam universalissimam*), which is to say according to the order of God to the creatures.[137]

Also here the subordination of the second cause is expressed with the notion of *instrumentum*. Just as the generator is the instrument of the sun, so is nature the tool of God.[138] God can be called the cause of every natural operation, since every instrument works through the power of the principal cause.[139]

An instrument does not work through the power of its own form, but through the movement by which it is moved by the principal cause. Essential to an instrument is its being a moved mover. It works "by the way of motion."[140] The mode of producing things through motion takes place

[136] *De pot.* 6, 1 ad 1; *S.c.G.* II, 22.
[137] *De pot.* 6, 1 ad 1. Cf. *S.Th.* I, 105, 6.
[138] *S.Th.* I-II, 1, 2: Tota natura comparatur ad Deum sicut instrumentum ad agens principale; 6, 1 ad 3; *In IV Sent.* 5, 1, 2; *S.c.G.* I, 44; III, 100; *De pot.* 3, 7.
[139] *De pot.* 3,7: Unum est causa actionis alterius, sicut principale agens est causa actionis instrumenti; et hoc modo etiam oportet dicere, quod Deus est causa omnis actionis rei naturalis.
[140] *S.Th.* III, 62, 1; *S.c.G.* II, 21: Instrumentum autem nunquam adhibetur ad causandum aliquid nisi per viam motus; est enim ratio instrumenti quod sit movens motum.

through the mediation of second causes (*mediantibus causis secundis*). But in the mode of production according to which a thing is brought into being absolutely, this cannot take place. That production occurs without motion "through a simple influx of being itself," which is to say, through "creation." Of this, God is the im-mediate cause.[141]

Because of this distinction it becomes understandable that Thomas posited two kinds of efficient cause (6.6.): a natural, and a divine that gives being as *Creator mundi*.[142] The act of creation is not "to nature." The Creator of the world is a "*supernatural* agent."[143]

The distinction in causality can also be indicated by the distinction of "cause of becoming" and "cause of being" which was made in the preceding section. The univocal agent is cause merely of becoming, the celestial body also of being, since it is cause of the form as such. Now that the analysis has been brought to a more universal level, it must be said that only the first cause is really "cause of being." According to the first proposition of the *Liber De causis*, every primary cause has a stronger influence on its effect than does the second cause (*Omnis causa primaria plus est influens super suum causatum quam causa secunda universalis*). Therefore God is more intimately present in all things than are the causes of motion. For He bestows upon things being, which is the innermost in each.[144] Beyond this principle of being one cannot question further. The resolution is at an end.

7.4. *Nature and creature*

With that the task has been brought to completion that was set at the close of chapter 4: to inquire into how the order of nature and that of creature are thought philosophically together. The point of departure for this further fathoming of Thomas's way of thought was the mode of knowing of the human intellect, the "way of reason" (ch. 5). In ch. 6 the "signs" were followed which show man the way towards what is ontologically prior. The discursion of reason is a regress to the origins from which motion and being are intelligible. The point of convergence of these resolutions was the notion of "act." In this chapter the reduction to the principles is made concrete. This analysis reveals how in Thomas's thought

---

[141] *De subst. separ.*, c. 10, 103.

[142] *In I Sent.* 7, 1, 1 ad 3.

[143] *De pot.* 3, 1 ad 1. Cf. *In II Sent.* 20, 1, 1 ad 4: ... a principio supernaturali esse.

[144] *In II Sent.* 1, 1, 4; *S. Th.* I, 8, 1: Esse autem est id quod est magis intimum cuilibet, et quod profundius omnibus inest: cum sit formale respectu omnium quae in re sunt ... Unde oportet quod Deus sit in omnibus rebus, et intime; *S. Th.* I, 105, 5; *In II Phys.*, lect. 6, 195.

the Greek perspective of the origin, "out of nothing comes nothing," is
united with that of the integral coming forth of being from God, "creation
out of nothing." Yet at the same time a number of questions arise.

In the first place, there is a question concerning the resolution to the
intrinsic causes. The principles of the motion and of the being of things
are matter and form. Both are nature, but these principles are not of equal
value ontologically. The form is the nature "more" than matter is, for
every thing is more what it is when it is in act; the form is something
"divine." Is it, however, still possible to call *one* of the two natural principles "divine" if in a further analysis the composite being is reduced to the
'esse', which is the proper effect of God? What does this mean for the
structure of (created) being? Thomas speaks of a "twofold composition,"
but is this solution not too "simple"?

In the resolution to the extrinsic causes Thomas finds successively: the
"particular nature," the univocal agent whose causality extends to a
single individual; the "universal nature," the celestial body which is the
cause 'per se' of the specific nature; and, finally, the Creator of the world,
who is the cause of being as being. As a result of its commencement at nature, the movement of thought is cosmo-centric. The celestial spheres are
an integral part of Thomas's world picture. But does the way of creation
actually agree with this orientation? To create is not "to nature"; the act
of creation is a deed of love and goodness. The "universal nature" intends
the species, which is preserved through the coming to be and passing away
of the individuals. But is this subordination of the individual to the species
also the meaning of the individual in the original relation to the Creator?
And what about man? Is his place on the way of the creature not entirely
different from the place which he has in the cosmic order of nature?[145]

Thomas's resolution to (universal) nature and Creator demands further reflection. As a basis for such reflection we can use a passage from
De pot. 3, 7 that can be viewed as a resumé of his analysis.

> The higher the cause the more common and more efficacious it is; and the
> more efficacious the cause, the more deeply does it penetrate into its effect,
> and the more remote the potentiality from which it brings that effect into act.
> Now in every natural thing we find that it is a being, a natural thing, and
> of this or that nature. The *first* is common to all beings, the *second* to all natu-
> ral things, the *third* to all the members of a species, while a *fourth*, if we take
> accidents into account, is proper to this or that individual. Accordingly this
> or that individual thing cannot by its action produce another individual of
> the same species except as the instrument of that cause which bears upon

---

[145] Cf. J.B. Metz, *Christliche Anthropozentrik, Über die Denkform des Thomas von Aquin*
(Munich, 1962). On the extent to which it is legitimate to speak of "anthropocentrism"
in Thomas, see 8.4. and 8.5.

the whole species and, besides, upon the whole being of the inferior nature. Wherefore no action in these lower bodies attains to the production of a species except through the power of the heavenly body, nor does anything produce being except by the power of God. *For being itself is the most common first effect* and more intimate than all other effects: wherefore it is an effect which it belongs to God alone to produce by his own power.[146]

7.4.1. *'Concursus'*

This text is characteristic of Thomas's endeavor to understand the intelligible structure of reality through an analysis that embraces both nature and creation. In this continuity lie the specific character and grandeur of Thomas's thought, but likewise the problems peculiar to his way of thought. These can be indicated in three respects, which point back to the sections in ch. 3 (3.7.3. – 3.7.5.) in which we began the investigation of the 'concursus': intelligibility, the hierarchical order of the causes, and the complexity of being.

(1) All men by nature desire to know. Science is the perfection of man as man. The discursive reason proceeds from a particular to a more universal consideration of being. "The common intention was to reduce a multiplicity to unity, and variety to uniformity, insofar as that was possible" (*De verit.* 5, 9).

A typical consequence of this movement of thought is the order in the natural thing, which is mentioned in *De pot.* 3, 7: the first is what is common to all beings, the last is what is proper to this or that individual. Science, however, does not deal with singulars (*scientia non est de singularibus*). Intelligibility is incompatible with individuality, because this is tied to materiality. The particular is, because of its matter, contingent. The intellect is directed towards the universal form, which is what is permanent in particular things. The horizon of "definitive" knowledge is the specific essence. Thinking and being are congruent, for the intention of nature is directed towards the species, not towards the individual.

In proceeding beyond the natural origination towards creation, this movement of thought is continued. So Thomas argues that the divine

---

[146] *De pot.* 3, 7: Quanto enim aliqua causa est altior, tanto est communior et efficacior, et quanto est efficacior, tanto profundius ingreditur in effectum, et de remotiori potentia ipsum reducit in actum. In qualibet autem re naturali invenimus quod est ens et quod est res naturalis, et quod est talis vel talis naturae. Quorum *primum* est commune omnibus entibus, *secundum* omnibus rebus naturalibus; *tertium* in una specie; et *quartum*, si addamus accidentia, est proprium huic individuo. Hoc ergo individuum agendo non potest constituere aliud in simili specie nisi prout est instrumentum illius causae, quae respicit totam speciem et ulterius totum esse naturae inferioris. Et propter hoc nihil agit ad speciem in istis inferioribus nisi per virtutem corporis caelestis, nec aliquid agit ad esse nisi per virtutem Dei. *Ipsum enim esse est communissimus effectus primus* et intimior omnibus aliis effectibus; et ideo soli Deo competit secundum virtutem propriam talis effectus.

work of creation intends primarily what is most perfect in the thing, namely, the 'species specialissima' (4.4.2.). The idea of creation, too, comes to
stand under the regime of the universal—it is the origin according to
which being, taken in its generalness, is 'per se' granted to things. "Being," the "first intelligible" (*S. Th.* I, 5, 2), must be reduced to the
"highest intelligible" (*S.c.G.* I, 102), God, who is Being itself.

The most universal effect must be reduced to the most universal cause.
"Being" is however not merely the most general but the act of all that is.
Thus we saw in 5.4.1. that the priority of being in knowledge is motivated
not only by its universality but also by its actuality. In this latter, ontological approach 'esse' is just what is proper to every thing. "The 'esse' of
each thing is something proper to it, and distinct from the 'esse' of every
other thing" (*De pot.* 7, 3). In line with this thought is Thomas's statement
that being and individual being coincide: *unumquodque secundum idem habet
esse et individuationem.*[147] But this statement has remained an isolated one;
we shall see later that this ontological view does not succeed in displacing
the universalistic one, since the desire to know proceeds by putting what
is individual aside.

(2) Philosophy desires to know the causes of things. The natural desire
is fulfilled if the first, universal cause of everything is known, which is not
composed of cause and effect like the "second causes."[148]

This dynamics towards intelligibility presupposes a hierarchy in causality. This order is based on the degree of actuality: "the order of agent
causes is to be understood according to their order in actuality" (*De pot.*
5, 8). We found in this chapter an ascending series of three causes: particular nature, universal nature, and the Creator of the world. The manner
in which this hierarchy is summarized in *De pot.* 3, 7 confirms the "cosmocentrism" of Thomas's thought. The particular nature is the instrument of the celestial body, which in its own turn is the instrument of the
divine power.

To the series of causes is applied the model of "first" and "second"
cause. But is the divine action adequately thought and philosophically intelligible through the indication of *first* cause? For it is striking that this
model is applied not exclusively to the relation of God and nature but
equally to the order of the heavenly body to the univocal agent. That suggests that God as first in the hierarchy is a more "efficacious" cause (cf.
De pot. 3, 7) than the second, to be sure, but not essentially different from

---

[147] *De anima* q. un., a. 1 ad 2.

[148] *Super Ioannem* cap. 1, lect. 11, 212: ... quod (desiderium naturale) non potest im-
pleri nisi scita et cognita prima universali omnium causa, quae non est composita ex effectu et causa, sicut causae secundae.

it—does the first proposition of the *Liber De causis* not say that *every* primary cause (*omnis causa primaria*) has a greater influence on the caused than does a second cause?

This framework of thought cannot do justice to the incomparableness of the divine action, for "God is not cause like the other efficient causes. . . . He is the transcendent and all-surpassing Source of all causality."[149] Certainly Thomas does not want to detract in any way from this idea. He constantly underscores that creation differs from every mutation and requires "another mode of causing." Therefore he also uses the term "*supernatural* agent,"[150] to typify both God's creating and God's miraculous works outside the natural order. But even if the mode of causing of the first cause goes "beyond" nature, the terminology itself still suggests a hierarchical continuity within causality that finds expression in theses such as "every agent effects something similar to itself."

In the resolution towards the causes there is an unproblematical transition from the (natural) causality of motion to the causality of being or—historically speaking—from the second phase of the categorical consideration of being to the third phase of the transcendental view. The constantly recurring argument for this transition is the thesis, which Thomas also mentions in *De pot.* 3, 7: the higher a cause, the greater the extent of its causality and the generalness of its effect. Now "to be" is more universal than "to be moved" (*esse autem est universalius quam moveri*), since some beings are immobile. Therefore, according to *S.c.G.* II, 16, above the cause that acts through motion there must be that cause which is the first principle of being. The cause of being differs from that of motion through a more universal effect. In this manner creation can appear as a "higher" moment in the quest for intelligibility. But this continuity has a reverse side.

Significant in this respect is the manner in which Thomas reasons in *Quodl.* III, 3, 6, for example. What is brought forth by creation can only be caused by the first cause. The reason for this is again the gradation of causes proportionate to the generalness of their effects, a thesis which Thomas here expressly ascribes to the neo-Platonists. Now a form realized by a cause is more universal as it is more proximate to the "first subject." This "first subject" is posited to be the proper effect of God, but in Thomas's exposition it remains unclear what this "first subject" is. In 7.4.3. we will see that the lack of clarity is closely connected with the course of his analysis. The effect of the universal cause must bear upon

---

[149] A. Hayen, *La communication de l'être*, vol. 2, p. 86.
[150] See for this term A. Deneffe, "Geschichte des Wortes 'supernaturalis,'" *Zeitschrift für katholische Theologie* 46 (1922), pp. 337–60.

what the particular cause "presupposes" for its operation and so goes "beyond" nature.

(3) In accordance with the order of the causes is the order of the effects.[151] With the resolution to the extrinsic causes corresponds, as is evident from 7.2. and 7.3., the inner multiplicity of the caused being. But does this being, through the Neoplatonic thesis of a hierarchical series of agents, not threaten to become an accidental unity of diverse components?[152] It is in order to guarantee the substantial unity of the effectuated that Thomas bases himself on the notions of act and potency.

Every action is a process of assimilation; "every agent effects something similar to itself." The assimilation to the agent is by act; typical for the agent is that it actuates something. Whenever in a thing two components are found, one of which is the "complement" of the other, then these two are related to each other as potency to act. For something is completed by its proper act.[153]

With the order of efficient causes corresponds the order of intrinsic principles. Matter has of itself incomplete being; the specific form is the complement of the essence, is the act of matter.[154] The 'esse' is the complement and therefore the act of every existing substance.[155] Through "being" itself, the created substance is assimilated to God.[156] For "being" itself is "the most common effect" (*De pot.* 3, 7) and therefore the proper effect of God. This analysis accounts for the fact that there is in Thomas a "twofold composition" of potency and act, and it explains why the structure of that which is must be threefold: 'subjectum – essentia – esse'.

"Being" is the complement, the "act of acts"; it is the moment in that which is that corresponds with the resolution towards the first cause. Act is always the act of something: "Act, as such, is referred to potency" (*S.c.G.* II, 53). Thereby arises the problem of the "other": "being" is

---

[151] *De pot.* 3, 7: Invenimus, secundum ordinem causarum esse ordinem effectuum, quod necesse est propter similitudinem effectus et causae.

[152] Cf. *De subst. separ.*, c. 11.

[153] *S.c.G.* II, 53: In quocumque enim inveniuntur aliqua duo, quorum unum est complementum alterius, proportio unius ad alterum est sicut proportio potentiae ad actum; nihil enim completur nisi per proprium actum.

[154] Cf. *De principiis naturae*, c. 1: Materia habet esse ex eo quod sibi advenit, quamvis de se habet esse incompletum; *S.c.G.* II, 54: Forma est principium essendi, quia est complementum substantiae; *In De div. nomin.* c. 4, lect. 6, 360: Omnis enim essentia . . . habet complementum per formam.

[155] *S.c.G.* II, 53: Ipsum autem esse est complementum substantiae existentis; *Quodl.* XII, 5, 1: Esse est complementum omnis formae, quia per hoc completur quod habet esse . . . Et quia esse est complementum omnium, inde est quod proprius effectus Dei est esse.

[156] *S.c.G.* II, 53: Assimilatio autem cujuslibet substantiae creatae ad Deum est per ipsum esse.

"outside the essence"; it is diversified by something that is outside 'esse' (*S.c.G.* II, 52). Matter and form "are," considered in themselves, in some manner, before they are actuated.[157] This problem emerged in the analysis of the transcendentals "being" and "true" in the form of a double metaphysical reduction (4.5.2.). It can, now that the resolution has been thought to its end, be elucidated even more sharply.

Creation presupposes nothing. God is the integral Origin of things; through creation He brings forth the whole subsisting being (*totum ens subsistens*) (*De pot.* 3, 1). Since however in the quest for intelligibility this being is analyzed into its parts, it is said: "the substances themselves are caused by the fact that they have being (*esse*) from another" (*S.c.G.* II, 53). Along this way of thought the question must then arise—and necessarily in this form—of the relation of "created being" to the other principles of being, namely, matter and form, which are both "nature." That relation will be unfolded in the next sections.

7.4.2. *The work of nature and creation*

In *De pot.* 3, 8 is raised the question: "Whether creation is mingled with the work of nature" (*Utrum creatio operi naturae admiscetur*).[158] Concerning this question there have been different opinions, Thomas states in his response. The root (*radix*) of all these opinions would appear to have been one and the same principle, namely, that nature cannot make anything "out of nothing."

"Some" were of the opinion that the forms preexist in matter. Generation is then the extraction of one thing from another, in which it was latent. The action of the natural agent is purely accidental; it consists only in this, that what was hidden is brought out into the open. This is Anaxagoras's doctrine of the 'latitatio formarum': the forms are in a hidden way actually present in matter (cf. 7.1.1.2.). This view arose, in Thomas's judgment, from ignorance concerning matter (*ex ignorantia materiae*) (*S.Th.* I, 45, 8); Anaxagoras did not manage to make a distinction between potency and act. The form preexists in matter in potency and not in act. For if it did not preexist in potency, it would become out of nothing; if the form already preexisted actually, it would not become at all, since what is does not become.

"Others" maintained that the forms cannot proceed from matter, for

---

[157] Cf. *De subst. separ.*, c. 8, 89: Materia quidem secundum se considerata, secundum modum suae essentiae habet esse in potentia ... Ipsa vero res composita in sui essentia considerata, iam habet formam esse.

[158] See also *In VII Metaph.*, lect. 7; *S.Th.* I, 45, 8; 65, 4; *In II Sent.* 1, 1, 4 ad 4.

matter becomes no part of the form. They were therefore forced to say that
the forms become out of nothing. Nature however lacks any such capacity. The cause of the generation of the forms must be a "supernatural
agent"; becoming needs to be reduced to an extrinsic *Dator formarum*. This
is the doctrine of Avicenna: natural forms flow from the lowest of the
spiritual substances. The operation of the natural agent consists only in
its preparing and disposing matter for the reception of the forms. Some
"modern thinkers," Thomas observes, have followed Avicenna in this
view and identified God with this separated substance.[159] The forms
come to be *per viam creationis* (*S.c.G.* III, 69); with the work of nature is always mingled creation. This view arose, in Thomas's judgment, from ignorance concerning form (*ex ignorantia formae*). The error of Avicenna and
his followers is that they considered the natural form as a 'quod est', as
a subsisting thing, and sought of such a thing the becoming. But form is
a 'quo est', that whereby a thing is. Only that becomes, properly speaking, which is able to be, and this is the composite of form and matter, the
subsisting thing, not the form.[160]

Therefore it is better, so Thomas says, to follow the 'via media' (*De virtutibus in communi*, q. un., a. 8) of Aristotle. He asserted, namely, on the
one hand that the forms preexist in the potency of matter and on the other
hand that they are brought to act by a natural agent. The form is not
generated by nature out of nothing but is educed (*educitur*) from the potency of matter.[161] One sees too that in the process of becoming, univocity
rules: every agent effects something similar to itself. The same specific
form which is to be acquired in the generated composite is found to be actually in the generator.[162] It does not make sense to leave the generator
out of consideration in becoming and to seek only an extrinsic cause that
is pure form, a separate substance. The thesis that "nothing becomes out
of nothing" by nature does not prevent one from saying that substantial
forms come to existence by the action of nature. In its operation creation
is not mingled.

Thus with respect to the production of natural forms there are three
different ways. According to the first, that of Anaxagoras, their origin is

---

[159] See for these 'moderni', who connected Augustine's doctrines with those of Avicenna: E. Gilson, "Pourquoi saint Thomas a critiqué saint Augustin," *AHDLMA* 1
(1926/7): 5–127.

[160] *De pot.* 3, 8: Res enim naturalis generata dicitur esse per se et proprie, quasi habens
esse, et in suo esse subsistens; forma autem non sic esse dicitur, cum non subsistat, nec
per se esse habeat. Cf. *S. Th.* I, 65, 4; *S.c.G.* III, 69; *De virtutibus in communi* q. un., a. 11.

[161] Cf. *De pot.* 3, 9: Omnis forma quae exit in esse per generationem, vel per virtutem
naturae, educitur de potentia materiae; 5, 1 ad 5.

[162] Cf. *De pot.* 6, 3.

wholly intrinsic; according to the second, that of Avicenna, wholly extrinsic; according to the third, that of Aristotle, partly intrinsic, partly extrinsic. And these divergent approaches go back to fundamentally different philosophical options. For this diversity presents itself not only with respect to the production of forms but equally with respect to the origin of science and virtue (*Secundum quod diversificati sunt aliqui circa productionem formarum naturalium, ita diversificati sunt circa adeptionem scientiarum et virtutum*).[163] According to "some," science and virtue are by nature innate to man. Man's task is only to clear away possible hindrances to their practice. This was the opinion of Plato. According to "others" the origin of virtue and science is wholly extrinsic. Thus Avicenna maintained that the intelligible forms in our mind proceed from an intelligence, that they are due to an action of an agent intellect separate from man. Here too Aristotle took a middle position: science and virtue are implanted in us by nature, insofar as we possess the aptitude to acquire them (*secundum aptitudinem*), but not in their perfection. There preexist in us certain "seeds" (*semina*) of science, namely, the first conceptions of the intellect. By nature our intellect knows the first intelligibles, such as "being" (cf. 5.4.2.); from these seeds, science develops.

And this opinion is according to Thomas to be preferred, since just as with respect to the natural forms the virtue of the natural causes is not eliminated, so too with respect to the becoming of science this efficacy (*efficacia*) is preserved.[164] On the contrary, any conception à la Avicenna excludes the proximate causes; all effects are attributed to first causes.[165]

Things are active through an intrinsic principle of motion. Here in Thomas we find the originality of nature legitimated. On that basis some have, indeed, spoken of Thomas's "naturalism" (cf. 3.4.).[166] More than the Augustinian school, Thomas emphasizes the autonomy of the natural. Things have a density and operation of their own, and they have that precisely through their nature. Because of this originality Thomas did not take the way of symbolist thought (6.3.3.). The creature is not first of all a "sign" of something else but a "thing" with a stability of its own, with intrinsic principles, from which an "absolute" or "natural" necessity follows. Against Platonizing thought, especially in the form of Avicennism, the Aristotelian concept of nature retains its polemical import. Not only the sun generates man; in man himself there is the power of generating man. The same holds true for the order of knowledge, in the becoming

---

[163] *De virtutibus in communi* q. un., a. 8. See also *De verit.* 11, 1; *S. Th.* I-II, 63, 1.

[164] *De virtutibus in communi* q. un., a. 8.

[165] *De verit.* 11, 1.

[166] See, e.g., P. Vignaux, *La Pensée au Moyen Age*, 2nd ed. (Paris, 1948), p. 116.

of science: not only does a higher intellect illuminate the human mind; the human intellect has a "natural light" that is of itself sufficient for knowing certain intelligible truths. For these there is required no further illumination.[167] By the natural light of reason the existence of God and the creation of the world can be demonstrated.

God's action does not eliminate the natural. There is a 'concursus' of first cause and second cause: "God *and* nature ... make what is better in the whole."[168] This "and" is according to the judgment of H. VOLK—and in this he does not stand alone—the basic form of Catholic thought, the distinctive feature in comparison with the Reformational conception.[169] From the Protestant side it is noted that in Roman Catholic thought, "to the natural order is attributed a certain degree of independence with respect to its Creator."[170] The distinction between mediate and immediate acts of God "entails acceptance of a split world-order and at the very least puts God in a dual relation to his creation."[171] A certain corroboration of this is provided by the earlier analysis of the relation between nature and miracle (7.1.1.3): the miracle is a breaking through of the natural order. This determination suggests that nature would have a persistence of its own with respect to the Origin. Has Thomas, as W. ULLMAN suggests,[172] effected an "Umwertung aller Werte" and paved the way to secularization?

Some occasion for this question definitely exists, given, e.g., the manner in which E. PRZYWARA speaks of the "fundamental law of the second causes" (*Grundgesetz der 'causae secundae'*). This guarantees "the impenetrable world of the creatures, which have a being and action of their own and therefore manifest God's being and God's action only indirectly." Thomas, "with the iron, impenetrable demarcation of the law of the 'second causes,'" became the savior of "science and culture in their proper nature

---

[167] Cf. *S. Th.* I, 79, 4; *S. Th.* I-II, 109, 1.

[168] *S. Th.* I, 48, 2 ad 3: Deus et natura et quodcumque agens, facit quod melius est in toto.

[169] H. Volk, "Christus und Maria," in *Gesammelte Schriften*, vol. 1 (Mainz, 1967), p. 143. Cf. M.F.J. Marlet, *Grundlinien der kalvinistischen "Philosophie der Gesetzesidee" als christlicher Transzendentalphilosophie* (Munich, 1954), pp. 129ff.

[170] M.C. Smit, *Christendom en Historie*, p. 103. Cf. English trans.: *Writings on God and History*, vol. 2: *The Relation between Christianity and History in the Present-day Roman Catholic Conception of History*.

[171] M.C. Smit, *Het goddelijk geheim in de geschiedenis*, p. 10. Cf. English trans.: "The Divine Mystery in History," in *Writings on God and History*, vol. 1, ch. 4.

[172] W. Ullmann, "Some Observations on the Medieval Evaluation of the 'Homo Naturalis' and the 'Christianus,'" in *L'Homme et son destin d'après les penseurs du moyen âge* (Louvain and Paris, 1960), p. 149; p. 150: "The way to Humanism, therefore, in its philosophic and scientific form may be reckoned to have been paved by Thomas, through his emancipating the Man of Nature."

and dignity." Must Thomas not be acknowledged "as father of the modern conception of culture, science, and vocation," in which science and culture are ends in themselves, detached from every religious objective?[173]

For a correct assessment of Thomas's position it is of importance to see what motives are involved in it. In *De pot.* 3, 7 he wants to show that God works in every operation of nature. "Some"—Thomas refers to Islamic theologians, of whom Maimonides makes mention—have understood this in the sense that every natural operation must be so ascribed to God that nature does nothing at all by its own power. The natural thing is, so it may be said in anticipation of the terminology of Malebranche, only the "occasional" cause. But this view is according to Thomas opposed to sense perception (*repugnans sensui*). It is also repugnant to reason (*repugnat etiam rationi*): if natural things are capable of nothing, the forms and forces with which they are endowed would be to no purpose, would be vain. It is contrary too, finally, to the divine goodness (*repugnat etiam divinae bonitati*), which is self-communicative. In this thought the counter-argumentation reaches its culmination. In the motive of the divine goodness we find a first relativizing of the "cosmocentrism" of Thomas's way of thought. The model (see 7.1.1.2.) he uses of the generator, which is the cause of the natural movements of the heavy and light, is inadequate for understanding the relation of God and nature.

The autonomy of the natural is not a sign of God's insufficiency but rather of His goodness. Avicenna's conception, in which everything is ascribed to the first cause, "eliminates the order of the universe, which is woven together through the order and connection of causes. For the first cause lends from the eminence of its goodness not only to the other things that they are, but also that they are causes."[174] To withdraw from things their own proper actions is derogatory to the divine goodness (*S.c.G.* III, 69), which communicates the dignity of causality to creatures. God makes the world free to activity. A "competitive" scheme is foreign to Thomas's intention. At the close of *S.c.G.* III, 21 he refers to a saying of pseudo-Dionysius (*De caelesti hierarchia*, c. 3): "There is nothing more divine in things than to become a co-operator with God" (*omnium divinius est Dei cooperatorem fieri*). Immediately following this reference is a citation from the Apostle Paul (I Cor. 3:9): "We are God's coadjutors."

The real problem is therefore not the "and" as such ("God *and* nature"), but the relation of God and creature. Unsatisfying, as we saw

---

[173] E. Przywara, *Religionsphilosophische Schriften* (Einsiedeln, 1962), pp. 190, 199.
[174] *De verit.* 11, 1. See also *S. Th.* I, 22, 3; 23, 8 ad 2. Cf. E. Gilson, *The Spirit of Mediaeval Philosophy*, ch. 7: "The Glory of God" (pp. 128–47).

earlier (6.6.), is Thomas's way of working out precisely that relation: being created is an accidental category. When GILSON writes that "a world of efficacious second causes, such as that of Aristotle, is worthy only of a God whose causality is essentially goodness,"[175] then the question is how far this world is thought relationally. How "radically" is the relation to the Origin rooted in the nature of created being? How are nature and creature connected ontologically?

The natural principles are twofold: matter and form. Nature has an operation that is proper to it. This cannot however be *ex nihilo:* consequently, it must be *ex praesuppositione.*[176] This pre-supposition is creation: "Creation is not mingled in the works of nature, but is presupposed for the operation of nature."[177] What does this pre-supposition mean?

7.4.3. *Matter as creature*

"Out of nothing comes nothing." This conviction dominates Greek thought about the origin and nature of things. Therefore Aristotle acknowledged as principle matter, which is ungenerated and incorruptible, and which as being in potency is a middle (*medium*) between absolute non-being and being in act (cf. 7.1.2.: "Matter is the nature").

When in *De pot.* 3, 1 the question is raised: "Whether God can create something out of nothing," the first and most obvious objection is the thesis of natural thought:

> God cannot act counter to a common conception of the mind, for instance, that a whole is not greater than its part. ... Now according to the Philosopher a common conception of the philosophers was that out of nothing comes nothing. Therefore God cannot make something out of nothing.[178]

Ex nihilo nihil fit. That is the objection of the philosophers, which denies creation as a possibility beforehand. On the basis of that objection, so Thomas writes in his commentary on the *Phys.* (VIII, lect. 2, 973), Averroës had controverted what the Christian faith holds about creation. The "axiom" of the philosophers seems more satisfying to natural thought,

---

[175] E. Gilson, "Pourquoi saint Thomas a critiqué saint Augustin," p. 127, n. 1.

[176] *De pot.* 3, 8: Operatio naturae non potest esse ex nihilo, et per consequens oportet quod sit ex praesuppositione.

[177] *S. Th.* I, 45, 8. Cf. ad 4: Operatio naturae non est nisi ex praesuppositione principiorum creatorum: et sic ea quae per naturam fiunt, creaturae dicuntur.

[178] *De pot.* 3, 1 obj. 1: Deus enim non potest facere contra communem animi conceptionem, sicut quod totum non sit maius sua parte ... Sed, sicut dicit Philosophus, communis conceptio ex sententia Philosophorum fuit, quod ex nihilo nihil fiat. Ergo Deus non potest de nihilo aliquid facere. Cf. *S.c.G.* II, 16 (at the end); *S.Th.* I, 45, 2 ad 1.

oriented as it is to the inner-worldly coming to be that always requires a substratum.

Primary matter turns up again and again as the opponent of the integrality of the idea of creation. Is it not an antinomy that God is the Creator of matter, since matter is the principle of imperfection?

> The same thing cannot be a principle both of perfection and of imperfection. Now imperfection is found in things. . . . Since then God is the principle of perfection, we must of necessity reduce imperfection to some other principle: and this can only be matter. Therefore things must of necessity have been made from matter of some kind, and not out of nothing.[179]

Matter is pure potency. How then can it be a terminus of creation, as every operation terminates in an act?[180] God is the first active principle, matter the first passive principle. "Therefore God and primary matter are two principles divided against each other, neither of which is from the other" (*S. Th.* I, 44, 2 obj. 2). But it is just in this text that Thomas sketches the history of philosophical reflection about the origin of being in order to show that primary matter does not stand outside God's creating causality, is not an "independent co-ordinate principle with Him."

HEIDEGGER has written that Christian dogmatics denies the truth of the statement *ex nihilo nihil fit*. In doing so it gives to the "nothing" the sense of the complete absence of being outside the divine being, a position which HEIDEGGER sums up in the formula: *ex nihilo fit—ens creatum*. The "nothing" becomes now the antipode of the real being, of the 'summum ens'.[181] Is it however correct to say that Christian "dogmatics" has denied the truth of *ex nihilo nihil fit?* Aquinas notes explicitly in a number of places that this statement is true, but not without provisos. It holds for a certain level of reality: "The common opinion of the philosophers, namely, that out of nothing comes nothing, is true (*habet veritatem*) as regards that becoming which they considered" (*S.c.G.* II, 37).[182]

The best look at Thomas's view we gain in his Commentary on the *Metaph.* (XII, lect. 2, 2437); there he endeavors to clarify the sense that "nothing" has when Aristotle still acknowledges that generation is a "mutation from non-being to being". Thomas points in that context to

---

[179] *De pot.* 3, 1 obj. 14: Non potest esse idem perfectionis et imperfectionis principium. In rebus autem imperfectio invenitur . . . Cum ergo perfectionis principium sit Deus, oportebit imperfectionem in aliud principium reducere. Sed non nisi in materiam. Ergo oportebit res ex aliqua materia esse factas, et non ex nihilo.

[180] *Ibid.* 3, 5 obj. 3.

[181] *Was ist Metaphysik?* (1929), p. 25.

[182] Cf. also *S.c.G.* II, 16 (end): . . . ex nihilo nihil fit, quod quidem in particularibus agentibus verum est.

the ambiguity of "non-being" since in some cases it does indeed acquire in Aristotle an ontological status. "Non-being is said in three ways" (*Dicitur enim non ens tripliciter*). It can in the first place signify "matter," which is in itself not a being in act, but a being in potency. From such a non-being (i.e., a non-actual) proceeds the generation 'per se' (cf. 3.2.). Further, non-being can mean the "privation," which is considered in some subject. From such a non-being proceeds the generation 'per accidens', insofar, namely, as the becoming begins from a subject to which the privation happens. Finally, it can signify what in no way is (*quod nullo modo est*). From such a non-being can proceed no generation, since out of nothing comes nothing—and then follows a decisive addition—*secundum naturam*.[183]

They are but two words, yet with this qualification Thomas distances himself from what is called "the sum total of Greek wisdom."[184] Creation is radically different from every process of becoming. Not as HEIDEGGER writes "ex nihilo *fit* . . . ens creatum" but "ex nihilo *creatur* ens." When at the end of *Phys.* I Aristotle proves that matter is ungenerated, Thomas adds in his commentary, almost in passing: "but this does not exclude that matter comes to be through creation."[185] One might almost gain the impression from the offhandedness of this remark that it involves only a slight nuance. But it can be clear from Thomas's version of the history of the question of being that this is not correct. Generation and corruption are inner-worldly, categorical changes, which Thomas places in the second, and thus not final, phase. Corresponding well with this is his reply to the objection "out of nothing comes nothing" in *De pot.* 3, 1 ad 1: This was the common opinion of the philosophers of nature, since they considered only the "natural agent," that acts through movement and therefore always requires a subject of movement. But this by no means applies to the "supernatural agent."

"Out of nothing comes nothing." This dictum is true of *particular* agents but has no place "in the first emanation from the *universal* principle of things."[186] The Philosopher is speaking of generation, the particular becoming; primary matter may not be subject to it, but that is for Thomas not ultimate. He wants to question primary matter with regard to its origin, according to the coming forth of things from the universal principle

---

[183] Cf. *De pot.* 3, 8: . . . *per naturam* ex nihilo nihil fit.

[184] H. Dooyeweerd, *A New Critique of Theoretical Thought*, vol. 1, p. 180.

[185] *In I Phys.*, lect. 15, 139: Sed ex hoc non excluditur quin per creationem in esse procedat.

[186] *S. Th.* I, 45, 2 ad 1: Ex nihilo nihil fieri . . . locum non habet in prima emanatione ab universali rerum principio.

of being.[187] The final conclusion of the history of the question of being in
S. Th. I, 44, 2 is: "And thus it is necessary to say that also primary matter
is created by the universal cause of things."

We find confirmed in the reduction of matter as *creature* what we observed in general earlier in the continuous dynamics towards intelligibility: the
regime of the universal. But in this transition from the particular causality
of generation and motion to the universal causality of being is not that disregarded which would have to render problematical the continuation of a
primary matter within a metaphysics of creation? Primary matter cannot
be brought forth by nature; it can therefore only be created by God: "God
is Himself the cause of matter, which cannot be caused (*non est possibilis
causari*) except by creation" (*S.c.G.* II, 22). Thomas's reasoning bears,
quite typically, the character of an 'argumentum per impossibile'. If
primary matter is not produced by creation, how then is it to be accounted
for?

This reasoning is unsatisfactory because it remains so external. The
status of what is presupposed on the basis of the thesis 'ex nihilo nihil fit'
is confirmed through the 'creatio ex nihilo'. In Thomas's dealing with
matter as creature it becomes clear that creation transcends nature, but
that in doing so creation remains strongly tied to the perspective of nature.
The "presuppositions" of the causality of motion come to determine the
framework within which the universal causality of creation acquires content. In this approach Thomas is too little alive to the implications contained in the createdness of matter. Does Thomas, it can be asked, in
preserving the notion of primary matter in a world created "out of nothing," do so in a truly critical way?[188]

Here too the hierarchical gradation in causality is a constantly recurring argument that Thomas advances for the createdness of matter. The
higher a cause is, the further its causality extends. Now, what is a substratum in things is always more universal than that which informs it. Therefore the more something is a substratum in things, the higher its cause.
Therefore the "first subject" must be the effect only of the first cause.
This "first subject" is primary matter, to which the causality of the second causes does not extend.[189] Nature presupposes matter, which is

---

[187] *S. Th.* I, 44, 2 ad 1: Philosophus in I Phys. loquitur de fieri particulari . . .; nunc
autem loquimur de rebus secundum emanationem earum ab universali principio essendi.
A qua quidem emanatione nec materia excluditur, licet a primo modo factionis exclu-
datur. Cf. *De pot.* 5, 1 ad 11; *S. Th.* I, 46, 1 ad 3.

[188] This aspect usually receives too little attention in studies of the medieval concept of
matter; that is the case, e.g., in the collection of studies edited by E. McMullin, *The Concept
of Matter in Greek and Medieval Philosophy* (Notre Dame, 1965), pp. 303ff.

[189] *In De div. nomin.* c. 4, lect. 2, 296: Considerandum est, secundum Platonicos, quod
quanto aliqua causa est altior, tanto ad plura se extendit eius causalitas. Unde oportet quod
id quod est primum subiectum in effectibus, idest materia prima, sit effectus solius primae

effected by the universal cause. Matter is the principle of individuation: "Forms . . . are individuated by matter, which cannot be in another since it is the first subject."[190] The particular agent accordingly always presupposes that on the basis of which its effect subsists as an individual.[191] Since God is the cause of matter, He is also the cause of the individual.

This order in the argumentation is typical: to the fore stands not that God creates individual beings, but that He creates matter. The argumentation is dominated by the "presupposition" for the work of nature. As the operation of art presupposes the operation of nature, since art works on that which has already been constituted in being by nature (3.3.2.), "so the operation of nature presupposes the creative operation of God" (*opus naturae praesupponit opus Dei creantis*), for nature receives its matter from God through creation.[192] Above the causality of nature is to be posited a more universal causality, which provides for matter.[193] Accordingly J. STUFLER concludes that "God through creation gives only matter, which is informed by the second causes."[194]

Here arises, however, a serious difficulty, which we alluded to in 7.4.1. For earlier we saw repeatedly that the proper effect of God is *ipsum esse*.

> The first effect is being itself, which is presupposed for all other effects, and which itself does not presuppose any other effect. Therefore the giving of being as such must be the effect of the first cause alone, by its own power.[195]

But if the proper effect of God is *ipsum esse*, how can He be said to give only matter through creation? FABRO attempts to escape this difficulty by regarding both, matter and being, as termini of the causality of creation. "The Thomist conception of creation presents two principles of created nature, which are the exclusive termini of divine causality: *materia prima* and *esse*."[196] Yet, why this duality, why this twofold metaphysical reduction,

---

Causae quae est bonum, causalitate secundarum causarum usque ad hoc non pertingente; *S. Th.* I, 65, 3; *De subst. separ.*, c. 10, 104; *In De causis*, lect. 1; *In VIII Phys.*, lect. 2, 974.

[190] *S. Th.* I, 3, 2 ad 3. Cf. *De spirit. creat.* q. un., a. 1: Materia prima recipit formam contrahendo ipsam ad esse individuale.

[191] *S.c.G.* II, 21: Omne igitur agens finitum praesupponit ad suam actionem hoc unde causatum suum individualiter subsistit.

[192] *S.c.G.* III, 65.

[193] Cf. *In De causis*, lect. 1; *De quat. opp.*, c. 4; *In II Sent.* 1, 1, 3 ad 5.

[194] *Gott, der erste Beweger aller Dinge*, p. 79; cf. 72: "Was Gott durch seine eigene Kraft, d.h. durch Erschaffung gibt, ist nur das Potenzielle oder Substrat."

[195] *De pot.* 3, 4: Primus autem effectus est ipsum esse, quod omnibus aliis effectibus praesupponitur et ipsum non praesupponit aliquem alium effectum; et ideo oportet quod dare esse in quantum huiusmodi sit effectus primae causae solius secundum propriam virtutem.

In the same text however one can also read: Solius primi agentis erit . . . aliis omnibus secundis agentibus materiam ministrare. Cf. *S.c.G.* III, 66; *Comp. Theol.* I, 68.

[196] *Participation et Causalité*, p. 358.

which is comparable with the one we found earlier with respect to the 'essentia' and 'esse'?

The duality is possible because what is considered in the resolution is the diversity, not however the unity of the analyzed moments of that which is. Yet the duality is impossible if Thomas's statement is taken seriously to the effect that "nothing can be added to *esse* that is extraneous to it, since nothing is extraneous to it except non-being, which can be neither form nor matter" (*De pot.* 7, 2 ad 9). Matter too cannot be added to being as something extraneous to it, for matter is not non-being. It thereby loses its "original" character.

Matter has the character of being (*S.c.G.* II, 16: "primary matter is in some way, for it is potentially a being"). This may be a "weak being" (*De verit.* 3, 5 ad 1), an imperfect being, but that does not change the fact that matter participates in the nature of being (*natura entis*).[197] Whatever in some way participates in being needs to be reduced to what is essentially being, as its cause. Through the idea of participation Thomas can relate matter as creature to the Origin more intrinsically than was possible through the idea of "presupposition." The being in potency that matter has belongs to it by virtue of participation in the first being.[198] Even the "weak being" of primary matter is an "imitation" of the first being; as "being," matter has a likeness to God.[199]

For this relation of matter to the Origin Thomas can appeal to Aristotle himself. For into this train of thought fits well the idea of *Metaph.* II, the causality of the 'maximum' (cf. 4.3.1.).

> Aristotle proves in *Metaph.* II that what is "maximally" true and "maximally" being is the cause of being of all existing things. From this it follows that the being in potency which primary matter has is derived from the first principle of being, which is "maximally" being.[200]

Whatever is imperfect derives its origin from what is perfect, the pure act.[201] That holds even for primary matter, which as pure potency is

---

[197] Cf. *S. Th.* III, 75, 4 ad 3. Thomas distances himself from the Platonic conception, which fails to distinguish matter from privation and therefore places it in the order of non-being. See *In De div. nomin.* c. 3, lect. 1, 226 and *S. Th.* I, 5, 3 ad 3.

[198] *De subst. separ.*, c. 8, 89: Materia, secundum se considerata, secundum modum suae essentiae habet esse in potentia, et hoc ipsum est ei ex aliqua participatione primi entis; *De pot.* 3, 1 ad 12; *S. Th.* I, 14, 11 ad 3.

[199] *De verit.* 3, 5 ad 1.

[200] *In VIII Phys.*, lect. 2, 974: Probat enim [Aristoteles] in II Metaph., quod id quod est maxime verum et maxime ens, est causa essendi omnibus existentibus: unde hoc ipsum esse in potentia, quod habet materia prima, sequitur derivatum esse a primo essendi principio, quod est maxime ens.

[201] *De pot.* 5, 1 ad 11: Materia dicitur ingenita, quia non procedit in esse per generationem: ex hoc tamen non removetur quin a Deo sit; cum *omne imperfectum oporteat a perfecto originem trahere.* Cf. *S. Th.* I, 4, 1 ad 2; *In II Sent.* 3, 3, 3 ad 2; *S.c.G.* II, 16.

most distant from God; it is the outer limit, as it were, of being.[202]

Yet this approach, too, to the createdness of matter continues to have something unsatisfying about it. For matter, like form, is not a subsisting thing (*quod est*).[203] In the preceding section about the operation of nature an important point in Thomas's argumentation against Avicenna was that only that becomes, properly speaking, which is able to be, i.e., the composite of form and matter, which subsists in its being. Likewise, that is created to which being properly belongs, namely, the subsisting things: *proprie vero creata sunt subsistentia*.[204] If now the name "creature" is taken in the stricter sense, "for only that which subsists" (*De pot.* 3, 3 ad 2), then it cannot be said of that which has no subsistence that it is created as such. This consideration holds for primary matter, for it "does not exist by itself in nature" (*S. Th.* I, 7, 2 ad 3). A subsisting first matter is in itself an absolute impossibility. Therefore Thomas does not shrink from saying that it cannot be produced even by the divine omnipotency.[205]

Primary matter is not created 'per se' but is "con-created" (*con-creata*) with the subsistent composite.[206] For if all that belongs to the being of the thing is created, then this must also include what is potential in it.[207] The implication of this con-creation is that primary matter was not created altogether formless, nor under any one common form, but under distinct forms (*sub formis distinctis*).[208]

This conclusion eliminates an "original" feature of primary matter; it is not the indeterminate "other," the antipode of pure act.[209] Yet with respect to the ontological status of first matter there continues to be a certain tension in Thomas's thought. In *S.c.G.* I, 43 he reasons from the infinite potentiality of primary matter towards the infinite actuality of God. In *S.c.G.* II, 16, which deals with "creation out of nothing," he asserts—in keeping with the conclusion just reached that matter is under distinct forms—that "diverse things have diverse matters." So matter is diversified in the spiritual and corporeal substances, in the celestial and sublu-

---

[202] *S. Th.* I, 115, 1 ad 4: Id quod maxime distat a Deo, est materia prima; *In III Sent.* 14, 1, 4: Materia prima ... tenet ultimum gradum in entibus.

[203] *S.c.G.* II, 54: Materia non potest dici quod est, sed ipsa substantia est id quod est.

[204] *S. Th.* I, 45, 4.

[205] *Quodl.* III, 1, 1.

[206] *De quat. opp.*, c. 4; *De pot.* 3, 1 ad 12: Unde neque materia neque forma neque accidens proprie dicuntur creari, sed concreari. Proprie autem creatur res subsistens, quaecumque sit.

[207] *S. Th.* I, 44, 2 ad 3.

[208] *S. Th.* I, 66, 1. Cf. *S. Th.* I, 84, 3 ad 2.

[209] That also comes out expressly in the consideration of Duns Scotus: Because matter is *terminus creationis*, it is not purely potency but has a positive being and consequently a certain actuality (*Opus Oxoniense* II, d. 12, q. 1, no. 11).

nary. "Hence there is no one matter which is in potency to universal being" (*Non est igitur una materia quae sit in potentia ad esse universale*). There is
no matter that is proportionate to the causality of God. Is it still possible
then to cling to a matter that is infinite, pure potency?

Matter has actual being through the substantial form. Because of its
reception of the form, matter participates in being (*materia ex hoc quod recipit
formam, participat esse*).[210] We are thereby referred to the origination of the
form.

7.4.4. *Being is consequent upon form ('Esse consequitur formam')*

Form is the nature "more" than matter is (7.1.3.). For a thing has its
nature only when it has its form. Through the form it is constituted in its
species and completed in its essence. Through the form it is in act: "it is
proper to the essential form that it gives to matter being absolutely."[211]

The relation of the form to the Origin Thomas approaches in various
ways, just as he does in the case of matter. Already in 4.1.1. we saw that
he brings the diversity of forms to unity through a reduction to the divine
exemplar, which is identical with the divine essence. The exemplary
causality, the divine art, creates the forms and natures of things. This creation is also expressed in terms of participation in essence: the form is "a
divine likeness that is participated in things." Because however the forms
themselves "co-exist" rather than "exist" and to be created belongs
properly to a subsisting thing, it is better in the end to say that the form
is "con-created."[212]

In the dialectics of form and matter 'per viam naturae', being is always
linked with form. The form is "cause of being." "It is striking," according
to J. DE VRIES, "just how closely Thomas again and again links form and
being. How often is it not said: 'The form gives being'! ... Yet I have to
admit that I have never yet found an interpretation of these texts that has
satisfied me."[213] Indeed, how are these texts to be reconciled with the
idea, emphatically advanced so often by Thomas, that the 'esse', the
proper effect of God, is the act of very form? "All forms are consequent
upon being itself" (*Omnes formae sequuntur ipsum esse*).[214] I believe,
however, that the investigation of Thomas's resolution has now put the key
to his understanding of being into our hands.

(1) The form is the cause of being in the absolute sense (1.2.): "the form

---

[210] *De anima* q. un., a. 6.
[211] *De anima* q. un., a. 9.
[212] *S. Th.* I, 45, 4; 45, 8.
[213] *Grundbegriffe der Scholastik* (Darmstadt, 1980), p. 80.
[214] *De quat. opp.*, c. 1.

gives being.'' This is an Aristotelian formulation, but in Thomas it appears in a new perspective on the origin. For in Thomas "giving of being" is also the description of "creation." That suggests that here we reach the 'concursus' of the way of nature and the way of creation, that here lies the point where God and nature come together. Is the form not "something divine" in things?

(2) That which is created is "that which is," that which subsists in its being (7.4.3.). 'Esse', however, which actuates all that which is, does not subsist. "Being" signifies something complete and simple but not something subsisting" (*De pot.* 1, 1). When in the *Liber De causis* it is said: "The first of created things is being" (*Prima rerum creatarum est esse*), Thomas explains (cf. 5.4.1.) that the word "being" does not refer to that which is created but to the proper nature of the object of creation. For creation is the emanation of all being.[215]

To express this distinction between that which subsists and being Thomas likes to use Boethius's distinction of 'quod est' and 'quo est' (cf. 1.4.2.). The second proposition of his writing *De hebdomadibus* is: "Being and that which is are different." For "being" itself is not yet, but that which is is when it has received the form of being (*forma essendi*).

(3) Only in God is there identity. God has not received being but is His being, hence is called *Esse subsistens*. In all other things the act of being inheres in something other, whereby the 'esse' acquires subsistence but is at the same time determined and contracted (cf. 3.6.2.). For all that is in another is in it according to the mode of the receiver.[216] What God is in a universal and infinite way is in created being in a particularized and finite way, i.e., through participation. Thus in order to understand the subsistence of the created in its being, we must follow the order of inherence.

(4) Here we find a 'duplex ordo' (cf. 3.7.2.); it is presented in *De subst. separ.*, c. 8:

> A twofold order is found in a substance composed of matter and form. One is the order of the matter to the form, and the other is the order of the composite thing itself to the *esse* participated in. For the *esse* of a thing is neither its form nor its matter but something coming to the thing through the form.[217]

Where the first order, that of the matter to the form, is concerned, matter

---

[215] *S. Th.* I, 45, 4 ad 1.

[216] *S.c.G.* I, 43: Omnis actus alteri inhaerens terminationem recipit ex eo in quo est; quia quod est in altero est in eo per modum recipientis.

[217] *De subst. separ.*, c. 8, 89: Invenitur igitur in substantia composita ex materia et forma duplex ordo: *unus* quidem ipsius materiae ad formam; *alius* autem ipsius rei jam compositae ad esse participatum. Non enim est esse rei neque forma eius neque materia ipsius, sed aliquid adveniens rei per formam.

is the cause of the form insofar as it takes up and sustains the form, is the "principle of substanding." The substantial form is the act of matter, is the "principle of subsisting."[218] The composite has through the form unity and identity, discreteness and perfection (2.3.). "The mode of every substance composed of matter and form is according to the form (*secundum formam*) through which it belongs to a determinate species" (*De subst. separ.*, c. 8, 89).

(5) The second order is that of the composite nature to being. For the *esse* is neither the form nor the matter but something that comes to the thing through the form. Through the complement of the form, the substance is a suitable subject for the 'esse', is apt to take up being.[219] The form is the 'medium' in the acquisition of being, because the composite would not be if the form did not inhere in matter.[220]

In the order of inherence it therefore holds: "Being is consequent upon form" (*Esse sequitur formam; De quat. opp.*, c. 1), "is consequent upon nature" (*S. Th.* III, 17, 2 ad 1). The form is prior to, is the cause of being, because it is only by means of the form that the *esse* can realize itself in a thing. "The form is said to be the principle of being, because it is the complement of the substance, whose act is being."[221] By means of the form, the being that is taken up becomes the being proper to this thing and is contracted to a determinate mode of being. The composite is "participating through its form in being itself from God according to a mode proper to it" (*De subst. separ.*, c. 8, 88).

The 'esse' is that whereby the substance is actuated, that whereby it is called "being" (*ens*). In the order of the acts, "being" is prior to the form.[222] Each thing is completed by participating in being, by its participation in the first act. "The 'esse' is the complement of every form, because through it, whatever has being is completed, and everything has being when it is in act; so no form is, except through being."[223] The 'esse' is the act of acts, "the most formal of all things" (*maxime formale omnium*).[224]

---

[218] *S. Th.* I, 29, 2 ad 5: Materia est principium substandi et forma est principium subsistendi; *De verit.* 28, 7: Materia causa est formae aliquo modo in quantum sustinet formam, et forma est aliquo modo causa materiae in quantum dat materiae esse actu; *In I Sent.* 23, 1, 1.

[219] Cf. *De spirit. creat.* q. un., a. 1.

[220] *De quat. opp.*, c. 1: Ideo forma est medium in acquirendo esse ipsi materiae et ipsi composito, quia ipsum coniunctum non esset nisi forma inhaerens esset materiae.

[221] Cf. *S.c.G.* II, 54.

[222] *De quat. opp.*, c. 1: In ordine enim principiorum formalium primum est esse, quia esse est primus actus . . . ; ideo omnes formae sequuntur ipsum esse in ordine actuum sive principiorum formalium.

[223] *Quodl.* XII, 5, 1.

[224] *S. Th.* I, 7, 1. Cf. I, 4, 1 ad 3; *S.c.G.* I, 23.

Being and form are inseparable. That which belongs to a thing 'per se' is necessarily in it always (2.1.1.). Now, ''being is consequent upon form through itself'' (*esse per se consequitur formam*). For each thing has being insofar as it has form. Therefore being can in no way be separated from form.[225] That was also the reason why the immaterial substances have being necessarily and have no contingency, no potency to non-being, within themselves (6.3.2.).

Through the concurrence of the intrinsic principles ''the complete being in itself, subsisting in its own being'' (*De ente*, c. 7) is constituted, that is, the substance (2.1.2.). In its subsistence the finite being becomes like its origin, the 'Esse subsistens'. This Being brings forth, through creation, the thing together with all its principles; ''from these principles the thing is constituted in its 'esse', which is the object of creation.''[226] How then can one still speak of a ''double creation'' (FABRO)?

(6) The way of the discursive and historical reason ends in the idea of creation. This movement of thought is an analysis of being into 'subjectum' (with which is connected the moment of subsistence)—'essentia'— 'esse'. It is the inner tendency of the resolution that what Thomas somewhere (*De verit.* 21, 1 ad 4) calls ''the thing according to its entire being'' (*res secundum totum esse suum*) is differentiated into simple components that ''complement'' each other through inherence: ''in substances composed of matter and form we find these three: matter, form, and being itself.''[227]

This ascending triad of matter-form-being is in conformity with the three phases in Thomas's history of the question of being. This history is unfolded by him to show that both matter (*S. Th.* I, 44, 2) and the essential form (*De subst. separ.*, c. 9) are also originated. It is necessary, according to the second basic text, ''to preconceive another origin of things,'' namely that of ''being itself.'' In the conception of this origin beyond the mode of becoming by which form comes to matter lies at once the basis for the ascending order of the principles and for the natural origination. The reduction of that which is must be adequate to the de-duction.

(7) There is a ''twofold cause of being'' (*duplex causa essendi*), namely the form, whereby something is in act, and the agent, which effects being in act.[228] The form ''gives being.'' Its causality is ''formal,'' not how-

---

[225] *De anima* q. un., a. 14: Id quod per se consequitur ad aliud, non potest removeri ab eo ... Manifestum est autem quod esse per se consequitur formam; unumquodque enim habet esse secundum propriam formam; unde esse a forma nullo modo separari potest; Cf. *S.c.G.* II, 55; *S. Th.* I, 75, 6.

[226] *De quat. opp.*, c. 4. Cf. *S. Th.* I, 45, 4 ad 2.

[227] *De anima* q. un., a. 6.

[228] *In De causis*, lect. 26.

ever "productive"; the form does not cause being as an efficient cause.[229] The efficient cause of being absolutely, the creating cause, is God. 'Esse' is the effect that is proper to Him. "Being is 'per se' consequent upon the form of a creature, supposed however the influence of God" (*S. Th.* I, 104, 1 ad 1). In this twofold giving of being, intrinsic and extrinsic, categorical and transcendental causality join. For the being of the thing produced depends on the efficient cause to the degree to which it depends on the form itself of this thing.[230] What does this mean for the structure of the act of creation?

> God effects natural being in us through creation, without any intermediary agent, *yet nonetheless through the mediation of a formal cause.* For the natural form is the principle of natural being.[231]

The creation of that which is has only God as Origin; it cannot be mediated by another efficient cause. Creation does, however, have a formal 'medium'. The first cause gives being by means of the form. In the descending series of principles, being supposes the specific form, which also is given by God. This last giving fits in with the idea of the "divine art," which effects the natures of things, and with the mode of participation, which concerns the essence, namely, the participation in the divine exemplary form. The form is the principle of natural being. Therefore Thomas can say (see 3.7.2.: "Duplex ordo") that "created being is not through something other whenever 'through' means the intrinsic formal cause; but whenever it means the efficient cause, then what is created is through the divine being and not 'per se.'"[232]

The form is the 'medium' in which the way of nature and the way of creation concur. In this 'concursus' the being that is given by God is at the same time from an intrinsic principle. God is the universal cause of being itself in all things. This causality is not something external to the effect but penetrates deeply into it (*profundius ingreditur in effectum; De pot.* 3, 7). For being is what is innermost in things. God therefore works intimately in everything. It is for this reason, so Thomas says, that in Holy

---

[229] *S.c.G.* II, 68; *S. Th.* I, 3, 4; *De ente,* c. 5: Non autem potest esse quod ipsum esse sit causatum ab ipsa forma vel quidditate rei, dico sicut a causa efficiente; quia sic aliqua res esset causa sui ipsius.

[230] *De pot.* 5, 1: Secundum hoc ergo esse rei factae dependet a causa efficiente secundum quod dependet ab ipsa forma rei factae.

[231] *De verit.* 27, 1 ad 3: Esse naturale per creationem Deus facit in nobis, nulla causa agente mediante, sed tamen *mediante aliqua causa formali,* forma enim naturalis principium est esse naturalis.
Likewise in *De caritate* q. un., a. 1 ad 13: Deus esse naturale creavit sine medio efficiente, *non tamen sine medio formali.* Nam unicuique dedit formam per quam esset.

[232] *In I Sent.* 8, 1, 2 ad 2.

Scripture the operations of nature are attributed to God.[233]

That which is is itself "from another," is dependent subsistence. The meaning of being *is* twofold. This is the ultimate reason why there is in Thomas the twofold sense of questioning, the two tracks of predication ('per se' and 'per participationem'), the distinct modes of causing, the intrinsic and extrinsic measures of truth.

(8) Through its form the thing has a relation to the first principle of being,[234] has con-formity to the divine exemplar. Because of this conformity Thomas can continue to call the formal principle "something divine in things." Through its form each thing has an active being of its *own*, a 'virtus essendi'.[235] "Supposed" for the form is matter as subject. It is the outermost limit in the deduction of being from God. Matter has an imperfect and incomplete being.

This order of the principles constitutes in that which is a dynamics which is of importance for a more comprehensive conception of being. For matter is related to form and form to being as potency to act. Matter desires by nature the perfection of the form; each thing tends towards the 'esse'. The act is the end of the potency. This process of actualization is the way of nature and of creature. Consideration of the 'finis' (chapter 8) will bring the "hodo-logy" to completion and enables us to establish a final motive of Thomas's way of thought.

---

[233] *S. Th.* I, 105, 5: Et propter hoc in sacra Scriptura operationes naturae Deo attribuuntur, quasi operanti in natura.

[234] *In De causis*, lect. 25: Res autem composita ex materia et forma non habet esse nisi per consecutionem suae formae; unde *per suam formam* habet habitudinem ad primum essendi principium.

[235] *De pot.* 5, 4 ad 1: Nam quantum unicuique inest de forma, tantum inest de virtute essendi.

CHAPTER EIGHT

FINIS

Every movement attains its fulfillment in the end. The *end* of the movement is called *finis*; for the 'finis' is "the terminus of motion, and is as such
opposed to the principle of motion" (*In I Metaph.*, 4, 71), is "the ultimate
in being" (*In V Metaph.*, 3, 782).

The 'finis' is not only the end, the ultimate, but also the *goal* towards
which the dynamics is directed and in which the movement comes to rest.
The terminus determines. It is that "for the sake of which" something occurs, is what as such is strived for. The final end is *first* in the intention
of the agent and has for that reason the aspect of a "cause."[1] The goal
to be realized is the prior that motivates the agent (6.5.3.). The final cause
is the cause of the agent, not with respect to its being but with respect to
its causality. The agent effects that matter takes up the form and that the
form perfects matter. Consequently, the end is also the cause of the inner
causality of matter as matter and of form as form. In the fabric of the
causes, the final cause has the primacy; it is "the cause of causes."[2]

The 'finis' is end and goal, since it is appetible and therefore has the
character of *good*. "The good is what all desire" (8.1.). Something is
desirable insofar as it is perfect and in act. In the teleo-logy the hodo-logy
of nature and creature attains its meaning and fulfillment. For in the finality the circular structure of their movements and ways becomes manifest.
Origin and end are identical. The way of nature (8.2.) and the way of
creature (8.3.) are a circulation that is completed by the human desire to
know (8.4.).

Circular movement is the most perfect of all movements. To the circulation motive is attached an ideal of perfection. There is a concurrence of
the movements in the dynamics towards perfection, in which the origin
becomes the end. Every being strives in its own way to become God-like.
"Perfect" has the character of "ultimate." In this perfectionism may be
found the ultimate 'ratio' of Thomas's way of thought (8.5.).

8.1. *"The good is what all desire"* (*'Bonum est quod omnia appetunt'*)

The motive of the way and of the movement is the 'finis'. For the concept

---

[1] *In I Metaph.*, lect. 4, 71; *S. Th.* I–II, 1, 1 ad 1: Finis, etsi sit postremus in executione,
est tamen prius in intentione agentis. Et hoc modo habet rationem causae.
[2] *De principiis naturae*, c. 4; *In V Metaph.*, lect. 2, 775; lect. 3, 782; *S.c.G.* III, 17; *De verit.*
28, 7; *S. Th.* I, 5, 2 ad 1.

"end" is identical with the concept of "good." "'Good' and 'end' have the same nature, since the good is that which all desire."[3] *Bonum est quod omnia appetunt.* This is the manner in which Aristotle defines the good at the beginning of his *Ethica Nicomachea.* To understand correctly the essence of good, one must notice the peculiar character of this determination: it is a definition from the effect of what is to be defined. The good is reckoned among the primary things (*bonum numeratur inter prima*) and can therefore not be defined by reduction to something prior. It can only be elucidated through something consequent (*per posteriora*), through something dependent upon it, through its proper effect.[4]

Through the effect, the cause is revealed. The definition of "good" as "what all desire" does not mean to say that something is good merely insofar as it is desired, but rather the opposite; it indicates the moving principle of the appetite, which is the essence of good itself.

> The essence of good consists in this, that it is something desirable (*appetibile*). Hence the Philosopher says: "The good is what all desire." Now it is clear that a thing is desirable only insofar as it is perfect, for all desire their own perfection. But everything is perfect insofar as it is in act.[5]

This text from *S. Th.* I, 5, 1 shows that there is a formal identity of "end"—"good"—"perfect"—"act." On the basis of it the meaning of the teleology and the general conditions of the finality can be clarified.

8.1.1. *Being and good are convertible ('Ens et bonum convertuntur')*

The mark of the good is its desirability. Something is desirable insofar as it is perfect. Something is perfect insofar as it is in act. From this it follows that "being" and "good" are convertible. This conclusion is the outcome of Thomas's argument in *S. Th.* I, 5, 1:

> Therefore it is clear that a thing is perfect so far as it is a being (*ens*); for being (*esse*) is the actuality of everything . . . Hence it is clear that good and being are the same really. But good expresses the aspect of desirableness, which being does not express.[6]

---

[3] *In II Metaph.*, lect. 4, 317: Remota autem causa finali, removetur natura et ratio boni: eadem enim ratio boni et finis est; nam bonum est quod omnia appetunt, ut dicitur in I Ethic.; *S.c.G.* III, 16; *S. Th.* I, 5, 4.

[4] *In I Ethic.*, lect. 1, 9. Cf. K. Riesenhuber, *Die Transzendenz der Freiheit zum Guten*, 39ff.

[5] *S. Th.* I, 5, 1: Ratio enim boni in hoc consistit, quod sit aliquid *appetibile*. Unde Philosophus dicit quod 'bonum est quod omnia appetunt'. Manifestum est autem quod unumquodque est appetibile secundum quod est *perfectum*; nam omnia appetunt suam perfectionem. Intantum autem unumquodque est perfectum, inquantum est *in actu*.

[6] *Ibid.*: Unde manifestum est quod intantum est aliquid bonum, inquantum est ens; esse enim est actualitas omnis rei . . . Unde manifestum est quod bonum et ens sunt idem

Every being is as such good. In "good" we find for the third time a transcendental property. The investigation in chapters 1 through 3 was directed towards "being," which is not a genus but which transcends the categories. In chapter 4 we saw: "Being and true are convertible." Now the convertibility of "being" and "good" is asserted. "Being," "true," and "good" are interchangeable 'secundum rem'; these terms refer to what is really identical, they refer to the same subject or supposit.[7] "True" and "good" are not, however, simply synonymous with "being." They add something to it qua concept that is not expressed by the term "being" itself. What "true" adds is the intelligibility, the relation to the intellect; the "extra" of "good" is the aspect of desirableness or appetibility (*ratio appetibilis*).[8] Since the good has the character of end, it is the last in the analysis.

(1) "True" expresses the 'convenientia' of being with the intellect, "good" the 'convenientia' with the appetite (cf. 4.1.2.). Knowledge is a process of interiorization. Its terminus, the true, is in the intellect itself. The order of the appetite is precisely the reverse: its terminus, the good, is in the things. So there is in the acts of the soul a kind of circle. The extramental reality moves the intellect; the thing apprehended ("the true") moves the appetite; and this tends towards that whence the process started.[9]

Earlier (5.1.) we found that there is a circulation in man, namely in his process of knowing. The way of reason begins from the one and simple, namely being, in order to end in the one. Now, the circle concerns the activity of both man's faculties. In this "inclusive" activity of knowing and willing lie implications for the understanding of being.

(2) In chapter 3 we saw that "being" (*ens*) in Thomas becomes threefold; it is the composite of 'subjectum-essentia-esse'. "True" refers in the structure of being primarily to the essence or species, for it is through the essence that a thing is knowable. It is striking that "good" is related especially to the 'esse', as can already be inferred from the cited text in *S. Th.* I, 5, 1. Something is desirable insofar as it is in act. "Being itself has the aspect of good."[10] So "true" and "good" add, qua con-

---

secundum rem, sed bonum dicit rationem appetibilis, quam non dicit ens. Cf. *S. Th.* I, 5, 3.

[7] Cf. *S. Th.* I, 16, 4: Verum et bonum supposito convertantur cum ente; *De verit.* 21, 2: Ens et bonum convertantur secundum supposita.

[8] Cf. *S. Th.* I, 16, 3: Sicut bonum convertitur cum ente, ita et verum. Sed tamen sicut bonum addit rationem appetibilis super ens, ita et verum comparationem ad intellectum.

[9] *S. Th.* I, 16, 1; *De verit.* 1, 2. Cf. *De pot.* 9, 9.

[10] *De verit.* 21, 2. Cf. *De malo* 1, 1: Ipsum esse maxime habet rationem appetibilis; *S.c.G.* I, 37: Esse igitur actu boni rationem constituit; *De verit.* 21, 3.

cept, determinations to "being" which correspond to those which the 'essentia' and the 'esse' entail with respect to the 'subjectum'. This correspondence must imply that the meaning of being as the whole of 'subjectum-essentia-esse' only opens up in the integral activity of the human faculties.

(3) "There is the same disposition of things in being and in truth" (4.3.1). Whatever is (true) in any way is reduced to the first being and to the maximally true, namely, God. The relation to the Origin must be understood as participation. The same line of thought we find in the transcendental "good." "There is the same disposition of things in goodness and in being" (*Eadem est dispositio rerum in bonitate et in esse; S. Th.* I–II, 18, 4).

S. Th. I, 5 has as subject: "On good in general"; every being is as such good. Next, in I, 6, the subject is: "The goodness of God." Goodness belongs to God as well, and in the highest measure; He is as pure act the highest Good (art. 2). Indeed, from the Neoplatonic tradition as it is adopted by pseudo-Dionysius, it must be said that "good" is the first among the divine names, since to the "good" primarily belongs the "aspect of causing."[11]

Only God is good "essentially" (I, 6, 3); for He is his being, and "everything has so much good as it has being (*esse*)."[12] All else is good through participation, through derivation from what is good essentially. The good of things is created: "All the good that is in things has been created by God."[13] The communication of the divine goodness extends to the lowest substances. Material creatures have, however, a "more obscure participation in the good." Because of their materiality the clarity of the divine goodness is darkened in them.[14] Primary matter itself is the limit of the extension of goodness. It is merely being in potency; yet it does participate in the good to a certain extent, namely, by its ordination to, or aptitude for, the good.[15] All created reality is and is good, because it participates by means of assimilation in the first Good.

Every thing is said to be good in virtue of an inherent form, which is its own goodness. But next, so Thomas claims, it may be held with Plato that every thing is said to be good in virtue of the exemplary form ("Idea") of the Good.[16] Every thing is good in virtue of the uncreated

---

[11] Cf. *In De div. nomin.* c. 3 and c. 4, lect. 1.

[12] *S. Th.* I–II, 18, 1.

[13] *S. Th.* I, 22, 1.

[14] *In De div. nomin.* c. 4, lect. 16, 501.

[15] *S. Th.* I, 5, 3 ad 3: Sed tamen participat aliquid de bono, scilicet ipsum ordinem vel aptitudinem ad bonum. Et ideo non competit sibi quod sit appetibile, sed quod appetat.

[16] Cf. *De verit.* 21, 4: Quantum ad hoc opinio Platonis sustineri potest.

goodness, which is the exemplary, effective, and final cause of all goodness. "And so of all things there is *one* goodness, and yet *many* goodnesses"
(*S. Th.* I, 6, 4). There is a categorical multiplicity, for a thing is good in
virtue of an intrinsic cause, its form. But this multiplicity is to be related
to the unity of the Origin; the inherent goodness is a likeness to the divine
goodness.

(4) It is proper to the transcendental "good," however, to constitute a
dynamism in the creature. Precisely because "good" has the character of
final end, the good is for the finite not just something to be but also something to be done. That can be elucidated by pointing out two further
differences between divine and creaturely goodness.

"Being" and "good" are convertible. Yet there is a difference between
"being absolutely" (*ens simpliciter*) and "good absolutely" (*bonum simpliciter*), for "good" adds something to the concept of being. "Being"
properly signifies that something is in act; something is therefore said to
have "being absolutely" insofar as it is primarily distinguished from that
which is only in potency. And this act is the substantial being of each
thing. Therefore it is by its essential principles that something is said to
have "being absolutely"; but by acts added to substantial being, a thing
is said to have "being in a certain sense" (*secundum quid*). With regard to
"good" the reverse is true: good expresses perfection and has consequently the character of being "ultimate" (*rationem ultimi*). Hence what has being "absolutely" is good only "in a certain sense" (*secundum quid*), for insofar as it is in act it has some perfection. A thing is said to be good
"absolutely" when through the ultimate act it has attained its complete
perfection.[17]

Only God has his goodness in a manner which is one and simple, namely, in the fullness of his Being.[18] All finite beings have their perfection not
in one but attain their goodness through a multiplicity of acts. For no creature whatsoever are "to be" and "to be good absolutely" identical.[19]
From this follows still another difference between divine and creaturely
goodness. The creature is good in virtue of the ordering towards something else, which is its last end; its perfection consists in its attaining an
end that lies outside itself. God is not ordered, however, towards any end
outside himself.[20]

---

[17] *S. Th.* I, 5, 1 ad 1.
[18] *S. Th.* I–II, 18, 1.
[19] *S.c.G.* III, 20: Non igitur cuilibet creaturarum idem est esse et bonum esse simpliciter, licet quaelibet earum bona sit in quantum est; Deo vero simpliciter idem est esse
et esse bonum simpliciter.
[20] *S. Th.* I, 6, 3; *In De div. nomin.* c. 4, lect. 1, 269; *S.c.G.* III, 20; *De verit.* 21, 5.

The other side of the non-identity of "being" and "being good absolutely" in finite things is an ontological dynamics, a "natural desire" towards a more complete actuality.

8.1.2. *"Nature" – "appetite" – "natural desire"*[21]

The good is the final end of the appetite, and likewise its origin. For the good arouses desire,[22] gives rise to the appetite, and in so doing becomes the end. The proper influence of the final cause is to be strived after and desired (*appeti et desiderari*).[23] Desire is a movement that is directed towards overcoming the non-identity with the end. It aims at the good in order to obtain it in reality. That which desires has the end whereby it is made perfect outside itself (cf. 1.1.). Once the perfection is possessed, the desire comes to rest. The end of the movement is there where its beginning was.[24]

Bonum est quod omnia appetunt. "Everything" tends or inclines towards the good. Thus "appetite"—a term that suggests conscious, psychic activity—must be taken here in a broad, ontological sense. It indicates the tendency of a thing towards an end.[25] And indeed, this tendency towards the good is preferably elucidated by Thomas, as is clear from the following text, via the movement of the elementary bodies.

Every being tends towards its own good. Specifically different things have different ends. In general, however, it can be said that in order to reach an end there are three prerequisites:

> ... namely a nature proportionate to that end, an inclination which is a natural appetite for that end, and a movement towards the end. Thus it is clear that in the element earth there is a certain nature by which being in the center is suitable to it, and consequent upon this nature there is an inclination to the center according to which earth naturally tends to such a place ...; and so when there is no obstacle, it is always moved downward.[26]

---

[21] Cf. J. Laporta, "Pour trouver le sens exact des termes 'appetitus naturalis', 'desiderium naturale', 'amor naturalis', etc. chez Thomas d'Aquin," *AHDLMA* 40 (1973), 37–95.

[22] *In I De anima*, lect. 1, 3: Bonum rei est illud, secundum quod res habet esse perfectum: hoc enim unaquaeque res quaerit et desiderat.

[23] *De verit.* 22, 2: Influere causae finalis est appeti et desiderari.

[24] *S. Th.* I–II, 26, 2: 'Appetitivus motus circulo agitur', ut dicitur in III De Anima (c. 10): appetibile enim movet appetitum, faciens se quodammodo in ejus intentione; et appetitus tendit in appetibile realiter consequendum, ut sit ibi finis motus, ubi fuit principium.

[25] *In I Ethic.*, lect. 1, 11: Quod omnia appetunt, non est intelligendum solum de habentibus cognitionem, quae apprehendunt bonum ... Ipsum tendere in bonum, est appetere bonum. Unde et omnia dixit appetere bonum, inquantum tendunt ad bonum. Cf. *De verit.* 22, 1.

[26] *De verit.* 27, 2: Scilicet *natura* proportionata ad finem illum; et inclinatio ad finem

The end can only arouse desire when this good is suitable (*conveniens*), is proportionate, to the thing. "Something is only affected by what corresponds in some way to its nature."[27] Determinative of what is appetible for a being is its nature. For nature is the principle of motion. The first condition for the attainment of an end is therefore a *nature* that is proportionate to it.

What is meant by this proportion to the end? Nothing other than that in the principle a certain beginning of the end (*inchoatio finis*), an orientation, pre-exists.[28] A movement towards an end is only possible when the terminus in some way determines the movement. In the explanation of nature as principle we already encountered this ordering towards the end. For in 7.1.1.2. we saw that the heavy bodies are moved by nature, because in virtue of an inner principle, their form of heaviness, they have an inclination towards their natural place, where they rest.

The second prerequisite for the attainment of an end is an inclination towards it, which is called *natural appetite*. What underlies this appetite is an anticipatory unity of the nature in which it is rooted and of the end towards which it tends. The foundation of the inclination towards the good is an affinity, a "connaturality," whereby the good desired pre-exists in the appetite, as the act in the potency. The good causes the inclination, because it arouses in the striving an affection towards itself, which Thomas—even at the level of the inanimate—calls love (*amor*) and complacency (*complacentia*): "the connaturality of the heavy body to the middle ... can be called natural love" (*S. Th.* I–II, 26, 1). Through love, a thing inclines to the end that is connatural to it.[29]

It belongs to love to move towards union (*S.c.G.* I, 91: *amoris est ad unionem movere*); it is the principle of the appetite, which aims at the completion of the union. From the complacency follows the movement towards the appetible, which is the *desire*.[30] This desire is called "natural" since it arises from the nature of that which tends, from an intrinsic principle. Things are led towards their final ends not through violence but

---

illum, quae est naturalis *appetitus* finis; et *motus* in finem. Sicut patet quod in terra est natura quaedam, per quam sibi competit esse in medio; et hanc naturam sequitur inclinatio in locum medium, secundum quam appetit naturaliter talem locum . . .; et ideo, nullo prohibente, semper deorsum movetur.

[27] *S. Th.* I, 63, 2. Cf. I–II, 27, 1: Unicuique autem est bonum id quod est sibi connaturale et proportionatum; *De verit.* 22, 1 ad 3; *S.c.G.* III, 3; *De spe*, q. un., a. 1 ad 8: Bonum proportionatum movet appetitum; non enim naturaliter appetuntur ea quae non sunt proportionata.

[28] *De verit.* 14, 2.

[29] See for the natural love *In III Sent.* 27, 1, 2 and *S. Th.* I–II, 26, 1.

[30] *S. Th.* I–II, 26, 2: Ex hac complacentia sequitur motus in appetibile, qui est desiderium.

through love. They have in themselves a principle of the inclination
towards what is suitable to them.[31]

The natural appetite is the "ordering of things according to their proper
nature to their end."[32] This "natural" appetite is distinguished from the
"sensitive" appetite which follows not the natural form of that which
desires but the form of its sense knowledge, and from the "rational"
appetite, which is called the will (*voluntas*).[33] "To a rational nature it is
proper to tend to an end by directing itself towards that end."[34]

This distinction could suggest—and some texts in Thomas do give that
impression[35]—that the "natural appetite" must be taken in opposition to
the other appetites and hence would be found only in things that are
devoid of knowledge. That this interpretation is incorrect,[36] however,
can be made clear by recalling the exposition on the definition of nature
(7.1.1.4.). Nature is the principle of motion in that in which it is *primo* and
per se. This addition effects that nature has always to be related to the subject, of which it is primarily the principle of motion. In this relation nature
again and again acquires different specifications. Characteristic of the
differentiation is that nature's "determination to one thing" becomes the
less restrictive the more the form dominates matter. Yet in this hierarchical order, as we saw in the exposition in question, that which comes first
is always preserved in what comes later. Nature is the immovable foundation and principle of all other processes. This definition of nature is determinative for the correct understanding of the "natural" appetite, since
nature is the root of this appetite.

"Natural" is what belongs 'per se' to a being. What is not 'per se' in
a being is reduced to what belongs 'per se', i.e., "by nature," to it. Therefore "the appetible that is strived for by nature is the principle and foundation of all else that is appetible."[37] Now in the order of what is appetible, the end is the principle of what leads to the end. Just as all knowledge
is to be reduced to principles which the intellect knows "naturally," so are
all acts of the will to be reduced to what is willed "naturally," the ultimate

---

[31] Cf. *De verit.* 22, 1; *In De div. nomin.* c. 4, lect. 11, 449: Amor autem est sicut motus
naturalis simul ab intimo procedens.

[32] *In I Phys.*, lect. 15, 138. Cf. *De verit.* 25, 1.

[33] See, e.g., *S. Th.* I, 59, 1; 60, 1; I–II, 26, 1.

[34] *S. Th.* I–II, 1, 2.

[35] *S. Th.* I, 19, 1: Et haec habitudo ad bonum, in rebus carentibus cognitione, vocatur
appetitus naturalis; I, 59, 1.

[36] Cf. *De verit.* 22, 5 ad 6 (in contr.): Voluntas dividitur contra appetitum naturalem
cum praecisione tantum, id est qui est naturalis tantum, sicut homo contra id quod est animal
tantum; non autem dividitur contra appetitum naturalem absolute, sed includit ipsum,
sicut homo includit animal.

[37] *De verit.* 22, 5. Cf. *S. Th.* I–II, 10, 1.

end, namely, happiness. The natural appetite of the will (*voluntas ut natura*) is the condition of the possibility for performing voluntary acts, the basis of the "voluntary appetite."[38] This basic act of willing (*velle et amare*), over which man has no dominion, is called by Thomas "natural desire." "In the process of rational appetite, which is the will, the principle has to be that which is naturally desired" (*S. Th.* I–II, 1, 5). To what does the natural desire tend?

8.1.3. *"The end corresponds with the principle"*

Since the good is what all things desire, it has character of end. The 'finis' is "the cause of causes." Causality therefore belongs primarily to the good.[39] Given this coherence it becomes understandable why Aristotle posits that the first Principle moves as "being loved," as final cause. For only so is it capable of moving something without being moved. The end can set in motion without itself requiring a prior mover (6.5.3.). "The appetite is a moved mover, but the appetible is an unmoved mover" (*De pot.* 6, 6).

The causality of the good consists in the communication of its perfection. It belongs to the essence of the good to be self-diffusive (*bonum est diffusivum sui esse*). This definition of the good is of Neoplatonic provenance and pertains originally to the One, which is the essential Good. It is ontologically broadened by Thomas, however, to include every being. Moreover, he does not want to conceive this emanation as a necessity of nature. Therefore Thomas understands the self-communication of the good not in the sense of an efficient but in the sense of a final cause. "The good is said to be diffusive in the manner of a final cause, as it is said that the end moves the efficient cause."[40]

The end moves the agent. In the resolution to the principles in chapter seven we found a hierarchy in efficient causality: "particular nature," "universal nature," and "the Creator of the world." This order is based on the degree of actuality and the efficacy resulting from it. Every agent acts for the sake of an end and a good. Now we saw in the preceding section that there must be a "proportion" between what strives and its end. There must therefore be a gradation in final ends proportionate to the degrees of efficient causality.[41] The higher an agent is, the more uni-

---

[38] See *De verit.* 22, 5; *S. Th.* I, 60, 2; 82, 1; *De caritate* q. un., a. 1: Omnes actus voluntatis reducuntur, sicut in primam radicem, in id quod homo naturaliter vult, quod est ultimus finis.

[39] *In De div. nomin.* c. 1, lect. 3, 87; *S. Th.* I, 49, 1.

[40] *In I Sent.* 34, 2, 1 ad 4. Cf. *S. Th.* I, 5, 4 ad 2; *De verit.* 21, 1 ad 4.

[41] *In I Ethic.*, lect. 9, 108.

versal the good for the sake of which it acts. The generator strives for the good of the species, the celestial bodies for a more universal good, and God, finally, "for the good of all being." The order of ends corresponds with the order of agents.[42] This correspondence rests on the actuality of both. Every agent acts insofar as it is in act. What has the character of an end is perfect. Something is perfect insofar as it is in act.

The counterpart of the resolution to the extrinsic causes is in the caused being an inner multiplicity of 'subjectum—essentia—esse', components that relate to each other as potency and act. Also the order in finality of the effected being is governed by the regime of the universal. Everything, so Thomas says, inclines by nature more towards what is common than towards what is its particular good. For nature never intends the particular as such, but for the sake of something else, the perfection of the species. On that basis Thomas concludes: "And much more has everything a natural inclination towards what is the absolutely universal good (*bonum universale*)."[43]

In this natural desire towards perfection, the principle from which the thing originated becomes the end. For the good of the effect is the assimilation to the efficient cause. By desiring its good, the effect turns itself back towards its principle. "All that is caused reverts upon its cause through desire."[44] For each thing it is desirable to be united with its origin, since it is in this that the perfection of each thing consists (1.7.). The dynamics of reality is a circulation, since the end corresponds with the principle.[45]

This order of finality must now be made more concrete. The movement towards the end will not only show correspondence with the reduction to the principle in chapter 7; it will also complete the hodo-logy. What remains to be examined is how the way of nature comes to an end and how it is enclosed in the circular movement of the creature. That will also bring us to the close of our investigation of Thomas Aquinas's way of thought.

---

[42] *De malo* 1, 1: Ordo autem finium est sicut et ordo agentium. Quanto enim aliquod agens est superius et universalius, tanto et finis propter quem agit, est universalius bonum; *S.c.G.* III, 24.

[43] *S.Th.* I, 60, 5 ad 3.

[44] *In De div. nomin.* c. 4, lect. 2, 296; c. 1, lect. 3, 94. Cf. *S.Th.* I, 6, 1: Perfectio autem et forma effectus est quaedam similitudo agentis, cum omne agens agat sibi simile; unde ipsum agens est appetibile, et habet rationem boni; hoc enim est quod de ipso appetitur, ut ejus similitudo participetur.

[45] *S.Th.* I–II, 2, 5 ad 3: Quia finis respondet principio ... Cf. *In II Sent.* 38, 1, 1: Eodem ordine res referuntur in finem quo procedunt a principio.

8.2. *"Nature" and "end"*

8.2.1. *'Natura est via in naturam'*

Nature acts for the sake of something, and this end is nature itself. This is the heart of the idea of finality that Thomas finds in Aristotle.[46] The Stagirite advances in *Phys.* II, 8 (lect. 12–14) a series of arguments for the teleology of nature. These arguments can be gathered into three clusters. We have encountered each of these reasonings before, but now they come to stand in a final perspective.

(1) The first argument, based on the stability in nature, is directed against the mechanistic conception of Empedocles. According to his view nature does not act for an end; there is in the process of nature only blind necessity. What appears to be for an end is only the outcome of natural selection. Through coincidence certain organisms were so constituted that they could maintain themselves. Others lacked such an adaptation and perished.

Over against this view Aristotle asserts that all natural things come to be always or as a rule in a given way. That is not the case in that which comes to be by chance. Only what happens by way of exception is casual (cf. 3.3.1.). The regularity in nature can therefore not be accounted for through chance but must be reduced to an operation for an end. The constancy must as such be intended, must come forth, so Thomas too says, *ex intentione finis.*[47]

To deny the teleology in nature is to do away with the concept of "nature." "For that is said to be according to nature which is continuously moved by an intrinsic principle until it reaches an end." This continuous movement does not proceed from an arbitrary beginning to an arbitrary terminus but always from the same principle to the same end. This end can only be accounted for from the intention of nature (*ex intentione naturae*). The view that nature does not act for an end is *contra rationem naturae.*[48] There is an identity between the natural and the teleological.

What proves most that nature operates for an end is that from the action of nature the best possible always follows. This thought, which Thomas formulates in his commentary on *Phys.* II, 8, is merely implicit in Aristotle's text.[49] But certainly Aquinas grasps here Aristotle's basic conviction concerning finality. The end is identical with the good. That is why it is strived after.

---

[46] Cf. A. Mansion, *Introduction à la physique aristotélicienne*, pp. 251ff.
[47] *Phys.* II, 8, 198 b 34ff. (lect. 13, 256). Cf. *De verit.* 5, 2.
[48] *In II Phys.*, lect. 14, 267 (*Phys.* II, 8, 199 b 14ff.).
[49] *In II Phys.*, lect. 12, 252.

(2) Another argument employed by Aristotle in support of natural finality identifies the end with the form. It runs as follows: nature is said in two ways, namely, of matter and form. The form is the end of generation. Since it belongs to the essence of the end that all the rest is for the sake of it, nature as form must be the final cause.[50] This reasoning is the same as one of the arguments used in *Phys.* II, 1 to show that not only matter but also form is "the nature" (7.1.3.). Nature in the sense of generation is *via in naturam*. Every coming to be is towards something, namely, the form. Therefore the terminus and end of the process must be the nature as form. And the form is the nature "more" than matter is, for each thing is more what it is when it has its end in it (*entelecheia*) than when it is in potency.

The form which gives the act is what is desirable, is the end of matter. The "natural desire" of the being in potency comes to an end in this perfection. The more an act is more final and perfect, the more is the appetite of matter inclined to it. This idea is worked out by Thomas in a special way in *S.c.G.* III, 22: the appetite of matter must tend towards the most perfect act to which matter can attain, as to the ultimate end of generation. The highest form to be found in things subject to generation and corruption is that of man. It is to this act that matter tends as its ultimate form.[51]

Nature is 'finis', and this end is the essential form. Cohering with this teleology is the axiology of form in ancient thought. The form is "something divine, is the best and desirable" (6.5.1.). The form is what is appetible, for it is the act of each thing. The form is as such good; it is "the good of nature" (*bonum naturae*).[52]

(3) A third argument is based on the imitation of nature by art. Now it is evident that production by art is directed towards an end. Hence there must equally be finality in natural generation. For in both productions the later stages relate to the earlier stages in the same way.[53] This argument confirms the interpretation given in 3.3.2. of the thesis "art imitates nature": it is an expression of an identical logos in the becoming of things. There is a structural agreement between the operation of nature and the operation of art: both are marked by an intelligible order, both are for an end.

---

[50] *Phys.* II, 8, 199 a 30ff. (lect. 13, 260).

[51] *S.c.G.* III, 22: Ultimus igitur generationis totius gradus est anima humana, et in hanc tendit materia sicut in ultimam formam.

[52] *S.c.G.* III, 20; *S. Th.* I, 19, 1: Quaelibet autem res ad suam formam naturalem hanc habet habitudinem, ut quando non habet ipsam, tendat in eam; et quando habet ipsam, quiescat in ipsa. Et idem est de qualibet perfectione naturali, quod est bonum naturae.

[53] *Phys.* II, 8, 199 a 15ff. (lect. 13, 258).

Nature advances in an orderly way from the one to the other. Via certain means it arrives at an end.[54] "Nature does nothing in vain."[55] This finality is the most manifest in the lower animals. They act not through deliberation but "by nature." Yet it is for an end that the swallow builds its nest and the spider spins its web.[56]

The occurrence of deviations in natural becoming is not incompatible with the teleology. They even occur in the operations of art: the grammarian, too, sometimes writes incorrectly. And no one will deny that art acts for an end. Monstrous births are the exception to the rule, are deviations from the norm, *peccata naturae*. That "mistakes"—literally, "sins"—can be spoken of in what is natural confirms rather that nature acts for an end. For 'peccata' presuppose an order with respect to the good.[57]

Nor can it be urged as an objection against teleology that nature does not deliberate about its end. The reply has the form of an "argument from the stronger" (*locus a maiori*). Even art does not deliberate; the cither player certainly does not ponder about what strings he will move! Even the voluntary and intelligent agent (sometimes) does not deliberate; hence even less so the natural cause.[58] The decisive distinction between nature and art does not lie here. They differ only in that nature is an intrinsic, art an extrinsic principle of motion.[59] It was also precisely this distinction that was advanced in 3.3.2. and 7.1.1.1. respecting the division of these causes 'per se'.

Yet just from the vantage point of final causality this distinction cannot fully satisfy and Aristotle's speaking of the "intention" of nature demands further explanation. In *Metaph.* VII, c. 7—a central text for the division of the causes of generation (see 3.3.1.)—he states that in production by art there are really two movements. First, there is a noetic process, a deliberation which proceeds from the mental form (species) that is to be realized and concerns the means to attain the end. Then follows the making (*factio*), the realization of the intended form in matter. In natural production there is only an equivalent of the latter movement, namely, the generation, which proceeds from the species in the generator. It is on the basis of that process that nature is distinguished as intrinsic principle

---

[54] *In VIII Phys.*, lect. 3, 993: Natura est causa ordinationis. Videmus enim naturam in suis operibus ordinate de uno in aliud procedere; *De occultis operibus naturae.*
[55] Aristotle makes this statement in, among other places, *De anima* III, 12 and *Politica* I, 1.
[56] *Phys.* II, 8, 199 a 20ff. (lect. 13, 259).
[57] *Ibid.*, 199 a 33ff. (lect. 14, 263).
[58] Cf. *De principiis naturae*, c. 3.
[59] *Phys.* II, 8, 199 b 26 (lect. 14, 268).

from art. Should consideration be given to both processes of art, however, then the emphasis would come to fall on the fact that nature has not consciousness either of its goal or of the means of attaining it. It intends its end without "foreseeing" it as such.

For Aristotle that nature acts for an end is not at all problematical. This striking feature in his conception of natural finality can only be understood by recalling once again that the concept of nature has a polemical function against Plato's expositions in the tenth book of the *Nomoi* (cf. 3.4.3.). For Plato the material nature is reducible to the soul and what belongs to it: mind and art. The World-Soul is the principle of movement. Plato's definition of the Soul is transferred by Aristotle, as we saw, to 'physis'. Nature is defined as the principle of movement, acts itself for an end. It has, however, no knowledge of the end. It is at this point that Thomas considers further the finality of nature.

8.2.2. *"Nature" and "providence": "All naturally desire the good"* (*'Omnia naturaliter bonum appetunt'*)

What strives after an end must be in some way determined to it. Otherwise there would be no reason why the agent would tend towards just this rather than some other terminus. That determination must proceed from the intention of the end. The end can only motivate the agent if it already pre-exists in the agent. This presence cannot be, however, according to the natural mode of being of the end; for then the agent would already possess the intented, and the movement would come to rest. The end must be present in what strives as *intentio*, that is, as "intelligible species." This representation is the essence of knowledge.[60] The determination of the agent must be through an intellect that determines the end for the action. An end can only be intended when the end as end is known, together with the means to it.[61]

Science as such is however not yet an active cause. Science signifies an intelligible form that remains in the knower. The terminus of the cognitive process resides in the one who understands. For the intelligible form to become a principle of action, there must be added to it the inclination to the known end or good.[62] That is the essence of the will. For the act of

---

[60] Cf. for the coherence of the two ways of 'intentio' *De verit.* 22, 12.

[61] *In III Sent.* 27, 1, 2: Intendere autem finem impossibile est, nisi cognoscatur finis sub ratione finis, et proportio eorum quae ad finem in finem ipsum; *In II Sent.* 25, 1, 1: Determinatio autem agentis ad aliquam actionem, oportet quod sit ab aliqua cognitione praestituente finem illi actioni.

[62] Cf. *In I Sent.* 38, 1, 1; *De verit.* 2, 14: Scientia inquantum scientia, non dicit causam activam ...; et ideo a scientia numquam procedit effectus nisi mediante voluntate, quae

the will is nothing other than "an inclination consequent on the form understood" (*S. Th.* I, 87, 4). Willing presupposes knowledge, and because the object of the will is the good, "good presupposes the true" (*De verit.* 21, 3). Inclination to a good requires understanding of what is loved.

Intending an end is possible only when the end is known. What has knowledge of an end is able not only to move itself towards an end but also to direct other things towards it. Therefore, something can be ordered towards an end in two ways. First by itself (*per seipsum*), as is the case with man, who knows the end as end. Secondly, by another (*ab altero*), if that which tends to an end lacks knowledge of the end. In this way an arrow is directed by an archer to a determinate end.[63]

Now natural things have no knowledge of an end. Their fixed course shows, however, that their movement is governed by some reason.[64] Hence they presuppose something else, an intellect, whereby they are directed towards their end: "it is necessary that for the natural agent the end and the necessary means to the end are predetermined by some higher intellect" (*S. Th.* I, 19, 4).

Natural things are not directed towards their end, however, as the arrow by the archer. The arrow is moved without acquiring from the mover a form in virtue of which the tendency is suitable to it; the inclination of the arrow is, in other words, violent. But all natural things are ordered to a good that is suitable to them. They have in themselves a principle in virtue of which their inclination is *natural*. They are not merely led to their appropriate ends but go themselves towards them in a certain sense.[65] This natural principle has been implanted in them by the divine intellect, by the divine Wisdom, which has established nature (*a sapientia instituente naturam, In III Sent.* 27, 1, 2).[66] The movement of natural things towards an end differs from a violent movement because what these things receive from God is precisely their nature.[67]

In this reduction of natural finality, various moments from the analysis of nature as principle in chapter 7 come up again; indeed, their philosophical meaning only now emerges fully, because the movement is a dynamics towards the end. Definitive for nature as "principle of motion"

---

de sui ratione importat influxum quemdam in volita; *S. Th.* I, 14, 8.

[63] *De verit.* 22, 1; *In III Sent.* 27, 1, 2; *S. Th.* I–II, 1, 2.

[64] *S. Th.* I, 103, 1 ad 1.

[65] *De verit.* 22, 1: Et per hunc modum omnia naturalia, in ea quae eis conveniunt, sunt inclinata, habentia in seipsis aliquod inclinationis principium, ratione cuius eorum inclinatio naturalis est, ita ut quodammodo ipsa vadant, et non solum ducantur in fines debitos. Violenta enim tantummodo ducuntur, quia nil conferunt moventi.

[66] Cf. *De verit.* 5, 2; *S. Th.* I–II, 26, 1.

[67] *S. Th.* I, 103, 1 ad 3.

was that this principle is intrinsic. This insight underlay the differentiation from other principles, such as "violence." "Violence" means that a thing is moved to something to which it has of itself no inclination. Besides, we find here again the distinction beween intrinsic principle of movement and self-movement. This difference was explained in 7.1.1.2. via the movement of the elements, the light and heavy bodies. None of them moves itself. Yet they are moved naturally, since in virtue of an intrinsic principle they have an inclination and dynamis to their proper places. And according to the model of this motion, which is reducible to an extrinsic cause, the generator, and an intrinsic principle, Thomas understood the relation of God and nature. An external cause moves naturally only when it causes an intrinsic principle of motion in the movable thing. In this manner God operates in nature. For He endows things with the forms and powers that are the inner principles of their motions.

This 'concursus' of God and nature receives its complete meaning from the finality. Natural things go towards their end in "cooperation" with their intellective ordainer through a principle that is implanted in them.[68] What occurs by nature needs to be reduced to an intelligent cause. "Since nature works for a determinate end under the direction of a higher agent, whatever is done by nature must also be reduced to God (*etiam in Deum reducere*)" (*S. Th.* I, 2, 3 ad 2). That reduction constitutes Thomas's "fifth way" to the existence of God. Whatever lacks knowledge cannot move towards an end, unless it be directed by some being endowed with knowledge and intelligence. "Therefore some intelligent being exists by whom all natural things are directed to their end; and this being we call God."

Nature is God's "instrument," is directed by Him to the end that He wills and intends.[69] God has, however, no other end of His will than Himself. He Himself is essentially good. Therefore everything is inclined by nature to the good, in such a manner that each thing has a principle whereby it tends to its good. Hence one must say, so Thomas claims, that all naturally desire the good (*omnia naturaliter bonum appetunt*).[70]

The natural inclination is always good. For it is implanted by God. Nothing natural is wrong. To say that the natural inclination is not right is to derogate from the Author of nature.[71] "God and nature ... make

---

[68] *De verit.* 22, 1: Naturalia vadunt in finem, in quantum cooperantur inclinanti et dirigenti per principium eis inditum.

[69] Cf. *S. Th.* I–II, 1, 2; *In XII Metaph.*, lect. 12, 2634: Ipsa natura uniuscuiusque est quaedam inclinatio indita ei a primo movente, ordinans ipsam in debitum finem.

[70] *De verit.* 22, 1.

[71] *Quodl.* I, 4, 3; *S. Th.* I, 60, 1 ad 3: Dicere ergo quod inclinatio naturae non sit recta, est derogare auctori naturae.

what is better in the whole" (*S. Th.* I, 48, 2 ad 3). Because of this "coope-ration", Thomas can also give a deeper meaning to Aristotle's statement that "nature does nothing in vain" (8.2.1.). Something is in vain if it is ordained towards an end to which it does not attain.[72] Now, the natural desire cannot be in vain, for everything is ordained to its end by the divine intellect.[73]

Because the operation of nature presupposes an intellect that predeter-mines the end of nature, the "work of nature" is called "the work of an intelligent substance" (*opus intelligentiae*).[74] Against this background it be-comes understandable that Thomas draws a conclusion at the end of his commentary on *Phys.* II, 8 that goes much further than Aristotle's exposi-tion of the agreement in finality between nature and art intends. "There-fore it appears that nature is nothing other than the 'ratio' of some art, namely, the divine, which is implanted in things whereby they are moved to the determined end" (*In II Phys.*, lect. 14, 268). Nature is founded in the divine art (cf. 4.3.2.).

The natural order is a providential order. This connection Thomas makes expressly in a passage in his commentary on the *Physica* which serves to introduce his exposition of the finality of nature:

> Nature belongs to the class of causes that work for an end. This is of impor-tance for the question of providence. For what lacks knowledge of the end does not tend towards the end unless it be directed by a being that knows, as the arrow by the archer. Thus if nature acts for an end, it must be or-dained by some intelligent being. This is the work of providence.[75]

Whoever denies the existence of the final cause denies providence. For providence concerns the ordering of things to their ends, is "ratio or-dinandorum in finem." The order to the end that nature has it has not of itself but from another (*ab alio*). Therefore nature has need of Provi-dence, whereby such an order is established in it.[76]

---

[72] *S. Th.* I, 25, 2: Frustra est quod ordinatur ad finem, quam non attingit.

[73] *In II De caelo*, lect. 16, 442: Natura autem nihil facit irrationabiliter neque frustra, quia tota naturae operatio est ordinata ab aliquo intellectu propter finem operante; lect. 8, 91; *In I Ethic.*, lect. 2, 21; *S.c.G.* III, 156: In operibus Dei non est aliquid frustra, sicut nec in operibus naturae; hoc enim natura habet a Deo.

[74] Cf. *De verit.* 3, 1: Operatio naturae, quae est ad determinatum finem, praesupponit intellectum, praestituentem finem naturae, et ordinantem ad finem illum naturam, ra-tione cuius omne opus naturae dicitur esse opus intelligentiae. See also ch. 4.3.2, n. 100.

[75] *In II Phys.*, lect. 12, 250.

[76] *De verit.* 5, 2 and ad 10. Cf. *S. Th.* I, 22, 1.
This is the philosophical background of the identification of the natural and the providential orders, which occupies such a central place in various recent documents of the Roman Catholic Church, especially in the encyclical *Humanae Vitae* (25 July 1968) con-cerning birth control. The manner however in which the concept of nature is used here deserves closer critical investigation.

8.2.3. *Nature and circulation*

Nature is the end of generation. The coming to be ends in the *species* or *essentia*, which is therefore called nature.[77] From the "hodology" of natural movement follows an ontology that revolves around the essence. For in the terminus of the way towards being, the meaning of "nature" becomes coextensive with "substance" or "essence."[78] In the essence lies the intelligibility of that which is. Nature is consequently also the terminus of definitional thinking. The last meaning of nature in the process of signification (cf. 6.5.2) is of a logical order: "nature is the specific difference which informs each thing." For the specific difference is what determines the substance of the thing.[79]

Through its essential principles, the thing is perfected in itself in such a way that it subsists.[80] These principles are its first perfection; from them results the "aspect of true."[81] Something is perfect insofar as it is in act. "The first act" is "the form and integrity of a thing" (*S. Th.* I, 48, 5). Insofar as something is perfect and is in act, it is good. The first "good of nature" (*bonum naturae*) is the essential principles.[82]

Now we found in 8.1.1. that although "being" and "good" are convertible, "being absolutely" and "good absolutely" are not identical. By its essential principles something is "being absolutely." But good has the aspect of perfect and consequently of ultimate. A being is only "good absolutely" when through the ultimate act it has attained its complete perfection. "Everything desires by nature to be complete in goodness (*esse completum in bonitate*)" (*De verit.* 22, 7). While good in itself, the being strives towards complete goodness, by which it is related as it should be to everything outside itself (*ut debito modo se habent ad omnia quae sunt extra ipsum*),[83] by which it is perfected in relation to other things.

---

[77] *In V Metaph.*, lect. 5, 822: Species et substantia dicitur natura, quia est finis generationis. Nam generatio terminatur ad speciem generati; *De unione verbi incarnati* q. un., a. 1; *S. Th.* III, 2, 1.

[78] *In V Metaph.*, lect. 5, 823: Et ex hoc secundum quamdam metaphoram et nominis extensionem omnis substantia dicitur natura; quia natura quam diximus quae est generationis terminus, substantia quaedam est... Ratione autem istius modi distinguitur hoc nomen natura inter nomina communia.

[79] Cf. *In I Sent.* 43, 1, 1: Finis vel terminus multipliciter dicitur... Dicitur alio modo finis quantum ad essentiam rei, sicut ultima differentia constitutiva est ad quam finitur essentia speciei. Unde illud quod significat essentiam rei vocatur definitio vel terminus.

[80] *De verit.* 21, 5: In seipso autem aliquid perficitur ut subsistat per essentialia principia.

[81] *De verit.* 1, 10 ad 3. Cf. *S. Th.* I, 71, 1: Prima quidem perfectio est, secundum quod res in sua substantia est perfecta. Quae quidem perfectio est forma totius, quae ex integritate partium consurgit; III, 29, 2.

[82] *S. Th.* I–II, 85, 1.

[83] *De verit.* 21, 5.

The non-identity of "being" and "good" is found to be connected with the manner in which the relationality of things is thought. Here too there becomes perceptible in Thomas's philosophical analysis a tendency that we noticed earlier in his reflection on creation as a relation (6.6.): what comes first is the subsistence; the relatedness to others is subsequent, ontologically speaking. This order to the other is a perfection that is in addition to the act whereby the being subsists in itself and remains essentially identical with itself. The thing desires a fuller actuality of being by acts added to the essence. Complete goodness must therefore consist in a perfecting in the accidental order (*secundum vero accidentale dicitur aliquid bonum simpliciter*).[84]

From the preceding it follows that two ends must be distinguished. First there is the end of generation, which is identical with the specific form whereby the thing is completed in itself; secondly, there is the end of the thing generated, which is to say that whereby the thing has its ultimate perfection. And the first end, nature, is directed to the second: "The thing's nature, which is the end of generation, is further ordained to another end, which is either an operation, or some product of operation, to which one attains by means of operation."[85] This final order provides further clarification of the conditions, analyzed in 8.1.2., prerequisite to attaining an end: "nature" – "appetite" – "natural desire."

The nature is the essence through which and in which that which is has being. The essence, however, is preferably called "nature" insofar as it is the origin of the capacity for further completion. The term "nature" "seems to mean the essence of a thing as directed to its proper operation" (*De ente*, c. 1). In the notion of *nature* are combined the stability and dynamics of that which is. It is the inner principle of the movement towards the end that is connatural to it.

Every being acts insofar as it is in act. It is in act through its form or nature. Every agent is therefore active in virtue of and in accordance with its formal principle (6.5.3.). From the form follows first of all an inclination to the operation that is suitable to the thing.[86] This inclination is the *natural appetite* towards the end.[87] Nature is the principle from which a being's inclination to the good that suits it emanates.

---

[84] *Ibid.*

[85] *S. Th.* I–II, 49, 3: Natura rei, quae est finis generationis, ulterius etiam ordinatur ad alium finem, qui vel est operatio, vel aliquod operatum, ad quod quis pervenit per operationem.

[86] Cf. *S. Th.* I–II, 94, 3; *S.c.G.* IV, 19: Res autem naturalis per formam qua perficitur in sua specie habet inclinationem in proprias operationes et proprium finem, quem per operationes consequitur; quale enim est unumquodque, talia operatur et in sibi convenientia tendit; *S. Th.* I, 5, 5; *In II De anima*, lect. 5, 286.

[87] *In III Sent.* 27, 1, 2; *De malo* 3, 3; *De verit.* 25, 1.

From the inclination follows the movement towards the end. "Movement" is to be taken here in a broad sense. For 'motus', strictly speaking, is "an act of an imperfect subject" (6.5.1.), which is to say of a being in potency. In question here, however, is an "act of that which is perfect", the movement of a being in act, which is called "operation". The operation is the ultimate end of the thing, its second perfection, from which the "aspect of goodness" arises.[88] Activity is the complementary act according to which the thing attains its complete goodness. The operation is the perfect or "second act" which is desired by every being as end.[89] "For the less perfect is always for the sake of the more perfect. Consequently, just as the matter is for the sake of the form, so the form which is the first act is for the sake of its operation, which is the second act; and thus operation is the end of the creature" (*S. Th.* I, 105, 5).

The most natural work (*opus naturalissimum*)[90] is "to generate." Therein the agent communicates its own perfection to others. Becoming is a process of assimilation. The end is the specific nature, which was the principle. These considerations again show, in a deepened manner, that the way of nature comes to an end in a *circulation* (cf. 3.4.1.). From, through, and to nature proceeds the movement. Through the natural circulation, reality is preserved. The intention of nature is directed to the permanent, to the good of the species.[91]

8.3. *"All naturally desire God" ('Omnia naturaliter appetunt Deum')*

The inclination of nature to an end must be aroused by a good that is different from and outside it. For the operation is the completion of the thing, because in this act it relates itself to something other. The last end to which a thing is directed is the most desired (*unumquodque maxime desiderat suum ultimum finem*; *S.c.G.* III, 25), for the ultimate is the first in the order of the appetible.

This end can only be the divine goodness.[92] After Thomas has shown in *S.c.G.* III, 16 that the end of everything is a good, he advances in cap. 17 a series of arguments for the thesis that "all things are directed to one

---

[88] *De verit.* 1, 10 ad 3: Secunda perfectio est operatio, quae est finis rei, vel id propter quod ad finem devenitur... Ex parte secundae consurgitur in ipsa ratio bonitatis, quae consurgit ex fine; *S. Th.* I, 73, 1; III, 29, 2.
[89] *In II De caelo*, lect. 4, 334: Quaelibet enim res appetit suam perfectionem sicut suum finem, operatio autem est ultima rei perfectio ... operatio autem est actus secundus, tamquam perfectio et finis operantis; *S. Th.* I, 48, 5; I–II, 3, 2.
[90] *In II De anima*, lect. 7, 312.
[91] *Ibid.*, 316.
[92] *S. Th.* I, 44, 4: Divina bonitas est finis omnium rerum. Cf. *In De div. nomin.* c. 10, lect. 1, 858.

end, which is God." These arguments are applications of basic ideas familiar to us from earlier expositions. Thomas bases himself on, among other things, the causality of the 'maximum', the highest good; on the greater efficacy of the first cause in every genus of causes; and on the subordination of the particular to the universal. This last argument contends that the particular good is directed to the common good as its end, for the being of the part is for the sake of the being of the whole. Now the supreme good, namely God, is the common good, since the good of all things depends on Him. But the good whereby each thing is good is the particular good of that thing. Therefore all things are directed to one good, namely God, as their end.[93]

This argument especially is characteristic of Thomas's way of thought. The ascent of the particular to the universal good is again attended with a resolution of the finite being to God. This continuous progression is possible through the transcendental unity of the good. Therefore Thomas, upon establishing that everything by nature loves the good of its species more than it loves its own individual good, is able to go on directly: "And much more has everything a natural inclination towards what is the absolutely universal good" (S. Th. I, 60, 5 ad 3). This universal good is what is good essentially, God. All else is good through participation, therefore a particular good, a reflection of the first Good.[94]

Everything by nature desires God. In every desired object He is desired, for a thing is only desirable if it participates in the highest Good.[95] The things which are as it were dispersed, insofar as they are ordained to their own different ends, are gathered in the directedness to this final end.[96] Also with respect to the end, diversity is reduced to unity. That everything by nature tends towards the good (8.2.2.) means ultimately: "All naturally desire God."[97] Because God is the universal good, every creature naturally loves Him more than it does itself.[98]

The end corresponds to the principle (8.1.3.). The ultimate end of

---

[93] S.c.G. III, 17, Praeterea.

[94] S. Th. I, 103, 2: Bonum autem universale est quod est per se et per suam essentiam bonum, quod est ipsa essentia bonitatis; bonum autem particulare est quod est participative bonum; In De div. nomin. c. 1, lect. 3, 95: In omni autem bono particulari refulget Primum Bonum, ex quo habet quodlibet bonum quod sit appetibile.

[95] In De div. nomin. c. 10, lect. 1, 857.

[96] Ibid., c. 4, lect. 3, 316ff.

[97] De verit. 22, 2. Cf. S. Th. I, 6, 1 ad 2; I, 44, 4 ad 3: Omnia appetunt Deum ut finem, appetendo quodcumque bonum.

[98] Quodl. I, 4, 3: Manifestum est autem quod Deus est bonum commune totius universi et omnium partium eius. Unde quaelibet creatura suo modo naturaliter plus amat Deum quam seipsam; S. Th. I, 60, 5 and ad 1; ad 4: Deus, secundum quod est universale bonum, a quo dependet omne bonum naturale, diligitur naturali dilectione ab unoquoque; I–II, 109, 3 ad 1.

everything is the first principle of things, in which is every perfection of being.[99] Desiring its perfection, every creature naturally turns back towards its Principle. In order that the universe of creatures may attain its ultimate perfection, it is necessary that creatures return to their principle.[100] "So a certain circulation is found in things, for egressing from the good, they tend towards the good."[101] The way of the creature is a circular movement of egress and regress; principle and end are identical. The basis of this identity is the goodness of the Origin: "The divine goodness reverts everything upon itself."[102] With the transcending of nature towards being as creature, the motive of circulation acquires a theological dimension and the Aristotelian finality is taken up in the Neoplatonic 'eros' towards the 'Archè'.

How is God the end of everything? Not as an end that is merely prior in the intention of the agent and that is to be established by its action. God is not an end to be effected or caused but an end to be acquired.[103] The ultimate end towards which all the creaturely moves is to be like God, to be assimilated to God.[104] Everything tends towards God *per viam assimilationis (S.c.G.* III, 25).

Wherein is the likeness to God acquired? In the previous section we noticed that everything is perfected by its own operation. Activity is the second act, whereby that which is acquires its complete goodness. Therefore the creaturely tends to the divine likeness through its operation.[105] It makes no difference, so Thomas asserts in *S.c.G.* III, 24, whether one says "things work for an end" or "they tend to the divine likeness" or "they tend to their own perfection." Because by tending to their own perfection, they tend to a good, since a thing is good insofar as it is perfect. And according as a thing tends towards a good, it tends to the divine likeness, since something is assimilated to God insofar as it is good. Now a particular good is appetible insofar as it bears a likeness to the first goodness. Therefore a thing tends to its own good because it tends to the divine likeness, and not vice versa.

Through its operation, every being is directed to the final end—in

---

[99] *S. Th.* I–II, 2, 5 ad 3: Quia finis respondet principio, ex illa ratione probatur quod ultimus finis est primum principium essendi, in quo est omnis essendi perfectio.

[100] *S.c.G.* II, 46. Cf. ch. 1.7.2.

[101] *In IV Sent.* 49, 1, 3, 1. Cf. *S. Th.* I, 64, 3.

[102] *In De div. nomin.* c. 4, lect. 1, 280: Divina enim Bonitas convertit omnia ad seipsam.

[103] *S.c.G.* III, 18; *Comp. Theol.*, 103.

[104] *S.c.G.* III, 19: Omnia igitur tendunt, sicut ad ultimum finem, Deo assimilari.

[105] *Ibid.* III, 19 and 20. Cf. *In II Sent.* 38, 1, 2: Finis autem proprius uniuscujusque rei, per quem in finem ultimum ordinatur, est sua propria operatio.

various ways, however, according to the diversity of operations.[106] In the first place, every thing tends in its operation towards the preservation of its being. "Being" is what is the most desired by all; 'esse' is the most perfect. "Being itself" is a likeness of the divine goodness; God, namely, is subsisting Being itself. "Insofar therefore as things desire being, they desire implicitly the likeness with God, and God."[107] In this order to the end appears the agreement with the analysis of the principles. In the inner multiplicity of what is, that of 'subjectum – essentia – esse', "being" refers to God, the Creator of the world (7.3.).

This assimilation to God in the preservation of being can be directly correlated to the cosmological circulation. This way of the creature *is* the natural circulation. The two movements come together. For nature is directed to the permanence of the species. Therein it tends towards the likeness with the divine being. Through the preservation of the species in generation, natural things take part, according to the measure of their possibility, in the divine and immortal. The operation of nature tends "to the likeness of the divine perpetuity" (*in similitudinem divinae perpetuitatis*).[108]

In the second place, every being tends through its operation towards the communication of its form, towards the diffusion of its goodness. It is a sign of its perfection when a thing is able to produce its like. Through its operation the one thing becomes the cause of another. Therein the thing "tends towards the likeness of the divine causality" (*in similitudinem divinae causalitatis*).[109] In the causal activity, in the giving of being, the thing completes itself and is assimilated to God.

In the regress of things to God there is therefore another order than in their egress. Creation is the exclusive act of God; it is not "mediated" by any agent. But in the regress of what is created, there are intermediary causes.[110] It is consequently only in the order towards the final end that the hierarchy of moving principles established in chapter 7 gains its justification. The cycle of natural generation whereby things become Godlike is reducible to the continuous and circular movement of the celestial body, the "universal nature." The end of its movement, intended by a spiritual substance, is also to acquire the divine likeness in causing the coming to

---

[106] *S.c.G.* III, 22: Diversimode tamen secundum diversitatem operationis.

[107] *De verit.* 22, 2 ad 2: Ipsum esse est similitudo divinae bonitatis; unde in quantum aliqua desiderant esse, desiderant Dei similitudinem et Deum implicite. Cf. *S.c.G.* III, 19; *S.Th.* II–II, 34, 1 ad 3.

[108] *Comp. Theol.*, 103, Cf. *In II De anima*, lect. 7, 314.

[109] *Comp. Theol.*, 103; *S.c.G.* III, 21: Ergo in hoc etiam res intendunt divinam similitudinem ut sint aliis causae.

[110] *De pot.* 3, 4 ad 1; *S.Th.* III, 6, 1 ad 1.

be and passing away of the sublunary things.[111]

The assimilation to God in causality is likewise the ultimate meaning of the 'concursus' of first cause and second cause that we found in 7.4.2. ("The work of nature and creation"). Thomas's argumentation against the view that nature does nothing by its own power and that everything must be ascribed to the first Cause culminates in the motive of the divine goodness. This is detracted from by those who deny to things their proper operations. For the first Cause lends to things from the eminence of its goodness not only that they are, but also that they are causes. By communicating to other things the perfection that they have received, they contribute to the execution of God's providential order and realize their likeness to the divine perfection. Their operation is a co-operation. In this context stands Thomas's reference (at the end of *S.c.G.* III, 21) to the saying of pseudo-Dionysius: "There is nothing more divine in things than to become a co-operator with God."

In the assimilation to God through perpetuity and causality the circular movement remains, however, imperfect. For things tend through that activity towards God only implicitly. In their natural ends they do not discern the attraction of the last End. Only in the rational nature is the circulation perfect. This creature alone is able to attain through its activity God himself.[112] Only man can reduce the proximate ends "by the way of resolution" (cf. 6.4.) to God himself; man is able to tend expressly to his Origin.[113] The rational creature is "capable of God", because it alone can know and love Him "explicitly."[114] Intellectual beings tend towards God *per viam cognitionis* (*S.c.G.* III, 25). By knowledge they become God-like. With that, the connection is made with the start of our study: the phenomenon of the natural desire to know.

---

[111] Cf. the excursus on celestial movement which Thomas inserts into his account of finality in *S.c.G.* III, 22–24. On the ultimate end of celestial movement, the fulfillment of the number of the elect, see: *De pot.* 5, 5 and *Comp. Theol.*, 171.

[112] *In IV Sent.* 49, 1, 3, 1: Haec autem circulatio in quibusdam perficitur creaturis, in quibusdam autem remanet imperfecta. Illa enim creaturae quae non ordinantur ut pertingant ad illum primum bonum a quo processerunt, sed solummodo ad consequendam ejus similitudinem qualemcumque, non perfecte habent hanc circulationem; sed solum illae creaturae quae ad ipsum primum principium aliquo modo pertingere possunt; quod solum est rationabilium creaturarum.

[113] *De verit.* 22, 2: Omnia naturaliter appetunt Deum implicite, non autem explicite... Unde sola rationalis natura potest secundarios fines in ipsum Deum *per* quamdam *viam resolutionis* inducere, ut sic ipsum Deum explicite appetat.

[114] *De verit.* 22, 2 ad 5; *Quodl.* X, 8.

8.4. *The super-natural fulfillment of the natural desire in man to know*

8.4.1. *The supernatural end of the "vision of God"*

"All men by nature desire to know." This desire is the dynamics of man towards the complete actualization of his being. The desire to know is the ontological ordering of man to the good that suits his nature. That is also evident from the three "a priori" arguments which Thomas advances in support of Aristotle's statement (*In I Metaph.*, lect. 1). Pro memoria (cf. 1.6.2. and 1.7.): each thing naturally desires its own perfection (*perfectio*); each thing has an inclination to its proper operation (*operatio*); for each thing it is desirable to be united with its origin (the motif of the *circulatio*). In this reasoning the various elements of finality analyzed in this chapter thus far come together and culminate in the Neoplatonic desire towards the Principle.

The ultimate perfection of a rational nature is called happiness (*beatitudo*); and hence it is that it is naturally desired. Through happiness the desire comes to rest; it is the final end of human life.[115] Now, man is man through his intellect. Therefore the natural desire that is constitutive for man is directed towards knowing. Science is the perfection of man as man.

Science intends clarification of being. Science is the knowledge of the causes and truth of things. The ultimate end must be what is the most perfect in this operation. An operation is more perfect according as its object is the more perfect. The ultimate end of human desire is therefore knowledge of the most perfect intelligible, which is to say the first being, the maximally true and through itself necessary, namely God. Man desires by nature, as his ultimate end, to know the first cause.[116]

In this knowledge he attains his final perfection. To know God is man's happiness, for this is the operation of his highest faculty with respect to the most intelligible object, whereby man is united with his principle and the circle is closed. In man's desire to know, the circulation is perfect, the re-duction is adequate to the ontological de-duction. Because in man the gifts God gives to creatures come together (5.1.) and because man is the ultimate act of generation to which matter tends (8.2.1.), in the union of human nature with the first Principle the entire creation comes, through a circulation, to its conclusion.[117]

---

[115] *S. Th.* I, 62, 1: Nomine beatitudinis intelligitur ultima perfectio rationalis seu intellectualis naturae; et inde est quod naturaliter desideratur, quia unumquodque naturaliter desiderat suam ultimam perfectionem; *S. Th.* I, 26, 2; I–II, 2, 4; *S.c.G.* I, 100.

[116] *S.c.G.* III, 25.

[117] *S.c.G.* IV, 55: Homo etiam, quum sit creaturarum terminus, quasi omnes alias creaturas naturali generationis ordine praesupponens, convenienter primo rerum principion unitur, ut quadam circulatione perfectio rerum concludatur.

Man's natural desire does not come to rest when the first cause is known "in some way."[118] "If the human intellect knows ... of God only that he is (*an est*), then its perfection does not yet reach the first cause absolutely, and there still remains in it the natural desire to inquire into the cause" (1.9.).[119] Man's beatitude can only consist in the contemplation of God's essence, in the *visio Dei*, in the knowledge of the first cause, in which the answer to the question "what it is" is seen. Gradually, that reveals itself to the intellect to which its movement was oriented from the outset: "Every intellect desires naturally to see the divine substance" (*S.c.G.* III, 57).

In 5.3.4. ("The 'distress' of philosophy") the pressing question however arose: Can human life actually attain happiness, i.e., reach its highest perfection through union with the Origin? For man is not able to know immaterial substances essentially. The intelligible to which the human intellect can extend 'secundum naturalem viam' (*De verit.* 18, 2) are those forms that are abstracted by the agent intellect from the phantasms. The natural light of reason extends no further than the quiddities of sensible things. Philosophical consideration therefore does not arrive at the essence of the first cause. There appears to be an unbridgeable discrepancy between the terminus of the ascending way of "reason" and the vision of God.

That forces Thomas to distinguish a *twofold* end: "man's beatitude is twofold" (*S. Th.* I–II, 3, 6). Thomas even speaks of a "twofold ultimate perfection of the rational or intellectual nature" (I, 62, 1), a "twofold *ultimate* human good" (*De verit.* 14, 2).[120] The one end is proportionate to human nature, is connatural: man can attain it through his natural principles. For the acquisition of this good, the natural powers are sufficient. This end is the happiness of which the philosophers have spoken: the contemplation of the divine as it is possible for man, that is, an imperfect contemplation. Beyond that is yet another good, the perfect happiness, which consists in the vision of God. This end exceeds human nature; it goes beyond the proportion and the faculty of each created nature; it is connatural only to God Himself. Man cannot attain this end through his natural powers. These are inadequate to obtain it, yes, to think and desire it.[121]

---

[118] *Comp. Theol.*, 104: Non igitur naturale desiderium sciendi potest quietari in nobis, quousque primam causam cognoscamus, *non quocumque modo*, sed per ejus essentiam.

[119] *S. Th.* I–II, 3, 8.

[120] See further for the twofold end: *S. Th.* I, 23, 1; I–II, 5, 5; 62, 1; *De verit.* 27, 2; *De virtutibus in communi* q. un., a. 10.

[121] *De verit.* 14, 2: Ad ipsum obtinendum vires naturales non sufficiunt, nec ad cogitandum vel desiderandum; *S. Th.* I–II, 114, 2.

The vision of God's essence is quite literally *super*-natural: it is "the ultimate and supernatural end" (*S. Th.* I, 75, 7 ad 1); "the supernatural
good" (I – II, 110, 2); "the supernatural beatitude" (I – II, 62, 1). If man
is to attain happiness, his intellective power must be fortified by a new,
supernatural disposition.[122] Man can reach the supernatural end only
through a supernatural agent, God. This action of God is absolutely
gratuitous, is pure grace (*gratia*).[123] The vision becomes a connatural end
for man if through God's goodness, through God's gracious action, some
principles are added to his nature whereby man is elevated above his
nature.

> Since each thing is ordered towards its end by some operation, and since the
> means must be in some manner proportionate to the end, of necessity there
> must be in man certain perfections whereby he may be ordered to his super-
> natural end, and these perfections must surpass the power of man's natural
> principles. Now this cannot be, unless certain supernatural principles of
> operation be infused into man by God, over and above the natural prin-
> ciples.[124]

Now that Thomas's way of thought has been brought to a close and to
the end, a grave apory seems to arise. For in the first place, how can the
supernatural end of the vision of God be the terminus of man's natural
desire? For a natural inclination is directed to the good that is connatural
to a thing (cf. 8.1.2.): "the proportionate good moves the appetite; for
what is not proportionate is not naturally desired."[125] The vision of God,
however, exceeds the proportion of each created nature. In the second
place, every thing has by nature one end. "In the process of the rational
appetite, which is the will, the principle must be that which is naturally
desired. Now *this must be one* because nature tends only to one thing"
(*S. Th.* I – II, 1, 5). Yet Thomas speaks, as we have just seen, of a twofold
ultimate end of man. Are these statements mutually reconcilable?

This question touches the deepest "motive" of Thomas's way of
thought, for the end motivates the movement. If there exists duality in it,
it means that the twofold directedness is primordial. Does this not lead to

---

[122] *S.c.G.* III, 53; *S. Th.* I, 12, 5.
[123] *S. Th.* I, 62, 2: Nulla creatura rationalis potest habere motum voluntatis ordinatum
ad illam beatitudinem, nisi mota a supernaturali agente; et hoc dicimus auxilium gratiae.
[124] *De virtutibus in communi* q. un., a. 10: Et quia unumquodque ordinatur ad finem per
operationem aliquam; et ea quae sunt ad finem, oportet esse aliqualiter fini proportionata;
necessarium est esse aliquas hominis perfectiones quibus ordinetur ad finem supernaturalem, quae excedant facultatem principiorum naturalium hominis. Hoc autem esse non
posset, nisi supra principia naturalia aliqua supernaturalia operationum principia homini
infundantur a Deo.
[125] *De spe*, art. 1 ad 8.

human existence breaking up into two orders, a natural and a supernatural?

8.4.2. *'Duplex ordo'?*

The natural desire towards the vision of God is one of the most controversial themes of Thomas's thought.[126] The interpretation of Cajetan (1469–1534), *the* commentator on the *Summa Theologiae*, is consistently Aristotelian. Every natural desire is directed towards the good which suits the nature and which the nature is able to assimilate through its own power. Consequently, nature does not tend towards that which it is not able to attain. "The natural desire does not exceed the power of nature."[127] The vision of God goes beyond the proportion of human nature and is therefore not the terminus of the natural desire. Its final end is the knowledge of God, which can be obtained from the created effects. This is the happiness that is possible for man as man. Only when supernatural principles are added to nature does the vision of God become desirable and connatural to man. For this elevation there is in man himself no intrinsic capacity, but only a *potentia oboedientialis*, a notion we have encountered earlier, in the discussion of "Nature and miracle" (7.1.1.3.). Cajetan uses the term to express that the relation of nature to the gracious elevation is merely a "non-repugnance." In this (restricted) sense man is in potency to the supernatural end.[128] Such an explanation in fact denies that the human directedness towards the vision is natural.

Sylvester of Ferrara (1474–1528), *the* commentator on the *Summa contra Gentiles*, shares Cajetan's view that the natural desire cannot be directed towards what exceeds the range of nature's action. Yet their interpretations diverge. Sylvester acknowledges that Thomas relates the natural desire to the vision, but he denies the supernatural character of the object. The vision towards which the natural desire is directed is the knowledge of God as first cause, not the contemplation of His essence. This can only be the object of a supernatural desire.[129]

To both interpretations is common that any positive directedness of

---

[126] Cf. B. Meyer, *De eerste levensvraag in het intellectualisme van St. Thomas van Aquino en het integraal-realisme van Maurice Blondel* (Roermond and Maaseik, 1940); H. de Lubac, *Surnaturel, Études historiques* (Paris, 1946), pp. 429–80.

[127] *Comment. in S. Th. S. Thomae* I–II, 3, 8, n. 1: Naturale desiderium non excedit vim naturae, nec est ad supernaturalem operationem.

[128] *Ibid.*, I, 1, 1, n. 9: Vocatur autem potentia obedientialis, aptitudo rei ad hoc ut in ea fiat quidquid faciendum ordinaverit Deus. Et secundum talem potentiam, anima nostra dicitur in potentia ad beatitudinem pollicitam, et finem supernaturalem.

[129] *Comment. in S.c.G.* III, 51, n. 4.

nature to the gracious communion with God is absent. This conception became the prevalent one in the "schools."[130] Human-being is thought as a *natura pura*, directed towards a natural perfection. To this order of life, which is closed in itself, is added a supernatural end. "Supernatural happiness is not required by nature because for nature it is not necessary."[131] The order of nature and the order of grace are sharply separated from each other. They appear as two strata, the one superimposed upon the other, which interpenetrate as little as possible.[132]

Against such an extrinsic relation opposition has arisen from many sides during the course of the present century.[133] "The thesis of the *surnaturel plaqué* means a theological schizophrenia which in our culture has facilitated the fatal division between an ever more irrelevant Christianity and an ever more secularized civilization."[134] Instead of the idea that nature is merely the substratum of grace, emphasis is placed on their inner relatedness. Human-being is as such destined for the supernatural.

A first striking aspect of the reaction against "extrinsicism" is the appeal to Thomas Aquinas. E. SCHILLEBEECKX argues: "Thomas did not know the dualism of a natural and super-natural final end: he knew only one destination for man, namely, to come to God."[135] What is given expression in this citation is a general tendency. The adherents of the "newer" conception want to get back behind the commentators of the "schools" to what they consider the authentic view of the historical Thomas: to be truly human is only possible "by God's grace."

The pioneering study, published in 1946, was H. DE LUBAC's *Surnaturel, Études historiques*. He too arrives at the conclusion that for Thomas there is only one, supernatural destination of man: "because for St. Thomas 'beatitude' without any other determination is always supernatural and can only be supernatural."[136] To the essence of human nature belongs the being called by God to community with Him. The way in which DE LUBAC elaborated this thesis encountered, however, serious criticism.

[130] Cf. J.H. Walgrave, *Geloof en Theologie in de crisis* (Kasterlee, 1966), pp. 213ff.

[131] B. Meyer, "Natuurlijk en bovennatuurlijk geluk," in *Theologische opstellen ... aan G. van Noort* (Utrecht, 1944), p. 160.

[132] Cf. K. Rahner, *Schriften zur Theologie* IV, 5th ed. (Einsiedeln, Zurich and Cologne, 1967), p. 212.

[133] Cf. M.C. Smit, *De verhouding van Christendom en Historie* (Kampen, 1950), pp. 40ff.; B. Wentsel, *Natuur en Genade. Een introductie in en confrontatie met de jongste ontwikkelingen in de Rooms-Katholieke theologie inzake dit thema* (Kampen, 1970).

[134] J.H. Walgrave, "Tweeheid en eenheid van de christelijke levensvisie," in *Welvaart, welzijn, geluk* (Hilversum, 1960), p. 44.

[135] "Arabisch-Neoplatoonse achtergrond van Thomas' opvatting over de ontvankelijkheid van de mens voor de genade," *Bijdragen* 35 (1974): 307.

[136] *Surnaturel* (Paris, 1946), p. 255. Cf. H. de Lubac, "Duplex hominis beatitudo (St. Thomas, I–II, q. 62, a. 1)," *Recherches de Science religieuse* 35 (1948): 290–99.

Is the unconditional ordering of nature to supernatural union with God still compatible with the gratuitousness of grace? Is the supernatural not so absorbed by nature that fulfillment of the natural desire becomes a claim? But in that case it is impossible to maintain that the gift of God is grace, that is, is gratuitous.

For K. RAHNER[137] too the directedness towards the supernatural end is an inner, ontologically constitutive element of concrete man. In order that the character of grace as a free gift may be secured, however, even this directedness, this "supernatural existential," must be gratuitous. For this reason RAHNER considers it legitimate to continue to speak of a "pure nature," if only as a residual concept acquired by subtracting the "supernatural existential" from the concrete nature. Man's dynamic directedness towards the supernatural he would construe as a 'potentia oboedientialis' though not in the sense of a pure non-repugnance, as in Cajetan's interpretation, but more positively. Man, according to RAHNER, is not completely known in his essence until his nature is understood as "obediential potency" for grace. This means that human nature is directed to the supernatural destination, without, however, having any claim to the fulfillment of this potency.

In this summary, brief though it may be, of the modern interpretations of the "natural desire" there is—besides the appeal to Thomas—a second striking aspect to be noticed: the dialectics in the relation of nature and grace. On the one hand, against a dual order one insists on the one ultimate end of man. Yet on the other hand, in order to secure the gratuitousness of grace one still invokes the idea of a "pure nature."

Is there a coherence between the two aspects? Or in other words, does Thomas's view of man's final end contain a latent dualism? In order to answer this question, we must first examine how the fulfillment of man's natural desire is possible. After the circular movement from and to the Origin has been closed, we will then endeavor to come to a closing judgment (8.5.). In this rounding off, the different ways that have been followed in this study will come together, will "concur."

8.4.3. *"Two things concur towards the perfection of the lower nature"* (*'Duo concurrunt ad perfectionem naturae inferioris'*)

Man's natural desire is for Thomas a special case of the natural appetite found in all that is creaturely. "All naturally desire God" (8.3). Everything tends in its own manner to be alike unto God. The regress to the

---

[137] "Über das Verhältnis von Natur und Gnade," in *Schriften zur Theologie* I, pp. 323–45; "Natur und Gnade," in *ibid.* IV, pp. 209–36.

Origin is in the case of a rational nature a special one: it is "explicitly" strived after, it happens *per viam cognitionis*. Man's perfection is to be assimilated to God through knowledge.

With respect to the final end of the natural desire to know, Thomas makes three affirmations. First, the assimilation is of course not perfect in a knowledge of God whereby man knows of Him only that He is. Secondly, the vision of God is a supernatural happiness. This end exceeds the proportion of the created nature; it is not attainable through the natural powers. Finally, the natural desire cannot be in vain (cf. 8.2.2.). Therefore one has to say that it is *possible* for the intellect to see God's essence.[138] Consequently, for Thomas the question of true happiness comes to focus entirely on the conditions of the possibility of bridging the disproportion between end and means.

Because man's special reduction to the Origin is at issue, reflection on the possibility of the vision of God must proceed from the nature of man. Man is man through his intellect. As such he has a transcendental openness: "the human soul is in a sense all things." The convertibility of "being" and "true" (4.1.1.) involves man's having the capacity to come together with every being. The divine essence is therefore not in such a sense outside the faculty of the created intellect as to be absolutely foreign to it. For something is knowable, insofar as it is a being. Now what is maximally "being" is also the most "true": "there is the same disposition in being and in truth" (4.3.1.). Therefore God is the better known "according to nature." The divine essence is however outside the faculty of the created intellect as exceeding its power.[139] There is an incongruence between what is better known "according to nature" and what is better known "in reference to us." Our intellect relates to the most intelligible as does the eye of the bat to the light of the sun: the lucidity exceeds the capacity to see (cf. 5.5.).

From this distinction is to be understood Thomas's speaking of a twofold end, although with that the last word on the duality has not yet been said. From the viewpoint of acquisition, a difference must be made between the end that can be reached through the natural powers and the end that is given through grace. From the viewpoint of completion, there is just one beatitude. The ultimate perfection is the vision of God, the

---

[138] *S.c.G.* III, 51: Quum autem impossibile sit naturale desiderium esse inane ... necesse est dicere quod *possibile* est substantiam Dei videri per intellectum; *S.c.G.* III, 48. See also 5.3.4.

[139] *S.c.G.* III, 54: Divina enim substantia non sic est extra facultatem intellectus creati, quasi aliquid omnino extraneum ab ipso ... Nam divina substantia est primum intelligibile, et totius intellectualis cognitionis principium. Sed est extra facultatem intellectus creati, sicut excedens virtutem ejus.

knowledge of the essence of the highest intelligible whereby the desire of an intellectual nature is fully satisfied. All the rest is at the service of this end.

Thomas's distinction of two ultimate ends has turned out in the course of history to be fraught with far-reaching consequences: the integral unity of human existence threatens to be broken up by it. It would have been better if he had consistently maintained the terminology he uses in one place (*De virtutibus in communi*, q. un., a. 12): the good that is "the ultimate end" and the good that is "for the sake of the end." In this manner his real intention appears to much fuller advantage. There is one destination to which man is ordained. This ultimate end is in a certain way (*quodammodo*) supernatural, insofar, namely, as man cannot attain it through his own power (*S. Th.* III, 9, 2 ad 3).

If on account of man's transcendental openness the vision of God is not foreign to his nature,[140] then man is in potency to the contemplation of God.[141] Of what character is this potency?

Immediately we are inclined to think here of the so-called 'potentia oboedientialis'. For this notion was unfolded by Thomas in a discussion akin to the one carried on in this section: the question of the *possibility* of the miracle in relation to nature (cf. 7.1.1.3.). The miracle, namely, is an effect which is produced by a supernatural cause and which falls outside the order of created nature. In order to escape the consequence that the divine works of wonder would be violent, Thomas introduces into nature alongside the passive principle yet another capacity, the "obediential potency." This potency is inherent to the creaturely condition: every creature obeys God by receiving into itself what the Creator has ordained. It is a potency to an act that cannot be realized by a natural agent.

Is this potency now not the capacity in man for the vision of God? For man can attain this end only through a supernatural cause, God.[142] The commentators of the "schools" and modern interpreters like K. RAHNER have indeed viewed man's receptivity to grace as an "obediential potency." In this manner man's inner directedness towards his supernatural destination is strongly minimalized. For the "obediential potency" is a

---

[140] Cf. *S. Th.* II–II, 2, 3: Natura autem rationalis, inquantum cognoscit universalem boni et entis rationem, habet immediatum ordinem ad universale essendi principium.

[141] *S. Th.* III, 9, 2: Homo autem est in potentia ad scientiam beatorum, quae in visione Dei consistit.

[142] Cf. *ibid.* III, 11, 1: Est autem considerandum quod in humana anima, sicut in qualibet creatura, consideratur duplex potentia passiva: una quidem per comparationem ad agens naturale; alia vero per comparationem ad agens primum, qui potest quamlibet creaturam reducere in actum aliquem altiorem, in quem non reducitur per agens naturale; et haec consuevit vocari potentia obedientiae in creatura.

general creaturely potency to what God wishes to do in things in a miraculous way. Thomas's view of the natural desire in man involves however more than this minimum conception.[143]

As one of the characteristics of the miracle Thomas mentions that "in the receiving nature there is no natural order to the susception of it [the miracle], but only (*sed solum*) an obediential potency to God" (*In IV Sent.* 17, 1, 5, 1). But of the vision of God he affirms precisely that it is "according to man's nature."[144] This perfect happiness is the end of the (intellectual) nature (*naturae finis*).[145] Thomas understands the receptivity to gracious elevation to the vision of God not as a general 'potentia oboedientialis' but as a potency of *human* nature, which is to say as an *intrinsic* aptitude. "The capacity for grace is consequent upon the rational nature as such."[146]

Of importance for a more searching understanding of this natural directedness is what Thomas writes in *In Boeth. De trin.* 6, 4 ad 5: "For even though by nature (*naturaliter*) man is inclined to his ultimate end, he cannot reach it by nature (*naturaliter*) but only by grace." This dual use of "nature" is the key to the correct interpretation of Thomas's conception.

Nature is an intrinsic principle of motion. In the analysis of it we saw (7.1.1.2.) that Thomas divides this origin into an active principle and a passive principle. A thing has therefore by nature two dynamics: the one is determined by its own activity, the other is owing to the influence of a higher nature (*natura superior*). This concurrence in the perfection of a nature Thomas sets out in *S. Th.* II–II, 2, 3:

> Wherever one nature is subordinate to another, we find that two things concur towards the perfection of the lower nature, one of which is according to that nature's proper movement, while the other is on the basis of the movement of the higher nature.[147]

This 'concursus' Thomas elucidates with an example, which he takes, as usual, from the movement of the elements. Water has a proper movement towards its natural place, the center. But thanks to the influence of its higher nature, the moon, it also has a movement around the center by ebb and flood. In the hierarchically structured universe the natural order is

---

[143] Cf. E. Schillebeeckx, "Arabisch-Neoplatoonse achtergrond," pp. 303ff.

[144] *S. Th.* III, 9, 2 ad 3.

[145] *S. Th.* I, 62, 1.

[146] *De malo* 2, 12: Talis habilitas (ad gratiam) naturam rationalem consequitur in quantum huiusmodi.

[147] *S. Th.* II–II, 2, 3: In omnibus naturis ordinatis invenitur quod *ad perfectionem naturae* inferioris *duo concurrunt*: unum quidem quod est secundum proprium motum; aliud autem quod est secundum motum superioris naturae.

that each thing is perfected, which is to say is assimilated to God, from within and from the higher. Otherwise than in the egress of things, in the regress the lower is reduced to God by the higher (cf. 8.3.).

When Thomas now writes that man *naturaliter* inclines towards the ultimate end, he means to say that man by nature (as passive principle) tends towards the vision of God. When he subsequently affirms that man cannot *naturaliter* attain this end, then nature must be understood in the sense of active principle. The natural powers have no proportion to it. For his final fulfillment man needs the operation of a higher nature. "By nature" man has the aptitude for receiving it.[148]

8.4.4. *The elevation to supernatural being: "Grace"*

By the higher nature man is brought into proportion to his end. By God's grace the vision of God becomes a good that suits man's nature (in the active sense). This 'concursus' is worked out by Thomas in strict parallelism with natural finality. "It is necessary that by God some principles are added to man by which he may be so ordered to supernatural beatitude, as he is ordered to his connatural end by his natural principles."[149]

For the attainment of an end three things are required, as we saw in 8.1.2. First, a "nature" or form that is proportionate to the end; next, an inclination towards that end, called "natural appetite" or "love"; finally, the movement, the desire towards the good that is loved. Moreover, in the case of a rational nature, knowledge of the end is required for a voluntary movement. An end can really be intended only when it is known as end (8.2.2.). That man may be ordered actively to the supernatural end, he must be perfected in these four respects. "There is infused into man by God, to enable him to perform acts ordered to eternal life as their end: first, grace (*gratia*), by which the soul has a certain spiritual being (*spirituale esse*); and then, faith (*fides*), hope (*spes*), and charity (*caritas*)," the three so-called theological virtues.[150]

Gratia is the ontological perfecting of human nature with respect to the final end. Through the gift of grace man is elevated above his nature: "grace is ... a perfection that elevates the soul to a supernatural being" (*ad quoddam esse supernaturale*; *De verit.* 27, 3). Through grace not a new substance is infused, but to man's substantial form a supernatural form is

---

[148] *De virtutibus in communi* q. un., a. 10 ad 2: Habet homo a natura aptitudinem ad recipiendum.
[149] *S. Th.* I–II, 62, 1. Cf. *In III Sent.* 23, 1, 4, 3.
[150] *De virtutibus in communi* q. un., a. 10. Cf. *De verit.* 27, 2; *S. Th.* I–II, 62, 1.

added; grace is therefore an accidental perfection.[151] In virtue of it, the rational nature is disposed to unite itself with God. For this new form deifies, effects a deification. Man attains to participation in the divine nature; Thomas sees this idea confirmed by the words of II Peter 1:4: we are made "partakers of the divine nature." Grace is "participation in the divine nature" (*participatio divinae naturae*). Hence only God can be the efficient cause of it—*solus Deus deificat*—just as only fire can make something fiery.[152] Following Boethius (*De consolatione philosophiae* III, 10), Thomas accordingly calls the blessed "gods by participation."[153]

It is noteworthy that Thomas interprets the supernatural gift of grace as participation in God, while earlier the gift of being by creation was identified with participation (3.6.2.). The relation between these two participations, natural and supernatural, Thomas does not elaborate systematically. J. AUER says in explanation: "Thomas certainly does not wish with this 'participation in the divine nature' to develop a complicated system concerning the possibilities and limits of man's participation in the communicable divine attributes; otherwise, he definitely would have unfolded this term thoroughly in his grand theology."[154] But this conclusion cannot satisfy. It cannot satisfy, especially because in his elaboration of the theological virtues Aquinas consistently carries the supernatural participation through. We must therefore inquire expressly into the meaning of this twofold divine communication (see 8.5.4.).

Fides is the perfecting of the human intellect with respect to the final end.[155] For this can only be strived after if it is known. Through the knowledge of faith, man is enlightened concerning what surpasses his natural knowledge. This perspective determines the opening of the *Summa Theologiae* (I, 1, 1). It was necessary for man's salvation, so Thomas claims, that there should be a doctrine revealed by God, besides the

---

[151] *S.c.G.* III, 150: Finis in quem homo dirigitur per auxilium divinae gratiae est supra naturam humanam. Ergo oportet quod homini superaddatur aliqua *supernaturalis forma* et perfectio, per quam convenienter ordinetur in finem praedictum; *S. Th.* I–II, 110, 2 ad 2: Et quia gratia est supra naturam humanam, non potest esse quod sit substantia aut forma substantialis: sed est *forma accidentalis* ipsius animae.

[152] *S. Th.* I–II, 112, 1: Donum autem gratiae excedit omnem facultatem naturae creatae: cum nihil aliud sit quam quaedam participatio divinae naturae, quae excedit omnem aliam naturam. Et ideo impossibile est quod aliqua creatura gratiam causet. Sic enim necesse est quod solus Deus deificet, communicando consortium divinae naturae per quamdam similitudinis participationem, sicut impossibile est quod aliquid igniat nisi solus ignis; *S. Th.* I–II, 62, 1 (with the reference to II Peter 1).

[153] *S. Th.* I–II, 3, 1 ad 1. Cf. I, 108, 5.

[154] *Die Entwicklung der Gnadenlehre in der Hochscholastik* II (Freiburg, 1951), p. 238.

[155] *De virtutibus in communi* q. un., a. 10: Per fidem intellectus illuminetur de aliquibus supernaturalibus cognoscendis, quae se habent in isto ordine sicut principia naturaliter cognita in ordine connaturalium operationum; *De verit.* 14, 2.

philosophical disciplines. For man is directed to God as to an end that surpasses the grasp of his reason. Therefore by the Word of God is revealed
the truth that is indispensable for man to arrive at his destination. Where
the way of reason terminates, the way of faith opens the prospect of the
fulfillment of man's desire to know in the vision of God (cf. 5.3.4.).

Through the supernatural knowledge of faith, man participates in the
divine knowledge.[156] The infused light of faith is a "seal of the first
truth" (*sigillatio primae veritatis*). In 5.4.2. we saw that Thomas employs an
expression here which he likewise applies to the innate light of the intellect, whereby the first intelligibles are known to us. The natural light
of reason is "a participation in the divine light" (*S. Th.* I, 12, 11 ad 3).
As with the ontology (of nature and grace), we find in knowledge (of
reason and faith) a twofold participation.

Caritas and *spes* perfect the will with respect to the supernatural
good.[157] "All naturally desire God." Each creature loves God by nature
more than it loves itself. There is a natural love (*amor*) to God as the Origin
and End of things. Union with God as He is in Himself exceeds, however,
the natural inclination of the will. Through the gift of charity the will is
assimilated to this end, ordered to God as object of beatitude, and a
spiritual union is established.[158] This love is a participation in the divine
love.[159]

From love to God follows the desire for union with Him. Through hope
this movement of the will is made more perfect. Hope provides certainty
that the good to which the desire is directed, the beatific vision of God,
is attainable.[160] Through the theological virtues man is ordered to the
supernatural union with God, which begins in faith, strives for completion
in hope, and is borne by charity.

---

[156] *S. Th.* I–II, 110, 4: Per potentiam intellectivam homo participat cognitionem divinam per virtutem fidei.

[157] *De virtutibus in communi* q. un., a. 10: Per spem autem et caritatem acquirit voluntas
quamdam inclinationem in illud bonum supernaturale ad quod voluntas humana per
naturalem inclinationem non sufficienter ordinatur.

[158] *S. Th.* I, 62, 2; *S.c.G.* III, 151. On the distinction between 'amor' and 'caritas': *De
spe* q. un., a. 1 ad 9; *S. Th.* I–II, 109, 3 ad 1.

[159] *S. Th.* I–II, 110, 4: Secundum potentiam voluntatis (homo participat) amorem
divinum, per virtutem caritatis; *De caritate* q. un., a. 2 ad 15: Caritas non est virtus hominis
in quantum est homo, sed in quantum per participationem gratiae fit Deus et filius Dei.

[160] *S. Th.* I–II, 62, 3: Voluntas ordinatur ad illum finem et quantum ad motum inten-
tionis, in ipsum tendentem sicut in id quod est possibile consequi, quod pertinet ad spem;
S.c.G. III, 153. See also the special treatises which Thomas devoted to hope and to charity:
De spe and *De caritate*.

On the difference between 'spes' and 'desiderium': *De spe*, q. un., a. 1. When Thomas
affirms in some texts (see n. 121) that man is not capable by nature of desiring the 'visio',
this 'desiderium' must not be understood as the basic act of willing but as the 'intentio',
that is, the will that has the means to attain the end (cf. 8.2.2.).

The whole of God's work of grace is interpreted by Thomas in terms of the motif of circulation. The final end is proportionate to the first agent, since principle and end of the universe are identical.

> Therefore, just as the first action, whereby things come to being, namely creation, is by God alone . . . so likewise the conferring of grace, whereby the rational mind is immediately joined with the ultimate end, is by God alone.[161]

Just as the things are brought to being by a supernatural agent, not out of necessity but by His will, so likewise they are carried to their perfection by the grace of the supernatural cause. Just as God through creation makes things participate in being, so likewise through re-creation He makes the rational creature a partaker of the divine nature. Just as God effects natural being through creation, without any intermediate agent, yet nonetheless through the mediation of the natural form (7.4.4.), so likewise God effects supernatural being without any intermediate agent, yet nonetheless by means of a created form, grace.[162]

8.5. "Perfect": What has attained its end

In this study we have investigated Thomas Aquinas's way of thought and endeavored to fathom its motives. The intelligibility of being which science seeks is determined by a twofold origination, the ways of nature and creature. Now that the way of thought has come to its end, the hodology can be rounded off.

The "ways" of the human desire to know, of nature and of creature, are in each case a circulation (8.5.1.). There is in the motif of the circle an ideal of perfection (8.5.2.). The ways concur in the dynamics towards perfection. In this coming to be perfect is to be sought the ultimate ratio of Thomas's way of thought: the Christian life is the super-natural perfecting of the natural order. "Grace perfects nature" (8.5.4.).

In the background of the process of perfection there is still another circulation, that in God Himself (8.5.3.). It is given little attention in interpretations of Thomas, although Aquinas himself says that the coming forth of the three divine Persons is the 'ratio' of every subsequent process.

---

[161] *De verit.* 27, 3: Et ideo, sicut prima actio, per quam res in esse exeunt, scilicet creatio, est a solo Deo . . . ; ita gratiae collatio, per quam mens rationalis immediate ultimo fini coniungitur, a solo Deo est.

[162] *Ibid.* 27, 1 ad 3: Esse naturale per creationem Deus facit in nobis nulla causa agente mediante, sed tamen mediante aliqua causa formali: forma enim naturalis principium est esse naturalis. Et similiter esse spirituale gratuitum Deus facit in nobis nullo agente mediante, sed tamen mediante aliqua forma creata, quae est gratia; *In II Sent.* 26, 1, 1 ad 4.

His reflection on this divine circulation can open a new perspective for interpreting the circulation of the creature.

8.5.1. *Threefold circulation*

From the viewpoint of the 'finis', it appears that the three ways we followed are governed by the motif of circulation. To show the continuity of their ends, we shall first recapitulate the three circular movements.

(1) The first circulation is the way of nature, which is explicated philosophically with Aristotelian concepts. It features the following characteristics.

The intention of nature is directed to the good of the *species*. There is an eternal return of the same, not numerically but qua specific form. End is the *essentia* or *natura*. Connected with this finality are a certain order of questioning, directed to the "what" question (*quid est*); and a certain way of knowing, namely, definitional thinking.

The movement towards nature is the *generatio*, the first, etymological meaning of "nature." It is a transition from potency to act, for "out of nothing comes nothing." But ontologically prior to potency is act. A thing is brought forth through what is synonymous. "Man generates man"— Aristotle's dictum—is characteristic for the identity of origin and end on the way of nature.

There is in the natural thing a non-identity of 'subjectum' and 'essentia'. The particular subject is not the specific nature but has it. This non-identity arises from the composition of matter and form. Because the form is taken up in matter, it is contracted and particularized.

Matter and form are both "nature." In this manner the different traditions of ancient thought are synthesized. The form is however the nature "more" than matter is. For each thing is more what it is when it is in act than when it is in potency. The form is something divine in things. Therefore there is a "natural desire" of matter towards the form.

(2) The second circular movement is the way of the creature. Being created is being from and to God. This 'via' features the following characteristics.

It is a "supernatural" origin, an origin called by Thomas *emanatio*, or also indicated with the Judaeo-Christian idea of *creatio ex nihilo*. This coming forth he interprets metaphysically in terms of the Neoplatonic notion of "participation."

All the creaturely is marked by the distinction of 'essentia' and 'esse'. No creature whatsoever *is* its being; the 'esse' is "outside the essence." The two components are related to each other as potency and act. Because "being" is taken up in the essence, it is contracted and specified.

Since creation is a "higher" origin, there is a 'concursus' of the ways of nature and creature. Accordingly, for Thomas the structure of things has become more complex, namely threefold: 'subjectum—essentia—esse'. That which is is constituted through three principles, which complete each other through inherence. First, there is the order of the matter to the form; next, that of the composite thing itself to the 'esse', which is the "act of acts." In this "twofold order" lies a first crux of the 'concursus'. It came to light in what we called the problem of the "other" and in the metaphysical reduction of the different components.

The reverse side of the participation is the natural desire in things towards the Origin. Everything by nature desires God. For He is absolutely identical; as pure Act He is being, true, and good essentially. All the creaturely turns itself by nature back towards the Source whence it has originated.

The return to God is realized in an imperfect manner in the first circulation. Nature tends towards the likeness to God through its causal activity, which is directed towards the perpetuation of the species. But the assimilation to God in this circulation of nature, which is reducible to the celestial movement, remains deficient. Things tend in it only "implicitly" towards God. Only the rational nature, man, is able to attain to God Himself through knowledge. In man alone, who because of his material and spiritual nature is the "middle" of the universe, is the circular movement perfect. With that, the connection is made with the third circulation.

(3) The ontological dynamics proper to man is the desire to know, the natural desire to know the cause, truth, and necessity of things. The final end of man, his beatitude, consists in knowing the essence of the highest intelligible, in the vision of God. Through this knowledge the circular movement of the creature, the return to the Origin, is closed. In this completion becomes evident too the "anthropocentric" turn of Thomas's thought.

8.5.2. *Circulation and perfection*

The circulation is the first and most perfect of all movements because it connects the end with the beginning (cf. 6.5.3.). Principle and end are identical. Contained in the motif of circulation is a model of perfection, an ideal of completeness. The definition of "perfect" in Aristotle's *Physica* is: "that which has nothing outside itself" (*cuius nihil est extra ipsum*).[163] "Perfect" has the character of "complete": nothing can be added to it

---

[163] *Phys.* III, c. 6, 207 a 9 (lect. 11, 385).

(*perfectum dicitur cui non potest fieri additio*). This perfection is the mark of the circular movement.[164] Because the ways of nature, creature, and man are each circular, all three also concur in being processes of perfection.

The term 'per-fectum' expresses, as Thomas himself signalizes, the end of a movement: "That which has not been made (*factum*) cannot properly be called perfect" (*S. Th.* I, 4, 1 ad 1). So movement was defined (6.5.1.) as "the imperfect act" of an "imperfect subject": what is moved is, precisely because it is mobile, not yet complete but tending towards a perfection. Perfect is what attains to its end (*perfectum est quod attingit ad finem ejus*);[165] the perfect is the ultimate. The *finis* of each thing is its perfection; then its potency has been brought to act. Insofar as something is in act, it is good. There is an identity of "perfect" with "end"—"good"— "act."[166] The conditions of the perfect are that it is determinate and absolute, not dependent on something else; it is self-sufficient (*per se sufficiens*).[167] The model of this independence is the substance.[168]

The perfect is by nature prior to the imperfect, since act has priority over potency (cf. 6.7.).[169] All that is imperfect takes its origin from what is perfect (*omne imperfectum trahit originem a perfecto*).[170] The perfect is *principium*; from it (the so-called "ex"-structure) is derived all else. Insofar as something is perfect, it is active, operative as a cause.[171]

Desire is the basic structure of perfectionism. "All desire their own perfection" (*S. Th.* I, 5, 1). There is a natural desire of the imperfect towards the perfect. "A thing is perfect insofar as it attains to its principle" (*S. Th.* I, 12, 1). End is the reduction to the origin. In the natural appetite for perfection, that from which a thing has originated becomes the end. "The end corresponds with the principle" (8.1.3.).

The way of *nature* proceeds from the imperfect to the perfect. The end of generation is the form, the specific nature. What has come to its end

---

[164] *In De caelo*, lect. 4, 43. Cf. *In V Metaph.*, lect. 8, 871: Perfectum est enim et totum, cui nihil deest: quod quidem contingit lineae circulari. Non enim potest sibi fieri additio, sicut fit lineae rectae.

[165] *De perfectione vitae spiritualis*, c. 1; *In De div. nomin.* c. 1, lect. 2, 47; *In X Metaph.*, lect. 5, 2028.

[166] *S. Th.* I, 5, 1 (cf. section 8.1., above); 4, 1 ad 1: In his quae fiunt, tunc dicitur aliquid perfectum cum de potentia educitur in actum; *S.c.G.* III, 16: Finis igitur uniuscuiusque rei est ejus perfectio. Perfectio autem cujuslibet rei est bonum ipsius.

[167] *In V Metaph.*, lect. 19, 1044; *In I Ethic.*, lect. 9, 112.

[168] Cf. *In IV Metaph.*, lect. 1, 543.

[169] *In I De caelo*, lect. 4, 41; 44.

[170] *In I Sent.*, prol. Cf. *In I De caelo*, lect. 21, 216: Ab eo quod est perfectissimum, fit derivatio ad alia quae sunt minus perfecta.

[171] *In II Sent.* 34, 1, 3: Nihil agit nisi secundum quod est in actu; nihil autem est in actu nisi secundum quod formam vel perfectionem aliquam habet; unde oportet quod omne quod agit, agat inquantum perfectum est; *In De div. nomin.* c. 3, lect. un., 227.

is in act and perfect. Something is therefore perfect when it has its form, when it possesses its nature completely.[172] To the species nothing can be added; the specific forms are "like numbers" (2.3.). Through its essential principles, the thing is perfected in itself. The first perfection is "the form of the whole, which results from the integrity of its parts" (*S. Th.* I, 73, 1).

"By way of generation and time" the potential and the imperfect come first. Different, though, is "the order of perfection or of the intention of nature." By nature the perfect is prior to the imperfect.[173] "Nature begins from perfect things."[174]

It is a sign of the perfection of the thing that it is active, that it communicates its good to other beings. The second perfection is the operation or something that is effected by it (8.2.3.). The intention of nature is directed to the perfection of the species, to its permanence. Through the circulation of nature, the imperfection of the particular, its contingency and lack of intelligibility, is overcome.[175]

The way of the *creature* concurs with the way of nature in the ideal of perfection. This 'concursus' results from the hodo-logy, which consists in the ontology of act and potency (6.7.). For something is perfect insofar as it is in act.

Terminus of the creation is 'esse'. This Thomas understands as "the actuality of all acts." In the same breath he can add: "and for this reason it is the perfection of all perfections" (*De pot.* 7, 2 ad 9). For "being" is related to every perfection as its perfecting act.[176]

HE WHO IS is according to Thomas's judgment the most proper name of God. One of the arguments he advances for this, borrowed from Jerome, is: the words of Exodus reveal the perfection of the divine being. Perfect is, namely, "what has nothing outside itself." Of human being it cannot be said that it has nothing outside itself. It is in part already past, in part still future. It is otherwise, however, with the divine being: God

---

[172] *In V Metaph.*, lect. 21, 1087: Forma est finis in generatione. Perfectum enim dicitur quod habet finem . . . Unde patet, quod perfectum est quod habet formam; *In I Polit.*, c. 1 b; *In VII Phys.*, lect. 6, 920: Cum autem aliquid habet complete suam naturam, tunc dicitur esse perfectum.

[173] *S. Th.* I, 85, 3 ad 1.

[174] *De verit.* 18, 2: Natura a perfectis principium sumit; *De pot.* 3, 10; *S. Th.* II–II, 1, 7 ad 3: Natura a perfectis sumit exordium: quia imperfecta non ducuntur ad perfectionem nisi per aliqua perfecta praeexistentia.

[175] *De anima* q. un., a. 18; *In I De caelo*, lect. 19, 197: Singula autem individua rerum naturalium quae sunt hic, sunt imperfecta; quia nullum eorum comprehendit in se totum quod pertinet ad suam speciem; *S. Th.* I, 79, 9 ad 3: Contingentia . . . habent imperfectum esse et veritatem; *De subst. separ.* c. 12, 111.

[176] Cf. *S. Th.* I, 4, 1 ad 3: Ipsum esse est perfectissimum omnium; comparatur enim ad omnia ut actus.

is eternally present and has therefore His entire being perfectly.[177] For
God, the perfection of identity obtains completely.

As subsistent Being itself God contains within Himself "the whole perfection of being." For according to the mode of their being, the things are
perfect. To God belongs the entire virtue, or power, of being (*tota virtus
essendi*). Therefore He is universally perfect. He is per-fect not because He
has come to the completed act but because He is complete actuality.[178]

As such God is "infinite." This connection of infinity with perfection
appears to involve a turnabout with respect to ancient thought. For according to the Greeks, constitutive for perfection is the 'finis', the determination, the de-finition. The infinite is imperfect since indeterminate.
Nullum igitur infinitum et interminatum est perfectum (*In III Phys.*, lect. 11,
385). For Thomas there lies however in the 'esse' a bridge from this model
of perfection of the definition to infinity as perfection. Greek thought
about perfection must be understood from the intrinsic principles of
matter and form. The infinite potentiality of matter is determined
through the form. This determination is a perfecting, regarded on the part
of matter. At the same time, however, the form is determined by the
matter to the form of this one particular thing. That contraction of the
universality of the form is something imperfect. Now, Thomas's analysis
of that which is recognizes as a component, besides matter and form, the
'esse', which is the most formal of all things (7.4.4.). Being is the most
universal, it has nothing outside itself by which it can be confined; it is
the most perfect, is in itself unlimited and infinite (*S.c.G.* I, 43). The
divine being is not received in something other, whereby it is contracted.
God is consequently infinite and perfect.[179]

The most perfect being (*perfectissimum ens, De pot.* 3, 5) is the origin of
the other beings. This coming forth is called "creation." Creation acquires, from the perspective of perfection, almost the character of an ontological "fall" (cf. 3.6.2.: "Creation and participation"). It is a "descent"
from unity to *diversity*;[180] from the 'maximum' to a hierarchical more or
less; from the fullness of being (the being 'per essentia') to that which
participates; from the infinite to the *finite*, that is contracted to a particular
mode of being; from the simple to the *composed*; from the perfect to the

---

[177] *In I Sent.* 8, 1, 1.
[178] *S.c.G.* I, 28; *S.Th.* I, 4, 2.
[179] See *S.Th.* I, 7, 1: Illud autem, quod est maxime formale omnium, est ipsum esse
... Cum igitur esse divinum non sit esse receptum in aliquo ... manifestum est quod
ipse Deus est infinitus et perfectus.
  Cf. for the opposition between 'perfectum' and 'infinitum', which is excluded with
respect to God: *In De div. nomin.* c. 13, lect. 1, 964.
[180] *S.c.G.* IV, 1 (cf. section 4.4.1., above).

imperfect. The creatures have an imperfect being, because they only participate in being.[181]

From this follows the natural desire towards the Perfect. Everything tends by nature to the highest Good, God, as ultimate end. The ultimate perfection of creatures is the return to their principle. Because of this regress Thomas understands the way of the creature not, as is currently prevalent, as a straight line, but as a circulation (1.7.2.).

Only in *man* is this circulation realized perfectly. His highest operation, his second perfection, is to know. The intellect is, according to Thomas, more elevated than the will. For knowledge perfects the knower in himself. And it is simply more perfect to have the nobility of another thing in oneself than, as in willing, to be directed towards a noble thing outside oneself (4.1.1.). Among all perfections the greatest is to be intelligent, for a thing is thereby "in a certain sense all things," is capable of assimilating all perfections.[182] Science is the perfection of man as man.

The ultimate perfection of man is to be assimilated to God through knowledge. His beatitude consists in the knowledge of the essence of the "most perfect intelligible."[183] Then there is nothing more to inquire or to desire. Then man is united with his Origin.

Yet here we come upon another crux in the 'concursus', upon another 'duplex ordo' (8.4.2.). The perfect knowledge of God, the vision of God, is a *super*-natural perfection for man. This end is only connatural to God Himself. So that man may be proportionate to the vision of God, he must be elevated above his nature. This order is connected with still another circulation, the one in the higher nature. It is therefore necessary to take this circulation into consideration first.

8.5.3. *The circulation in the divine*

Thomas speaks of yet a fourth circulation, namely, in God. In God Himself there is a circular movement, the eternal process of the Persons. This was not noted earlier because it is no longer understandable philosophically. That God is triune, that the one divine being unfolds itself in a plurality of Persons, cannot be grasped by human reason but

---

[181] *S.c.G.* I, 28: ... participant esse per quendam particularem modum et imperfectissimum. Cf. I, 32: Omne quod participatur determinatur ad modum participantis, et sic partialiter habetur, et non secundum omnem perfectionis modum.

[182] *S.c.G.* I, 44: Inter perfectiones autem rerum potissima est, quod aliquid sit intellectivum; nam per hoc ipsum est "quodammodo omnia," habens in se omnium perfectionem.

[183] *De verit.* 18, 1; *S.c.G.* III, 25.

is knowable only through Christian faith.[184] Just this process, however, this divine circulation is, as we shall see, the basis of the other movements.

The God of Christian faith is active and productive.[185] The activity in question Thomas endeavors to clarify, like Augustine, through an analogy with the two immanent operations that are found in the spiritual human nature, namely, intellection and volition. From both of these, something comes forth within the divine.[186]

The process of "understanding" has not been completed until the intellect conceives in itself that which is understood, a conception which is called "inner word." Between the Word conceived by God and the word conceived by man, however, substantial differences do exist. This word is in God only one, for not by many acts but by one act does He understand everything. Moreover, the word conceived by God is identical with His essence, since in God to be and to understand are the same. As (co-essential) "Word" the Son proceeds, who is distinguished from the Father in being "from another." The relationships of Paternity and Filiation, which are real in the divine, cannot be accidents but are subsistent. These subsisting relationships constitute the Persons. The process of "volition" is completed in the love to something. This love is in God one, for by loving His goodness He loves all else. Moreover, God's love is identical with His essence, since in God to will and to be are the same. As "Love" binding Father and Son together proceeds the Spirit.

The order of understanding and willing is such that both acts are completed in a circle (8.1.1.). But in God this is otherwise than in man. Man's intellectual knowledge is derived from the external things; his volition tends towards an external end. In God this circle is closed within Himself (*in Deo iste circulus clauditur in se ipso*).[187]

Father, Son, and Spirit have the same divine nature. Yet distinct properties are ascribed to each of the Persons. This is not so because they are proper to one Person—they are, rather, common to the entire Trinity—but because they have a greater resemblance to what is proper to the one Person than they have to what is proper to another. These properties are attributed in virtue of "appropriation."[188]

Already in the analysis of truth (at the end of chapter 4), we saw that truth is ascribed to the second Person. Through the circulation in the

---

[184] Cf. *De pot.* 9, 5: Pluralitas personarum in divinis est de his quae fidei subiacent, et naturali ratione humana nec investigari nec sufficienter intelligi potest.

[185] *In De div. nomin.* c. 1, lect. 2, 57: Et dicit quod invenimus Deum laudari sicut Trinitatem ad manifestandum supersubstantialem fecunditatem trium personarum.

[186] See besides *S. Th.* I, q. 27ff. especially also *De pot.* 9, 5 and 9, 9.

[187] *De pot.* 9, 9. Cf. *S.c.G.* IV, 26.

[188] *De verit.* 7, 3: Appropriare nihil est aliud, quam commune trahere ad proprium.

divine the order of the transcendentals is now more fully manifested in the Persons. "Being" (or "one") belongs by appropriation to the Father. "True" belongs to the Son, since it resembles what is proper to the Son: for this proceeds as the "Word," which refers to the process of the intellect. "Good" belongs to the Spirit, for this proceeds as Love; and the object of love is the good.[189]

The good is the terminus of the immanent operation. For something is first understood as true; it is subsequently desired as good. From here begins the operation towards the outside. Now, goodness is appropriated to the Spirit. From this it can be accepted that the process of the divine Persons extends no further. With the coming forth of the Spirit, the divine circulation is closed. The circle is the perfect figure, because nothing can be added to it. What follows in the divine works is accordingly no part of the inner divine life, is outside of the divine nature: the coming forth of the creaturely.[190]

The eternal coming forth of the Persons is the foundation of every subsequent process. This idea Thomas expresses in the prologue to the first book of his commentary on the *Sententiae*. "Just as the branch is derived from the stream, so also is the temporal process of the creatures derived from the eternal process of the Persons. What is first, namely, is always the cause of what is later, as the Philosopher (in *Metaph.* II) says. Therefore the first process is the cause and reason of every subsequent process."[191] The order of origin within the divine is the archetype of the work of creation. "The Person proceeding in God proceeds as the principle of the production of creatures."[192]

If the process in God is the foundation of all other movements and this process is only knowable through Christian faith, then this knowledge will also be the basis for understanding the creaturely. "The Trinity is the heart of Christianity."[193] For many present-day Christians this article of faith has become problematical; for the primitive Christian church the Trinity was the core of the Christian confession. That the God of Christian faith is a triune God, Father, Son and Holy Spirit, is for writers such

---

[189] Cf. *De verit.* 1, 4 sed contra (5); 1, 1 sed contra (5); 7, 3.

[190] *De pot.* 9, 9 ad 14: Unde ex hoc ipso quod bonitas Spiritui sancto appropriatur, convenienter accipi potest quod processio divinarum personarum ultra non porrigitur. Sed quod sequitur, est processio creaturae, quae est extra naturam divinam; *ibid.*, ad 15.

[191] *In I Sent.*, prol.: Sicut trames a fluvio derivatur, ita processus temporalis creaturarum ab aeterno processu personarum ... Semper enim id quod est primum est causa eorum quae sunt post, secundum Philosophum; unde primus processus est causa et ratio omnis sequentis processionis.

[192] *S. Th.* I, 33, 3 ad 1. Cf. *In I Sent.*, dist. 2, divisio textus: Exitus enim Personarum in unitate essentiae, est causa exitus creaturarum in essentiae diversitate.

[193] H. Bavinck, *Gereformeerde Dogmatiek* II, 4th ed. (Kampen, 1928), p. 251.

as Augustine, Bonaventure, and Eckhart such a living reality that their thought about the structure of the creation and the meaning of human existence has been profoundly influenced by it.

Regarding Thomas's philosophy, however, a trinitarian interpretation is highly unusual. That is understandable, since his treatise on the triune God remained a somewhat isolated exposition. For that reason his idea of God is rather abstract and impersonal. Yet in the background of Thomas's thought, as with all medieval writers, the Trinity does play a role. An important indication is that he understands the divine process as a circulation—how important this motif is in Thomas's work we have seen in the preceding section and throughout our study—and that he considers this circular movement the basis of the other movements. Thus a trinitarian interpretation of Thomas's thought about that which is finds support in his work. Such an interpretation can also, I believe, be made fruitful for further thought about (the problematics of) his philosophy. That is consistent with what we established earlier, in the "middle" of our investigation (4.5.2.). For there we saw that the double metaphysical reduction (of 'esse' and 'essentia'), with which different forms of participation are connected, becomes meaningful when viewed in terms of the work of the triune God.

(1) The knowledge of the divine Persons, so Thomas judges, is necessary for a correct view of the creation of things.[194] For thereby we understand that God did not produce things by necessity or out of need. We can extend this thought still further. Thereby light is also cast upon the threefold causal relation of God to the creatural as efficient cause, exemplary cause, and final cause. He is these in virtue of one and the same, His being act.[195] Every agent effects something that is like itself; therefore the principle of the action can be considered from the effect. To create is to cause the being of things. To create therefore belongs to God according to His 'esse', which is identical to His 'essentia'. This is common to the three Persons. Hence to create is not proper to any one Person. Yet the divine Persons, according to the nature of their procession, have a causality in relation to the creation of things. God the Father made the creature through His Word, which is His Son; and through His Love, which is the Holy Spirit. In that sense the processions of the Persons are the foundation for the coming forth of the creature.[196] In virtue of appropriation the efficient cause is related to the Father; the exemplary cause to the Son, the Truth; and the final cause, whereby the things are brought

---

[194] *S. Th.* I, 32, 1 ad 3.
[195] *De pot.* 7, 1 ad 3.
[196] *S. Th.* I, 45, 6.

to their proper end, to the Holy Spirit, the Goodness.[197]

(2) Every effect represents its cause in some way. In all the creaturely is something that must be reduced to the divine Persons as cause, is a trace of the Trinity (*vestigium Trinitatis*).[198] In the created is found 'principium', 'medium', and 'finis'. According to this triad the Persons are represented.[199] "Principle" of the thing is the subsistence in its own being, which is reducible to the emanation from the Father. "Middle" is the specific form, which is reducible to the art of the Son. "End" is the order to some other thing, which is reducible to the love of the Spirit.[200]

With this triad corresponds the threefold structure of that which is: 'subjectum—essentia—esse'. Different from each other (*aliud*) in the creatures are "what subsists in its own nature," "essence," and "being." This complex structure is the counterpart of the analysis whereby Thomas seeks to understand reality as nature ('essentia') and creature ('esse'). This 'duplex ordo' formed a crux in his reduction to the Origin. Precisely at this point a more comprehensive notion of the creaturely can be developed through a trinitarian interpretation. The Tri-une causality makes it possible to see in the different components of being the unity of what is caused.

There is in the creature the trinity of being subsistent (principle), being what (middle), and being act (end). They agree in the 'esse', which is a being from, through, and to God and constitutes the way of the creature (the second circulation). The "subject" is dependent subsistence, the "essence" is the expression of the formal diversity established by the divine art, and "being" (as act) is reference to the Final End. There is unity in the relation to the Origin.

(3) Regarding the Scholastic doctrine of the relation J. DE VRIES has correctly remarked that it "is still very much in need of further elaboration."[201] It is therefore of great philosophical importance that Thomas in his exposition of the Trinity advances a new elaboration of the concept of relation. We referred to it already in 4.3.3. in the discussion of the "relationlessness" of God, Thomas's view that in God there is no real relation to the creature.

In the divine circulation are original relations that are subsistent: "In God relation and essence do not differ in being but are one and the same"

---

[197] See for this "appropriation": *S. Th.* I, 45, 6 ad 2; I, 39, 8. Cf. *De pot.* 10, 2 ad 19: Filius est sufficiens ratio processionis temporalis creaturae ut verbum et exemplar; sed oportet quod Spiritus Sanctus sit ratio processionis creaturae ut amor.

[198] *S. Th.* I, 45, 7.

[199] *In I Sent.* 3, 2, 2.

[200] Cf. *S. Th.* I, 45, 7; 93, 6; *In I Sent.* 3, 2, 2; *De verit.* 1, 4 sed contra (5); *De pot.* 9, 9.

[201] *Grundbegriffe der Scholastik*, s. v. "Beziehung," p. 38.

(*in Deo non est aliud esse relationis et esse essentiae sed unum et idem*; *S. Th.* I, 28, 2). Being and relation ("being-to-something-other") belong "originally" together. This idea has remained outside of Thomas's metaphysics of creation. Yet it is this model of relation that can be made fruitful for a renewed reflection on creaturely being, since it can provide the instigation for a different ontology. The relation to God is not something added, being created is not an accidental relation, as Thomas claimed (6.6.). "In Him we live and move and have our being," according to Paul's words at Athens (Acts 17:28). For the creature, to be is to be in relation. From this idea it becomes possible to view also the circular movement of egress and regress as a concrete history of salvation (see the closing section).

(4) In man—in the triad 'anima – intellectus – voluntas'—the Trinity is represented in a special way, namely, according to the same kind of operation (*secundum eamdem rationem operationis*) (*De pot.* 9, 9). For in him are found the processes of intellection and volition; therefore man, who is a person, is the image of the Trinity (*imago Trinitatis*).[202] This idea breaks through the ancient cosmocentrism in the most radical manner. Only man is capable, in his acts of understanding and willing, to close the way of the creature.

With this (third) circulation is expressed that only one motive moves man as 'viator'. Man is as image of God destined to one end, namely, the beatific communion with God.[203] This one motive must, to a greater extent than is customary in Reformational circles, be given prominence in assessing Thomas's thought. This driving force should be aknowledged before Thomas's elaboration of man's being-unto-God, a second crux in his way of thought, is considered critically.

8.5.4. *"Grace perfects nature"*

Communion with God Thomas qualifies as man's super-natural end. To attain this end man needs "grace". The 'duplex ordo' of the "natural" and "supernatural" has left deep marks in tradition. It has profoundly influenced thought about the meaning of the Christian existence and the salvation of man. To this very day the fundamental point of controversy between Rome and the Reformation is often considered to be their different views of the relation of nature and grace.[204]

---

[202] *S. Th.* I, 45, 7; I, 93, 6; *De pot.* 9, 9; 10, 1 ad 5.

[203] Cf. *S. Th.* III, 9, 2: Est enim creatura rationalis capax illius beatae cognitionis, inquantum est ad imaginem Dei.

[204] Cf. G. E. Meuleman, "Natuur en genade", in *Protestantse verkenningen na Vaticanum II* (The Hague, 1967), pp. 65–88; B. Wentsel, *Natuur en genade* (Kampen, 1970), p. 3.

That to be truly human is only possible by God's grace is a primal Christian idea. What is crucial, however, is that "grace" is understood by Thomas as the ontological perfecting of nature to a super-natural being. Between this coming to be perfect and the "supernaturalism" there is a direct coherence. Both have a clearly philosophical background: Thomas's way of thought, in which the originations of nature and creature are brought together in a hierarchy. To accomplish this concurrence it is necessary to overcome the closedness and autonomy of the Aristotelian concept of 'physis'. Nature must be opened up for a reality which is "supernatural". The term 'supernaturalis', of Neoplatonic provenance, Thomas uses to signify a divine operation that surpasses the operation of nature, namely, creation and miracle.[205] In the desire for the perfecting final end, the degree of assimilation to God determines the mutual relations of the circular movements. In this 'concursus' towards the perfect there arises, as we shall see, an inner necessity to understand also the divine grace to man as supernatural.

By nature man turns himself back towards God, his Origin. The natural desire in man is a desire to know, for science is the perfection proper to him. The fulfillment of this desire in the vision of God is however no longer natural. To render this understandable Thomas appeals to a general cosmological thesis: "Two things concur towards the perfection of the lower nature" (8.4.3.). In the perfecting of a nature there go together its own activity and the influence of a higher nature, which fulfills the passive potencies. Yet this thesis can not satisfy. For man is distinguished from the other creatures precisely by his being ordered to an end that exceeds his natural faculties.[206]

B. MEYER speaks of the "tragedy of human thought." "For where the circle which things pass through closes, there ends the power of reason to penetrate independently into those things worthy of knowing for which man by nature has the highest interest."[207] The "tragedy" is the incapacity of the rational nature to realize its perfection—"perfect is what has nothing outside itself." It is to be asked however if the human drama is not much more radical than that.

It is here that a trinitarian interpretation can lead to a deeper penetration. Man is the image of the Trinity: in him are found the processes of

---

[205] Cf. J. Auer, "Inwieweit ist im 13. Jahrhundert der Wandel des Begriffes 'supernaturalis' bedingt durch den Wandel des Naturbegriffes?" in *La Filosofia della natura* (Milan, 1966), pp. 331–49.

[206] *S.c.G.* III, 147: Hoc autem inferioribus creaturis non competit, ut scilicet ad finem pervenire possint qui eorum facultatem naturalem excedat; *S. Th.* I–II, 109, 5 ad 3; *In IV Sent.* 43, 1, 1, 3.

[207] "Het participatiebegrip in de Thomistische circulatieleer", p. 67.

intellection and volition. Yet can then the triad 'anima—intellectus—voluntas' in man be integrated in terms of just *one* of the faculties of the soul, the intellect?[208] The consequence of it is an intellectualistic narrowing of man's integral being. The perfection of the Christian life is that man is one with God; that happens, so Thomas acknowledges, in charity. "Et ideo *secundum caritatem* specialiter attenditur perfectio vitae christianae" (*S. Th.* II–II, 184, 1). Through this relational reality par excellence, charity, the circular movement of egress and regress comes to stand in a concrete economy of salvation. For instead of the natural *conversio* towards God is not rather the *aversio* characteristic for man?

Nature as creature is taken up in the history of salvation. The redemptive-historical concept of nature, which goes back to Augustine,[209] knows two "states" of man, integral and fallen. "We may speak of man in two ways: first, in the state of integral nature (*naturae integrae*); secondly, in the state of corrupted nature (*naturae corruptae*)."[210] Is not this corruption, this fall the radical obstacle to human happiness?

The primary effect of the original sin Thomas sees in man's being deprived of grace, the special gift of God to the rational nature. Another effect of the fallen state is that man is wounded in his natural faculties.[211] But here a distinction needs to be made. The first perfection of nature—the constitution whereby a thing is completed in itself—remains untouched by sin. What is affected is the second perfection, the ordering to the operation. The inclination to the good, which suits the nature, is diminished. It is however not destroyed entirely, because the root of the inclination, the nature, always remains.[212] "Sin does not diminish nature" (*S. Th.* I – II, 85, 2). Nature remains after the Fall intrinsically good. *Naturalia manent integra*.[213]

Against this inner consistency the Reformation reacted. Thus Luther writes in his commentary on Genesis 3: the original justice "was so truly

---

[208] Cf. *S. Th.* 1, 3, 1 ad 2: Secundum intellectum et rationem, quae sunt incorporea, homo est ad imaginem Dei.

[209] Cf. the commentary by F.-J. Thonnard on Augustine's writing *De natura et gratia*, in *Oeuvres de St. Augustin* 21, pp. 614–22.

[210] *S. Th.* I–II, 109, 8. Cf. 109, 2: Natura hominis dupliciter potest considerari: uno modo, in sui integritate, sicut fuit in primo parente ante peccatum; alio modo, secundum quod est corrupta in nobis post peccatum primi parentis.

[211] Cf. *S. Th.* I–II, 85, 3 and *De malo* 2, 11 on the four "vulnera naturae ex peccato consequentia."

[212] Cf. *S. Th.* I–II, 85, 1; 2: Non tamen potest totaliter consumi, quia semper manet radix talis inclinationis; *De malo* 2, 12: Numquam tamen totaliter tolletur, propter permanentiam subjecti in quo radicatur talis habilitas.

[213] *In De div. nomin.* c. 4, lect. 19, 541; *In II Sent.* 3, 4 ad 5: Bona naturalia, prout in esse naturae absolute considerantur, remanent integra post peccatum. Cf. B. Quelquejeu, "Naturalia manent integra," *Revue des sciences philos. et théol.* 49 (1965): 640–55.

natural that it was Adam's nature to love God, to believe God, to acknowledge God (*ita ut natura Adae esset diligere Deum, credere Deo, agnoscere Deum*) . . . Likewise, after man fell from justice into sin, it is also correct and true to say that the natural is not whole but is broken by sin." Man in his being has averted himself from God "so that he flees and hates Him and desires to be and to live without Him."[214] Human nature itself is corrupted.

This statement is to those who are schooled in Thomas's thought incomprehensible. How, if nature itself is touched by the corruption, can man still be man? A good example is GILSON's attitude. In his inaugural address, *Le Moyen Age et le naturalisme antique*, he concludes that Protestantism by definition can have no philosophy since it teaches the radical corruption of nature. "Here . . . the opposition of the Reformation to medieval philosophy appears in its true light. Since there is no nature any more, how then could there still be a philosophy of nature?"[215] The essential result of the Christian philosophy of the Middle Ages is a deeply considered affirmation of a goodness intrinsic to nature.[216]

GILSON touches upon something here that deserves serious attention. Does the religiously motivated opposition to the tendency towards autonomy not entail as a dangerous counterpart the dissipation of the reality proper to the created? It is the consistency of the creature that Thomas has emphasized in his philosophizing about nature within the circular movement of egress and regress. GILSON however has misunderstood the basic intention of the Reformation. He has insufficiently discerned—not accidentally, since Thomas also does not elaborate this moment in his philosophy—that in the Reformational view, following the Augustinian tradition, the nature of man is his essentially relational mode of being. *Fecisti nos ad Te.* Being human is being unto God.[217]

This relation cannot be undone by sin but it can be perverted by it. It is over against sin that the Reformation has set grace. Grace is the act of God that *restores* and liberates nature. The second Person of the Trinity, the Word, became flesh in order to show man the way back, the conversion to God. This last thought is also given expression by Thomas in the structure of his *Summa Theologiae*: the first part will deal with God, the second with the rational creature's movement towards God, the third with

---

[214] *In Gen. 3*, in *Martin Luther's Werke, Kritische Gesamtausgabe*, vol. 42 (Weimar, 1911), p. 124.
[215] *Arch. d'Hist. doctrinale et littéraire du Moyen Age* 7 (1932): 19.
[216] E. Gilson, *The Spirit of Mediaéval Philosophy*, p. 420.
[217] Cf. the fair and open discussion of the Reformers, "the last of the great medieval figures," in J. H. Walgrave, *Geloof en Theologie in de crisis*, pp. 148ff.

Christ, Who as man is our way of tending to God (*via est nobis tendendi in Deum*) (I, 2, prol.).

The view that nature itself remains untouched by sin, that nature in itself is perfect, must however have consequences for Thomas's conception of grace. To begin with: "Grace presupposes nature" (*gratia praesupponit naturam*). Nature is "the preamble" to grace.[218]

> Nature is to beatitude as first to second, because beatitude is superadded to nature. But the first must always be preserved in the second.[219]

Nature is as bearer and subject of grace "more essential" to man.[220]

The reverse side is that grace is not forgiveness of sin, does not restore nature to communion with God, but is the elevation of nature. "Grace perfects nature" (*gratia perficit naturam*). Grace relates to nature as the perfection to the perfectible. Grace does not eliminate nature but rather perfects it. Illumination through faith does not destroy reason but is rather the completion of it.

> The gifts of grace are added to nature in such a way that they do not destroy, but rather perfect it. Therefore, the light of faith, which is gratuitously infused into us, does not destroy the light of natural reason, which is implanted in us by God.[221]

The communion with God by grace must become *super*-natural. Grace is a perfection that elevates man to a "supernatural being"; faith is the supernatural completion of human reason with regard to the terminus of the circular movement. The elevation of man through the supernatural form is a deification. Through it man becomes partaker of the circulation that is in God Himself (8.5.3.), in the intratrinitarian divine life. Man's soul participates through grace in the divine nature, the intellect becomes

---

[218] *S. Th.* I, 2, 2 ad 1: Sic enim fides praesupponit cognitionem naturalem, sicut gratia naturam; *De verit.* 27, 6 ad 3: Gratuita praesupponunt naturalia; *In Boeth. De trin.* 2, 3: Natura praeambula est ad gratiam.

[219] *S. Th.* I, 62, 7: Natura ad beatitudinem comparatur, sicut primum ad secundum; quia beatitudo naturae additur. Semper autem oportet salvari primum in secundo.

[220] *S. Th.* I–II, 94, 6 ad 2: Gratia, etsi sit efficacior quam natura, tamen natura essentialior est homini, et ideo magis permanens.

[221] *In Boeth. De trin.* 2, 3: Dona gratiarum hoc modo naturae adduntur quod eam non tollunt, sed magis perficiunt; unde et lumen fidei, quod nobis gratis infunditur, non destruit lumen naturalis rationis divinitus nobis inditum. Cf. *S. Th.* I, 1, 8: Cum igitur gratia non tollat naturam, sed perficiat, oportet quod naturalis ratio subserviat fidei; *In III Sent.* 13, 11 ad 2: Gratia est perfectio naturae; *S. Th.* I, 2, 2 ad 1: Sicut gratia (praesupponit) naturam, et ut perfectio perfectibile; *De verit.* 27, 6 ad 1: Gratia ... perficit tamen esse naturale, in quantum addit spirituale; 14, 10 ad 9: Fides non destruit rationem, sed excedit eam et perficit.

through faith partaker of the divine knowledge, the will through charity partaker of the divine love.[222]

On account of this coming to be perfect Thomas distinguishes a twofold participation. On account of this motive it also becomes necessary to speak of a twofold communication of God to the creature. One is common, whereby He gives to things their natural being—Thomas speaks of "natural creatures" (*creaturis naturalibus*); the other is special, whereby He draws the rational creature above its nature to a participation in the supernatural, divine good.[223]

"Perfectionism is a basic feature of European thought. Its history, and the various forms and shapes it has assumed in the course of time, has not yet been written," observes K. KUYPERS in his study of Kant.[224] In that history stands also the thought of Thomas Aquinas. He sees reality governed by a continuous dynamics towards perfection, in which the earlier is always preserved in the later: the way of nature towards the permanent "essence"; the way of the creature towards "being," "the perfection of all perfections," in which God is strived after implicitly. Only the way of human knowing tends explicitly towards God.

Here "perfectionism" in Thomas assumes a special shape. Not through philosophy but through faith and grace is man perfected. The Christian life is the completion of the natural order. *Gratia perficit naturam.* This "Christian" perfection is super-natural and consequently holds within it a latent duality. Grace presupposes nature, in itself perfect. In creation man was established as perfect in the perfection of nature; to this through God's grace perfections are added.[225]

However, one does not betray Thomas's thought when on the basis of the circulation in the divine one gives a different 'ratio' to the creaturely movement of egress and regress. For in Thomas's reflection on the trinitarian faith of the one, Catholic church a concept of relation is unfolded in which being and relation are "originally" one. Therein lies a more integral meaning of his penetrating view of the circulation. Therein lie still unconceived possibilities for thinking through with Thomas the being and movement of the creature in its egress from the Origin and in its regress by grace. Such philosophizing is oriented to the perfection of the being-itself in the being-to-something-other ("good").[226] Is this dynamic relationality not also inspired by Jesus' words (Matthew 5: 48), cited more

---

[222] *S. Th.* I–II, 110, 4.
[223] *Ibid.* I–II, 110, 1 and 2.
[224] *Immanuel Kant* (Baarn, 1966), pp. 122–23.
[225] *In Boeth. De trin.* 3, 1 ad 2.
[226] Cf. J. Bauer, "Fragen eines evangelischen Theologen an Thomas von Aquin," in *Thomas von Aquin 1274/1974*, ed. L. Oeing-Hanhoff (Munich, 1974), pp. 172ff.

than once by Thomas: "Be you perfect as also your heavenly Father is perfect"?[227]

---

[227] Cf. *S.c.G.* I, 28; *S. Th.* I, 4, 1 sed contra.

EPILOGUE

The torrent of publications about Thomas Aquinas that was started by the commemoration of the seven-hundredth anniversary of his death (1974) continues unabated. Yet one who surveys this flood of literature is soon overcome by doubt that it represents any genuine renewal. Is Thomas still a vital, formative force in philosophical thought? The *élan* with which people turned to Thomas for decades after the encyclical *Aeterni Patris* (1879) seems to have ebbed away. Many studies have a predominantly historical character. Thomas has become a figure of the past, for some has even become passé.

In the growing remoteness to Thomas in Roman Catholic circles, a number of factors play a role. One of these is the reaction, understandable in itself, against an ecclesiastical "sanctioning" that meant "conserving". Yet one cannot ignore the intellectual tradition without damaging himself. What this medieval devisor has bequeathed us still sets one thinking. For Thomas inquires into the first and original, which touches what is inner in things, the "mystery" of their "being." The study presented here seeks, along seldom trodden paths, to provide a dynamic picture of his thought.

Our aim was to develop an interpretation of the inner coherence and direction of Thomas's philosophizing. This objective was pursued by following his way of thought and by seeking to fathom the motives of his quest for intelligibility. Now that this inquiry has been brought to an end, it turns out that our investigation of Thomas's way of thought has proceeded according to the order of the transcendentals "being," "true," and "good." Their logical order, which Thomas sketches, is that "being" is the first and that "the true" and "good" come after it, in this order. For, so he argues in *S. Th.* I, 16, 4, "knowledge naturally precedes the appetite." "Being" is the first, "good" the ultimate.

From the triad "being"—"true"—"good," their convertibility, and their conceptual nonidentity a number of coherences can be brought to light that were not always signalized or worked out by Thomas himself. They are nonetheless most illuminating for the movement of Thomas's thought, and also for the course of our investigation. These coherences show that in what has preceded, a multiplicity of themes has been traversed according to a definite pattern.

(1) In chapters 1 through 3 inquiry is made into that whereby being is "being" (*ens*). The intelligibility sought is dominated by a twofold origination, the ways of nature and of creature. Nature motivates the mode of

questioning, the mode of predicating, and the mode of causing, which are directed to the definitive *essentia*. Through the essence or quiddity, that which is has being. For Thomas, however, that which is is not yet accounted for radically by the natural origin. Being as being requires a supernatural origin, creation. Creation motivates another mode of questioning, mode of predicating, and mode of causing which are directed to the *esse*. As a result, the structure of that which is has become in Thomas threefold, namely, 'subjectum – essentia – esse'.

The complex structure of that which is comes to expression in the transcendentals. Transcendentals are convertible with each other. Yet they are not synonymous terms, for they differ conceptually. The transcendentals "being" (*ens*) and "thing" (*res*) express in their conceptual nonidentity the very complexity of that which is. That which is, as viewed in its essence or quiddity, is called "thing"; as viewed in its *esse*, it is called "being." "Being" is convertible with "thing," so Thomas says, insofar as "being" signifies the entity of a thing, according as it is divided by the ten categories (*S. Th.* I, 48, 2 ad 2). It is noteworthy that the categories, the first contractions of being, are related to being in the sense of "thing," that is, to being in its quidditative aspect. For that reason the "if" question could not be separated from the "what" question (1.3.4.).

The transcendental "thing" we encountered earlier, and it is important to recall its context. In 6.3.3. we observed that Thomas did not take the path of symbolist thought. To his mind the creature is not first of all a "sign" of something else but a "thing": it has an intelligibility of its own. The transcendentality of "thing" expresses Thomas's emphasis on the proper nature of creatures.

(2) In the concurrence of the ways of nature and creature there arose the problem of the "other": being (*esse*) is outside the essence. How can that which is through this difference then still be one? That is only possible (7.4.4.) if the one component is the complement of the other, that is, if the components are related to each other as potency and act. In this manner essence and *esse* are related to each other. Act and potency constitute the hodo-logy (6.7.). The novelty of Thomas's interpretation is his understanding of being as act. The term *ens* is taken from the act of being. This guarantees the unity of what is composite. Insofar as something is, it is one. This unity is expressed by the transcendental "one" (*unum*). "Being" and "one" are convertible, but what "one" adds to "being" is the indivision (*S. Th.* I, 11, 1). "One" expresses that which is as viewed in the integrity of its components. We find here a corroboration of Thomas's statement that "thing" and "one" express determinations which pertain to every being in itself (4.1.2.).

(3) In chapter 4 the question of truth was raised. "True" expresses the intelligibility of that which is. "Being" and "true" are convertible. What "true" adds to "being" is the order to another being. "True" and "good" belong to the relational transcendentals: they express determinations which pertain to every being in relation to the human being. This "anthropocentrism" becomes manifest in *De verit.* 1, 1, where Thomas relates "true" and "good" to the two human faculties. "True" expresses the order of being to the intellect, "good" the relation to the appetite. Human being is characterized by a transcendental openness, for the soul has the aptitude to accord with every being. The human faculties have therefore a transcendental directedness. The object of the intellect is "being" and "true" in general; the object of the will, which is the rational appetite, is "good" in general. To the triad 'anima – intellectus – voluntas' in man corresponds the triad 'ens – verum – bonum'.

In *De verit.* 21, 1, where Thomas discusses the convertibility of "being" and "good", he establishes yet a further connection. The "true" and the "good" are related there to the different components of being itself. The "true" is connected with the specific essence, the "good" with the *esse.* "True" and "good" express "being" according to the determinations which the 'essentia' and the 'esse' entail with respect to the 'subjectum'. So a parallelism appears between the triad 'ens – verum – bonum' on the one hand and 'ens' as the composite of 'subjectum – essentia – esse' on the other hand, while the former triad was just shown to correspond with 'anima – intellectus – voluntas'. These correspondences indicate that the meaning of being as the oneness of 'subjectum – essentia – esse' can only be understood from the integral activity of the human faculties.

(4) The connection of the true with the essence or species is corroborated by Thomas's way of truth. The truth of things must be reduced to the first exemplary cause. This causality concerns primarily the "ideality" of things, their quiddity. Therefore the question of truth was important for another aspect of the problem of the "other" in the structure of that which is, namely, the problem of the relation of the essence of things to the Origin. This relation becomes problematical when it is said that *esse* is the proper effect of God, that it is the terminus of creation. Thomas's way of truth showed that the essential diversity of things must be reduced to the exemplary cause, which is the Truth itself.

(5) Human being has an openness to all that is; "the soul is in a certain sense all things." This capacity is realized in knowledge, that is, in the science of the causes, the truth, and the necessity of the thing. Man's natural desire to know was from the outset another line in our investigation.

Man's knowledge comes about "by the way of reason" (ch. 5). Characteristic of reason is that it is discursive: it proceeds from one item to another. The principle of the discursion is the notion of "being." It is that which is first known, for "being" is included in every concept.

The quest for intelligibility proper to man is "the way of resolution" (6.4.), the reduction to the ontologically prior. The movement of the discursive and historical reason occurs in three phases. Firstly, that which is is considered as *this* being, as particular subject, the cause of which is the "particular nature." Secondly, it is considered as *such* being, that is, viewed in its essence, of which the cause is the "universal nature." Finally, it is considered as *being*, that is, viewed in its *esse*, of which the cause is the Creator. "Being" is therefore also that "to which the intellect resolves all conceptions" (*De verit.* 1, 1).

Man's transcendental openness entails that the way of reason has a circular structure. Starting from being, it terminates in the consideration of being. In the metaphysical consideration of being as being, the return is "complete".

(6) "Being" and "good" are convertible. Yet "good" adds something to "being," namely, the relation to the appetite. "Good" expresses perfection and has consequently the character of being "ultimate." The notion of "good" is identical with "end" (ch. 8). Precisely because "good" has the aspect of end, it is proper to the transcendental "good" to constitute a dynamism in the creature. This dynamism comes to expression in the natural desire towards perfection, towards a more complete actuality of being. This completion concerns the faculties and powers of a thing, it consists in its activity or operation.

A thing is perfect insofar as it attains to its principle. Principle and end are the same. One of the most prominent features of our investigation is that it shows that the motif of circulation is of essential importance for Thomas's view of reality. The ways of nature, of creature, and of the human desire to know are in each case a circulation. The circular movement is the most perfect movement, because it connects the end with the beginning. Nothing can be added to it.

The final end, to which a thing is directed in its activity, cannot be anything other than that which is essentially good, the divine goodness. That from which the things originate turns out to be their final end. In this circulation the way of nature has its place. The natural circulation is directed towards the permanence of the species. Through this perpetuity nature tends to the likeness with the divine being. In the circular movement from and towards God, a special position pertains, however, to the human being. Owing to his transcendental openness, man alone is able to refer himself explicitly to his Origin. Only he addresses himself expressly to God in his acts of knowing and loving. It is in the rational creature that the circulation of reality is perfectly completed.

The ultimate end of man's desire to know is the vision of God. This end cannot be attained by the metaphysical consideration of being. It is a supernatural good. Because "good" is preceded by "being" and "true," man must be elevated with respect to his 'anima – intellectus – voluntas', that the vision of God may become connatural to him. "Grace" perfects the soul, "faith" the intellect, "hope" and "charity" the will. Christian life is the fulfillment of the natural order.

(7) The result of Aristotle's exposition in *Metaph.* II is the thesis: "There is the same disposition of things in being and in truth" (4.3.1.). On the analogy of this thesis Thomas himself frames the statement: "There is the same disposition of things in goodness and in being" (8.1.1.). A hierarchical order can be found in being, the true, and good. Whatever is in any way and is true and is good is to be reduced to the first Being, to the maximally True and to the ultimate Good, namely, God. The causal relation of God to the world is therefore threefold. He is 'causa efficiens', 'exemplaris', and 'finalis'. With this threefold causality Thomas connects the triad of transcendental determinations 'ens (or: unum) – verum – bonum'.

This coherence of the transcendentals with the divine causality makes clear that the "anthropocentrism" in Thomas's doctrine is to be specified: man is marked by a transcendental openness, certainly, is "in a certain sense all things," but not in a constitutive sense. It is typical of the medieval approach to inquire into the origin of being, into the ground of the truth and goodness of things. This origin and ground is conceived as "creation." Every being is true and good because it is thought and willed by the Creator. The relational character of the transcendentals "true" and "good" is ultimately founded in the relation to the divine intellect and will.

The divine foundation of the transcendentals is connected by Thomas with the circulation in God Himself, the eternal coming forth of the Persons. "Being" (or: "one") is attributed by appropriation to the Father, "true" to the Son, and "good" to the Spirit. This connection with the divine Trinity provides the basis for developing a trinitarian interpretation of that which is creaturely. In the conceptual nonidentity of the transcendentals 'ens – verum – bonum' the threefold structure of that which is comes to expression. Viewed in the light of the Triune causality, the different components of that which is concur into a unity.

"Being," "true," and "good" are not only common names but also divine names. The relation of what is common to what is proper to the Transcendent is conceived by Thomas in terms of "participation." He subscribes to Aristotle's criticism of this Platonic idea by stating that there are no separate, self-subsisting Forms of natural things. But Thomas, in the prologue to his commentary to pseudo-Dionysius's *De divinis nominibus*, recognizes the legitimacy of this doctrine with regard to what is most common. Only in the case of transcendental forms can a first be posited which is the perfection essentially and as such subsistent. All else must consequently be understood as participation in this perfection. Against this background it becomes understandable that Thomas conceives "creation" preeminently as "participation."

The doctrine of the transcendentals is found to have an important, integrating function in Thomas's way of thought. In man's quest for intelligibility, the transcendentals present a comprehensive perspective on nature and creature. Their circular ways come to an end in the return to the Origin, in which "being," "true," and "good" are perfectly one.[1]

---

[1] Since completing my doctoral dissertation I have dealt with the medieval doctrine of the transcendentals in a number of studies. With regard to Thomas, reference may be made to: "Het zijnde en het goede zijn omkeerbaar, De betekenis van een Scholastieke stelling," in Th. van Velthoven, ed., *Zin en Zijn, Metafysische beschouwingen over het goede*, Baarn, 1983, pp. 32–45; *Medieval Reflections on Truth, 'Adaequatio rei et intellectus'*, inaugural address, Amsterdam, 1984; "The Convertibility of Being and Good in St. Thomas Aquinas," *The New Scholasticism* 59 (1985): 449–70; "Transzendental versus kategorial: Die Zwiespaltigkeit von Thomas' Philosophie?" *Vivarium* 24 (1986); "Die Transzendentalienlehre bei Thomas von Aquin in ihren historischen Hintergründen und philosophischen Motiven," in *Thomas von Aquin. Sein Leben, sein Werk und seine Zeit in der neuesten Forschung*, Miscellanea Mediaevalia, vol. 19, Berlin, 1987 (forthcoming).

BIBLIOGRAPHY

1. Writings by Thomas Aquinas

Where possible, use is made of the critical edition: *Opera Omnia iussu Leonis XIII edita cura et studio Fratrum Praedicatorum* (Rome, 1882-).
For a complete listing of the various editions, see J.A. Weisheipl, *Friar Thomas d'Aquino* (Oxford, 1974), pp. 355–404.

We consulted the following English translations:

De ente: On Being and Essence. Trans. A. Maurer. Toronto, 1968.
De pot.: On the Power of God. 3 vols. Trans. English Dominican Fathers. London, 1932–34.
De spirit. creat.: On Spiritual Creatures. Trans. M.C. Fitz Patrick. Milwaukee, 1949.
De subst. separ.: Treatise on Separate Substances. Trans. F.J. Lescoe. West Hartford, Conn., 1963.
De verit.: On Truth. 3 vols. Trans. R.W. Mulligan. Chicago, 1952–54.
De virtutibus in communi: On the Virtues in General. Trans. J.P. Reid. Providence, R.I., 1951.
In Boeth. De trin: Division and Methods of the Sciences (q. 5–6). Trans. A. Maurer. Toronto, 1953.
In Ethic.: Commentary on the Nichomachean Ethics. 2 vols. Trans. C.I. Litzinger. Chicago, 1964.
In Metaph.: Commentary on the Metaphysics of Aristotle. 2 vols. Trans. J.P. Rowan. Chicago, 1961.
In Phys.: Commentary on Aristotle's Physics. Trans. R.J. Blackwell et al. New Haven, 1963.
In Post. Anal.: Commentary on the Posterior Analytics of Aristotle. Trans. F.R. Larcher. Albany, N.Y., 1970.
Quodl.: Quodlibet Questions 1 and 2. Trans. S. Edwards. Toronto, 1983.
S.c.G.: On the Truth of the Catholic Faith. 5 vols. Trans. A.C. Pegis. New York, 1955–57.
S. Th.: Summa Theologiae. 60 vols. Trans. the English Dominicans. London, 1964– .

2. Other Sources

ALBERT THE GREAT
Opera Omnia. Edited by A. Borgnet. Paris, 1890–1899.
ARISTOTLE
Opera. Ed. Academia Regia Borussica. Berlin, 1831–1870.
Aristotle's Metaphysics. Oxford, 1924. A revised text with introduction and commentary by W.D. Ross.
Aristotle's Physics. Oxford, 1936. A revised text with introduction and commentary by W.D. Ross.
Aristoteles, Physikvorlesung. Trans. H. Wagner. Berlin and Darmstadt, 1967.
Aristotle's Physics I and II. Trans. with an introduction and notes by W. Charlton. Clarendon Aristotle Series. Oxford, 1970.
Aristote, Physique II. Trans. with a commentary by O. Hamelin. 3rd ed. Paris, 1972.
Aristotle's Prior and Posterior Analytics. A revised text with introduction and commentary by W.D. Ross. Oxford, 1949.
AUGUSTINE
Oeuvres de saint Augustin. Bibliothèque augustinienne. Paris, 1947– .
De doctrina christiana. Edited by W.M. Green. Corpus scriptorum ecclesiasticorum latinorum, vol. 80. Vienna, 1963.
De trinitate. Edited by W.J. Mountain and F. Glorie. Corpus christianorum, vols. 50 and 50 A. Turnhout, 1962.

AVERROES
In librum V Metaphysicorum Aristotelis Commentarius. Edited by R. Ponzalli. Bern, 1971.
AVICENNA
Opera philosophica. Venice, 1508.
Avicenna Latinus—Liber de Philosophia prima sive Scientia Divina. Edited by S. van Riet. Louvain and Leiden, 1977.
BERNARD OF CLAIRVAUX
Opera. Edited by J. Leclercq and others. Rome, 1957–1977.
BOETHIUS
The Theological Tractates. Edited by H.F. Stewart and E.K. Rand. London and Cambridge (Mass.), 1962.
BONAVENTURE
Opera Omnia. Edited by P.P. Collegii S. Bonaventurae. Claras Aquas, 1882–1902.
CAJETAN
Commentaria in Summam Theologiae Aquinatis. Editio Leonina. Rome, 1888–1903.
DIONYSIUS THE AREOPAGITE
Opera Omnia, Migne, PG 3 and 4.
DUNS SCOTUS
Opera Omnia. Editio Vaticana. Rome, 1950–.
Quaestiones subtilissimae super libros Metaphysicorum Aristotelis. In *Opera Omnia*, vol. 7. Edited by L. Wadding. Lyon, 1639.
ECKHART
Die lateinischen und deutschen Werke. Edited by the Deutsche Forschungsgemeinschaft. Stuttgart, 1936–.
GILBERT DE LA PORRÉE
"Expositio in Boethii Librum contra Eutychen et Nestorium." Edited by N.M. Häring. *Archives d'Histoire Doctrinale et Littéraire du Moyen-Age* 21 (1954): 241–357.
HUGH OF ST. VICTOR
Didascalicon. Edited by C.H. Buttimer. Washington, D.C., 1939.
ISIDORE OF SEVILLE
Etymologiarum sive Originum libri XX. Edited by W.M. Lindsay. Oxford, 1911.
JOHN OF SECHEVILLE
De principiis naturae. Edited by R.-M. Giguère. Paris, 1956.
LIBER DE CAUSIS
O. Bardenhewer. *Die pseudo-aristotelische Schrift über das reine Gute, bekannt unter dem Namen 'Liber de Causis'.* Freiburg i.Br., 1882.
"Edition établie à l'aide de 90 manuscrits avec introduction et notes par A. Pattin." *Tijdschrift voor Filosofie* 28 (1966): 90–203.
PARMENIDES
H. Diels. *Die Fragmente der Vorsokratiker*, vol. 1. 9th ed. Berlin, 1960. Pp. 217ff.
PETER LOMBARD
Libri IV Sententiarum. Edited by P.P. Collegii S. Bonaventurae. Grottaferrata, 1971–.
PLATO
Opera. Edited by J. Burnet. Oxford, 1900–1907.
PROCLUS
C. Vansteenkiste. "Procli elementatio theologica translata a Guilelmo de Moerbeke." *Tijdschrift voor Philosophie* 13 (1951): 263–302; 491–531.
ROBERT GROSSETESTE
Commentarius in VIII libros Physicorum Aristotelis. Edited by R.C. Dales. University of Colorado Press, 1963.
SYLVESTER OF FERRARA
Commentaria in Summam contra Gentiles S. Thomae Aquinatis. Leonine edition. Rome, 1918–1930.

3. Secondary Literature

AERTSEN, J.A. "'Uit God zijn alle dingen', Enkele overwegingen bij de 700ste sterfdag van Thomas van Aquino." *Philosophia Reformata* 39 (1974): 102–55.

——, "Der wissenschaftstheoretische Ort der Gottesbeweise in der *Summa Theologiae* des Thomas von Aquin." In *Mediaeval Semantics and Metaphysics, Studies dedicated to L.M. de Rijk*. Edited by E.P. Bos. Nijmegen, 1985, pp. 163–93.

ALCORTA, J.I. "El concepto de naturaleza en Santo Tomas." In *La filosofia della natura nel medioevo*. Milan, 1966, pp. 465–70.

AMORIM ALMEIDA, R. DE *Natur und Geschichte. Zur Frage nach der ursprünglichen Dimension abendländischen Denkens vor dem Hintergrund der Auseinandersetzung zwischen Martin Heidegger und Karl Löwith*. Meisenheim, 1975.

ANDERSON, J.F. *The Cause of Being. The Philosophy of Creation in St. Thomas*. St. Louis and London, 1952.

ARMSTRONG, A.H., ed. *The Cambridge History of Later Greek and Early Medieval Philosophy*. Cambridge, 1970.

AUBERT, J.-M. *Philosophie de la nature, Propédeutique à la vision chrétienne du monde*. Paris, 1965.

AUER, J. *Die Entwicklung der Gnadenlehre in der Hochscholastik*. Vol. 2: *Das Wirken der Gnade*. Freiburg, 1951.

——, "Inwieweit ist im 13. Jahrhundert der Wandel des Begriffes 'supernaturalis' bedingt durch den Wandel des Naturbegriffes?" In *La filosofia della natura nel medioevo*. Milan, 1966, pp. 331–49.

BARENDSE, B.A.M. "Over de graden in het zijn." *Tijdschrift voor Philosophie* 11 (1949): 155–202. Also in *Zich door het leven heendenken, keuze uit het werk van Prof. Dr. B.A.M. Barendse O.P.*. Edited by Th. van Velthoven. Kampen, 1982, pp. 42–75.

——, "Intersubjectief verkeer en lichamelijkheid; De bemiddeling van het lichaam." In *Lichamelijkheid*. Utrecht and Brussels, 1951, pp. 85–119. Also in *ibid.*, pp. 76–97.

——, *Thomas van Aquino: Een geloof op zoek naar inzicht*. Baarn, 1968.

BAUR, J. "Fragen eines evangelischen Theologen an Thomas von Aquin." In *Thomas von Aquin 1274/1974*. Edited by L. Oeing-Hanhoff. Munich, 1974, pp. 161–74.

BERGER, H.H. "Der Partizipationsgedanke im Metaphysik-Kommentar des Thomas von Aquin." *Vivarium* 1 (1963): 115–40.

——, "Ousia en deelhebbing, Aristoteles' opvatting over identiteit." *Tijdschrift voor Filosofie* 25 (1963): 706–78.

——, *Op zoek naar identiteit*. Nijmegen and Utrecht, 1968.

——, *Zo wijd als alle werkelijkheid, Een inleiding in de metafysiek*. Baarn, 1977.

BERNATH, K., ed. *Thomas von Aquin*. Vol. 1: *Chronologie und Werkanalyse*. Wege der Forschung, vol. 188. Darmstadt, 1978.

BLANCHETTE, O. "The Four Causes as Texture of the Universe." *Laval Théologique et Philosophique* 25 (1969): 59–87.

BLUMENBERG, H. "Augustins Anteil an der Geschichte des Begriffs der theoretischen Neugierde." *Revue des Etudes Augustiniennes* 7 (1961): 35–70.

——, *Der Prozess der theoretischen Neugierde*. Revised ed. of *Die Legitimität der Neuzeit*, part 3. Frankfurt am Main, 1973.

BOEHM, R. *Das Grundlegende und das Wesentliche, Zu Aristoteles' Abhandlung "Über das Sein und das Seiende" (Metaphysik Z)*. The Hague, 1965.

BRINKMANN, H. *Mittelalterliche Hermeneutik*. Tübingen, 1980.

BRUGGER, W. "Sprachanalytische Überlegungen bei Thomas von Aquin." *Theologie und Philosophie* 49 (1974): 437–63.

BRUNNER, F. "Le conflit des tendances platoniciennes et aristotéliciennes au moyen-âge." *Revue de Théologie et de Philosophie* 5 (3rd series) (1955): 179–92.

——, "Über die Thomistische Lehre vom Ursprung der Welt." *Zeitschrift für philosophische Forschung* 16 (1962): 251–58.

BUCHER, Z. "Die Natur als Ordnung bei Thomas von Aquin." *Salzburger Jahrbuch für Philosophie* 19 (1974): 219–38.

CHENU, M.-D. *Introduction à l'étude de Saint Thomas d'Aquin*. 2nd ed. Montreal and Paris, 1954. Eng. trans.: *Toward Understanding St. Thomas*. Chicago, 1964.

——, "Nature and Man: The Renaissance of the Twelfth Century." In *Nature, Man and*

Society in the Twelfth Century. Chicago, 1968, pp. 1–48.

———, "The Symbolist Mentality." In *ibid.*, pp. 99–145.

———, "S. Thomas innovateur dans la créativité d'un monde nouveau." In *Tommaso d'A-quino nella storia del pensiero,* vol. 1 (= Atti del Congr. Intern. 1974 Tommaso d'Aquino nel suo settimo centenario). Naples, n.d., pp. 39–50.

CHENU, R., ed. *L'homme moderne et son image de la nature.* Neuchâtel, 1974.

COLLINGWOOD, R.G. *The Idea of Nature.* Oxford, 1945.

COURTÈS, P.C. "L'être et le non-être selon St. Thomas d'Aquin." *Revue Thomiste* 67 (1967): 387–436.

DECLOUX, S. *Temps, Dieu, Liberté dans les commentaires aristotéliciens de St. Thomas d'Aquin. Essai sur la pensée grecque et la pensée chrétienne.* Brussels, 1967.

DELFGAAUW, B. *Thomas van Aquino.* Bussum, 1980.

DELHAYE, Ph. *Permanence du droit naturel.* Analecta Mediaevalia Namurcensia. Louvain, 1960.

DENEFFE, A. "Geschichte des Wortes 'supernaturalis.'" *Zeitschrift für Katholische Theologie* 46 (1922): 337–60.

DIEMER, J.H. *Natuur en wonder.* Amsterdam, 1963.

DIPPEL, C.J. "De inconsistentie tussen scheppingsgeloof en natuurbegrip." In *Geloof en natuurwetenschap,* vol. 1. Edited by C.J. Dippel and J.M. de Jong. The Hague, 1965, pp. 182–232.

DOIG, J.C. *Aquinas on Metaphysics: A Historico-doctrinal Study of the Commentary on the Metaphysics.* The Hague, 1972.

DOLCH, H. *Kausalität im Verständnis des Theologen und der Begründer neuzeitlicher Physik. Besinnung auf die historischen Grundlegungen zum Zwecke einer sachgemässen Besprechung moderner Kausalitätsprobleme.* Freiburg, 1954.

DOOYEWEERD, H. "De vier religieuze grondthema's in den ontwikkelingsgang van het wijsgeerig denken van het Avondland." *Philosophia Reformata* 6 (1941): 161–79.

———, *Reformatie en scholastiek in de wijsbegeerte,* vol. 1. Franeker, 1949.

———, *A New Critique of Theoretical Thought,* vol. 1. Trans. David H. Freeman and William S. Young. Amsterdam and Philadelphia, 1953.

———, *Roots of Western Culture: Pagan, Secular and Christian Options.* Trans. John Kraay. Toronto, 1979.

DÜMPELMANN, L. *Kreation als ontisch-ontologisches Verhältnis.* Freiburg and Munich, 1969.

DUINTJER, O.D. *De vraag naar het transcendentale, vooral in verband met Heidegger en Kant.* Leiden, 1966.

DURAND, G. "L'Occident iconoclaste, Contribution à l'histoire du symbolisme." *Cahiers internationaux de symbolisme* 2 (1963): 3–15.

DIJKSTERHUIS, E.J. *De mechanisering van het wereldbeeld.* Amsterdam, 1950. Eng. trans.: *The Mechanization of the World Picture.* Oxford, 1961.

ECKERT, W.P., ed. *Thomas von Aquino, Interpretation und Rezeption.* Walberberger Studien, vol. 5, Mainz, 1974.

ELDERS, L. *Aristotle's Theology: A Commentary on Book XII of the Metaphysics.* Assen, 1972.

ENGELHARDT, P. "Zu den anthropologischen Grundlagen der Ethik des Thomas von Aquin; Die Enthüllung des mass-gebenden Lebenszieles durch das desiderium naturale." In *Sein und Ethos.* Edited by P. Engelhardt. Mainz, 1963, pp. 186–212.

FABRO, C. "Intorno alla nozione 'tomista' di contingenza." *Rivista di Filosofia Neoscolastica* 30 (1938): 132–49.

———, *La nozione metafisica di partecipazione secondo S. Tommaso d'Aquino.* 2nd ed. Turin, 1950.

———, *Participation et Causalité selon St. Thomas d'Aquin.* Louvain and Paris, 1961.

———, "The Intensive Hermeneutics of Thomistic Philosophy: The Notion of Participation." *The Review of Metaphysics* 27 (1974): 449–91.

FLASCH, K. "Ars imitatur naturam. Platonischer Naturbegriff und mittelalterliche Philosophie der Kunst." In *Parusia, Festgabe für J. Hirschberger.* Frankfurt am Main, 1965, pp. 265–306.

———, *Die Metaphysik des Einen bei Nikolaus von Kues, Problemgeschichtliche Stellung und systematische Bedeutung.* Leiden, 1973.

FOREST, A. *La structure métaphysique du concret selon St. Thomas d'Aquin.* Paris, 1931.

FROMM, H.; HARMS, W.; AND RUBERG, U., eds. *Verbum et Signum. Beiträge zur mediävistischen Bedeutungsforschung, Studien zur Semantik und Sinntradition im Mittelalter.* Munich, 1975.

GADAMER, H.-G. *Wahrheit und Methode, Grundzüge einer philosophischen Hermeneutik.* 4th ed. Tübingen, 1975.

GEIGER, L.-B. *La participation dans la philosophie de St. Thomas d'Aquin.* Paris, 1942.

———, "Saint Thomas et la métaphysique d'Aristote." In *Aristote et Saint Thomas d'Aquin.* Louvain and Paris, 1957, pp. 175–220.

GEVAERT, J. *Contingent en noodzakelijk bestaan volgens Thomas van Aquino.* Verhandelingen van de Koninklijke Vlaamse Academie voor Wetenschappen, Klasse der Letteren, vol. 27, no. 58. Brussels, 1965.

GHISALBERTI, A. "La concezione della natura nel commento di Tommaso d'Aquino alla 'Metafisica' di Aristotele." *Rivista di Filosofia Neoscolastica* 66 (1974): 533–40.

GILSON, E. *La philosophie de saint Bonaventure.* Paris, 1924.

———, "Pourquoi saint Thomas a critiqué saint Augustin?" *Archives d'Histoire Doctrinale et Littéraire du Moyen-Age* 1 (1926–27): 5–127.

———, "Réfexions sur la controverse St. Thomas – St. Augustin." In *Mélanges Mandonnet,* vol. 1. Paris, 1930, pp. 371–83.

———, "Le moyen-âge et le naturalisme antique." *Archives d'Histoire Doctrinale et Littéraire du Moyen-Age* 7 (1932): 5–37.

———, *The Spirit of Mediaeval Philosophy.* New York, 1940.

———, "La possibilité philosophique de la philosophie chrétienne." *Revue des Sciences Religieuses* 32 (1958): 168–96.

———, *Introduction à la philosophie chrétienne.* Paris, 1960.

———, *Being and Some Philosophers.* 2nd ed. Toronto, 1961.

———, "Notes pour l'histoire de la cause efficiente." *Archives d'Histoire Doctrinale et Littéraire du Moyen-Age* 29 (1962): 7–31.

———, "Prolégomènes à la 'Prima via.'" *Archives d'Histoire Doctrinale et Littéraire du Moyen-Age* 30 (1963): 53–70.

———, *Le Thomisme, Introduction à la philosophie de saint Thomas d'Aquin.* 6th ed. Paris, 1965.

GRABMANN, M. *Die theologische Erkenntnis- und Einleitungslehre des hl. Thomas von Aquin auf Grund seiner Schrift in Boethium de Trinitate.* Freiburg, Switzerland, 1948.

GREGORY, T. "La nouvelle idée de nature et de savoir scientifique au XIIe siècle." In *The Cultural Context of Medieval Learning.* Edited by J.E. Murdoch and E.D. Sylla. Dordrecht and Boston, 1975, pp. 193–218. (Proceedings of the First International Colloquium on Philosophy, Science and Theology in the Middle Ages).

GRIJS, F.J.A. DE *Goddelijk mensontwerp, Een thematische studie over het beeld Gods in de mens volgens het Scriptum van Thomas van Aquino.* 2 vols. Hilversum and Antwerp, 1967.

———, "Mensenmacht, Enige aantekeningen bij 'De Regno' van Thomas van Aquino." *Bijdragen* 35 (1974): 250–97.

GUARDINI, R. *Die Sinne und die religiöse Erkenntnis. Zwei Versuche über die christliche Vergewisserung.* Würzburg, 1950.

HAPP, H. *Hyle, Studien zum Aristotelischen Materie-Begriff.* Berlin and New York, 1971.

HAYEN, A. *L'intentionnel dans la philosophie de St. Thomas.* Louvain, 1942.

———, *La communication de l'être d'après Saint Thomas d'Aquin.* Vol. 2: *L'ordre philosophique de Saint Thomas.* Paris, 1959.

———, "Aqua totaliter in vinum conversa: philosophie et révélation chez saint Bonaventure et saint Thomas." In *Die Metaphysik im Mittelalter.* Miscellanea Mediaevalia, vol. 2. Berlin, 1963, pp. 317–24.

HAYES, Z. *The General Doctrine of Creation in the Thirteenth Century, with Special Emphasis on Matthew of Aquasparta.* Munich, Paderborn, and Vienna, 1964.

HEIDEGGER, M. *Vom Wesen der Wahrheit.* 3rd ed. Frankfurt am Main, 1954.

———, "Vom Wesen und Begriff der 'Physis', Aristoteles' Physik B, 1." In *Wegmarken.* Frankfurt am Main, 1967, pp. 309–72.

———, *Sein und Zeit.* 12th ed. Tübingen, 1972.

HEIMSOETH, H. *Die sechs grossen Themen der abendländischen Metaphysik und der Ausgang des Mittelalters.* 5th ed. Stuttgart, 1965.

HELLER, B. *Grundbegriffe der Physik im Wandel der Zeit.* Braunschweig, 1970.

HENGSTENBERG, H.E. *Sein und Ursprünglichkeit; zur philosophischen Grundlegung der Schöpfungslehre.* Munich, 1958.

HENLE, R.J. *Saint Thomas and Platonism.* The Hague, 1956.

HIRSCHBERGER, J. *Geschichte der Philosophie,* vol. 1. 9th ed. Basel, Freiburg, and Vienna, 1974.

HOENEN, P. *La théorie du jugement d'après St. Thomas d'Aquin.* 2nd ed. Rome, 1953.

HOLLAK, J. "Wijsgerige reflecties over de scheppingsidee; St. Thomas, Hegel en de Grieken." In *De eindige mens?* Edited by C. Struyker Boudier. Bilthoven, 1975, pp. 89–103.

INCIARTE, F. *Forma formarum, Strukturmomente der thomistischen Seinslehre im Rückgriff auf Aristoteles.* Freiburg and Munich, 1970.

JALBERT, G. *Nécessité et contingence chez St. Thomas d'Aquin et chez ses prédécesseurs.* Ottawa, 1961.

JOLIVET, R. *Essai sur les rapports entre la pensée grecque et la pensée chrétienne.* New ed. Paris, 1955.

KAULBACH, F. *Der philosophische Begriff der Bewegung, Studien zu Aristoteles, Leibniz und Kant.* Cologne and Graz, 1965.

KELLER, A. *Sein oder Existenz? Die Auslegung des Seins bei Thomas von Aquino in der heutigen Scholastik.* Munich, 1968.

KLUXEN, W. *Philosophische Ethik bei Thomas von Aquin.* Mainz, 1964.

——, "Thomas von Aquin: Das Seiende und seine Prinzipien." In *Grundprobleme der grossen Philosophen,* vol. 1. Edited by J. Speck. Göttingen, 1972, pp. 177–220.

——, ed. *Thomas von Aquin im philosophischen Gespräch.* Freiburg and Munich, 1975.

KREMER, K. "Die Creatio nach Thomas von Aquin und dem Liber de Causis." In *Ekklesia, Festschrift für Bischof dr. Matth. Wehr.* Trier, 1962, pp. 321–44.

——, "Der Apriorismus in der Erkenntnismetaphysik des Thomas von Aquin. *Trierer Theologische Zeitschrift* 72 (1963): 105–16.

——, *Die neuplatonische Seinsphilosophie und ihre Wirkung auf Thomas von Aquin.* Leiden, 1971.

——, "Der Schöpfungsgedanke und seine Diskussion in der Gegenwart." In *Denkender Glaube.* Edited by J. Hirschberger and J.G. Deninger. Frankfurt am Main, 1966, pp. 150–89.

——, "Wer ist das eigentlich—der Mensch? Zur Frage nach dem Menschen bei Thomas von Aquin." *Trierer Theologische Zeitschrift* 84 (1975): 73–84; 129–43.

KREMPEL, A. *La doctrine de la relation chez Saint Thomas, Exposé historique et systématique.* Paris, 1952.

LAPORTA, J. "Pour trouver le sens exact des termes 'appetitus naturalis', 'desiderium naturale', 'amor naturalis', etc. chez Thomas d'Aquin." *Archives d'Histoire Doctrinale et Littéraire du Moyen-Age* 40 (1973): 37–95.

LAUBENTHAL, R. *Das Verhältnis des heiligen Thomas von Aquin zu den Arabern in seinem Physikkommentar.* Kallmünz, 1934.

LE BLOND, J.M. *Logique et méthode chez Aristote. Etude sur la recherche des principes dans la physique aristotélicienne.* Paris, 1939.

LEGRAND, J. *L'univers et l'homme dans la philosophie de saint Thomas.* Paris and Brussels, 1946.

LEINSLE, U.G. *Res et signum. Das Verständnis zeichenhafter Wirklichkeit in der Theologie Bonaventuras.* Munich, Paderborn, and Vienna, 1976.

LEISEGANG, H. "Physis (natura) als philosophisch-wissenschaftlicher Begriff und terminus technicus." In *Real-Enzyklopädie der classischen Altertumswissenschaft,* 39. Halbband (XX/1). Stuttgart, 1941, pp. 1130–64.

LENOBLE, R. *Esquisse d'une histoire de l'idée de nature.* Paris, 1969.

LITT, Th. *Les corps célestes dans l'univers de Saint Thomas d'Aquin.* Louvain and Paris, 1963.

LONERGAN, B.J. *Verbum, Word and Idea in Aquinas.* Notre Dame, 1967.

LORENZ, R. "Die Wissenschaftslehre Augustins." *Zeitschrift für Kirchengeschichte* 67 (1955–56): 29–60; 213–51.

LOTZ, J.B. *Martin Heidegger und Thomas von Aquin: Mensch –Zeit –Sein.* Pfullingen, 1975.

LUBAC, H. DE *Surnaturel. Etudes historiques.* Paris, 1946.

MAIER, A. *An der Grenze von Scholastik und Naturwissenschaft.* 2nd ed. Rome, 1952.

MANNSPERGER, D. *Physis bei Platon.* Berlin, 1969.

MANSION, A. *Introduction à la physique aristotélicienne.* 2nd ed. Louvain and Paris, 1946.

MANSION, S. *Le jugement d'existence chez Aristote.* 2nd ed. Louvain, 1976.

MANTHEY, F. *Die Sprachphilosophie des hl. Thomas von Aquin und ihre Anwendung auf Probleme der Theologie.* Paderborn, 1937.

MARITAIN, J. *Distinguer pour unir ou les degrés du savoir.* Paris, 1932.

MARROU, H.-I. *Saint Augustin et la fin de la culture antique.* 4th ed. Paris, 1958.

MAURER, A. "St. Thomas and Henry of Harclay on Created Nature." In *La Filosofia della natura nel medioevo.* Milan, 1966, pp. 542–49.

MCINERNY, R.M. *The Logic of Analogy: An Interpretation of St. Thomas.* The Hague, 1961.

MCMULLIN, E., ed. *The Concept of Matter in Greek and Medieval Philosophy.* Notre Dame, 1965.

MEEHAN, F.X. *Efficient Causality in Aristotle and St. Thomas.* Washington, D.C., 1940.

MERTENS, J. "Functie en wezen van de intellectus agens volgens St. Thomas." *Tijdschrift voor Filosofie* 36 (1974): 267–322.

METZ, J.B. *Christliche Anthropozentrik, Über die Denkform des Thomas von Aquin.* Munich, 1962.

MEULEMAN, G.E. "Natuur en genade." In *Protestantse verkenningen na Vaticanum II.* The Hague, 1967, pp. 65–88.

MEYER, B. *De eerste levensvraag in het intellectualisme van St. Thomas van Aquino en het integraalrealisme van Maurice Blondel.* Roermond and Maaseik, 1940.

———, "Nieuw licht over een oud beginsel: 'Het natuurlijk verlangen kan niet ijdel zijn.'" *Bijdragen* 4 (1941): 255–98.

———, "Het participatiebegrip in de thomistische circulatieleer." In *Verslag van de tiende algemene vergadering der vereeniging voor thomistische wijsbegeerte.* Nijmegen, 1944, pp. 55–68. (Supplement of *Studia Catholica*).

———, "Natuurlijk en bovennatuurlijk geluk." In *Theologische opstellen . . . aan G. van Noort.* Utrecht, 1944, pp. 148–61.

MEYER, H. *Natur und Kunst bei Aristoteles. Ableitung und Bestimmung der Ursächlichkeitsfaktoren.* Paderborn, 1919.

———, *Die Wissenschaftslehre des Thomas von Aquin.* Fulda, 1934.

———, *Thomas von Aquin, Sein System und seine geistesgeschichtliche Stellung.* Paderborn, 1938.

MICHAUD-QUANTIN, P. "Notes sur le hasard et la chance." In *La filosofia della natura nel medioevo.* Milan, 1966, pp. 156–63. Also in *Etudes sur le vocabulaire philosophique du Moyen-Age.* Rome, 1970, pp. 73–84.

MITTERER, A. *Die Zeugung der Organismen, insbesondere des Menschen nach dem Weltbild des hl. Thomas von Aquin und dem der Gegenwart.* Vienna, 1947.

MONTAGNES, B. *La doctrine de l'analogie de l'être d'après Saint Thomas d'Aquin.* Louvain and Paris, 1963.

MOSER, S. "Der Begriff der Natur in aristotelischer und moderner Sicht." *Philosophia Naturalis* 6 (1960): 261–87.

MÜLLER, A., PFÜRTNER, S.H., AND SCHNYDER, B., eds. *Natur und Naturrecht, ein interfacultäres Gespräch.* Freiburg (Switserland), 1972.

NICOLAS, M.-J. "L'idée de nature dans la pensée de Saint Thomas d'Aquin." *Revue Thomiste* 74 (1974): 533–90.

NOBIS, H.M. "Frühneuzeitliche Verständnisweisen der Natur und ihr Wandel bis zum 18. Jhrt." *Archiv für Begriffsgeschichte* 11 (1967): 37–58.

———, "Die Umwandlung der mittelalterlichen Naturvorstellung, ihre Ursachen und ihre wissenschaftsgeschichtlichen Folgen." *Archiv für Begriffsgeschichte* 13 (1969): 34–57.

NUCHELMANS, G. *Wijsbegeerte en taal.* Meppel, 1976.

OBERMAN, H.A. *Contra vanam curiositatem. Ein Kapitel der Theologie zwischen Seelenwinkel und Weltall.* Zurich, 1974.

O'BRIEN, M.C. *The Antecedents of Being, An Analysis of the Concept "de nihilo" in the Philosophy of St. Thomas: A Study in Thomistic Metaphysics.* Washington, D.C., 1939.

OEING-HANHOFF, L. *Ens et Unum convertuntur; Stellung und Gehalt des Grundsatzes in der Philosophie des hl. Thomas von Aquin.* Beiträge zur Geschichte der Philosophie und Theologie des Mittelalters, XXVII, 3. Münster, Westfalen, 1953.

———, "Die Methoden der Metaphysik im Mittelalter." In *Die Metaphysik im Mittelalter.* Miscellanea Mediaevalia, vol. 2. Berlin, 1963, pp. 71–91.

———, "Mensch und Natur bei Thomas von Aquin." *Zeitschrift für katholische Theologie* 101 (1979): 300–315.

O'FLYNN BRENNAN, S. "Physis, The Meaning of 'Nature' in the Aristotelian Philosophy of Nature." *Thomist* 24 (1961): 383–401.

OWENS, J. *The Doctrine of Being in the Aristotelian Metaphysics: A Study in the Greek Background of Mediaeval Thought.* 2nd ed. Toronto, 1963.

———, "Aquinas as Aristotelian Commentator." In *St. Thomas Aquinas Commemorative Studies*, vol. 1. Toronto, 1974, pp. 213–38.

PANIKKAR, R. "La novedad que en el concepto de naturaleza introduce el Christianismo." *Tijdschrift voor Philosophie* 13 (1951): 236–62.

———, *El concepto de naturaleza, Analisis historico y metafisico de un concepto.* 2nd ed. Madrid, 1972.

PAQUÉ, R. *Das Pariser Nominalistenstatut. Zur Entstehung des Realitätsbegriffes der neuzeitlichen Naturwissenschaft (Occam, Buridan und Petrus Hispanus, Nikolaus von Autrecourt und Gregor von Rimini).* Berlin, 1970.

PATTIN, A. *De verhouding tussen zijn en wezenheid en de transcendentale relatie in de tweede helft der XIIIe eeuw.* Verhandelingen van de Koninklijke Vlaamse Academie voor Wetenschappen, Klasse der Letteren, no. 21. Brussels, 1955.

PEGHAIRE, J. *Intellectus et Ratio selon St. Thomas d'Aquin.* Publications de l'Institut d'Etudes Médiévales d'Ottawa, vol. 6. Paris and Ottawa, 1936.

PEGIS, A.C. "Some Permanent Contributions of Mediaeval Philosophy to the Notion of Man." *Transactions of the Royal Society of Canada* 46, series 3 (June 1952): section 2, pp. 67–78.

PEPERZAK, A. *Der heutige Mensch und die Heilsfrage: eine philosophische Hinführung.* Freiburg, 1972.

PERSSON, P.E. *Sacra doctrina; Reason and Revelation in Aquinas.* Oxford, 1970.

PETERS, J. "De wijsgerige waarde van St. Thomas' participatieleer." In *De vraag naar het zijn.* Selected writings of J. Peters, edited by H.H. Berger, C.E.M. Struyker Boudier, and Th. van Velthoven, Kampen, 1984, pp. 69–90.

———, *Metaphysica, Een systematisch overzicht.* Utrecht and Antwerp, 1967.

PETTER, D.M. DE "De oorsprong van de zijnskennis volgens Thomas van Aquino." In *Begrip en werkelijkheid, Aan de overzijde van het conceptualisme.* Hilversum and Antwerp, 1964, pp. 94–135.

———, *Naar het metafysische.* Utrecht and Antwerp, 1972.

PHILIPPE, M.-D. *Une philosophie de l'être est-elle encore possible?* 5 vols. Paris, 1975.

PIAZZA, L. *Mediazione simbolica in S. Bonaventura.* Vicenza, 1978.

PIEPER, J. *Die Wirklichkeit und das Gute.* Leipzig, 1935.

———, *Wahrheit der Dinge. Eine Untersuchung zur Anthropologie des Hochmittelalters.* 4th ed. Munich, 1966.

———, "Wahrheit der Dinge—ein verschollener Begriff." In *Festschrift für Leo Brandt.* Edited by J. Meixner and G. Kegel. Cologne and Opladen, 1968, pp. 417–29.

———, "Kreatürlichkeit. Bemerkungen über die Elemente eines Grundbegriffs." In *Thomas von Aquin 1274/1974.* Edited by L. Oeing-Hanhoff. Munich, 1974, pp. 47–71.

PRZYWARA, E. *Religionsphilosophische Schriften.* Einsiedeln, 1962.

PUNTEL, L.B. *Analogie und Geschichtlichkeit.* Vol. 1: *Philosophiegeschichtlich-kritischer Versuch über das Grundproblem der Metaphysik.* Freiburg, Basel, and Vienna, 1969.

QUELQUEJEU, B. "'Naturalia manent integra'. Contribution à l'étude de la portée, méthodologique et doctrinale, de l'axiome théologique 'Gratia praesupponit naturam.'" *Revue des Sciences Philosophiques et Théologiques* 49 (1965): 640–55.

RABEAU, G. *Species, Verbum. L'activité intellectuelle élémentaire selon St. Thomas d'Aquin.* Paris, 1938.

RAEYMAKER, L. DE *Vergelijkende studie over de betekenis van het "Zijn" in de metafysiek van Avicenna en die van Thomas van Aquino.* Brussels, 1955.

RAHNER, K. *Geist in Welt. Zur Metaphysik der endlichen Erkenntnis bei Thomas von Aquin.* 3rd ed. Munich, 1964. Eng. trans.: *Spirit in World.* Montreal, 1968.

RATZINGER, J. "Der Wortgebrauch von natura und die beginnende Verselbständigung der Metaphysik bei Bonaventura." In *Die Metaphysik im Mittelalter.* Miscellanea Mediaevalia, vol. 2. Berlin, 1963, pp. 483–98.

REGIS, L.-M. "Analyse et synthèse dans l'oeuvre de saint Thomas." In *Studia Mediaevalia in honorem R.J. Martin.* Brugge, 1948, pp. 303–30.

RENARD, A. *La querelle sur la possibilité de la philosophie chrétienne.* Paris, 1941.

RIESENHUBER, K. *Die Transzendenz der Freiheit zum Guten. Der Wille in der Anthropologie und Metaphysik des Thomas von Aquin.* Munich, 1971.

———, "Der Wandel des Naturbegriffs vom Hochmittelalter zur frühen Neuzeit." In *San Bonaventura maestro di vita francescana e di sapienza Christiana,* vol. 2. Edited by A. Pompei. Rome, 1976, pp. 607–25.

RIESSEN, H. VAN *Wijsbegeerte.* Kampen, 1970.

RINTELEN, F.J. VON "Die Frage nach Sinn und Wert bei Thomas von Aquin." *Rivista di Filosofia Neoscolastica* 66 (1974): 682–739.

ROBBERS H. "Natur im Blickfeld der Philosophie und Theologie." *Studium Generale* 7 (1954): 294–98.

———, *Antieke wijsgerige opvattingen in het Christelijk denkleven.* Roermond and Maaseik, 1959.

ROBERT, J.-D. "Note sur le dilemme: 'Limitation par composition ou limitation par hiérarchie formelle des essences.'" *Revue des Sciences Philosophiques et Théologiques* 49 (1965): 60–66.

ROBINSON, R. *Definition.* Oxford, 1954.

ROHNER, A. *Das Schöpfungsproblem bei Moses Maimonides, Albertus Magnus und Thomas von Aquin, Ein Beitrag zur Geschichte des Schöpfungsproblems im Mittelalter.* Beiträge zur Geschichte der Philosophie und Theologie des Mittelalters XI, 5. Münster, 1913.

RIJK, L.M. DE "Die Bedeutungslehre der Logik im 13. Jahrhundert und ihr Gegenstück in der metaphysischen Spekulation." In *Methoden in Wissenschaft und Kunst des Mittelalters.* Miscellanea Mediaevalia, vol. 7. Berlin, 1970, pp. 1–20.

———, *Middeleeuwse wijsbegeerte, Traditie en vernieuwing.* Assen and Amsterdam, 1977. French trans.: *La philosophie au moyen âge.* Leiden, 1985.

———, "On Ancient and Mediaeval Semantics and Metaphysics." *Vivarium* 15 (1977): 81–110; 16 (1978): 81–107; 18 (1980): 1–62.

SALLMANN, K. "Studien zum philosophischen Naturbegriff der Römer." *Archiv für Begriffsgeschichte* 7 (1962): 140–284.

SANGUINETI, J.J. *La filosofía de la ciencia según Santo Tomás.* Pamplona, 1977.

SCHADEWALDT, W. "Natur–Technik–Kunst." In *Hellas und Hesperien,* vol. 2. Zurich and Stuttgart, 1970, pp. 497–512.

———, "Die Begriffe 'Natur' und 'Technik' bei den Griechen." In *ibid.,* pp. 512–24.

SCHILLEBEECKX, E. "Arabisch-Neoplatoonse achtergrond van Thomas' opvatting over de ontvankelijkheid van de mens voor de genade." *Bijdragen* 35 (1974): 298–308.

SCHMIDT, R.W. *The Domain of Logic According to Saint Thomas Aquinas.* The Hague, 1966.

SCHULTZ, W. "Die Natur in der Deutung des Abendlands." *Zeitwende, die neue Furche* 33 (1962): 80–97; 162–73.

SECKLER M. *Das Heil in der Geschichte. Geschichtstheologisches Denken bei Thomas von Aquin.* Munich, 1964.

SEECK G.A., ed. *Die Naturphilosophie des Aristoteles.* Wege der Forschung, vol. 225. Darmstadt, 1975.

SEIDL, H. "Bemerkungen zu Erkenntnis als Massverhältnis bei Aristoteles und Thomas von Aquin." In *Mass, Zahl, Zahlensymbolik im Mittelalter.* Vol. 1. Miscellanea Mediaevalia, vol. 16/1. Berlin, 1983, pp. 32–42.

SELVAGGI, F. "Il concetto di natura in Aristotele e S. Tommaso." In *Scritti in onore di C. Giacon.* Padua, 1972, pp. 259–76.

SERTILLANGES, A.D. *La philosophie de St. Thomas d'Aquin.* 2nd ed. Paris, 1940.

———, *La philosophie morale de St. Thomas d'Aquin.* Paris, 1942.

———, *L'idée de création et ses retentissements en philosophie.* Paris, 1945.

SMIT, M.C. *Het goddelijk geheim in de geschiedenis.* Kampen, 1955.

———, *De verhouding van Christendom en Historie in de huidige Rooms-Katholieke geschiedbeschouwing.* Kampen, 1950.

———, *Writings on God and History.* 2 vols. Edited by H. Van Dyke. Trans. H.D. Morton. Toronto, forthcoming.

SOLAGUREN, C. "Contingencia y creación en la filosofia de Duns Escoto." In *De doctrina Ioannis Duns Scoti,* vol. 2. Acta Congressus Scotistici Internationalis Oxonii et Edimburgi 11–17 sept. 1966 celebrati. Rome, 1968, pp. 297–348.

SOLMSEN, F. *Aristotle's System of the Physical World: A Comparison with His Predecessors.* Ithaca, N.Y., 1960.

———, "Nature as Craftsman in Greek Thought." *Journal of the History of Ideas* 24 (1963): 473–96.

STEENBERGHEN, F. VAN *La philosophie au XIIIe siècle.* Louvain and Paris, 1966.

———, "La philosophie de la nature au XIIIe siècle." In *La filosofia della natura nel medioevo.* Milan, 1966, pp. 114–32.

STEINBÜCHEL, Th. *Der Zweckgedanke in der Philosophie des Thomas von Aquino.* Beiträge zur Geschichte der Philosophie und Theologie des Mittelalters, XI, 1. Münster, 1912.

STOECKLE, B. *"Gratia supponit naturam." Geschichte und Analyse eines theologischen Axioms.* Rome, 1962.

STUFLER, J. *Gott, der erste Beweger aller Dinge. Ein neuer Beitrag zum Verständnis der Konkurslehre des hl. Thomas von Aquin.* Innsbruck, 1936.

TONQUÉDEC, J. DE *La critique de la connaissance.* Paris, 1929.

TROELTSCH, E. "Die Bedeutung des Begriffs der Kontingenz." In *Gesammelte Schriften,* vol. 2. 2nd ed. Tübingen, 1922, pp. 769–778. English trans. s.v. "Contingency," in *Encyclopaedia of Religion and Ethics,* vol. 4. Edited by James Hastings. Edinburgh and New York, 1911; rpt. ed. 1935, pp. 87–89.

TUGENDHAT, E. *TI KATA TINOS, Eine Untersuchung zu Struktur und Ursprung aristotelischer Grundbegriffe.* Freiburg and Munich, 1958.

ULLMANN, W. "Some Observations on the Medieval Evaluation of the 'Homo Naturalis' and the 'Christianus.'" In *L'homme et son destin d'après les penseurs du moyen-âge.* Actes du premier Congrès intern. de Philos. Médiévale. Louvain and Paris, 1960, pp. 145–51.

ULMER, K. "Die Wandlung des naturwissenschaftlichen Denkens zu Beginn der Neuzeit bei Galilei." *Symposion* 2 (1949): 289–350.

———, *Wahrheit, Kunst und Natur bei Aristoteles, Ein Beitrag zur Aufklärung der metaphysischen Herkunft der modernen Technik.* Tübingen, 1953.

VANSTEENKISTE, C.M.J. "Situation des études thomistes." *Bijdragen* 35 (1974): 118–28.

VELTHOVEN, Th. VAN *Ontvangen als intersubjectieve act.* Amsterdam, 1980. Inaugural address.

VERBEKE, G. "Le développement de la connaissance humaine d'après saint Thomas." *Revue Philosophique de Louvain* 47 (1949): 437–57.

———, "Man As a 'Frontier' According to Aquinas." In *Aquinas and Problems of His Time.* Louvain, 1976, pp. 195–213.

———, "Introduction doctrinale." In *Avicenna Latinus, Liber de Philosophia prima sive Scientia Divina.* Edited by S. van Riet. Louvain and Leiden, 1977, pp. 1–122.

VERES, T. "Eine fundamentale ontologische Dichotomie im Denken des Thomas von Aquin." *Philosophisches Jahrbuch* 77 (1970): 81–98.

VERGOTE, A. "Intellektualisme en Volontarisme. De antinomieën van het finalistisch goedheidsbegrip bij Aristoteles en Thomas van Aquino." *Tijdschrift voor Philosophie* 17 (1955): 477–522.

VIGNAUX, P. *La pensée au Moyen-Age.* 2nd ed. Paris, 1948.

VOGEL, C.J. DE *Antike Seinsphilosophie und Christentum im Wandel der Jahrhunderte.* Baden-Baden, 1958.

——, "Plato, Aristoteles en het ideaal van het beschouwende leven." In *Theoria, Studies over de Griekse wijsbegeerte.* Assen, 1967, pp. 154–71.

——, "De Griekse wijsbegeerte en het Christelijk scheppingsbegrip." In *Theoria, Studies over de Griekse wijsbegeerte.* Assen, 1967, pp. 188–202.

VOLK, H. *Gesammelte Schriften,* vol. 1. Mainz, 1967.

VOLLRATH, E. "Aristoteles: Das Problem der Substanz." In *Grundprobleme der grossen Philosophen,* vol. 1. Edited by J. Speck. Göttingen, 1972, pp. 84–128.

VOS, H. DE *Beknopte geschiedenis van het begrip natuur.* Groningen, 1970.

VRIES, J. DE *Grundbegriffe der Scholastik.* Darmstadt, 1980.

WALGRAVE, J.H. *Geloof en theologie in de crisis.* Kasterlee, 1966.

——, "Het natuurverlangen naar de Godsaanschouwing bij Thomas van Aquino." *Tijdschrift voor Filosofie* 36 (1974): 232–66.

WALLACE, W.A. *Causality and Scientific Explanation,* vol. 1. Ann Arbor, 1972.

WEIDEMANN, H. *Metaphysik und Sprache, Eine sprachphilosophische Untersuchung zu Thomas von Aquin und Aristoteles.* Freiburg and Munich, 1975.

WEIER, W. "Seinsteilhabe und Sinnteilhabe im Denken des hl. Thomas von Aquin." *Salzburger Jahrbuch für Philosophie* 8 (1964): 93–114.

——, *Sinn und Teilhabe. Das Grundthema der abendländischen Geistesentwicklung.* Salzburg and Munich, 1970.

WEISHEIPL, J.A. "The Concept of Nature." *The New Scholasticism* 28 (1954): 377–408.

——, "Natural and Compulsory Motion." *The New Scholasticism* 29 (1955): 50–81.

——, "'Omne quod movetur ab alio movetur' in Medieval Physics." *Isis* 56 (1965): 26–45.

——, "'Quidquid movetur ab alio movetur': A Reply." *The New Scholasticism* 42 (1968): 422–31.

——, *Friar Thomas d'Aquino, His Life, Thought, and Work.* New York, 1974.

——, "The Axiom 'Opus naturae est opus intelligentiae' and its Origins." In *Albertus Magnus, Doctor Universalis 1280/1980.* Edited by G. Meyer and A. Zimmermann. Mainz, 1980, pp. 441–64.

WENTSEL, B. *Natuur en Genade. Een introductie in en confrontatie met de jongste ontwikkelingen in de Rooms-katholieke theologie inzake dit thema.* Kampen, 1970.

WEYERS, O. "Contribution à l'histoire des termes 'natura naturans' et 'natura naturata' jusqu'à Spinoza." *Vivarium* 16 (1978): 70–80.

WHITEHEAD, A.N. *The Concept of Nature.* Cambridge, 1920.

WIELAND, W. *Die aristotelische Physik, Untersuchungen über die Grundlegung der Naturwissenschaft und die sprachliche Bedingungen der Prinzipienforschung bei Aristoteles.* 2nd ed. Göttingen, 1970.

WIELE, J. VANDE "Le problème de la vérité ontologique dans la philosophie de saint Thomas." *Revue Philosophique de Louvain* 52 (1954): 521–71.

——, "'Res' en 'ding', Bijdrage tot een vergelijkende studie van de zijnsopvatting in het Thomisme en bij Heidegger." *Tijdschrift voor Filosofie* 24 (1962): 427–506.

——, *Zijnswaarheid en Onverborgenheid. Vergelijkende studie over de ontologische waarheid in het Thomisme en bij Heidegger.* Leuven, 1964.

WILPERT, P. *Das Problem der Wahrheitssicherung bei Thomas von Aquin. Ein Beitrag zur Geschichte des Evidenzproblems.* Münster, Westfalen, 1931.

WIPLINGER, F. *Physis und Logos. Zum Körperphänomen in seiner Bedeutung für den Ursprung der Metaphysik bei Aristoteles.* Freiburg and Munich, 1971.

——, *Metaphysik, Grundfragen ihres Ursprungs und ihrer Vollendung.* Freiburg and Munich, 1976.

WOLFSON, H.A. "The Meaning of *ex nihilo* in the Church Fathers, Arabic and Hebrew Philosophy, and St. Thomas." In *Studies in the History of Philosophy and Religion*, vol. 1. Cambridge, Mass., 1973, pp. 207–21.
WOODBRIDGE, F.J.E. *Aristotle's Vision of Nature*. New York and London, 1965.
ZIMMERMANN, A. "Die 'Grundfrage' in der Metaphysik des Mittelalters." *Archiv für Geschichte der Philosophie* 47 (1965): 141–56.
ZUM BRUNN, E. "La 'métaphysique de l'Exode' selon Thomas d'Aquin." In *Dieu et l'Etre, Exégèses d'Exode 3, 14 et de Coran 20, 11–24*. Paris, 1978, pp. 245–69.

INDEX RERUM

and grace, 365–6, 370–1, 384ff.
integral/corrupted, 386
and intelligibility, 9, 30, 131,
   134–5, 239
intrinsic principle, 102, 262, 279–83,
   294
and matter, 262, 297–300, 301
meanings of, 79, 261–3
and miracle, 290–2
modern concept of, 25, 77
and motion, 234, 261–3, 269–70
naturans, 309–10
and necessity, 236ff.
and providence, 353
and truth, 152–3
universal, 308–9
is the way towards nature, 4, 105, 301,
   348
Necessary (Necessity), 230, 240, 241ff.,
276
   absolute, 235, 237, 242, 306
   and cause, 237ff.
   natural, 238, 239, 282
   in a certain respect, 238
Nothing, 95, 114, 251, 325–6
   out of nothing comes nothing, 95,
      112, 120, 300, 320, 324–7

One (Unity), 73, 119, 145, 173–4, 175,
254, 318, 392
Operation, 356, 358
Opposition, 257, 258–9, 272
   relative, 156, 170, 257
Origin, 2, 10, 12, 47ff., 104, 113ff., 130,
210, 270, 272

Participation, 79ff., 85, 113, 118–9, 132,
161, 176, 183–5, 224, 245–6, 303–4,
311, 329, 335, 371, 389, 395
   and causality, 119
   through composition, 138, 183, 185
   and creation, 123–7
   in the divine nature, 371–2
   through formal hierarchy, 184–6
   two modes of, 87–8
Passion, 148, 156, 169, 266, 274
Perfect (Perfection), 38, 82, 174–5, 261,
338, 375–6, 389–90
   and creature, 377ff.
   and finite, 68, 378
   first, 354, 386
   grades of, 75, 174
   and nature, 376–7
   second, 356, 386
Perpetuity, 106, 108, 247, 267, 269, 298,
359

Phantasm, 225–6
Physics, 229, 237, 253–4
Potency, 95, 107, 136–7, 245–6, 251–2,
259–60, 263–6, 273, 276–8, 289, 318,
319
   first/second, 285–6
   and matter, 260, 299
   obediential, 291–2, 364, 366, 368–
      9
Predicament, 58–60, 145, 259, 392
   and motion, 258
Predication, 27, 54ff., 74, 86ff., 96, 136,
158
   analogical, 61, 86, 125
   equivocal, 61
   and generation, 92, 96–7, 102–3,
      299
   through identity, 26
   per essentiam/per participationem, 55,
      64, 68, 80ff., 83ff., 113, 136
   per se/per accidens, 54, 57–8, 65–7,
      86ff., 97, 136, 235, 295
   two tracks of, 89–91, 253
   univocal, 61, 68, 99
Principle, 10ff., 27, 293
Privation, 8, 257
Providence, 353

Question(-ing), 12ff., 23ff., 45ff., 108
   another mode of, 22, 46ff., 214
   four questions, 13
   "if", 19ff., 24–5, 31, 49, 51–3,
      59, 88, 116, 220–1, 271
   "katallel" structure, 16, 27, 31, 47
   of the middle term, 14–5, 70
   twofold sense of, 50–3
   "what", 18–9, 21ff., 25ff., 31, 49,
      51–3, 59, 64, 88, 116, 238
Quiddity, 29
Quo est/Quod est, 29, 47, 85, 320, 332

Reason, 191ff., 210–1, 228–9, 230
   discursive, 192–6
   and faith, 201ff., 209–10, 212ff.,
      227
   historical, 196ff.
   imitates nature, 194, 228
   and intellect, 195–6, 218–9, 253–4
Relation, 89, 147–8, 156–7, 168–70,
265, 274–5, 355, 383–4
   accidental, 169, 275
   of God to the creature, 168–70
   mixed, 155, 168
   subsisting, 169, 380
Resolution, 16, 79, 113, 144, 198, 252ff.,
271ff., 275, 298, 360, 394